The Superstitious Muse:
Thinking Russian Literature Mythopoetically

Studies in Russian and Slavic Literatures, Cultures and History
Series Editor: Lazar Fleishman

The Superstitious Muse:
Thinking Russian Literature
Mythopoetically

DAVID M. BETHEA

Boston
2009

Library of Congress Cataloging-in-Publication Data

Bethea, David M., 1948-
The superstitious muse: thinking Russian literature mythopoetically /
David M. Bethea.
    p. cm.
Includes bibliographical references and index.
ISBN 978-1-934843-17-8 (hardback)
1. Russian literature — History and criticism. 2. Mythology in literature.
3. Superstition in literature. I. Title.
PG2950.B48 2009
891.709—dc22
                    2009039325

Copyright © 2009 Academic Studies Press
All rights reserved

ISBN 978-1-61811-812-7

Book design and typefaces by Konstantin Lukjanov©
Photo on the cover by Benson Kua
Published by Academic Studies Press in 2009
28 Montfern Avenue
Brighton, MA 02135, USA
press@academicstudiespress.com
www.academicstudiespress.com

For Kim

Contents

	Preface: David M. Bethea	9
	Introduction: Caryl Emerson (Mythopoetics Meets the Living Person: How David Bethea Balances the Body and the Muse)	17

I. Part One: Russian Literature: Background, Foreground, Creative Cognition

1. The Mythopoetic "Vectors" of Russian Literature — 27
2. Mythopoesis Writ Large: The Apocalyptic Plot in Russian Literature — 41
3. Mythopoesis and Biography: Pushkin, Jakobson, and the Secret Life of Statues — 101
4. The Evolution of Evolution: Genes, Memes, Intelligent Design, and Nabokov — 127
5. Relativity and Reality: Dante, Florensky, Lotman, and Metaphorical Time-Travel — 149
6. Whose Mind is This Anyway? Influence, Intertextuality, and the Legitimate Boundaries of Scholarship — 167

II. Part Two: Pushkin the Poet, Pushkin the Thinker

7. Of Pushkin and Pushkinists — 185
8. Biography (with Sergei Davydov) — 205
9. Pushkin's Mythopoetic Consciousness: Apuleius, Psyche and Cupid, and the Theme of Metamorphosis in *Eugene Onegin* — 227
10. "A Higher Audacity": How to Read Pushkin's Dialogue with Shakespeare in *The Stone Guest* — 249
11. Stabat Pater: Revisiting the "Monumental" in Peter, Petersburg, and Pushkin — 265
12. Slavic Gift Giving, the Poet in History, and Pushkin's *The Captain's Daughter* — 281
13. Pushkin's *The History of Pugachev*: Where Fact Meets the Zero-Degree of Fiction — 301

III. Part Three: Reading Russian Writers Reading Themselves and Others

14. *Sorrento Photographs*: Khodasevich's Memory Speaks — 323
15. Nabokov's Style — 337
16. Sologub, Nabokov, and the Limits of Decadent Aesthetics — 347
17. Exile, Elegy, and Auden in Brodsky's "Verses on the Death of T. S. Eliot" — 363
18. Joseph Brodsky and the American Seashore Poem: Lowell, Mandelstam, and Cape Cod — 381
19. Joseph Brodsky's "To My Daughter" (A Reading) — 391
20. Brodsky, Frost, and the Pygmalion Myth — 405
    Index — 421

Note on Transliteration

Transliterating modern Russian is always a thorny issue, as any single method (e.g., "Library of Congress") universally applied is going to create problems with a book's implied readership. In the following essays the author has merged two systems in an attempt to recognize the competing needs of the general academic reader and the specialist scholar. In text as text, whether in the body of the essay or in the footnote, proper names are rendered less formally: "Yury," not "Iurii," "Olga," not "Ol'ga," "Solovyov," not "Solov'ev," "Petrushevskaya," not "Petrushevskaia"; in text and bibliographical material cited from the Russian, the situation is reversed, and the Library of Congress system (without diacriticals) is used consistently throughout: Iurii Lotman, "Ideinaia struktura Kapitanskoi dochki." When common practice supports a westernized version of a well-known figure's name, "Tsar Nicholas" for example, I have adopted that version in the text and in the narrative portions of the footnotes.

Preface

First, a disclaimer — let us call it a "caveat emptor" statement. I trust I am not being coy or self-serving when I say, with my conventional WASP upbringing and social instincts, I find it rather awkward to speak *in propria persona*, to discuss my work "in general," outside the comfort zone of a book project's governing concept and shape. Over the years I have said often to colleagues and graduate students that there is no system of ideas, no school or movement, I feel competent to create or, what is probably at some level an analogous response, encourage others to follow. Formalism and structuralism, "secondary modelling systems," psychoanalysis, Freud, Jakobson, Bakhtin, Bloom, Lotman, Dawkins — these movements and individuals have all provided important grist for my mill, but that grist has always seemed to me to some significant degree insufficient, and this in full knowledge of the fact that, in terms of sheer intelligence, erudition, and conceptualizing ardour, my contributions are small potatoes when placed alongside what has been achieved by these proper names. If someone tells me that he or she admires or has learned something from my work, my initial reaction is embarrassment (obviously not everyone's intentions are suspect, but what does one do with praise, other than gain some modicum of confidence that perhaps in the given case you got some things right). To those who don't agree with my premises or how I use them in my books and articles I am also indebted: in many ways you are my ideal readers because I have your negative reactions ringing in mind ("why bother?" "this is not serious") when I try to formulate something speculative and empirically unprovable. In any event, I am genuinely grateful if anyone reads my work, especially in these times.

I have come closest to explaining how I think and how I organize ideas and build arguments in the "polemical" introductions to my books on Brodsky (*Joseph Brodsky and the Creation of Exile*, 1994) and Pushkin (*Realizing Metaphors: Alexander Pushkin and the Life of the Poet*, 1998). But these "vectors" were there earlier as well:

in the thoughts on how Khodasevich used Pushkin (*Khodasevich: His Life and Art*, 1983) and in the "structuralism with a human face" (the late Efim Etkind's phrase) I tried to apply to an alternative tradition and sub-genre of modern Russian prose I called "apocalyptic fiction" (*The Shape of Apocalypse in Modern Russian Fiction*, 1989). In each case I was trying to isolate cultural patterns, but then add something to the strict structural component—how the pattern took on flesh and blood, how it entered into historical and biographical context, how it happened once and then changed in the hands (brains) of the next individual or next cultural kin group. In all these instances I have consciously mixed what is purely descriptive, "scholarly" and supposedly "scientific," with what is not: the use of metaphor, metaphorical thinking, associative leaps in understanding that are colored not simply by logic but also by emotion. Why?

The danger of delving into metaphorical thinking is that you can never be sure the metaphors are not merely your own and that you are offering an "impressionistic" picture of events that might have transpired otherwise. Also, if we take into account—which move is itself a mirage, as the ideas themselves spread into our brains like viruses—recent decades' pulverizing of the self, the author, and the very concept of intentionality, then what does it matter to address the issue of biography (we can never know what Pushkin was thinking anyway) or the links between biography and cultural artifacts (any attempt to explain how the one interacts with the other is nothing more than a quixotic exercise in putting Humpty-Dumpty back together again). But it seemed to me that, if one read one's subject carefully enough, and if one tried to focus more on their metaphors (the creation and use of which I will be referring to in these pages as "mythopoesis") than on one's own, then the effort did not have to be futile.

There was also another important factor affecting my thinking: desire. So much of contemporary discussion and analysis of "desire" in culture is—no mystery here!—a desire-killer. Obviously I am not complaining about how scientists measure what is happening in the brain and elsewhere when someone sees or thinks about something that to them is desirable. No, I am speaking about the lit-crit tendency, diagnosed powerfully by people like Mark Edmundson, to assume we have explained something when we look at Shakespeare's language and descend (the Freudian subterranean episteme), like psychic spelunkers, into the subconscious depths only to reveal what is hidden there. We identify what the desire means through this blindness-reveals-insight activity; we, as it were, explain to Shakespeare what he really meant when he penned such and such. Yet the moment someone trundles in Freudian or Lacanian language, especially Lacanian, which is infinitely able to hide behind its own ambiguity, the desire being discussed is nowhere to be found. As an aside, we should never forget that what to Saussure (and everything that followed out of Saussure) was purely arbitrary, the connection between the *signifié* and *signifiant*, was by no means arbitrary in the same way to Darwin (and everything that followed out of Darwin): for the latter natural selection did not have an identifiable end-goal, and yet the adaptations to species that arose over time did so in response to environmental pressures, with the result that the species (if it survived) grew more complex, better able to function in its environment. (Of course it has been eloquently argued by those such as Stephen J. Gould that some organisms, parasites for instance, can evolve by becoming simpler.) Language may evolve, but we can't say with intellectual honesty that the changes arising in a language make the user of that language more "fit." When a de Man or a Derrida focuses on the infinite difference-making quality of language, the capacity to refine and refine without capturing a wholeness always in retreat, they are the modern avatars of Saussure. Darwin and the way his followers might look at language as a key factor, but not the only factor, in how *Homo sapiens* evolves stand outside the Saussurean frame.

My idea, which as I say I am not confident in calling a methodology, is to try to track desire as something made up of both thought (what one wants) and emotion (how much and why one wants it). If, for example, to cite my piece on Pushkin, Jakobson, and the statue-come-to-life motif, we look at (speculate, if you wish) why Pushkin might have experienced such superstitious dread when he created *The Stone Guest* on the eve of his marriage, we come much closer to what was really happening — and a practicing poet like Akhmatova, which is no coincidence in this case, sensed something like this before me — than Jakobson's brilliant, structurally precise, though (for this reader) sterile classic. In my rendering I try to recoup, inasmuch as this is feasible, the metaphorical logic of Pushkin's superstitious dread: how it traced back to his youth and early poems (above all *The Gabrieliad*), his view of himself as a physical and emotional being, his guilt about his betrayal of beauty (in his Russian way beauty was both an aesthetic and ethical category), and his eerie sense, as he prepared to marry a supreme beauty, that the statues that were on the verge of animation in the play were isomorphic (and isochronic, hence the feeling of mental expansion, of various mythopoetic forms living through you at one time) with the bliss of a statuesque beauty come to life (Natalie) and the fear that the lucky lover must now pay dearly for all those husbands he has "killed" by stealing their wives and making fun of it. Desire needs resistance, abrasion, personal investment, risk, for it to be genuine, not ersatz, desire. It cannot reside in structural terms alone.

There is more to the issue of "desire" though, and for me that is what makes pursuing this line of thought rewarding. Too long we, including the writer of these lines, have remained in the comfort zone of literary studies, which is now, or has been for some time, morphing steadily into cultural studies. I would not want to say anything invidious about cultural studies: the most I would venture is that the democratizing (if that's the right word) thrust of the movement has encouraged practitioners to look for patterns outside of "high" culture and "great" authors and cultural figures. There is a significant mixing, of genre, media, cultural layer and audience, taking place that is part and parcel of late postmodernism, or post-postmodernism. Philology, classical literary study, has the reputation, whether deserved or not (personally I suspect deserved), of being stale and stuffy. Theory as it applies to "high" culture seems less in evidence if not totally exhausted, and much of the impetus to look at things cultural these days comes from adjacent disciplines, such as anthropology, history, philosophy, and psychology.

For the past few years I have been spending part of every spring in Oxford (UK). This year (2009) is, as many know, the bicentennial of the birth of Charles Darwin. In science, with the possible exception of Einstein's relativity theory, no discovery has had a greater impact on how we view ourselves in the modern world than natural selection. Darwin's "finches," with their different beaks adapted for alternative means of food gathering on the different islands of the Galapagos, have become not only a vivid illustration of this core discovery, that species are not unchanging and designed once and for all by God, but can adapt over time and diverge from a common ancestor under environmental pressures. That discovery has set us on a path that is, curiously, as metaphoric as it is metonymic and taxonomical. Let me explain. Recently I attended in Oxford a lecture by a bright young zoologist who specialized in a small subset of the multitude of bird species found in the Amazon rainforests (in this instance in Peru). The zoologist explained that there were more different species of birds (thousands) in this relatively small area where she had been conducting her research than in any other place on earth. What was fascinating was that the subspecies that the young scientist studied did not communicate with family members or close relatives through any learned bird signals or songs. Apparently, the possibilities for mating were so richly available that the birds never had to depend on anything other than their original inherited "hard-wiring" to produce offspring and get on with their bird lives. But when these same or similar birds were tracked north and found on other continents with less inviting habitats, which meant that the competition for mates was more demanding, the birds that produced vocal signals only through genetic coding morphed into birds that were capable of learning signals and songs from parents. This may not be anything to write home about for the scientists that study birds at the level of my young zoologist, but the message is clear for those of us who try to make sense of culture, including literature. Biologically, learning begins as the need to find a mate in more competitive circumstances. However, there is a quantum leap between one's genes telling one's brain to find a way to replicate themselves and the "culture" (because those birds that learn from parents to sing in a certain way are participating in a rudimentary form of culture) that produces Dante's *Commedia*. Rote learning, as we move higher and higher up the taxa (or further and further laterally across the taxa, as Darwin-Gould might say), becomes learning imbued with ever increasing desire, not simply with the sex drive per se, which we must assume is an evolutionary constant, but with the sort of value added that produces, in the right time-space, a *Commedia* or a *Hamlet* or a *Eugene Onegin*. That is why we need, on the cultural side, more attention paid to how metaphorical thinking actually works, when looked at in all the striations (Mandelstam actually compares it to trying to run across a jagged watery football field of Chinese junks) of its historical dimensionality.

Broadly speaking, what I mean by "mythopoesis" is how the poetic impulse creates and is created by story. When I discuss questions of tradition and group perception, such as my studies of apocalyptic thinking in Russian literature, the focus is more on the transmission and modification of large cultural patterns. Individual biography, while not disappearing entirely, by necessity takes a back seat. The focus, however, shifts and the understanding of how the poet uses his own biography becomes central when we begin to examine individual instances. Pushkin, for if there was ever anyone genetically and culturally wired up to be a poet it was he, did not make a practice of collecting fully rounded off stories into which he then inserted himself, disguised as this or that character, in his artistic works. The process didn't operate that simply or crudely. Rather, he adopted for himself certain signature mythoi — Pygmalion, Psyche and Cupid, Prodigal Son, Virgin Mary, Arion, etc. — fragments of which he would use from time to time to tell the story of his pilgrim soul's progress. It is important to note that the specific work that grows out of the mythopoetic nexus does not suggest the entire story is being lived through from beginning to end. Pushkin was smart enough, and constantly challenged enough by the harsh facts of his and others' existence, not to give himself wholly to any one explanation for his being. Most of the time his use of these plot fragments involves metamorphosis, a change his heart desires but makes known to itself as something difficult, fraught with obstacles, often potentially tragic obstacles. The part of the

Pygmalion story Pushkin uses for his own purposes at a specific point in his life is the need to create beauty and be loved by beauty at the same time, when it is clear to the beauty-maker that his enterprise is not inherently worthy of anything, especially the love of a beautiful creature for the person he really is. The Psyche and Cupid plot gave Pushkin the opportunity to try to understand what happens on the female side (the proverbial "what women want") when eros is experienced fully and for the first time. The Prodigal Son parable was what came to mind in connection with the deep need to be forgiven for past profligacy by the Good Father. And so on. These moments of great need drew Pushkin to try to imagine what exactly it was he was living through, and then these stories, or the parts of them that mattered, provided the best available answer, which itself became the words on a page we love. But because Pushkin was so through and through a poet, the process seemed to work both ways: it could also be that he was sitting and playing with the sound of words and then the mythic traces surfaced (the *poln / voln*, "full"/"waves" rhyme pair runs through a number of his 1820's poems about his own creative thinking, and makes the "pregnancy of thought/inspiration" idea and the "romantic element of water/birth" idea a logical starting point for Peter's creation myth — "Na beregu pustynnikh *voln* / Stoial on, dum velikikh *poln*" [On the shore of the desolate *waves* / He stood, *full* of great thoughts] — by the time we get to The Bronze Horseman). The point is both these tendencies were firing off each other at great speed and intensity.

The essays in this volume are divided into three parts: a more conceptual first part, a second part devoted to similarly conceived articles on Pushkin, and a third part focusing on how other writers (Khodasevich, Nabokov, Brodsky) read themselves and others. In general, while I composed these articles over a thirty year period with no conscious intention to house them under one conceptual roof, it seems to me that they do somehow "belong together." In the beginning of the first and second parts I decided to include pieces of a broader framing nature, studies that would address the questions "How can we look at Russian literature mythopoetically?" and "Can this mythopoetic tendency be tracked through history along one major current (apocalypse)?" (Part One); "How can we organize the history of Pushkin studies?" and "What are the primary contours of Pushkin's biography that would be relevant for a study like this?" (Part Two). The idea was that the information provided in these pieces would make some of the more speculative arguments in the later essays more plausible and "load-bearing." Although I have added new material in some places, cut in others, and where appropriate tried to bring the older pieces up to date, there is only one completely new essay: "The Evolution of Evolution: Genes, Memes, Intelligent Design, and Nabokov." For what it is worth, I consider this latter contribution an important (to me) later statement of how I perceive these matters and in that respect something the volume needs and would be much less representative without. Finally, when I did return to an older piece, as for example my 1980 essay on Khodasevich's *Sorrento Photographs*, I tried as a rule not to "write over" my previous self and start an entirely new and uncomfortably coy meta-dialogue with what has transpired in the secondary literature in the intervening years. While I'm a great fan of structures that seem to live and breathe on their own and to continue to create their own future as it were, a signature poem by Pushkin being a prime example, I also have no desire to get in the last word, since I do believe our larger role as teachers and servers of knowledge is to build on others and to make ourselves available for others to build on us.

To all those readers who have helped me knead my ideas into shape over the years, I thank you. I am especially grateful in the present instance to Caryl Emerson, who took time from a very full schedule to write an Introduction for this volume, and to Andrew Reynolds, my dear colleague at Madison, who has looked at (and proofread) this project in its various incarnations and who has been an ideal interlocutor and source of helpful information as I have attempted to think through the project's many challenges and issues. Any inadequacies in the following pages, and inadequacies of various stripes there will be despite one's good intentions, are entirely my own.

Madison/Oxford
March 2009

Mythopoetics Meets the Living Person: How David Bethea Balances the Body and the Muse

CARYL EMERSON

The entries in this volume cover a huge amount of territory, but even so represent only a portion of David Bethea's wide-ranging interests over the past three decades. One figure will serve as portal into these selected essays, arguably the fulcrum and inspiration for Bethea's mythopoetics: Alexander Pushkin. The shade of that great poet hovers over Bethea's other perennial companions: Vladimir Nabokov, Vladislav Khodasevich, Joseph Brodsky, Gavrila Derzhavin. From this magical zone of Russian writers with Pushkin at its core, one question will be central. How, and through what charmed intermediaries, does a poet create and then continue to live?

The two prongs of that question, primary creativity and posthumous life, address with equal urgency the poet (life as well as work) and the responsibility of the poet's "recuperators." The professional behavior of this latter category of cultural servant — the biographer, literary critic, cultural historian, editor, textologist, secondary or tertiary commentator — is deeply important to Bethea. Himself a master at close readings in biographical context (one third of the essays in this collection are happy evidence of this skill), he disavows any single method. To be sure, a distinguished group of theorists and cultural critics do serve Bethea as recurrent reference points: Harold Bloom, Sigmund Freud, Roman Jakobson, Mikhail Bakhtin, Yury Lotman, even in passing the "continentals" Julia Kristeva, Jacques Derrida, Helene Cixous. All are suggestive and all are found inadequate. But Bethea's own voice, or better his own "mythopoetic critical consciousness," cannot be traced back to any of them. Some hints are provided, however, in the way he circles warily around Pushkin. We can extract these hints from the opening paragraphs of one essay included here, on metamorphosis in *Eugene Onegin*.

In that essay, Bethea applauds Pushkin's instinctive move to mask the personal, and especially the painfully intimately personal, through two means. The first is lived experience through the concept of a code of honor. The second, operative in his poetic persona, is through "genre consciousness," that is, an awareness of what sort of message a given literary form can and should transmit. Writing about Pushkin and other poets, Bethea will scrupulously respect these constraints. Allow one's subject matter to breathe, to hide its face, to drape and mystify itself. Be attentive to "vectors": the poet's use of multiple points of view, for example, to complicate his own subjective perspective or to organize a fictional world that is alive on its own terms. (These terms are different for each genre, of course, and part of the genius of Pushkin is his ability to challenge the reader to identify which type of world is in force.) But inevitably the critic is drawn to those subjective moments in a poet's lived experience that are "fraught with certain life choices and heightened by fear and anxiety."[1] At those times the pressure is on to save oneself, or find oneself, through one's creativity.

This risk-laden, heated-up terrain is Bethea's point of departure. But his concerns are not solely for the life of the poet. Our own lives and livelihoods also hang in the balance. Bethea has long sought analogies between the incipient creative spark born in the poet's imagination and the creative vision painstakingly reassembled by the poet's disciples and later by scholars, who strive to keep the most vital parts of their hero alive by judiciously re-animating them from outside or from beyond. Guidelines here are intuitive and few. Bethea addressed just this problem in his 2004 keynote address to the AATSEEL Annual Convention: "Whose Mind is This Anyway?" — with a subtitle naming the more slippery components of the answer: "Influence, Intertextuality, and the Boundaries of Legitimate Scholarship." In that speech, Bethea examined Yury Lotman's recuperation of Karamzin and Pushkin as acts almost of "co-creation," analogous to the intentional risks taken by Pushkin to re-animate his own life at crucial junctures, especially the feverishly productive Boldino autumn of 1830 preceding his marriage and his debut in prose. Bethea ex-

[1] See Chapter 9 of the present volume, "Pushkin's Mythopoetic Consciousness: Apuleis, Psyche and Cupid, and the Theme of Metamorphosis in *Eugene Onegin*," 228.

plains that it is practically impossible to catch Pushkin, perfect poet, speaking directly of himself. The scholar in search of Pushkin's authenticity must look elsewhere for intent: at his superstitions, his love objects, the moments of sudden, Pygmalion-like metamorphosis that he sets up or (when they happen by chance) that he accepts and instantly incorporates into his fate. Or as Bethea puts the matter in lapidary fashion, we can glimpse the poet as human being and not as a literary pose in two exemplary situations: by the "authenticity of what one wishes for in one's unhappiness coming to life," and by "the sort of love that doesn't question the past or the motives of the supplicant."[2] In terms of the intimate access required, this is a staggering agenda. What are the proper tools to bring to such a project? Which methods are decent, which invasive and indecent? How might scholarly critics acknowledge their own subjectivity (for to deny it, however we aspire to the ideals of an objective science, is surely fraudulent in all but the most quantified study of metrics or external biographical fact), while at the same time not obscuring the poet with our own passionately needy face?

[2] See chapter 6 of the present volume, "Whose Mind is This Anyway? Influence, Intertextuality, and the Legitimate Boundaries of Scholarship," 182.

Bethea's theater of operations, like Lotman's, can be vast. In his entry on Literature in Nicholas Rzhevsky's 1998 *Cambridge Companion to Modern Russian Culture* (excerpted here as chapter 1 of Part One), he posits nine "vectors" that govern the "ecosystem" of the Russian literary semiosphere. Perhaps Bethea's most ambitious attempt to objectivize the critical impulse is that phase of his research invoking the ancient, impersonal tropes of metamorphosis and apocalypse, two chronotopic changes of state that would appear to function above the level of personal agency. But this is a smokescreen, for the person of the poet and the anguish of the critic who loves the poet are never wholly muffled or displaced. Again and again, Bethea returns to the problem, or the challenge, of intentionality and creative autonomy. If Harold Bloom has remained vital in Russian criticism during the last two decades, it is largely thanks to Bethea's continued willingness to interrogate and circulate his terms. By and large Bethea does not approve of Bloom's suspicious, imperious, quasi-Freudian categories and invokes them as cautionary or negative examples — but he does take them seriously. Where Bethea goes beyond both Bloom and the mega-structures of the apocalypse is his realization, crystallized in his 1998 book *Realizing Metaphors: Alexander Pushkin and the Life of the Poet*, that a poet (a critic, a human being) can be more individual, more inspired, more open to revelation, in fact more free when struggling within the constraints of a given code, prejudice, ideal, or superstition. The Superstitious Muse.

The matter is not trivial, for Bethea is himself a strong critic and fully aware of it. He understands the desirability of disciplining the love or need that motivates a "professional other" in pursuit of literary genius. He also adores his subject matter, trusting its holistic wisdom and unique "mythopoeticizing consciousness" over any single explanatory system that might be invoked to read it. In Bethea's work there is no hint of a "hermeneutics of suspicion"—except, perhaps, toward other strong critics. We see the professional recuperator straightforwardly doing his job: he gazes upon the poet, paraphrases the energy found there (through metaphor, citation, biographical context, juxtaposition with other poems or poets), passes authoritative judgment on the creative corpus, and prepares it for further life. But a volume like this is vulnerable. Bringing together scholarship on many different topics and persons from various years, collapsing the time-space, contextual noise, and complex evolution of the critic into a series of consecutive chapters, "selected essays" as a genre inevitably reveal the enduring passions of the critic. What is the enduring passion here? I suggest that at the heart of David Bethea's life's work so far has been an inquiry into the mysterious chemistry of authentic transmission. Not influence or tradition but specifically—technically— transmission: from poet to poet, from poet to critic, from poets and critics and scholars to new generations of readers. Bethea has tried out several systems of thought in his pursuit of this phenomenon, from the most sentimental to the most scientific, most recently involving the language and logic of evolutionary biology (genes, memes, memeplexes; see Part One, Chapter 4). He has accumulated a repertory of hybrid approaches to the challenge of transmission that bear his signature. In my role as secondary critic, I suggest that they can be divided into four approximate categories: governed respectively by Bakhtin, Lotman, metamorphosis, and evolution. What links them all, in my view, is the Pushkinian device of a sudden "unexpected intersection" of several different planes.

What does the world feel like at one of these intersections? It is an aha! experience, or as Bethea would say: pure poetry. We think we know the story we are reading. The characters inside that story think they know it too; they are counting on a comfortable denouement. But suddenly—and this happened with Marya Gavrilovna in "The Blizzard" while she was watching Burmin obediently on his knees before her—the conventional plot stops, twists, breaks open, and reveals a deeper (if no less miraculous) truth. Hero and heroine are disoriented and for a moment they forget their lines. Fate, so gorgeously designed that it resembles predestination, steps into the space opened up by risk and chance. Remarkably, the biogenetic model for transmission that is currently freshest in Bethea's mind pays unspoken homage, in scientific terminology, to this moment in the *Belkin Tales*. But let us begin with the least hard-core-scientific of Bethea's models for transmission, acknowledged by him as worthy but by no means fetishized: the Bakhtinian-dialogic.

Many acts of cultural transmission are open, reciprocal, and intensely personal on both sides. As communicative exchanges designed to change each interlocutor incrementally over time, such acts usually take the form of interpersonal dialogues of words or gestures that can be tracked metonymically—if often meanderingly. Earnestness of emotional content and freedom of plot are dominant over symmetrical form. We recognize in such patches of communication the familiar bedrock of our everyday life as well as the appeal of the psychological novel ("A reaches out to B; B turns toward or away from A; A responds with joy or despair," etc.). But this prosy, full-access Bakhtinian model, with its asymmetries, transparent presumption of authorial honesty, and bleak linear fate, does not really persuade a critic like Bethea who, in Pushkinesque fashion, cannot help seeing little nascent poems everywhere. (Indicative of this helplessness is a very early and very interesting essay by Bethea: "Structure versus Symmetry in *Crime and Punishment*," 1982). Bethea has written astutely on Pushkin's prose, especially *The Captain's Daughter* and the *History of Pugachev*—but readers will not find in these discussions a thorough-going prose consciousness on either side of the artwork. This is appropriate when analyzing Pushkin the prose-writer (at least in his short stories and novel fragments; what to do with the late-breaking scraps of prose drama from Pushkin's pen present another problem). Always the non-prosaic is shown to be somewhere embedded in the narrative, either in a literal phonic rhyme or in a "situation rhyme," and these symmetries serve as the infrastructure of the whole.

Bethea's Bakhtin is best displayed in the segment on Yury Lotman in the 1998 book *Realizing Metaphors*. At stake is dialogism versus structuralism, Bakhtin versus Lotman, even though that antinomy was eased during the final years of Lotman's life. Bakhtin is implicitly appreciated there for his wisdom about novelistic prose (which are also Pushkinian wisdoms: chatter, new ideas, pace and openness of event). But the great dialogist is useful primarily as a counter-balance and friendly other to a critic much closer to Bethea's heart, Yury Lotman himself. Lotman is a great Pushkinist, Bethea argues, precisely because he understands, as Bakhtin was reluctant to do publicly as a philosopher, that transmission procedures can be standardized, collective, mechanistic, apparently authorless, governed by codes of rhythm, rhyme, and honor rather than by the fact (or the illusion) of dialogues or the "honest" unstylized confession. To do commerce with such "pre-made" messages does not suggest impersonal enslavement by a ready-made code, however — quite the contrary. Precisely because a poet is so practiced in seeking his creativity within formal (that is, "unfree") structures is he competent to "wrestle with codes," to forge his individuality against their constraints. Thus, Bethea writes, "Bakhtin appeared less original, less 'himself,' when the topic was Pushkin" rather than, say, Dostoevsky or Tolstoy. Unmediated self-expression intuitively strikes Lotman (and Bethea too) as something inherently unpoetic.

Here too the tasks of poet and critic can be seen to coincide. Pushkin's supremely poetic era tested itself against formal, not Realist-era-ethical, codes. Extraordinary self-discipline is required to handle the hottest, most vulnerable, most vital subject matter in a respectful manner. Thus does Bethea so admire the neoclassical side of Pushkin that resists the Romantic (or Tolstoyan-Realist) confessional mode. "Pushkin doesn't tend to 'open up' the way subsequent generations do,... he *doesn't perceive the need to* — i.e., that need is not a category of cognition. Meaning comes from a different sort of friction."[3] The "different sort of friction" is precisely the life wrestling with the code. And wrestle it must, because for Pushkin, any public or Tolstoy-style invitation to unmediated intimacy would be incompatible with a poet's honor and could only compromise the potency of a poet's word. What applies to the perfect poet applies also to the model code of behavior governing the literary critic. Therefore the structuralist in Lotman had no trouble grasping a poet like Pushkin, who could "fully acknowledge the arbitrariness of a fixed form and yet willingly adopt that form to generate energy and construct a life that is, well, open."[4] Among the essays in the present volume that work with this model (not freedom within structure but freedom precisely because of structure) is Bethea's probing exploration of Dante and Florenskian space, originally appearing in a volume honoring Lotman.

[3] David M. Bethea, *Realizing Metaphors: Alexander Pushkin and the Life of the Poet* (Madison: University of Wisconsin Press, 1998), 38.

[4] Ibid., 131.

The third category of critical approach is on the border between "life" and the monument: the metamorphosis of Pygmalion's statue. Here the moment of revelation, of desire made real, is actually embodied, not in plot (as happened with Marya Gavrilovna and Burmin in "The Blizzard") but in tactile, responsive physical material. As Bethea stresses in his essay on Apuleius, Psyche, Cupid, and metamorphosis in *Eugene Onegin*, this is the magical moment when the muse comes alive. She does so in the zone of "unnatural union" (unexpected intersection). She can console and caress the creator, or, as in Tatiana's case, she can be satisfied with a "knowledge of eros." Here we connect with an important anchor in Bethea's own metaphysics, Pushkin's definition of inspiration. It is deeply neoclassical and, one might also say, "cognitive." Inspiration is not ecstasy felt by the poet (something in that closed economy must have struck Pushkin as obscenely self-focused and out of control — for although Pushkin is erotic beyond our tools to measure it, he is always somehow humorous, outward-looking and thus chaste; this point Bethea emphasizes often). Genuine inspiration is also a category of transmission, perhaps the only foolproof one: the ability of the poet to absorb and then to sustain, through a mastery of form, his own aha! experience, his own burst of new ideas:

"Inspiration is the disposition of the soul to the most lively reception of impressions and consequently to the quick grasp of concepts, thus facilitating their exposition." The poet is a prophet to the extent that he is an educator and a sage.

Bethea's most recent work on cultural transmission has opened a fourth category, a tribute and update of Yury Lotman's "semiosphere." This is his fascinating foray into the Intelligent Design debates, first published in this volume, which bring on board for literary consideration Richard Dawkins's memes, memeplexes, and Bethea's signature term enriching both, "metamemetics". Nabokov's butterflies are the putative cause, of course, but Bethea triumphantly configures the argument so that inspiration — in Pushkin's exalted sense — wins out over any Darwinian concept. Even memetics "cannot do justice to a complex cultural artifact as the latter is presently understood in the scientific literature," Bethea insists. "A religion or a political ideology... creates memes and memeplexes that as a rule do not generate new information, do not spur cognitive discovery. They are learned, repeated, personalized. What they do is compactly replicate tradition as something closed and provide strategies (coping mechanisms) for surviving in a given environment."[5] Here we have it: mere coping mechanisms versus the genuine risk-taking required for true creativity. And we are back to Alexander Pushkin in Boldino, 1830, saving his life at the fountain of art.

[5] See chapter 4 of the present volume, "The Evolution of Evolution: Genes, Memes, Intelligent Design, and Nabokov," 140.

In closing, let me comment on two difficulties of Bethea's ambitious agenda. The first is one of medium. I would add to Bethea's "Bloomian" list another anxiety that I believe is inherent in his critical project, one that will grow more pronounced as the nature of cultural recuperation shifts in the academy. This is the fact that for better or worse, professional recuperators of literary genius must also work with words. Thus the task of the poetic critic differs from the duty of those who recuperate the person or works of a composer, choreographer, dancer, actor, visual artist, architect, photographer, filmmaker — critical fields that have boomed in twenty-first century academic humanities. For those non-print media critics, words are only an approximate and partial means for transmitting their subject matter, which are pitches, rhythms, gestures, volumes, colors, the movement of bodies, harmonies, and melodies through time and space. Even the most poetically gifted commentators in these disciplines will readily acknowledge that the aesthetic experience they are describing cannot be remotely duplicated by mute letters of the alphabet lined up blackly on a white page. For the non-print media critic, there must be some measure of relief in such a realization: since I am not expected to sculpt (or sing, or mime, or dance) my response to this magnificent artwork, put down my pale verbal account of it and go experience the real thing. But for literary critics, whose fate it is to deal with words on words, there is this terrible overlap of substance. Our expressive tools are the same as the poet's. Thus the dialogue we conduct with our subject matter is dangerously intimate, inevitably in competition across a border of shifting voice-zones, tantalizing echoes, even copy-cat rhythms. And it would seem that no verbal borders are more dangerous and delicate to negotiate than the subfield Bethea has created and now furnishes so handsomely: literary mythopoetics. One careless move, one crude touch, and the vectors of the poet's own creativity are distorted or betrayed. Here is anxiety worthy of the name.

In an almost throwaway line at the beginning of his brief entry on "Nabokov and Blok" for Vladimir Alexandrov's *Garland Companion to Vladimir Nabokov* (1995), Bethea betrays his grasp of this fragile complexity. Harold Bloom is brought in and (as usual) severely modified to the point of outright discrediting. Khodasevich and Bunin were acquaintances for Nabokov, Bethea notes, colleagues in emigration, real people and thus manageable — but Blok was a different dimension, distant, to be studied and not talked with, "Blok never existed for Nabokov on the same plane...," which "only underscores how literary and thus complicated this relationship was." Bethea too has written in depth about contemporary poets still alive, "real people and acquaintances" such as Joseph Brodsky, in addition to classics from another age (Khodasevich and Pushkin). The anxieties he confronts are present on different planes, but never absent. Can we ever do the poet justice, can we keep him alive, without leaving the alien trace of our own instruments on his body?

The second difficulty is related to the first but focuses on a different aspect of the critic-midwife's duties. Readers want to receive the real poetic thing — but not only as a closed artifact inducing the shock of the sublime. The work of art must feel like an open, living structure that can stimulate our own creativity. Only in this way can it generate new life. Bethea would insist that poets of genius expect no less of their audiences. But transmission this ambitiously conceived raises a second set of concerns within the master question posed in my opening paragraph. What is this "real thing," in content and form? What does it mean to call it creative fiction? Why do poets so often shape their lives with the same desperate degree of artifice as they shape their poems? What can the poet's biographer learn from these struggles? And finally, why does the obligation to inherit, master, alter, and transmit dearly-won aesthetic form weigh so heavily on a poet like Pushkin, a "man of letters rather than a man of the sword or tsar's confidant," who "had to create a space for himself in Russian history, a space that would be defined not by martial deeds but by words which brought, over time and often against the wishes of the reigning powers, an inner freedom and an inner sophistication to their readers and listeners"?

This reminder of Pushkin's anxieties over cultural transmission and potential audience is a chord also heard in Bethea's own work, most intensely in the pieces he published around the poet's bicentennial. "To start with the obvious," Bethea wrote in a volume from 1999 subtitled *A celebration of Russia's best-loved writer*, "Poetry as we know it is dying." *Realizing Metaphors* opens in the same way: "Poetry as we know it is dying. Literally."[6] [6] *Realizing Metaphors,* At any given time, I suppose, some aspect of the humanities is said to be dying, so the regnant phrase here is "as we know it." Pushkin surely made the same lament during that first Boldino autumn of 1830, and frequently thereafter, as he felt his own aristocratic, poetry-based literary culture give way to the crude vagaries of the market and the cruder machinations of ill-educated rivals and censors. Does David Bethea feel the same way today, ten years later? That is for readers to decide as they sample the rich assortment of insights provided in this volume, but I am provoked to suggest that he would not. Poetry simply embeds itself in new forms and people develop new ways of registering its power.

PART I
Russian Literature: Background, Foreground, Creative Cognition

Chapter 1 The Mythopoetic "Vectors" of Russian Literature[1]

Any national literature is to some significant extent a mirror held up to its people's collective countenance: its myths, aspirations, national triumphs and traumas, current ideologies, historical understanding, linguistic traditions. But it is also more than that—more than a reflection in the glass of what has come before and what is now, even as one glances into it, passing from view. It is, in a real sense, generative of new meaning, and thus capable of shaping that countenance in the future. For the society that takes its literary products seriously, the text of a novel or poem can be a kind of genetic code[2] for predicting, not concrete outcomes or actual progeny, but something no less pregnant with future action: the forms of a culture's historical imagination. The variations seem limitless, and yet how is it we are able to determine any given work of literature is clearly identifiable as Russian? Why could Flaubert's Emma Bovary in some sense not be imagined by the great realist who created Anna Karenina? How is Dostoevsky's

[1] Originally appeared as part 1 of the essay/chapter "Russian Literature," in *Cambridge Companion to Modern Russian Culture*, ed. Nicholas Rzhevsky (Cambridge: Cambridge University Press, 1998), 161–204.

[2] See Chapter 4 in Part 1 of the present volume with its discussion of how genes and "memes" work together to create an individual's and a culture's views of itself.

Marmeladov both alike, but more importantly, unlike Dickens's Micawber? What, in short, can be shown in a mirror that *speaks back*?

Few societies have been more dependent on their literature for overall meaning (social, psychological, political, historical, religious, erotic) than the Russia of the modern period (1800 to the present). For a variety of reasons we will touch upon in the pages to follow, Russians have turned repeatedly to their literature as the principal source of their national identity and cultural mythology. But this relationship to the written word is a two-edged sword. It gives Russian literature both a high seriousness that can be genuinely inspiring and at times an intrusive didacticism that can be annoying to a more pluralistic (or "secular") Western audience. Regardless of one's orientation as reader, however, Russian culture is unthinkable without this literature — and not only the great novels of Tolstoy and Dostoevsky out of which Westerners have for decades constructed their own versions of "Russianness." The purpose of the present study is to acquaint the non-specialist reader with the basic cultural contours necessary to read and understand this literature, including its formative influences and salient themes. Along the way, and where appropriate, I will also discuss how certain important Russian writers and cultural figures creatively engage aspects of contemporary Western thought. The goal here cannot be historical thoroughness or authoritative canon-formation, but rather a reasonably accurate readerly orientation — that is, an attitude toward the subject that takes its cultural values seriously and tries to understand its various verbal traces in their proper context.

Formative influences, salient themes

In recent times, culture has been compared to a kind of "supraconsciousness" hovering over the physical globe in a circumambient cloud. It manipulates on a massive scale the same communicative codes that every human being operates in his/her individual world. Building on discoveries in cell biology, organic chemistry, and brain science, the Russian theorist and literary scholar Yury Lotman has devised the term "semiosphere" to capture this notion of human communication writ large as cultural ecosystem: the place where intracranial brain function (i.e. the relationship between right and left hemispheres), meaning production, and the shapes and symbols we project onto (or extract from) the external world coalesce into our collective organism's psychic drive for growth and discovery. That this site is a metaphor, a product of language and therefore invisible like the atmosphere over the earth, does not make it any less "real" to those constructing meaning out of their interactions with others. In this regard, literature has traditionally been seen as a rich source of communication (i.e. new information) because, potentially, many different codes and "languages" (in the sense of stylistic registers, dialects, idiosyncratic speech patterns, etc.) can coexist and be artfully juxtaposed within its boundaries.

Modern Russian literature, as I have already intimated, has played a dynamic, even crucial role in the larger "ecosystem" of Russian culture. To appreciate this role, let us propose another metaphor—an interior photograph, or what neurosurgeons call a CAT scan, of the Russian literary "brain." This figure of speech is, of course, inexact, in that it registers likeness more than difference (as all metaphors do); and it cannot do justice to subtle changes over time or to the historical specificity of certain phenomena. Still, as a means of isolating global psychic tendencies that become, as it were, imprinted on the larger social organism's memory, it is not without heuristic value. Exceptions to these tendencies exist, to be sure, some of them very significant, but the fact that these exceptions take the tendencies into account (i.e. they thwart them or undermine them but they do not *ignore* them) means that this psychic mapping is not invisible. Why these tendencies and not others have become salient in the Russian context is buried deep in the past, and is as much a question of cultural mythology (Russians' sacred legends about themselves and about their destiny as a people) as of history *per se*. The list could of course be expanded, but the following seem a good place to start:

   (1) Religious sensibility (*dukhovnost'*)
   (2) Maximalism
   (3) Writer as secular saint
   (4) Heterodox literary forms
   (5) Belatedness
   (6) Literature as social conscience
   (7) Problem of personality (*lichnost'*)
   (8) Space-time oppositions (East/West, old/new)
   (9) Eros-cum-national myth

(1) *Religious sensibility.* Perhaps the first and arguably the most important formative influence/psychological trait to come to mind is Russian culture's

pervasive spirituality (*dukhovnost'*) and, correlatively, the written word's traditionally sacred status. Russia (Kievan Rus') was Christianized under Prince Vladimir in the year 988, and from roughly that point until well into the seventeenth and eighteenth centuries, the entire notion of literature as a secular form of pleasure or edification was largely moot. There were saints' lives (*vitae*), sermons, chronicles, and even epics (e.g. *The Igor Tale*), but what is interesting from a modern vantage is that the category of "fiction" (i.e. a self-contained world wholly created through words that is understood by its reader to be artificial, hence "untrue") came late to Russian literature. Indeed, it can be argued that much of the attraction of the great works of Russian literature is due to this tendency of reader reception/perception: Russian "fictions" about the world are more "real" than the real-life context into which they are read and absorbed. Russian writers have long operated under the conviction that they are writing, not one more book, but versions, each in its way sacred, of The Book (Bible). Thus, when some modern Russian writers have taken a militantly materialist, anti-spiritualist approach to reality, the fervidness and single-mindedness of their commitment to new belief systems often suggest a replay of various medieval models of behavior, replete with the latter's thematics of conversion. Likewise, Leo Tolstoy's anti-clericalism and his sharp criticism of Orthodox dogma and ritual are, significantly, not in the name of Voltairean enlightenment and urbane secularism but in that of a *new* religion, which came to be known as "Tolstoyanism."

One of the attributes of this religious sensibility that continues in the shadow life of some of the most influential Russian poems, novels, and dramas is the transposing of medieval forms of sacred writing (especially hagiography) to later secular works. Examples include Ivan Turgenev's "Living Relics," Nikolai Chernyshevsky's *What Is to Be Done?*, Fyodor Dostoevsky's *Idiot* and *The Brothers Karamazov*, Sergei Stepnyak-Kravchinsky's *Andrei Kozhukhov*, Maksim Gorky's *Mother*. What the *vita* requires is that the personal become sanctified, monumentalized, subsumed within the impersonality of holiness, which means—if one considers how much the modern novel in the European and Anglo-American "bourgeois" traditions depends on individual, concrete examples of an open, *developing* biography and history (e.g. the *Bildungsroman*)—that in many instances the Russian novel will be acting against prevailing trends in Western practice. Saintly behavior can be actively submissive (the "meek" model of the martyred brothers Boris and Gleb) or defiantly subversive (the "holy warrior" model of Alexander Nevsky), but what it cannot be is consciously concerned with its own needs as a separate ego with a merely personal mission.

Another important attribute of the literary expression of Russian spirituality is the latter's emphasis on what might be termed, after the pioneering work of the mathematician-priest Pavel Florensky, liminality or "iconic space." The icon, with its physical materials (painting on wood), its other-worldly, two-dimensional figures, and its notion of divine authorship (the icon painter is merely the instrument of the higher power), is not perceived by the viewer as a representation of holiness, but as holiness itself: when the penitent individual kisses the icon, he or she as it were steps *through* its frame from the realm of the profane to the realm of the holy. There is no middle ground or expandable space *en route* to this miraculous transformation, just as the icon itself cannot be understood in Western terms of mediation (i.e. the three-dimensional figures that, increasingly, as a result of the Renaissance, stood in for humanity in representational paintings). One could argue that when a writer such as Dostoevsky describes heroes and situations — Myshkin before the picture of Nastasya Filippovna and the Holbein painting of Christ; Alyosha Karamazov recalling his half-crazed mother in the context of an icon of the Virgin — that are constructed around the psychological dynamics of liminality, we are in the presence of this same iconic space: the space of religious conversion (or, in its demonic opposite, the space wherein all faith is lost).

Likewise, the reason the *iurodivyi* (holy fool, fool-in-Christ) is such a potent figure in Russian literature, from Alexander Pushkin's character who says to the tsar what no one else dares (*Boris Godunov*) to Yury Olesha's Ivan Babichev who tells campy versions of Gospel parables to the drunks and outcasts of Soviet society (*Envy*), is because he captures in one person, with great economy and expressive force, this principle of iconic liminality. He voluntarily humiliates himself, thus re-traversing Christ's path, in order to, as it were, rub society's nose in its own pride and exclusionary logic (ostracizing the "pure" from the "impure"). By plunging into the midst of "polite society" naked or with the carcass of a dog strapped to one's waist, the *iurodivyi* forces the issue of his own degradation and marginalization.[3] And the reader must make a choice: is this simply a fool or a fool whose antics reveal the workings of divine wisdom? Do I judge and join the ranks of the modern Pharisees or do I imitate Christ and celebrate the carnival logic of role-reversal, laughter, and folly?

3   See Harriet Murav, *Holy Foolishness: Dostoevsky's Novels and the Politics of Cultural Critique* (Stanford: Stanford University Press, 1992).

(2) *Maximalism*. Russian spirituality has a powerful maximalist streak, a fact which should not seem surprising in light of the tragic character of Russian history. "There are," as the philosopher Nikolai Berdyaev once wrote in *The Russian Idea*, "two dominant myths which can become dynamic in the life of a people — the myth about origins and the myth about the end. For Russians it has been the second myth, the eschatological one, that has dominated."[4] Likewise, some of the best known works in modern Russian literature, works like Pushkin's *Bronze Horseman*, Nikolai Gogol's *Dead Souls*, Dostoevsky's *The Devils*, Gorky's *Mother*, Andrei Bely's *Petersburg*, Alexander Blok's *The Twelve*, Evgeny Zamyatin's *We*, Andrei Platonov's *Chevengur*, Mikhail Bulgakov's *The Master and Margarita*, and Boris Pasternak's *Doctor Zhivago*, have possessed a "deep structure" of biblical/apocalyptic or utopian myth. Meaning is sought in a dramatic, usually violent, "right-angled" resolution: either God the Author, standing outside/beyond, decides to put a flaming end (*ekpyrosis*) to his story (human history), or else mankind, realizing that it is the sole author (God is dead) and that perfectibility on earth is possible, devises its own ideal polis (a secular City of God) as a conclusion to history's plot.[5] In either case, whether meaning comes from without or from within, an equals sign is placed between "revelation" (the final truth) and "revolution" (violent social/political upheaval). Indeed, not only charismatic popular leaders (Stenka Razin, Emelyan Pugachev), whose rebellions were inevitably portrayed as apocalyptic scourges striking at the godless state with its "new" religion, but Peter the Great himself, perhaps the most famous of all tsars, was viewed among some segments of the populace (e.g. the Old Believers) as the Antichrist and among others (e.g. Pushkin) as an arch-revolutionary.

But it is not only historical conditions that have forced on Russians this maximalist mentality. One can argue that the very structure of their religious imagination has in a way guaranteed certain outcomes. For example, Russian holy men and religious thinkers have traditionally shown great impatience with any axiologically neutral or "middle ground" — from the Purgatory of the Catholic Church, where one can gradually (cf. the notion of "progress") atone for one's sins *en route* to Paradise, to the notion of "middle class values," where one can see to one's individual well-being even as those less fortunate are excluded or allowed to become invisible. Likewise, it has been traditional for Russians to evince a profound skepticism for the rhythms of everyday life (*byt*): it seems this quotidian space/time can only, with great difficulty, "mean." Furthermore, as Lotman

---

4   Nikolai Berdiaev, *Russkaia ideia* (Paris: YMCA, 1946), p. 35

5   David M. Bethea, *The Shape of the Apocalypse in Modern Russian Fiction* (Princeton: Princeton University Press, 1989), 3–61.

and others have shown, Russians, and perhaps Slavs in general, have felt that such compromising notions as "negotiation" and "agreement" (*dogovor*) are the province of the devil, whereas in the Western tradition of Roman law and the Catholic church such concepts were more or less unmarked: i.e. one could "arrange" one's position (or one's loved ones') in the other world by doing good deeds, making donations, etc. in this one. But as in Florensky's iconic space, where any believer can instantaneously step through the frame from the profane to the holy, this concept of agreement, or "giving with strings attached," has often proved anathema to the "all or nothing" Russian religious mind. It is by no means strange in this context, therefore, that Russian culture has produced a number of modern thinkers, most notably Vladimir Solovyov and Nikolai Fyodorov, whose ambitious visions for the realized transfiguration of humanity are virtually unimaginable in the West. Solovyov, for instance, made the case for a theocratic marriage of Western and Eastern Christian churches, while Fyodorov assayed nothing less than the actual biological (as in molecule by molecule!) resurrection of our ancestors. Moreover, these and other philosophers (including the already mentioned Florensky) exerted considerable influence on modern writers: their ideas surface in modified form in the works of Gorky, Fyodor Sologub, Blok, Bely, Vladimir Mayakovsky, Bulgakov, Platonov, Nikolai Ognyov, Nikolai Zabolotsky, Pasternak, etc.[6]

(3) *Writer as secular saint*. Because Russian society was slow to adopt the worldly ways of the West and because the written word was carefully scrutinized and censored by church and state (its "sacred" status thereby implicitly recognized and controlled), the writer in general and the poet in particular became a secular saint and, very often, a martyr (or suffering "holy fool").[7] The Ur-text in this regard was Pushkin's 1826 poem "The Prophet" ("Prorok"), whose speaker has his formerly sinful tongue ripped out by a six-winged Seraph (the source is Isaiah) and whose words are henceforth meant to "burn the hearts of people" with their message. The list of "martyred" writers is very long and the role of "suffering for the faith" must be acknowledged as one of the truly defining traits of the Russian literary imagination: Vasily Trediakovsky, Alexander Radishchev, Pushkin, Mikhail Lermontov, Gogol, Chernyshevsky, Dostoevsky, Blok, Velimir Khlebnikov, Nikolai Kliuev, Evgeny Zamyatin, Isaak Babel, Osip Mandelstam, Anna Akhmatova, Marina Tsvetaeva, Bulgakov, Pasternak, Alexander Solzhenitsyn, Varlam Shalamov, Andrei Sinyavsky, Joseph Brodsky. Even famous suicides — Alexander Radishchev, Sergei Esenin,

---

6   See Irene Masing-Delic, *Abolishing Death: A Salvation Myth of Russian Twentieth-Century Literature* (Stanford: Stanford, 1992).

7   Marcia Morris, *Saints and Revolutionaries: The Ascetic Hero in Russian Literature* (Albany: State University of New York Press, 1993).

Mayakovsky, Tsvetaeva — did not "simply" kill themselves but were written into this larger martyrology (i.e. they were "killed" by society/the state). The Russian writer became a lightning rod (or scourge) in a society that was anything but "civil" and in a faceless, sprawling bureaucratic state (tsarist, then Soviet) that had little respect for individual rights and the rule of law.

How did this martyrology work, what were its psychic mechanisms? In the poet Vladislav Khodasevich's phrase (borrowed again from Pushkin), Russian society and its writers entered into a kind of fatal contract, or "bloody repast" (*krovavaia pishcha*). It was a contract with little of the spirit of compromise about it. The poet/martyr was persecuted and eventually killed (like Christ) because of his service to a higher ideal (Russian culture, the Russian poetic word), while society played the role of Pontius Pilate or the Roman soldiers at the foot of the cross. The persecutors could not, according to this logic, act otherwise. By bringing the sainted figure to his death they were fulfilling a larger dispensation: giving the Christ-figure the chance *to redeem them* through his sacrifice. Even those who survived persecution (Akhmatova, Pasternak) or those who emerged alive from the hell of the camps (Solzhenitsyn, Shalamov) did so with the martyr's aureole intact and the myth of their semi-religious witness confirmed. Hence one of the more fascinating questions of Russian literary studies is how poets have seemed to fashion their own "fated" ends (Pushkin's is again the archetypal example) out of this contract with their wayward, needful flock. Rather than meekly accepting God's will, as in the famous *vita* of the murdered brothers (and first "passion sufferers") Boris and Gleb, the Russian poet has tended to model his life on that of the indomitable and "plain-speaking" Archpriest Avvakum, who was burned alive with his sectarian followers in 1682 for not accepting the official faith of the church and state.

(4) *Heterodox literary forms*. Russian writers have developed a reputation in the West for their eccentric understanding of literary form. Henry James, for example, in a famous phrase that captured well his and other contemporaries' puzzlement at the extravagant shape of Russian novels, called the latter (he was discussing Tolstoy's *War and Peace*), "loose baggy monsters." However, the issue goes deeper than James and his tradition could have imagined. From at least the time of Gavrila Derzhavin, Nikolai Karamzin, and Pushkin (late eighteenth, early nineteenth centuries) right up until the recent work of Solzhenitsyn and Sinyavsky, Russian literature has produced major exemplars that both take into account Western genre systems and boldly use those same systems against themselves in order

to create something distinctly Russian. Here we must keep in mind two factors: (a) the Russians' need not merely to copy/imitate Western forms but to make something their own, and (b) the fact that Western trends (schools of thought, current "-isms," etc.) were not, beginning with the modern period, imported and assimilated in strict chronological sequence, but often mixed together in a heady, asynchronous brew (see no. 5 below). Thus, Russian writers were intensely aware of the fact of their belatedness and of their need to outstrip (or remake in their own image) existing models in order to arrive as equals at the "feast" of European culture. In most cases their frustration of genre expectations could not be called naive. The list of great works of Russian literature that are also generic "misfits" is astonishing, in some sense a logical extension of that same maximalism ("doing the impossible" and "undoing the expected") observable in the national identity, with its spiritual strivings: Derzhavin's jocular odes ("Felitsa"), Karamzin's belletristically shaped history (*History of the Russian State*), Pushkin's novel-in-verse (*Eugene Onegin*), Gogol's novel-*poema* (epic poem) (*Dead Souls*), Chernyshevky's anti-novelistic novel (*What Is to Be Done?*), Dostoevsky's novel-memoir (*Notes from the Dead House*), Tolstoy's monstrous historical novel (*War and Peace*), Pasternak's novel-plus-poetic-cycle (*Doctor Zhivago*), Solzhenitsyn's "experiment in literary investigation" (*The Gulag Archipelago*). Also adding to this hybridization is the fact that several of Russia's most celebrated creative writers have either tried their hands at professional historiography (Karamzin, Pushkin) or openly competed with academic historians in their attempts (neither wholly fictional nor non-fictional) to reconstruct the past (Tolstoy).

(5) *Belatedness*. Russian writers, thinkers, and cultural figures have long grappled with their country's belated status *vis-à-vis* the West. Due to a variety of factors, no doubt the most important being the Mongol invasion and occupation of the Russian lands from the thirteenth through the fifteenth centuries, Russia did not benefit directly from the two most seminal movements of modern humanistic thought: the Renaissance and the Reformation. Over and over again in later centuries Russians were faced with the dilemma of how to "catch up" with Europe. Some saw Russia as hopelessly backward and doomed to outsidership (Pyotr Chaadaev), others saw their country's anomalous position as an opportunity to avoid Europe's mistakes (Alexander Herzen), and still others turned this very lack into nothing less than a salvational mission, a scenario in which Russia "saved" Europe from barbarism in order that Europe could now learn from this supreme gesture

of Christian love and sacrifice (Dostoevsky). Whatever the case, it is clear that Russian writers could not ignore this time-lag: it had to be dealt with and in some way "overcome." Virtually all the major movements in Russian thought and culture of the nineteenth century, beginning with the debates between the Slavophiles and Westernizers (late 1830s-1840s), addressed this problem of belatedness, placing either a plus or a minus sign over the "other" values and institutions that had been forcibly foregone or those that were "ours" and indisputably native. When Western movements, such as classicism, romanticism, realism, symbolism, did come to Russia, it was often with the sense that there was something profoundly artificial about their application to the Russian context (an autocratic/ bureaucratic state with a tiny oppositional intelligentsia surrounded by a huge and illiterate peasant mass). One of the problems of belatedness was that Russians often felt they were "playing" at being Westerners and that this was sinful: e.g., the boyars whom Peter tried to force to wear Western dress thwarted the emperor by wearing hair-shirts underneath the new fashions.

(6) *Literature as social conscience.* As Nadezhda Mandelstam once wrote about the role of poetry in Russian culture, "People can be killed for poetry here [in Russia] — a sign of unparalleled respect — because they are still capable of living by it."[8] She was of course speaking not only about poetry (and literature) in general, but also about the work of her husband, Osip Mandelstam, one of the great poets of the twentieth century, who died in a Stalinist labor camp because his writing was judged to be a crime against the state (and more crucially an affront to its leader). The point is that, ironically, the state has shown — until very recently — "unparalleled respect" through its relentless persecutions of its writers because its attempts to silence them has only further emphasized the roar of independent protest in their written words. And because the state has not only not protected the individual, but made a mockery of any notion of basic human rights, it has traditionally been literature's job to serve as social conscience: advocate for the downtrodden (peasant, "little man" *chinovnik*/bureaucrat, factory worker, women and children) and critic of the despotic tsarist regime, with its instruments of power (censorship, secret police, court system, labor camps). It is this tendency to give voice to concerns, however partially muffled by censorship and "Aesopian" encodings and circumlocutions, that were incapable of being uttered through other social institutions that has given Russian literature its strong didacticism and sense of moral rectitude. It is arguable that this same urge to use "literature" (broadly defined) in

8 Nadezhda Mandelstam, *Hope Abandoned*, trans. Max Hayward (New York: Atheneum, 1974), 11.

the service of social change has always been present in Russian culture, but its rise in modern times is usually associated with the name of the great *raznochinets* critic Vissarion Belinsky and his literary journalism of the 1830s and 1840s. The questioning titles of works by various leading practitioners of the "Belinskian line" speak forcefully of this notion of literature as conscientious opposition to the status quo: Alexander Herzen's novel *Who Is to Blame?* (1847), Nikolai Dobroliubov's essays "What Is Oblomovism?" (1859) and "When Will the Real Day Come?" (1860), Nikolai Chernyshevky's novel *What Is to Be Done?* (1863).

(7) *Problem of personality (lichnost')*. Closely related to Russian literature's function as social conscience (no. 6) is the problem of *lichnost'* (personality, personhood). If the tradition of Belinsky and the civic critics relentlessly exposed the negative sides of Russian existence (what the state had denied its citizens in terms of basic dignity and self-respect), then the concern on the part of many other writers was to find a positive content—expressed in the search for a "positive hero" (*polozhitel'nyi geroi*)—for *lichnost'*.[9] Russian literature of the nineteenth and twentieth centuries is heavily populated by personality "types": the "superfluous man" (*lishnii chelovek*) who is gifted and often "noble" (in both senses) but has no historically viable arena for action and thus repeatedly suffers a loss of will (Alexander Griboedov's Chatsky, Turgenev's Rudin, Ivan Goncharov's Oblomov); the "new man" of the 1860s (and then of the Soviet period), who is precise, unsentimental, scientific, materialist, but who inevitably must wait for society to "catch up" to him (Turgenev's Bazarov, Chernyshevsky's Rakhmetov, Gorky's Pavel Vlasov); and the "strong woman" who is often made to represent Russia's hidden potential and who possesses the courage and resolute idealism that the weaker male characters lack (Pushkin's Tatiana Larina, Goncharov's Olga Ilyinskaya, Fyodor Gladkov's Dasha Chumalova, Bulgakov's Margarita). Again, in a way that suggests a religious/"maximalist" as opposed to secular/"skeptical" approach to the written word, the Russian reading public has often made a direct, prescriptive link between the portrayal of charismatic activity in fiction and the rules for behavior in phenomenal reality outside the text. As is the case with Florensky's iconic space, the word does not stand in, metaphorically, for the person, but is the person, his most real, sacred trace.

(8) *Space-time oppositions (East/West, old/new)*. From the time of its earliest formation Russia has faced the problem of how to view itself in the "history of nations" (e.g. which version of Christianity, Eastern or Western, should it

[9] See Rufus Matthewson, *The Positive Hero in Russian Literature* (Stanford: Stanford University Press, 1973).

choose for itself?). Many of the turning points in its history and many (if not most) of its cultural monuments have centered on the issue of whether this increasingly vast and diverse country and its people are "Western," "Eastern," or some significant, new combination of the two. But what has not been, until recently, sufficiently commented upon is how another opposition, the temporal old/new, is simultaneously embedded in the spatial East/West. In other words, these oppositions, which are necessary for constructing meaning, can in certain highly charged situations be viewed as extensions of each other. Their respective values (plus/minus, good/bad, we/they) can change depending on the circumstances, but that they are implicated in each other in the Russian historical imagination seems by now beyond doubt.

To mention a few prominent examples: Hilarion, in his early "Sermon on Law and Grace" (c. 1037–50), likens the "new" faith of the Russians to the enfranchised bride Sarah (hence to New Testament grace) but the "old" faith of Byzantium to the handmaiden Hagar (hence to Old Testament law). Several centuries later, the Archpriest Avvakum would reverse these values during the Great Schism (*raskol*) of the 1660s—i.e., the "new" Nikonian reforms imposed by the church/state were now perceived as the province of the Antichrist and a betrayal of the Old Belief. Likewise, Moscow's role as Third (and last) Rome, with its tsar as *basileus* (the emperor who was simultaneously spiritual and secular leader of the Christian realm), became clear when Constantinople (the "Second Rome") fell to the Ottoman Turks in 1453. And Peter the Great's reforms, including his spelling with a foreign alphabet, his passion for Western architecture, and his new calendar, galvanized the Old Believer sectarians precisely because these innovations conflated and made interchangeable the unholy categories of new/Western: they demonstrated that this tsar could not be the true *basileus* and so had to be an impostor, which is to say, the Antichrist. In recent centuries these binaries have become especially marked in Russia's myth-saturated geography: the "old," more native city of Moscow versus the "new," more Western city of St. Petersburg. Generally speaking, Russian cultural and political figures, and writers *a fortiori*, tended to face the problematic present by either looking to a positive future ideal (a modern urban or technological utopia emerging out of new/Western ideas) or to a positive past ideal (an archaic village utopia—the peasant *mir/obshchina*—emerging out of old/native ideas).

(9) *Eros-cum-national myth*. The pagan roots of Russian/Slavic culture were not forgotten with the coming of Christianity. Indeed, as the scholar Boris

Uspensky has indicated, those roots were often "remembered" *through inversion* in the forms of the adopting mythology: the pre-Christian gods became the devils of the Russian Christian world (e.g. Volos/Veles-à-*volosatik* or "wood goblin"). In this respect, one of the inevitable developments in the mythologization of Russian time and space by its writers and thinkers is that the pagan concept of "Mother Earth" (*mat' syra zemlia*) and the Christian concept of "Holy Russia" (*Sviataia Rus'*: the term was first used in the sixteenth century by Prince Andrei Kurbsky in his correspondence with Ivan IV) were telescoped—again, made extensions of each other. As a result, perhaps the greatest of all modern Russian literary plots, expressed in a stunning variety of works over the past two centuries, involves the rescuing/redeeming of a heroine, who represents the country's vast potential, by a Christ-like paladin. The logic of the fairy tale and the logic of the Christian hierogamy (the marriage of the Lamb and the Bride in Revelation) join hands. This indicates that the national Russian myth has, at its core, become profoundly eroticized and at the same time strangely sublimated/abstracted: personal love cannot have meaning outside this higher calling. Pushkin's Tatiana, Dostoevsky's Nastasya Filippovna, Tolstoy's Anna Karenina, Solovyov's Sophia, Blok's Beautiful Lady/Stranger, Bulgakov's Margarita, Pasternak's Lara —all these heroines, and more, have their fates linked with Russian history (broadly speaking), primarily in its tragic incarnation. Many of them die for their love. In a sense their lives and loves cannot have a happy ending until the right "Prince Charming" appears in a historical context that is ready for him—and this, given the belatedness of Russian culture, is almost never. Even the great women poets, Tsvetaeva and Akhmatova, participate as suffering wives, mothers, and lovers in the tragedy that is Russian historical time: Tsvetaeva's roles as Amazonian freedom fighter (it is she who must rescue the swain) and as archetypal heroine trapped in male role-playing (Ophelia, Gertrude, Phaedra); Akhmatova's realized metaphor of Suffering Mother in *Requiem* (her first husband the poet Nikolai Gumilev executed by firing squad, her close friend Mandelstam dead in a Stalinist camp, her own son Lev also serving time in prison). In sum, the erotic theme in Russian literature has traditionally been played for infinitely more than the stakes of bourgeois love and family happiness. If the heroine is portrayed as some combination of heavenly mother and earth-bound demiurge — e.g. the Stranger is both streetwalker and other-worldly enchantress, Margarita is both the spirit of hope/forgiveness and a witch who flies naked, Lara is both a Mary Magdalene figure and an image of Russia waiting to be reborn—then the hero is also just as likely to appear as Christ-like paradox: the leader of marauding Red Guard disciples as androgynous apparition (*The Twelve*), the poet-doctor Zhivago as weak-willed Red Cross Knight, the Master as great artist who is also hopelessly paranoid and on the verge of insanity.

With some notable exceptions (e.g. Pushkin), therefore, Russian literature of the modern period is plagued with its own special brand of cultivated repression or "Victorianism." Sex for its own sake, as a source of bodily pleasure, or sex merely for the sake of procreation, to produce children, can be equally "insulting" to the quixotic Russian truth-seeker. By the same token, the number of influential writers and thinkers (Solovyov, Fyodorov, Blok, Bely, Mayakovsky, etc.) who felt the act of copulation to be essentially humiliating and/or the prospect of biological children frightening is striking. The rare exception of someone such as the philosopher Vasily Rozanov, whose championing of sex and family life in their everyday, non-hieratic guises was scandalous for its time, only proves the general rule. The fear was not so much sin, as in the Catholic and Protestant West, but cosmic indifference, meaninglessness. Perhaps the strongest condemnation of the "demonic" source of erotic pleasure in all Russian literature belongs to Tolstoy in his novella *Kreutzer Sonata*, who in typical maximalist fashion would prefer celibacy, and hence the end of the human race itself, to "sex without meaning."

Postscript

Obviously, over the last two decades, with the fall of the Soviet Union, the coming (and partial going under Putin) of *glasnost'*, and the shift among large segments of the reading (and viewing) public toward popular culture and mass-media and away from the high culture that served as the conscience of the intelligentsia, the "vectors" I have outlined above no longer operate with the same potency they did for much of the nineteenth and twentieth centuries. To be sure, they are still there, in the half-light of TV shows, movies, contemporary art and music, journalism, but more often than not their mythopoetic valences are the object of parody and postmodern play. Even so, they remain useful in defining "classical" Russian literature, and should that literature ever re-emerge in the future in some "post-postmodern" guise, where historical circumstances demand a different sort of re-engagement with the cultural roots of prior centuries, they will doubtless play their part.

Chapter 2 — Mythopoesis Writ Large: The Apocalyptic Plot in Russian Literature[1]

> As far as I know, this [statue of Lenin in front of the Finland Station] is the only monument to a man on an armored car that exists in the world. In this respect alone, it is a symbol of a new society. The old society used to be represented by men on horseback.
>
> —Joseph Brodsky, "A Guide to a Renamed City"

Myth

Humankind has always lived in time, but it has not always lived in history. Archaeologists and anthropologists provide countless examples of societies, "ancient" in time or "primitive" in development, where time was experienced mythically rather than historically, where only those details of life that fit into and recapitulated the master plot of a sacred tale were

[1] Originally appeared as "Introduction: Myth, History, Plot, Steed" in *The Shape of Apocalypse in Modern Russian Fiction* (Princeton: Princeton University Press, 1989), 3–61.

worthy of remembrance.² The British social anthropologist Bronislaw Malinowski defined myth as

> ...not merely a story but a reality lived. It is not of the nature of fiction, such as we read today in a novel, but it is a living reality; believed to have once happened in primaeval times, and continuing ever since to influence the world and human destinies... Myth is to the savage, what, to a fully believing Christian, is the Biblical story of the Creation, of the Fall, of the Redemption by Christ's sacrifice on the Cross. As our sacred story lives in our ritual, in our morality, as it governs our faith and controls our conduct, even so does his myth for the savage.³

The phrases most operative in this passage are "a reality lived," "believed to have happened once in primaeval times," and "continuing ever since to influence the world and human destinies." "History," on the contrary, is perceived as the very opposite of myth—the desacralization of the past, the recording of events as they actually happened, without reference to some prefiguring master plot. What characterizes the "archaic" as opposed to the "modern" human being, according to Mircea Eliade, is that the former is able, through ritual, to return periodically "to the mythical time of the beginning of things" and thereby to abolish "concrete, historical time," whereas the latter, having been cut off from this Great Time through the gradual process of desacralization and secularization, must "make himself, within history."⁴ To cite just one example of how ritual served (and serves) as a shield against duration and chaos, the Babylonian New Year festival (*akitu*) is based on the story of an underwater "carnival" king (Tiamat) who destroys the status quo, humiliates the "real" sovereign (Marduk), and casts the participants back into a pre-time of deluge and darkness; virtually at the same time, and at the dawn of the new year, order is restored, chaos is reconfigured through the act of creation, and a sacred union (hierogamy), symbolizing the rebirth of the human being and the world, is celebrated. Here the parallels with the Christian sacrament of baptism (the ritual death of the old man followed by a new birth), which in earlier times took place on Easter and New Year's Day, are obvious.⁵

In the venerable confrontation between history and myth the Judaeo-Christian tradition has often been seen as a turning point. Put simply, the Old Testament prophets explained the vagaries of fate and the periodic debacles of the chosen people, the "remnant of Israel" (Zephaniah 3:13),

---

2   One of the best-studied examples of an older, indigenous culture that has taken on the structural models of Christian apocalyptic (imported via missionaries) is the Melanesian Cargo cult. See Peter Lawrence, *Road Belong Cargo: A Study of the Cargo Movement in the Southern Madang District, New Guinea* (Manchester: Manchester University Press, 1964), and Peter Worsley, *The Trumpet Shall Sound: A Study of 'Cargo' Cults in Melanasia* (London: MacGibbon & Kee, 1957).

3   Bronislaw Malinowski, *Magic, Science, and Religion* (New York: Doubleday, 1954), 100.

4   Mircea Eliade, *The Myth of the Eternal Return, or Cosmos*

not by relating these events to a continually recaptured great past but by re-placing them within a plot of *things to come*, as trials to be borne in order to make the Israelites worthy of their status and mission. "They [the prophets] insisted," writes Amos Funkenstein, "that God's immense, universal powers were manifested by the very plight of the chosen people: only God could employ the mightiest empires as 'rods of wrath' to purge Israel, while these empires were unaware of their role in the divine plan, of their objective role in history (Isaiah 10:5–7)."[6] One can immediately see the difference between this view of time and that, say, expressed implicitly in Hesiod's myth of declining world ages (Golden, Silver, Copper, Age of Heroes, Iron) and explicitly in Plato's doctrine of reciprocating cosmic cycles (the *Politicus*), where panplanetary conjunctions are linked with various terrestrial adversities to make a statement about the human being's continuous rise and fall as a moral being.[7] With the Judaeo-Christian tradition, humanity had "entered" history (not of course yet history in the modern, secular sense) and that history had a straightforward movement and teleological coloring. The human being had also, as we learn in Genesis, *fallen* from privileged status in the Garden of Eden (the Judaeo-Christian "Great Time") *into* profane time and an imperfect world, and there was no way back.

The figure whose interpretation of the biblical plot from a Christian standpoint was most influential for the Western Roman Catholic tradition was St. Augustine (A.D. 354–435). Through his doctrine of the three stages of salvation (the *ante legem* before Moses, the *sub lege* during and after him, and the culminating — for this world — *sub gratia* initiated by Christ) and through his periodization of history into Six World Ages (with the Seventh located *outside* of time), he consolidated the "historiosophy" of the prophets and gave it a christocentric reading that was to dominate for centuries.[8] Pivotal to this reading was the conviction, expressed in *The City of God*, that the Christ example was unique, unrepeatable, and end-determined. As Funkenstein explains further,

> It is very clear that the apocalyptic tradition does not exclude eternal return, at times even alludes to it under the influence, perhaps, of Iranian tradition. Nor indeed does the Bible exclude eternal return — it simply is outside the horizon of biblical imageries. The *uniqueness* of history, or at least of its central event, became thematic only in the Christian horizon. Against Origen's theory of world succession, Saint

and History, trans. William R. Trask (Princeton: Princeton University Press, 1954), ix. Cf. in this regard Engels' remark in a letter to Ernst Bloch that "We *make our history ourselves*" (my emphasis; cited in Raymond Williams, *Marxism and Literature* [Oxford: Oxford University Press, 1977], 85).

5   Eliade, *Myth of Eternal Return*, 55–59.

6   Amos Funkenstein, "A Schedule for the End of the World: The Origins and Persistence of the Apocalyptic Mentality," in *Visions of Apocalypse: End or Rebirth?*, ed. Saul Friedlander et al. (New York: Holmes and Meier, 1985), 46.

7   Harald A.T. Reiche, "The Archaic Heritage: Myths of Decline

Augustine insisted that Christ came only *once* for all times. The difference is rather that while the apocalyptic writer takes his proof from Scripture and history, the Greek philosopher relies on astronomical-cosmological speculations.[9]

So with the Judaeo-Christian model the Great Time of the past (the Garden of Eden) was cast into the future (the New Jerusalem), and the steady organ bass of apocalyptic thinking came gradually to drown out the Greek music of the spheres.[10] Ironically, the figure of the circle, distinct from that of the repeating cycle, was not eliminated entirely, since the New Jerusalem not only replaced but was a return to the lost garden as a reward for trials suffered in the name of the faith, the shape of history becoming, in Karl Löwith's apt formulation, "one great detour to reach in the end the beginning."[11]

But what is meant precisely by the term "apocalyptic thinking" and how does it relate to the "bookish," "scribal" nature of the revealed message? There are so many apocalypses and so many non-biblical myths of the End that this is no easy question to answer. In an effort to locate certain finite transhistorical categories, such scholars of myth as Franz Cumont and Eliade have been apt to cast their narratives all the way back to ancient Iranian legends about an end of the world by fire, which then, presumably, migrated westward—the *ekpyrosis* that occupies a central position in the religious systems of Stoicism, the Sibylline Oracles, and Judaeo-Christian literature.[12] Biblical scholars, however, seem to be more restrained in their application of terminology; they draw a sharp line between "eschatology," or knowledge of the end (*eskhaton*), which any culture may announce it possesses, and "apocalypticism," or the "distinctive form of teaching about history and its approaching End" found in the Judaeo-Christian tradition.[13] It may clarify matters, therefore, to view apocalypticism as "a species of the genus eschatology," with the implication that there is "an important difference between a general consciousness of living in the last age of history and a conviction that the last age itself is about to end, between a

and End in Antiquity," in *Visions of Apocalypse: End or Rebirth?*, ed. Saul Friedlander et al. (New York: Holmes and Meier, 1985), 27–29.

8   Marjorie Reeves, "The development of apocalyptic thought: medieval attitudes," in *The Apocalypse in English Renaissance Thought and Literature*, ed. C.A. Patrideas and Joseph Wittreich (Ithaca: Cornell University Press, 1984), 41.

9   Funkenstein, "A Schedule," 50; see also Jaroslav Pelikan, *Jesus Through the Centuries*

(New Haven: Yale University Press, 1985), 21–33.

10   The ancient Greek interest in astrological signs and configurations continued in the Christian tradition well into the Middle Ages and is prominent in such writers as Dante.

11   Karl Löwith, *Meaning in History: The Theological Implications of the Philosophy of History* (Chicago: University of Chicago Press, 1949), 183.

12   Franz Cumont, "La fin du monde selon les mages occidentaux," *Revue de l'Histoire des Religions* (Paris) (January-June 1931): 29–96; cited Eliade, *Myth of Eternal Return*, 124.

13   Bernard McGinn, "Early Apocalypticism: the ongoing debate," in *The Apocalypse in English Renaissance Thought and Literature*, ed. C.A. Patrides and Joseph Wittreich (Ithaca: Cornell University Press, 1984), 6. Cf. also "Apocalypticism in its Jewish origins is distinguishable from two related terms common in biblical theology and the history of religions: *eschatology* and *prophecy*. Apocalypticism is a

belief in the reality of the Antichrist and the certainty of his proximity (or at least of the date of his coming), between viewing the events of one's own time in the light of the End of history and seeing them as the last events themselves."[14] In this regard, the "wholesale invasion of Persian religious ideas into post-exilic Judaism as the determining factor in the rise of apocalypticism are now generally discounted," having been supplanted by more plausible "gradualist" theories about the interaction of Canaanite mythology and Near Eastern Wisdom traditions with indigenous Judaism (or Judaisms) as it existed in the Hellenistic world.[15] Thus the "genre" of the apocalypse, according to those who have examined it most closely, is now believed to have arisen in the third and second centuries B.C. under the impulse of a Jewish nationalism, which was itself a natural outgrowth of, rather than a radical departure from, the "proto-apocalyptic" phases associated with the Canaanite and Wisdom antecedents.

The Revelation of John, or the Apocalypse, as it is known by its Greek name, is only one of a number of extant apocalyptic texts, some from the Intertestamental period and entirely Jewish in origin (I Enoch, Daniel), others from Christianity's first century (the synoptic Gospels, I and II Thessalonians), and others still from the later Patristic tradition (Shepherd of Hermas, Testament of the Lord, Apocalypse of Peter, Vision of Paul). Still, the Apocalypse of John, which is now generally thought to have been written c. 90–95 A.D., has become the most famous (or notorious) of all apocalypses, the one most laymen have in mind when they speak of *the* Apocalypse. And it in turn has become the text that has most palpably influenced our Western views of history as a plot with: (1) a beginning by divine fiat (the creation), (2) a tale of early catastrophe (the fall of Adam and Eve), (3) a later privileged moment of crisis (the incarnation, crucifixion, and resurrection), and (4) a final crescendo with awesome dénouement (the *Parousia*, or Second Coming, of Christ, followed by the replacement of the old world by a "new heaven and new earth").[16] Narratologically speaking, the Apocalypse, which both comes *at the end* of the Bible and tells *of the*

species of the genus eschatology, that it, it is a particular kind of belief about the last things—the End of history and what lies beyond it. Scriptural scholars have used the term *apocalyptic eschatology* to distinguish the special teachings of the prophets. (Apocalyptic eschatology may be seen as equivalent to the frequently used term *Apocalyptic*, formed in imitation of the German *Apocalyptik*.) Valuable as the distinction may be in the realm of biblical studies, the picture will obviously become blurred in later Christian history when elements of both forms of eschatology will frequently be mingled" (Bernard McGinn, *Visions of the End: Apocalyptic Traditions in the Middle Ages* [New York: Columbia University Press, 1979], 3–4).

14 McGinn, *Visions of the End*, 3–4.
15 McGinn, "Early Apocalypticism," 14.
16 M.H. Abrams, "Apocalypse: theme and variations," *The Apocalypse in English Renaissance Thought and Literature*, ed. C.A. Patridea and Joseph Wittreich (Ithaca: Cornell University Press, 1984), 343–44.

end of human history, allows that history to have a coherent and meaningful *beginning* and *middle* because it provides a fitting conclusion.[17] Hence, while some scholars still argue that apocalypticism as a balance of myth, method, and way of life existed only for about two hundred years (or until the early Christians grew tired of "standing on tiptoes")[18] in the shadow of disconfirmation), most will agree with Funkenstein that "the fascination with historical time and its structure was the most important contribution of the apocalyptic mentality to the Western sense of history."[19] Precisely how the Johannine conclusion, with its elaborate figures and haunting codes, dovetails with the real events of contemporary history has been a source of endless debate, and no less endless carnage, from the beginning. It has left its signature on page after page of Christian history, constituting the vast "underthought" of orthodoxy and millenarian heterodoxy (Manichaean, Messalian, Paulician, Bogomilian, Patarian, Albigensian) alike.[20]

What do all apocalypses have in common, how are we able to speak of them as a distinct genre? A 1979 volume of *Semeia* answers the question in the following way: "Apocalypse" is a genre of revelatory literature with a narrative framework, in which a revelation is mediated by an otherworldly being to a human recipient, disclosing a transcendent reality which is both temporal, insofar as it envisages eschatological salvation, and spatial, insofar as it involves another, supernatural world."[21] In the broadest terms, a member of the elect is deeply troubled by the affairs of his church in this world. It may be the pseudonymous Daniel, one of the *maskilim* or wise teachers, who must try to make sense of the persecution of the Jews under the Hellenizing program of Antiochus IV Epiphanes (167–164 B.C.), a kind of "proto-Antichrist";[22] or it may be John, sent into exile on the island of Patmos by the Emperor Domitian (A.D. 81–96), who must try to find justification for similar persecution of the early Christians by Rome. The seer is allowed to understand through an apocalypse, a "disclosing" or "uncovering," which translates into a series of visions of the glorious End. Hence the various magnificent figures, such as the four beasts of Daniel 7 or the beast rising out of the sea of Revelation 13, have *ex eventu* referents in history (i.e., the Babylonians, Medes, Persians, Greeks, Romans), but at the same time are colorful, compelling, and abstract enough to provide ready-made source material for subsequent "seers." The Whore of Babylon could be the Roman Empire in one epoch and the Church of Rome in another; the beast could be *Nero redivivus* in one context and a concupiscent pope, later called an "Antichrist,"[23] in another.

[17] Frank Kermode, *The Sense of an Ending: Studies in the Theory of Fiction* (New York: Oxford University Press, 1967), 5–8.

[18] Pelikan, *Jesus*, 24.

[19] Funkenstein, "A Schedule," 49, 57.

[20] Frank E. and Fritzie P. Manuel, *Utopian Thought in the Western World* (Cambridge: Harvard University Press, 1979), 48.

[21] John J. Collins, "Introduction: Towards the Morphology of a Genre," *Semeia* 14 (1979): 9.

[22] McGinn, "Early Apocalypticism," 8.

[23] In the New Testament the name "Antichrist" does *not* appear in Revelation, but only in I and II John.

What is significant is that the tribulations of the profane present, of *human beings in history*, are rendered understandable and therefore bearable by reference to a suprahistorical intelligence (God) who, standing *beyond* the Beginning and the End, sends His messenger (the angel of Revelation 1:1) to one of His faithful (the "servant John") with a divine preview of history's "Finis"—that spatial metaphor for a non-temporal paradise called the New Jerusalem. Just as Christ's life culminated in a triadic pattern of trial-crucifixion-resurrection, so now does the life of humanity, that is, universal history, promise to culminate in a similar pattern (thus the *Second Coming* of Christ) of present crisis-coming judgment-final vindication.[24]

As the *Semeia* volume shows, the genre of apocalypse has numerous permutations: it may contain a review of universal history up to the present moment of crisis or it may involve a purely personal eschatology; the revelation itself may be presented in the form of a vision or a speech or a dialogue; the seer may go on an otherworldly journey (a Judaeo-Christian version of the utopian *topos*)[25] or may be visited in his or her realm, etc. Yet whatever the particular variations, certain basic elements, what might be termed the epistemological "deep structure" of apocalypse, hold firm: (1) history is a unity or totality *determined* by God but at the same time so configured as to allow humanity, or more precisely, a member of the elect, to choose between Christ and Antichrist, between the truth coming from beyond and the mirage of worldly power, well-being, etc. that passes for truth in the here and now; (2) the moment of decision has arrived and the initial stage in the climactic pattern of crisis-judgment-vindication has begun; and (3) this coming End is viewed as tragic and retributive for those who have chosen not to uphold the faith and as triumphant for those who have.[26] Above all, the apocalypticist mentality and its scribal expression in the genre of apocalypse imply the interplay

---

24 McGinn, "Early Apocalypticism," 9.

25 It is of course moot to argue which impulse came first—the apocalyptic or the utopian. After all, Plato's presentation of his ideal republic, which Thomas More used as an important point of departure in his text, antedates the appearance of Christian apocalyptic. The foremost American scholars of utopia, Frank and Fritzie Manuel, isolate and historicize the utopian urge in the following way:

"Utopia is a hybrid plant, born of the crossing of a paradisaical, otherworldly belief of Judeo-Christian religion with the Hellenic myth of an ideal city on earth. The naming took place in an enclave of sixteenth-century scholars excited about the prospect of a Hellenized Christianity. While we may loosely refer to ancient and medieval works with some utopian content as utopias, the Western utopia is for us a creation of the world of the Renaissance and the Reformation... But the relation of the utopian to the heavenly always remains problematic. Utopia may be conceived as a prologue or foretaste of the absolute perfection still to be experienced; it then resembles the Days of the Messiah or the Reign of Christ on earth of traditional Judaism and Christianity, with the vital addition of human volition as an ingredient in the attainment of that wished-for state. Or the utopia, though originally implanted in a belief in the reality of a transcendental state, can break away from its source and attempt to survive wholly on its own creative self-assurance. Whether the persistence of the heavenly vision in a secularized world, if only in some disguised shape, is a necessary condition for the duration of utopia is one of the unresolved questions of Western culture" (Manuel and Manuel, *Utopian Thought*, 15–17).

26 McGinn, "Early Apocalypticism," 4–6, 10–12.

of spatio-temporal *oppositions* and of one's place within them: old/new, here/there, determinism from beyond/free choice from within, the historically mired Whore of Babylon/the ahistorical New Jerusalem, etc. The perceived resolution of all opposition comes, logically enough, at the climax of the Book of Revelation. The Beast, the symbol of benighted power in this world, brings about the destruction of the Whore of Babylon (originally Rome), "the great harlot... with whom the kings of the earth have committed fornication" (Revelation 17:1–2). Against this sense of tumultuous discord is presented the marriage of the Lamb and the Bride, Christ and the "holy city... coming down out of the heaven from God" (Revelation 21:10). In effect, the final vision of the Christian hierogamy has achieved a kind of narrative optical illusion —a view of the "outside" of history from the "inside," a projection of an all-encompassing and all-resolving "then" from the vantage of a beleaguered "now."

The record of how, time and again, the apocalypticist urge provoked historical confrontation in the West is immense, and can only be touched on in these preliminaries. Suffice it to say that of all the individuals who attempted to transpose the principal figures and codes of the Johannine text to the terms of contemporary reality, two were pivotal to the course of Western apocalypticism —St. Augustine and Joachim of Fiore (1145–1202). In his classic *The Pursuit of the Millennium*, Norman Cohn has written a social history of the volatile fit between the apocalyptic plot and its numerous adaptations among sectarian movements of Northern and Central Europe during the Middle Ages. Whatever the sects (Tafurs, Flagellants, Taborites) and whatever the social basis for their unrest (religious fervor during the Crusades, fear of the Black Death, deteriorating economic conditions in feudal Europe), the pattern was uniform: these were the saving remnant whose role it was to usher in the End and inherit a renovated kingdom. In this context, the Bishop of Hippo's earlier declaration that the millennium, that is, the thousand-year period of Revelation 20:1–6 during which Satan would be temporarily bound and the martyrs would reign with Christ over the world,[27] was coterminous with the reign of the church did little to dissuade what was often a rag-tag band of wanderers, itself socially disenfranchised, that saw that church as a haven of simony, voluptuousness, and the spirit of Antichrist. Officially, then, this move to legitimize the historical church as the only "City of God" on earth had enormous ramifications, not the least of which was to defuse the urgent need to look for a future Golden Age, since apparently it was

---

[27] "In a strict sense, millenarianism, or chiliasm, was originally limited to a prophetic conviction, derived from a commentary on the fourth verse of the twentieth chapter of the Apocalypse of John, to the effect that Christ would reign for a thousand years on earth. The pivotal events of the transition to the days of the millennium were depicted in1 well-worn images of catastrophe: During a time of troubles empires crumble, there are titanic struggles of opposing armies, vast areas of the world are devastated, nature is upheaved, rivers flow with blood. On the morrow, good triumphs over evil, God over Satan, Christ over Antichrist. As existential experience the millennium of

already here. As we discover in *City of God* (xviii: 52–53), it is not our place to tease out a divine fretwork of apocalyptic signs from the welter of current affairs: these prophecies are, in R.A. Markus' summation of the Augustinian position, "not to be read as referring to any particular historical catastrophe, but to the final winding up of all history; and the time of that no man can know."[28]

But in the popular, sectarian consciousness, which could not help from noticing the disparity between the historical and ideal churches, the millenarian impulse remained strong. This is especially true after Joachim, a seminal mystic of the Catholic Middle Ages, reversed Augustinian doctrine and gave the people back their millenarianism with his triadic periodization of history: "Joachim's originality lay in his affirmation that the threefold pattern of history was as yet incomplete and that the work of the Holy Spirit, the Third Person, must shortly be made manifest in a further stage of spiritual illumination. Recasting the traditional Pauline pattern he expanded his famous doctrine of the three status in history: the first, beginning with Adam and ending with the Incarnation, has been characterized by the work of the Father; the second, beginning back in the Old Testament (to overlap with the first) and continuing until Joachim's own day, belonged to the Son; the third, with a double origin in the Old Dispensation and the New and about to come to fruition in the near future, would see the full work of the Holy Spirit completed. *Here was a magnificent programme of progress which offered an advance still to come within history.* Its novelty is well illustrated by the fact that Joachim departs decisively from the Augustinian tradition by placing the Sabbath Age of the World and the opening of the Seventh Seal of the Church clearly within history and identifying them with the third *status*."[29]

The thirteenth century, as Russia fell under the Mongol Yoke to the East, was a time of great eschatological fervor and anxiety in Europe. 1260 was, in the popular imagination, the year in which Joachim's prophecies were to come true, and the Franciscan Spirituals, whose apocalyptic hopes and fears are presented in Umberto Eco's novel *The Name of the Rose*, were to be the original inheritors of the third *status*. But as routinely happens in these matters, disconfirmation makes it possible for later generations to recalculate and retranslate the numbers and signs into their own "chosen" *status*. Thus Joachim's placement of this third age of the Holy Spirit *within* history was enormously influential for the development of

early Christianity is the counterpart of the Days of the Messiah in much of Jewish apocalyptic. The bout of violence reaches a grand climax, and then and only then is there peace—primitive priapic scenes are the inescapable analogy" (Manuel and Manuel, *Utopian Thought*, 46–47).

28 R.A. Markus, *Saeculum: History and Society in the Theology of St. Augustine* (Cambridge: Cambridge University Press, 1970), 152–54.

29 My emphasis; Reeves, "Medieval Attitudes," 49–50; see also Marjorie Reeves, *The Influence of Prophecy in the Later Middle Ages* (Oxford: Oxford University Press, 1969).

apocalyptic thought in the West. It surfaces, *mutatis mutandis*, in the programs of Müntzer, Campanella, Lessing, in the Third State of Auguste Comte, in Marx's Higher Stage of Communism, in Teilhard's Noösphere, as well as in countless nationalisms, from Savonarola's Florence to Hitler's Third Reich.[30] Even Columbus' discovery of a new world in 1492 (the year the old world was scheduled to end in Russia) is largely a product of this tradition.[31] And in the Russian context it can be seen in modern guise in the tripartite periodization of history advanced by such thinkers as Vladimir Solovyov and Dmitry Merezhkovsky.

History

It is difficult to imagine two students of Russian cultural history more unalike than the émigré philosopher Nikolai Berdyaev and the Soviet structuralist and semiotician Yury Lotman. Yet on one issue they are both in unequivocal agreement — the relentlessly *eschatological* shape of those cultural models (of history, of life, and of the two as presented in literature) that have been the focus of Russia's popular and literary imagination for centuries. Berdyaev — who was powerfully influenced by Dostoevsky and who came to maturity on the eve of the revolution, when the thought systems of various Christian mystics and Marxists were brought to a boil by the expectation of a new millennium — could still claim as late as 1946 that "Russians are either apocalypticists or nihilists. Russia is an apocalyptic revolt against antiquity... This means that the Russian people, according to their metaphysical nature and calling in the world, are a people of the end [*narod kontsa*]."[32] Lotman — who came to prominence in the 1960s as the leader of the Tartu School of structural poetics and who wrote a series of pioneering works on the thesis that art does not passively "reflect" life but actually provides models and norms that social life then tries to imitate and incorporate — argued that "The historical fate of Western thought... developed in such a way that, beginning with the Middle Ages and continuing up to recent times, the idea of progress occupied a dominant position in both scientific and social thinking, coloring the whole of culture for entire historical periods. On the other hand, in the history of Russian social thought there dominated, over the course of entire historical periods, concepts of an eschatological or maximalist type."[33] Whether both of these writers,

30 Manuel and Manuel, *Utopian Thought*, 33, 63.
31 Reeves, "Medieval Attitudes," 62 ff.
32 Nikolai Berdiaev, *Russkaia ideia*, (Paris: YMCA, 1946), 195.
33 Iu.M. Lotman and B.A. Uspenskii, "Spory o iazyke v nachale XIX v. kak fakt russkoi kul'tury," *Trudy po russkoi i slavianskoi filologii* 24 (1975): 173.

the one more "intuitive" and given to broad, unqualified generalization and the other more "contextualist" and given to a meticulous sifting of evidence, are "objectively" correct is ultimately beside the point, since they are continuing a dialogue about the *received* notions of Russia's past, present, and future that is central to any discussion of their country's historical identity.

The binary oppositions by which Russians have tended to define themselves from their first steps into literacy have had, according to Lotman and Boris Uspensky, a profound impact on the eschatological view of national history passed down through the centuries. In the Roman Catholic West earthly life was from very early on "conceived of as admitting three types of behavior [on the model of heaven-purgatory-hell]: the unconditionally sinful, the unconditionally holy, and the neutral, which permits eternal salvation after some sort of purgative trial. In the real life of the medieval West a wide area of neutral behavior thus became possible, as did neutral societal institutions, which were neither 'holy' nor 'sinful', neither 'pro-state' nor 'anti-state,' neither good nor bad."[34] In Russia, however, "duality and the absence of a neutral axiological sphere led to a conception of the new not as a continuation, but as a *total eschatological* change."[35] Of these oppositions, argue Lotman and Uspensky, none are more important than the fundamental temporal distinction between "old" and "new" and the fundamental spatial distinction between "east" and "west." These terms shift valence as times and audiences change. More central to our discussion, the very distinctions between space and time can overlap and interpenetrate, suggesting that in point of fact they are extensions of each other.[36]

This means that to a structuralist like Lotman what is determinative in Russian cultural history is the ongoing clash between "outsiders" and "insiders," between those of a "now" versus those of a "then" temporality. Indeed, a number of historians have analyzed the major turning points of Russian history—the Christianization of *Rus'* in 988, the period of the Mongol Yoke (1240–1480), the origins of the formula "Moscow the Third Rome" and the growth of religious nationalism in the late fifteenth and early sixteenth centuries, the Great Schism led by the Old Believers in the 1660s, and the

[34] Iu.M. Lotman and B.A. Uspenskii, "Binary Models in the Dynamics of Russian Culture (to the End of the Eighteenth Century)," *The Semiotics of Russian Cultural History*, ed. Alexander D. Nakhimovsky and Alice Stone Nakhimovsky (Ithaca: Cornell University Press, 1985), 32.

[35] My emphasis; ibid. Again, a Western observer, or "outsider," may wish to question the existence of a now almost mythical past of a "neutral axiological sphere" among medieval Catholics, especially if one considers the widespread appeal of the proto-revolutionary, millenarian heterodoxies—which decidedly did *not* admit any middle ground in questions of judgment and faith—studied by Cohn, but if by this the authors mean that, as a result of the Renaissance, Reformation, and Enlightenment, the notions of "progress" and a human-centered view of the world associated with the rise of a middle class came gradually to dominate—but never to eliminate entirely—the "either/or" mentality of apocalypticism in the West, then their formulation appears more defensible.

[36] See pp. 37-38 above.

Petrine reforms in the first quarter of the eighteenth century — in precisely these terms.[37] The cast of "outsiders" (Byzantium, Turko-Mongol Empire, Western Europe) may change and what is "traditional" or "iconoclastic" may fluctuate depending on the point of view of the speaker/participant, but Lotman and Uspensky's point is well-taken: Russia has tended to define itself by radically breaking, or at least *by seeing itself* as radically breaking, with an earlier period. This break is never, to be sure, as clean and final as the principals might imagine for the very reason that the earlier period which is supposedly overcome is preserved willy-nilly in the cultural memory as a necessary opposition. After 988, paganism was not forgotten but remembered because its gods became the devils of the "Christian" world (Volos/Veles→*volosatik* or "wood goblin") or because their previous function was preempted by a Christian counterpart (Volos/Veles→St. Blaise [Vlasy], St. Nicholas, St. George).[38] Whereas Hilarion, in his celebrated "Sermon on Law and Grace" (c. 1037–1050), likens the "new" faith of the Russians to the enfranchised bride Sarah and thus to *New* Testament grace but the "old" faith of Byzantium to the handmaiden Hagar and thus to *Old* Testament law, the archpriest Avvakum will, in another era, resort to a diametrically opposed system of contrasts. To the leader of the Old Believers, as we shall see shortly, the Nikonian reforms of the 1660s were a betrayal of sacred tradition; what was "unorthodox," including the three-figured sign of the cross, was a fall from a better past into the "now" of the Antichrist.

But to return to our topic, Russian history has been subject not only to the distant thunder of eschatology, which views any present *saeculum* in light of the *eskhaton*, but also to the specific tremors and oscillations of apocalypticism, which, like a kind of divine seismograph, shows history's explosive conclusion to be near and predictable as soon as the shape of current events are keyed to certain texts of Judaeo-Christian tradition. As suggested earlier, "eschatological" can imply any radical break with the past, while "apocalyptic" implies the salient features of Judaeo-Christian historiosophy: history is determined by God the author, the plot is now coming to a close in the rhythm of crisis-judgment-vindication, the figures of the Johannine and other apocalyptic texts have begun to appear to the "seers" of contemporary history, etc. Here the same opposition of old/new applies, but now it is given a narrower interpretation. In general, "eschatologists" may be dour or eupeptic, depending on which side of the break they place themselves and their generation.[39] That is to say, they may be either *apocalypticists*, if they see

---

[37] Dmitri Obolensky, "Russia's Byzantine Heritage," in *The Structure of Russian History*, ed. Michael Cherniavsky (New York: Random House, 1970), 3–28.

[38] B.A. Uspenskii, "Kul't Nikoly na Rusi v istoriko- kul'turnom osveshchenii," *Trudy po znakovym sistemam [Uchenye zapiski Tartuskogo Gos. Univ.]* 463 (1978): 86–140.

[39] Cf. Sergei Bulgakov in "Pravoslavnaia eskhatologiia": "Eschatologism may have two images [*dva obraza*], light and dark. The latter has its place when it arises as a result of historical fright and a certain religious panic: it was this sort [of eschatologism that was produced by] the Russian schismatics — the

the present *transitus* as an ultimate judgment "from beyond" on their fallen fellows (as well as a simultaneous vindication of their own faith), or *utopians* (or millenarians *avant le lettre*), if they see contemporary reality simply as a stage to pass through in order to reach that "no place" which passes for a terrestrial New Jerusalem. Thus, although there are countless permutations and no hard-and-fast laws in these matters, the apocalypticist tends to interpret the old/new opposition by making the first element positive (the original, pristine faith) and the second element negative (contemporary impiety and desecration), while the utopian tends to do the reverse, making a fetish of what is new, "enlightened," "advanced," such as technology (usually seen in Russia's case as coming from the West), and denigrating what is old, "superstitious," and "ignorant," such as religious tradition (usually seen in. Russia's case as indigenous).[40] Ultimately, however, the apocalypticist and utopian cannot be said to translate simply into opposite sides of one eschatological coin; they have radically different conceptions of what constitutes narrative authority in the historiographical process. To the one, this authority comes from God, who is outside human (hi)story; to the other, this authority comes from human beings, who can make themselves and their ideal POLIS within history, *if* only they really try.

While our focus in these pages is primarily the nineteenth century and that "prehistory" of Russian apocalyptic consciousness leading up to Dostoevsky and the modern period, I would like to dwell briefly on several episodes from earlier Russian history. These episodes loom large because over time they became a fertile source for the kind of end-determined,

self-immolators who wanted to destroy themselves in order to save themselves from the reigning Antichrist. But characteristic of eschatologism can be (and should be) a bright image with its impulse toward the Coming Christ. As we proceed in history, we come to meet Him [*idem k Nemu navstrechu*], and the rays [of light], emanating from His future coming to the world, can be felt... Thus the Second Coming of Christ is not only terrible for us, since He will come as our Judge, but also glorious, since He will come in His glory, and this Glory is also the glorification of the world and the fullness that has come to pass in all creation" (Sergii Bulgakov, prot. "Pravoslavnaia eskhatologiia," *Pravoslavie: Ocherki ucheniia pravoslavnoi tserkvi* [Paris: YMCA, 1985], 385).

[40] Utopians can, to be sure, select as a model a golden agrarian age in the past, but I have in mind those—Alexander Bogdanov and Alexei Gastev would be prime examples in the modern Russian context—who take the streamlined euchronia, the "high tech" urban center, as the destined goal of history. See the Manuels (*Utopian Thought*, 20) for the difference between "eutopia" and "euchronia": "In the bosom of a utopia of agrarian calm felicity a utopia of endless, dynamic change in science and technology was born. This switch to euchronia was heralded with the awakened sleeper of Sébastien Mercier's *L'An 2440* and with the utopian projections in the Tenth Epoch of Condorcet's *Esquisse*. The vision of a future society of *progrès indéfini* predominates through the emergence of Marx on the utopian landscape. Paradoxically, un-Christian utopia represented a resurgence of a strong millenarian, paradisaical, and apocalyptic current in secular form. The free rational choices of the Morean Utopian lawgiver or the Renaissance architect were abandoned to history: Utopia became less Hellenized and more Judeo-Christian. Older rhythms of thought from millenarianism and Joachimism were secularized, and translations of Judeo-Christian apocalyptic rhetoric into new forms became the stuff of the transformation." Again, on the parallels between utopia and apocalyptic paradise, see *Utopian Thought*, 33–63.

"right-angled" view of national history perpetuated by later writers, social theorists, and public figures. Moreover, they have striking similarities that gradually entered into the Russians' myths about themselves, their nation, and their ruler. The first has to do with the formula "Moscow the Third Rome," and, while generally traceable to the pronouncements of the Pskovian monk Philotheus in the early sixteenth century,[41] encompasses a larger series of dates and events: the Council of Ferrara-Florence (1438–39), the fall of Constantinople in 1453, the projected end of the world in 1492, the writings of Philotheus c. 1510–24, and the crowning of Ivan IV as tsar in 1547. The second involves the Great Schism of the 1660s and the Petrine reforms which followed in the early years of the eighteenth century. These two constellations of events are not only related to each other but are seminal to an understanding of Russia's historical identity *before* its writers of secular history, such as Karamzin, began to try to disentangle the myth from the reality. It was these myths, whose precise historical provenance was often forgotten or ignored, that those coming after either tried to live up to or to live down, but rarely reacted to neutrally.

An essential element of Byzantine ideology inherited by the Russians was the notion of *basileus*, of the emperor who is simultaneously spiritual and secular leader of his Christian realm.[42] Even though the *basileus* is largely a "messianic" concept,[43] it does have important ties with the Eastern Christian apocalyptic tradition through the *Revelations of the Pseudo-Methodius* (wr. late seventh century). According to the latter, there would appear a Last World Emperor, whose role it was to defeat the Ishmaelites (read Islam) and then journey to Jerusalem to hand over his crown to God, at which moment the time of the Antichrist would commence.[44] The *basileus* myth itself goes back to Constantine (288?–337), who united Christianity and imperial Rome during his reign and built a new capital in Byzantium, which was renamed Constantinople and which, from the latter part of the fourth century, came to be known as the

[41] Evidence for the emergence of the myth of Moscow the Third Rome can be found in texts that pre-date Philotheus' formulation, such as "The Tale of the White Cowl" (late fifteenth century), but it was Philotheus who first made the case explicitly and concisely ("Both Romes fell, the third endures, and a fourth there will never be" [cited in Sergei A. Zenkovsky, *Medieval Russia's Epics, Chronicles, and Tales* (New York: Dutton, 1974), 323]).

[42] The attributes "spiritual"/"secular" were originally not opposed, but merely different profiles of one divinely inspired countenance. See Michael Cherniavsky, "Khan or Basileus: An Aspect of Russian Mediaeval Political Theory," in *The Structure of Russian History*, ed. Michael Cherniavsky (New York: Random House, 1970), 65–79; and Obolensky, "Russia's Byzantine Heritage." For much of this discussion of Philotheus, I am indebted to Stremooukhoff's fine study of Moscow as the "Third Rome" (Dimitri Stremooukhoff, "Moscow the Third Rome: Sources of the Doctrine," in *The Structure of Russian History*, ed. Michael Cherniavsky [New York: Random House, 1970], 108–25).

[43] McGinn, *Visions of the End*, 28.

[44] Ibid., 70–73; see also Paul J. Alexander, *Byzantine Apocalyptic Tradition*, ed. Dorothy deF. Abrahamse (Berkeley: University of California Press, 1985), 13–60.

[45] According to the prophetic script of the pseudo-Methodius, Constantinople was to be liberated by the Last World

"New Rome." This second, "Eastern" Rome acquired additional status when the first, "Western" Rome was sacked by Alaric in 410. But by the fifteenth century Constantinople, which up to then had been successful at fending off Eastern marauders, was itself under imminent threat of falling to the Ottoman Turks. Its church delegates were eager to strike a bargain with a now renovated Rome at the Council of Ferrara-Florence. Moscow, on the other hand, which for some time had seen the rival Latinists as "old," "corrupt," "fallen," and "Western" (especially after the excommunication of Michael Cerularius, patriarch of Constantinople, and the resulting schism of 1054) interpreted the union as perfidy. The actual fall of Constantinople in 1453 became proof *a fortiori* both of God's displeasure and of the Russians' own elect status. Already profoundly under the spell of messianism through the imported concept of the *basileus*, Moscow was soon faced with the prospect of either liberating Constantinople (thereby fulfilling its role as the "fair-skinned tribe" in the prophetic script of the pseudo-Methodius)[45] or declaring itself the third and last Rome and its tsar[46] the *basileus*. When the end of the world did not occur in 1492 (the last year of the seventh millennium in the Byzantine calendar), Moscow was free to pursue the second alternative.

Strangely enough, the fall of Constantinople, the passing of the year 1492, *and* the rise of Moscow as the Third Rome were essentially a reading of the Christian plot or *mythos* into contemporary history, but with a different twist. History was not yet secularized, and thus its meaning had still to come from outside. What could be "apocalyptic," or a justification for negative happenings, in the case of Constantinople could also be "messianic," or a justification for "chosen" status, in the case of Moscow.[47] This distinction is borne out with remarkable vividness in the exegesis of Philotheus. Taking his cue from earlier remarks by Zosimius, metropolitan of Moscow, and borrowing his figures from the Apocalypse of Ezra,[48] Philotheus identifies the *third* head of the twelve-winged eagle (IV Ezra 12:23) with Moscow, which had recently coopted the two-headed eagle as its coat of arms. Yet Philotheus is also apparently aware that this image of a three-headed beast could have *negative* connotations, such as the *passing* of worldly empires on the model of Daniel's four beasts. Thus in the epistle "Against the Astrologers and the Latins" (c. 1524) he shifts his emphasis from the third head of the eagle to the Woman Clothed in the Sun (Revelation 12:2), whom he perceives as Russia fleeing into the desert

Emperor and his fair-skinned tribe, after which the final confrontation with the Antichrist would take place and the End of the world would follow (Sackur, *Sibyllinische Texte*, 89–94; cited McGinn, *Visions*, 75–76).

[46] The title began to gain currency under Ivan III (ruled 1462–1505).

[47] On the distinction between "messianism," "millenarianism," and "apocalypticism," see McGinn, *Visions* 28–36.

[48] The Apocalypse of Ezra was itself based in part on the Book of Daniel, an important Old Testament apocalyptic text. See Stremooukhoff, "Moscow the Third Rome," 113.

of true faith away from the false capitals of Rome and Constantinople. What is particularly striking about this case being made for Russia's manifest destiny is that Philotheus was arguing, like a Russian Augustine, against his native Pskovians, who saw Moscow as the seat of the Antichrist (Pskov had recently fallen under the rule of Vasily III, who deprived the ancient city of its rights and dispersed much of the population), and against the Latins, who maintained that the true Christian empire was still located in the West.

When Ivan IV had himself crowned tsar in 1547 amid much pomp,[49] he in effect consolidated the notion of Russia as holy empire and himself as *basileus*, which latter fact was soon recognized by the Eastern church. Indeed, beginning with the early sixteenth century scribal attempts were made to trace the Russian princely dynasties back to Augustus via his brother Prus, ruler of Prussia; this meant that these princes "were heirs of the two Romes not only spiritually or eschatologically, as they were for the monk Philotheus, but historically, virtually dynastically."[50] Moreover, the shift from saintly prince, with his filial, "Christ-like" role, to pious tsar, with his paternal, "God-like" one, was not lateral but *vertical*. It was, concludes Cherniavsky, "a raising of his functions to a higher, *apocalyptic* level; his person could not be made more exalted in any case."[51]

With the coming of the Great Schism in the next century, the terms of spatiotemporal opposition remain essentially the same, but their values are reversed. The questions of ritual and doctrine now, as in the cases studied by Cohn in Northern and Central Europe, have an ever stronger *social* undercurrent. It is as if the Pskovians' cries in the wilderness, which in their time were limited to one or two cities (Novgorod also experienced apocalyptic forebodings in the early sixteenth century), had spread to a larger area and begun to rival in resonance the voices of official doctrinal reason. The Old Believers, it should be recalled, made their case to a *significant* portion of the population, with as many as twenty percent of the Russians of the time joining their ranks and embracing the *political theology* of the Schism.[52] Above all, Avvakum and his followers were a sectarian movement that saw their golden age of harmony and piety in the past. As Berdyaev writes, "The Schism was a departure from history because history was controlled by the prince of this world, the Antichrist, who had penetrated to the upper levels of the church and state. The Orthodox kingdom was going underground. The

---

[49] This was, to be sure, not the first time that a Muscovite grand prince had borne the title but it was the first time that the crowning had been surrounded by such august celebration.

[50] Michael Cherniavsky, *Tsar and People: Studies in Russian Myths* (New Haven: Yale University Press, 1961), 42.

[51] Ibid., 40.

[52] Michael Cherniavsky, "The Old Believers and the New Religion," *The Structure of Russian History*, ed. Michael Cherniavsky (New York: Random House, 1970), 4–5.

genuine kingdom was the City of Kitezh [a popular version of paradise], located beneath the lake."[53] Hence the seventeenth century in general and the decade of the Schism in particular were times of great social upheaval, including the civil wars of the Time of Troubles, the peasant unrest in the 1630s, the town rebellions in the 1640s and 1650s, the Cossack uprisings in the 1660s and 1670s, and the *streltsy fronde* in the 1680s and 1690s. Indeed, it would be no exaggeration to say that the Schism and the Petrine reforms (which the Old Believers led the reaction against) were *the* moment in Russian history when the oppositions of old/new and east/west entered into a particularly fateful alignment with the Russians' myths about themselves and the governance of their state. The very facts of broad popular appeal and interpenetration of the political, social, and theological realms suggest that this time was perceived as a "turning point" not only for the Avvakumians but for all those coming later who, with the emergence of "historical consciousness" in the early nineteenth century, would wrestle with their country's identity as "Eastern" or "Western," as a renovation of a golden past or a radical thrust into an enlightened future. The replacement of Moscow the Third Rome by St. Petersburg, the secular Western city of the Antichrist, would become a central theme, for example, of *The Idiot* and *Petersburg*, two of the "apocalyptic fictions" to be treated in this study; both pre-1917, these works present imperial Russia fast entering a state of crisis and eclipse. Similarly, the fate of the original capital, renovated to its former status after the revolution, would be the subject of *The Master and Margarita* and *Doctor Zhivago*, novels that show the city as a parodic Whore of Babylon and a fallen (and ultimately risen) Third Rome, respectively.[54]

If the apocalyptic mood in medieval Russia never disappeared entirely, it reasserted itself with a vengeance in 1644, when the government printing office released the so-called *Book of Cyril*, which contained various South Slavic and Ukrainian apocalyptic writings. It was at approximately this same time that the monk Kapiton, founder of a hermitage in the north (Totma), first began to spread his theology—known pejoratively as *kapitonovshchina*—of flight from this world, imminent apocalypse, and self-immolation.[55] Kapiton's activities served as a prelude to those of the Old Believers three decades later; an important shift in political theology was augured by the claim, made by one of his followers, that Tsar Alexis (ruled 1645–76) was "not tsar but a horn of the Antichrist."[56]

53 Berdiaev, *Russkaia ideia*, 14.

54 Dostoevsky's The Idiot, Bely's Petersburg, and Pasternak's Doctor Zhivago are several of the texts analyzed in The Shape of Apocalypse (see note 1 above).

55 Cherniavsky, "Old Believers," 16.

56 Ia.L. Barskov, *Pamiatniki pervykh let russkogo staroobriadchestva* (St. Petersburg: Tip. Alexandrova, 1912), 333; see also P.S. Smirnov, *Vnutrennie voprosy v raskole v XVII veke* (St. Petersburg, 1898), 31 ff.

In this cryptic comment we already see the beginnings of an assault on the myth of *basileus* that will be carried far and wide by the Old Believers. The apocalyptic expectations of *kapitonovshchina* began to heat up again when the Patriarch Nikon decreed changes in church ritual in 1652–54. These reforms in ritual, which affected the way one made the sign of the cross, the number and manner of prostrations, and the hallelujah glorification, were not the first undertaken at the initiation of a tsar;[57] along with the abovementioned social tensions, however, their endorsement of Greek and South Slavic "purity" held the match to the powder keg of broad reaction. At first, the small group of Moscow preachers led by Avvakum was kept in check, but they persisted in their ecclesiastical rebellion. Attempts at compromise were rebuffed by the Avvakumians — the Fathers Avvakum, Fyodor, Lazar, and Epiphany — and the Patriarchal Council of 1666–67 passed intact the Nikonian reforms and declared the "old" practices and texts heretical. Those who continued to resist were anathematized, while the Avvakumians themselves were exiled to the far north (Pustozersk), where, in 1682, they were burned at the stake.

58.
PART I

This skeletal account gives little sense of how closely apocalyptic theology was intertwined with the Council's work and the subsequent fate of the Avvakumians and their converts.[58] The Schism forced the Old Believers to rethink the essential terms entering into their Russian understanding of the economy of salvation. If Moscow was turning its back on its heritage as the Third Rome, then there was only one conclusion to draw — it was not the holy but the *unholy* city, the seat of the Antichrist. Nikon and Tsar Alexis were precursors of the Antichrist, whose appearance was scheduled for 1666 (the date of the convening of the Council and a convenient cipher for the beast's number, 666 [Revelation 13:18]). Messianism was turned inside out into apocalypticism; Russia's manifest destiny as the New Rome and world savior was transformed into its manifest destiny as traducer of sacred (here "old") tradition, as the Antichrist. In the words of the Old Believer monk Avraamy, "There will no longer be any further delay; everywhere is Russia's last [moment], and from hour to hour worse things happen."[59]

57 Witness Ivan IV's well-known *Stoglav* Council in 1551.

58 To shift the context a little, the Great Reform movement — the West's version of the Schism — which originated in Luther's Germany a century and a half earlier and soon spread to Calvin's Geneva and Zwingli's Zurich, involved a quite similar apocalyptic theology. Only the terms, not perhaps unexpectedly, were reversed: the Wittenberg preacher (who, like Avvakum, was excommunicated in 1521 for insisting that popes and their councils can err) stood for "newness" — for a translation of the Bible into colorful German vernacular, for congregational singing, for lay reception of the eucharistic bread and wine, etc.; the traditions of the Roman Catholic church, especially those connected with the practice of granting indulgences were seen as "old" — as belonging to the temporal rather than the universal church, to the Antichrist rather than Christ. Of course Luther, like most late medieval Christians, fully believed that his children would live to see the Second Coming.

59 Barskov, *Pamiatniki*, 162.

By the late seventeenth century the Old Believer movement had spilled over into the impressionable, often uneducated public far beyond anything imagined by the original group of four. Numerous zealots were writing hundreds, if not thousands, of apocalypses of their own, preaching fiery sermons in the northern woods, and, when hemmed in too closely by the authorities (in 1684 it was made a *secular, state* crime, with punishment of death, to practice the schismatic faith), burning themselves alive to protest this world. Equally significant, these same *starovery* provided important ideological impetus for popular rebellion: consider, for example, the now generally acknowledged connection between the Old Believers and the revolt of Stenka Razin in 1670–71 and the uprising of the *streltsy* in 1682. And so, "beginning with the insurrection of 1682, every popular uprising in Russia—the continued *streltsy* troubles, the Cossack rebellions under Peter I (Azov, Astrakhan, Bulavin's uprising), and the climax of the great uprising of Pugachev under Catherine II—was fought under the banner of the Old Belief: the restoration of old rituals, icons, and books was inextricably connected with the program of massacring the aristocracy and abolishing serfdom."[60]

In other words, with the coming to power of Peter I (ruled 1682–1725), the fury of the Old Believers' apocalypticism reached its peak and the true *raskol* began. Peter, who spelled his name with a foreign alphabet, was seen as the Antichrist incarnate; his city, with its Western architecture, its predominance of European spires over Orthodox cupolas, as un-Russian and thereby unholy; his new calendar, which "stole eight years from God," as a turning away from Biblical time; and his chosen title—*imperator* (emperor)—as the ultimate derogation of his sacred role as tsar. Peter's desacralization of Russia's past went much further than the shearing of boyars' beards—the number of variations on the Peter as Antichrist myth attests to this. But the main issue remained one of divine genealogy: as *basileus*, Peter was supposed to be God's appointed servant on earth; yet rather than accepting this role, he had made of himself a *zemnoi bog*, a god on earth.[61] It is indeed ironic that the Old Believers were so devoted to the "old," including the belief in their ruler as *basileus*, that they devised stories about Peter's changeling status. After all, to them this colossal figure of evil could not be both tsar *and* Antichrist.

The seventeenth century was not only a time of great turmoil for the myth of the tsar as *basileus*, however. It was also the time when the second great myth, that of "Holy Russia" (*Sviataia Rus'*) and her

60 Cherniavsky, "Old Believers," 20. To glance ahead for a moment, both Blok and Bely, in the years leading up to 1917, would become fascinated by the tradition tying together apocalypticism, revolution, and sectarian heterodoxy. After 1917, writers such as Pilnyak and Platonov would translate the same apocalypticist-sectarian nexus into Bolshevik legend: the former's *okhlomony* (Mahogany) and the latter's Chevengurians are in fact modern Old Believers who are attempting to keep the faith of the revolution alive in times of compromise and "secularization" (the NEP—New Economic Policy).

61 Ibid., 33.

people (*narod*), first gained wide currency as something independent of, and indeed in many ways opposed to, the myth of the tsar.[62] As Alexander Solovyov first established, the term "Holy Russia" initially appeared in Prince Andrei Kurbsky's correspondence with Ivan IV as an *indictment* of the tsar's action — the émigré prince lamented that Ivan had "dishonored [himself] and the holyrussian land."[63] But only with the Time of Troubles (*Smutnoe vremia*) in the early seventeenth century, when Russia was without a tsar and had to preserve its Orthodox essence intact against Polish Catholic intervention, did the term gain popular acceptance and begin to appear in numerous folk songs and epics:

> Russia was "Holy Russia" because it was the land of salvation, expressed in its icons, saints, people, and ruler. But the historical origin of the term indicates its concrete limits: "Holy Russia" was what remained, during the Time of Troubles, after Tsar and State and church hierarchy were gone; it was the concentrated essence of Russia, visible when the form of Russia was destroyed. Hence, both on the transcendental and concrete levels "Holy Russia" was an absolute, immutable, because the land of salvation could not change except catastrophically, nor could the Russian essence change without losing itself.[64]

Here was a spatial myth that existed "no-place" but was capable of sustaining those like the Old Believers as they confronted the specter of tsar turned Antichrist and the Third Rome turned Whore of Babylon. Where, one might ask, could this "Holy Russia" be found? It could be found in the *narod*, in the villages and monasteries, lower gentry and simple folk that kept the faith alive when the tsar was absent and the Poles were at the gates of Moscow. So too could it be found in those preachers in the northern woods who burned themselves alive because their tsar had disappeared and because the only way back to the past, to the underwater kingdom of Kitezh, was through fiery death. Thus "Holy Russia," though born of a specific time and place, became something nonhistorical, transcendental. *Rus'*, the name for "old" Russia, could be *Sviataia*, "Holy," but the *Imperiia*, "Empire," could only be *Rossiiskaia*, a secular "Russian" formed from the "new" noun *Rossiia*.[65] And it was between these two essentially opposing myths, that of the tsar and that of the people of "Holy Russia," that the intelligentsia, the group of educated Russians who were located

[62] It could conceivably be argued that the notions of "Russian Land" (*russkaia zemlia*), dating back to Kievan times, and "Holy Russia" are analogous. Here, however, the operative term is holy, which was first joined with *Rus'* in the sixteenth century, in Kurbsky's correspondence. Paszkiewicz links the older term *Rus'* and the Christian religion, but without the specific use of *sviataia* (Henryk Paszkiewicz, *The Origin of Russia* [New York: Philosophical Library, 1954], 12).

[63] *Russkaia Istoricheskaia Biblioteka*, vol. 31, *Sochineniia Kniazia Kurbskago* (St. Petersburg, 1914), 134; cited in Cherniavsky, *Tsar*, 107.

outside either myth,⁶⁶ found themselves when, returning obsessively to the question of Russia's identity, they made cultural history in the nineteenth century.

It would be futile to try to define with any precision "Holy Russia" and its ephemeral boundaries within the *narod*. What can be proposed is that the term, as a cultural model, inevitably raises issues of mythical, as opposed to historical, time. Each of its later champions — Khomyakov, Zhukovsky, Vyazemsky, Tiutchev, Dostoevsky, Fyodorov, Berdyaev — was forced to accommodate a contingent, problem-ridden present by casting back to this nonhistorical past or by projecting it into the future. Moreover, the moment in Russian cultural history at which this all-important opposition became actual and operative, entering into the very structure of the Russian language, was again the seventeenth century, the same epoch-making period of the Schism. The Soviet scholar A.M. Panchenko has demonstrated that, beginning with the second half of the seventeenth century, one can add to the already familiar oppositions of old/new and foreign/domestic the new opposition of mythical time/secular history. This may seem, *prima facie*, simply another variation on the old/new antinomy, but Panchenko thinks otherwise. The grounds for argument between Nikon and Avvakum were not necessarily tradition and innovation in a true *historical* sense (since in matters of ritual and doctrine almost any scriptural source can be adduced to buttress the priority and hence the authority of one's argument); on the other hand, the grounds for argument between the traditionalists and the new teachers of imported baroque culture who came to prominence during the reigns of Tsars Alexis and Peter could, and probably did have, considerable import for the development of Russian historical consciousness. In this case, the polemic between the Old Believers and such "New Enlighteners" as Simeon of Polotsk, Silvester Medvedev, Stephan Yavorsky, and St. Dimitry of Rostovsk was not so much over doctrine — though that was the pretext — as over *historical time*. "It was not a historiographical but a historiosophical argument — an argument about a historical ideal, about historical distance, about the interrelation between man and time, about eternity and the perishable, about the past, present, and future."⁶⁷

Using an approach not unlike Lotman's, Panchenko breaks these two conceptions of time into the medieval, that valorized by the Old Believers, and the proto-modern, that valorized by the New Enlighteners. The first sees

64 My emphasis: Cherniavsky, *Tsar and People*, 116.

65 Ibid., 119.

66 Generally speaking, the intelligentsia saw themselves as belonging neither to the tsar's reactionary government nor to the *narod*'s difficult daily life and customs. See below.

67 A.M. Panchenko, "Istoriia i vechnost' v sisteme kul'turnykh tsennostei russkogo barokko," *Trudy otdela drevnerusskoi literatury* 34 (1979): 191.

"human existence, taken *in toto*, as an *echo of the past* — more precisely, of those events from the past which are identified with eternity."[68] This "echo" is intimately bound to the Orthodox understanding of weekly and yearly cycles, each of which "renews," in small or large scale, the resurrection of Christ. Within the family circle (or "cycle"), the same echo principle was at work: individual members, as descendants, were often given names from one semantic "family" to underscore the belief that their role was to recapitulate the "clannish fate" (*rodovaia sud'ba*) of their ancestors. Here the renewal is never innovative, never a break with the past, but always a reconfirmation of human contact with eternity. In other words, Panchenko's revealing analysis is in remarkable accord with what Eliade has written about sacred time in archaic or primitive societies. The future does not yet exist (hence the Apocalypse for the Old Believers is *now*) because the profane present is constantly annulled in favor of a periodic return to eternity. According to Orthodox ritual, the "man who fasts, confesses, and takes communion each time 'renews himself.' That is, he purifies himself of sinful [outer] layers, grows closer to the ideal. 'Renewal' is a kind of 'aging' [*odrevlenie*: lit: 'making ancient'] of man, in which the qualities of the ideal show through with greater clarity."[69]

For the New Enlighteners, however, many of whom had been through the Kiev Academy and were influenced by Polish (that is, "Western," post-Renaissance) models, historical time was not something to be banned; rather it was something to be learned and understood. These were men of books and libraries, whereas Avvakum was a man of one book in principle and few books in practice. When, for example, the latter was blessed early in his career by a confessor, the formula used included "by *the* [apocalyptic!] Book of Ephrem the Syrian."[70] This is not to say that the culture of the Old Believers was one of ignorance and obscurantism, as Simeon and his colleagues would submit, but simply that the book, like the icon, was something sacred, immutably true, in no need of duplication. The book, and the Great Time of which it told, possessed human beings; human beings did not possess the book. With the Enlighteners, on the other hand, the Russian, to use again Eliade's formulation, *entered* history as secular time. To be sure, this was not seen by them as a "fall" into history — quite the opposite, since Russia was being raised out of the darkness — but it would seem so to later, more nostalgic, generations. These scholars "proclaimed the idea of a *unified, civilized* time, removing, in effect, the distinction

68   My emphasis: ibid.
69   Ibid., 192.
70   Cited in Panchenko, "Istoriia i vechnost'," 194.

between eternity and perishable existence"; history became "'interesting' in and of itself, independent of its relation to God, eternity, and the soul"; and history, most importantly, no longer "predetermined the fate of [one's] descendants, their earthly existence. The past was dead."[71]

Not fortuitously, the gradual emergence of secular literature, as well as of its disguised forms in the works of those still closely associated with the church, marked this shift in historical consciousness. Simeon's verse play written in the 1670s provide compelling evidence of the change in process. The first, about Nebuchadnezzar, would appear by its title to be an adaption of the church ritual then referred to as *chin peshchnogo deistva* (lit. "rite of the furnace action").[72] It was this ritual, which took place at Christmastime and symbolically recalled the immaculate conception (just as the youths were not burned in the furnace, so was the Virgin not harmed by the fiery Holy Spirit entering her natural body), that the tsar himself had traditionally participated in. Now, however, it was subject to ban, and consequently Simeon's play has none of this symbolic overlay. In fact, the principal focus of the play is the "comedic" (plays at this time were called *komedii*), "verisimilar" historical parallels between the ancient king and the current Tsar Alexis. Hence the *faith* (*vera*) implicit in the Christmas ritual (*chin*) was being eroded by the *culture* of the "comedy."[73] The similarities (and differences) between Nebuchadnezzar and Alexis served to indicate how *future* generations would interpret the deeds of the present tsar. History began to stretch out into the future, to appear endless. Even questions of the Last Judgment, which so vexed the Old Believers, became more personal than collective, more "literary" than "literal." The numerous works of the Russian baroque that deal with the Apocalypse—the "Pentateugum" of Andrei Belobotsky and the anonymous "Staircase to Heaven" are two of the best known—do so thematically rather than ritually. Conversely, the actual ritual during Shrovetide—when the patriarch wiped clean the icon of the Last Judgment in the Uspensky Cathedral (the act of "renewal") and blessed and sprinkled water over the tsar—was abolished. Like Augustine defending his church and faith against the apocalypticists, St. Dimitry, one of the New Enlighteners, could claim: "To us the Last Judgment is more personal [*komuzhdo svoi*] than general, and as for the time itself of the terrible judgment day, it is not for us to ask. It is enough to believe that it will come… but when it will come, do not inquire… about that day and hour no one knows."[74]

---

[71] Panchenko, "Istoriia i vechnost'," 195.

[72] See Simon Karlinsky, *Russian Drama from its Beginnings to the Age of Pushkin* (Berkeley, CA: University of California Press, 1985), 1–14. The actual title read: *Of the King Nebuchadnezzar, the Golden Calf, and the Three Youths Not Burned in the Furnace*.

[73] Panchenko, "Istoriia i vechnost'," 196.

[74] *Rozysk o raskol'nicheskoi brynskoi vere* 62; cited in Panchenko, "Istoriia i vechnost'," 198.

Russia's transition from theocratic to secular state was obviously more complex and continuous than our schematic retelling of it allows, yet in the final analysis there is no minimizing the vast significance of the Petrine reforms and the figure of Peter himself. Nineteenth-century social thought and historiography abound with comparisons, optimistic and pessimistic, utopian and apocalyptic, that interpret the present and predict the future by attempting to solve the riddle of the Petrine Sphinx. Even such a respected historian as S. M. Solovyov considered Peter "*the* hero of Russian history, probably the only hero, and the last one... [He] concludes the epic period of Russian history and opens the era of civilization for Russia... The change under him was most radical: from epic to history — from prehistory to history proper. Only since Peter has Russia become an 'historic' nation."[75] This is a gross oversimplification, as most modern historians would now admit, but again, as a cultural model and narrative *mythos* to be strenuously rejected (the Slavophiles) or equally strenuously embraced (the Westernizers), it maintained its potency into the nineteenth century and, in some cases, beyond.

Thus flanked by an "enlightened" vanguard whose task it was to legitimize the tsar's role, the Petrine myth emerged in its purest form as a tale of long overdue change — not evolutionary, but revolutionary, not ameliorative, but total, instantaneous, seemingly *ex nihilo*, and of course eschatological. Antiokh Kantemir proclaimed that through the "wise commands" of Peter Russia had become, "*in a moment's time,*" "a new people."[76] And just as Simeon had earlier compared Alexis to Nebuchadnezzar, so now Feofan Prokopovich compared Peter to Saint Vladimir, the Christianizer and "enlightener" of Russia, in his tragicomedy of the same name.[77] "New" suddenly had a positive valence, as it had for Hilarion, and what was "old"— including the obstreperous Orthodox priests thinly disguised as "pagan sorcerers" in Prokopovich's play — was ignorant and evil.[78] In effect, the notions of progress and enlightenment championed by the new cultural spokesmen carried with them the spatial image of futurity, the *put'* (path) that was to become the root metaphor for directing and marshalling the "historical present" (ultimately a *contradictio in adjecto*) in the collective imagination of the emerging intelligentsia. What was totally "new" or "reborn" had to go somewhere, to look for something. Disenfranchised by Peter's meritocracy and table of ranks and raised on a steady diet of "progressive" European principles, the hereditary nobility (*stolbovoe*

[75] Cited in Georges Florovsky, "The Problem of Old Russian Culture," *The Structure of Russian History*, ed. Michael Cherniavsky (New York: Random House, 1970), 127.

[76] My emphasis; Antiokh Kantemir, *Sobranie stikhotvorenii* (Leningrad: Sovetskii pisatel', 1956), 75. Compare, for example, the following lines about Stalin written by the Georgian poet N. Mitsishvili in the mid-thirties and translated by Pasternak: "You have achieved the unachievable: / You have remade [*peresozdal*] people's minds and souls, / Your hand with sickle has covered a continent, / And with hammer has gone to the ends of the earth"

dvorianstvo) were to become leading members of the intelligentsia and the creators of the new literature. Not only did they see their own power and wealth ebbing away, they were forced to witness the decline of their peasants, the principal victims in this political and economic realignment.[79] "The Russian nobleman of the nineteenth century normally lacked strong roots in any particular area and had no real feeling of attachment to a specific locality and to a family estate on which his ancestors had lived for generations... There is little evidence of the attachment to and the ties with the ancestral home which characterized the mentality of the western nobleman."[80] Reared by nursemaids and tutors who had no "rights" to him, sent to a school which offered a completely Western education, the young nobleman grew up with a distinctly rationalistic and didactic cast of mind, neither totally Muscovite nor French, but one that obviously anticipated that of the nineteenth century *intelligent*.[81] In a word, the educated nobleman of the eighteenth century found himself *"doubly cut off*: from his own people's past, which he had learned to scorn and reject, and from Western Europe, which had not yet fully accepted him and of which he still did not feel the equal."[82]

The almost hypnotic attraction of the *put'*, with its spatialization of temporal desire, is an essential ingredient in the messianic and apocalyptic roles that the nineteenth-century intelligentsia assigned to the long-suffering *narod*. It was felt that the various roads, paths, and ways invoked to describe Russian historical time should in the end, and *at the end*, have a destination. With remarkable ingenuity, the present was overcome by finding some popular trapdoor to a sacred — usually pre-Petrine — past or by scaling the ladder of Western, post-Enlightenment knowledge to a brighter future. Yet in either case the *temporal* ideal was equally removed, equally *distant* from the *intelligent* "outsider." Berdyaev, whose own work grew out of the late nineteenth-century tradition, resorts to the same matrix of images (spatiality standing in for temporality) when he states with characteristic aplomb that "Russians

(*Poéty Gruzii v perevodakh B.L. Pasternaka i N.S. Tikhonova*, ed. N. Mitsishvili (Tiflis: Zakgiz, 1935), 85–86).

77 Lotman and Uspenskii, "Binary Models," 52–56; see also Karlinsky, *Russian Drama*, 24–29.

78 It is significant that the opponent of the pagan sorcerers is not a churchman but a Greek philosopher. See Karlinsky, *Russian Drama* 26.

79 Iu.M. Lotman, "Ideinaia struktura 'Kapitanskoi dochki', "*Pushkinskii sbornik* (Pskov:

Pskovski Gos. Ped. Institut, 1962), 3–20.

80 Marc Raeff, "Home, School, and Service in the Life of the Eighteenth-Century Russian Nobleman," in *The Structure of Russian History*, ed. Michael Cherniavsky (New York: Random House, 1970), 295–307.

81 Henry L. Roberts, "Russia and the West: A Comparison and Contrast," in *The Structure of Russian History*, ed. Michael Cherniavsky (New York: Random House, 1970), 256.

82 My emphasis; Marc Raeff, "Russia's Perception of Her Relationship with the West," in *The Structure of Russian History*, ed. Michael Cherniavsky (New York: Random House, 1970), 262–63.

are *beguny* [a sect whose name means "runners," those running from this world] and bandits. And Russians are wanderers [*stranniki*] in search of God's truth."[83] It is only a short step from this account of the sectarian genesis of Russian restlessness and "flight" to a *general* spatialization of the urge for temporal reintegration experienced by all great Russian writers:

> Russians always thirst for another life, another world; they always experience displeasure at what is. There belongs to the structure of the Russian soul an eschatological directedness. The urge to wander [*strannichestvo*] is a very characteristic Russian phenomenon, and as such unknown to the West. The wanderer walks the boundless Russian land and never settles down [*osedaet*], never becomes attached to anything. The wanderer searches for the truth, for the Kingdom of Heaven; he is directed into the distance. The wanderer has no abiding earthly city, but is directed toward the City-to-Come [*Grad Griadushchii*]. The people [*narodnyi sloi*] have always singled out from their midst such wanderers. Yet in spirit the most creative representatives of Russian culture — Gogol, Dostoevsky, L. Tolstoy, Vl. Solovyov, and all the revolutionary intelligentsia — have also been wanderers. There exists not only a physical, but a spiritual urge to wander. This is the inability to be at ease with anything finite, the directedness toward what is infinite. But this is also an eschatological directedness, an expectation that there will be an end to all that is finite, that a final truth will be revealed, that in the future some sort of extraordinary occurrence will take place. I would call this a messianic sensibility, to an equal degree characteristic of those [coming] from the people [*narod*] and of those of higher culture. Russians are, to a greater or lesser extent, consciously or unconsciously, chiliasts. Westerners are much more sedentary [*osedlye*], more attached to the perfected forms of civilization; they value their present and are more concerned with the successful management of the earth.[84]

As is often the case, Berdyaev's generalizations could be relegated to the musty files of *Geistesgeschichte* were it not for the influence such notions had on leading nineteenth century thinkers, who in turn, with their own mix of mythos- and political agenda, cast an imposing shadow on the

---

83   Berdiaev, *Russkaia idela*, 10.
84   Ibid., 199.

"authors" of the revolution at the turn of the twentieth century. One need only recall how attached Lenin was to his executed brother's copy of *What Is to Be Done?* (1863),[85] itself a kind of utopian fairy tale with an ideal future (cast in the present) and a plucky Cinderella (Vera Pavlovna) who wins both her prince and her happy kingdom (a Russian version of the Fourierian phalanstery) in the bargain. From the late eighteenth to the early twentieth century nearly every major historian, philosopher, and author (as well as countless minor ones) tried to come to terms with the familiar old/new, east/west oppositions, and, as social tensions increased and anarchy and revolution became more probable, they saw the conclusion to the historical plot rise into view either as a utopian triumph devoutly to be wished or as an apocalyptic *ekpyrosis* (great fire) or *kataklysmos* (great flood) anxiously to be awaited.

The most prominent landmarks are now commonplace in the annals of intellectual and cultural history and can be touched on here in telegraphic fashion:

(1) the Masonic "catastrophists" (Semyon Bobrov, Matvei Dmitriev-Mamonov, A. M. Kutuzov, Sergei Shirinsky-Shikhmatov) and other proto-Decembrists who forecast an end to the Russian Empire either by flood or by fire,[86] and who set down a tradition to be reworked by Pushkin, Vladimir Pecherin, Vladimir Odoevsky, Mikhail Dmitriev, and others;

(2) the preaching of St. Seraphim (1759–1833) about another order of time beyond this world and his prediction that the visit of a tsar to a nunnery would initiate a period of great upheaval and carnage;[87]

(3) the heated debate over the "old" and "new" styles in Russian literature carried on by the Shishkovites and Arzamasians in the early years of the century;

(4) the broad interest in history spurred by many things: the defeat of Napoleon in 1812, the monumental work of Karamzin that followed, the sharp disagreements in print between Pushkin and Polevoy over the authority of the great historiographer in the post-Decembrist Uprising years, the spate of historical studies that appeared in the 1830s and that derived authority either from the idealism of Hegel and Schelling (Polevoy, Ivan Kireevsky, Pogodin) or from the skepticism of Niebuhr and Von Ranke (Kachenovsky), the emergence into prominence of the historical novels of Bulgarin, Lazhechnikov, Zagoskin, and, in general, the dogged search for a legitimate national identity promoted during the reign of Nicholas I (ruled 1825–55);

---

85 The title was to reappear as one of Lenin's most important reinterpretations of Marxist doctrine.

86 For the poetic treatment of the great flood (*kataklysmos*) and great fire (*ekpyrosis*) see, e.g., Bobrov's "The Fate of the Ancient World" (1789?) and Dmitriev-Mamonov's "Fire" (1811?).

87 The visit would turn out to be made by Nicholas II in July 1903 and was seen to usher in the two revolutions. See Katerina Clark and Michael Holquist, *Mikhail Bakhtin* (Cambridge, Mass.: Harvard University Press, 1984) 133–34, 372.

(5) Chaadaev's famous critique, from the viewpoint of conservative French Catholic philosophy (de Bonald, de Maistre), of Russia's past (or absence thereof: "Isolated from the world, we have given nothing to the world; we have taken nothing from the world; we have not added a single idea to the mass of human ideas; we have contributed nothing to the progress of the human spirit"[88]), his premonition that some great turning point was at hand and that the establishment of the Kingdom of Heaven upon earth was imminent, and his radical *volte-face* in *Apologie d'un fou* (1836), when the lack of an historical past is suddenly transformed into the promise of a future ("the future is ours"[89]);

(6) the search by the Slavophiles (chiefly Ivan Kireevsky, Alexei Khomyakov, and Konstantin Aksakov) for an ideal past in the concepts of *sobornost'* (the spirit of "free unity") and *obshchina* (the peasant commune), their desire to project that past into the future as the *telos* of Russian history, and their radical rejection of the Catholic and Protestant West—the one's "unity without freedom" (i.e., socialism) and the other's "freedom without unity" (i.e., the "egoism" of Max Stirner);

(7) Belinsky's provocative *mot*, echoing Chaadaev's earlier historical claims, that "we have no literature";[90]

(8) Herzen's nagging fear of revolution ("This lava, these barbarians, this new world, these Nazarenes who are coming to put an end to the impotent and the decrepit... they are closer than you think"[91]), his skepticism about apocalypse and historical destiny ("history is all improvisation, all will, all extempore"[92]), his disenchantment with 1848, and yet his hope, during the period of "Russian Socialism," that his country — especially the Eastern frontier of Siberia — in its "newness" and "openness," could save the world from the corruption and philistinism of the European bourgeoisie;

(9) Bakunin's translation of Left Hegelianism into the joy of destruction (recall his notorious "Die Lust der Zerstörung ist auch eine schaffende Lust" [The desire for destruction is also a creative desire]) and total negation of the past;

(10) Dostoevsky's neurotic hatred of Switzerland, his falling out with Turgenev over the subject of Germany versus Russia, his savage parodies of the "men of the sixties," his anxiety over the rising tide of anarchy, terrorism, and *nechaevshchina*, and his predictions, especially in sections of *Diary of a Writer* written in the 1870s, that the Antichrist was afoot and

---

88 Peter Chaadaev, *Philosophical Letters, and Apology of a Madman*, trans. and intro. Mary-Barbara Zeldin (Knoxville: University of Tennessee Press, 1969), 41.

89 Ibid., 175.

90 V.G. Belinskii, *Polnoe sobranie sochinenii*, 13 vols. (Moscow: Akademiia Nauk SSSR, 1953–59), 1:22.

91 A.I. Gertsen (Herzen), *Sobranie sochinenii v tridtsati tomakh* (Moscow: Akademiia Nauk SSSR, 1954–65), 6:58–59.

92 Ibid., 6:34–35.

the End was near ("The Antichrist is coming to us! He is coming! And the end of the world is near — nearer than they think"[93]);

(11) Leontiev's conservative scorn for equality, progress and enlightenment, his rejection of drab and tasteless European dress and habits, his eerie sense of living at the edge of an abyss, his legendary desire to "freeze Russia lest she rot," and his conviction that "we suddenly, from the depths of our state bowels [*gosudarstvennye nedra*]... will give birth to the Antichrist" and "will end history, destroying humanity in a bloodbath of universal equality";[94]

(12) Fyodorov's utopian attempt, in *The Philosophy of the Common Cause* (1906, 1913), to render apocalyptic retribution "from beyond" unnecessary through a program of universal brotherhood, scientific discovery, and literal resurrection — molecule by molecule — of one's ancestors;

(13) Vladimir Solovyov's conviction near the end of his life that the twentieth century would be "an epoch of last great wars, civil disorders, and revolutions," that would reign, and that as a result of a universal intermixing of East and West there would emerge a "superman... a great thinker, writer, and public figure," whose activities on the stage of history would appear as a kind of photographic negative, or anti-image, of Jesus Christ.[95]

These are just a few of the moments that, taken together, gave our novelists the overwhelming sensation of apocalypse and *Endzeit*. I do not mean to suggest that there is a direct or simple correlation between these ideas themselves and the structure (as opposed to the themes per se) of the novels under discussion, but only that certain assumptions about the meaning of Russian history — it is meaningful because it is ending soon, and any ending, whether punitive or expiative, confers meaning — can also be made about the meaning of Russian history and individual biography as presented in narrative fiction. The time has come, however, to look more closely at what this means.

Plot

We have been speaking primarily of Russian history and the views of participants/spectators as to that history's alleged beginning and end. As we move to a discussion of fictional narrative and its presentation of a *Russian* apocalypse, it would be well to state several givens. First, as Arthur Danto has rigorously argued, there is a fundamental difference between historical crisis as viewed (or "lived") by a participant (say,

---

93 V.V. Timofeeva (Pochinkovskaia), "God raboty s znamenitym pisatelem," *F.M. Dostoevskii v vospominaniakh sovremenikov*, ed. V.V. Grigorenko et al (Moscow: Khud. lit., 1964), 2:170.

94 Konstantin Leon'tev, "Nad mogiloi Pazukhina," *Sobranie sochineniia* (Moscow: Izd. V.M. Sablina, 1912–13), 7:425.

95 Vladimir Solov'ev, *Tri razgovora* (New York: Chekhov, 1954), 193, 199.

Avvakum) and that same crisis as viewed by the historian (say, Michael Cherniavsky) looking back and narrating it.[96] The participant *projects* an ending, but the historian knows that that is how things turned out; the participant is still "inside" (hi)story, but the historian is by definition "outside" it, located temporally and spatially at that much invoked "meta-" level whence he or she can presumably, objectively and dispassionately, describe and therefore explain how the chronicle of events became history, how, in formalist terms, the "fable" (*fabula*) became a "plot" (*siuzhet*), the "story" (*histoire*) a "discourse" (*discours*).[97]

Thus it is the historian's special role to generate, in Danto's terminology, "narrative predicates"— those statements which, when applied to objects, "do so only on the assumption that a future event occurs," and which are seen as "retrospectively *false*... if the future required by the meaning- rules of these predicates fails to materialize."[98] Such narrative predicates make a special claim on the future, but it is a future only from the viewpoint of the participant. From the viewpoint of the historian it is *already past*: e.g., "Lenin's arrival at the Finland Station *would* [a modal the participant might have hoped for but could not know for certain] unify the revolutionary movement and contribute to the collapse of the Provisional Government." On the other hand, while the historian can narrate the past, he or she *cannot* narrate the future; the very closedness of the past (the historian is located outside it) implies that the future is open and that, in this new context, the historian must trade the role of narrator for that of participant/spectator (he or she is inside and part of that which is still unfolding). "*The very structure of narrative*," concludes Danto, "entails the openness of the future, for only then can it in any way depend upon the present."[99]

So much has been written about the essential isomorphism of historical and fictional narratives[100] that we tend to overlook the more basic difference between the narrative predicates characteristic of them.[101] The historian, if consistent and not given to narrating what cannot, *historically*, be known, is limited to a description of the past, meaning that his or her "meta"- viewpoint is only privileged vis-à-vis the participants of those already accomplished events and "turning points" at issue. To *know* the End from one's own viewpoint, from *one's present*, is to break the rules of a narrative predicate, and therefore to posit what for the *historical* narrative is an impossibility. "If the knowledge of the narrator [historian] were made available to the characters [participants, spectators], the structure of

---

96 Arthur Danto, *Narration and Knowledge* (New York: Columbia University Press, 1985), 342–63.

97 Seymour Chatman, *Story and Discourse: Narrative Structure in Fiction and Film* (Ithaca, Cornell University Press, 1978), 19.

98 Danto, *Narration and Knowledge*, 349–50.

99 Ibid., 353.

100 Both historical and fictional narrators select out and "prefigure" their material, both tell "stories," even if one is, based primarily on "fact" and the other, with varying degrees of subterfuge, embraces its fictionality, etc. A fine distillation of the argument is found in

narration would be destroyed."[102] Danto is assuming, as indeed he must, that there is no higher viewpoint *outside* of and enclosing the historian's future which can be known and narrated as history. Yet this very stricture, essential to the integrity of historical narration, does not necessarily bind the unfolding of fictional narrative. Perhaps the most fundamental, ahistorical argument advanced by the "apocalyptic fictions" we will be examining is that narrators, like historians, do stand in a position of "metacognitive" superiority to their characters, *but* these characters can, if sensitive to the signs/symbols in these stories, know ("intuit") what their narrators know. This is not of course historical knowledge as Danto would define it, but to the characters (and to their narrators and authors) it *is* knowledge (one would probably have to call it "mystical" or "revelatory") nonetheless.[103]

In other words, the protagonists of these novels, who in several cases write versions of their own stories, may be paradoxically characterized not only as "chroniclers" but, in a sense, as "historians"—they are given, by their narrator or author, a *foreknowledge* of the future *from the present*. Located on the inside, they are vouchsafed *aperçus* that could come only from the outside. And, strange to say, not only does this not destroy narrative, it makes it rich and mystifying. We are constantly presented with Escher-like optical illusions, with narrative hierarchies that, like staircases climbing upward and simultaneously back into themselves, are both circular *and* open. For just as in fiction a character can have knowledge that by rights should only belong to the narrator (the Master "knows" that the stranger at Patriarchs Ponds *is* the Devil),

---

Suzanne Gearhart, *The Open Boundary of History and Fiction* (Princeton, NJ: Princeton University Press, 1984), 3–28, but see also Roland Barthes, "Historical Discourse," in *Structuralism: A Reader*, ed. and intro. Michael Lane (London: Jonathan Cape, 1970), 145–55; Leo Braudy, *Narrative Form in History and Fiction* (Princeton: Princeton University Press, 1970); W.B. Gallie, *Philosophical and Historical Understanding* (New York: Schocken Books, 1968); Lionel Gossman, "History and Literature," in *The Writings of History: Literary Form and Historical Understanding*, ed. Robert H. Canary and Henry Cozicki (Madison: University of Wisconsin Press, 1978), 3–39.; J. Hillis Miller, "Narrative and History," *ELH* 41(1974): 455–73.; and Hayden White, *Metahistory: The Historical Imagination in Nineteenth-Century Europe* (Baltimore: The John Hopkins University Press, 1973). Gearhart's book is useful for its non-flamboyant discussion of the contributions of many of the chief participants in this dialogue, including Louis Althusser, Roland Barthes, Arthur Danto, Paul de Man, Jacques Derrida, Michel Foucault, W.B. Gallie, Claude Lévi-Strauss, and Hayden White.

101 Cf. Bakhtin's position on the difference between novel and history as explained by Michael Holquist in Mikhail Bakhtin, *The Dialogic Imagination*, ed. Michael Holquist and trans. Caryl Emerson (Austin: University of Texas Press, 1981): "But histories differ from novels in that they insist on a homology between the sequence of their own telling, the form they impose to create a coherent explanation in the form of a narrative on the one hand, and the sequence of what they tell on the other. This templating of what is enunciated with the act of enunciation is a narrative consequence of the historian's professional desire to tell 'wie es eigentlich gewesen ist' ["how it really was"]. The novel, by contrast, dramatizes the gaps that always exist between what is told and the telling of it, constantly experimenting with social, discursive and narrative asymmetries (the formal tetralogy that led Henry James to call them 'fluid puddings'" (xxviii).

102 Danto, *Narration and Knowledge*, 356.

103 To "narrate the world" in this way is to do something

so too can the narrator, circumscribed by the work's beginning and end, have knowledge that should only belong to the author. Such then is the epistemological Phrygian Cap coming between the narrative hierarchies of historiography and fiction writing. The novel can play with, indeed be obsessed by, the meaning of history, but it can also freely undermine the logic of the narrative predicate without which historiography is impossible.

At this point I would like to offer a rough typology of a sub-genre of the modern Russian novel which I call the "apocalyptic fiction." Along the way I will also suggest why certain current assumptions about novelistic form in general and narrative in particular do not always account for the "structure" of these works, which routinely question their own limits as verbal art only to posit a non-verbal (or non-verbalizable) meaning lying *beyond*. This is to say, in the first place, that an apocalyptic fiction is not an apocalypse, but a modern equivalent of one, a kind of sacred text or version of *the Book* through which the character and the narrator and, by implication, the reader — all in their separate, self-enclosed realms — are made privy to a "secret wisdom" from another space-time. For our purposes the following characteristics might be selected out as determinative in apocalyptic fiction: (1) a canonical subtext that plays an important role both thematically and structurally in the parent text (in our case the Apocalypse of John); (2) a living tradition with which the work enters into dialogue and against which it asks to be read (i.e., the work is not an isolated phenomenon); (3) an apocalyptic "set" or predisposition to read current historical crisis through the prism of the Johannine structures and figures (here, the Revolution as eschatological turning point to be either anticipated or retrospectively evaluated);[104] and (4) an apocalyptic plot whose "deep" or mythological structure in modern novelistic terms is a recapitulation of the essential movement of the Johannine text.

Rather than looking at these novels through the either/or optic of structuralism or poststructuralism — that is, they are *either* self-regulating, self- inscribing linguistic units whose "anatomies" can be classified and dissected with the appropriate narratological *langue* (Tomashevsky, Barthes, Todorov, etc.) *or* they are generic anarchists whose chief *raison d'être* is to subvert convention and tradition and to exist in what Bakhtin would call a zone of maximum openness with reality — we will see them as verbal forms that are *simultaneously aware of their openness and*

very similar to what Karl Solger and Friedrich Schlegel discussed and Ludwig Tieck, E.T.A. Hoffmann, and Heinrich Heine practiced under the rubric of "Romantic Irony." The romantic ironist, however, sees the character as the author's plaything, just as a human being is a puppet held up by a mocking deity's strings. To put it another way, the boundary-line between story and teller, narrative and narrator, is to be crossed only by "the fully-conscious artist whose art is the ironical presentation of the ironic position of the fully-conscious artist" (D.C. Muecke, *Irony* [London: Methuen, 1970], 20). Yet for these Russian writers and the tradition they were creating,

closedness, and of the boundary between *Wahrheit* and *Dichtung*. As Frank Kermode has aptly remarked, these are the fragile "fictions of concord," the "plots of, or against, the world and time" that, neither pure reality nor pure myth, fully acknowledge the modern world's skepticism about holistic pattern and yet somehow are able to provide form enough to make sense of our lives.[105]

Let us now examine more closely the various elements of an apocalyptic fiction. To begin with, each of the novels in question alludes significantly to the Johannine text. These allusions are not merely thematic overlay, that is, their function is not limited to drawing the reader's attention to the fate of individual Russian heroes and Russian history caught at "biblical" turning-points or crises. Rather, we are invited to view the mythic "zone" of novelistic space (i.e., the themes, figures, and passages taken from Revelation) and the realistic "zone" of novelistic space (i.e., the openness and contingency of contemporary life and history) as being in profound dialogic interaction. It is not simply that the mythic zone subsumes and determines the realistic zone in a straightforward and simplistic allegory or that the realistic zone upstages and undermines the authority of the mythic zone in an irreverent parody, but that genuine meaning — what it really signifies to experience apocalypse and revelation *in our time* — must be sought in a full-scale and honest confrontation between the two.

Myshkin cannot be understood only — if at all — as the triumphant Christ of the Second Coming; nor can the manifest weaknesses of the Master or Yury Zhivago be explained away by calling them Christ figures; nor can we disentangle *Petersburg*'s plot (in both senses of the word) by acknowledging the very real parallels planted there between the Bronze Horseman and the Antichrist. If the Christian myth does have the last word in these works, *enclosing* the aimless flux of chronos in a higher pattern, it is not an easily won victory. Rogozhin murders Nastasya Filippovna and Myshkin goes mad; Dudkin murders Lippanchenko and Nikolai Apollonovich almost blows up his father; the Master and Margarita die at the hands of the same Pilate who executed Yeshua when they drink the gift of his poison wine; Sasha Dvanov follows his fisherman father into Lake Mutevo and suicide; and Yury Zhivago dies a broken man, having lived the last years of his life in the house of a former servant, while Lara disappears into the camps and their orphan daughter is left to fend for herself. In each case, to read these heroes' and heroines' actions

---

the narrative hierarchy does not have to be in the shape of a closed and vicious circularity.

[104] Frank Kermode, "Apocalypse and the Modern," in *Visions of Apocalypse: End or Rebirth?* ed. Saul Friedlander et al. (New York: Holmes and Meier, 1985), 86.

[105] Frank Kermode, *The Sense of an Ending: Studies in the Theory of Fiction* (New York: Oxford University Press, 1967), 59; "Apocalypse and Modern," 101.

within history (or history as represented as narrative) is to read them as failure. Yet to conclude from this that the primary function of the apocalyptic subtext is parodic is, as most readers would readily affirm, to misinterpret something very basic. What Pasternak's title character says in high seriousness could be applied (with certain reservations) to the entire tradition we are investigating: "All great, genuine art resembles and continues the Revelation of St. John: it always meditates on death and thus always creates life."[106]

The question of tradition in these novels is potentially vexed for the simple reason that they can be said to form a conscious and coherent whole only from our position "on the outside," and then presumably only with a good deal of typological tampering. "Conscious" and "coherent" to which historian, which narrator? Julia Kristeva's concept of *intertextualité* ("the transposition of one or more *systems* of signs into another") is useful in this connection only if one is interested in isolating the boundaries of the novel as *textual system* and then demonstrating how, in time, those same boundaries are contaminated and "transposed."[107] As even the casual reader can see, these five novels do not form an "intertext" in the sense of master grid of biographical influence or literary provenance. The lines of influence are more tangled than that and in any case may go back further, often to Pushkin and Gogol, who were perceived in this tradition as mediators between Russia's "epic past" and the modern historical present. For example, Dostoevsky alludes prominently to Pushkin in *The Idiot*; Bely to Pushkin, Gogol, Dostoevsky and others in *Petersburg*; Platonov to Dostoevsky in *Chevengur*; Bulgakov to Pushkin, Gogol, and Dostoevsky in *Master and Margarita*; and Pasternak to Pushkin and the Symbolists in *Doctor Zhivago*. It is probably more accurate to say that these Russian novelists were reacting to the unique injunctions of their moment and to the sense of national crisis that had to be narrated and "domesticated" into meaningful structures for them personally. Their eccentric novelization of history brings to mind such celebrated Western apocalypticists as Robert Musil and D. H. Lawrence; the latter's view of historical epochs as a neo-Joachimist triad dominated by "Law," "Love," and the "Comforter" is uncannily similar to the ideas of Vladimir Solovyov and Merezhkovsky, just as his urge to translate an apocalyptic fervor into personal myth is rivaled only by that of Andrei Bely. Any quasi-Proppian analysis which advances a "master plot" at the expense of the "living" and changing

---

[106] Boris Pasternak, *Doctor Zhivago*, trans. by Max Hayward and Manya Harari (New York: Signet, 1958), 78.

[107] Julia Kristeva, *Desire and Language: A Semiotic Approach to Literature and Art*, ed. Leon S. Roudiez, trans. Thomas Gora et al. (New York: Columbia University Press, 1980), 15.

aspects of the tradition cannot do justice to the existence in history, the historicity, of these forms.

What can be said without oversimplifying the case about the tradition of apocalyptic fiction on Russian soil is the following:

(1) the already mentioned eschatological orientation in cultural consciousness, which had its genesis in earlier centuries and which assumed an ever greater prominence with the rise of historiosophical/historiographical debate in the nineteenth century, was still experienced as real and vital by these writers and was incorporated into the structure of their fictions.[108] All of these works provide compelling cases of how context, text, and subtext interact, since in them the authors borrow from given bodies of Russian messianic or eschatological thought and adapt them to their own purposes — for Dostoevsky, it was the Slavophiles; for Bely, Vladimir Solovyov; for Bulgakov, Pavel Florensky; for Platonov and Pasternak, Nikolai Fyodorov.

(2) In terms of richness and breadth of apocalyptic literature, there is nothing to compare in the Russian context with the Symbolist period and with the theme of "last things" in the many novels, stories, poems, essays and philosophical causeries of Vladimir Solovyov, Dmitry Merezhkovsky, Vasily Rozanov, Valery Briusov, Maximilian Voloshin, Alexei Remizov, Alexander Blok, Andrei Bely, and others. Indeed, it could be said without exaggeration that the "new" Soviet literature and the doctrine of Socialist Realism that it eventually engendered were logical — if often forced — extensions of this culture of "last things," and that the long-awaited *transitus* from old to new, end to beginning, then to now, was not only historically determined, as many wished to believe, but also predetermined by this essentially Christian myth, ancient, potent, yet ever mutable.[109] And

(3) taken together, these five works represent various responses of the novel form (from roughly 1860 to 1960) to the central apocalyptic event of modern Russian consciousness, which they either predict or "prophesy,"

[108] As an aside one could mention the intelligentsia tradition of defining the perceived boundaries of epochal change with the help of certain root spatial and temporal metaphors: Radishchev's *Journey from St. Petersburg to Moscow*, Herzen's *From the Other Shore* and *Endings and Beginnings*, Turgenev's *On the Eve*, Chernyshevsky's "The Russian at the Rendezvous," Dobrolyubov's "When Shall the Real Day Come?" Bely's *The Beginning of the Century* and *Between Two Revolutions*, Vyach. Ivanov's *Furrows and Boundaries*, etc.

[109] This connection is especially clear in the "salvation programs," the plans to achieve secular, *physical* immortality, that surfaced either explicitly or implicitly in many Soviet works. Irene Masing-Delic, in her *Abolishing Death: A Salvation Myth of Russian Twentieth-Century Literature*, (Stanford: Stanford University Press, 1992), identifies a number of texts, including Khlebnikov's *Ladomir*, Ognyov's "Eurasia," and Zabolotsky's *Columns* and *The Triumph of Agriculture*, where this theme of the literal overcoming of death is prominent.

as in the cases of Dostoevsky and Bely, or look back on with the wisdom of disconfirming hindsight, as in the cases of Platonov, Bulgakov, and Pasternak.

It has long been maintained that as the idea of history as divinely inspired human activity with an imminent conclusion from without gave way to the idea of history as secular progress with an immanent conclusion here on earth the historical "plot" was constantly modified to include an ever wider and disparate reality. This plot, asserts Kermode, made its way not only into our histories but into our fictions — secular humanity's answer to *the Book*. In *Natural Supernaturalism* M.H. Abrams has further contributed to the discussion by demonstrating that the vast history of apocalyptic literature in the West reached its highwater mark during the period of the French Revolution: the millenarian enthusiasm and hopes for a new age found in the early works of the English and German romantics (especially Blake, Southey, Wordsworth, Coleridge, Schelling, Hölderlin, and Hegel) were severely tested in the wake of Jacobin terror. The end of history as they knew it — which *should* have come with the revolution but did not — was dealt with not by rejecting apocalypticism out of hand but by turning to an *artistic re-visioning* of reality which was able to accommodate the specter of disconfirmation. Thus, the central distinction between much of the earlier and later works of these poets and historians (from Wordsworth's *Descriptive Sketches* to his *Prelude*, from Coleridge's *Religious Musings* to his *Rejection: An Ode*, from Blake's *Marriage of Heaven and Hell* to his *Jerusalem*, etc.) involved a shift in emphasis from an "apocalypse of revolution," or a universal eschatology achieved through sudden and violent political means, to an "apocalypse of consciousness,"[110] or a personal eschatology achieved through the agency of the poetic imagination. For the romantics of the post-revolutionary era the New Jerusalem was to be achieved, in Abrams' words, "not by changing the world but by changing the way we see the world."[111] And without ignoring important cultural differences, I would also propose that

[110] Cf. M.H. Abrams' statement (*Natural Supernaturalism* [New York: Norton, 1971], 332) on the English and German romantics before the French Revolution and the Russian symbolists before the October Revolution: "[Their works] are written in the persona of the visionary poet-prophet, 'the Bard,' who present, past, and future sees; they incorporate the great political events of their age in suitable grandiose literary forms, especially the epic and 'the greater Ode'; they present a panoramic view of history in a cosmic setting, in which the agents are in part historical and in part allegorical or mythological and the overall design is apocalyptic; they envision a dark past, a violent present, and an immediately impending future which will justify the history of suffering man by its culmination in an absolute good; and they represent the French Revolution (or else a coming revolution which will improve on the French model) as the critical event which signals the emergence of a regenerate man who will inhabit a new world uniting features of a restored paradise and a recovered Golden Age."

[111] Abrams: *Natural Supernaturalism*, 347 and "Apocalypse: Theme and Variations," in *Apocalypse in English Renaissance Thought and Literature*, ed. C.A. Patrides and Joseph Wittreich (Ithaca: Cornell University Press, 1984), 363.

for Russian apocalypticists like Bulgakov and Pasternak, who wrote *after* 1917 and who had to make sense of the revolution's excesses and failings, this same shift to a personal eschatology and to an artistic, as opposed to a political, revisioning of reality is readily apparent.

Finally, as far as tradition is concerned, it can be argued that these works, and others like them, constitute a resilient set of counter-models to the Socialist Realist classic, and this may be one reason why they have become the tradition to be studied in the Western academy. Katerina Clark has described how certain elements of the Socialist Realist "master plot" can adapt to historical context and still remain cohesive (e.g., a hero's being historically "spontaneous" [*stikhiinyi*] or "conscious" [*soznatel'nyi*] can be characterized as positive or negative depending on the time and place of writing[112]). What the Socialist Realist classic is able to do with a remarkable economy of means is to "fabulize" a Marxist view of history by manipulating certain powerful and hallowed mythical categories: the Bolshevik hero, such as Gleb Chumalov, has been in touch with an epic past — he participated in 1917, performed legendary feats of heroism at the front, and knows people, like Shibis, who *saw* Lenin. And this contact with a sacred past confers the "right stuff" on Gleb; it allows him to confront and overcome a problem-ridden present (NEP) and make his way toward, but never actually to, the *telos* of communism. Likewise, *Mother* freely borrows the semantics of religious conversion to generate enthusiasm for the indisputable destiny of Gorky's Marxist "elect." Our primarily "Christian" authors, on the other hand, incorporate into their narratives a different view of history. Because meaning is not immanent or historically determined (that is, it does not come "from within"), it must be generated by comparing the *disjunction* between character and narrator, narrator and reader, and ultimately reader and God. What prevents dramatic irony in the Socialist Realist classic (the narrator does not play with character or reader because "enlightenment" is not relative and because "realism" implies a maximum proximity to history and a maximum distance from fiction), is precisely what makes meaning so richly polysemous in these relentlessly unrealistic works about the climax of Christian history. Here too we find characters "from beyond," as shall be suggested in more detail in a moment, but their function, in terms of the purpose or goal of history, is entirely different.

What are the essential elements of the "apocalyptic plot" and how do they relate to the works under discussion? First, each of these novels in a

---

[112] Katerina Clark, *The Soviet Novel: History as Ritual* (Chicago: University of Chicago Press, 1981), 46–67.

fundamental way is about *the End*. A number of contemporary critics have made studies of the device of closure in the modern novel, with the implication that, regardless of strategies for sealing off, or leaving open, a narrative,[113] the entire structure of a work is inevitably "end-determined," that is, it is emplotted backwards, from, as it were, its "Finis" to its "Once upon a time..." Yet it is not enough to say that these works are simply end-determined; both on the level of biography and on the grander level of Russian history, their narratives invoke the shadow of the biblical End. They are a search — and herein the spatial metaphor of the "path" or "road" (*put'*) necessarily enters discussion — for the meaning of the *Russian* apocalypse. Their heroes' and heroines' stories are Russia's stories, and in much the same way as the reader of the Socialist Realist classic is urged to draw analogies between the fate of a member of the elect and the country at large (that is, there is an unmistakable homology between development of a Bolshevik hero and the shape of Marxist historiography), so too is the reader of these works drawn to see a connection between personal death and the end of national, even world history. Not for nothing does each of these novels conclude, and most begin, with a crucial death: Marie and Nastasya Filippovna in *The Idiot*, Lippanchenko and Nikolai's parents in *Petersburg*, Sasha Dvanov's father and Sasha himself in *Chevengur*, Berlioz and the Master and Margarita in *The Master and Margarita*, and Yury's mother and father and Yury himself in *Doctor Zhivago*. As we proceed closer to 1917 (that is, from Dostoevsky to Bely), this parallelism between personal and national ends becomes more and more fraught with anxiety (and more and more formally complex). As suggested, however, those works written after 1917 (*Chevengur*, *Master and Margarita*, and *Doctor Zhivago*), when the connection between revelation and revolution has been disconfirmed and a qualitatively new era has *not* begun, still make comparisons between personal and national history, but use different strategies in order to avoid a literal prediction of the end of Russian history within time (e.g., Menippean satire/"mock apocalypse" in the case of *The Master and Margarita*, the secularization of the apocalyptic through Fyodorovian philosophy in the cases of Platonov and Pasternak).

To speak of the apocalyptic plot in narrative terms is also to make certain assumptions about the shape of Christian *Heilsgeschichte*. Despite their considerable variety, sophistication, and lack of orthodoxy (or Orthodoxy), these authors' views of history share a concern with those of the biblical prophets about the nature, compass, and narrative presentation of

---

113 E.g., the relation of end to beginning and middle may be "circular" or "parallel" or "incomplete" or "tangential," etc. See Marianna Torgovnik, *Closure in the Novel* (Princeton: Princeton University Press, 1981), 3–19, as well as Alan Friedman (*Turn of the Novel* [New York: Oxford University Press, 1966]), D.A. Miller (*Narrative and Its Discontents: Problems of Closure in the Traditional Novel* [Princeton: Princeton University Press, 1981]), and David Richter (*Fable's End* [Chicago: University of Chicago Press, 1974]).

the End — what would it look like from "here" or from "there"? how can its projected significance be read backwards to provide meaningful pattern in one's life now? what in this conclusion to history's plot is "fictitious" — the result of an insufficiently informed reading of the signs — and what is "real" — the result of a truly *higher* understanding? If scholars of biblical texts such as Collins can speak of the "genre" of apocalypse in descriptive terms, then perhaps we can speak of a subset of the modern novel which takes the core elements of the biblical genre and adapts them to its own hybrid form. Among the assumptions about the narrative shape of history that enter into the biblical genre and that are relevant to our discussion are the following:

(1) History is determined by God's plot, but the individual is free to choose between positive and negative fields of action within that plot. In narratological terms, this means that characters are limited both as "actants" once they act and as verbal constructs once their action is described, but that they can free themselves from this epistemological prison and, as it were, unwrite their biographies once they know what the narrator/author does.[114]

(2) The latter, tumultuous stage of history which these modern novelists as "prophets" are describing follows the same *triadic pattern* of crisis-judgment-vindication found in Revelation and other canonical apocalypses. However, whereas the initial stages of crisis and judgment are usually self-evident, the final stage of vindication may not be, and depends on whether a higher authorial viewpoint of all-embracing unity and resolution — the novelistic equivalent of the biblical marriage of the Lamb and the Bride — can be posited from "within" the text.

(3) History is a *totality*, and its movement from beginning to end is also a *return* — from a paradise of innocence (the Garden of Eden) to a paradise *earned* through suffering (the New Jerusalem).[115] In each of these novels the period of innocence or grace is "not of this world" and is experienced as a separate, enclosed epic past which took place prior to the principal action and which preceded the hero's and/or heroine's "fall into" history: Myshkin's "fairy tale" romance with Marie in Switzerland and Nastasya Filippovna's idyllic life at Otradnoe before the seduction by Totsky; Nikolai Apollonovich's dashing presence as an Ivan Tsarevich before his attempted rape of Sophia Petrovna; the Kitezh-like realm that Sasha's father goes to look for in Lake Mutevo and that, as the symbol of what separates parent from child, haunts and simultaneously moves Sasha forward in

---

[114] A compelling example of this situation is presented in the mock apocalyptic ending to Nabokov's *Invitation to a Beheading*.

[115] This movement, by the way, which is both a progression and a return, evokes the image of the romantic spiral, an image alluded to either explicitly or implicitly in several of the works under discussion and serving in them as an important structural principle. For more on the romantic spiral, see Abrams, *Natural Supernaturalism*, 183–87.

his search for the Bolshevik City of the Sun; the Master's and Margarita's life with their novel and the lottery money before the work is finished and "crucified" by the literary establishment; Yura's adolescent notions about sex before he sees the frightening galvanism joining Komarovsky and Lara, and Lara's own virginal symmetry and beauty before these are shattered by the lawyer's "Roman" ethic. This paradise lost is then projected into the future, beyond the present crisis (and its boundaries as "text"), as the *telos* of personal and national history; if it is to be recaptured at all, it is only *at the end*, through suffering and death (compare, for example, the final resting place of the Master and Margarita *outside* history and the salvational status of the *late* Yury Zhivago's poetry). And

(4) an understanding of history, which all apocalypses profess to provide, is possible only by looking for signs — in artistic terms, symbols — of God's will in the otherwise baffling "text" of current events. Such "revelations" normally involve a conflation of narrative's mythical and realistic "zones": the buffoon Lebedev reading a central passage from Revelation to a brooding Nastasya Filippovna; the half-literate Styopka regaling the alcoholic Dudkin with popular versions of the Second Coming. Too marked to be dismissed as parody, they might better be seen as those charged moments when another, authoritative voice from beyond intrudes into the text to speak of the End.

Another salient element of the apocalyptic plot is the messenger from a different temporality and spatiality who announces/reveals to the characters of this world that the end is at hand. To recall the basic terms of Collins' definition: "'Apocalypse' is a genre of revelatory literature with a narrative framework, in which *a revelation is mediated by an otherworldly being* to a human recipient, disclosing a transcendent reality which is both temporal, insofar as it envisages eschatological salvation, and spatial, insofar as it involves another, supernatural world." In the Johannine text itself, this messenger is the angel of God who provides the prophet with his vision and who takes his place "betwixt-and-between" the heavenly and earthly realms. The fact that the angel appears from somewhere outside history to a member of humanity trapped within history (and mortality) is the very essence of the revelation (*apokalypsis*). These novels also provide such a mediating figure, although often thinly disguised in what remains of a "realistic" tradition. Logically enough, his appearance in the lives of other characters usually raises questions of his or their sanity.

---

116 Bakhtin, on the other hand, would undoubtedly argue that the notion of human dialogue outside of time is literally inconceivable, a *contradictio in adjecto*. To speak of a Voice from outside time is, according to him, to release the listening hero (and reader) into a kind of "audiencelessness" (impossible) or "neotvetstvennost'" (unresponsiveness in various senses). Be this as it may, it is my contention that these novelists were attempting to project the narrative equivalent of just such an optical (or auditory) illusion. Their model for divine utterance is potentially non-binding with regard to the speaker's time and space (what has been said can be

In *The Idiot*, this figure is the title character, that passionate advocate of beginnings (his offer of marriage at Nastasya Filippovna's birthday party) and ends (his thoughts on execution) who has come to fallen Petersburg and to life "in the middle" with his epileptic visions of an existence outside time; in *Petersburg*, it is the Bronze Horseman (and the Unicorn), who announces to the lesser characters that their end, and that of Russia, is imminent; in *Chevengur*—Sasha's father, who, having plunged into the lake, already knows the secret of death for which his son spends the entire novel searching; in *Master and Margarita*—Woland, who knows that there is a historical Jesus, a Satan, and an existence beyond death (which he brings Berlioz) and whose appearance sets off the race around the streets of Moscow that lands Ivan (a modern-day St. John?) in Rimsky's asylum; and in *Doctor Zhivago*, this figure is the mysterious Evgraf, the "angel of death," who, "as though falling from the skies," appears to Yury during his bout with typhus, helps to raise him, like Lazarus, from the dead, and at the same time encourages him to write poetry, the most tangible evidence of Zhivago's "talent for life." All these figures, then, come from or have access to a different temporality, and it is their role to enter history ("life in the middest") with messages, often cryptic or difficult to translate into the logic of everyday speech, about eschatological salvation ("life at the end").

What this also means, to subvert for a moment Bakhtin's logic with regard to novelistic discourse, is that this voice is not merely that of any other, whose status is equal and equally contingent, but that of *the Other*, whose status is transcendent and uniquely resonant.[116] It is true that Myshkin's efforts to follow this voice and forego judgment only bring judgment with a vengeance; then again, to think this way is to judge him and the other protagonists *within history, within the text*. The voice that speaks to Myshkin during his epileptic aura, before his falling sickness, or to Homeless each Easter season when the injection, his symbolic crucifixion, releases him from his nightmare and puts him back in touch with a radiant and calm Master and Margarita, or to Yury at the moment of poetic inspiration when he becomes St. George and the wolves closing in on the house at Varykino become the dragons of history, is the voice from *outside* time. And while it does not ignore the reality principle,[117] it does, contrary to Bakhtinian theory, suggest that human dialogue can be inscribed in divine monologue, that diachrony can unfold within a synchronous pattern.

unsaid) in precisely the way that *human* dialogue is not.

117 Again, it cannot be emphasized enough that all these characters are feckless in the eyes of history.

No sketch of the apocalyptic plot would be complete without mention of its chief protagonist and antagonist, Christ and Antichrist. As suggested earlier, none of these novels is a transparent allegory promoting literalist notions of the End. Instead they are hybrid forms that often apply principles of irony and parody to subvert the received wisdom (whether it be Christian or Marxist) of the Orthodox view. In the final analysis, however, they are not simply subversive or ironic but committed to a vision of their own, which is often mystical or quasi-gnostical and, in the cases of Bely, Bulgakov, and Pasternak, tightly linked with the gift of artistic creation.[118] The marked presence of Christ-like figures in nearly all of our novels — Myshkin ("Prince Christ"), the white Domino and Unicorn, the Master, Yury Zhivago — does *not* imply, at least in any obvious way, that these are versions of the triumphant Lord of the *Parousia* come to defeat the forces of the Beast and oversee the climax of human history.

The creators of these characters are too conscious of what history has wrought since Christ first made his appearance and supposedly conferred on time a unique meaning "from the end" to rely on the sort of "sudden relief expedition from the sky"[119] that appealed to the religious imagination of first and second century Christians. According to the typology set out by Theodore Ziolkowski in *Fictional Transfigurations of Jesus*, there is a danger in overinterpreting the "Christ-like" character in modern literature. If the features characterizing this hero do not add up to a consistently emplotted portrait, complete with the chief topoi, of the life of Jesus, then we are dealing with atmosphere and scattered allusion, but not with "fictional transfiguration." Thus, for instance, the majestic Pieter Peeperkorn in Mann's *The Magic Mountain* falls into the category of a modern transfiguration because his stay at the International Sanitorium Berghof has its climax in a parodic last supper and betrayal, while the character of Myshkin, for all its Christ-like qualities, does not.[120] Still, even if some of these Russian novels *do* have characters who come closer to a "transfigured" Christ,[121] this may not be what is ultimately significant. Ziolkowski's definition turns out to be too limited for our purposes, particularly when the chief focus in these Russian novels is on death, judgment, and *the end* of history. We are not here dealing with a simple paradigm of *Jesus redivivus* or *imitatio Christi* (examples of which abound in the ecstatic tradition of socialist literature), but with the Christ-like figure who must live near the end of his own and (in Dostoevsky and Bely at

---

[118] Platonov's work offers the clearest example of the collision of utopian and apocalypticist worldviews and, as the product of a proletarian dreamer deeply disenchanted by NEP, can rely on no higher belief in the transcendent value of language; it is thus unique in its pessimism and dark use of parody.

[119] Rufus Jones, *The Eternal Gospel* (New York: Macmillan Co., 1938), 5.

[120] Theodore Ziolkowski, *Fictional Transfigurations of Jesus* (Princeton: Princeton University Press, 1972), 3–6, 104–5.

[121] E.g., not only does the Master share many of Yeshua's traits, but his burning

least) his nation's history. None of these characters is the avenging Lamb of Revelation, the eerie field marshal on white charger come to scatter the forces of the unrighteous. Each must bear the judgment of history, his cross, and each must try to deal with what the end means for his time. Yet by now it should be obvious that if there is a way out, if history is to be transfigured, and if the humiliated Christ is to become victorious, it is through *the Book*.

Conversely, all those figures in these novels whose purpose it is to bring judgment are in essence fictional incarnations of the view that history, after Hegel and Marx, is its own highest court.[122] They are punishers, avenging horsemen, not Christ-like but Antichrist-like figures. Among them we find Rogozhin, who is associated in the dream of Ippolit (the "unleasher of horses") with the beast of Revelation and with the great dumb *mashina*, the "iron horse" and its relentless ride, that crushes the most beautiful being in the world; the Bronze Horseman, who pours his molten essence into Dudkin, the second Evgeny, and bids him kill Lippanchenko; Kopyonkin, the quixotic knight of the revolution, who kills out of comradely feelings and whose Proletarian Strength, the Bolshevik Rosinante, tramples everything underfoot; Pilate, the Rider of the Golden Spear, who executes Yeshua against his wishes and who threatens Cayaphas with a flood of Arab horsemen; and Strelnikov, the executioner, who from his armored train strikes out against the enemies of the revolution.

Steed

Mention of the avenging horseman brings us to the final element of the apocalyptic plot — the means it has at its disposal for propelling itself forward, for moving, as fictional history, from beginning to middle to end. Since all of these novels, as apocalyptic templates, begin in a time of the manuscript is obviously linked with the crucifixion of the historical Jesus.

[122] "Hegel's program was avowedly theological, was seen by him specifically as a regrounding of Christian revelation within the newly glimpsed limits of an intelligible human history. Thus, for instance, God brooding over the abyss becomes in Hegel Being in that moment of identity before its first self-estrangement through negation, and thus the Biblical creation of the universe becomes the process of self-estrangement through which Being splits off from itself into a realm of brute matter, *and thus Apocalypse becomes the reconciliation of all contradiction and the abolition of all differences in an Absolute Spirit that, in a last negation of negation, resumes all things into itself*... For Hegel, the notion of reality unfolding through contradictions and rising to ever-higher levels until Spirit at last becomes conscious of itself constituted no new Revelation but only (and here was the originality of Hegelian philosophy as he saw it) Revelation in its *immanent* form. History *discovering its own meaning from the inside*, humanity grasping itself not as the arbitrary creation of some absent sky-deity but the Spirit gradually becoming manifest to itself" (my emphasis; William Dowling, *Jameson, Althusser, Marx: An Introduction to 'The Political Unconscious'* [Ithaca: Cornell University Press, 1984], 44–45).

of crisis, their starting points are not the biblical garden, but a time much closer to the Johannine climax. This proximity to catastrophe has important implications for the form their stories take. What will be suggested, following but not necessarily agreeing with Bakhtin, is that these novelists need some concrete way to visualize the rapid and ominous passage of time in space. To make a pun that Bely (if not my reader) would approve of, they need to find a way to translate theodicy, or a justification of God's plot in the face of recalcitrant reality, into "the odyssey," or the journey down history's road. Bakhtin's term for this artistic translation is the *chronotope* (lit: "time-space"), that is, the place(s) in the text where the novelist seeks to "materialize time in space," to work out an equation for the spatialization of human temporal desire within the terms permitted by one's historical context. For Bakhtin the chronotope is much more than a traditional generic rubric; it is, as Caryl Emerson has recently pointed out, a "category of consciousness," an "assumption about the workings of time and space" that every author must make in seeking to "totalize" his or her world. It always contains an element of *evaluation* that tethers it to the author's "here" and "now" and, in this sense, it *cannot be transcended*.[123] Perhaps the most obvious way — at least to the Western mind — for the novel as personal/national history to show movement is through the time-honored figure of the road, which in modern times of doubt, anxiety, and irony tends to be beset by all manner of thresholds, crossroads, borders, and spatio-temporal choices.

All of our novels are dominated by the haunting presence of a "threshold city," the end of history's road or the place where all paths converge as history prepares for eschatological change. Thus the two prerevolutionary novels are set in the doomed imperial capital of Petersburg and the three postrevolutionary novels are set either in the "fallen" Third Rome of Moscow or in the beclouded *Civitas Solis* of Chevengur. These cities are the precise focal points where, to apply Eliade's terminology, the "profane center" (e.g., the Whore of Babylon) and the "sacred center" (e.g., the New Jerusalem) meet, where the modern seer, straddling two different temporalities, catches glimpses of an otherworldly order in the midst of worldly chaos and revolution. Related to this phenomenon of mythical centering is what the structural anthropologist Edmund Leach, analyzing the binary elements of biblical narrative, defines as "liminality" — that is, the rules governing the *limen*, the place "betwixt-

---

123 Caryl Emerson, *Boris Godunov: Transpositions of a Russian Theme* (Bloomington: Indiana University Press, 1986), 5–6; see also Pavel N. Medvedev, *The Formal Method in Literary Scholarship*, trans. Albert J. Wehrle (Baltimore: Johns Hopkins University Press, 1978), 129–30.

and-between" the sacred and profane where the prophet experiences revelation:

> Fined down to its essentials the argument [about *thresholds*] runs something like this. Uncertainty generates anxiety, so we avoid it if we can. The categories of language cut up the world into unambiguous blocks. The individual is either a man or a beast; either a child or an adult; either married or unmarried; either alive or dead. In relation to any building I am either inside or outside. But to move from one such clear state to its opposite entails passing through an ambiguous 'threshold,' a state of uncertainty where roles are confused and even reversed. This marginal position is regularly hedged by taboo.
>
> This finding clearly has an important bearing on my general topic of the relevance of anthropology to biblical studies. *For, after all, mediation between opposites is precisely what religious thinking is all about.*
>
> Thresholds, both physical and social, are a focus of taboo for the same reason that, in the Bible, inspired sacred persons, who converse face to face with God, or who, in themselves, have attributes which are partly those of mortal man and partly those of immortal God, *almost always experience their inspiration in a 'betwixt and between' locality, described as 'in the wilderness,' which is neither fully in This World nor in The Other.*[124]

The means that these Russian novelists find to place their heroes in a sacred-tabooed zone "betwixt-and-between" are rather obvious: Myshkin's idiocy and sexual ambivalence, Nikolai's androgynous status and Dudkin's alcoholic delirium, Sasha Dvanov's role as dreamy *durak* (as opposed to *umnik*), the Master's insanity, Yury's moments of illness and inspiration. More importantly, this state of social or psychological or artistic liminality is also associated with *sites* steeped in the Russian eschatological tradition.[125] It is, for example, at just such a sacred-profane site that Nastasya Filippovna must choose between the opposing versions of time represented by her prospective grooms, Myshkin and Rogozhin; or that Apollon Apollonovich, Nikolai Apollonovich, Dudkin, Lippanchenko, and Sophia Petrovna must learn what it means to be "doomed irrevocably" by the retributive horseman; or that the Chevengurians must labor to build a new life whose result is mass death; or that the Master and Margarita must experience first

---

[124] Edmund Leach and D. Alan Aycock, *Structuralist Interpretations of Biblical Myth* (Cambridge: Cambridge University Press, 1983), 15–16.

[125] The one exception being Chevengur, which follows a popular utopian model.

crucifixion, then resurrection at the hands of their artistic child; or that Yury, on the eve of the revolution, must look for his Christmas star in the same candle in the window that Lara has asked Pasha Antipov to light as she sets out to shoot Komarovsky, the cause of her "fall."

What is equally intriguing, however, is that in these apocalyptic fictions, in these novels that progress by (fore)telling the end, the journey down history's road is accelerated and foreshortened, for we are near the end and about to reach it. Taking their cue from perhaps the best-known of all passages — Revelation 6:1–8, which depicts history's movement through four stages of horse and rider — these novelists develop elaborate symbolic networks around the image of the horse and its modern counterpart, the train ("the iron horse"). I would like to propose that the horse is a powerful visual tool in the hands of these verbal artists precisely because it is capable of telescoping in one economical image several traditions (the imperial, the folkloric, the religious) and because its inherent qualities (speed, beauty, elemental forces, comradeship, martial prowess) make it an ideal symbol for eschatological transit, for the tumultuous "ride" from one space-time to another.[126]

86. Imperially, the steed sets the ruler or the aristocratic knight (*eques*) apart from the common people. If the ancient Egyptians discerned something undignified about seating their ruler on horseback and thus preferred the chariot, the Greeks had no such scruples and in fact placed great emphasis on horsemanship. One aspect of Alexander's "greatness" that has come down to us was his prowess on horseback (it was said that his horse Bucephalus would accept no other rider), including his discomfiting of Darius from his chariot as depicted in a famous mosaic. The steed continued to acquire significance, becoming the attribute not simply of the *eques*, but, especially during the Roman Empire, of the emperor: witness the famous equestrian monument to Marcus Aurelius first erected on the Capitol as a symbol of his majesty and authority and later preserved during the Christian era only because

---

126 In my treatment of the imperial and folkloric equine traditions I have relied extensively on the following sources: D.N. Anuchin, "Sani, lad'ia i koni, kak prinadlezhnosti pokhoronnago obriada," *Trudy Imperatorskogo Moskovskogo Arkheologicheskogo Obshchestva* 14 (1890): 83–226; H.W. Janson, "The Equestrian Monument from Cangrande della Scala to Peter the Great," in *Sixteen Studies* (New York: Harry N. Abrams, 1974), 159–187; R. Lipets, *Obrazy batyra i ego konia v tiurko-mongol'skom epose* (Moscow: Nauka, 1984); George Levitine, "The Problem of Portraits, Late Allegory, and the Epic of the Bronze Horseman," in *The Sculpture of Falconet*, trans. Eda M. Levitine (Greenwich: New York Graphic Society, 1972), 51–60; Robert N. Watson, "Horsemanship in Shakespeare's Second Tetralogy," *English Literary Renaissance* 13 (1983): 274–300. See also A. Bartlett Giamatti, "Headlong Horsemen: An Essay in the Chivalric Epics of Pulci, Boiardo, and Ariosto," in *Italian Literature: Roots and Branches*, ed. Giose Rimanelli and Kenneth John Atchity (New Haven: Yale University Press, 1976), 265–307; V.V. Ivanov, "Opyt istolkovaniia drevneindiiskikh terminov, obrazovannykh ot asva-'kon'," in *Problemy istorii iazykov i kul'tury narodov Indii* (Moscow: Nauka, 1974); Gertrude Jobes, *Dictionary of Mythology, Folklore, and Symbols* (New York: Scarecrow, 1962), 789–91; L.P. Potapov, "Kon' v verovaniiakh i epose narodov Saiano-Altaia," *Fol'klor i etnografia* (Leningrad: Nauka, 1977), 3:164–178; Beryl Rowland,

it was rechristened "Constantine" (thus linking the notion of papacy to empire) and moved to the Lateran. After a hiatus of almost a millennium, the equestrian reemerged in the monuments of Donatello, Verrochio, Bologna, Mochi, and Bernini, and in the sketches of Leonardo. Particularly noteworthy about the Renaissance treatment is the fact that the *concetto* (the conceit or "spark" for the entire project) for the *Reiterstandbild* underwent gradual change: the horse and rider were slowly separated as part of an ensemble decorating a ducal tomb (e.g., that of Cangrande [1330] in Verona); the *eques* now no longer had to be a sovereign, but could be a mere *condottiere*, or captain of mercenary forces (e.g., Donatello's *Gattamelata* [1448–50] in Padua); and the steed became more animated and full of latent power to the point that, in Leonardo's sketches and especially in Bernini's sculpture of Constantine the Great (1654–70), it finally reared up on its hind legs. Bernini's equestrian monument occupies such a prominent place in this genealogy because it is located on the Scala Regia (the main landing of the Vatican), thereby forming the first image of papal authority that a visitor encounters, and because Constantine is presented at that moment of revelation — the "moving stasis" of the rearing horse captures this *concetto* perfectly — when he sees the cross in the sky and prepares himself to conquer in its name.

This first completed statue of the rearing horse became, significantly, the model for the Louis XIV equestrian monument at Versailles, which in turn would influence Falconet as he worked on the Bronze Horseman for Catherine.[127] When Bernini's statue arrived in France, Louis' advisers urged that the rock support on which the statue rested be reconfigured in a representation of flames: at the time it was felt to be politically wiser to play down the imperial connotations and to recast the horseman in the role of a latter-day Marcus Curtius hurling himself into the abyss to save his earthquake-riven capital. Ironically, however, the earthquake was not to be forestalled, and in the wake of 1789 all royal equestrian statues in France save this one (which was conveniently located across the lake from the palace in a far corner of the park) were destroyed. And it is a double if not triple irony that Falconet, who supposedly despised Bernini, returned to the master's *concetto* (the rock rather than the flames) and that his statue of Peter the Great would have such an hypnotic effect on generations of the Russian intelligentsia faced with a similar specter of revolution.[128]

"The Horse and Rider figure in Chaucer's Works," *University of Toronto Quarterly* 35 (1965–66): 249–59; I.D. Sirotina, "Obraz konia v russkom, altaiskom i iakutskom geroicheskom épose," *Sibirskii fol'klor* (Novosibirsk: Novosibirskii gos. ped. institut, 1980), 41–61.

[127] Bernini had virtually finished the statue of Louis before he (Bernini) died, but since it underwent various changes once it reached French hands (see below), it is the sculptor's terracotta *bozzetto* which most accurately preserves his intentions.

[128] Janson, "The Equestrian Monument," 157–89.

Bernini had originally wished to represent Louis on a rocky summit, "in full possession of that Glory which... has become synonymous with his name,"[129] an idea which Falconet felt was justifiably transposable to the Russian context. Moreover, the snake being trampled underfoot was an allegory for defeated envy. But the Russian time-space in which this bronze "text" was erected quickly changed meaning. The tsar as modern Marcus Aurelius did not arguably mean much to the Russians,[130] but the tsar as Christ-like St. George slaying the serpent (the pagan forces) of history did. Long before this, in the late sixteenth century, foreigners visiting the court of Ivan the Terrible's son Fyodor Ivanovich mentioned the existence of "a golden medal portraying St. George mounted on a horse," which was worn on the sleeve or hat of the recipient as a sign of "the highest honor that can be bestowed for any service whatsoever."[131] In any event, the *apocalyptic* connotation of the horse and rider is very much in evidence on one of the extant flags of Ivan the Terrible, where we find Christ mounted on a white charger, surrounded by twenty-seven angels on horseback, and escorted by the archangel Michael with his winged steed. The official order of St. George, the most popular of all Russian military medals and the only tsarist decoration to survive (in altered form, of course) into Soviet times, was instituted in 1769, that is, some thirteen years before the unveiling of Falconet's statue on Petersburg's Senate Square. So while Peter had done his best to secularize the imperial iconography, it retained a religious referent after his death, even perhaps in Falconet's borrowed *concetto*. To subsequent generations the Moscow horseman could be seen as having moved —

129 Ibid., 166–67.

130 Wacław Lednicki (*Pushkin's "Bronze Horseman"* [Berkeley, CA: University of California Press, 1955], 33–34) shows that Falconet, in his correspondence with Catherine and Diderot, openly *opposed* a recreation of the original Marcus Aurelius. He much preferred the idea of "Peter-the-pacifist" and "Peter-the-legislator," with outstretched hand in a *protective* gesture (*main protectrice*). Nevertheless, in the court's efforts to legitimize Peter's role by tying the tsar to an older classical model, the connection with the Moscow horseman (St. George) was not avoided, especially in later generations (Blok, for example, was to compare specifically the rival horsemen: see Sergei Hackel, *The Poet and the Revolution: Aleksandr Blok's "The Twelve"* [Oxford: Oxford University Press, 1975], 41). Moreover, the fact that Falconet's equestrian was *rearing* (as opposed to the original Marcus Aurelius on the Capitoline) gave the monument an energy and *dynamic* relation to its surrounding space which was of course not lost on Pushkin. Here the main issue is not what Falconet or Catherine intended, but what those coming after read *into* the statue and its present context as cultural myth. For an excellent (though not entirely objective) discussion of Pushkin's understanding of Falconet's work, see Lednicki, *Pushkin's 'Bronze Horseman,'* 25–42. Pushkin's view of the dynamic between rider and steed is given a structuralist interpretation in Alexander Zholkovsky, *Themes and Texts: Toward a Poetics of Expressiveness* (Ithaca: Cornell University Press, 1984), 69–75.

131 These words belong to Giles Fletcher, an envoy of England's Queen Elizabeth I who visited Russia during the reign of Fyodor Ivanovich. See V. Durov, *Russkie i sovetskie nagradnye medali* (Moscow: Gos. Istoricheskii Muzei, 1977), 4. It is intriguing to note that on some of these medals there was simply a horseman, *without the defeated dragon*, or a *unicorn*. Some scholars attest that the dragon *came later*—that is, after the solitary horseman — during the late fifteenth century, when Moscow was considering the significance of the fall of Constantinople and adopting as state emblem the two-headed eagle. For more on the history of the St. George medal and order on Russian soil, see A.B. Lakier, *Russkaia*

against his will — to the city of Peter, St. George as having traded his lance for an arm pointed imperiously into Russia's future, and the serpent impaled by the lance as having become a snake trampled underfoot by the tsar's steed.[132]

Whether its rider was Christ or Antichrist, the majestic steed became *the* symbol of Russia rearing up into the space between the old and the new. If writers like Pushkin did not, for reasons of artistic temperament or historiosophical conviction, choose to make the connection between the monument and the apocalyptic *end* of Russian history (that connection would be established later), the reason was not, as we have seen, for any lack of eschatological tradition.[133] Peter could be viewed in opposite ways: by enlighteners as a St. George stamping out ignorance and obscurantism so that Russia could leap into a better future; by sectarians as a man-god who had betrayed his role as tsar to become emperor and hence Antichrist. But regardless of one's *a priori* beliefs about the direction of Russian history, Peter on horseback came to signify a radical and total shift in time-space relations, the visual equivalent of his new calendar. That this tradition was later undermined by other equestrians, notably Paolo Trubetskoy's satiric monument to Alexander III in which Peter's spirited charger comes to resemble a hippopotamus, should not be seen as a serious challenge to, but as confirmation of, the remarkable potency of Falconet's work, which from Pushkin's poem on retained a mythical status, either positive or negative. The statue of a triumphant Lenin arriving at the Finland Station *on his armored car (bronevik)* is of course further evidence that even the Soviets felt

geral'dika, 2 vols. (St. Petersburg, 1855), 1:228–31, 290–91; and N.N. Speransov, *Zemel'nye gerby Rossii* (Moscow: Sovetskaia Rossiia, 1974), 25–26.

132 As I argue in "The Role of the *Eques* in Puškin's Bronze Horseman," the confrontation(s) between Peter and Evgeny in Pushkin's poem in fact revolves around their opposing roles as "pagan" versus "sacred" riders. When in the first confrontation, for example, Evgeny is frozen astride a stone lion (the heraldic symbol of Yury Dolgoruky, founder of *Moscow*), which in turn stands guard over one of Petersburg's *new* houses (instead of over the *vetkhii domik*, the "little old house" of Parasha, Evgeny's fiancée), it can be said that the hero's various attributes as "Moscow horseman" have been undercut and parodied by their transference to the seat of the Bronze Horseman, the new city's all-powerful *kumir* (idol) and cruel tutelary spirit. See David M. Bethea, "The Role of the *Eques* in Puškin's *Bronze Horseman*," in *Puškin Today*, ed. David M. Bethea (Bloomington: Indiana University Press, 1993), 99–118.

133 Pushkin, who was a highly irreverent Voltairian in his youth (the anti-religious element persists in his work only until about 1826) did not have what we would call today an apocalyptic "turn of mind." But he did take for granted that his readers and correspondents would have some knowledge of the last book of the Bible. There are in all five indisputable mentions of the apocalypse in Pushkin's literary works (including drafts) and letters: see A.S. Pushkin, *Polnoe sobranie sochinenii*, ed. V.D. Bonch-Bruevich et al., 17 vols. (Moscow: Akademiia Nauk SSSR, 1937–1959), 1:162–63, 3:860, 12:174, 13:29, 14:121. Most of these references are parodic, that is, Pushkin tended to use them in a comic rather than serious context, referring to himself during the first Boldino autumn (1830), for example, as sending regards from his "Patmos" (letter to M. P. Pogodin of November 1830 in 14:121). On another occasion, Pushkin includes an allusion to the Pale Horse of Revelation in a draft of the poem "Verses composed during a night of insomnia" (Stikhi, sochinennye noch'iu vo vremia bessonnitsy, wr. 1830), but then removes it, presumably because he did not want the elements of this mythological system to invade his art on a serious level.

compelled to tap into a later, but transparently similar, version of the imperial equestrian.

Underlying our discussion of Falconet's and Pushkin's horsemen is another, larger issue. The Western tradition of equestrian statuary takes its roots from the notion of controlling, of "reining" in, a wild and passionate "body politic." The centaur is half brute beast; Euripides' Hippolytus (like his namesake in Dostoevsky's *The Idiot*) lives up to his etymology as an "unleasher of horses"; and, perhaps most influential, Plato's *Phaedrus* presents the human soul in the allegorical guise of a chariot driven by reason and drawn by noble and ignoble horses — all these images have created a context in which countless writers depict royal heroes as both "reining" and "reigning."[134] Among the ancient and modern authors who have adopted the Platonic metaphor or its correlate myth of the overproud Phaeton, one might mention Philo Judaeus, Plutarch, Augustine, Prudentius, Dante, Ariosto, Chaucer, Luther, Sidney, Spenser, Bunyan, Burton, Herbert, Jonson, and especially Shakespeare.[135] Whether presenting the fatal error of Macbeth's vaulting ambition in an image of Phaeton, or equating the loss of Richard II's solar (regal) status to Bolinbroke's mastery of his (Richard's) roan Barbary, or implying that Hal has come of age when he "uncolts" Falstaff and defeats his rival horseman of the "hotspur," Shakespeare returns incessantly to what he perceives as a necessary parallelism between ruling one's own passions and ruling those of the people.[136] This, after all, is the notion of noble horsemanship from which, etymologically and culturally, the *chivalric* tradition grew. He who could control his own steed and unhorse his opponent was the ideal knight; and victory in combat was all the evidence needed to establish nobility and status. Hence in Western literature as in statuary it was essential *to keep distinct* the notions of horseman and horse, rider and ridden.

In Russia, however, where a tsar such as Peter was associated by a significant segment of the population with what was *new* and *revolutionary* and the people with what was *old* and *orthodox*, this Western formula could not be so easily transplanted. If Catherine and her German "enlighteners" could insist, on viewing Falconet's work as an expression of Peter's proud design to control the elements (and, by implication, the wild force of the people), then those of another generation could also see the tsar as that figure which, by turning Russia westward and upsetting the *status quo*, unleashed rather than reined in the passions of his

[134] Watson, "Horsemanship," 275.
[135] Watson, "Horsemanship," 275–79; see also Giamatti, "Headlong Horses"; and Rowland, "The Horse and Rider figure." Even Freud felt "spurred on" by the metaphor when comparing the roles of ego and id: "One might compare the relation of the ego to the id with that between a rider and his horse. The horse provides the locomotive energy, and the rider has the prerogative of determining the goal and of guiding the movements of his powerful mount towards it", Sigmund Freud, *New Introductory Lectures on Psychoanalysis*, trans. W. J. H. Sprott (New York: Norton, 1933; cited in Watson, "Horsemanship," 276).

people. As Pushkin himself remarked in a plan (1830) for a work about the nobility: "Pierre I est tout à la fois Robespierre et Napoleon (la révolution incarnée)" — "*Peter I is at one and the same time Robespierre and Napoleon (the revolution incarnate).*"[137] This very issue of Peter's unreining/unbridling became, among others, a focus in *The Bronze Horseman* for Pushkin's quiet polemics with his friend, the great Polish poet Adam Mickiewicz.[138] The latter had recently, in the *Digression* of Part III of *Forefather's Eve*, criticized his "Muscovite friends" — singling out "the bard of the Russian people" — for their chauvinistic response to the Polish uprising of 1830–31. And one of his chief images for describing his (the oppressed Pole's) version of Russian history is that of Peter's steed racing out of control: "His charger's reins Tsar Peter *has released*; / He has been flying down the road, perchance, / And here the precipice checks his advance."[139] Pushkin, with his genius for absorbing the most disparate viewpoints and making them his own, implies an answer to Mickiewicz in his introduction (Peter is magisterial and in control) *at the same time* that he makes "a crack... in the smooth surface of panegyrism" in the story that follows.[140] The link between a natural and social unleashing is never stated in the poem, and yet this buried kinship is, to "gallop" ahead of ourselves a moment, one reason — perhaps the reason — why a Western formula signifying imperial order became in time a Russian formula signifying *apocalyptic chaos*. Thus it will be our argument that Pushkin's *Bronze Horseman*, drawing as it does from sculptural, iconographic, and heraldic traditions which join Marcus Aurelius and St. George, Europe and Russia, not only marks the moment of maximal equipoise in the fictional depiction of Russian history but also is itself, with its unique stand-off of styles and thematics (eighteenth-century "panegyric"/nineteenth-century "realistic")[141] and counterpointing of introduction and narrative sections, a perfect formal expression of that balance.[142] Peter and his city are both splendid *and* cruel, and therein lies the enigma of Pushkin's masterpiece.[143]

---

136 Watson, "Horsemanship," 277ff.

137 Pushkin, *Polnoe sobranie sochinenii*, 12:205; see also Lednicki, *Pushkin's 'Bronze Horseman'*, 30–31.

138 Depending on context and audience, Pushkin's attitude toward his country could be both condemnatory and patriotic, just as his view of Peter's place in history was a complex mix of fascination and repugnance.

139 Translated and cited in Lednicki, *Pushkin's 'Bronze Horseman'*, 29; my emphasis.

Lednicki (*Pushkin's 'Bronze Horseman*," 28–30) also suggests further that Mickiewicz's image of the unreined steed owes a debt to Pushkin's earlier poem "To Licinius," where the over-proud hero (and by implication Russia) is threatened with a fall because he can no longer control his chariot.

140 Lednicki, *Pushkin's 'Bronze Horseman'*, 52.

141 For the shift from panegyric (Kantemir, Trediakovsky, Sumarokov, Lomonosov, Derzhavin, etc.) to realistic (Gogol, Dostoevsky, etc.) treatment of Peter and his city, see N. Antsyferov, *Dusha Peterburga* (Petersburg: Brokgauz-Efron, 1922).

142 Lednicki, *Pushkin's 'Bronze Horseman,'* 49–50.

143 Later commentators on the meaning of the city's mounted *genius loci*, including Dostoevsky, will ignore the capital's splendor — or see it in decline and foreground its cruel, tyrannical side.

The question of the folkloric roots of the equine image is admittedly more vague and indeterminate, shrouded, as it were, in the mists of the popular memory/collective unconscious. Here its chief expression in the nineteenth-century literary tradition is found not in Pushkin but in Gogol, whose celebrated panegyric on Russia's destiny in the context of a troika ride had an immense impact on later generations of writers, including a strikingly apocalypticist reworking in Blok. Folklorically, the horse has always possessed distinct connotations. There is, to begin with, the most obvious — the *bogatyrskii kon'* (hero's steed) of epic poem and folktale, the brave, wise, and prophetic friend of Ilya or Dobrynya that leaps over mountains with the speed of an arrow and tramples the enemies of sacred Russia.[144] Less well-known but equally potent source material for the popular imagination is the practice, widespread and ancient, of killing and burying a horse with its master. D. Anuchin, the eminent late nineteenth-century Russian anthropologist who examined primitive burial mounds (*kurgany*) in Slavic countries, came to the conclusion (echoed more recently by Eliade) that the horse is "pre-eminently the funerary animal."[145] The horse is buried with its master not only to show respect but also to give the deceased a way of traveling to the other world. This notion of conveyance is reinforced in the tradition of the sledge (*sani*), which carries the individual from an earthly home to the final resting place and which also is drawn by the horse.[146] Similarly, the figure of a horse's head or "little horse" (*konek*) was placed on a Russian peasant's hut to protect the family within from disaster and their flock from disease or infertility.[147] If the *konek* was smashed by others or fell apart on its own, it meant that either death or some great misfortune was in store for the head of the household. Finally, in the peasant consciousness, and in its modern representation in the works of such poets as Esenin and Kliuev, the horse's head was the symbol of the popular cosmos (*izbianyi kosmos*), of the link between the sun ("there") and the earth ("here"), and of motion upward and outward into unknown regions.[148] Therefore, the horse not only had important ties with the ritual of sacrifice and burial but also with the mythical *put'* (path) joining the little world of the peasant's hut to the great world beyond.[149]

Beyond this, however, the horse has long had another, darker side in the popular consciousness — that associated with the "Scythian" marauder. It is at this point that the Russian tradition comes close to the generally positive or romanticized images of the Argentinian gaucho and the

[144] Lipets, *Obrazy*, 124–249.
[145] Anuchin, "Sani, lad'ia i koni," 83–226; Eliade, *Myth of Eternal Return*, 67.
[146] The barque or boat (*lad'ia*) also suggests a "crossing-over" — cf. the river Styx and the ferryman Charon of Greek mythology — but without the help of a horse.
[147] P.A. Rovinskii, "Zemlia i volia," *Chernogoriia v ee proshlom i nastoiashchem* (St. Petersburg: Tip. Imp. Akademii Nauk, 1897), 438.
[148] Cf. Eliade's statement, in *Shamanism: Archaic Techniques of Ecstasy* (Princeton: Princeton University Press, 1964), 470, that the horse "facilitates the

American cowboy, with the important difference that the latter horsemen were seen to "open up" (but not civilize) parts of their countries, while the Mongols imposed their "yoke" on a flourishing Kievan state. All of these roving men on horseback stood for something quite different from the chivalric tradition — volatile, unrestrained movement, freedom coupled with lawlessness, a nomadic lack of culture. As we see in the poems of such modern "Scythians" as Voloshin and Blok (in the latter especially the "chivalric" and "Mongol" notions of horse and rider often alternate and compete), the revolution conjured up past ghosts of mounted chaos sweeping into "European" Russia from the East. Ironically, as Blok maintained in the tortured logic of his essays, if its purpose was to bring down the corrupt edifice of European civilization, this "second coming" of Russia's Eastern origins was not without its cathartic truth. The "pagan" as opposed to "chivalric" horseman came to be an important *prefiguring* element in the intelligentsia's quest to understand its "Russianness." Russians, as Berdyaev said so often, needed a *put'* (path) of their own, regardless of where that path led; they were *stranniki*, wandering truth-seekers, and they despised the "sedentary" (*osedlyi*) European. Borges' eulogy of the gaucho and of the latter's doomed attempt to conquer time and history by conquering space comes eerily close to certain "Scythian" passages in Zamyatin[150] and others and indicates to what extent this popular myth of wanderlust is not unique or indigenous:

> The figure of the man on the horse is, secretly, poignant. Under Attila, the "Scourge of God," under Genghis Khan, and under Tamerlane, the horseman tempestuously destroys and founds extensive empires, but all he destroys and founds is illusory. His work, like him, is ephemeral. From the farmer comes the word "culture" and from cities the word "civilization," but the horseman is a storm that fades away.[151]

To presume from the above that Gogol's Chichikov is a nineteenth-century Genghis Khan come to rape and pillage in a provincial backwater is,

trance, the ecstatic flight of the soul to forbidden regions."

149 Vasilii Bazanov, *Sergei Esenin i krest'ianskaia Rossiia* (Leningrad: Sovetskii pisatel', 1982), 70–77.

150 "The essence of the spiritual revolutionary was captured by Zamjatin's description of the Scythian: 'Over the green steppe speeds alone a wild horseman with streaming hair — the Scythian. Where is he speeding? Nowhere. Why? For no reason. He speeds simply because he is a Scythian, because he has become one with the steed, because he is a centaur, and because freedom, solitariness, his steed, the wide steppe are most dear to him.' The galloping Scythian symbolized freedom, unending movement, and solitariness — freedom to reject the present in the name of the distant future, unending movement as a guarantee of man's progress in the face of universal philistinism; and solitariness because the spiritual revolutionary and heretic was always an isolated figure who stood apart from the masses" (A.M. Shane, *The Life and Works of Evgenij Zamjatin* [Berkeley: University of California Press, 1968], 18). See also the description of the centaur, of one who "has become one with the steed," in *We* when D-503 looks down at the world beyond the Green Wall from within the spaceship Integral.

151 Jorge Luis Borges, "Stories of Horsemen," *New Republic* (19 May 1982): 8.

prima facie, not a little far-fetched. He is cultured (albeit superficially), his background is urban, he has a passion for order — in short, all the terms in Borges' formula are reversed. Yet everything that Chichikov creates and destroys is *illusory*. And more important, it is when Chichikov disappears into the wide-open spaces at the end of part one that Gogol's narrator abandons himself to lyrical ruminations on the troika and Russia's destiny and we enter a strange and privileged narrative space in the text.[152] Here the horse-drawn troika (the Russian chariot) symbolizes the shift from everyday time (the provincial town) to epic time (the grand *openness* of Russia's future). We are meant to "cross over" with Chichikov (he is indeed a kind of mock-epic Charon) and rise above this world (he is also, at a higher level, a kind of Elijah). At the same time, Gogol's imperatives exhort us to enter into the sheer nervous excitement of the ride, the combination of pleasure *and* fear that the passenger feels as the troika and Russia hurtle into the future. Thus, along with Pushkin's poetic treatment of Falconet's statue, Gogol's folk-inspired apotheosis of the troika becomes another potent image of eschatological change to be adopted and reworked by later writers.

It is, to be sure, a risky enterprise to extrapolate a shape for Russian cultural history from scattered examples of the equine motif. The term "Trojan horse" means something quite different to us than it did to the Greeks, just as the horse that brought death to Prince Oleg in the Primary Chronicle is not — because of the *context* in which it is presented — the horse of Pushkin's adaptation. I would like to propose, however, that many nineteenth-century Russian writers combined myth and realism in their use of the horse and that this intentional modal confusion suggests that the abovementioned traditions were very much alive. We have already discussed Pushkin and Gogol, and, while space does not permit further treatment of them here, there are other examples in their work that lend credibility to our assumptions.[153] To turn our attention elsewhere, Chatsky, the famous hero of Griboedov's *Woe from Wit* (1833), does not merely ask

---

[152] For more on the poetics of space in Gogol, see Iu. Lotman, "Problema khudozhestvennogo prostranstva v proze Gogolia," *Uchenye zapiski Tartuskogo gosudarstvennogo universiteta* 209 (1968): 5–50.

[153] In Pushkin one could cite, for example, his poetic reworking of the legend of the prophetic Oleg and his important lyric "The Devils." In the first work it is predicted that the prince will die because of his steed, so Oleg cautiously remains apart from the horse until after the latter is dead. The prophecy comes true, however, and the connotation of equine-inspired doom is realized when Oleg, come to visit the remains of his faithful friend, is fatally bitten by a snake lying in wait in the horse's skull. "The Devils" describes how the speaker's sleigh is caught in a snowstorm and how the horses, frightened by the eerie atmosphere, lose their way. The animals' wild movements and lack of a road/destination *could* symbolize several things at this juncture of Pushkin's career (1830), not the least of which being his own troubled feelings about his forthcoming marriage. Gogol often used some form of horse-drawn conveyance as a *way out* of a difficult situation: Podkolyosin in *Marriage* makes a quick exit in a carriage rather than proceed to the altar, and the tormented Poprishchin in "The Diary of a Madman" imagines his escape from madness and the terrible conditions of the asylum in terms of a heavenly bound troika (another Elijah motif). The equine motif also appears at the end of the story "The Carriage"

for his carriage at the end of the play; rather, he exclaims that "he is no more a rider" whose destination is Moscow and that he is going into the world to look for a more worthy residence. His departure is thus a direct appeal to the audience, a kind of "crossing-over" into their space-time and into their notion of Russia's historical *put'*. In other words, Griboedov uses, *before* Gogol, the formula of an equine exit from a fallen world.

In Lermontov's poetry and prose a spirited horse is repeatedly associated with a beautiful maiden: both horse and maiden may be destroyed (or "broken" or "run to death") by the speaker's or protagonist's passionate but fickle nature. One obvious example of this appears in *A Hero of Our Time* (1840), where Bela's death is inextricably linked first with Pechorin's cynical horse-trading and then with his efforts to "break" her, and where his loss of Vera finds an objective correlative in the death from exhaustion of his horse. A remarkably similar case can be found in Turgenev's "First Love" (1860), when Vladimir is shattered by the discovery that his father is having an affair with Zinaida, the object of his impossible adolescent infatuation. Indeed, in this instance passion becomes something much more than innocent horseplay; it is a galvanic force that binds "rider" to "mount" (the father is repeatedly referred to as a formidable horseman who *curbs* Zinaida much as he curbs his mare Electric) in a sadomasochistic duel until the moment when a blow delivered by his riding crop shows the unsuspecting boy the depth of their attraction. (It may well be that the sophisticated and well-read Turgenev was playing with a modern version of the Renaissance simile that linked the sex act with a man's domineering position "in the saddle.") And of course the most celebrated example of this cruel male horsemanship belongs to Tolstoy, whose elaborate description of the horse race in *Anna Karenina* (wr. 1873-77) makes an unmistakable connection between Vronsky "in the saddle" on the mare Frou-Frou, breaking her back with his careless riding, and Vronsky in relation to Anna, "crushing" her so much that she hurls herself beneath a train.[154]

and the fragment "Rome," but its demonic connotations are perhaps most evident at the end of "Nevsky Prospect": "When the entire city [Petersburg] is transformed into thunder and flash, myriads of carriages careen off bridges, postilions shout and jump off horses, and the devil himself lights the streetlamps for the sole purpose of showing everything in an unreal guise" (N.V. Gogol', *Polnoe sobranie sochinenii*, ed. N.L. Meshcheriakov et al., 14 vols. [Moscow-Leningrad: Akademiia Nauk SSSR, 1937-52], 3: 46).

As a folk symbol of Russia on the move, the troika was invoked regularly by members of Pushkin's pleiad: see, e.g., the spirited poem "Again the Troika" by Vyazemsky. Other writers (primarily poets) who developed the equine motif at this time, or earlier, include: Batiushkov ("The Song of Harold the Brave"), Bestuzhev-Marlinsky ("Saatyr"), Derzhavin ("The Chariot"), Küchelbecker ("Sviatopolk," "Rogday's Hounds"), Kozlov ("The Nocturnal Ride"), Krylov ("The Rider and the Steed"), Zhukovsky ("The Song of the Arab [Sung] over the Grave of his Horse," "Svetlana," "Lenora," "The Knight Rollon").

[154] For more on the connection between the steeplechase and the train ride in *Anna Karenina*, see my discussion in *The Shape of Apocalypse*.

In *Crime and Punishment* (1866), Raskolnikov's terrifying dream of the mare beaten to death by a peasant is modeled on a similar description in Nekrasov's long poem *About the Weather* (wr. 1863–65). Nekrasov and Dostoevsky replace the powerful male steed (*kon'*) of folklore with the bedraggled nag (*kliacha*) — this female horse symbolizes the silent (non-verbal), long-suffering Russia of Lizaveta, Sonya, and the *narod*. While "aristocratic" writers like Lermontov, Turgenev, and Tolstoy tend to conflate the curbing, breaking, or destroying of a high-strung mare with the "painful pleasure" of romantic love, Dostoevsky and Nekrasov, though in their own ways sadomasochistic, expand the mare image into a more "popular" horse, one not ridden by a privileged rider but compelled to draw a heavy burden in the workaday world. In fact, only with Dostoevsky does the horse (and its modern version the train) begin to assume a definite and indisputable *apocalyptic* resonance; Russian history has now entered a new and ominous stage, and for the first time personal and national ends are embodied in variations on the same image cluster. Finally, two notable equine allusions are provided by Leskov and Chekhov in the latter part of the nineteenth century. In Leskov's "Enchanted Pilgrim" (1873) Ivan Flyagin is a *koneser* (or "connoisseur" of the *kon'* — the pun is Leskov's), an expert tamer of horses, an extravagant drinker and male specimen of epic proportions, and a saintly and sinful *strannik*;[155] Chekhov's description of a popular world falling apart in an orgy of drunkenness and ignorance ("The Peasants" [1897]) is again symbolized by a horse, crazed by a fire and running out of control.

---

155 See Hugh McLean, *Nikolai Leskov: the Man and His Art* (Cambridge: Harvard University Press, 1977), 241–55.

156 An excellent introduction to the mythic connotations of the horse and train in nineteenth-century Russian literature is found in Stephen L. Baehr, "The Troika and the Train: Dialogues Between Tradition and Technology in Nineteenth-Century Russian Literature," in J. D. Clayton, ed., *Issues in Russian Literature Before 1917* (Columbus: Slavica, 1989), 85–106. Baehr's study provides numerous examples of how the horse and train were perceived as opposing concepts (old/new, traditional/modern, natural/mechanical, etc.) in both the popular and the educated imagination. Particularly pertinent to our survey are his comments about the various reworkings of the Bronze Horseman myth into railway terms: Vyazemsky's "Pyotr Alekseevich" (1867), a poem in which the tsar's mount becomes an "imperial tender" and his title "crowned engineer" (*ventsenosnyi mashinist*); or Nekrasov's "The Railroad" (1864), another poem about, among other things, the abused and forgotten workers who haunt the Moscow-Petersburg railroad as it is built by Count Pyotr Andreevich Kleinmichel (a surrogate for Nicholas I): the ghosts of these "little men" come to utter their "threatening exclamations" in much the same way that Evgeny, in Pushkin's poem, once uttered his demented challenge to the equestrian statue. For additional discussion on the theme of the railroad in nineteenth century Russian literature, see Wolfgang Gesemann, "Zur Rezeption der Eisenbahn durch die Russische Literatur," in *Slavistische Studien zum VI Internationalen Slavistenkongress in Prag, 1968*, ed. Erwin Koschmieder and Maximilian Braun (Munich, 1968), 349–71; and M.S. Al'tman, "Zheleznaia doroga v tvorchestve L.N. Tolstogo," *Slavia* 34 (1965): 251–59.

157 A more appropriate model of course, and one which actually surfaces in the text of *The Idiot*, is *Don Quixote*, a work which parodies and "novelizes" the by then dated model of the chivalric quest. It also plays an important role in Platonov's *Chevengur*, which focuses on the Bolshevik quest for a new and better world. See Chapter 3

Dostoevsky's work suggests itself as a turning point in this tradition and a logical point of entrance because several of his major works, and *The Idiot* in particular, witness a joining of the notions of biblical end and the current direction of Russian history in the image cluster of the horse/train.[156] Personal tragedy expands into imminent national tragedy, and the metaphorical ride of Nastasya Filippovna, who is, on a mythical level, Russia "the fallen bride," is repeatedly presented as a composite of the third and fourth horses of Revelation (6:5–8) and of the railroad network that is poisoning the "waters of life" (7:17, 8:10, 21:6). Living in a later, more skeptical time, and fearing that the "religion" of rationality that the "men of the sixties" had imported from the West would lead to universal destruction, Dostoevsky reverses the terms of the chivalric epic—the genre in which a poet like Spenser could still equate England's progress toward a New Jerusalem of ideal governance with a knightly quest on horseback.[157] Now the rider does not hold the reins but is driven by a diabolical machine toward the terminus of death. In such apocalyptically oriented writers as Dostoevsky and Leontiev, the train, with its domination over horse-drawn conveyance in the second half of the nineteenth century, gradually becomes the equivalent of the Petrine steed: it is once again the victory of the false "new" over the genuine "old," of godless European enlightenment over orthodox, organic Rus'.[158] The train is so threatening as a symbol of doom (in the popular consciousness it was given not the neutral name *poezd*, but the marked one, *mashina*—the ultimate machine and handiwork of the Antichrist[159]) because it moves, like "atheistic" logic, along iron rails without any higher reason for being

("*Chevengur*: On the Road with the Bolshevik Utopia") of *The Shape of Apocalypse*, 145–85.

158 American writers and thinkers experienced some of the same reservations about the incursion of the machine world—especially the train—into pristine America, although, to be sure, there seems to have been more sheer fascination with the idea of progress and less of Russia's apocalyptically-tinged fears. See Leo Marx's classic *The Machine in the Garden: Technology and the Pastoral Ideal in America* (New York: Oxford University Press, 1964), 194–98, 209–16, 227–65. Of all American writers, Hawthorne was probably the one most mesmerized by the mythological aura surrounding the appearance of the iron horse in his country: see, e.g., his chapter "The Flight of Two Owls" in *The House of Seven Gables* as well as his story "The Celestial Railway."

159 For example, in a "physiological sketch" ("Zheleznaia doroga mezhdu Peterburgom i Moskvoi" [The Railroad between Petersburg and Moscow]) that appeared in volume 54 of the journal *The Contemporary* (*Sovremennik*) for 1855 (43–71), the author ("S") repeatedly refers to the train as a *mashina* and dwells on the fears of his passengers toward the new form of transportation: "'Oh, tell me, please, isn't it dangerous to ride on the railroad?' asks a stout lady" on the very first page (43). A related, but popular (*narodnyi*) fear of the train is expressed by the character Fyoklushka in A. Ostrovsky's play *The Storm* and by one of Tolstoy's peasants in *War and Peace*. For more on the railroad motif and its "chronotopic" possibilities, see Chapter One ("*The Idiot*: Historicism Arrives at the Station") of *The Shape of Apocalypse*, 62–104.

and because it reaches its destination, which in these apocalyptic fictions is often associated with death, with only a mechanical explanation of how it got there. Since the train is perceived as a self-enclosed ensemble of origin/destination, coach, rails, and telegraph,[160] the passenger feels cut off from nature and the outside world and begins to experience the space-time of the journey in *relative* terms.[161] Moreover, the shift from individual, aristocratic rider to collective, driven passengers (Dostoevsky was again one of the first to stress this melting-pot atmosphere of "many-voicedness" in his description of a third class coach) makes the train a perfect "vehicle" for the expression of tumultuous social change.[162] The train continues to be a powerful, and often apocalyptically colored symbol for both the popular and literary imagination well into the twentieth century: there is, for example, Esenin's famous race between flesh-and-blood colt and iron horse in "Sorokoust"; Mandelstam's blending of the notions of music and iron, of a passing age rent by the screeching of train whistles, in his poem "Concert at the Station"[163]; Artyom Vesyoly's duel between bull and train in *Russia Drenched in Blood*; Andrey Platonov's and fellow proletarians' fervent belief that the train, as quintessential machine, would be the liberating force in the new Soviet era; V. Ilenkov's metaphor of Soviet society as train and the party as the "driving axle" in the novel by the same name;[164] and in the latter decades of the twentieth century there is Solzhenitsyn's description of the dismantling of "true-timbered" (*kondovaia*) Russia and the demise of its best representative in terms of a railway accident ("Matryona's Homestead"); and Venedikt Erofeev's tragicomic tale, punctuated with allusions to Revelation, of another doomed train-ride into alcoholic oblivion and death (*From Moscow to the End of the Line* [*Moskva-Petushki*]).

Thus, perhaps more than any other single ingredient of the apocalyptic plot it is the "chronotopic" picture of the horse/train that has had the most far-reaching implications for the *shape* of our various authors' thinking as *inscribed* in the movement of the different stories. Following Dostoevsky's lead, Bely, Platonov, Bulgakov, and Pasternak return, *mutatis mutandis*, to this image cluster as a way into the larger issue of how to conceptualize ("emplot") the movement of history—is it, for instance, linear, circular, or spiralic? It is presumably not fortuitous that, together with that of the train, the image of the horse has remained one of the most durable and rich in all Russian literature and culture: witness its prominent place (usually in some form of the chivalric, folkloric/Scythian,

---

160 The telegraph was added at a later point to aid in communication and prevent accidents.

161 See Wolfgang Schivelbusch, *The Railway Journey: Trains and Travel in the 19*[th] *Century*, trans. Anselm Hollo (New York: Urizen Books, 1980). In general Schivelbusch is a rich source of information on how the nineteenth century European perception of space and time was radically changed by the presence of the train. He also provides numerous examples of the train in popular and elitist literature of the time.

162 In the "physiological sketch" referred to above there is a good deal made of the different

or apocalyptic *topos*) in the works of Blok, Bely, Voloshin, and other Symbolists; in Esenin, Kliuev, and the peasant poets; in Shershenevich, Mariengof, Gruzinov, and the Russian Imagists. The list could go on to include Mandelstam, Tsvetaeva, Babel, Sholokhov, the émigré poet Vladimir Korvin-Piotrovsky — even Vs. Ivanov, Efim Dorosh, I. Gudov, and other converts to high Stalinist Socialist Realism.[165] And one most remarkable recent example, Joseph Brodsky's poem about the black horse, has been shown by the Soviet scholar O.V. Simchenko to trace its ancestry to Anna Akhmatova and her recollection of 1936, the eve of the great purges: "Life [placed] us at the reins [lit. 'under the bridle' — *pod uzdy*] of a Pegasus that [was] somehow reminiscent of the Pale Horse of Apocalypse or the Black Horse of the verses [i.e., Brodsky's] that [were] yet to be born."[166] To be sure, not all of these writers employ the equine image within the explicit semantic field of "apocalypse," yet such a meaning may not be far off, especially if the given passage raises the issue of the shape and direction of Russian history and the end-time of the revolution. In this larger sense, one may go so far as to say that the Russian tradition of apocalyptic fiction is a unique metaphorical "unbridling" or "unreining" of those same relentless cultural categories (old/new, East/West, pagan/orthodox) that had pursued the collective consciousness of the intelligentsia for centuries.

In the West, perhaps for the reasons advanced by Berdyaev and Lotman, or perhaps because the potent combination of national myth and fanatic millenarianism driving the human imagination down "history's road" came to be questioned sooner, few modern writers of the "large form" (especially after the Great War) enter into the living tradition of "apocalyptic fiction" as I have tried to define it.[167] Only someone like D.H. Lawrence, whose novels are considered by many to go against the grain of Anglo-American modernism, rivals these Russian novelists in his persistent telescoping of personal, national, and biblical myths of the End (and Beginning). Let us then close our introductory remarks with Lawrence, who apparently

classes (first, second, and third) on the train and their respective attitudes, from boisterous to reserved, toward the journey. Dostoevsky was clearly laying claim to this recent phenomenon in his vivid presentation of the third class coach carrying Myshkin, Rogozhin, and Lebedev in the opening pages of *The Idiot*.

163 See discussion, e.g., in Omry Ronen, *An Approach to Mandel'štam* (Jerusalem: The Magnes Press, 1983), xvii–xx.

164 Katerina Clark, "Little Heroes and Big Deeds: Literature Responds to the First Five-Year Plan," in *Cultural Revolution in Russia, 1928–1931*, ed. Sheila Fitzpatrick (Bloomington: Indiana University Press, 1978), 190–91.

165 Clark, *Soviet Novel*, 139, 277. For specific examples of the equine motif in the works of the symbolists, see Chapter Two ("*Petersburg*: The Apocalyptic Horseman, the Unicorn, and the Verticality of Narrative"), in *The Shape of Apocalypse*, 105–44..

166 Cited in O.V. Simchenko, "Tema pamiati v tvorchestve Anny Akhmatovoi," *Izvestiia AN SSSR: Seriia iazyka i literatury* 44 (1985): 506.

167 This is not to say that the apocalyptic theme fades from Western literature (and culture) after World War I. On the contrary, it is quite evident in the works of modern drama — witness the plays of Girandoux, Ionesco, Beckett, Genet, and others (see Maurice Valency, *The End of the World: An Introduction to Contemporary Drama* [New York: Schocken, 1983], 419–37). And it is present in prose works from recent decades, such as Pynchon's *Grav-*

had his own "Scythian" streak and who too felt compelled to seat his apocalyptic fervor "in the saddle"[168]:

> Horses, always horses! How the horse dominated the mind of the early races, especially in the Mediterranean! You were a lord if you had a horse. Far back, far back in our dark souls the horse prances. He is a dominant symbol: he gives us lordship: he links us, the first palpable and throbbing link with the ruddy-glowing Almighty of potence: he is the beginning even of our godhead in the flesh. And as a symbol he roams the dark underworld meadows of the soul. He stamps and threshes in the dark fields of your soul and mine. The sons of god who came down and knew the daughters of men and begot the great Titans, they had "the members of horses," says Enoch.
>
> Within the last fifty years man has lost the horse. Now man is lost. Man is lost to life and power — an underling and a wastrel. While horses thrashed the streets of London, London lived...
>
> But the rider on the white horse is crowned. He is the royal one, he is my very self and his horse is the whole *mana* of a man. He is my very me, my sacred ego, called into a new cycle of action by the Lamb and riding forth to conquest, the conquest of the old self for the birth of the new self...
>
> The true action of the myth, or ritual-imagery, has been all cut away. The rider on the white horse appears, then vanishes. But we know why he has appeared. And we know why he is paralleled at the end of the Apocalypse by the last rider on the white horse, who is the heavenly son of Man riding forth after the last and final conquest over the "kings." The son of man, even you or I, rides forth to the small conquest; but the Great Son of Man mounts his white horse after the last universal conquest, and leads on his hosts.[169]

ity's *Rainbow*. Nonetheless, the underlying faith in a *Christian* resolution to the biblical plot has become increasingly untenable, and what is now called "apocalyptic" is more and more the *end as nothingness* (an especially vivid theme in, say, Beckett). It is my argument that Russian writers such as Bulgakov and Pasternak fall more into a Christian tradition of *Apocalyptik* that is perhaps anachronistic by Western standards.

168 Compare, for example, the following passage from Lawrence's *Apocalypse* and the passionate scene of Ursula and the horses at the conclusion of *The Rainbow*.

169 D.H. Lawrence, *Apocalypse* (New York: The Viking press, 1932), 125–28.

Chapter 3

Mythopoesis and Biography: Pushkin, Jakobson, and the Secret Life of Statues[1]

Schools in the "human sciences" are bound virtually by their own phylogenetic principles to undermine and supersede their predecessors rather than disinterestedly, patiently, build on them. A prior school has to be razed and then a new one erected on the same spot, with the "school board" quickly forgetting the attractions and the still usable space of the now nonexistent building. Students get bussed to the new school without any knowledge (unless some teachers tell them so) that they are walking the halls of a place that once looked much different. The prior school is precisely not "refurbished" or "updated," not given a new heating system or graced with a handsome new wing, but torn down and rebuilt in some entirely new way. This, I take it, is what Lydia Ginzburg had in mind when she wrote in her notebook in 1927 that "I find extremely unpleasant both in myself and in my comrades that satisfaction with one's own bold steps and that pathos of broad horizons. When entering any cultural activity (science, art, philosophy), one ought to remember: what is easy is bad (just as when entering a shop one remembers that what is cheap is

---

[1] Originally "Jakobson: Why the Statue Won't Come to Life, or Will It?" in David M. Bethea, *Realizing Metaphors: Alexander Pushkin and the Life of the Poet* (Madison: University of Wisconsin Press, 1998), 89–117.

bad). To acquire theoretically broad horizons and universal acceptance [*vsepriiatie*] is much easier than constructing and using a system of fruitful limitations [lit. 'conditions of one-sidedness,' *odnostoronnosti*]."[2] Where a *school of thought* is concerned, which depends greatly on the works *and personality* of its first thinker, it seems simpler to begin anew with the "theoretically broad horizons" than to use the already existing "system of fruitful limitations." Here Freud's notion of oedipal struggle — destroying and seemingly wiping away the existence of a controlling father — really does appear to be the operative principle.

I say all this by way of introducing the thought of Roman Jakobson, the great structural linguist, whose work only a generation ago was the cornerstone of every major Slavic program in the country (if not the world) and whose emphasis on the "Slavic word" (the interlocking systems of languages, cultures, folklores, verse forms, etc.) was the heart of "philology" as it was then practiced. How times have changed, how linguistics with its "system of fruitful limitations" has become a stepchild discipline, how the mention of "philology" makes the contemporary student's (and perhaps his faculty advisor's) eyes glaze over! Jakobson is a truly remarkable example of the sort of human science school razing I have just been describing. Just as Freud's psychoanalytic metaphors (primarily archaeological) have remained and even thrived while the scientific basis of his findings has been in constant dispute, Jakobson's strictly descriptive structuralist terminology has not been superseded in the realm of (linguistic) science even as his presence (if not his reputation per se) in current debates about the humanities and "whence literary studies?" has been reduced to what can only be called a spasmodic blip on our culture's radar screen. Moreover, essentially the same thing can be said about the relative reputations in the west of Bakhtin and Lotman: the former, primarily a philosopher, offers ways (and alluring vocabularies) for making literature not an object of study but a *place* where *subjects and subjectivities* interact; the latter, on the other hand, clearly Jakobson's equal in the field of semiotics and one of the most fertile minds of the second half of the century, hews to the descriptive, scientific/"enlightenment" episteme perfected by his illustrious predecessor, and *for that reason* continues to be less well known.[3]

But why is this, why are we so much more apt to *listen* to Freud and Bakhtin, to try to glean the vectors behind their thought, and yet to *ignore* Jakobson and Lotman, to reduce them to the "mere" structuralist and

---

2   Lidiia Ginzburg, *Chelovek za pis'mennym stolom* (Leningrad: Sovetskii pisatel, 1989), 55.

3   Freud, Bloom, Jakobson, and Lotman were the four theoretical "prisms" through which (and against which) I constructed a way of "vectoring in" on Pushkin's poetry in my *Realizing Metaphors* book (see note 1 above), hence the mention of their names prominently in this essay, whose focus is Jakobson and his study of Pushkin's sculptural myth (originally section 5 of part 1 of the book).

semiotician? The cruder response is that Freud and Bakhtin allow us, relatively painlessly (unless we are sufficiently self-aware and scrupulous), to enter into dialogue with our texts and with their now silent authors. That is of course more intriguing, more inherently interesting. Jakobson and Lotman require us to know a great deal more before we speak and then to speak about what we do know in a way that is not itself a subjective, that is, metaphorical, embrace of its own subjectivity. Jakobson, for example, would not have used Mandelstam's flying machine metaphor (from "Conversation about Dante") in a manner that suggested that this kind of thinking was not something to be "studied" (analyzed) but something to be "lived" (experienced); rather, he would have described what Mandelstam was doing as an example of the (note the depersonalization) "poetic *function*": "The poetic function projects the principle of equivalence from the axis of selection into the axis of combination. Equivalence is promoted to the constitutive device of the sequence."[4] It makes no difference whether it is Jakobson's famous "I like Ike" example (internal rhyme) or the flying machine metaphor of Russia's greatest twentieth-century poet: both exhibit the same principle of language drawing attention to its own simultaneity (i.e., the coexistence of different "axes"), to its ability to say more than one thing at the same time. One doesn't need such slippery notions as "charisma" (the personality in and around the words) to talk about "poetry" in terms of the poetic function: one can merely say that "verse [as an orientation] actually exceeds the limits of poetry, but at the same time verse always implies the poetic function."[5] The poet can be "beside himself"[6] if he wants to, but language can't, and it is the latter (or so it seems! —see below) that is the only thing we can accurately describe and study. "Poetry" and "metalanguage" (the language that talks about poetic functions) are simply mirror inversions of one another, the former building on the principle of pure equation (simultaneity), the latter building on the principle of pure sequence (difference). Absolutely everything Jakobson says about texts (poetic and otherwise), messages, and the retrieval of information encoded therein—the speech event, the different functions of language (referential, expressive, conative, metalingual, etc.), study that is diachronic versus study that is synchronic, the dominant, verse organization, rhythm versus meter, sound symbolism, lexical versus grammatical tropes, etc.—is couched in a (meta)language that remains on this side of the scientific divide, that resolutely refuses to be "turned on," that

4 Roman Jakobson, in "Linguistics and Poetics," *Language in Literature*, ed. Krystyna Pomorska and Stephen Rudy (Cambridge: Harvard University Press, 1987), 71.

5 Jakobson, "Linguistics and Poetics," 72.

6 See Susan Stewart, "Lyric Possession," *Critical Inquiry* 22.1 (Autumn 1995): 35.

describes the poetic function at work but will not itself be contaminated by the "poetic." The one glaring exception is an article that is itself framed by its own hortatory trope, the brilliant "On a Generation That Squandered Its Poets" (1931), which is Jakobson's homage to his own youth (the formalist-futurist symbiosis) and to the suicidal poet of the revolution (Mayakovsky) who more than any other symbolized the impossibility of embodying a revolutionary poetic over time. But this, one hastens to add, is only the exception that proves the rule.

There is an essential paradox in Jakobsonian thought, which I have likened to the statue that refuses to come to life. It is fascinating that this man, who was clearly a genius, returned in his last years to the "trans-sense" verse (zaum*nye stikhi*) of his youth not simply as object of study, but as something belonging to his own once-open past, as he filled the summer air of his Peacham, Vermont dacha with the hilarious sounds of gods run wild (or was it beasts?).⁷ This is not another banal tale of the *poete manqué*—for how many poems, even some great ones, are worth the *quality* of Jakobson's mind in its verbal traces?—but a case of one legendary hero, say Achilles, trying at the end of his quest to have a go at being, if only in jest, a very different type of hero, say Odysseus. The one's (analytical) muscles, as awesome as they are, cannot in certain situations stand in for the other's (poetic) craftiness. And the result is burlesque, something recognizably both more and less than Khlebnikov. Jakobson is at his best, which is for this reader routinely astounding, when he is describing a general situation in language acquisition, or its opposite, language loss: aphasia, with its "similarity disorder" (the loss of the metalinguistic function, the inability of the speaker to select the right word — "knife" becoming "fork" — for the right slot) versus its "contiguity disorder" (the loss of the surrounding grammatical framework of "relations"— conjunctions, prepositions, etc. — so that the speaker begins to forget inflections and to talk in a "telegraphic style").⁸ Such articles really do have the aura of "science" about them. Likewise, Jakobson is compelling

---

7   A stimulus to Jakobson's thoughts and reminiscences about his own "trans-sense" verse was an article he was writing during the 1979 summer season in Vermont: entitled "Zaumnyi Turgenev" (Supraconscious Turgenev), it retold and analyzed with considerable panache an anecdote about how the great prose writer had resorted to screaming out a *zaumnyi* list of feminine Russian nouns ("Radish! Pumpkin! Mare! Turnip! Peasant Woman! Kasha! Kasha!") when confronted with a too orderly, ritualized, and masculinized setting at an exclusive London eating club (see Jakobson, *Language in Literature*, 262–66). The story of the early Jakobson as aspiring futurist poet is found in Bengt Jangfeldt, ed., *Jakobson-Budetlianin* (Stockholm: Almqvist & Wiksell, 1992; Acta Universitatis Stockholmiensis, Stockholm Studies in Russian Literature, 26). My thanks to Jakobson's biographer the late Stephen Rudy for this information.

8   "Two Aspects of Language and Two Types of Aphasic Disturbance" (1956, in collaboration with Morris Halle), in *Language in Literature*, 95–114.

and very much still "usable" today when he enters on the terrain of "how relations in one area *interact* with relations in another": his move (with Tynianov) in 1928 away from the excesses of early Formalism toward the more historicized and dimensionalized concept of "system" ("The history of a system is in turn a system"[9]) of the Prague School, or his identification of the "dominant" (*dominanta*) as a way of properly focusing attention in a historical context, of bringing together the diachronic and synchronic realms.[10]

Above all, however, this greatest of structural linguists is "on top of his game" when he analyzes a poem that itself draws meaning from *grammatical* (i.e., strictly relational) categories: the readings of Pushkin's two short lyrics "I loved you" ("Ia vas liubil," 1829) and "What is there in my name for you" ("Chto v imeni tebe moem," 1830) in "Poetry of Grammar and Grammar of Poetry," for example.[11] These readings succeed so admirably, they seem to "deliver" a meaning that is completely adequate in this case to the exhaustiveness of the formal analysis, because they relate to a virtually "imageless poetry"[12] and because their compensatory play with pronouns (personal and interrogative) so totally overwhelms and in effect takes the place of the "axis of selection." There is a geometric elegance to these readings—the author even suggests that what geometry is for the visual arts grammar is for the verbal arts[13]—that foregrounds beautifully Jakobson's genius (but not necessarily Pushkin's). If one could put it this way, Roman Jakobson is the "Deep Blue" of poetic analysis: his way of looking at things as *relations* of abstract chess pieces on a chess board has no equal in its realm, where the category of "poetry" can be more or less subsumed into the category of "system" and "artificial intelligence." "Deep Blue" can defeat the world's greatest chess player, for it has no equal when it comes to abstract *relational* strategy, but it could never create something with the ontological status of a poem because it has no biography and no personality, only "on" and "off" switches. And even if it could simulate what a "good" poem would sound and look like, something essential (the relation of the "life" to the "art," which even "poets without biographies" possess as a consciously adopted absence) would be left out. Achilles cannot become Odysseus.

Jakobson's Achilles' heel makes itself felt most palpably in those exhaustive structural analyses of poems—Baudelaire's "Les Chats" and Shakespeare's sonnet 129 ("Th' expense of Spirit")[14]— where the strictly relational categories and the "geometric" qualities of form (say, symmetries of

9 "Problems in the Study of Language and Literature" (1928, with Yury Tynianov), in *Language in Literature*, 47–49; this quotation is taken from p. 48.

10 "The Dominant" (from unpublished Czech lectures on Formalism given in Brno in 1935), in *Language in Literature*, 41–46.

11 Jakobson, "Poetry of Grammar and Grammar of Poetry" (1960), in *Language in Literature*, 121–144.

12 Ibid., 129.

13 Ibid., 133.

14 Jakobson, "Baudelaire's 'Les Chats'" (1962, with Claude Lévi-Strauss) and "Shakespeare's Verbal Art in 'Th' Expense of Spirit" (1970, with L. G. Jones), *Language in Literature*, 180–197 and 198–215.

person, gender, nasal vowels, rhyme words, etc., in and among lines and stanzas) do not seem to bring the reader closer to a "feel" for the artistic structure and its ability to generate meaning. Whether lines 7 and 8 of "Les Chats," those referring to the cats' unwillingness to serve ("L'Érèbe les eût pris pour ses coursiers funèbres, / S'ils pouvaient au servage incliner leur fierté"), form a chiasmus-like pivot between two sestets and whether the configuration of the sonnet is ultimately tripartite or bipartite seem questions better suited to the reader-qua-chess-player type. Only on the very last page of the article, when Jakobson and Levi-Strauss link up the cats, the Sphinx, the principle of the "feminine" in the context of the "supervirility" of the poem's grammatical gender, and the poet as the one who is capable of bringing these notions to life and endowing them with graceful movement, does the structure begin to be successfuly "semanticized." But it seems too little too late, something akin to trying to get from "here" to "there" by casting a rope across a chasm the width of the Grand Canyon. It is not this sexiest of poets who needs to be "delivered" from the piece's final words and purported feline message, "the scholar's austerity,"[15] but the authors themselves. What Helen Vendler has written contra Jakobson's reading of Shakespeare's sonnet 129 could be applied with equal validity to the analysis of "Les Chats" and indeed to all Jakobsonian texts where the object of study is an *internal system of relations*:

> Jakobson had hoped, it is clear, to find a useful method that could be applied to all poems, or at least to very many poems. In this method, one compares all possible combinations of parts: odd strophes against even strophes, early strophes against late strophes, outside strophes (beginning and end) against inside strophes (middle), pre-center strophes against post-center strophes, quatrains against couplet, middle two lines against the lines preceding them and following them. This method, so extraordinarily bizarre when applied to a poem, does not I think yield useful interpretations, and the linguistic features remarked by Jakobson could be described independently of his binary method. The method militates against any notion of *the evolution of feeling* in the poem, any progressive expansion or contradiction of thought, and especially in this poem, the *indispensable sequence of emotional logic* which makes the poem a whole. The linearity of

15   Jakobson, "Baudelaire's 'Les Chats'," 197.

the poem is wholly lost sight of, and the many small points of suspense and climax ignored.[16]

In other words, the statue remains itself, a frozen system of symmetries; it does not come alive.

In 1937, the centennial of Pushkin's death, Jakobson wrote perhaps his greatest work as literary scholar: originally published in Czech, "The Statue in Pushkin's Poetic Mythology" was translated into English, equipped with a host of photographs, and reissued in 1975 as *Puškin and His Sculptural Myth*.[17] The study is remarkable because it shows, in a very striking way, both the power and the limitations of the author's structural linguistic episteme. On the positive side, it demonstrated for the first time, on a sampling of a great many texts, that the theme of sculpture was absolutely crucial to the poet's personal mythology. More to the point, however, it isolated with considerable elegance and conceptual power such "magnetized" issues as: (1) when the theme (the "destructive statue") first began to become foregrounded as a subject in its own right (i.e., near the time of Pushkin's marriage); (2) how concerns arising in Pushkin's private life (i.e., his continual difficulties with money and his questionable reputation as freethinker and borderline radical) that stood athwart the path to his marriage could be seen to be reworked as plot "invariants" in three important works of the 1830s, *The Stone Guest* (*Kamennyi gost'*, 1830), *The Bronze Horseman* (*Mednyi vsadnik*, 1833), and "The Fairy Tale of the Golden Cockerel" ("Skazka o zolotom petushke," 1834), that also represented the poet's final efforts in these respective genres (drama, narrative poem, fairytale); (3) how this notion of graven image had a very real (not merely "metaphorical") biographical resonance for Pushkin that went back to his Lyceum days (e.g., the monuments in the parks at Tsarskoe Selo that celebrated some of the empire's victories during Catherine's "Golden Age" and that implicated the poet's own relatives) and that continued into his year of courtship (1830) (and beyond) with the repeated reference in his correspondence to the "bronze grandmother" (a bust of Catherine belonging to the Goncharov family) that he believed he would have to have melted down and sold in order to produce sufficient dowry funds in order to get married; (4) how the reversible idea of "the statue that comes to life" and "the human being that turns to stone" seems to have been one with which Pushkin became increasingly obsessed, especially with the onset of his married years; and (5) how the plot

16   Helen Vendler, "Jakobson, Richards, and Shakespeare's Sonnet CXXIX," in *I.A. Richards: Essays in His Honor* (New York: Oxford University Press, 1973), 179–98; this passage is from pp. 197–98 (my emphasis).

17   Roman Jakobson, *Puškin and His Scuptural Myth*, ed. and trans. John Burbank (The Hague-Paris: Mouton, 1975). The version I am using here ("The Statue in Puškin's Poetic Mythology") is based on the Burbank translation, slightly revised, and is found in Jakobson, *Language in Literature*, 318–67.

invariant in each case is what we might call today a "triangulated" (after Girard) relation involving a woman and competing lovers, one usually a husband (with his "rights") and the other a potential seducer or "kidnapper" of the woman who may be endowed with a different kind of power (i.e., political). It would seem that any reader of Jakobson's study must come to the conclusion that he has made some major, if not seminal, discoveries and that he has caused us to read "Pushkin" in a new and exciting way.

But has he? I would argue that this otherwise foundational work suffers, from my point of view fatally, from the same structuralist "bricolage," the same inability to glean in proper perspective *the evolution of feeling* and *the indispensable sequence of emotional logic*, that we noted above in Vendler's response to the Jakobsonian reading of Shakespeare's sonnet 129. Which is to say, Jakobson is brilliant at isolating "structure," but he seems next to helpless at showing the "dominant" as an organizing figure of emotion, as a way of understanding *how* structure interacts with feeling in order to tell its own story. Jakobson's calcified binaries can't tell the tale that arises out of their flesh-and-blood tensions. His way of presenting how Pushkin's biographical and aesthetic concerns interact is, despite the disclaimers,[18] extremely mechanical. All he can do is protect the new world of his structuralist discoveries by planting the flag of his own scientific "colonizing": he is against both "vulgar biographism" and "vulgar autobiographism,"[19] which seems to mean any of the "noise" he comes upon that cannot be pressed into the service of his binaries. It is not, I would argue, the "repeated correspondences between a [biographical] situation and the work,"[20] i.e., the so-called invariants, that attract us to Pushkin and his "life of the poet," although to see that they are there is necessary to comprehend what is taking place, but rather the *difference* (the "story") those invariants generate when they are placed in contact with new, unpredictable information. It is this more telling (in various senses) story, this constant shuttling

---

18 "The analysis of poetic language can profit greatly from the important information provided by contemporary linguistics about the multiform interpenetration of the word and the [biographical] situation, about their mutual tension and their mutual influence. We do not wish mechanically to derive a work from a situation, but at the same time, in analyzing a poetic work, we should not overlook significant repeated correspondences between a situation and the work, especially a regular connection between certain common characteristics of a poet's several works and a common place or common dates; nor should we overlook the biographical preconditions of their origin if they are the same" (Jakobson, "Statue in Puškin's Poetic Mythology," 320).

19 Ibid.

20 Ibid.

21 I take, for example, Pushkin's statement in the voice of one of his favorite heroes (Petrusha Grinev) to be closely reflective of his own feelings: "I hope the reader will forgive me, for he probably knows from experience how easy it is for people to fall into superstition, however great their contempt for unfounded beliefs may be" (A.S. Pushkin, *Polnoe sobranie sochinenii*, ed. B.V. Tomashevskii, 10 vols. [Leningrad: Nauka, 1977–79], 10:269; Alexander Pushkin, *The Complete Prose Fiction*, trans. and intro. Paul Debreczeny [Stanford: Stanford University Press, 1983], 276; these two sources will be referred to subsequently as "*Pss*" and "*CPF*"). Recent scholarship suggests that it was during the Mikhailovskoe exile

back and forth between what is fixed and what is free in life and art, *both of which always already implicate each other*, that Jakobson's model cannot replicate. To narrate this story successfully one cannot simply describe, one must evaluate, interpret in such a way that emotional coloring perforce enters the picture. For just as Chomsky's transformational grammar (another type of structuralism) works neatly for the simple declarative sentence, but quickly becomes unwieldy, a virtual skyscraper of embedded rules, when a complex and emotionally nuanced (i.e., potentially "poetic") utterance is diagrammed, so too are Jakobson's invariants both too much (they see structure where structure is not necessarily meaningful) and not enough (they don't convey the poet's awe and enchantment before the idea of *living form*). Moreover, Jakobson's own ideological vectors, which are not by the way a priori or "scientifically" arrived at, cause him, when they do surface to shape the material, to see Pushkin as more atheist/nonbelieving ("iconoclastic" in terms of the graven image myth) and more inherently radical (his complicated feelings toward Alexander and Nicholas) than he was in fact, especially later in life. This is a not insignificant distortion, about which I will be speaking more in a moment. Therefore, despite his remarkable findings, Jakobson is not I would say successful at *realizing* the sculptural metaphor in the larger context of the poet's personal mythology.

It will be the task of the remainder of this essay to show how Jakobson's findings (together with some additional ones) might be used to bring Pushkin's statue back to life. Let us begin again by opening, in a manner that is precise and not arbitrary, the hermeneutic circle to Pushkin's own cultural context: to repeat, from his earliest days the poet was deeply superstitious, a tendency that seems to have played to his pagan, popular side and to his sense that there are signs in the world (and in his own biography) that he may interpret but over which *he has* no control.[21] Equally if not more important, after a certain point (1826 and

(1824–26) that the actual theme of *sud'ba* (fate), as a concept suffused with superstitious dread and bearing a message of cosmic retribution for past sins, began actively to enter Pushkin's lyrics. A. F. Belousov was the first to explore the notion of a superstition-laden fate in Pushkin's post-1825 lyrics in his "Khudozhestvennyi smysl stikhotvoreniia A. S. Pushkina 'Zimnii vecher,'" *Prepodavanie literaturnogo chteniia v Estonskoi shkole* (Tallin: Tallinskii Pedagogicheskii Institut, 1981), 6–27. Belousov shows that a cluster of poems, "Winter Evening," ("Zimnii vecher," 1825) "To [My] Nanny" ("Niane," 1826), "Gift futile, gift accidental" ("Dar naprasnyi, dar sluchainyi," 1828), "Foreboding" ("Predchuvstvie," 1828), "Devils" ("Besy," 1830), and "Verses composed at night during insomnia" ("Stikhi, sochinennye noch'iu vo vremia bessonnitsy," 1830), are united into an informal cycle by several factors: (1) they are composed (with the sole exception of "To Nanny") in a trochaic meter that has "folk" connotations; (2) several feature the presence of an old woman spinning or knitting (cf. the Parcae); (3) they seem obsessed by the viciously circular movement of snow or leaves and, especially, by the recurrence of an uncertain but ominous noise that the lyrical speaker strains, but fails, to comprehend. It is through this notion of gathering dread, which appears to commence in Mikhailovskoe alongside the poet's newfound respect for sincere religious faith (see next note), that time and history shed their playful ("salon") guises and become "irreversible" in Pushkin.

"The Prophet" ["Prorok"] can be cited as watersheds[22]) he *stops* treating Christian thematics in his work with Voltairean irreverence. Why this is so is a matter of some speculation, but his own humiliating exile in the south and then in Mikhailovskoe, the dismal failure of the Decembrist uprising and the sad fate of implicated friends and classmates, and his own maturation as thinker and writer must all have been factors. In other words, rather than the on/off switch of Jakobsonian binaries, what we have with the "sacred"/"demonic" space of superstition and religion is a rather large fuzzy band of pure feeling or awe governed by "forms" ("rites" in the case of religion) that are not susceptible of analysis or direct cognition. This, I submit, is where we must start in order to try to understand Pushkin's sculptural myth, because it is this sacred space that he traduced in the Voltairean exuberance of his starting out. Hence, it is not the statue per se that we find in the early verse as an example of the demonic, but the "shade" or the "specter" (*ten'*), which only over time takes on three-dimensional form. In Pushkin's early poetry, say "Recollections at Tsarskoe Selo," monuments such as the Kagul obelisk and Chesma column function purely as links to the historic past (again, the heroic age of Catherine), to the poet's own family history (the Pushkins as warriors), and to the sacred site-in-the-making of his schooling and friendships (the Lyceum). Such graven images are perceived as exclusively, benignly *commemorative* — they are the tangible evidence of the "immortality" of brave and glorious deeds. The fact, for example, that Derzhavin, the Russian poet with greatest claim to a historic biography, and the one who wanted to see his own bust among those of Catherine's favorites at Tsarskoe Selo, is present at this soon to be mythopoeticized inauguration of Pushkin's career must be viewed as enormously significant. But the statue itself does not become a serious fact of Pushkin's personal, and what is more important, erotic mythology until the prospect of his marriage to Natalya Goncharova. In this Jakobson is certainly right.

---

22 Actually, the watershed years are 1824–26, i.e., those coterminous with Pushkin's northern exile in Mikhailovskoe. The thematic links between the ninth poem in the cycle "Imitations of the Koran" ("Podrazhaniia Koranu"), "And the weary wanderer grumbled at God" ("I putnik ustalyi na boga roptal," wr. November 1824), and "The Prophet" (wr. September 1826) show how Pushkin's ideas regarding the high calling of the poet were evolving in these years of his greatest, most soul-searching isolation. Although humor, scabrousness, and an unwillingness to moralize directly will be features of Pushkin's work right into the 1830s, there is not a shred of the strictly "Voltairean" element, i.e., the "atheistic" mocking of religious sensibilities, after 1826. I take my trajectory for Pushkin's treatment of religious themes here from Sergei Davydov, "Puškin's Easter Triptych," in *Puškin Today*, ed. David M. Bethea (Bloomington: Indiana University Press. 1993), 44–45.

But what exactly does this mean in terms of the *indispensable sequence of emotional logic* surrounding the poet's "created life"? What was going on in and around his words and their experiential residue to precipitate this shift to the "embodied ghost," the destructive statue, or, to borrow Jakobson's terms taken from Russian ethnology, from *lekan* (statue as pure "external representation") to *ongon* (an "incarnation of some spirit or demon").[23] Here I think we might start with "To a Young Widow" ("K molodoi vdove", 1817), a poem written during the Lyceum period:

> O priceless friend!
> Is it to be forever that you shed tears,
> forever that you summon
> from the grave your dead spouse?
> Believe me: from cold sleep
> the prisoners of the grave cannot be awakened.[24]

This little piece of silliness (only extracted here), which was not published in Pushkin's lifetime, was written fully thirteen years before *The Stone Guest*, yet it already displays certain structural attributes of the later drama, especially the notion that the speaker's challenge is to woo not just anyone, but precisely the young wife of a dead husband. In this case, the fetching widow was a certain Marie Smith, née Charon la Rose, who was visiting at the home of the Lyceum's director, E.A. Engelhardt. What is important to understand is that *already* the schoolboy Pushkin must maintain his independence against all forces, living and dead, and that in order for him to get to his happiness (a night with Marie Smith) he must *get by* a dead, hence potentially ghostly,[25] rival. But that rival has certain legitimate claims on the object of affection, claims which, when we look at issues of the "Muse" and poetic tradition that are engaging Pushkin simultaneously, have to do with the other's (for our purposes, Derzhavin's[26]) *earned* position as a genuinely historical figure. Thus, in order to establish his bona fides (and "be born," as it were) as artist and lover, the young Pushkin must willingly mock, and as it turns out in the

---

23 Jakobson, "Statue in Puškin's Poetic Mythology," 322.

24 *Pss*, 1:214. The original reads: «О бесценная подруга! / Вечно ль слезы проливать, / Вечно ль мертвого супруга / Из могилы вызывать? / Верь мне: узников могилы / Беспробуден хладный сон». The link between the "enraged jealous one [*razgnevannyi revnivets*, i.e. spouse] of the very early "K molodoi vdove" and the *komandor* of *The Stone Guest* is first mentioned in Anna Akhmatova, "'Kamennyi gost'," Pushkina," *Sochineniia* [Munich: Inter-language Literary Associates, 1968], 2: 272.

25 At the end of the poem the speaker refers to the absent husband as a *zavistlivaia ten'* (envious shade) who (he hopes!) won't come back from the dead. *Pss*, 1:215.

26 In *Realizing Metaphors* I made the point here that the speaker's mocking of the dead husband in the poem is analogous to Pushkin's metaliterary mocking of a great deceased precursor like Derzhavin because in each case the young aspirant must remove the male authority figure in order to woo successfully the female incarnation of beauty (the "young widow" in the poem, the Muse in the case of Pushkin's historical positioning vis-à-vis Derzhavin). The superstitiously colored mocking of Derzhavin comes in the early, and unpublished, "Ten' Fonvizina" (Fonvizin's Shade, 1815). See Bethea, *Realizing Metaphors*, 137–72.

most provocative sacrilegious terms (here hinted at with the imperative of the verb "to believe," *ver*), those others already fixed in place—whether husbands, whose wives he eagerly pursues, or dead poets, whose muses he willingly woos away. And his challenges are particularly bold and fraught with risky (i.e., superstition-laden) consequences when they join jokes at the expense of the other world with the notion of "dead" + "husband/lover." The speaker who says at the end of "To a Young Widow" "No, a jealous one full of rage / Will not emerge from the eternal darkness"[27] is, as we might put it today, whistling in the dark.

The next stage in the psychic evolution of this ghost story occurs at the end of a poem that later in life Pushkin would have done anything to take back. But then to take it back would have meant that he wouldn't have been "Pushkin":

> But days fly by, and time, imperceptibly,
> flecks with gray my head,
> and serious marriage will unite me
> at the altar with an amiable wife.
> Wonderful comforter of Joseph!
> I beseech you, on bended knee,
> O defender and protector of cuckolds,
> I beseech — so bless me,
> Grant me lack of care and humility,
> Grant me patience again and again,
> Tranquil sleep, and confidence in my spouse,
> In my family peace and love for my neighbor.[28]

Written in 1821 in Kishinev at the height of Pushkin's Voltairean phase, *The Gabrieliad* is, despite its great charm, truly one of the most brazenly sacrilegious pieces ever penned, in Russia or elsewhere. It is also at its very center about infidelity: about as conscious of what she was doing as the apple eaten by her primordial mother, Mary was such a ripe and available piece of fruit ("Ah, how that Jewess was lovely!"[29]) that not to pluck her was itself a sin. And so each, first the serpent, then a weak-willed Gabriel, and finally the holy spirit (the dove) itself, has his/its way with her, but God, the ultimate patriarch and husband figure, all-knowing in other respects, is ironically kept in the dark about the escapades of the generous "virgin." It is this playfulness that Pushkin, through his speaker in "The Last Relative of Jeanne d'Arc," clubs in his old teacher and author of *La Pucelle* (just as Gabriel kicks Satan in the groin in *The*

---

27 *Pss*, 1:215. The original reads: «Нет, разгневанный ревнивец / Не придет из вечной тьмы».

28 *Pss*, 4:119. The ending of "Gavriiliada" (1821) reads in the original: «Но дни бегут, и время сединою / Мою главу тишком посеребрит, / И важный брак с любезною женою / Пред алтарем меня соединит. / Иосифа прекрасный утешитель! / Молю тебя, колена преклоня, / О рогачей заступник и хранитель, / Молю — тогда благослови меня, / Даруй ты мне блаженное терпенье, / Молю тебя, пошли мне вновь и вновь / Спокойный сон, в супруге уверенье, / В семействе мир и к ближнему любовь».

Gabrieliad), when he says three weeks before his fatal duel with d'Anthès that "Modern history knows no subject more touching, more poetical, than the life and death of the heroine of Orléans, and now look to what use he [Voltaire] has put his inspiration! With his satanic breath he blows on the sparks smoldering in the ashes of the martyr's pyre, and, like some drunken barbarian, dances around his amusing fire. He is like the Roman executioner who adds defilement to the mortal torments of the maiden." Pushkin could not help himself from authoring his sacrilegious joke at the time, but then after the fact, once he had set this "ontological rhyme" in motion in his life, he realized he had trod upon sacred territory, territory dear to many countrymen, who were after all Russians and not French, and territory that was the source of "poetry" of another sort. Yet I would even go so far as to say that the "after the fact" is a bit of an optical (or "scholarly") illusion, since there is the sense in almost everything Pushkin wrote that he *knew* what he was doing (not merely cognitively, and not merely emotionally, but precisely cognitively and emotionally at the same time, which has no other name than *poetic* knowledge). The passage above begins *as a prayer* — "Amen! Amen!" — that the speaker utters, challengingly, into the just concluded space of his elaborate off-color joke. He enjoys making fun of the ultimate cuckold if the prize, the apple waiting to be plucked, is worth it. But then, as always with Pushkin, he puts the shoe on the other foot. He, only twenty-one, projects forward to his own future days as husband and prays to the comforter and protector of cuckolds that he too, in the name of family peace and quiet, be kept in the dark about his wife's extracurricular activities. "Grant me lack of care and humility, / Grant me patience again and again, / Tranquil sleep, and confidence in my spouse, / In my family peace and love for my neighbor" is precisely *not* what will be given to the intensely jealous future husband of Natalya Nikolaevna, *and he knows it*.[30] Indeed, given the poet's self-mutilating call in the post-watershed "Prophet" to have a six-winged seraph tear out "my sinful tongue, / both cunning [*lukavyi*,

---

29 «Ах, как была еврейка хороша!» (*Pss*, 4:117).

30 For the record, Pushkin could be consumed by feelings of jealousy, especially when he sensed that the object of his desire was deliberately toying with his passionate need in the presence of a rival. See, in this respect, the consciousness of the speaker in the poem "Will you forgive me my jealous dreams" ("Prostish' li mne revnivye mechty," 1823), in *Pss*, 2:146, which was supposedly written under the influence of the poet's feelings for Amalia Riznich. On the other hand, Pushkin, like the Othello to whom he often implicitly compared himself, was trusting by nature. If during the last months of his life he came to experience overpowering jealousy toward his rival Georges d'Anthès, who continued to make public display of his feelings for Mme. Pushkina, he as far as we know never questioned the intentions, the implicit rectitude, of his "Madonna-like" wife. Thus the jealousy that would come back to haunt the poet was directed at the end not toward the "spouse" in whom he lacked "confidence," but rather toward the "neighbor" who was threatening, in public, to shatter the "family peace."

in popular tradition 'from the Evil One'] and full of idle speech,"[31] one can only imagine how Pushkin saw these lines coming back to haunt him.

Our third example brings us to the watershed years and to the premonition that the shade is about to be embodied as the retributive statue. In *Boris Godunov* (wr. 1824–25), we find a Pushkin who is well into "living down" the lessons of Byronic romanticism and is now interested more in *Russian* history, Karamzin, Shakespeare, and a notion of time that is maximally risk-laden and nonreversible. Here the primary shade or specter is the one haunting Tsar Boris and his claims to legitimacy. Yet even that shade, renegade priest Grigory Otrepev-cum-arisen Tsarevich, has its own shade to worry about. In the famous scene at the fountain, the Pretender, clearly the most "Pushkinian" character in the play and the one closest to the status of "poet in history,"[32] declares in frustration to his exquisitely cool fiancée, Marina Mniszek,

> Don't torment me, charming Marina,
> Don't tell me that it is my [high] office, and not myself,
> that you have chosen...
> ...
> No! Enough!
> I have no wish to share with a corpse
> a lover belonging to him.[33]

Marina is a Polish (i.e., alluringly western) amalgam of Juliet on the balcony and Lady Macbeth uttering her dark visions of power into the ear of her spouse. She is also described externally, in the scene immediately preceding this one, as a "marble nymph: eyes, lips, without life, without a smile."[34] In other words, her beauty is potentially statuesque, and the one way the Pretender can bring that beauty to life as erotic feeling is through the assumed presence of a rival, that of the murdered Tsarevich, to whom she believes, or wants to believe, she is betrothed. It is only when the Pretender *becomes* the Tsarevich, when he enters sufficiently into his role as proud scion to make that role believable—a fact Pushkin underscores brilliantly by switching the stage direction from "Pretender" to "Dimitry (proudly)"—that the Polish ice goddess begins to melt. But then again, this is another sort of infidelity, since it is, in Pushkin's rendering, the Tsarevich (or his power) that Marina loves but it is the Pretender with whom she will eventually sleep.

The Boldino autumn of 1830, that tremendously fertile and anxiety-laden eve of the poet's marriage, provides the next series of examples. It is during this year, and especially during this autumn, of courtship that

---

31 *Pss*, 2:304: «грешный мой язык, / И празднословный и лукавый».

32 "I believe in the prophecies of poets" (*Ia veruiu v prorochestva piitov*), says the Pretender to a poet at one point (*Pss*, 5:236).

33 *Pss*, 5:242–43: «Не мучь меня, прелестная Марина, / Не говори, что сан, а не меня / Избрала ты... / Нет! Полно! / Я не хочу делиться с мертвецом / Любовницей ему принадлежащей».

34 *Pss*, 5:238: «Да, мраморная нимфа: / Глаза, уста, без жизни, без улыбки».

we for the first time come face to face with the full presence of the sculptural myth. Here it must be said that Jakobson and his descriptive method are both stunningly correct and immensely helpful — the very building blocks on which those coming after can erect their versions of a "truer" story. Even so, however, some significant adjustments are in order. First, there is the deadly erotic play in *The Stone Guest* with *statuia* (statue) and *stat'* (to stand erect): in scene iii, Don Guan mocks his rival's gender by calling the man embodied in the static form *ona* (*statuia* is feminine in Russian), and then he invites him to stand erect — the ultimate insult — at his wife's chamber door while he himself is taking his pleasure within.[35] What is distinctly Pushkinian about this encounter with the fixed other (i.e., "dead" + "husband" → "statue"/embodied ghost) is that the plainly superstitious hero, as opposed to the more cowardly and down-to-earth Leporello, decides to carry out his fatal plan (the assignation) even *after* the *komandor*'s graven image has nodded to him. In other words, the utterer of the challenge knows at some level, just as he did in The *Gabrieliad*, its cost. Yet no matter what, this man with a reckless past, who, as Akhmatova pointed out, is a poet not only "in love" but in the more conventional sense,[36] will have his chance at rebirth[37] at the feet of his initially chaste but eventually desiring beauty.[38] As Donna Anna says, in lines that resonate unmistakably with Tatiana's famous rejection of Onegin, written contemporaneously:

> Diego [i.e., Don Guan in disguise], stop [your talk]: I sin
> listening to you — I am forbidden to love you,
> a widow must be faithful even to the grave...[39]

And as Guan retorts,

> Don't torment my heart,
> Donna Anna, with eternal mention
> [lit. "remembrance," *pominan'e*]
> of your husband. You have punished me enough,
> even though it could be that I deserve execution.[40]

An important shift has taken place here along with the notion that the statue is retributive: not only is Guan in competition with the dead husband (actually, the husband that he killed), but the rights of that husband are

---

35 To be sure, the unprefixed *stat'* is not the same verb in Russian for "to have an erection" (*vstat'*, *vstavat'*) or "to be erect" (*stoiat'*), but the root is identical and, given the context, it seems clear that Pushkin is playing off these meanings.

36 "Don Guan is a poet. His verses, transposed to music, are sung by Laura, and Guan himself calls himself an 'improvisatore of the love song'" (Akhmatova, "'Kamennyi gost'" Pushkina," 2:260).

37 *Pss*, 5:347: "It seems to me I have been reborn entirely" (*Mne kazhetsia, ia ves' pererodilsia*).

38 Cf. the psycho-erotic evolution of "No, I do not prize" ("Net, ia ne dorozhu"), in *Pss*, 3:356.

39 *Pss*, 5:343: «Диего, перестаньте: я грешу / Вас слушая, — мне вас любить нельзя, / вдова должна и гробу быть верна...».

40 *Pss*, 5:343: «Не мучьте сердца / Мне, Дона Анна, вечным поминаньем / Супруга. Полно вам меня казнить, / Хоть казнь я заслужил быть может».

legitimately *sacred* and not to be tampered with. That's where the embodiment comes from, since it is Pushkin's own body that is about to step into the role of the potentially ridiculous *komandor*. Hence it is the *husband*, and not the father, as in other versions of the Don Guan story, who comes to protect the honor of Donna Anna;[41] hence it is the striking *difference* between the massive physical monument, with its static grandeur, and the dead man's tiny, seemingly insect-like[42] stature in real life that draws the attention of the ironic, though still admiring ("He was proud and bold and possessed a stern spirit"[43]) Guan; hence it is that, for all the Spanish decor and the synecdochic mention of lemon and bay trees, a more accurate parallel for Laura and her guests would be, as Akhmatova also divined, some scene from Pushkin's days as a Petersburg "scapegrace," seated gaily among "members of the 'Green Lamp' society who are dining at the home of some celebrity of the time, such as [the actress Alexandra] Kolosova, and discussing art";[44] and hence it is that all the demonic/atheistic connotations in the drama are, strangely enough, associated not with the graven image of Orthodox loathing but with the "godless" man who is about to take what is not his in the name of love.[45] In this respect, I believe that Akhmatova's evaluation of the ultimate meaning of *The Stone Guest*, coming as it does through a poet's sensibility, possesses a kind of spiritual acuity that cannot be even hinted at in the midst of all Jakobson's findings:

> And so, in the tragedy *The Stone Guest* Pushkin is punishing himself — his young, carefree, sinful self, and the theme of jealousy from beyond the grave (i.e., the fear of it) sounds as loudly here as the theme of retribution.
>
> Therefore, a careful analysis of *The Stone Guest* brings us to the firm conviction that behind [these] externally borrowed names and situations we have, in essence, not merely a new reworking of the universal legend of Don Guan, but a profoundly personal, original work by Pushkin, the basic character of which is determined not by the sujet of the legend, but by the personal lyrical feelings, inextricably bound to real-life experience, of Pushkin himself.
>
> Before us is the dramatic embodiment of the inner personality of Pushkin, the artistic exposing-to-view [*obnaruzhenie*] of that which tormented and captivated the poet.[46]

41 Mentioned in Akhmatova, "'Kamennyi gost' Pushkina," 262.

42 Don Alvar is described as a "dragonfly" (*strekoza*) impaled on Guan's sword (*Pss*, 5:332); Pushkin was known among his Arzamas brethren as the "cricket" (*sverchok*).

43 *Pss*, 5:332: «... а был / Он горд и смел — и дух имел суровый».

44 Akhmatova, "'Kamennyi gost'" Pushkina," 265.

45 "The shameless, godless Don Guan" (monk), "Your Don Guan is an atheist [*bezbozhnik*] and a scoundrel" (Don Karlos), etc. Guan's reputation as an *Ateista fulminado* is mentioned at least four times

This explains, and beautifully, Pushkin's feelings toward his own version of Guan, but even that is not enough to account for the massive "simultaneity" of this situation. For the poet is both Guan and the jealous husband-cum-statue. That is the point. There is a reason he is willing, even now, to hurl challenges at his own image of future pain and humiliation. It has to do with the actual beauty, Natalya Goncharova, at whose altar he is willing to sacrifice everything. For the image of stone (marble) also is associated with her, or at least with her image in the tragedy, almost as much as with the jealous statue guarding her virtue. Recall, for example, what the seductive (or is it genuinely worshipful?) Guan says to her at the pedestal of her husband's monument:

> It is only from afar that I with reverence
> look on you when, bending down quietly,
> you strew your black locks onto the pale marble —
> and it seems to me then that secretly
> an angel has paid a visit to this tomb,
> [and] in my troubled heart I can then no longer
> find prayers [i.e., Guan is playing the role of monk].
> I marvel wordlessly
> and think: happy is he whose cold marble
> is warmed by her heavenly breath
> and watered by the tears of her love....[47]

This, I would say, is the missing second element in Pushkin's intricately realized sculptural metaphor, what we have been referring to elsewhere as his "Pygmalion myth"[48]: it is both what the stone will do to him (it will come for him as his death) and what it will do *for* him (it will bring him back to life even as he seems to be the one doing the touching and the creating). Pygmalion was, in Ovid's poetic rendering, the legendary king of Cyprus who, disappointed in love ("Pygmalion loathed the vices given by nature / To women's hearts"), created a statue of such beauty ("Meanwhile he carved the snow-white ivory / With happy skill; he gave it a beauty greater / Than any woman's") that he became enamored of it ("The sculptor / Marveled, and loved his beautiful pretense") and prayed to Aphrodite to give him a wife resembling his creation.[49] But poets shouldn't ask to have their prayers answered: Aphrodite not only heeded the supplicant, but gave Pygmalion precisely *his own statue* come to life:

in the play: see discussion in Akhmatova, "'Kamennyi gost'' Pushkina," 264.

46 Ibid., 273.

47 *Pss*, 5:333: «Я только издали с благоговеньем / Смотрю на вас, когда, склонившись тихо, / Вы черные власы на мрамор бледный / Рассыплете — И мнится мне, что тайно / Гробницу эту ангел посетил, / В смущенном сердце я не обретаю / Тогда молений. Я дивлюсь безмолвно / И думаю — счастлив, чей хладный мрамор / Согрет ее дыханием небесным / И окроплен любви ее слезами».

48 See *Realizing Metaphors*, 10–33 and below.

49 The translation is Gilbert Highet's, as found in

> When he returned [from the festival of Aphrodite],
> he went to his ivory image,
> Lay on its couch and kissed it. It grew warm.
> He kissed again and touched the ivory breast.
> The ivory softened, and its carven firmness
> Sank where he pressed it, yielded like the wax
> Which in the sunlight takes a thousand shapes
> From moulding fingers, while use makes it useful.
> Pygmalion was aghast and feared his joy,
> But like a lover touched his love again.
> It was a body, beating pulse and heart.
> Now he believed and in an ardent prayer
> Gave thanks to Venus: pressed his mouth at last
> To a living mouth. The maiden felt his kiss —
> She blushed and trembled: when she raised her eyes
> She saw her lover and heaven's light together.[50]

This metamorphosis feels eerily like the speaker's reaction to the gift of eros in the very private "No, I do not prize."[51] But isn't our detective work here simply another case of figurative language run wild, for what could it mean, *really*, to claim that Pushkin-Pygmalion had, in his disenchantment over his amorous past, fallen in love with his own creation and had prayed for a wife resembling what he had made? I think not. During this very same Boldino autumn Pushkin wrote, as it turns out mainly for himself, a series of responses to his critics ("Refutation of Criticisms"/["Oproverzhenie na kritiki"]). In this quite personal essay format, while defending himself against various ad hominem attacks in the periodic press referring to his physical appearance, his genealogy, and what some with unseemly glee saw to be the waning of his talent, he decided to "explain himself," with tetchy sarcasm and a sturdy sense of amour propre. He told his imaginary reader that, contrary to the simpleminded opinion of his critics, it was logical and

---

Latin Poetry in Verse Translation, ed. L.R. Lind (Boston: Houghton Mifflin, 1957), 164–65. The Latin originals for these quotes read: "Quas quia Pygmalion aevum per crimen agentis / viderat, offensus vitiis, quae plurima menti / femineae natura dedit, sine coniuge caelebs / vivebat thalamique diu consorte carebat"; "interea niveum mira feliciter arte / sculpsit ebur formamque dedit, qua femina nasci / nulla potest, operisque sui concepit amorem" (Ovid, *Metamorphoses*, 2 vols., with an English translation by Frank Justus Miller [Cambridge: Harvard University Press, 1951], 2:80–82).

50 Lind, ed., *Latin Poetry in Verse Translation*, 165. The original reads: "ut rediit, simulacra suae petit ille puellae / incumbensque toro dedit oscula: visa tepere est; / admovet os iterum, manibus quoque pectora temptat: / temptatum mollescit ebur positoque rigore / subsidit digitis ceditque, ut Hymettia sole / cera remollescit tractataque pollice multas / flectitur in facies ipsoque fit utilis usu. / dum stupet et dubie gaudet fallique veretur, / rursus amans rursusque manu sua vota retractat. / corpus erat! saliunt temptatae pollice venae. / tum vero Paphius plenissima concipit heros / verba, quibus Veneri grates agat, oraque tandem / ore suo non falsa premit, dataque oscula virgo / sensit et erubuit timidumque ad lumina lumen / attollens pariter cum caelo vidit amantem" (Ovid, *Metamorphoses*, 2:82).

51 See Pushkin's intimate lyric about his wife and how her cool, statuesque beauty comes

psychologically convincing to have Maria, his lovely young heroine in *Poltava* (1828), fall in love with the gloomy and aging hetman Mazepa. Why? Because "love is the most capricious of passions," because there happen to be myths about such miraculous reversals, *including Ovid's story of Pygmalion*, that inspire us with their own special poetry, and because, to cite another example that for Pushkin was close to home, "Othello, the old moor, captivated Desdemona with stories about his wanderings and battles."[52] Here too Pushkin was talking, obliquely but nonetheless unmistakably, about himself and his own situation as potential Pygmalion and potential Othello. If the statue might be coming for him as repayment for past sins (his Guan incarnation), then in return for this fatal barter he could enjoy ("Pygmalion was aghast and feared his joy"[53]) the sensation of the black tresses on his stone flesh (his statue incarnation, or the end of his protean movement) and the equally, if not more, arousing sensation of the cool marble coming to life (as Ovid's ivory had melted into warm, pliable wax) at the sculptor's touch.

Even so, even granting that the poet might have been thinking of one of Ovid's metamorphoses as he was writing furiously during that Boldino autumn, is there a concrete sense in which some*thing* created can, because it is adored so much and because it so seems to have a life of its own, become some*one*? Not Natalie by herself, but the statue that predated her and into which she seemed to have entered? Yes. There are, it turns out, two other contemporaneous texts that show how powerfully and seemingly alchemically Pushkin was *realizing* this double-sided sculptural metaphor in the year of his courtship. The first involves his letter to Natalie's mother (N. I. Goncharova), dated 5 April 1830, on the occasion of their betrothal; the second the final, eighth (originally the ninth) chapter of *Eugene Onegin*, which he was also finishing that fall. The letter, which I quote virtually in full, reads:

---

to erotic life under his touch in "Net, ia ne dorozhu miatezhnym naslazhden'em," in *Pss*, 3:356. Discussed in *Realizing Metaphors*, 11–17.

[52] *Pss*, 7:132. The other Ovidian transformations/matings that Pushkin mentions on this page all involve *women* - Leda, Philyra, Pasipha, and Myrrha - a fact that would make the example of Pygmalion even more significant. Ovid of course had been an important early interlocutor (the "poet as exile") in Pushkin's work: see, e.g., "To Ovid" (K Ovidiiu, 1821), *Pss*, 2:62–64. Pushkin had at least three different editions of Ovid, two French and one Latin, in his library as catalogued by Modzalevsky: (1) *Amours mythologiques, traduits des Metamorphoses d'Ovide par De Pongerville*, 2d ed. (Paris, 1827) (no. 1231 in catalogue); *Oeuvres completes d'Ovide*, ed. "imprimee sous les yeux et par les soins de J. Ch. Poncelin" (Paris, 1799) (no. 1232 in catalogue); and *Publii Ovidii Nasonis opera*, ed. "recognovit, et argumentis distinxit J. A. Amar" (Paris, 1822) (no. 1233 in catalogue). See B. L. Modzalevskii, "Biblioteka A. S. Pushkina," *Pushkin i ego sovremenniki. Materialy i issledovaniia* 9–10 (1910): 304.

[53] Akhmatova correctly surmises that what Pushkin fears is not death but the *loss of happiness*, which he knows his too tormented heart cannot withstand. He repeatedly describes his wish for marriage and family life as his try *for happiness*. Akhmatova, "'Kamennyi gost' Pushkina," 267 (see n. 24, above).

When I saw her for the first time, her beauty was just beginning to be noticed in society. I fell in love with her; my head began to whirl; I asked for her hand. Your answer, all vague as it was, gave me a moment of delirium. I departed the same night for the army. You ask me what I was doing there? I swear to you that I do not know at all, but an involuntary anguish was driving me from Moscow. There I would not have been able to bear either your presence or hers. I wrote you. I hoped, I waited for an answer — it did not come. The errors of my first youth presented themselves to my imagination. They were only too violent, and calumny had added to them further; talk about them has become, unfortunately, widespread. You might have believed it; I dared not complain, but I was in despair.

What torments awaited me on my return! Your silence, your cold air, Mlle. Natalie's reception of me, so nonchalant, so inattentive... I did not have the courage to explain myself, I went to Petersburg with death in my soul. I felt I had played a rather ridiculous role; I had been timid for the first time in my life, and timidity in a man of my age could hardly please a young person of your daughter's age [Natalie was eighteen at the time of the Pushkins' marriage in February 1831]. One of my friends [i.e., Vyazemsky] went to Moscow and brought me back a kind word which restored me to life, and now when those gracious words which you have been so kind to address to me should have overwhelmed me with joy [i.e., news that the proposal was being looked on favorably] — I am more unhappy than ever. I shall try to explain.

Only [force of] habit and a long [period of] intimacy could win for me your daughter's affection. I hope in time I can awaken in her feelings of attachment toward me, but I have nothing with which to please her [in the sense of "giving pleasure," "je n'ai rien pour lui plaire"] If she consents to give me her hand, I shall see only the proof of the calm indifference [*la tranquille indifférence*] of her heart. But surrounded as she will be [in society] with admiration, with homage, with enticements, will this calmness last? She will be told that only unfortunate fate has prevented her from forming other ties, more fitting, more brilliant, more worthy of her — perhaps such remarks may be sincere, but she will assuredly believe them to be so. Will she not have regrets? Will she not regard me as an obstacle, as a fraudulent ravisher [*un ravisseur frauduleux*]? Will she not take an aversion to me? God is my witness that I am ready to die for her, but that I should die to leave a dazzling widow, free to choose a new husband tomorrow — this idea is hell.

Let us speak of finances; I set little store on that. Mine have sufficed me up to the present. Will they suffice me, married? Not for anything in the world would I bear that my wife should come to know privations, that she should not go where she is invited to shine, to amuse herself. She has the right to insist upon it. In order to satisfy her, I am ready to sacrifice to her all my tastes, all the passions of my life, a mode of life quite free and quite reckless. Still, will she not murmur if her position in society is not as brilliant as that which she deserves and which I would wish for her?[54]

I find this document to be one of the most remarkable, and poignant, examples in all world literature of a great and proud artist exposing his own vulnerabilities and displaying his readiness to shed all the outward trappings of a previous identity in order to have a "try at happiness" — love, family, domestic life — which, we recall, he *already suspected to be doomed*. Pushkin, to repeat, was someone who was fastidiously guarded about his feelings. Only his desperate situation (he had in recent years already been rejected several times by other young ladies, including a first time by Natalie and her mother[55]), together with the relative freedom of a "noneroticizable" female correspondent and the glorious limitation of his idiomatic French, could have made him so fully place his cards on the table. This is not Don Juan, the man who claimed that his wife was his "113th love," but the man who correctly suspects that one day in the not so distant future he will be nothing more than a dragonfly caught on the rapier of a younger, more desirable opponent. With all his verbal gifts, with all his protean genius he is willing to sacrifice in her name, he has nothing of value to offer to the other side. What he has earned in the eyes of society, which is what concerns the mother, is a bad name. He sees this and he knows it. He can worship at the altar of this beauty, he can hope that one day it will be well disposed toward him, but he knows in his heart that this maiden's *tranquille indifférence* (the attitude of a statue) will not be (for her) the same as pleasure, desire,

---

54 Alexander Pushkin, *The Letters* trans. and intro. J. Thomas Shaw (Madison: University of Wisconsin Press, 1967), 405–6; *Pss*, 10:217–18.

55 Technically speaking, Natalie's mother did not reject Pushkin during his initial suit for her daughter's hand; what she did was *not accept* that suit, which is to say, she did not completely "shut the door," but at the same time she continued to look about for a more attractive prospect.

love: "I have nothing with which to please her." And he doesn't (and as far as we know he never will) *resent this in her*: it is not her fault. If anything, it is his. The extent to which Pushkin sees everything and even now, at the moment in his life when he is most exposed and most needful, resolutely refuses to write himself into the role of the victim simply takes the reader's breath away. If the source of inspiration can exist in a document that is not, strictly speaking, aesthetically shaped, then this is it.

The final chapter of *Eugene Onegin* provides us the example we need of the female statue come to life—what in Pushkin's erotic mythology might be called not the destructive, but the grace-bearing, *ongon*. It is important to keep in mind here the details of Ovid's plot: Pymalion creates a statue of such charm that he falls in love with it, but it is only through prayer (to Aphrodite in Ovid, to God in Pushkin's Madonna poem[56]) followed by the intercession of the other that the statue comes to life. At the beginning of chapter 8, the speaker lists all the incarnations of the Muse in his works up to that point, and then, as he brings Onegin together with Tatiana for the story of their second round of meetings and his obsessive infatuation, we are introduced to his (the speaker's) current, and what will turn out to be ultimate, version of the Muse—the village miss (*uezdnaia baryshnia*) become the comme il faut society princess.[57] The metamorphosis of Tatiana is so shockingly total and unaccountable that many have faulted the author for failing to realize the *novelistic* expectations of this finale. But then Pushkin was writing a novel in verse, which is a "devil of a difference," as he said. I would like to suggest, therefore, that the psycho-erotic structure of this last chapter replicates certain crucial aspects of the Pygmalion myth as they apply to Pushkin's situation: (1) the change in Tatiana as she navigates the treacherous waters of high society makes her beauty now superior to, because alive and somehow coming from within, that of marble ("She sat at a table / with the brilliant Nina Voronskaya, / that Cleopatra of the Neva; / and in truth you would have to agree, / that Nina, *with her marble beauty* / could not outshine her neighbor, / although she was dazzling"[58]); (2) Onegin, the narrator's Byronic alter ego and rival for the affections of Tatiana, is struck dumb, paralyzed, virtually turned to stone himself by this change he cannot explain ("But Onegin could find / no traces of the former Tatiana. / He wanted to start up a conversation with her / and— and he couldn't. She asked / whether he had been here for a long time,

---

56 See *Pss*, 3:166.

57 A reading of Tatiana that mounts a spirited and well-reasoned challenge to her status as Muse is Caryl Emerson, "Tatiana," in *A Plot of Her Own: The Female Protagonist in Russian Literature*, ed. Sona Stephan-Hoisington (Evanston: Northwestern University Press, 1995), 6–20.

58 *Pss*, 5:148: «Она сидела у стола / С блестящей Ниной Воронскою, / Сей Клеопатрою Невы; / И верно б согласились вы, / Что Нина мраморной красою / Затмнить соседки не могла, / Хоть ослепительна была».

whence he was coming / and whether it might be from their parts? / Then she turned to her husband / a weary glance, and glided away... / And he [Onegin] remained there motionless"[59]); and (3) the general who is Tatiana's husband and Onegin's relative is there in the background as the necessary third party — not a shade, not an avenging statue himself, but simply a decent man who has *earned*, through his deeds as a warrior, a place of honor in society and to whom the statue-come-to-life is faithful even if she does not love him. In this reversal of the *Stone Guest* plot (this Donna Anna does not yield to the lover's words), Pushkin places the husband in the virtuous and now departing wife's boudoir at the climactic moment when the failed hero freezes on the spot: "She left. There stands Evgeny / as though thunderstruck."[60] The only hint of the husband's vulnerability — not developed in the plot — are the war wounds fixed on by the Freudians. But the general need not be a Russian Jake Barnes. Rather he is, in the psychological space of the poem, together with the thoughts of the narrator who is clearly "on his side," that everyday other into whose hands is committed the living statue. In other words, the general (who is bound by the storyline) + the narrator (who possesses the mythopoetic sensibility "behind the scenes") = Pushkin-Pygmalion *after the fact* of Aphrodite's gift. In terms of the poet's erotic mythology, there is no more story to tell — it passes beyond the veil, and almost (but not entirely) from view, into the privacy of the Pushkins' domestic life.[61]

In conclusion, in my reworking of Jakobson's findings I have been stressing how all the different aspects and details — some random, others "bio-aesthetically" shaped — of Pushkin's sculptural mythology came together on the eve of his marriage to produce poems, dramas, prose writings, doodlings, and other verbal artifacts seemingly "alive" with their own haunting prescience. And, to be sure, the myth of the graven image come to life did not disappear from the poet's work after the Pushkins' wedding. It did, however, fuel itself on a different sort of economy: now Pushkin

59 *Pss*, 5:149: «Но и следов Татьяны прежней / Не мог Онегин обрести. / С ней речь хотел он завести / И — и не мог. Она спросила, / Давно ль он здесь, откуда он / И не из их ли уж сторон? / Потом к супругу обратила / Усталый взгляд; скользнула вон... / И недвижим остался он».

60 *Pss*, 5:162: «Она ушла. Стоит Евгений / Как будто громом поражен».

61 I say "not entirely" because out of political considerations (i.e., tsarist censorship), Pushkin was not allowed to become a completely *private* citizen. As he writes to his wife in a letter of 18 May 1834 after he has become angered by the intrusion of the postal censors into his domestic sphere: "Look, little wife [*zhenka*]. I hope that you won't give my letters to anybody to make copies of. If the post has unsealed a husband's letters to his wife, then that's its affair. But there is one unpleasant thing in that: the privacy of family relationships, intruded upon in a foul and dishonorable manner. But if you are to blame, then that would be painful for me. Nobody must know what may take place between us; nobody must be received into our bedroom. Without privacy there is no family life" (*Pss*, 10:377; *Letters*, 652).

was concerned not so much with winning a Madonna (that prayer had been granted), but with protecting the modest domesticity that he did possess and with returning to the values and figures of the eighteenth century with a view to how he might be measured against them when his time, sooner or later, came. To put it rather crudely, Pushkin wanted to demonstrate again and again, over a broad swath of genres, how the power of the poet and the power of the tsar were and were not commensurate, and how Russia needed them both to move forward out of her troubles. As the poet wrote to his wife several months after completing *The Bronze Horseman* and while gathering material for his history of Peter: "And suddenly I shall cast a bronze monument that can't be dragged from one end of the city to the other, from square to square, from alley to alley."[62] In other words, the "material" quality of his legacy was always on his mind during these years. On the other hand, he continued to be superstitious about any graven image *in his own likeness* (as opposed to his wife's): "Here [in Moscow] they want a bust of me to be sculpted," he complains in another letter of the mid-1830s to Natalia Nikolaevna, "but I don't want it. Then my Negro ugliness would be committed to immortality in all its dead immobility."[63] Any attempt to translate the poet's monument into something fixed and three-dimensional is understood instinctively to belong to the semantic field of the "demonic."

In this respect, *The Bronze Horseman* and "The Fairy Tale of the Golden Cockerel" are indeed, as Jakobson copiously argued, deep-structural siblings to *The Stone Guest*, although he didn't push the parallelism (the difference in sameness) quite far enough. In the more realistically motivated narrative poem, where the poet's contest with his greatest rival (Peter as both creative and destructive historical force) must be given a more or less "verisimilar" outcome, the now *déclassé* hero and little man is destroyed along with his sweetheart and dreams of domesticity. The statue come to life is that of the titanic tsar trying to protect his legacy — the city, the empire — the cost of which is the "happiness" of the unprepossessing subject. In the peculiarly Pushkinian fairy tale, on the other hand, where the power and legacy of the adviser to Tsar Dadon are presented with a kind of "dream" logic, the astrologer-castrate (*zvezdochet-skopets*) is betrayed by the tsar, but it is *his* statuette-cockerel, as small as Peter's monument is large, that whirls into motion and gets, so to speak, the last word. The adviser and his magic helper

62 Pushkin, *Letters*, 654; *Pss*, X:379. The letter was written no later than 29 May 1834, that is, very close to Pushkin's birthday (26 May).

63 Pushkin, *Letters*, 767; *Pss*, X:452. The letter was written between 14 and 16 May 1836. For a revealing early self-portrait that touches, even in 1814, on some of the same themes (e.g., *Vrai singe par sa mine*), see "Mon Portrait," in *Pss*, I:80–81.

64 Anna Akhmatova, "Posledniaia skazka Pushkina," *Sochineniia*, ed. G. P. Struve and B. A. Filippov (Munich: Inter-language Literary Associates, 1968), II:197–222. The reading of "The Fairy Tale of the Golden

are heeded only so long as they serve Tsar Dadon, which by 1834, as Akhmatova was the first to demonstrate in another article,[64] likely alludes to Pushkin's role as post-Karamzinian "court historian" and to his ambiguous feelings toward Alexander and Nicholas. At the same time, the astrologer is *castrated*, which is Pushkin's *addition* to Irving's "The Legend of the Arabian Astrologist,"[65] and thus symbolically denied direct access to power (but not to desire). In other words, read back into Pushkin's biography, the imposed position of aging *kameriunker* made him more of a *jester* (he constantly refers in private to his uniform as his "fool's motley") than a distinguished confidant. All the fairy-tale character wants in return for his kingdom-saving counsel is the one request he has coming to him, the "maiden, the Tsarina of Shemakha" (*devitsa, Shamakhanskaia tsaritsa*), but it is this request that Dadon, himself now struck by the maiden's beauty, denies. For a poet as sensitive to logosemantic play as this one is, is it any wonder that "*petushok*" (cockerel) can be anagrammatically decoded as *Pushkin*? Yes, the wonder-working *zvezdochet* is struck down by the tsar's phallic staff (*zhezl*), but then the *petushok*, which could only be the poetic/historical "truth" that exists independent of its author, comes to life and avenges, *after the fact*, the injustice. If Nicholas will ignore the implicit message of *The History of Pugachev*, then he will do so at his own risk. Thus, just as in his own doodles of himself Pushkin caricatures or even *disfigures* his laurel-enshrouded human likeness, so too does he *refigure* himself as a fantastic bird elsewhere: the sketch, for example, of what may well be this very same cockerel that was bizarrely inserted into the manuscript of

Cockerel" as political satire, initiated by Akhmatova in the early 1930s, has become in recent years the work's dominant mode of interpretation, although very rarely (if ever) can it be said (and one has to assume that Akhmatova herself would not have said it) that Pushkin's artistic design is politically or, ideologically motivated *tout court*. Perhaps the most extreme example of this tendency (fairy tale = political cryptotext) is found in Andrej Kodjak, "Skazka Pushkina 'Zolotoi Petushok,'" in *American Contributions to the VIII International Congress of Slavists* (Columbus: Slavica, 1978), II:332–74. For an outstanding recent study of "The Golden Cockerel," with thorough exposition of the scholarly debate and of the tensions between folkloric and nonfolkloric (i.e., literary, biographical, etc.) sources, see V.E. Vatsuro, "'Skazka o zolotom petushke': Opyt analiza siuzhetnoi semantiki," *Pushkin: Issledovaniia i materialy* 15 (1995): 122–33.

65 First noted in Jakobson, "Statue in Puškin's Poetic Mythology," 328. The theme of the "compensatory" interrelations between worldly power (wealth, status) and artistic power (inspiration), with the striking variable of castration (the absence of sexual potency) added in, seems to have been on the poet's mind, for obvious reasons, in his last years. See, for example, his 1835 off-color poetic joke (not intended for publication) "Once a violinist came to a castrato" (K kastratu raz prishel skrypach), in *Pss*, 3:322. Another possible subtext here was Pavel Katenin's poem "An Old True Story" (Staraia byl'), which, in a gesture of prickly "friendship," the bilious archaist dedicated to Pushkin and sent to him in 1828. In that work Katenin presents a competition between a "Greek castrate" (*ellin-skopets*) and an old "Russian warrior" (*russkii voin*) over who can best create a song to honor Prince Vladimir. Although the competition is won without a fight by the Greek, Katenin's ironic point is that the post-December 1825 Pushkin (i.e., the castrated Greek) is too willing to sing the praises of autocracy (here the allusion is to Pushkin's advice, perceived by some as too close to flattery, that Nicholas follow the generous impulses of his great forebear Peter, as presented in "Stanzas" ["Stansy," 1826]), while

The History of the Village Goriukhino.⁶⁶ Vadim Vatsuro's astute conclusion about the "Golden Cockerel" — "Pushkin makes the 'magical helper' an autonomous figure and very nearly the genuine hero of his fairytale narration" — is, in this reader's opinion, wrong in one crucial respect. No, the impression that "evil is punished, but good does not triumph" is a false one, since it is not the life of the astrologer (or the tsar) that the logic (the embedded desire) of the tale would or should preserve, but the message — the (poetic) truth will out — of the statuette.⁶⁷ Likewise, the poet will make every effort, throughout his own ultimate self-sculpting in "Exegi monumentum," to undo both the tsar's (the "other" Alexander's) and the poet's (Derzhavin's) literalism and boastfully three-dimensional immortality.⁶⁸ To repeat, Pushkin's immortality, if he has any choice in the matter, will be of the *nerukotvornyi* (not made by hand) variety. And the maiden, the occasion for the conflict? Well, she simply disappears.

---

the still "disgraced" Katenin (i.e., the old Russian warrior in exile on his estate) is content to remain silent. By the mid-1830s Pushkin may have agreed with Katenin's "castrate" label with regard to his historical person (hence the wry reinvocation of the insult), but not with regard to the power of his word (the *petushok*). See the illuminating discussion of the Katenin-Pushkin competition in Iu. Tynianov, *Arkhaisty i novatory* (Leningrad: Priboi, 1929), 160-77.

66 See *Pss*, 6:119. There is considerable debate about when precisely Pushkin wrote *The History of the Village Goriukhino* (*Istoriia sela Goriukhina*), although most scholars now agree it was probably during the first Boldino autumn (1830). It is also hard (if not impossible) to determine when Pushkin made his sketch of the fantastic bird and inserted it into the manuscript of his mock history. One thing is certain, however: as M.P. Alekseev first established, Irving's *A History of New York* was one of Pushkin's sources for *The History of the Village Goriukhino;* and likewise, after Akhmatova's discovery it has become impossible not to take into account "The Legend of the Arabian Astrologist" as Pushkin's primary textual point of departure in "The Fairy Tale of the Golden Cockerel." Thus, even if Pushkin didn't know Irving's legend in 1830, when we think he was working on *The History of the Village Goriukhino*, he still could have done the sketch a few years later (based on Akhmatova's chronology) and then interleaved it after the fact, as a kind of mnemonic trace of the cockerel's "power" and message, in his own (in various senses, i.e., Boldino=Goriukhino) history.

67 Vatsuro, "'Skazka o zolotom petushke'," 133.

68 Pushkin's "I have erected for myself a monument not made by hand" ("Ia pamiatnik sebe vozdvig nerukotvornyi," wr. 1836) uses Derzhavin's famous "Monument" ("Pamiatnik," 1795; orig. "K muze. Podrazhanie Goratsiiu"), itself a "copy" of Horace, as its point of departure and chief dialogic partner. The interplay between physical monuments, such as the original Alexandrine column honoring the Emperor Diocletian and the new Alexander Column commemorating the twentieth anniversary of Tsar Alexander I's victory over Napoleon (and unveiled in 1832 on Palace Square in St. Petersburg at a ceremony Pushkin demonstrably did not attend), and spiritual monuments, the most obvious in this case being the "Alexandrines" not-made-by-hand of "I have erected," are very much on the poet's mind in the last years of his life. See Bethea, *Realizing Metaphors*, 217–34.

Chapter 4

The Evolution of Evolution: Genes, Memes, Intelligent Design, and Nabokov[1]

> He told me about the odours of butterflies — musk and vanilla; about the voices of butterflies; about the piercing sound given out by the monstrous caterpillar of a Malayan hawkmoth, an improvement on the mouselike squeak of our Death's Head moth; about the small resonant tympanum of certain tiger moths; about the cunning butterfly in the Brazilian forest which imitates the whirr of a local bird. He told me about the incredible wit of mimetic disguise, which was not explainable by the struggle for existence (the rough haste of evolution's unskilled forces), was too refined for the mere deceiving of accidental predators, feathered, scaled, and otherwise (not very fastidious, but then not too fond of butterflies), and seemed to have been invented by some waggish artist precisely for the intelligent eyes of man...
>
> Nabokov, *The Gift*[2]

Many of us know this famous passage from The Gift. Quite aside from its stylistic fireworks it has served as exhibit #1 in the ongoing debate about where Nabokov comes down on the issue of intelligent design (ID) and evolutionary theory. Depending on one's epistemological point of

---

[1] I would like to take this opportunity to thank my distinguished colleague at Madison, Vilas Professor of Philosophy Elliott Sober, for his invaluable insights into the Neo-Darwinian-Intelligent Design debate.

[2] Vladimir Nabokov, *The Gift* (London: Penguin, 2001), 105, Vladimir Nabokov. *Sobranie sochinenii russkogo perioda v piati tomakh*, vol. 4 *1935–1937: Priglashenie na kazn', Dar, Rasskazy, Esse*), (St. Petersburg: Simpozium, 2000), 294. I will be referring to both these editions in the following pages. *Dar* was written between 1933 and January 1938 (mainly in Berlin), published serially in *Sovremennye zapiski* in 1937–38 (without

departure, readers have tried now for some time to "get at" VN's strategy for mixing and matching scientific and artistic observation. According to this strategy the artist must be able to observe and name the phenomenal world like the naturalist, the naturalist must be able to integrate different planes of reality like the artist, and somewhere in between — is it random? is it conscious? — an event takes place that is profoundly creative. VN's creations, like the fantastically tinted and drawn-to-perfection butterflies, many with real genera but playful, imaginary species, that he conjured out of thin air to inscribe first editions of his work to Vera, all bear the imprint of his "ludic logo."[3] Of VN's many commentators, Brian Boyd has had the most to say on this topic, with others like Stephen Blackwell and Victoria Alexander adding to and refining our knowledge. Be that as it may, the subject is by no means exhausted, nor is it likely to be any time soon. In the pages to follow I would like to join in the conversation.

First of all, let us restate the givens. Nabokov is a one-of-a-kind phenomenon; that is, in his terms, which he insisted upon with his playful arrogance, a cunning butterfly in a Brazilian forest that can imitate the whirr of a local bird. Translation: he can, or seems to be able to, communicate beyond his species' voice zone, the *nom de plume* "Sirin" being from the start conceived as *rara avis*. If one describes VN's case not metaphorically but supposedly factually, objectively, he is a genius. (Likewise, he might add

the controversial chapter four biography of Chernyshevsky), and printed in its complete form as a separate book only in 1952 by the Chekhov Publishing House. It was then rendered into English as *The Gift* by Dmitri Nabokov and Michael Scammell (with final revisions by Nabokov himself) and published by Putnam in 1963. "Father's Butterflies," which will be the subject of discussion in different parts of this essay, has been assigned a "very likely" time of writing by Brian Boyd of spring 1939 ("Vtoroe dobavlenie k 'Daru'," *Zvezda* 1 [January 2001]: 86); as one of the tantalizing roads not taken, the piece was written in Russian after the initial appearance of *Dar*, in connection with a planned edition of the novel in two volumes, later aborted, but before VN had emigrated to America (May 1940) and decided for certain to become an American writer.

3 Kurt Johnson and Brian Boyd, "Verochka Verochka: Amusing the Muse," in Sarah Funke, *Vera's Butterflies: First Editions by Vladimir Nabokov to His Wife*, ed. Glenn Horowitz (New York: Glenn Horowitz Booksellers, 1999), 14.

4 A phenotype is "the total of all observable features of a developing or developed individual (including its anatomical, physiological, biochemical, and behavioral characteristics). The phenotype is the result of interaction between the genotype and the environment." A genotype is "the set of genes of an individual." Ernst Mayr, *What Evolution Is* (New York: Basic Books, 2001), 286, 289.

5 "Meme" as a term was first coined by Richard Dawkins in his 1976 *The Selfish Gene*: "The new soup is the soup of human culture. We need a name for the new replicator, a noun which conveys the idea of a unit of cultural transmission, or a unit of *imitation*. 'Mimeme' comes from a suitable Greek root, but I want a monosyllable that sounds a bit like 'gene'. I hope my classicist friends will forgive me if I abbreviate mimeme to *meme*... It should be pronounced to rhyme with 'cream'. Examples of memes are tunes, ideas, catch-phrases, clothes fashions, ways of making pots or of building arches" (Richard Dawkins, "Memes: The New Replicators," *The Selfish Gene* (Oxford: Oxford UP, 2006; first ed. 1976), 192; the phrase "pattern of neuronal wiring-up" is found on 323. "Meme" took on a life of its own after its inaugural usage, eventually appearing in the OED as a lexical item of recognizable currency — an instance of where the "meme" actually became itself ("metamemetics?"). See Richard Dawkins, "Chinese Junk and Chinese Whispers: From the Foreword to *The Meme Machine* by Susan Blackmore," in *A Devil's Chaplain: Selected Essays* (London: Phoenix, 2004), 141–42. "Memeplex," or meme complex (another Dawkins coinage), has also been used

with his everpresent linguistic consciousness, if you take out the "i/I" he becomes only a "genus," a type.) To those of us who read his novels, chess problems, and lepidopterological studies the man's phenotypic presence on earth between 1899 and 1977 seems not only a stroke of genetic and environmental good luck.[4] We want to believe there is more, perhaps a kind of *unnatural* selection. This notion of uniqueness, "chosenness," simultaneously partakes of the romantic poet as genius figure (*poet bozh'ei milost'iu*) going back to Pushkin in the Russian tradition, another thing of which VN was keenly aware. Such arch classification, where the exhibit is not merely *homo sapiens*, but some marked subspecies of the latter (*homo scribens, homo ludens*), may have been VN's point, at least publicly, but can we really say with intellectual honesty it is the point now, in the time-space in which the man's creations continue to exist after his passing? On the one hand, we have the cultural (here high cultural) argument: genius is noticed, mediocrity is invisible. The "meme" that is a robust VN idea and the "memeplex" that is a VN novel are then replicated (obviously not faithfully!) in our brains as "patterns of neuronal wiring-up" that get passed on via cultural transmission.[5] On the other hand, we have the scientific argument: the information from genetic material travels *only in one direction*, from the DNA-bases (ACGT) and codons that specify a certain amino acid or code for (or against) protein synthesis

frequently in scientific literature to describe how memes "cooperate" with each other (by analogy to genes) in order to construct more elaborate cultural systems which then protect and preserve their legacy in a given cultural environment: "Just as selfish genes group together for mutual protection, so whenever memes can propagate better as part of a group than on their own they form co-adapted meme complexes, or memeplexes. Memeplexes include languages, religions, scientific theories, political ideologies and belief systems such as acupuncture or astrology. Like memes, memeplexes spread as long as there is some reason for them to be copied. Some are true or useful, others are copied despite being false" (Susan Blackmore, "Meme, Myself, and I," *New Scientist* (13 March 1999): 40–44; digital web version: www.susanblackmore.co.uk/journalism/NSmeme%201999.htm). Dawkins rightly sees problems with the concept of "memeplex" and has attempted to address them in his subsequent essays and books: 1) that the fidelity present in the replication of a very complex cultural artifact is understandably rather low (what does it mean when we "replicate" for ourselves and others the units of culture that comprise *The Gift*, for example); 2) that what exactly memes are made of—they can't, for example, be located on double-helix strands of DNA à la the Watson-Crick experiment—is still puzzling and all too vague (although neurobiologist Juan Delius has suggested to Dawkins what a meme might look like in the brain); and 3) the replication that goes in duplicating a tool (an obvious example when discussing, say, how "Mousterian" and "Aurignac" cultures worked for Neanderthals and Cro-Magnons) or learning a religion (why most children share the religious systems of their parents is because that is what they are taught from earliest childhood, before they understand what it is they are learning) is not the same as that involved in understanding, *and using*, a system that seems, in its complexity, to model life itself. Dawkins, "Chinese Junk and Chinese Whispers," 143–46. For more on memes and memetics, see Daniel Dennett, *Consciousness Explained* (Boston: Little Brown, 1991) and *Darwin's Dangerous Idea* (New York: Simon and Schuster, 1995); H. Bloom, *The Lucifer Principle* (Sydney: Allen & Unwin, 1996); R. Brodie, *Virus of the Mind* (Seattle: Integral Press, 1996); A. Lynch, *Thought Contagion: How Belief Spreads Through Society* (New York: Basic Books, 1998); J.M. Balkin, *Cultural Software* (New Haven: Yale UP, 1998); Robert Aunger, *The Electric Meme* (New York: Simon and Schuster, 2002); Kevin Laland and Gillian Brown, *Sense and Nonsense* (Oxford: Oxford UP, 2002); Stephen Shennan, *Genes, Memes, and Human History* (London: Thames and Hudson, 2002).

to individual neural pathways that then help (or don't help) one interact with the environment. Phenotypes cannot speak back to (chemically code in reverse) genotypes.[6]

What if, though, simply for the sake of argument we placed VN and his thinking about the art-science divide back into the evolutionary process, but the evolutionary process writ large. By "writ large" I do not mean sociobiology, which as brilliantly as it is presented by Wilson still has a clear scientific bias and does not — cannot? — do justice to the linguistic complexity of a Nabokov novel or a Mandelstam poem. Rather what I have in mind is attempting to understand terms like "reproductive viability," "survival," and "fitness" both literally and figuratively, in the sort of broad sense that would do justice to the most complexly constructed cultural artifact. It is a truism but one worth repeating: scientific discourse, which is primarily metonymic, and poetic discourse, which is primarily metaphoric, are always already at odds. Their ways of framing the world cancel out each other. If we mix the integrative aspect of poetic language with the classificatory precision of scientific language, as VN does in the famous *Dar* passage, what we get is a new subspecies of discourse, one that may be enchanting, but one which we already know beforehand practicing scientists will not accept as probative. Such language is never proving one thing, unless that one thing is many things, many ways of looking at and experiencing and mentally processing the world, at once. And yet, this may not be an obstacle. It could be an evolutionary stimulus. Here I suspect Dawkins is a more trustworthy guide than Wilson: "We are built as gene machines and cultured as meme machines, but we have the power to turn against our own creators. We, alone on earth, can rebel against the tyranny of the selfish replicators."[7] Is there a way to look at this "rebellion" as itself potentially evolutionary? In this respect, VN's way of thinking may be "memetically wired-up" to survive, and to help us survive, which is presumably the same thing. It is a question that is in the hands, or brains, of the cultural replicators. Culture and biology co-evolve, only cultural evolution takes place much faster and can happen within one generation and in Lamarckian (horizontal) as well as Darwinian (longitudinal) ways. When poets like Mandelstam and Brodsky talk about the warp speed of their metaphorical thinking they are really talking about how cultural evolution is happening inside them — they feel like they are the vessels for their "immortal memes" just as we, à la Dawkins, are the mortal shells for our immortal genes.[8]

I will return to these issues of the meme and memeplex as they relate to creative consciousness in the case of VN at the end of this essay.

[6] As Daniel Dennett cleverly frames it, genetics can, with its error-correcting enzymes, fix its own "typos," but only culture can respond to semantic norms and thereby make right what hackers call "thinkos." Daniel Dennett, "From *Typo* to *Thinko*," in Stephen C. Levinson and Pierre Jaisson, eds., *Evolution and Culture* (Cambridge, MA: MIT Press, 2006), 139.

[7] Dawkins, *The Selfish Gene*, 201.

A Slight Detour into the Intelligent Design Debate

To better get our bearings it may help to make a detour to the scientific end of the spectrum. Scientists regularly use metaphors to explain their theories without necessarily acknowledging that the linguistic transfer at the heart of metaphor (this = that) is *poetic* in provenance. It is a knight's move, as VN might say. When a ID biochemist like Michael Behe argues for the "irreducible complexity" of the flagellum that appears on certain bacteria to propel them around, he claims that the 40-different-proteins-selected-in-the-exact-sequence come together to produce a miniature "outboard motor."[9] His point against hard-core Darwinism is that the flagellum as it exists is a distinct functional advantage and that to miss any part of it or to select that part out of sequence would result in no functional advantage at all — hence how can that flagellum come into existence gradually, through random selection (i.e. the so-called co-option theory, where one organ or body part can take up an alternate function)? This would seem to be the old argument, now writ small, about the human eye, which William Paley famously compared to an intricately designed watch: isn't it simpler, more logical, to see here the handiwork of a higher power than the organ's incremental evolution — what functional advantage is there to possessing part of an eye? — from a light-sensitive freckle?[10] Behe would counter by saying that he has broken the cell down to such a submicroscopic level of irreducible complexity that the only way to understand what is revealed to be inside Darwin's "black box" is through the presence of an external agent (or Agent).

But whether or not classical Darwinism has a response (it does) is again at some level irrelevant, because Behe and his colleagues revert to a *metaphor* (outboard motor), and a mechanical one at that (since what is mechanical always seems less "soft," less "poetic"), to convince the audience that the flagellum must have been intelligently designed. This

---

[8] Mandelstam gives his version of the speed and "launching" quality (its sense of slingshot reversibility) in the following passage from "Conversation about Dante" (notice the flying metaphors that will come up later in our discussion of Nabokov — see below): "Metaphorical thought in Dante, as in all true poetry, is accomplished with the aid of a property of poetic material that I suggest we call reversibility or recurrence. The development of a metaphor can be called development only in a provisional sense. And indeed, imagine an airplane that in full flight designs and launches another airplane (disregarding the technical impossibility of this). In just the same way, this flying machine, though absorbed in its own flight, nonetheless succeeds in assembling and launching a third. To make my comparison even more precise, let me add that the assembly and launching of these technically inconceivable new machines produced during flight is not an ancillary or secondary function of the flying machine, but is a most necessary appurtenance and part of the flight itself, and no less a condition of its possibility than the manipulability of the steering unit or the unimpaired functioning of the motor." Osip Mandel'shtam, "Razgovor o Dante," *Sochineniia v dvukh tomakh*, comps. S. Averintsev and Nerler, vol. 2 (Moscow: Khudozhestvennaia literatura, 1990), 229–30.

[9] For Behe's now well-known and still controversial "irreducible complexity" argument see his *Darwin's Black Box* (New York: Free Press, 1996). The flagellum

incredibly intricate gadget has parts that are called bushings, hooks (universal joints), stators (studs, rings), rods (drive shaft), and so on.[11] Curiously, opponents of ID don't point to the figurative element in Behe's explanation, for apparently calling something that tiny and organic an outboard motor is not a problem for scientific logic. Rather, the crux of the issue always comes down to whether the flagellum is "designed" (i.e. God put it there, which assertion if accepted creates its own real problems in terms of how to discuss these matters in school curricula) or whether it randomly "happened," through vast periods of time we can scarcely wrap our minds around and through countless genetic false starts and "homologous" moves that finally resulted in this tiniest of motors. For the neo-Darwinians the power the ID crowd calls God is a force they see continually making mistakes, some of which become useful in different contexts. Functionally advantageous body parts are not always perfectly ticking watches; they can also be something more ad hoc and tentative, like Stephen J. Gould's panda's thumb — an appendage that works "just well enough" given the circumstances.

This debate gets even more interesting, and for us more relevant, if we proceed deeper into the thickets of the great Darwin-Mendel synthesis of the 1940's. One of the most powerful theories in the history of evolutionary study involves another metaphor, Sewall Wright's notion of "adaptive landscape." Although Wright is usually grouped with famed population geneticists J.B.S. Haldane and Ronald Fisher, his primary area of expertise was physiological genetics. Focusing less on how the selection of beneficial genes increases their frequency among large, genetically varied populations and more on how complex genetic interactions take place within small, genetically restricted populations, Wright arrived at the idea, in a 1932 paper, that an organic population is best conceived as *a landscape* with hills and valleys, the higher points being areas of greater Darwinian fitness and the lower points or valleys being areas of declining fitness. Put simply, Haldane's and Fisher's sophisticated mathematical models plotted the paths toward greater fitness in a dominant population in a given environment. Wright's special insight, on the other hand, addressed what happens when smaller populations located along the downslopes and border areas of fitness "hills" branch out into other groupings and descend into "valleys" of diminishing viability. In Edward Larson's telling,

> Natural selection should drive populations up toward peaks of fitness... but could not fully account for one species

---

argument is found on 69–73. Frank Sherwin, for example, calls the flagellum a "constant-torque, liquid-cooled, proton-motive force-powered rotating motor." See www.icr.org/article/3465/.

10 See Edward J. Larson, *Evolution* (New York: The Modern Library, 2004), 91–92, 207.

11 Behe, *Darwin's Black Box*, 71.

branching into many. Branching would require subpopulations of organisms to travel down from their current peaks of fitness, across valleys of relative unfitness, and back up other peaks of fitness — all through a process of incremental genetic variation... If the subpopulation were small enough and subject to intense inbreeding (which stimulates genetic interactions and brings out recessive traits), then selection might not operate to maximize its adaptive fitness. In his [Wright's] metaphor, the subpopulation would move downhill and begin wandering across the valley. Wright called the phenomenon "genetic drift."[12]

Clearly, Wright is not suggesting that something other than natural selection is drawing these subpopulations into valleys where there is less chance of future group survival. Nor is he implying that increased inbreeding along with the production of more recessive traits is in any way purposeful. Still, what is important here is that it is again a *metaphor* that is used to explain the otherwise unexplainable. Presumably no actual hills and valleys are involved in the selection of genes for greater fitness.

It is factors closer to home, however, that make the metaphorical logic at the center of Wright's theory possibly pertinent for the Nabokov of the 1930's. First, it was the Russian geneticist and evolutionary biologist Theodosius Dobzhansky, who emigrated to America in 1927, that became enamoured by Wright's adaptive-landscape metaphor when hearing him at a genetics congress in 1932 and that, thereafter collaborating with Wright and developing his ideas further, may be a missing Russian link underlying aspects of the scientific thinking in *Dar* and "Father's Butterflies."[13] And second, the notions of an "adaptive landscape" and "genetic drift" sound very reminiscent of, and close in chronological inception to, the "lawless fantasy" advanced by Konstantin Kirillovich in "Father's Butterflies: Second Addendum to *Dar*" (see below). Dobzhansky's first major book, *Genetics and the Origins of Species*, appeared in 1937, as VN was completing *The Gift* but before he wrote "Father's Butterflies." Not only was he one of the major players (the so-called "four horseman") in the evolutionary synthesis of the 1940's, Dobzhansky was a world leader in refining the concept of "species" through greater taxonomic and morphological precision — one of VN's keenest interests once he joined the Museum of Comparative Zoology at Harvard in the 1940's. By the same token, Dobzhansky's signature stance of foregrounding the vast genetic diversity within a given species, so that recessive genes and alleles

12 Larson, *Evolution*, 230.

13 Before emigrating from Russia Dobzhansky was influenced by the great Moscow geneticist Sergei Chetverikov, pioneer of the principle that "recessive mutations create hidden reservoirs of genetic diversity within populations on which selection can act when conditions warrant" (Larson, *Evolution*, 232). These ideas seem also to have played into VN's thinking. See below.

become significant in their own right in explaining aspects of speciation, would surely have appealed to the VN opposed to the domination of the predictably unfit by the predictably fit ("the rough haste of evolution's unskilled forces"). Both deeply believing in a Russian Orthodox Christian worldview and insistent that anti-evolutionary arguments made from a position of Protestant creationism were wholly unscientific, Dobzhansky was the sort brilliant, original, seemingly paradoxicalist yet no-nonsense thinker respected by VN. Indeed, having an intuition that there is a force "on the outside" guiding our moral impulses (cf. the "to whom it may concern" of VN's speculations) yet unwilling to use that intuition to distort the evidence "from the inside," Dobzhansky and VN seem epistemological kindred spirits. That the "other world" worked through the rigorous laws of evolutionary science in ways that could not be fully parsed was not a problem for either of them. VN corresponded with Dobzhansky in 1954 (how much previous to that he knew the celebrated scientist's work we can only speculate).[14] Dobzhansky was nominated for a Nobel Prize in 1975, shortly before his death, but did not receive it.

Creative Thinking in VN's Version of ID

To return now to the citation with which we opened this essay, VN-Fyodor tells us that some butterflies have "voices," which is a more anthropomorphic way of saying that they can communicate by sound. Another butterfly is "cunning." The psychological trait belongs to the insect, and regardless of whether the speaker is being playful or serious or both, it *forces us to think*.[15] Gathering narrative momentum, VN-Fyodor claims that the "mimetic disguise" which is a butterfly's means of protecting itself against predators possesses "incredible wit," another attribute of a sophisticated consciousness. Then he comes to the argument from design, that is, to the point in the telling where the only logical conclusion, if we take into account the value added of the design's potential for conveying information vis-à-vis a predator's possible awareness of the information it needs to capture its prey, is that the scene "seems to have been invented [note the *seems to have been*] by some waggish artist for the intelligent eyes of man." Now, an up-to-date expert on evolutionary theory, say a Stephen J. Gould, would characterize VN's logic here is as "quaint" and

[14] This correspondence is cited in Boyd et al., eds., *Nabokov's Butterflies*, 332. Kurt Johnson and Steve Coates (50) write that Nabokov followed Dobzhansky's work with critical interest.

[15] Dawkins, on the other hand, will provocatively call a gene "selfish," knowing full well that genes have no concept of self. His text, though, while captivatingly written and routinely resorting to metaphor to illustrate things, is not primarily a poetic/artistic text; in this respect, it never tries to say two things at once, as in a pun, where the ambiguity itself can be real and meaningful. See, e.g., Dawkins's elequent call for clarity in in truth-telling

"old-fashioned," inasmuch as, writing in the 1930's, VN did not have the benefit of the Darwin-Mendel synthesis, the Watson-Crick discovery of the structure of the DNA double helix, and of course recent decades' fast-moving developments in the areas of genomics and speciation study. We don't have the necessary fossil evidence, Gould would submit, but if we did, and if we could take into account all the possible mutations over many millions of years, statistically speaking we would have a better chance of coming to the "waggish artist's" version of the butterfly's wing than we would by claiming it is the work of a higher intelligence. Simple systems develop into more complex systems, not the other way around. At the same time, to repeat, an ID creationist like Behe might assert that the design was put there by God (which is indeed one way of reading VN's logic) and that getting to this point, so seemingly pregnant with meaning to our eyes, through a process of random selection is perversely "secular." I suspect something else is going on here that falls between Gould and Behe. The space for creative thinking that VN was carving our for himself over his entire life depended neither on a narrowly Christian God nor on a strictly Darwinian gradualist evolutionary trajectory. The metaphysical speculation in "Father's Butterflies" about "spherical speciation" (Konstantin Godunov-Cherdyntsev's "daring" theory — see below) need not be correct in a probative scientific sense for it to be correct in a creative one. What do I mean here? I do not mean that VN was ever in favor of sloppy thinking. This we know. He famously preferred the bottom-up approach to cognizing when it came to making formulations about what is "real" in reality, as he says in *Strong Opinions*: "As an artist and a scholar I prefer the specific detail to the generalization, images to ideas, obscure facts to clear symbols, and the discovered wild fruit to the synthetic jam."[16] Be that as it may, it does not follow that VN's vaunted ability to observe precisely was itself flawless: witness the cases, reversed by subsequent lepidopterists, where his overly refined categorizing fervor split subspecies of "Blues" into incorrect new species. Brian Boyd, who knows more about how VN thought in time and about time than anyone, writes in his Introduction to *Nabokov's Butterflies* that "It seems likely that, had [Nabokov] begun serious work on mimicry, he would have found sufficient evidence of purely physical explanations to be forced to abandon his dearly held metaphysical speculations."[17] What I believe, however, is that the "purely physical explanations" we have at our disposal now would have caused VN to revise, to think further, but not necesaarily

and writing in "Postmodernism Disrobed," *A Devil's Chaplain*, 55–62.

16 Vladimir Nabokov, *Strong Opinions* (New York: McGraw-Hill, 1973), 7.

17 Brian Boyd, "Nabokov, Literature, Lepidoptera," in *Nabokov's Butterflies*, ed. Brian Boyd and Robert Michael Pyle (Boston: Beacon, 2000), 20.

to "abandon his dearly held metaphysical speculations." At least not completely. Sometimes mistakes can be creative — the happy, chance "mutations" that push cognition further.

On a scientific level, what would a non-gradualist, non-Christian creationist evolutionary development look like? And second, what relationship would this sort of development have to the artistic structure (the "memeplex") of a work like *The Gift*? As Victoria Alexander has recently argued, VN's core interest as a scientist was more in the laws of biological form that explain a species' drive for symmetry than in naming the "intelligence" (or random lack thereof) that put that drive there in the first place. (In general, if it could be put this way, VN was more concerned in seeing the "form" of life through its "content" rather than the other way around.) As an aside, today's scientists can identify the chemical make-up of the genes (the serotonin transporter [*SLC6A4*] and the arginine vasopressin receptor 1a [*AVPR1a*]) that appear more often among dancers, and we know in the distant past dance was one of the first forms of "culture" and that, through analogy with the animal world this activity was linked to mating ritual.[18] However, to say that today's "memetic" transmission of dance somehow plays a signficant role in reproductive viability is a long stretch indeed, just as linking any truly sophisticated cultural production, in a classic Freudian manner, primarily with an individual's childhood traumas involving biological parents, is cripplingly reductionist. Among the forms that most intrigued VN were the ones he called "non-utilitarian" — again, think of the dewdrop marking on the Blue's wing — which as we know is another way of saying "artistic," or, in terms of *The Gift*, "non-Chernyshevskian." Furthermore, it was the "reverse cause" situations, where the function of something is understood after the fact of its appearance, and where that appearance could not be predicted beforehand, that most fired his imagination. Thinking about "purpose" from all sides even if there is no purpose is a mind-expanding exercise. (This, as I will explain, also had important ramifications for VN's work as a creative writer.) Thus, according to Alexander, VN was in the "phylogenetic" company of nineteenth-century Kantian teleomechanists (those studying how parts shaped wholes) that then morphed into twentieth-century scientists, among them D'Arcy Wentworth Thompson, Alan Turing, Brian Goodwin and lepidopterist Frederik Nijhout, who investigated "the laws of biological form and pattern formation" and who "offered alternatives to an exclusively adaptationist evolutionary program."[19] For our purposes,

[18] See www.plosgenetics.org/article/info%3A:doi%2F10.1371%2Fjournal.pgen.0010042. *Mimicry*, Sante Fe Institute Working Papers, no. 01—10 —57 (Sante Fe, 2001), 8.

[19] Victoria Alexander, *Neutral Evolution and Aesthetics: Vladimir Nabokov and Insect*

it is Nijhout who (along with the aforementioned Dobzhansky) most complements VN's scientific thinking, since he has "examined butterfly wing patterns using nonlinear dynamics and theories of spontaneous formation."[20]

According to this line of thought, there are phenomena of resemblance in nature that are not explainable strictly in terms of adaptation and directionality. These are those knight moves ("nature's rhymes") that so appealed to Nabokov the artist. Among them we might find the following: 1) changes that are nonutilitarian *within a genus* (i.e. viceroys and monarchs that have come to share formal characteristics supposedly through a "convergence" — so-called Batesian mimicry — that confers adaptive advantage to the copying viceroy because it looks like the bitter-tasting monarch, except in this instance both the monarch *and* the viceroy are unpalatable to predators); 2) changes in gene sequences that could have arisen suddenly, through environmental factors such as heat shock (i.e. the similarity between a dead-leaf and a certain butterfly "phenocopy," where the lookalike remains a member of its original species and carries the genotype of its parents); and 3) changes that possess a resemblance across phyla but also serve no apparent purpose (i.e. the hummingbird and the hummingbird moth do not need, in a Darwinian sense, to look alike to promote reproductive viability or to avoid predators).[21] VN's best example of a Darwinian natural selection process that does not take place when we expect it to and that eventuates still in survival is the caterpillar of the Siberian Owlet moth that is found on the chumara plant, only the coloring of the insect's fetlocks and dorsal shape appears at the end of summer while the shrub blooms in May. Following the logic of adaptation, "nature [has] defraud[ed] one of the parties."[22] Thus, "natural selection alone could not," summarizes Alexander, "*create* a mimetic form by gradual fine-tuning. The form would have to appear suddenly as a definite resemblance since a non-resemblance that was an earlier stage for the resemblance would not be selected because of what it would eventually resemble."[23] Whether demonstrating how heat shock can affect genetic selection and hence pattern design even within one generation, or establishing a nymphalid "ground plan" that operates as a kind of Platonic starting point for controlling the stochastic process of pigment diffusion across a wing surface,[24] it seems there is sufficient scientific evidence to suggest that the nature/nurture, "blind watchmaker"/"waggish artist" debate is not yet dead. That evolution can be neutral and recessive genes

20 Ibid.

21 These examples in support of Kimura's theory of neutral evolution are provided by Alexander. See excellent discussion in Alexander, *Neutral Evolution and Aesthetics*, 10–11, 16–17, 18–23.

22 Boyd et al., eds., *Nabokov's Butterflies*, 222.

23 Alexander, *Neutral Evolution*, 10–11.

24 Ibid., 12.

can come into play in manners that challenge our thinking in no way proves that such developments are purposeful. It simply means that for some a purposefulness cannot be fully ruled out.

In the second half of this essay I would like to speculate on some of the ways VN's artistic strategies in *The Gift* might mimic his scientific writing and stimulate creative cognition. First, there is Fyodor's connection to Pushkin through his father and through his own study and contemplation of the poet.[25] "Pushkin entered his blood. With Pushkin's voice merged the voice of his father."[26] All three examples of unique individual are aligned through the notions of poetry, love, mortality, and *chance*. These three figures are linked through different "bloodlines"—one hereditary (genetic), the other cultural (memetic)—but Fyodor is the living example—the phenotype as it were—attesting to each bloodline's reality. The "Godunov" in the double surname could be attributed to the family's place in Russian history, but it could also hark back to Pushkin's play about dynastic succession and impostorship — a more likely scenario given the context. (Indeed, by analogy to earlier aristocratic families, like the Musin-Pushkins, VN has placed his hero in a genealogical force field between Pushkin on the one hand [Godunov], and the non-poetic Chernyshevsky [Cherdyntsev], on the other.) What Fyodor's father calls "nature's rhymes" and what Fyodor himself is searching for when he comes down with rhyming fever early in the book belong to a common weave.

Let me stop here for a moment to insert Dawkins's central metaphor for how one's genes together with one's responses to environmental pressures work together to create meaning, or at least the next move in a life one is trying to make meaningful:

> Think of the body as a blanket, suspended from the ceiling by 100,000 rubber bands, all tangled and twisted around one another. The shape of the blanket—the body—is determined by the tensions of all these rubber bands taken together. Some of the rubber bands represent genes, others environmental factors. A change in a particular gene corresponds to a lengthening or shortening of one particular rubber band. But any one rubber band is linked to the blanket only indirectly via countless connections amid a welter of other rubber bands. If you cut one rubber band, or tighten it, there will be a distributed shift in tensions, and the effect on the shape of the blanket will be complex and hard to predict.[27]

[25] On the Pushkin-V.D. Nabokov-K.K Godunov-Cherdyntsev father/son nexus in *The Gift* see Monika Greenleaf, "Fathers, Sons and Impostors: Pushkin's Trace in *The Gift*," *Slavic Review* 53.1 (Spring 1994): 140–58, and Maria Malikova, "V.V. Nabokov and V.D. Nabokov: His Father's Voice," in *Nabokov's World II: Reading Nabokov*, ed. by J. Grayson, A. McMillin, and P. Meyer (Basingstoke: Palgrave, 2002),15–26.

[26] Nabokov, *The Gift*, 4.
[27] Dawkins, "Genes Aren't Us," *A Devil's Chaplain*, 125.
[28] Dawkins, "Viruses of the Mind," *A Devil's Chaplain*, 151–72.

This is a wonderfully heuristic example of how a metaphor is used by a scientist to explain with simple logic something very complex. But what is missing are precisely the "memes." One's responses to environmental factors are, the more our species develops cognitively and linguistically, bound to translate into memes, those replicatable cultural patterns that we use to push farther and farther out not only into the space of the outer world but into, *whether it is "virtual" or not*, the inner space of the mind. Note that Dawkins stays on this side of the scientific divide by leaving the organization of environmental factors as something given, not developed further in his metaphorical logic. VN, and other "poets" and poetic thinkers, would take the metaphorical logic further. For VN, the blanket hanging from the 100,000 genetic and environmental rubber bands becomes a *magic carpet* that he propels backwards (memory) and forwards (imagination) to time- and space-travel in his "more real" virtual world. What facilitates (causes?) this sensation of being in many places and times at once is the metaphorical fabric of the language. Dawkins's metaphor must go only in one direction — it needs to preserve the semblance of Popperian falsifiability; VN's metaphor goes in multiple directions simultaneously — it only has to prove itself to itself. And if it proves itself to itself with sufficient success there is a good chance it will find itself in someone else's brain, via memetic "virus."[28]

To return to VN's text, the very structure of *The Gift*, with its blurring in and out of the "I" and "he" narrators and its tying-up of the plot by an Onegin stanza, itself a pseudo-genetic map for creating infinite meanings out of a single string (rhyme scheme), challenges us to understand it as "open" or "closed." Is this structure an optical illusion à la Escher, a Moebius strip modeling space as "outside" and "inside" at the same time (memetics)?[29] Or is it, through some ancient deep-seated psychic trace, the visual reproduction of that double helix of chemically paired on-off switches whose codes and mappings cannot transcend themselves (genetics)? Or is it some time-in-a-bottle encapsulation of the two? Do the spirals and spheres that imbed themselves in VN's speculations about sudden bursts of creativity trace back to Bely and the Symbolists' notions of revolutionary time, to Bergson's cloud of "creative evolution," or are these natural archetypes whose function in thought is akin to the "nymphalid ground plan" as starting point in wing design?[30] Pushing the analogy further, are rhyme words the memetic equivalent of genes, are their endings, which may not be meaningful in their own right, but which

29 The Moebius strip metaphor was coined by Omri Ronen. See Irena and Omri Ronen, "'Diabolically evocative': An Inquiry into the Meaning of a Metaphor," in *Slavica Hierosolymitana: Slavic Studies of the Hebrew Universi*-*ty* 6–7 (1981): 378. See also Sergej Davydov, *"Teksty-Matreški" Vladimira Nabokova* (Munich: O. Sagner, 1982), passim.

30 Another more recent example would be Lotman's concept of "explosion" [*vzryv*] in cultural evolution (Iurii Lotman, *Kul'tura i vzryv* [Moscow: Gnozis, 1992]). Cognitive scientists would probably call such natural archetypes "image schemas."

acquire meaning in combination with additional morphemic appendages, the memetic equivalent of alleles? This is where Dawkins, Dennett, Blackmore et al., despite the great attraction of memetics, cannot do justice to a complex cultural artifact as the latter is presently undertood in the scientific literature. A religion or a political ideology, with their various ideas, rituals, and cultural inculcation processes, create memes and memeplexes that as a rule *do not generate* new information, do *not spur* cognitive discovery. They are learned, repeated, personalized. What they do is compactly replicate tradition as something closed and provide strategies (coping mechanisms) for surviving in a given environment. VN's kind of writing (which is actually inaccurate to call it a "kind" because it is a class unto itself) provides coping mechanisms (although "coping" is a timid word for what it engenders) for surviving on the planet in general, if not beyond. Fyodor says of his father's prose, which he gets closer to by reading Pushkin, "the very body, flow, and structure of the whole work [i.e. *Butterflies and Moths of the Russian Empire*] touches me in the professional sense of a craft handed down. I suddenly recognize in my father's words the wellsprings of my own prose: squeamishness toward fudging and smudging [note Jakobson's poetic function], the reciprocal dovetailing of word and thought... and I doubt that the development of these traits under my frequently willful pen was a conscious act."[31] The process is presented as virtually physiological. Indeed, it may turn out some day in the not too distant future that the "body, flow, and structure" of a cultural construct are not simply figures of speech. As animal behaviorist N.K. Humphrey puts it,

> Memes should be regarded as living structures, not just metaphorically but technically. When you plant a fertile meme in my mind you literally parasitize my brain, turning it into a vehicle for the meme's propagation in just the way a virus may parasitize the genetic mechanism of a host cell. And this isn't just a way of talking — the meme, say, for "belief in life after death" is actually realized physically, millions of times over, as a structure in the nervous systems of individual men the world over.[32]

In "Father's Butterflies" we learn that Fyodor is fascinated by the exceptional flora and fauna of Russia that gets left out of popular German editions of butterfly atlases. The fact that Konstantin Kirillovich fills this lacuna with *The Butterflies and Moths of the Russian Empire*, itself a fiction, is VN's

---

[31] Boyd et al., eds., *Nabokov's Butterflies*, 210.
[32] Cited in Dawkins, *The Selfish Gene*, 192.

way of saying that the dumbing-down of history that was the Soviet regime and the tragedy that was the death of Fyodor's father (and VN's father) is undone by the life's work that lives on. "The bitterness of interrupted life is nothing compared to the bitterness of interrupted work: the probability that the former may continue beyond the grave seems infinite when compared to the inexorable incompletion of the latter."[33] The future is secretly embedded in one's work: that is why the latter is so crucial and that is what memetic time-travel in its most developed forms can feel like. There is, Sukhoshchokov tells us, "something seductive" in Pushkin's "fatal destiny"; he has a "special reckoning with fate"; his poetry is born out of his "tragic thought about the future"; "the triple formula of human existence — irrevocability, unrealizability, inevitability [again, the *poetic function*] — was well known to him"; "one could not find any other poet who peered so often — now in jest, now superstitiously, or with inspired seriousness — into the future."[34] VN is implying here, in a medium (novelistic prose) that permits it, that Pushkin's art is not only about how consciousness imagines the future, but how such a consciousness also is the future, and that this special knowledge comes from the fact that the poet's life is always already fatally marked. The death sentence (think of Pushkin's fears about marriage, his earlier challenges to cuckolded husbands in *The Gabrieliade* [*Gavriiliada*], etc.) unleashes poetic thinking — the most obvious example of this being the condemned André Chénier who calls forth both Pushkin in his great poem but also Cincinnatus in VN's novel.[35] Similarly, Konstantin Kirillovich, presumably sensing that he is marked in a way that his hero is, has a "secret" and a special "solitude"; he "go[es] off on his journeys not so much to seek something as to flee something, and... on returning, he realiz[es] that it [is] still with him, inside him, unriddable, inexhaustible."[36] Fyodor's father senses powerfully he is going to die prematurely, and the seemingly foreordained ways his life intersects his work and his work his life seems to prove this. Not for nothing does Fyodor imagine his father walking in and out of a rainbow and Pushkin seeing *Othello* (his signature Shakespeare play) at sixty; only art could create these other lives, with alternative futures, since life in history too often rules otherwise.

So much of what we have been discussing thus far relates to the idea of randomness, happenstance, and how one interprets the latter. In Russian, *sluchai* (chance, accident) and *sluchainost'* (randomness) can replicate themselves as coincidence or providential design through memetic, if not genetic, patterning. Here too Nabokov took his cue from Pushkin, who

33 Ibid., 234.
34 Nabokov, *The Gift*, 95.
35 See Sergej Davydov, "Nabokov and Pushkin" in Vladimir Alexanrov, ed., *The Garland Companion to Vladimir Nabokov* (New York: Garland, 1995), 488; and A. Dolinin, "Pushkinskie podteksty v romane 'Priglashenie na kazn'," *Instinnaia zhizn' pisatelia Nabokova* (St. Petersburg: Akademicheskii proekt, 2004), 214–30.

36 Nabokov, *The Gift*, 109.

was obsessed with the relationship between fate and chance in the last decade of his life. The hareskin coat that sets a "miraculous" sequence of events in motion in Pushkin's *novel* (and that Fyodor's mother wears as she goes to look for her husband on one of his expeditions[37]) can just as easily be a negative, fatal coincidence in Pushkin's history (*History of Pugachev*): for example, the cannon that Major Kharlov fires to raise the morale of his troops at Nizhne-Ozernaia Fortress scares off the allied troops coming to the rescue and allows Pugachev and his band to take the fort easily and continue to spread death and mayhem.[38] Pushkin sees *sluchai* as the single most defining trait of a Russian history which is otherwise misunderstood or ignored (much like the flora and fauna of the Russian Empire that Konstantin Kirillovich undertook to rescue in his lepidopterological studies). As Pushkin writes in his second review of Polevoy's *History of the Russian People* (*Istoriia russkogo naroda*) in one of those prose passages Fyodor's tuning fork (*kamerton*) responds to in order to capture perfect pitch:

> Guizot has explained one of the events of Christian history: *the European Enlightenment*. He discovers its embryo, describes its gradual development and, removing all that is separate, all that is extraneous, *random*, he delivers it to us through the dark, bloody, rebellious, and, finally, enlightening centuries. You [Polevoy] have understood the great merit of the French historian. But remember this as well: Russia has never had anything in common with the rest of Europe; her history requires a different [type of] thought, a different formula from those drawn out by Guizot from the history of the Christian West. Don't say "*It could not be otherwise.*" If that were so, then an historian would be an astronomer and the events in the life of humankind would be predicted in calendars, like solar eclipses. But providence is not algebra. The human mind, according to popular expression, is not a prophet, but a guesser; it sees the

---

[37] Nabokov, *The Gift*, 100. See Alexander Dolinin's commentary to 288 in *Dar* (668): «... заячий тулупчик из „Капитанской Дочки"...—то есть подобный тому заячьему тулупу, который Гринев в „Капитанской дочке" дарит Пугачеву (гл. 2). Этот начальный дар приводит в действие весь сюжетный механизм пушкинского романа, строящийся на ситуациях взаимного обмена дарами и расплаты, и в конечном счете вознаграждается судьбой. В главной теме „Дара" видны явственные параллели к теме судьбоносного дарения в „Капитанской дочке", чем, очевидно, и мотивируются многочисленные аллюзии на нее в тексте». See also Dolinin's notes to 191 and 280 (639, 663—65).

[38] A.S. Pushkin, *Istoriia Pugacheva, Polnoe sobranie sochinenii v desiati tomakh*, vol. VIII, *Avtobiograficheskaia i istoricheskaia proza* (Moscow: Akademiia nauk SSSR, 1958), 171.

general course of things and can draw out from that profound suppositions, often confirmed in time, but it cannot foresee chance — the powerful, momentary instrument of providence. One of the shrewdest men of the eighteenth century predicted the Chamber of French De puties and the potent rise of Russia, but no one predicted Napoleon or Polignac.[39]

VN plays constantly with the interweaving notions of chance, coincidence, and providence in *The Gift*. Konstantin Kirillovich's favorite line from Pushkin is "Tut Apollon ideal, tam Neobeia — pechal" (Here is Apollo — ideal, there is Niobe — sadness)," which comes from one of the poems ("To the Artist" ["K hudozhniku"]) Pushkin wrote during the last year of his life, when he sensed more than ever that his fate was now upon him, and which is filled with a mood of "happy sadness" and "sad happiness": "Grusten i vesel vkhozhu" (Melancholy and merry I enter) and "Veselo mne... Grusten guliaiu" (I feel jaunty... Sad I stroll).[40] The poet is pleased to walk among the sculptor B.I. Orlovsky's beautiful statues but he misses his friend Del'vig, who helped him get started on his life-long quest to, à la Pygmalion, bring verbal statues to life. Now, in Konstantin Kirillovich's mind, and in Fyodor's experience of the butterfly hunt, the cultural nexus of Pushkin's original words (statues, Greek myths) morphs into the naturalist nexus of the precisely observed "russet wing and mother-of-pearl of a Niobe fritillary" and "the small black Apollo."[41] Art and science come alive as cognitive extensions of each other.

Quoting Pushkin, but also rephrasing him, prodding his words onto another level of awareness, Konstantin Kirillovich says to an unidentified interlocutor in the closing lines of "Father's Butterflies," "Yes, of course it was in vain that he [Pushkin] said 'by chance' [*sluchainyi*], and by chance that he said 'in vain' [*naprasnyi*]."[42] The poem alluded to here (Gift futile, gift random [Dar naprasnyi, dar sluchainyi]), composed on the poet's birthday (May 26, 1828), was one of the saddest, most self-lacerating confessions in Pushkin's fully and fiercely lived creative life.

---

39 A.S. Pushkin, "Vtoroi tom 'Istorii russkogo naroda' Polevogo," *Polnoe sobranie sochinenii v desiati tomakh*, vol. VII, Kritika i publitsistika (Moscow: Akademiia nauk SSSR, 1958), 143–44.

40 A.S. Pushkin, "Khudozhniku," *Polnoe sobranie sochinenii v desiati tomakh*, vol. III, Stikhotvorenia 1827–36 (Moscow: Akademiia nauk SSSR, 1957), 365.

41 Nabokov, *The Gift*, 94.

42 Boyd et al., eds., *Nabokov's Butterflies*, 234. See also Brian Boyd, "'The Expected Stress Did Not Come': A Note on 'Father's Butterflies'," *The Nabokovian* 45 (Fall 2000): 23. I have corrected the translation made by Boyd and Dmitri Nabokov to show that the Russian here refers to "he" (Pushkin) rather than "I" (Fyodor's father). In Russian the omission of a personal pronoun can take place in a third person form of the verb (*skazal*), but the first person pronoun cannot be left out in the same situation. My thanks to Alexander Dolinin for pointing this out to me. See also discussion in Boyd, "Expected Stress," 26–28; Gennady Barabtarlo, "He Said—I Said: An Afternote," *The Nabokovian* 45 (Fall 2000): 29–30; and Dolinin, http://etc.dal.ca/noj/volume1/articles/DOLININ.pdf (11–12).

But the words here intimate, turning the original sequence of thought inside out as Fyodor, through his father, flies forward on his Moebius strip-cum-magic carpet, that the poet's gift is neither random nor futile — that is, despite the tragedy (for Pushkin, for Konstantin Kirillovich) it, the *dar*, is pulling him and his readers somewhere into the future. Konstantin Kirillovich's words trail off right at the moment when he is about to tell the interlocutor how his unparalleled knowledge of the plant and animal world dovetails with the "clergy's" (Metropolitan Filaret's) response to the poet's *cri de coeur*, this also a poem, but now in the form of an affirmation of the gift, when "Gift futile, gift random" first appeared in print in 1830. "The awaited final stress [u*dar*éniia] did not come," the son says of the father's utterance. This beat is the second element in the rhyme pair for which we are always searching. Indeed, as Alexander Dolinin has pointed out, the *dar* in the Russian word for "stress" is precisely where the beat does *not* fall.[43] And yet the second shoe does drop for VN, as it had for his precursors, in the last words of "Father's Butterflies": "and now I have suddenly remembered the title of the book."[44] The title of the book remains nameless, for it is Fyodor's (or rather VN's) business. This book, which is "difficult and strange" and whose "pages [seem] out of order," is Fyodor's companion as he thinks back to a world where his mother and father are still in the picture and he is growing as a conscious entity. My guess is this tome, the rhyme partner for which Fyodor has always and will always be waiting, is the book of life:[45]

How is it conceivable, in fact, that amid the huge jumble containing the embryos of countless organs (of which up to forty-three are currently represented), the magnificent chaos of nature never included *thought*? One can doubt the ability of a genius to animate marble, but one cannot doubt that one afflicted by idiocy will never create a Galatea [NB. the Pygmalion theme]. Human intelligence, with all its limitations and rights, inasmuch as it is a gift of nature, and a perpetually repeated

---

[43] A. Dolinin, "Tri zametki o romane Vladimira Nabokova Dar," in B. Averin et al., eds., V.V. Nabokov: Pro et Contra (St. Petersburg: Russkii Gumanitarnyi Institut, 1997), 598–99n.

[44] Boyd et al., eds. Nabokov's Butterflies, 234.

[45] Cf. the ending of the Chernyshevsky chapter in which his last words are quoted: "A strange business: in this book there is not a single mention of God." The narrator wryly then comments: "It is a pity that we do not know precisely *which* book he was reading to himself" (Nabokov, *The Gift*, 273; *Dar*, 475). Another possible subtext, suggested to me by my colleague Alexander Dolinin, is Shakespearean: "O God! that one might read the book of fate!" (II Henry IV, iii, 1, 45).

one, cannot fail to exist in the warehouse of the bestower. It may, in that dark storehouse, differ from the species in sunlight as a marble god is distinct from the convolutions of the sculptor's brain — but still it *exists*.[46]

Final Thoughts

Biological evolution works by trial and error. Cultural evolution seems to as well. The difference is that there is a feedback system in cultural evolution, and what we may call a "memotype," which by analogy to the phenotype is all the cultural patterns and meaning-generating structures collected in an individual at a given moment, can do a lot of "evolving" even in one lifetime. We are the mortal carriers of potentially immortal memes and memeplexes, but it is by no means simple replication that we do when we try to combine rigorous scientific logic (and evidence) with a linguistically sensitive, "poetic" logic that sees and experiences various levels of cognition simultaneously, all the while remaining open, rather than closed, to the lure of new information. Let us close this discussion with some final speculation about where VN was going with "Father's Butterflies" and how the "mistakes" he made in his thinking there turn out to be "true" in a way that is, memetically speaking, useful for our survival, broadly defined. The issue comes down to the strikingly close *metaphorical* parallels between the Wright-Dobzhansky concepts of "adaptive landscape" and "genetic drift" and Godunov-Cherdyntsev *père*'s theory of speciation (what biologists now refer to as "species concept"). First VN's text, which I have to quote at length because its "weave" is too dense to disentangle otherwise:

> By "species" he [Konstantin Kirillovich Godunov-Cherdyntsev] intends the original of a being, nonexistent in our reality but unique and definite in concept, that recurs ad infinitum in the mirror of nature, creating countless reflections; each one of them perceived by our intelligence, reflected in the selfsame glass and acquiring its reality solely within it, as a living individual of the given species. An aberration, or chance deviations are but the consequence of less "faithful" areas of the mirror, while the recurrent falling of a reflection on one and the same flaw may yield a stable local race, the idea of

[46] Boyd et al., eds. *Nabokov's Butteflies*, 219.

which tends toward the periphery of the circle, the center of which, in turn, is the idea of species. These races remain on the circumference of the species insofar as the spatial link (i.e., one with a locus on earth at a given point in time) between the type (i.e., the most precise sample at a given moment) and a local variant is supported by intermediate variations (that can manifest themselves as local races or chance deviations), in other words, so far as the species circle remains unbroken.[47]

What is fascinating about this passage (and those immediately following for several pages) is that we are witnessing the mind of genius who is trying to get to the future via metaphor but does not yet have the scientific knowledge and terminology to put that future into words. He is feeling his way toward the "hills" of fitness and the "valleys" of unfitness that Wright first brought to the world's attention as genetic landscape. Obviously his initial stab at defining species has problems, as the "original of a being, nonexistent in reality" sounds too much like a Platonic idea. But what he is trying to express, presumably, is something like the nymphalid "ground plan" cited earlier. On the other hand, he seems to get some important things right: those individuals with traits that mutated ("chance deviations") tend to migrate to the periphery of the circle (Wright would say they "drift" into "valleys"). And the "spatial link" joining peripheral members to the "original" in the center (i.e. the members closest to the ideal for VN, but simply more "fit" for Wright) through "intermediate variations" is also not that far off. The "mirror of nature" with its "countless reflections" sounds like some *Naturphilosophie* hocus-pocus, but here too we can give the author a partial passing grade because he is trying to come up with a more vivid, less pedestrian sounding version of "replicate." The main impasse arises, however, from the very meaning of species. Species can be defined typologically (taxonomically) and biologically, but trying to define the term by using both methods at once is verbally impossible, something like trying to write at the speed of light, or seeing waves and particles at the same time. Evolutionary biologists have split many hairs trying to ascertain precisely, in terms of an individual's phenotypic traits, where one species crosses the line into another. But if they forget the naming and focus on which groups can interbreed with one another they have a good pragmatic way to move forward. In the above passage VN, then, is attempting to use what he knows, his own temporally and spatially confined "memotype," to come up with something similar to

---

47 Boyd et al., eds., *Nabokov's Butterflies*, 216.

"adaptive landscape" and "genetic drift." Whether he knew Wright's and Dobzhansky's work is a tantalizing fact for us scholars, yet ultimately it is beside the point. The main message of the passage, its "meta-memetic" gist if you will, is that VN's metaphors, at this point in spring 1939, are too precious, too skeletal, to get as close as he needs to sense that some new rung in the (genetic-memetic) evolutionary ladder has slipped in place and he is ready to climb further. Here we might say that metaphorical thinking, if it tries to leap forward without sufficient experiential and probative ballast, ends up being ambiguous without being necessarily meaningful.

> In exactly the same way, the repetition of individual reflections in time (limited by the span during which a given species conserves its basic identity) may, if the process lasts long enough, generate certain modifications that, however, are just unanchored spatial variations, with which they may even coincide if we have come upon the species in its ideal period, i.e., at the moment of full harmony among its radial components.[48]

This is not the VN we know and love. Abstract, clanky and sprawling, these words as memetic replicators come painfully close to the postmodernist mumbo-jumbo scientists like Dawkins and Alan Sokal make fun of. Cultural evolution also works by trial and error.

The final point is: to what extent are we programmed by our memes the way we are programmed by our genes? What does Dawkins's provocative sentence "We, alone on earth, can rebel against the tyranny of selfish replicators" *mean*? It really means what it always has: genetics determines chemically aspects of our makeup, but those 100,000 rubber bands holding up the blanket that is "me" and twisted around each other in myriad ways are made not only of genetic material and "environmental factors."[49] Those environmental factors contain our acquired learning, which itself contains the "neuronal wiring up" of our memes and memeplexes. Those memes can act on us and through us when we reflexively buy what others have (simple replication), or watch a repeat on tv rather than read a new book (also simple replication), or use religious or political ideology to advance our version of reality, usually at the expense, sometimes lethal expense, of rival populations (simple replication yet again). Looked at this way, memetic replication could easily eventuate in the extinction of *Homo sapiens*, only in this instance we, and not a natural catastrophe, will have made ourselves dinosaurs. But what the best of VN's thinking in something like *The Gift* encourages us to do is *add productive* (literally

---

48 Ibid., 216–17.
49 Dawkins, *The Selfish Gene*, 125.

mind-expanding) change to replication, to try to see as much of the world as we can in all its vertical and horizontal, scientific and poetic, dimensions. Statues are butterflies, poets are lepidopterists.

Brilliant evolutionary biologists like Gould tell us that evolution is horizontal not vertical: humans are not "at the top" of the evolutionary ladder, but merely one species on one of the branches of the Darwinian tree that grows sideways. Likewise, some species can evolve into simpler, not more complex, forms (parasites). We may have superior symbolizing power (and larger brains) than the apes, but we do not exist separate from them in an evolutionary sense; we sit on contiguous branches — we ourselves are just another version of ape. This is not reason to despair, however. Quite the opposite in fact. In the nineteenth century philosophers of a certain type (Vladimir Solovyov is the most vivid example) tried to imagine what love, and more broadly, creative behavior, would be like without biology, without procreation. Obviously there is a quixotic element to such thinking that would elicit nothing but laughs from a sceptical, empirically driven, western educated twenty-first century audience. Yet perhaps what Solovyov was about was hurrying on cultural evolution (he of course wouldn't call it that), trying to see if the energy that goes into biological mating and the preservation of kith and kin could be somehow channeled into an expansion of mind and spirit. Most people today don't care to imagine how to live without biology. But is there a higher form of (pro)creation, and if there is what would it look like scientifically? Just as important, would it help our species to think there is, or think there could be? Is evolution truly the tyranny of the selfish replicator, genetic and memetic, or could it be a continual remaking and retesting of the rubber bands (again, *replication plus change, i.e. one's own memotypical input*): not that from which we only hang, as blankets, but that *with the help of which* we fly, metaphorically speaking, through time and space, through biology and culture, on a magic carpet of words, mind, and desire?

Chapter 5   Relativity and Reality: Dante, Florensky, Lotman, and Metaphorical Time-Travel[1]

Given his interest in complex semiotic structures and in a "semiosphere" whose ever ramifying interactions model the vast physical cosmos, it is not surprising that Yury Lotman paused in his writings to discuss the most elaborate of all texts, the worlds within worlds of Dante's *La Divina Commedia*. Indeed, these two authors seem almost made for each other, for their passion for meaning (and meaning making) against a moving backdrop of epistemology and geo- and astrophysics are uncannily similar. In *Universe of the Mind* Lotman juxtaposes the vertical journey of Dante the pilgrim and the horizontal journey of the curious, courageous, yet "morally indifferent" Ulysses as symbolic of the seam separating the medieval and the Renaissance worldview. Homer's "wily king of Ithaca," argues Lotman, "becomes in Dante the man of the Renaissance, the first discoverer and the traveller. This image appeals to Dante by its integrity and its strength, but repels him by its moral indifference. But in this image of the heroic adventurer of his time... Dante discerned something else, not just the features of the immediate future, the scientific mind and cultural attitudes of the modern age; he saw the coming separation of knowledge from morality, of discovery from its results, of science from

---

[1] This essay has been adapted from earlier versions: "Florensky and Dante: Revelation, Orthodoxy, and Non-Euclidean Space," in *Russian Religious Thought*, ed. Judith Deutsch Kornblatt and Richard F. Gustafson (Madison: University of Wisconsin Press, 1996), 112–31; and "Dante, Florenskii, Lotman: Journeying Then and Now Through Medieval Space," in *Lotman and Cultural Studies: Encounters and Extensions*, ed. Andreas Schonle (Madison: University of Wisconsin Press, 2006), 41–58.

the human personality."² Lotman's key point is that Ulysses' journey in Dante, if not in Homer, is only over *space* per se (however new and mysterious), that is, it embraces the notion of pure contiguity, whereas Dante the pilgrim's journey is down and up *symbolic space*, which is to say, space that is perceived as attached to meaning every step of the way and that is embodied textually through the logic of metaphor and transference. Thus Ulysses and his crew can see what eventually becomes Mount Purgatory before their shipwreck in the Southern Hemisphere but have no idea what it is (what it *means* — i.e., this place where there is supposedly no landfall) and will be unable to make their way to it. Hence, Dante the pilgrim and Ulysses the pagan traveler are "doubles" and "antipodes," just as their respective journeys are, in Lotman's reading, symmetrical yet antithetical.³

Curiously, however, Lotman does not come alone to his analysis of these two quintessential journeys in the *Commedia*. He too has a double and an antipode, as it were: the priest, philosopher, and mathematician Pavel Florensky, whose remarks in *Imaginary Spaces in Geometry* Lotman takes as his point of departure.⁴ Of all the possible commentators on Dante's work, Lotman singles out Florensky and his unique way of incorporating issues of faith and spatial poetics in a post-Einsteinian world as his initial and, as it turns out, only interlocutor in this section of *Universe of the Mind*.⁵ After citing at length a crucial passage from *Imaginary Spaces* in which Dante and Virgil are described as experiencing something like the "bending" of space as they climb the bulge of Lucifer's haunch in the *Inferno*, Lotman concludes that "Florensky in his eagerness to show how much closer to the twentieth century is the medieval mind than the mechanistic ideology of the Renaissance gets somewhat carried away (for instance the return of Dante to earth [*Paradiso*, I, 5–6] is only hinted at and there are no grounds for assuming that he travelled in a straight line); but the problem of the contradiction in the *Commedia* between real-everyday space and cosmic-transcendental space, which he highlights, is a crucial one, although the solution to this contradiction has to be sought in another direction."⁶ In other words, Florensky appears to have the correct conceptual instincts but has lost his bearings, so to speak, with the result that the "solution...has to be sought in another direction." We might say then, if we agree with Lotman, that the philosopher-priest is, despite his piety and heroic life, a kind of Ulysses (but ironically, *a faith-based, Christian* one) of

2 Iurii Lotman, *Universe of the Mind: A Semiotic Theory of Culture*, trans. Ann Shukman (Bloomington: Indiana University Press, 1990), 184.

3 Ibid., 183–85.

4 *Mnimosti v geometrii*, literally "Imaginaries in geometry." See discussion later in the essay.

5 Lotman, *Universe of the Mind*, 177–85.

6 Ibid., 179.

Dante studies — a bold but misguided traveler.[7] In this essay I expand on this dialogue between Lotman and Florensky about the meaning of spatial poetics in the *Commedia* and try to ascertain how Lotman's and Florensky's different readings of the Dantesque *viaggio* provide insights into their respective views of Russian culture. I will suggest that Lotman, with his Enlightenment orientation, saw himself commenting on Florensky (i.e., on Florensky reading Dante) in a manner analogous (but in a *reversely* symmetrical way) to Dante's own "correcting" of Ulysses' "amoral" navigation of pre-Christian space-time. Put simply, Dante the pilgrim is to the ultimately shipwrecked Ulysses of the *Inferno* (canto 26) as the Lotman of the *Universe of the Mind* passage is to the "overreaching" Florensky of *Imaginary Spaces*.

First, some additional background on Florensky. As recent studies have made abundantly clear, every crucial question of ontology had for Florensky an antinomial structure.[8] Whether he was speaking about icons, language, dreams, the creative process, non-Euclidean geometry, the interior of a cathedral, or even St. Sophia, he *visualized* two separate and seemingly self-canceling categories and then showed, against logic (*rassudok*), how these categories could suddenly occupy the same space in a privileged "crossover zone," what Steven Cassedy has termed, following Heidegger and Roman Ingarden, the "ontically transitional."[9] Thus we have the board, glue, gesso, and gold leaf of an icon, on the one hand, and the unmediated "Mother of God," on the other; or the composition (that which the artist, with the concrete materials at hand, *conceives* from his or her vantage) of a work of art, on the one hand, and its construction (that which the viewer *perceives* from his or her vantage), on the other, and so on. Florensky constantly asks the reader/viewer of his spatially arranged formulations to see two or more points of view *simultaneously*, to, as it were, look back from the far side and forward from the near. The icon is a sacred object because the viewer sees the boards qua boards *and* the Mother of God

---

[7] According to reports Florensky died a latter-day martyr's death in a Stalinist labor camp, where he had selflessly tended his fellow prisoners to the end.

[8] As Robert Slesinski has noted, an antinomy is, for Florensky, "an opposition whose terms remain incompatible in the logical order, but which find their resolution and, indeed, essential complementarity in the metalogical order." *Pavel Florenskii: A Metaphysics of Love* (Crestview: St. Vladimir's Seminary Press, 1984), 145.

[9] Steven Cassedy, "P.A. Florensky and the Celebration of Matter," in *Russian Religious Thought*, ed. Judith Deutsch Kornblatt and Richard F. Gustafson (Madison: University of Wisconsin Press, 1996), 101.

qua Mother of God; this is achieved by *stepping through the window of belief* where separation equals identification.

Pivotal to Florensky's antinomial thinking-cum-faith system is the notion of "sanctuarial barrier," the *limen* without which the philosopher cannot envision his crossover zone.[10] The iconostasis is an ideal expression of this precisely because of its flat surface and its function as a threshold separating sacred from nonsacred space. As Cassedy summarizes, "Florensky's method was always to start with a duality... and demonstrate the metaphysical inadequacy of that duality. The two members of a duality simply reflect each other and offer no chance for movement to a higher state. A third member is always needed to transcend this aporia, and the result is the completeness of trinity... What is remarkable, though, is how deeply entrenched in the pretrinitarian stage of his thinking Florensky's mind seems to be. It is as though he knew in good conscience that a Christian worldview required trinity for completeness, but put the third member of the trinity in its place almost by a kind of intellectual artifice."[11] Even Florensky's definition of a symbol partakes of the visually constructed figure of the crossover zone (here a "window") and reveals its author to be a true child of the Symbolist epoch: "A symbol is larger than itself... A metaphysical symbol is that essence whose energy bears within itself the energy of another, higher essence, and is dissolved in it; its joining with it and through it manifestly reveals that higher essence. A symbol is a window to another, not immediately given essence."[12] The symbol is neither "itself" (presumably the phenomenal reality of its "essence") nor the energy that is "larger than itself" (presumably the noumenal reality of the "higher essence"), but precisely both brought together through the image/iconic surface of the window.

This is where Dante and Florensky's discussion of the *Commedia* enter the picture. In 1921, on the six hundredth anniversary of the death of Dante, Florensky wrote a short but remarkably dense and provocative pamphlet

---

10   Ibid., 100–101.

11   Ibid., 108. To be fair to Florensky, he might respond, contra Cassedy, that the third member of the trinity appears not through "intellectual artifice" but through the mediating presence of the icon as it produces the "transcending vision" that draws the viewer across the threshold into its sacred space. Still, this aspect of the optical illusion and space-bending "crossover zone" (*perekhodnaia zona*) is crucial to many of Florensky's arguments and does seem to have a strong cognitive/mathematical quality to it. For relevant passages on Florensky's understanding of iconic space, see his "Ikonostas," *Bogoslovskie trudy* 9 (1972): 91–92, 96–99, 101–3.

12   Cited O.I. Genisaretskii, "Konstruktsiia i kompozitsiia v ikonologii P. A. Florenskogo," *Trudy VNIITE* (Seriia "Tekhnicheskaia estetika") 59 (1989): 47. Unless otherwise noted, the translations are mine.

in which he tried to prove that the latest theoretical discoveries in math and physics actually confirm what Christian mystics had for centuries been calling revelation — namely, that infinity could be knowable. His term for this was *aktual'naia beskonechnost'* (actual infinity). The booklet, which has since become a bibliographical rarity, was called *Imaginary Spaces in Geometry: The Expansion of the Domain of Two-Dimensional Images in Geometry* (*Mnimosti v geometrii: Rasshirenie oblasti dvukhmernykh obrazov geometrii*) and was published in 1922 by the Moscow publishing house Pomor'e. Several of the names that Florensky cites as sources for his ideas are well known in modern accounts of the geometry of space and anticipate in interesting ways Einstein's general theory of relativity: Carl Friedrich Gauss, Bernhard Riemann, and A.F. Moebius. In essence, what Florensky contends, contra Euclidean geometry and contra its variations in Leibniz, Newton, and Kant, is that the universe can and should be imagined as (in contemporary terminology) "a finite homogeneous galactic system."[13] That is to say, we can conceive of a universe that is both finite, in that it is bounded, *and* homogeneous, in that it has no fixed center. To put it another way, there is no other space beyond space, and yet space is not infinite. How can this be so? By seeing space as *curved*, as non-Euclidean, as having no properties *extrinsic* to itself by which to fix its dimensions, by imagining the intrinsic *relativity* of any position one is able to take in space. Those visual prompts, including Klein bottles, Moebius strips, and Escher drawings, that fascinate us because we cannot isolate their boundaries do so precisely by playing with or "bending" our perspective. From our three-dimensional space we look on their two-dimensional surfaces as optical illusions, for their bending does not pierce our space (i.e., it is not measurable outside itself) just as the Einsteinian 3-sphere cannot be *empirically* charted.

These are some of the ideas Florensky engages in his booklet. Intriguingly, the print by Favorsky decorating the cover of *Imaginary Spaces* is itself a kind of non-Euclidean geometrician's Moebius strip: it presents *two* sides of a plane — the left side, which is visible, and the right side, which is imaginary. Florensky asserts the integrity of the plane that can be seen from *both sides simultaneously*. Certain details from the visible side (the letter *O*) show up on the imaginary side, but fragmented, reversed in perspective, and, most important, bent or distorted. Here the author is suggesting, as on a chart, the essential curvature of space. Whereas

13 Cf. the "antinomy of space" in Kant's *Critique of Pure Reason*. Quotation from J.J. Callahan, "The Curvature of Space in a Finite Universe," *Scientific American* 235 (August 1976): 93.

the basic distinction in the Gauss-Riemann-Einstein model is a universe that is *finite and homogeneous*, that is, it has no fixed center (all galactic units being bounded equally by all other units) and thus no outer limit to be crossed over or pierced, the Orthodox and otherworldly Florensky still telescopes these antinomies in perhaps his most audacious crossover zone: "A shred of the real side, while located on the border of imaginary [space]... conveys the fluctuation of the geometrical figure at the point where it collapses through the plane, when it has not yet been fixed in place [or "determined," *opredelilas'*], being at once both real and imaginary."[14] If the modern scientist must conclude that "it is hopeless [that is, in the absence of extrinsic criteria] to imagine curved space as being mysteriously bent through a fourth dimension," no such doubts assail Florensky, for that is exactly what he is asserting that the intrinsic becomes extrinsic at this "crossover zone."[15] In short, Florensky, with the aid of Favorsky, has constructed what might be termed a *mathematical icon*: rather than the antinomies of boards versus Mother of God, we have the antinomies of three-dimensional versus four-dimensional space. When Florensky says of the cover sketch that it "does not merely decorate the book, but *enters* as a constitutive element into its *spiritual* make-up," he is asking his reader to step through that same *limen* of faith we have witnessed elsewhere.[16]

Florensky concludes *Imaginary Spaces* with an ingenious discussion of how Dante's work, in its presentation of the other world, was not only "ahead of contemporary science" but in fact startlingly prescient about notions such as the bending or breaking of space at conditions imaginary yet no less real — beyond the speed of light.[17] As we recall, this is the same passage that Lotman cites as his point of departure (both into Dante and from Florensky) in *Universe of the Mind*. Thus, the Russian scientist-priest anticipates by almost sixty years the work of such physicists and mathematicians as J. J. Callahan and Mark A. Peterson, who have argued in their publications that Dante's vision in the *Paradiso* of the harmonious interrelation between the heavenly spheres (which increase in size and turn more rapidly the higher the pilgrim goes) and the Empyrean (whose nine concentric circles decrease in size but, paradoxically, increase in rotating speed the closer they come to the blinding point of light at their center) is in fact a rather accurate replica of Einstein's "finite and homogeneous" galactic system known as the 3-sphere.[18] The reader is left with "the almost inescapable impression that [Dante] conceives

14   Pavel Florenskii, *Mnimosti v geometrii: Rasshirenie oblasti dvukhmernykh obrazov geometrii* (Moscow: Pomor'e, 1922), 63–64; cited in Lena Szilard, "Andrei Belyi i P. Florenskii," *Studia Slavica Hung.* 33 (1987): 233.

15   Callahan, "Curvature of Space," 94.

16   My emphasis; Florenskii, *Mnimosti*, 58; cited in Szilard, "Andrei Belyi i P. Florenskii," 232.

17   Florenskii, *Mnimosti*, 53.

18   Callahan, "Curvature of Space," 99.

of these nine angelic spheres [of the Empyrean] as forming one hemisphere of the entire universe and the usual Aristotelian universe up to the Primum Mobile as the other hemisphere, while he is standing more or less on the equator between them... Taken all together, then, his universe is a 3-sphere."[19] Or as Florensky himself formulates the paradox of relativity in his own strikingly similar terms, "Dantesque space is precisely like elliptical space. This [realization] sheds a sudden bundle of light on the medieval notion of the finite character of the world. But these ideas concerning geometry in general have recently received an unexpected concrete interpretation through the principle of relativity, and from the point of view of modern physics, universal space should be conceivable precisely as elliptical space and is acknowledged to be finite, just as time is finite, enclosed in itself... The realm of imaginary space is real, comprehensible, and in the language of Dante is called the Empyrean."[20]

Thus far we have been setting the stage for Lotman and his view of Dante's journey by focusing on Florensky as interlocutor, in particular the latter's antinomial thinking and his unique way of reading a non-Euclidean curvature in the space-time continuum into the "geometry of salvation" in the *Commedia*. Now I would like to bring into play Lotman's argument in *Universe of the Mind* by showing how it foregrounds, without explicitly saying so, the profound and irreconcilable differences between Dante's medieval Catholic worldview and Florensky's Symbolist-tinged Orthodoxy. Along the way I shall also demonstrate, with Lotman's help, how these competing faith systems implicate very different histories and — this is the central point — different ways of negotiating a "middle space" on earth.

I will begin by introducing two additional works by Lotman to support my argument. First, his well-known study of binary models of culture (coauthored with Boris Uspensky), from which the following passage is taken:

> In Western Catholicism, the world beyond the grave is divided into three spaces: heaven, purgatory, and hell. Earthly life is correspondingly conceived of as admitting three types of behavior: the unconditionally sinful, the unconditionally holy, and the neutral, which permits eternal salvation after some sort of purgative trial. In the real life of the medieval West a wide area of neutral behavior thus became possible, as did neutral societal institutions, which were neither "holy"

[19] Mark A. Peterson, "Dante and the 3-Sphere," *American Journal of Physics* 47 (1979):1033.

[20] Florenskii, *Mnimosti*, 48, 53.

nor "sinful," neither "pro-state" nor "anti-state," neither good nor bad. The neutral sphere became a structural reserve, out of which the succeeding system developed...

The Russian medieval system was constructed on an accentuated duality. To continue our example, one of its attributes was the division of the other world into heaven and hell. Intermediate neutral spheres were not envisaged. Behavior in earthly life could be either sinful or holy. This situation spread into extra-ecclesiastical conceptions: thus secular power could be interpreted as divine or diabolical, but never as neutral.[21]

This absence of a neutral space, *not only purgatory itself but any middle ground over which one makes one's way to the destination of salvation/ revelation*, has direct application, as we shall see, to Florensky's reading of Dante.

The second is an article in which Lotman advances the thesis that for Orthodox Slavs in general and for Russians in particular "a religious act has as its basis an unconditional act of self-giving."[22] This idea of religiously inspired behavior as being *one-sided* and *noncompulsory*, that is, as bearing no signs of an implied *quid pro quo*, will again be implicated in the possibility or impossibility of imagining an axiological middle space:

In the West the sense of agreement, though having its remote origin in magic, had the authority of the Roman secular tradition and held a position equal to the authority of religion; in Russia, on the other hand, it was felt to be pagan in character... It is significant that in the Western tradition an agreement as such was ethically neutral. It could be drawn up with the Devil... but one might also make agreements with the forces of holiness and goodness... [In the Russian context, however,] an agreement may only be made with a Satanic power or its pagan counterpart.[23]

Space opens up for interpretation/negotiation when one's acts, according to a rule or "agreement," can affect the response of the interlocutor, even when that interlocutor is God.

With these two works in mind, let us now turn to the relevant passages in *Universe of the Mind*. Lotman begins with the assertion that he will be "dwelling on the meaning of the spatial axis 'top/bottom' in Dante's created world."[24] That may be so, in that Dante's world is traditionally visualized along a vertical axis, yet it is also clear that Lotman's semiotic

[21] Iu.M. Lotman and B.A. Uspenskii, "Binary Models in the Dynamics of Russian Culture (to the End of the Eighteenth Century)," in *The Semiotics of Russian Cultural History*, ed. Alexander D. Nakhimovsky and Alice Stone Nakhimovsky (Ithaca: Cornell University Press, 1985), 31–32.

[22] Lotman, "'Agreement' and 'Self-Giving' as Archetypal Models of Culture," in Lotman and Uspenskii, *Semiotics of Russian Culture*, 125.

[23] Ibid., 126–27.

[24] Lotman, *Universe of the Mind*, 177.

approach owes much to an appreciation of a neutral axiological or "middle" space (one that is not inherently "right" or "wrong" but simply informative), and that its geometry is more Euclidean than non-Euclidean, more "filled in" and three-dimensional than "mind-bending" and "out of this world." That there is something to negotiate (i.e., space itself) is precisely what generates meaning in Dante and Lotman:

> So when Dante and Virgil move down the relative scale of the earthly "top/bottom" axis, that is, when they go deeper from the surface of the Earth towards its centre, they are at the same time in relation to the absolute axis rising up. The solution to this paradox is to be found in Dante's semiotics. In Dante's belief-system space has meaning, and each spatial category has its own meaning. But the relationship of expression and content is not an arbitrary one, unlike semiotic systems based on social conventions... The content, the meaning of the symbol is not bound to its expression by convention (as happens with allegory) but shines through it. The closer the text is placed in the hierarchy to the heavenly light which is the true content of medieval symbolics the brighter the meaning shines through it and the more direct and less conventionalized is its expression. The further the text is from the source of truth, then the more dimly will it be reflected and the more arbitrary will be the relationship of content to expression. Thus on the highest step truth is accessible to direct contemplation through the eye of the spirit, while on the lowest step truth is glimpsed through conventional signs. Because sinners and demons of different degrees use purely conventional signs they can lie, commit perfidy, treachery and deceit — all ways to separate content from expression. The righteous also converse with each other in signs but they do not put convention to ill use, and with recourse to the highest sources of truth they can penetrate into the conventionless symbolic world of meanings.[25]

This is a fascinating series of formulations when placed alongside the turning-point scene (Lucifer's bulge at the hip, discussed later) in Florensky. Basically Lotman is saying that, viewed semiotically, Dante the pilgrim's journey through the three realms of the afterlife is one continuous and uninterrupted force field, where the geo- and astrophysics of movement (first downward, then) upward against the

---

25   Ibid., 179.

gravitas of sin equals theodicy, or the morally responsible making of meaning in the universe created by God. Despite the claims of "symbolic space," this movement is not about right-angled visions and singular turning points. Choices in the path do not result in wholesale movements "in" or "out." Each step is equally meaningful in the amount of information it imparts. Wherever one is located along this journey's route, one's position vis-à-vis the "truth" as told (or shown) by the forever-fallen sinners, the purgatorial "works-in-progress," and the now-risen righteous is relative (but never amoral). The pilgrim moves along this axis as along a slide rule, and with the help of his various guides, he stops to experience/interpret the meaning of what he sees, understanding that that meaning is always dependent on the interlocutor's or actor's own orientation to the truth of his or her life as refracted through the spectrum of "conventional signs-holy symbols." By operating in a world where conventional signs can be manipulated out of selfish motives and no sign is inherently holy (i.e., reflective of a higher symbolics), the sinner shows himself or herself to be far away from the truth. Semiotics becomes the orienting tool or slide rule that shows the truth, good or bad, of each scene en route: "The solution to this paradox [how an axis can be both relative and absolute] is to be found in Dante's semiotics." Interestingly enough, however, the point in Lotman's narrative where we feel the greatest need for something akin to Florenskian mathematics specifically, the statement that "when Dante and Virgil move down the relative scale of the earthly 'top/bottom' axis, that is, when they go deeper from the surface of the Earth towards its centre, they are at the same time in relation to the absolute axis rising up" is also the point where space and meaning are the most problematic. For how can Dante and Virgil be moving up one axis (the absolute one) and down another (the literal, physical one) at the same time, without those axes in some way bending into each other? How can a journey be both straightforward and circular without a perspective on it that is simultaneously "inside" and "outside"? To be fair to Florensky and his iconism then, this is the moment when Lotmanian semiotics seems to appear "flattest" and most in need of the priest's mathematical mysticism.

Now, to return to Florensky and his Dante. What we find at the end of *Imaginary Spaces* is a different sort of journey entirely, and not only because Florensky is, in Lotman's words, "getting carried away." Something else is going on here, something having to do with the very nature of symbolic space:

> And so let us recall the path taken by Dante and Virgil. It begins in Italy. Both poets descend along the steep slopes of the funnel-shaped Inferno. The funnel culminates at the last, narrowest circle of the Lord of the Nether Regions [Vladyka preispodnei]. What is more, all the while during the descent down, a vertical position is maintained by both poets — their heads are turned in the direction of the point of departure, that is, toward Italy, and their feet toward the center of the earth. But when the poets reach approximately Lucifer's waist [poiasnitsa], they both suddenly *turn over* [perevorachivaiutsia], proceeding now with their feet toward the surface of the earth, whence they entered the subterranean kingdom, and with their heads in the opposite direction (*Inferno*, canto 34).[26] Having crossed the border... that is, having completed the path [down] and crossed the center of the world, the poets find themselves beneath the hemisphere, whose counterpart is the place "where Christ was crucified": they [now] rise up along the crater-shaped way [po zherloobraznomu khodu]... Mounts Purgatory and Zion, diametrically opposed to each other, arose as the result of that fall [namely, Lucifer's], which means that the path to heaven is directed along the line of Lucifer's fall but has an opposing meaning. In this way Dante constantly moves along a straight line and [comes to] stand in heaven, turned with his feet in the direction of his descent. But having looked out from there, from the Empyrean, at God's glory, in the end he finds himself, without any particular movement of turning back, in Florence. His journey has been a reality, but if anyone would deny the latter, then the least that can be said is that this journey must be acknowledged as a poetic reality, that is, as something conceivable and possible to imagine, which means it contains in itself the givens for an elucidation of its geometrical premises. And so, moving constantly ahead in a straight line and turning over once en route, the poet comes to his prior place in the same position in which he left it.[27]

[26] There is an apparent error in Florensky's text at this point: this scene takes place in canto 34, not 23, as indicated in *Imaginary Spaces* (46). I have made the change in the cited passage.

[27] Florenskii, *Mnimosti*, 45–47.

Note that whereas the physicists who speak of Dante's anticipation of the Einsteinian 3-sphere invariably single out the *Commedia*'s last book and the pilgrim's transit from the earthly to the heavenly spheres, Florensky fixes on a radically different "crossover zone": the end of the *Inferno* and Lucifer's waist or, more precisely, the seam where the thigh/loin meets the bulge of the hip/haunch.[28] Why, one wonders, does Florensky the priest focus on this particular turning point to make his case about non-Euclidean optical illusion qua revelation? It has been suggested by at least one memoirist that Florensky "was possessed rather by the spirit of cognition on a grand scale than by that of kindness and charity; Lucifer was closer to him than Christ."[29] But whether this interest in the depths of the *Inferno* (rather than the heights of the *Paradiso*) is a matter of will or of temperament ("Luciferian" pride) is an imponderable and need not concern us here. My own hypothesis is that the vividness, the sheer graphic element of sin, coupled with its idolatry of three-dimensional form and movement, was perceived by Florensky to be, precisely because it was fallen, more readily available to the world of the Inferno.[30] Thus, Florensky telescopes all the drama of the *Inferno* into this one point in space and time where opposites can be identities where the pilgrim and the guide can turn upside down and still walk upright, where their heads and feet can turn in a diametrically different direction, and yet they can still make forward progress in their journey, where Lucifer as the very symbol for the way down can suddenly provide an exit to the way up, and so on. One imagines Florensky taking a mathematician's pure delight in the elegant posing of these paradoxical movements. Somehow Dante makes his way ever forward, turns a somersault at one juncture en route, and arrives back at the original point of departure in the same position in which he left. Salvation becomes a Moebius strip, and the place where the outer surface joins the inner surface is the Prince of Darkness's "nether region."

Looking at this from the Lotmanian perspective, the fact that Florensky makes no mention of the tremendous learning process Dante experiences to reach Lucifer's hip is characteristic, as is the fact that he does not seem to notice that the underworld grows denser and, as it were, "fatter" (i.e., all the various pouches in the Eighth Circle and the rings in the Ninth Circle) the closer the two travelers get to the center of the earth (just as things will move more slowly the closer we get to the Earthly Paradise and the Empyrean later on).[31] According to

---

28 In the Italian: Quando noi fummo là dove la coscia / si volge, a punto in sul grosso de l'anche" (34.76–77); and in Lozinsky's translation: «Когда мы пробирались там, где бок, / Загнув к бедру, дает уклон пологий».

Florensky himself uses another translation (that of D.I. Min?), which foregrounds even more the notion of turning and crossing: «Когда же мы достигли точки той, / Где толща чресл вращает бедр громаду».

29 Leonid Sabaneeff, "Pavel Florensky—Priest, Scientist, and Mystic," *Russian Review* 20 (October 1961): 316–17.

medieval tradition, one's soul has two feet, the *affectus* (will, carnal appetite) on the left, which clings to the things of the earth, and the *apprehensivus* (intellect) on the right, which tries to perceive the good in a postlapsarian world. The pilgrim's steps as *homo claudus* have been measured out to the ethical centimeter by the Catholic notion of sin and retribution, that very specific adherence to the rightness of the *contrapasso* — the fitting of the punishment in hell to the unrepented sin on earth.[32] Thus, to cite the first few examples, those who refused to take sides in the battle between good and evil are, like the neutral angels, punished just beyond the Gates of Hell by chasing after banners that lead nowhere (they had no *telos* in life) and by being bitten by horseflies and wasps (they were themselves parasites of sorts) (canto 3); or the lustful, including the Symbolists' beloved Paolo and Francesca, are blown about like birds (just as their passions tossed them about in life) because they have forfeited their right to choose (canto 5, Second Circle); or Ciacco and the other gluttons, who gorged themselves and indulged in Florentine life, must now lie in the filthy and evil-smelling pigsty of the Third Circle and be flayed by the big-bellied Cerberus (canto 6), and so on. The number of circles in Minos the judge's tail tell each sinful soul his or her precise destination below.

But all these measurements and portionings out are, for the reasons outlined by Lotman, anathema to the spirit of Orthodoxy. To be punished in a way that fits one's misdeeds, just as to be rewarded in a way that fits one's spiritual *podvigi* (acts of heroism), is to engage in the *quid pro quo* that the Slavic world associates with magic (the domain of the devil), Roman law, and the Catholic Church. Here Florensky very much follows Dostoevsky and the Slavophiles. As he writes in "Gehenna," his eighth letter in *The Pillar*:

> I want to point out the decisive difference between the view expressed here... and the Catholic teaching about purgatory, where the person is saved *not in spite of, but thanks to, as a result of* the torments of purification. It is for this reason that, for the apostle Paul, what is saved is not the person in his entire makeup, but only "he himself" [*sam*], his God-given "about oneself" [*o sebe*], while according to

---

30 Florensky had ambivalent feelings about such vividness. See the discussion later in this essay.

31 Here Florensky is by no means alone or eccentric in his analysis. Considerable emphasis has been placed in the Russian tradition on Dante's so-called verticality, on the one moment of his transcendence rather than on the multitude of moments between any ultimate stepping across or over. See, e.g., M.M. Bakhtin, "Forms of Time and of the Chronotope in the Novel," *The Dialogic Imagination*, ed. Michael Holquist, trans. Caryl Emerson and Michael Holquist (Austin: University of Texas Press, 1981), 156–57.

32 Cf. "All sins, which Dante arranges in a strict hierarchy, have spatial attachment so that the weight of the sin corresponds to the depth of the sinner's position" (Lotman, *Universe of the Mind*, 180).

Catholic teaching it is the whole person who is saved, but only having bethought himself and changed for the better under [the influence of] the disciplined retribution of purgatory. The profoundly mysterious and suprarational metaphysical act of the separation of the two moments of being ("about oneself" and "for oneself" [dlia sebia]) is transformed, in the vulgar conception of Catholic purgatory, into something psychological, thoroughly understandable — into justification through suffering and education through punishment.[33]

One should not be surprised, having read such statements, to find Florensky not dwelling on the steps leading up to the way out of the Inferno: these latter would have smacked of the "false discipline," the "justification through torment," and the "edification through punishment" of Catholicism. It is not simply that these various mediating measures are too easily associated with the corruption of the historical church, with simony and the securing of one's place in the other world through negotiations in this one. Equally offensive to Florensky's mentality is the very notion that *there is or can be something in between*, that the "crossover zone" can be stretched out, arranged with signposts, made long or steep in its own right. Salvation is not a process but a freely given act that penetrates across a threshold and pulls one (*bends* one) from "here" to "there." In this Florensky joins hands with the Dostoevsky of *The Idiot*, whose hero tells the tale of the peasant who murders his friend for a silver watch *at the same time* that he genuinely asks God's forgiveness *radi Khrista* (for Christ's sake).

In another letter of *The Pillar*, Florensky explains the phenomenon of Sophia's wisdom by first describing taxonomically the three primary categories of Sophia icons (typified by the Novgorod, Yaroslavl, and Kiev "Sophias," respectively) and then explaining what the symbolism in these icons means. In this telling there is no plot, no storyline. Instead there are one-to-one correspondences (phrasal icons, as it were) on the order of "Sophia's wings = closeness to a higher world," or "the caduceus = theurgic power," or "the crown in the form of a city wall = Earth-mother/civitas."[34] One can only assume that a plot such as we have in the *Commedia*, where the salvation of one pilgrim soul is achieved through grace, to be sure, but also through the intricately calibrated blend of poetic footsteps in terza rima and physical footsteps through three massive realms of the afterlife, is already by definition too human-centered,

---

[33] Florenskii, *Stolp i utverzhdenie istiny. Opyt pravoslavnoi feodotsei* (Berlin: Rossica, 1929), 233.

[34] Ibid., 374–75.

too "secular," for Florensky's tradition. Beatrice, as the *Vita Nova* tells us, is the ninth most beautiful woman in Florence — certainly the kind of hair-splitting in the aesthetic/potentially erotic realm that Florensky would have absolutely no interest in. Likewise, whereas Dante is very careful about the various female intercessors, their precise positions vis-à-vis the Godhead, and even their individual qualities — recall that it is Mary who sends Lucia, who sends Beatrice — Florensky is apt to collapse the different incarnations of Sophia. To the poet who could not speak of feminine beauty, whether physical or spiritual, without remembering the lessons of *dolce stil nuovo* and the love poetry of Guinizelli and Cavalcanti, the following telescoping of Sophia would seem very strange indeed:

> If Sophia is all Creatures [/Creation], then the soul and conscience of Creation, Humankind, is chiefly Sophia. If Sophia is all Humankind, then the soul and conscience of Humankind, the Church, is chiefly Sophia. If Sophia is the Church, then the soul and conscience of the Church, the Church of Saints, is chiefly Sophia. If Sophia is the Church of Saints, then the soul and conscience of the Church of Saints, the Intercessor and Defender for all creatures before the Word of God... [that is,] the Mother of God... is once again chiefly Sophia. But the true sign of the Blessed Mary is Her Virginity, the beauty of Her Soul. It is this that is Sophia.[35]

This is a striking passage when juxtaposed with the notion of Christian beatitude in feminine form in the *Commedia*. As Zenkovsky first noted, how can Florensky's version of Sophia be at one and the same time "the pre-existent nature of creation," "the Church in its earthly aspect," and "creation that has been deified by the Holy Spirit"?[36] How can Sophia be both the "ideal personality of the world," that is, unfallen, and that world's Guardian Angel, a concept that presupposes there is some evil to guard against?[37] She cannot be, if any Christian plot or extended notion of theodicy is involved. The main point to keep in mind as we conclude this discussion of Catholic middle distance and Orthodox two-dimensionality (or apocalypticism) is that the former stresses the *analogous that is different* (Mary is like Lucia, who is like Beatrice, but still they are different), and the latter stresses the *different that is identical* (Sophia = Humankind = Church = Church of the Saints = Mother of God = Virginity). The former cannot help but create space, especially over time as the Church fathers

---

[35] Ibid., 350–51.
[36] See Florenskii, *Stolp*, 350.
[37] V.V. Zenkovsky, *A History of Russian Philosophy*, trans. George L. Kline, 2 vols. (London: Routledge & Kegan Paul, 1953), 2:889.

continued to weigh and measure the subtle differences on the path from secular to divine knowledge. The latter cannot help but consume and eliminate the potential for middle space.

I do not mean to suggest that Florensky's understanding of Dante is essentially flawed (not terribly useful information in the final analysis) but that it is to a significant degree culturally and historically determined and that it says as much about its author and his tradition as it does about its subject. How Florensky processes not only the idea of an axiological middle space (what is visually prompted in the *Commedia* by the *quid pro quo* activities of those doing penance on Mount Purgatory) but more centrally the multitude of steps down to the bulge at Lucifer's hip is what is interesting. In a word, he doesn't go "there." There simply is no way or path from secular to sacred love in Florensky. By the same token, Lotman's formulations have been especially useful and apposite in our discussion, if not without their own inbred "aporias" (e.g., they rigorously reject anything mystical or "mind-bending," surely an aspect of Dante's text that at some level needs to be reckoned with). Upon reflection one realizes that Dante is already, even in the early fourteenth century, deeply humanist (or at least on the way to becoming so: i.e., he unmistakably and personally eroticizes, even as he spiritualizes, his text), while Florensky, writing after the revolution and fully aware of how secular powers wield apocalyptic models, is deeply anti-humanist. Even as Florensky is clearly intrigued, as a mathematician, by Dante's non-Euclidean vision, he would appear to have little patience with the sensuous, concrete, quirky, almost palpable quality of Dante's imagery. As he writes in *The Pillar*:

> If the Protestant destroys Christ, then the Catholic wishes to dress himself in the likeness [*lichina*] of Christ. Whence the sensuous [*chuvstvennyi*] quality of the church service, its drama, its open altar (the altar a stage, the priest an actor), the plasticity, the sensuous music, the mysticism that is not of the mind but of the imagination/fantasy [*voobrazhatel'naia*], leading to a fixation on the stigmata (it is noteworthy that in the East there has been no such fixation…), the eroticism, the sense of hysterics, and so on. Whence too the Catholic mysteries, the processions, everything that operates on the imagination the action, the shameful display, but not contemplation, not thoughtful [*umnaia*] prayer.[38]

38 Florenskii, *Stolp*, 723n400.

Hence despite his connections to the tradition of St. John of Damascus and the eighth-century theologian's assertions that the material world is sacred and spirit bearing, Florensky leaves little room in his thinking for "matter," if by matter we mean a traditional love object in this world (i.e., "Beatrice" cannot cross over into "Sophia").[39] What he identifies as damning in the Catholic service are precisely those elements that gave Dante's poem its middle space and its love plot-cum-Christian history: its sensuous images, its potential eroticism, its drama and incipient orientation toward a three-dimensional realism, its openness (N.B. the lack of the iconostasis and the "ontically transitional"), its mysticism tinged with elements of a dark imagination.

But at the same time it would be remiss not to acknowledge the compelling, even poignant quality of Florensky's voyage, however wayward or Ulysses-like it might seem to our postmodern understanding, into uncharted territory. Unsatisfied with any logic that finds truth in three-dimensional space, Florensky pushes relentlessly backward into two-dimensionality (iconism) and forward into four-dimensionality (the Moebius strip, or "bendable" space). Unlike Dante's Ulysses, he is clearly not "morally indifferent," and like the pilgrim struggling upward against the weight of his own and others' fallen humanity, he fears a future "separation of knowledge from morality, of discovery from its results, of science from the human personality." He may have appeared to contemporaries as twentieth-century Russia's quintessential Renaissance man. But in reality his turn away from secularism and human-centeredness made him, as Lotman divined, the perfect medieval mind (and soul) for modern science and for the idea that movement beyond the speed of light is not only imaginable but meaningful. By the same token, Lotman's reading of Florensky's reading of Dante is itself incredibly revealing. In it we see *homo semioticus* clearly turning away from Florensky's neo-medievalism and toward a neo-humanism and neo-personalism quite new and heuristically useful for its own space-time. It is as though Dante's anxiety about the shift from the medieval to the Renaissance worldview is repeated in reverse perspective in Lotman's fear that Russian cultural space will never manage to shed its own obsessively binary, relentlessly "iconic" tradition — that is, will never make the transition to a fully embodied "Trinitarian" universe.[40] Thus, if the brilliant and fascinating Florensky might be dubbed the Ulysses of twentieth-century Russian spiritual culture, a figure whose oratorical

---

39 See Cassedy, "P. A. Florensky and the Celebration of Matter," 98–99.

40 See Lotman's very last sentences in *Culture and Explosion*, in which he asserts that it would be a "historical catastrophe" if Russia failed to adopt the "all-European ternary system and to renounce the ideal of destroying 'the old world to its foundation and then' building a new one on its ruins" ([Moscow: Gnozis, Publishing Group 'Progress,' 1992], 148).

flair inspired the sailors on board with the promise of landfall in the Southern Hemisphere (or in post-Einsteinian terms, existence beyond the speed of light), then Lotman is his total antipode, the prodigiously erudite yet modest teacher-exile whose "rage for order" is as humane as it is larger than life. Not Catholic (or Orthodox),—not even Christian, he is the closest thing Russian culture has to the Dante of twentieth-century semiotics.

Chapter 6

Whose Mind Is This Anyway? Influence, Intertextuality, and the Boundaries of Legitimate Scholarship[1]

On a green island amid the dark-blue sea there appeared a man. Here he decided to erect a temple. He broke up and carted blocks of marble, hewed them, cut capitals and friezes, erected columns and walls. But before doing that he constructed a temple in his imagination, and all that he erected in stone was simply the recreation of his already created ideal. This ideal was not something dead and immobile: in the head of the builder there swarmed designs, with the variants pressing in on each other, and the view from a hill or the form of a block of marble introduced corrections into the construction plans or into the figure of a god. The builder was both bound and free: this was not the first temple he had built, and in his wanderings over the years he had made the rounds of hundreds of structures created by other geniuses. He knew what was necessary to build a temple and to escape that knowledge was not in his power. But he also knew that another's experience not only helps, it binds. And what he wanted to create was a *free* temple, one that had never existed before. The building grew, but so too

---

[1] This paper was delivered as the keynote address at the annual AATSEEL convention in Philadelphia on December 29, 2004 and then published in *Slavic and East European Journal* 49.1 (Spring 2005): 1–17.

grew, and changed, the ideal, which was, inexplicably, ahead of the [original] conception.

What was the builder thinking about, what brought him to this island, what was he trying to say with his work, and whom was he addressing? The only way of understanding is to be one of those who tread with the builder along the difficult and dusty roads of his life, who think over his thoughts on long nights, who experience his losses and hopes, his grievous humiliations and high soaring[s] of the soul…

Centuries pass. The temple has fallen, become overgrown, its scattered parts covered with earth. And in its place has arisen a green hill.

On the green hill amid the dark-blue sea there appeared a man. He had with him books, maps, and a shovel. He decided to restore the temple. He dug, extracted and cleaned off pieces of wall and statuary, he laid out on the green sward shining fragments of marble. He was a scientist and he knew the value of prosaic labor. Prior to this he had surveyed the proportions of many different temples. He understood the language of drafts, so dry to the uninitiated, to those who demand results and don't want to know at what cost such results are obtained. And now, after everything the earth could disgorge had been retrieved, it was time to put the scattered pieces back together.

But in the man's hands are only pathetic shards: much is missing, for along the shore there had grown up an entire village, built out of the stones of the former temple, and dozens of columns had been crushed into gravel as a new highway was being laid. The man's work gets a name—"reconstruction." In order for the fragments to assume a unified form once again it is necessary to see the temple in the mind's eye in its integral wholeness. And here what is required is a marriage of the most precise calculation, the multitudinous "boring" skills of the professional, [on the one hand], and imagination, sometimes even fantasy [on the other]. As it happens reconstruction is never irrefutable, definitive: after all, what needs to be restored is not some run-of-the-mill barracks but the creation of an individual genius, and what needs to be divined is not simply what was done by the builder but also what was rejected by him, what he didn't want to do, or what he wanted to do but couldn't. That which was built is only part of that which wasn't, the realized only part of the unrealized. The work of the reconstructor is co-creation [*sotvorchestvo*]. In order for him to restore the temple he has to recreate the entire spiritual world of the builder. He has to *resurrect him [voskresit' ego]*.[2]

Many of you will recognize this passage as the opening to Yury Lotman's *The Creation of Karamzin* (*Sotvorenie Karamzina*). I have cited it to begin my talk today because I believe it is a good place to start a discussion of how we as scholar-critics may choose to situate ourselves vis-à-vis our subjects. I also think it is a good place to begin framing my larger topic, to wit, where we as readers can responsibly come down on the issue of what qualifies as "influence," with its post-Bloomian aura of individual psychological struggle and adaptation, and what as "intertextuality," with its decentering of the subject and its challenging of traditional textual boundaries. You will be pleased to know that this is not going to be an elegy for literary studies, as much as that discipline seems diminished and demoralized of late. Bewailing the way the cultural winds are blowing is not a very useful activity. Nor are my comments going to be a straight "theory" talk, an attempt to show how my sword is sharper than my adversaries', its blade dancing in the air with deadly accuracy like that of some rhetorical sushi chef. Some names will crop up—Taranovsky, Kristeva, Barthes, Riffaterre, Genette, Hirsch, Ricoeur, Bloom, and Lotman—but when they do the main point of emphasis will be the stance of the interpreter/thinker toward the text he or she is interpreting, not so much the "correctness" of the individual reading. I think the most useful thing I can do in a talk of this sort is to try to point out what seems to work best in the little scholarly corner of the world I occupy. But to do that I first need to turn back to Lotman on Karamzin and to the whole problem of "authorial intention."

Lotman was above all a teacher and enlightener. Particularly in later years his "secondary modeling system" method did not get in the way of his message. *The Creation of Karamzin* was published in 1987, just six years before the scholar's death. Lotman's allegory about literary research as an archaeological project, with the temple being the writer's inner life, has much to recommend it—I confess I for one am smitten by it—but let's interrogate it a bit, poke around the edges. First of all, the logic of the allegory suggests that the original genius of a builder had an *ideal* in his mind which he then made concrete in a specific idea or conception

[2] Iu.M. Lotman, *Sotvorenie Karamzina* (Moscow: Kniga, 1987), 11–12. Unless otherwise indicated all translations in the present essay are mine.

(*zamysel*). I'm not sure "ideal" is the right word here, since it sounds so hygienic and abstract; I suspect what Lotman means is that the creative person has an idea of the world, which is also an *idea of himself in the world*, that he then wants to *embody* (make as "real" as possible) in his work. Anyway, the ideal pulls the conception (*zamysel*) forward and forces it to change under the power of circumstance (the hill that is different from a neutral flat space, the block of marble that already asks to be chiseled in a certain way). Lotman, always logical, always lucid (this is his strength as well as his weakness), says that the writer "constructs" his inner life in the same way: beginning as "a person born with great capabilities" he decides "to create himself as a good writer."[3] That is the writer's *intention*. Moreover, Lotman, who knew his Bakhtin and whose semiotic thinking was always recoding one text's rules into another's, goes on to say that the original builder was both "bound and free [*sviazan i svoboden*]." Nevertheless, this genius builder, who knew very well how other temples were constructed, wanted to build something Lotman calls a *"free* temple" ("one that had never existed"), in other words, one that appeared more unique than alike. That is also, by analogy, the writer's *intention*.

Lotman does not downplay the gaps and indeterminacies in the restoration project. He says: "in the man's hands are only pathetic shards: much is missing, for along the shore there had grown up an entire village, built out of the stones of the former temple, and dozens of columns had been crushed into gravel as a new highway was being laid." Translation: there are certain questions that will never be fully answered, some information that may be lost irretrievably. Who was Pushkin's secret love (*utaennaia liubov'*)? Did she ever exist? But this doesn't stop the restorer. Lotman goes on to say in the following paragraphs that the author of a "novel of reconstruction" (*roman-rekonstruktsiia*)" does not have the right, as Tynianov did in his novels about Pushkin, Küchelbecker, and Griboedov, to place imagined speeches in the mouths of his heroes.

> He cannot fill in the absent fragments of columns with stones of his own making, no matter how certain he is that he has correctly guessed what is lost. His creative work [*tvorchestvo*] has a different nature and is carried out in a different sphere: his activity is directed toward the recreation of the integral ideal of personality (*vossozdanie togo tselostnogo ideala lichnosti*) which the hero of the biography created in his soul. This was the design according to which he constructed

---

3   Ibid., 12.

himself. We must discover, expose the design, to guess it out among others, from those that are possible and those that are impossible [...] and in so doing enliven the remaining fragments, confer meaning on them, force them to speak.⁴

Thus the scholar, à la Lotman, does not contrive (*izmyshliaet*), he searches and he compares (*ishchet, sopostavliaet*). What inspires him, launches him so to speak, is what is already there. There is no place is his *roman-rekonstruktsiia* for conjecture *domysel*, for the idea that does not already, because of the existing jagged edges of the fragment, connect up to the overarching design. And if imagination or invention (*vymysel*) do play a role (they do), it is a carefully pinioned one: based on the evidence, sensitively and plausibly parsed, of an existing document. Presented allegorically, Lotman's scholar-archaeologist is at best a kind of secondary or co-creator — hence the play on words in the title, the "Creation [*Sotvorenie*] of Karamzin" — a faithful accomplice who can, through sacrificing himself and giving himself over to his subject's original construction plans, get inside the head and heart of the departed *lichnost'*. Thanks to Lotman's meticulous sleuthing, the Karamzin of his inner biography comes alive as someone quite different from his sentimental heroes (he was anything but naïve) and as someone who created a cult of friendship (*iskusstvo nezhnoi druzhby*) but who himself was "extraordinarily chary of soulful outpourings"⁵ — all hard lacquered surface that only those closest to him got behind. Inside the pupil who bounced around Europe registering with wide-eyed wonder the great figures and events changing the world beyond his country's borders in *Letters of a Russian Traveler* was a shrewd and masterful teacher, someone in fact quite like his biographer. Indeed, it is the *difference* between one set of texts, the aestheticized structure of *Letters*, and another set of texts, the actual letters and documents relating to Karamzin's trip abroad, that lays bare the design (*plan*) by which Karamzin constructs himself, which in turn is a reflection of the implicit ideal (the "free temple"), of which Lotman spoke in his allegory.

Now, using Lotman's archaeological allegory as our starting point, let us consider the vexed issue of authorial intention. Ever since Wimsatt and Beardsley published their 1946 essay "The Intentional Fallacy" it has been something of a given in the critical literature that, in their words, a poem "is not the critic's own and not the author's (it is detached from the author at birth and goes about the world beyond his power to intend about it or control it). The poem belongs to the public."⁶ This cornerstone of New

4 Ibid., 13.
5 Ibid., 17.
6 J.A. Cuddon, *A Dictionary of Literary Terms and Literary Theory*, 3rd ed. (Oxford: Blackwell Reference, 1991), 452.

Critical thinking obviously did not appear out of nowhere but was itself a reaction to the naïve application of extratextual, and often extraliterary, information, beginning with details of the poet's biography, to how a poem works, and means, from the inside. What a poem means should be limited to what can be legitimately analyzed as belonging within the boundaries of its discrete aesthetic structure. In the intervening half-century the issue of intentionality has been further refined and contested, with epistemological thrusts that can be characterized as either centrifugal or centripetal. Painting with broad strokes, one could say that the centrifugal tendencies are most potently represented in Kristeva, whose early (1960s) deployment of the term "intertextuality"[7] built on the relational features of language from Saussurean structuralism and on the inherently social nature of dialogue in Bakhtin; Barthes then took matters further with his arch announcement of the "death of the Author"[8] and his argument that the new meanings generated by a reader's "play with the signifier" are their own pleasurable reward, a "liberation" from what had been authorial control.[9] Thus, Kristeva and Barthes, in their movement beyond the strict tenets of Structuralism, tenets which in their hermetic quality shared certain framing orientations with New Criticism, were the bellwethers for what became loosely known as Poststructuralism.

The contravening tendencies are most clearly represented in the work of such neo-structuralists as Riffaterre and Genette, who would like to keep the meaning of a poem still somehow stable and coextensive with its formal boundaries, but who also understand implicitly the power of intertextual codes to explain the "inside" from "without" (one system "recoding" another system, as Lotman would say) and have come up with their own terminology ("architext," "hypertextuality," "hypogram," "inter-text," "ungrammaticalities," "semiotic" vs. "mimetic"[10]) to keep discussion on the level of the specific text. The situation is, of course, further complicated, and oftentimes to a truly mind-boggling extent, by the intensely citational (*tsitatnyi*) nature of many modernist texts — just

---

7   Originally in Julia Kristeva, *La Révolution du langage poétique* (Paris: Seuil, 1974), 59–60. See discussion in Toril Moi, ed., *The Kristeva Reader* (Oxford: Basil Blackwell, 1986), 36–37.

8   Roland Barthes, *Image-Music-Text*, trans. Stephen Heath (London: Fontana, 1977), 124–48.

9   See Roland Barthes, *The Pleasure of the Text*, trans. Richard Miller (New York: Hill and Wang, 1975), 14, on the difference between a "text of bliss" (*jouissance*) and a "text of pleasure" (*plaisir*) as well as discussion in Graham Allen, *Intertextuality* (London and New York: Routledge, 2000), 90–91.

10   Gerard Genette, *Palimpsests: Literature in the Second Degree*, trans. Jane E. Lewin and Claude Doubinsky (Lincoln: University of Nebraska Press, 1997), 83–84; Michael Riffaterre, *Semiotics in Poetry* (Bloomington: Indiana University Press, 1978), 63–64; Allen, *Intertextuality*, 97–132.

11   Kiril Taranovsky, *Essays on Mandel'štam* (Cambridge: Harvard University Press, 1976), 18: "If we define the context as a set of texts which contain the same or a similar image, the subtext may be defined as an already existing text (or texts) reflected in a new one. There are four kinds of subtexts: (1) that which serves as a simple impulse for the creation of an image; (2) *zaimstvovanie po ritmu i zvučaniju* (borrowing of a rhythmic figure and the sounds contained therein); (3) the text which supports or reveals the poetic message of a later text; (4) the text which is treated

think about Mandelstam's and Eliot's poetry or Joyce's and Nabokov's prose. Is such allusion or reminiscence (what Taranovsky defines in a more precise way as "subtext"[11]) merely decorative or playful, or does it have some more significant role in, as it were, "emplotting" the author's stance to his material and to his life as seen through his work? I'll return to these issues briefly at the end of my talk.

The other very loud voice in this discussion of intentionality is of course Harold Bloom, who has come in the magnificent excess of his latest works to resemble more his hero Falstaff than any doubting Hamlet of postmodernism. Applying a Freudian optic of filial struggle against paternal domination, and shifting the terms of debate from biology to poetry, Bloom has forced readers to rethink the whole issue of influence. And indeed, with his astonishing recall of virtually the entire western canon and his love of romantic overstatement, Bloom has come closer than anyone in demonstrating the essential *psychomachia* at work in modern poetry — how a Milton challenges a Wordsworth and Keats; a Shelley a Browning and Yeats; an Emerson a Whitman and Stevens. Thanks to Bloom, no longer is the poet being influenced a passive receptacle of prior tradition; now that poet, in order be "born" in his context of belatedness, must overcome the past, his poetic father or fathers, by remaking it in his own image. And to become this strong poet in an overcrowded world he wields as his weapons what Bloom terms "revisionary ratios," the "swervings" from the precursor or the "emptyings-out" of his being before the fullness of the precursor's, so that he can recreate himself as something even greater than that with which he is competing. To be fair, Bloom has of course moved on in the decades since the original publication of *Anxiety of Influence* (1973), and it is true that today he tries on numerous occasions to challenge the very Freudian model on which he built his own, but it is too late.[12] He himself has become a captive of his own belatedness. Bloom's core arguments that poetry writing is itself a disease[13] and that after Dante

polemically by the poet. The first two do not necessarily contribute to our better understanding of a given poem. However, (2) may be combined with (3) and/or (4), and (3) and (4) may, in their turn, be blended. It is evident that the concept of context and subtext may overlap in cases of self-quotations and autoreminiscences."

12   Harold Bloom, *Breaking the Vessels* (Chicago: University of Chicago Press, 1982), 64: "The unconscious turns out alas not to be structured like a language, but to be structured like *Freud's* language, and the ego and superego, in their conscious aspects, are structured like Freud's own texts, for the very reason that they *are* Freud's texts. We have become Freud's texts, and the *Imitatio Freudi* is the necessary pattern for the spiritual life of our time." This sounds very much like the Derrida of *Mal d'Archive: une impression freudienne* (1995), translated by Eric Prenowitz as *Archive Fever: A Freudian Impression* (Chicago: University of Chicago Press, 1996). See Derrida, *Archive Fever*, 30–31.

13   "If influence were health, who could write a poem? Health is stasis" (Harold Bloom, *The Anxiety of Influence* [Oxford: Oxford University Press, 1973], 95).

western poetry as a celebratory "sharing with others" model is replaced by poetry as a solipsistic "being with oneself" model (Bloom 1973, 123) are in my judgment significantly wrong-headed, way too Freudian (culture = neurosis), and yet another example of the critic going over the top with his romantic bluster.[14] To say that the struggle that goes into writing a poem is a sign of disease is to look at the evolution of intelligent life in a rather perverse way. Likewise, to see the struggle with authority as being verbal or poetic *tout court*, as opposed to political or social or economic, is to exclude a very large portion of any person's, including a poet's, experience.

Now, in the second part of my talk let us see what happens on a practical level when we engage a set of specific texts by a specific author. My idea is to find out, given the givens, if we can get at a more workable understanding of intention. At the conclusion of my comments I will return to Lotman's notion of inner biography as an archaeological restoration project and I will suggest how the problem of intertextuality, influence, and authorial intention is itself profoundly historicized. My examples will come from Pushkin and they will involve two sources. First, his relationship with his greatest contemporary European rival Lord Byron, and second, two texts, one from pagan antiquity and one from the Bible (or biblical tradition in the arts), that are used by Pushkin to "read" his inner life against contemporary expectations (including the famous "Don Juan List" (*Don-zhuanskii spisok*) and to find a way through his Byronic apprenticeship to something beyond and unmistakably his own.

Example No. 1 is a planned article on the life of Byron that Pushkin began in 1835, but never finished.

> It is said that Byron valued his genealogy more than his creative works. A most understandable feeling! The brilliance of his ancestors and the honors he inherited from them elevated the poet; on the other hand, the fame that he acquired himself brought him petty insults, which often humiliated the noble baron, subjecting his name to the whim of rumor. [...] It is worth noting that Byron never mentioned the domestic circumstances surrounding his childhood, finding them humiliating. Little Byron learned to read and write at school in Aberdeen. In his classes he was among the worst students, distinguishing himself more in games. His school-fellows attest that he was a sportive, hot-tempered, grudge-bearing boy, always ready

---

14 Bloom, *Anxiety*, 123.

to fight and repay an old insult. [...] His first years, spent in meager circumstances not in keeping with his birth, under the supervision of a temperamental mother as unreasonable in her caresses as she was in her fits of anger, had a powerful influence on his entire life. [...] At the very moment of his birth Byron's leg was injured, and he remained lame his entire life. Nothing could compare with his rage on the occasion when Mistress Byron scolded him by calling him a *lame little boy* [*khromoi mal'chishka*]. Even though he was handsome he imagined himself to be a monster and avoided the society of people he didn't know well, as he feared their scornful glance. It was this flaw that strengthened his desire to distinguish himself in all exercises requiring physical strength and agility.[15]

Pushkin's Byronic apprenticeship, especially with regard to his Southern Poems written in the early 1820s, is now a commonplace in the scholarly literature and has been studied by Zhirmunsky and many others. There are also numerous instances in Pushkin's writing where he mentions Byron and his works directly and obviously, in a quite Bloomian way, attempts to distance himself from what Byron had already accomplished and what he, Pushkin, was doing that was different. Several well-known examples: his letter to Vyazemsky on the death of Byron where he extols the somber greatness of the latter's autobiographical heroes but criticizes his rapid decline and repetitiveness (June 24 or 25, 1824); his comments to Bestuzhev-Marlinsky about how his new novel-in-verse has "nothing in common" with *Don Juan* (March 24, 1825); his speaker's droll insistence at the beginning of *Onegin* that he is different from his Byronic hero and that some poets, as opposed to the creator of *Childe Harold*, can actually write about something other than themselves.[16]

But this 1835 passage, written late in life, is of an entirely different order. For it brings us as close as we can get to Pushkin actually talking about himself. (The loophole here is that he can talk about himself because he is talking about another.) Nearly every detail he singles out from his source (Thomas Moore) is something that, *mutatis mutandis*, affected him deeply as well: a noble ancestry that is ridiculed in the press (the Bulgarin episode where it was alleged the poet's African great-grandfather was purchased by Peter the Great for a bottle of rum); a childhood with little money and much domestic turmoil that was perceived as not in keeping with his heritage and that he preferred not to discuss; a very

---

15 A.S. Pushkin, *Polnoe sobranie sochinenii*, ed. V. D. Bonch-Bruevich et al., 17 vols. (Moscow: Akademiia Nauk SSSR, 1937–1959), 11:275–78. Referred hereafter as "*Pss*."

16 *Pss*, 13:99, 155; 6:29.

difficult and unpredictable mother; the "mark of Cain" that was Byron's clubfoot and Pushkin's "African" ugliness and that Pushkin's mother, like Byron's, would attack him with when she lost control of herself; the desultory performance at school coupled with the fierce urge to excel at sports and games; the sensitivity and the wounded *amour-propre* that caused both boys to get in trouble with their mates even though they were good-hearted and generous at base; etc., etc. Let it be said that in this passage Pushkin shows no fear of "imitating" Byron (again, the facts of Byron's life are technically not his, and that itself makes him feel safe, more "open" as it were). It is simply that he sees defining traits and circumstances that "explain" his own excesses and will to succeed to him. Are we being too Freudian here, parsing what is there by referring to what is not (Pushkin speaking in *propria persona*)? No, I don't think so. The details from Moore have too much potential for self-referentiality (there are others I could have cited), which may explain why Pushkin never went farther with the article. In any event, when in a matter of months the poet is lying on his deathbed and wracked with pain from the bullet lodged in his abdomen and the doctor tells him to scream out if it helps and the patient answers "*Net, ne nado, zhena uslyshit, i smeshno zhe eto, chtoby etot vzdor menia peresilil!* [No, I oughtn't, my wife would hear, and anyway it's ridiculous to let this nonsense get the better of me],"[17] he is, even at the end, the boy Byron refusing to be called *khromoi mal'chishka*.

However, Pushkin knew in his bones he could not be Byron, not even a Russian Byron. Despite some similar character vectors, their creative paths had to separate. At this point we both need Bloom and we need to guard ourselves against him. For Pushkin came to understand that there was something about his life as a poet and a Russian that could no longer work creatively with the Byronic model. It was not an issue of linguistic priority (Bloom's point) but of experiential truth — the truth of failed revolutionary movements (Byron's radicalism and Greek misadventure) seen from a "Russian" point of view and, as important if not more so, the truth of failed human relationships involving erotic love (the affair with Elizaveta Vorontsova) and male friendship (the trust placed in Alexander Raevsky). The chief lesson of Pushkin's southern sojourn was the pain of betrayal; and the chief creative lesson of that lesson was the inapplicability of the Byronic model of behavior (the demonic outcast) to Pushkin's metapoetic thinking after that. In *Eugene Onegin* especially, but in many other works

[17] Stella Abramovich, *Predystoriia poslednei dueli Pushkina* (St. Petersburg: Petropolis, 1994), 302.

as well, the main thrust after 1824 (when Pushkin leaves the south and goes to northern exile in Mikhailovskoe) is that the Byronic character, his "pose" to the surrounding world, is a dead end. The notion that the past has blighted and frozen one's feelings, that the English "spleen" can become the Russian *khandra*, is a psychological position that Pushkin can't live with. If women, say his own beloved Tatiana, fall in love with the Byronic hero, their warmth chasing his coldness, then it is a game he, whether narrator or lyric speaker, can no longer play. Neither does it translate into his actual biography (the Vorontsova-Raevsky triangle), however much aspects of that biography are themselves "aestheticized" (e.g., Pushkin and Raevsky used to refer to Vorontsova in their private language as "Tatiana"), nor does it translate into his treatment of life events in his art. From now on those characters in his works that are most alive are the ones who, while knowing the literary expectations of their behavior, act other than their role-playing would dictate, which fact makes them even more alluring, more aesthetically pleasing. This is especially true of Pushkin's women characters.

What model did Pushkin use to replace the Byronic one? For that we need to proceed to *Example No. 2*: an excerpt from one of the original opening stanzas of chapter 4 of *Eugene Onegin*. These stanzas were not included in the final version of the novel but were published separately as *Zhenshchiny* [Women] (wr. 1824–26 in Mikhailovskoe, pub. 1827). After describing in the hottest language how on the one hand his life has been "poisoned" by the *izmena* (betrayal) of the beautiful woman who seemed to love him, the speaker presents the other hand:

>То вдруг я мрамор видел в ней,
>Перед мольбой Пигмалиона
>Еще холодный и немой,
>Но вскоре жаркий и живой.[18]

>Then suddenly I saw in her that marble
>Which before Pygmalion's entreaties
>Is still cold and mute
>But is soon to be warm and alive.

Pygmalion was, in Ovid's poetic rendering, the legendary king of Cyprus who, disappointed in love ("Pygmalion loathed the vices given by nature / To women's hearts"), created a statue of such beauty ("Meanwhile he carved the snow-white ivory / With happy skill; he gave it a beauty greater / Than any woman's") that he became enamoured of it ("The

[18] *Pss*, 6:592.

sculptor / Marvelled, and loved his beautiful pretense") and prayed to Aphrodite to give him a wife resembling his creation. Aphrodite not only heeded the supplicant, she gave Pygmalion precisely *his own statue* come to life:

> [Pygmalion] went to his ivory image,
> Lay on its couch and kissed it. It grew warm.
> He kissed again and touched the ivory breast.
> The ivory softened, and its carven firmness
> Sank where he pressed it, yielded like the wax
> Which in the sunlight takes a thousand shapes
> From moulding fingers, while use makes it useful.
> Pygmalion was aghast and feared his joy,
> But like a lover touched his love again.
> It was a body, beating pulse and heart.
> Now he believed and in an ardent prayer
> Gave thanks to Venus: pressed his mouth at last
> To a living mouth. The maiden felt his kiss—
> She blushed and trembled: when she raised her eyes
> She saw her lover and heaven's light together.[19]

This, I would argue, becomes Pushkin's signature myth, the one he uses to "read" his creative life against the frozen emotion of Byronism.[20] He needs to be loved, not because he is a poet, but because he is a man. His prayers are not literary, they are real. The *khromoi mal'chishka* cannot get what he needs simply through an act of will; he needs help. And he gets this help from Ovid's pagan story of miraculous change (metamorphosis), where the goddess of love comes to the rescue, and the Bible's parallel story of prayers being answered, where the Christian goddess of love sends him, the undeserving sinner, his own Madonna. Which leads us to *Example Nos. 3 and 4*: first, an excerpt from an exceptionally private (and obviously never published) poem Pushkin wrote about his wife at the time of their marriage (1831):

> О, как мучительно тобою счастлив я,
> Когда, склоняяся на долгие моленья,
> Ты предаешься мне нежна без упоенья,
> Стыдливо-холодна, восторгу моему
> Едва ответствуешь, не внемлешь ничему
> И оживляешься потом все боле, боле —
> И делишь наконец мой пламень поневоле![21]

---

19 L.R. Lind, ed., *Latin Poetry in Verse Translation* (Boston: Houghton Mifflin, 1957), 164–65. The translation here is Gilbert Highet's. The original Latin is found in Ovid, *Metamorphoses*, trans. Frank Justus Miller, 2 vols. (Cambridge: Harvard University Press, 1951), 2:80–82. Pushkin had at least three different editions of Ovid, two in French and one in Latin, in his library as catalogued by Modzalevsky (B.L. Modzalevskii, "Biblioteka A. S. Pushkina: bibliograficheskoe opisanie," *Pushkin i ego sovremenniki. Materialy i issledovaniia* [1910] 9–10:304).

20 For more on Pushkin's use of the Pygmalion myth, especially around the time of his

> O, how tormentingly through you am I [made] happy,
> When, bending to my insistent pleas,
> You give yourself to me sweetly, without rapture,
> Modestly-cold, you barely respond
> To my ecstasy, you heed nothing,
> And then, more and more, you come to life,
> Until at last, involuntarily, you share my flame!

Note *la tranquille indifférence* of the statuesque Natalie, as Pushkin describes her in a letter to his future mother-in-law,[22] who comes to (erotic) life not because she wants to (*ponevole*), but because she feels his need (the *dolgie molen'ia*, longstanding pleas, which are related etymologically to prayers) and this turns the ivory of perfect form into the pliable warmth (the wax in Ovid) of human response.

Then there is the Christian counterpart, more suitable for the eyes of his bride, where the perfection (Perugino's Virgin, which was the occasion for the poem) loves because that is its essential nature, and where the sight of the *prechistaia*, "most pure," Madonna calls up in the poet's mind his own "*chisteishei prelesti chisteishii obrazets* [the purest model of purest charm]." *Example No. 4*:

> Исполнились мои желания. Творец
> Тебя мне ниспослал, тебя, моя Мадонна,
> Чистейшей прелести чистейший образец.[23]
>
> My desires have been fulfilled. The Creator
> Has sent you down to me, you, my Madonna,
> The purest model of purest charm.

Example No. 5 involves Don Guan's confession to Dona Anna at the end of *The Stone Guest* [*Kamennyi gost'*], right before he is confronted by the Commendatore and taken down to hell (these words were also written in the Boldino autumn of 1830, immediately before Pushkin's marriage, and never published in his lifetime):

> Так, Разврата
> Я долго был покорный ученик,
> Но с той поры, как вас увидел я,
> Мне кажется, я весь переродился.
>
> For all too many years
> I've been the most devoted slave of Lust;
> But ever since the day I saw your face
> I've been reborn, returned once more to life.[24]

impending marriage, see David Bethea, *Realizing Metaphors: Alexander Pushkin and the Life of the Poet* (Madison: University of Wisconsin Press, 1998), 89–117. Basically I argue, building on Jakobson's famous study but also departing from it, that at this fraught moment Pushkin was thinking of two statues come to life simultaneously: the female one representing grace and answering the lonely poet's needs and the male one representing punishment and come to claim the poet for his past sins. See Chapter 3 of the present volume.

21 *Pss*, 3:213.
22 *Pss*, 14:76.
23 *Pss*, 7:168.
24 *Pss*, 7:168.

The Pushkin of the Boldino autumn is concerned above all with the *unlikely in love*: the grizzled Mazepa who is loved by the young Maria (*Poltava*), the black warhorse Othello who is loved by the white and gentle Desdemona — both texts mentioned in another work of that same Boldino autumn ("Refutations of Criticisms").[25] For it is clear that the aging bridegroom and great-grandson of Peter's jealous blackamoor has much on his mind. The Boldino autumn is also the time when Pushkin returns to the Byronic model in three different genres with three different amorous configurations: the *prose tale*—Alexei Berestov who only pretends to be dark and brooding and wears a death's-head ring as an affectation but in fact is a good-natured lad who falls in love with the *maiden* Liza Muromskaya, herself quickly blossoming into much more than her role-playing in "Mistress into Maid" ("Baryshnia-krest'ianka"); *the novel-in-verse* — Onegin who, now exposed to the heroine as a mere "imitation," a "Muscovite in Harold's cloak," at last changes because of the change he notices in the *married* Tatiana; and *the dramatic sketch/"little tragedy"* — the *sushchii demon* (utter demon) and *pokornyi uchenik Razvrata* [devoted slave of Lust] who pays suit to the angelic *widow* in *The Stone Guest*.

In this respect, the story of Don Juan, who supplied Byron with one of his most notorious heroes and characteristic poses, is played out in *The Stone Guest* as yet another reworking of the Pygmalion myth ("Ever since I saw your face / I've been reborn" is the metamorphosis), with the following important differences. First, the statue come to life out of love undergoes a magnificently sacrilegious reversal: the "godless" (*bezbozhnyi*) Guan begins his seduction of Dona Anna by telling her, in the guise of a strangely voluble monk, that he would gladly take her husband's place in the grave if her "black tresses" would enfold the "pale marble" of his final resting place and her "heavenly breath" and "tears of love" would warm and water it.[26] In other words, the statuesque beauty, cool and chaste in her widowhood, unwittingly becomes the source of desire and the melter of marble. Second, Pygmalion's erotic creation is tragically counterbalanced in this season of dread by the animated statue of death (the humiliated husband come to take the miscreant down to hell for his past, and now present, crimes). That the living statue is the poet's own creation, so to speak, is confirmed in the other plot of love and marital fidelity being completed simultaneously: the concluding chapter eight (originally nine) of *Eugene Onegin*, where the village miss, Tatiana, undergoes a "miraculous" metamorphosis to *comme il faut* high-society princess *and* muse incarnate, so that her graceful

---

25 *Pss*, 11:158-59.
26 *Pss*, 7:154.

presence now outshines even that of the legendary Nina Voronskaya, with her marble beauty (*mramornaia krasa*).²⁷ In this transposition of the *Stone Guest* plot, Pushkin places the husband (the general), now neither dead nor cuckolded, in the virtuous and departing wife's boudoir at the climactic moment when the failed hero freezes on the spot: "She [Tatiana] leaves. There stands Eugene / As though thunderstruck."²⁸

Thus, in the erotic space of the Boldino autumn, as the poet contemplates being given Aphrodite's gift of his beautiful statue/muse come to life, he also imagines the full weight of his past crimes. Indeed, these crimes seem to be replayed when Guan, who being himself cannot help but enjoy an opportunity for male rivalry, *brings the other statue to life as well* by having Leporello invite it to take up its humiliatingly "erect" post and then refer to it, following the gender *statúia*, as *oná* (she)—the ultimate put-down. In this sense, the one statue ("female" grace) cannot exist without the other statue ("male" retribution) — hence the tragedy. As the ecstatic Guan says to this woman who has fallen for him despite his past, "It's true, isn't it, he [Guan] was described to you / As a villain, a monster; O, Dona Anna, / Rumor, perhaps, has not been altogether wrong, / [And] perhaps much evil weighs heavy / On his weary conscience."²⁹ What I am suggesting is that the Pushkin of *The Stone Guest* is *both* the Guan hoping to be reborn and the husband (his new role) protecting what is his by right. And his dialogic counterpart? She is *both* the pagan living statue that comes to know passion (Ovid) *and* the spiritualized Christian beauty that confers grace through compassion/mercy (Dona Anna become Madonna). When the recently married Pushkin wrote to Pletnev that "This state [marriage] is so new to me that it seems I have been reborn [*chto kazhetsia, ia pererodilsia*],"³⁰ he was repeating, with the same joyous surprise, the sentiments of his hero.

To conclude, the psychic mechanisms underwriting the works of the mature Pushkin lie somewhere between the Bloomian notion of influence ("strong," Oedipally challenged poets finding ways to say something new outside the shades/shadows of great precursors) and the depersonalized notion of intertextuality (a borrowing that is purely linguistic or "philological" and exists in the absence of poetic fears, resentments, and "dodgings"). Thus as Pushkin, in that exceptional Boldino autumn, passed from poet to prose writer, illicit paramour to lawful husband, dreamer of muses to one who had to live daily with a muse-like beauty come to life, he had as his best man the Byron who could no longer stand in for him, the Byron

27 *Pss*, 6:172.
28 *Pss*, 6:189.
29 *Pss*, 7:168.
30 *Pss*, 14:154–55.

who could be his foil but not his true self. That true self needed the help of a different set of texts (Pygmalion, Madonna), neither one situated in historical time, to read his way through the impasse, as personal and private as it was artistic and poetic, of his Byronic apprenticeship. Yes, Pushkin "overcame" Byron by creating something different, which is Bloom's point. But where Bloom gets it wrong is the strict Freudian nature of the struggle: Pushkin didn't turn to these other mythological or sacred texts because he was trying to defeat his rival; he turned to them because he needed to as a human being. The authenticity of what one wishes for in one's unhappiness coming to life or the sort of love that doesn't question the past or the motives of the supplicant is not usefully thought of as a literary pose or a concern for fame or external validation. The same scepticism holds for the fear of committing the intentional fallacy: how can we speak of these texts accurately without referring to aspects of Pushkin's biography outside them? There is no "art" that exists in noble, uncontaminated isolation from the "life." Even poets without biographies have them, only those biographies are conducted under a "minus sign" (think of Mallarmé the unapproachable dice-thrower or the Brodsky who tried so hard to pretend that the dramatic aspects of his pre-exile life were not important). Lotman is right: all we can do is to try to conduct the most meticulous restoration projects, keeping in mind that the only real unit of measure is a human life and to bring that life back one needs, again as Lotman tells us, both scholarly rigor and imagination.

We are fortunate in the case of Pushkin, a pre-modern, that the tension between intertextuality and influence tends to involve "plots" (the Pygmalion story), so that the relationship between a life outside the text and one inside it is always on the brink of being semanticized, animated as it were. When we come to the great modern poets, Mandelstam above all, pieces of prior texts (their "citational" quality) often seem to just be there, which may itself be a sign of Mandelstam's belatedness and his notion that to know him, the *raznochinets*, you have to know the books, not so much the personalities behind the books, on his bookshelf. But even this is overstatement: Dante, Villon, Pushkin, Charlie Chaplin — Mandelstam did read his story through theirs. In other words, to return to my own point of departure, intertextuality itself needs to be understood as historically situated. Mandelstam's life is so thoroughly embedded in, suffused with, literary and cultural texts that when he says "yesterday has not yet been born"[31] or "only the moment of recognition is sweet to

---

[31] Osip Mandel'shtam, *Sobranie sochinenii*, ed. B. A. Filippov and G. P. Struve, 3 vols (Washington and New York: Inter-Language Literary Associates, 1967–1971), 2:224.

us "(*I sladok nam lish' uznavan'ia mig*),"³² it is difficult if not impossible to know where to start with our notion of Bloomian competition. Again, where does life end and art begin? "*Vse bylo v star', vse povtoritsia snova*"³³ [Everything has been long ago, everything will happen again]: is the poet complaining or is he rejoicing?

Two final caveats, these from the hermeneutics people (i.e., those that study not interpretation per se, but the theory of interpretation). E. D. Hirsch urges us to keep track of the difference between the "meaning" of a verbal artifact, which is invariable, and its "significance," which involves "the relationship of verbal meaning to something outside this meaning" (i.e., a context), and which expands and changes over time.³⁴ The faculty that governs meaning is "understanding," while the faculty that governs significance is "judgment." In Hirsch's view it is criticism's task "to determine significance in texts."³⁵ Opposed to the line in the sand drawn by the intentional fallacy crowd and their postmodern adepts, Hirsch stoutly maintains that "*only authorial intent supplies a valid criterion for meaning*" and that "a valid interpretation is one that corresponds to the meaning represented by the text."³⁶ And Paul Ricoeur, who has been one of the most articulate opponents of the Freudian episteme, suggests that there are basically two, and only two, models of interpretation: the first, aligned with Rudolph Bultmann and his "hermeneutics of faith," attempts to "recapture or recollect meaning," and the second, aligned with Marx, Nietzsche, Freud and their "hermeneutics of suspicion," "tear[s] away masks and reveal[s] false consciousness."³⁷ In discussing these texts by Pushkin it has been my contention that their meaning may trace back to prior texts in Ovid and the New Testament (something we need to "understand"), but their significance cannot be appreciated without reference to Pushkin's failure as Byronic hero (a matter of "judgment"). Likewise, the sort of interpretation that gets closest to what Pushkin is about in these works is not the one that "tears away masks and reveals

---

32 Mandel'shtam, *Sobranie sochinenii*, 1:73.

33 Ibid.

34 Robert Holub, "Hermeneutics: Twentieth Century," in *The Johns Hopkins Guide to Literary Theory and Criticism*, ed. Michael Groden and Martin Kreiswirth (Baltimore: Johns Hopkins University Press, 1994), 381.

35 Holub, "Hermeneutics," 381. See the lucid discussion in E.D. Hirsch, Jr., *The Aims of Interpretation*. (Chicago: University of Chicago Press, 1976), 1–13 and 79–81, where he traces the relativism in much current theory and practice in literary studies to the basic distinction between Husserl's notion of "bracketing" (the very possibility of demarcation means we can make a division between meaning and context/situation) and Heidegger's contrasting idea of the "hermeneutic circle," which prevents any knowledge of the part from being apprehended without some pre-existing sense (preunderstanding) of the whole, hence the relativistic "creep" or "seepage."

36 Holub, "Hermeneutics," 381.

37 On Ricoeur's early use of the "school of suspicion" (*l'école du soupçon*) to describe Freud's hermeneutic stance, see Paul Ricoeur, *De l'interprétation: Essai sur Freud*. (Paris: Seuil, 1965), 40–44.

false consciousness" (i.e., the Freudian-Bloomian angle that focuses on Byron-induced anxiety) but the one that tries to "recapture or recollect [the original] meaning" (i.e., what Pushkin needed that the Byronic model couldn't supply).

PART II
Pushkin the Poet, Pushkin the Thinker

Chapter 7   Of Pushkin and Pushkinists[1]

Introductions to books and collections about Alexander Pushkin tend to begin, especially when their origin is not Russian, with *de rigueur* nods to the poet's massive presence in, and seminal influence on, the native culture. Such expository scaffolding falls under the category of preemptive advertising for a figure who, outside his context and more importantly outside his language, has difficulty translating. Thus, from the operas of Glinka, Tchaikovsky, Musorgsky and Rimsky-Korsakov to the stylish illustrations and set designs of Benois, Bilibin, and Dobuzhinsky; from endlessly anthologized paintings by Kiprensky and Repin to ghosts of allusion in better known works by Dostoevsky and Nabokov; from the fact that the tsar's summer residence (Tsarskoe Selo) was renamed after the poet because he once studied on its grounds to the fact that to this day countless schoolchildren across the land memorize pages of his verse by heart — all these phenomena point to why, as previous witnesses of the myth in the making have attested, Pushkin is "our everything" (Apollon Grigorev) and the indisputable "sun of [Russian] poetry" (V.F. Odoevsky). Yet, for all the Russians across the cultural and political spectrum who view their national poet as the equivalent of Dante, Shakespeare, Goethe, and Thomas Jefferson rolled into one, there are just as many in the English-speaking world who, nodding back in agreement with W.H. Auden, cannot see what all the fuss is about.

1 First appeared as Introduction to *The Pushkin Handbook* (Madison: University of Wisconsin Press, 2006), xvii–xlii. NB. since this piece was originally conceived as a frontespiece to *The Pushkin Handbook* as well as a historical survey of the discipline of Pushkin studies, I have left in place most of the formal "scaffolding" relating to the larger volume.

In this essay I propose to take a somewhat different tack. For those who already know and appreciate Pushkin, I will not presume to preach to the choir. (In any event, Pushkin does not need us; we need him. Or, to paraphrase Harold Bloom, who has put the source of his own anxious logic on the couch, it is our Russian Shakespeare who has invented our Russian human, and not the other way around.) For those who don't, I will not send them to Tchaikovky, nor will I try to impress readers with the magnitude of "our everything" by showing how it has inspired other arts and media, thereby talking around and about—but not really to—the one area that is Pushkin's absolute native realm: Russian poetry. What Pushkin accomplished in twenty short years in Russian poetry was to give his readers an inner world (its own sort of declaration of independence) that was to keep on giving. That world was not without its codes and formal constraints, indeed those constraints were a priori absolutely necessary and acknowledged as such, and yet it was a world that, once entered, pulled the visitor forward, creating cognition, cognizing creation. At each and every level of this constructed world, from its punctuation, prosody, and stylistic register to its expectations about genre, character, plot, theme, and authorship, it projected the tense hovering of a consciousness becoming ever more aware of itself and of choices that are made somewhere between fixity (the mold) and freedom (the open space of pure desire). It is this Pushkin, the Pushkin that has served as touchstone and launching pad for some of the most painstaking research and brilliant thinking by Russian intellectuals over the past two centuries, which I now set out to sketch in the following remarks.

Beginning from the middle of the nineteenth century and continuing up to the recent past there have been somewhere between fifty and sixty scholars (for simplicity's sake, I speak here of those *writing in Russian* and *no longer living*[2]) who could be classified as "serious" Pushkinists (those devoting the majority of their time and energy to Pushkin studies proper) or as authors (otherwise non-specialists) of important or "serious" monographs on the poet. These individuals can in turn be classified into groups based on their epistemological points of departure and scholarly traditions—in other words, on their ways of *coming at* the phenomenon of "Pushkin." Thus, in the second half of the nineteenth and early years of the twentieth centuries we find the "foundational" Pushkinists: such manuscript compilers, editors, and path-breaking biographers as P.V. Annenkov (1813–1887),[3] P.I. Bartenev (1829–1912), Ia.K. Grot (1812–1893), P.A. Efremov

2 For a survey of more recent Pushkin studies that takes into account work done in Russia and the west since the publication of *Pushkin. Itogi i problemy izucheniia* (Pushkin: Achievements and Problems in the Scholarship) in 1966, see the contribution by Svetlana Evdokimova and Vladimir Golstein in *The Pushkin Handbook*, 609–38.

3 Annenkov's edition of *Sochineniia Pushkina*, in seven volumes, was published in 1855–1857. It is often called the first *nauchnoe* ("scholarly," "critical") edition of the poet in the sense that the editor went to

(1830–1907), V.E. Yakushkin (1856–1912), and L.N. Maikov (1839–1900). Within this group Annenkov occupies a special place as editor of the first "critical"[3] collected works and author of *Materialy dlia biografii A.S. Pushkina* (Materials for the Biography of A. S. Pushkin, 1855), the traditional starting point for all those interested in the poet's life;[4] Bartenev, on the other hand, is Annenkov's foil — an early empiricist whose notion about the hard facts of Pushkin's life and works came in conflict with his rival's more narratively integrative and "emplotted" approach.[5] Grot is the great literary historian and academician who, among other things, culled important data about Pushkin's lyceum years.[6] Yakushkin made a detailed description of the contents of Pushkin's working notebooks housed in the Rumiantsev Museum in Moscow and compared his findings to those of Annenkov and Bartenev.[7] Maikov's role in this early cast of characters is particularly distinguished for the systematic way he arranged manuscripts and traced compositional histories for the first volume (the lyceum verse) of the first "academic" Pushkin,[8] while Efremov is the energetic editor of different late nineteenth and early twentieth century collections of the poet's works. Another visible turn of the century figure is S.A. Vengerov (1855–1920), whose famous "seminars" produced some of the most outstanding Russian literature scholars of the Soviet period. Vengerov edited a massively annotated and lavishly illustrated and produced "Silver Age" Pushkin with the help of the premier specialists (A.S. Iskoz [1880–1968], B.L. Modzalevsky [1874–1928], N.O. Lerner [1877–1934], M.O. Gershenzon [1869–1925], P.E. Shchegolev [1877–1931]) and writers (Briusov, Blok) of the day.[9]

great pains to gather materials, consult with still living family members and friends, and so on. In fact, however, the title of first genuine "academic" Pushkin, published under the auspices of the Imperial Academy of Sciences, is associated with the name L.N. Maikov. Unfortunately Maikov died having overseen only the first volume. See note #7 below.

4   *Materialy dlia biografii A. S. Pushkina* was the first volume in Annenkov's *Sochineniia Pushkina*. A second edition of *Materialy* appeared once more during Annenkov's lifetime, in 1873. See also his *Aleksandr Sergeevich Pushkin v Aleksandrovskuiu epokhu 1799–1826 gg.* (1874).

5   See Bartenev, *O Pushkine* (1992) for a collection of the scholar's major publications on Pushkin. Bartenev's "Rod i detstvo Pushkina" first appeared in *Otechestvennye zapiski* 11.2 (1853): 1–20; "Aleksandr Sergeevich Pushkin. Materialy dlia ego biografii" first appeared in the newspaper *Moskovskie vedomosti* in 1854 (#71, 117, and 119) and 1855 (#142, 144, 145); and "Pushkin v Iuzhnoi Rossii. Materialy dlia ego biografii, sobrannye P. Bartenevym. 1820–1823" first appeared in the newspaper *Russkaia rech'/ Moskovskii vestnik* in 1861 (#85–104).

6   See Ia.K. Grot, *Pushkin, ego litseiskie tovarishchi i nastavniki* (1887) and K. Ia. Grot, *Pushkinskii litsei (1811–1817)* (1911).

7   Iakushkin, "Rukopisi A. S. Pushkina, khraniashchiesia v Rumiantsovskom muzee v Moskve" (1884).

8   *Sochineniia Pushkina* (1899 —). This enterprise (producing the first serious "academic" Pushkin) was continued after Maikov's death by Yakushkin, P.O. Morozov (1854–1920), and N.K. Kozmin (1873–1942), but for various reasons it eventually foundered when a new generation of Pushkinists appeared on the scene after the revolution. In addition to being one of the first genuine experts on Pushkin manuscripts, Maikov was also an informed and perceptive source on the poet's biography. See his *Materialy dlia akademicheskogo izdaniia sochinenii A.S. Pushkina* (1902) and *Pushkin. Biograficheskie materialy i istoriko-literaturnye ocherki* (1899).

The first half of the twentieth century is dominated by a group that has been termed the "positivist" Pushkinists: the archivists, textologists, commentators, and manuscript editors—most significantly, Modzalevsky and his son Leonid (1902–1948), B.V. Tomashevsky (1890–1957) and M. A. Tsiavlovsky (1883–1947), but also others in valuable contributing roles such as D.D. Blagoi (1893–1984), S.M. Bondi (1891–1983), D.P. Yakubovich (1897–1940), N.V. Izmailov (1893–1981), Yu.G. Oksman (1895–1970), and G.O. Vinokur (1896–1947)—who built the modern institution of academic Pushkin studies. Of these, Modzalevsky is the most senior—a transitional figure with links going back to an earlier era. He is known as the motivating force behind the founding of Pushkinskii Dom (Pushkin House, the principal repository for Pushkiniana, including the poet's manuscripts and extant library, in Russia/Soviet Union) as well as an outstanding commentator (along with his son) on Pushkin's letters and diaries and an irreplaceable source on the period (he compiled an archive of some 300,000 note cards on figures related to the Pushkin age).[10] Tomashevsky stands out as the author of the single most authoritative (though at the time of his death still uncompleted) study of Pushkin's life and works, a specialist on the poet's prosody and verse structure, an important taxonomist of concepts central to Pushkin studies (see below), and perhaps the leading and most rigorous exponent of what became known as "Pushkin House" textology (that is, the idea that the preferred text of a work can be reconstructed from all the printed and manuscript copies and that this version, which is able to take into account issues of censorship and previous editorial distortions, can become authoritative even when the poet *published* a different version in his lifetime).[11] Tsiavlovsky, for his part, represents the third leg (what is not covered by either the elder Modzalevsky or Tomashevsky) of the strict empiricist approach—among other things, he and his wife T. G. Tsiavlovskaya-Zenger (1897–1978) spent decades compiling their *letopis'* (chronicle) of Pushkin's life (also uncompleted at the time of their deaths, despite its basis in more than 20,000 note cards), with its pinpointing in time and space of the poet's and his friends' whereabouts, the writing of his and their works (and their internal repetitions and echoes), relevant epistolary exchanges, contemporaneous reactions in the press, and so on.[12] As with so much else during this period of Soviet-style "scientific" scholarship, the Tsiavlovskys' magnum opus did not "connect the dots" between chronicle and narrated biography (although they had many fascinating hunches and potential discoveries they shared among themselves in the pri-

9 *Pushkin*, 6 vols. (St. Petersburg: Brokgauz-Efron, 1907–1915).
10 See, e.g., Modzalevskii, "Biblioteka A. S. Pushkina" (1910), *Dnevnik A. S. Pushkina 1833–1835* (1923), and [Pushkin's] *Pis'ma*, 3 vol. (1926–1953).
11 Among Tomashevsky's most important contributions are *Pushkin: Kniga pervaia (1813–1824)* (1956) and *Pushkin: Kniga vtoraia. Materialy i monografii (1824–1837)* (1961); his "small" Academy edition (in 10 vols.) of the collected works (1949); and *Pushkin: Raboty raznykh let* (1990). Useful information about Soviet textology, including bibliographical references to

vacy of their diaries and correspondence), the implied message being such speculation was either "unscholarly" or "untimely" (as in before its time).

A word should also be said at this point about the publication of the "large" Academy *Polnoe sobranie sochinenii* (Complete Works) from 1937 to 1949, in 17 volumes, with the final reference tome appearing a decade later in 1959.[13] Earlier in the 1930's different trial editions had prepared the way for this huge event: with essentially the same editorial nucleus or some combination thereof (the Tsiavlovskys, Oksman, Tomashevsky, Bondi, Vinokur, and a few others), there appeared one after the other the 6-volume "Krasnaia niva" (Red Cornfield) edition (1930), five 6-volume "gikhlovskie"[14] editions (1931–1937), a 9-volume (small format) "Academia" edition (1935–1936), and a 6-volume "Academia" edition. It was in these various editions that the basic corpus of Pushkin's texts was worked out. And it was during this same period that, under the general editorship of Yakubovich and accompanied by extensive annotations from leading scholars, the seventh volume (Pushkin's drama) of the proposed "large" Academy edition was produced in another trial print run (1935).[15] In any event, when it finally came out the "large" Academy edition displayed all the signal strengths (as well as weaknesses) of the Soviet textological school and was to many that tradition's crowning glory. Its appearance at the height of the Stalinist purges with subsequent volumes coming out during the war years was itself without question a heroic feat that those looking on from the outside can never fully appreciate. On the one hand, the infamous decision by Stalinist bureaucrats to pare away commentaries and contextualizations to a skeletal minimum (i.e., the 1935 "Yakubovich" model was dropped) was a significant loss: here the ostensible reasoning went that it would be a crime (how literal the metaphor in this case!) to lard the words of Russia's national poet on the occasion of the centennial of his death with "needless" information—i.e., we want to read "Pushkin and not Pushkinists." In fact, the real message was that Pushkin scholars and Pushkin studies were themselves under the control of the Party and the new complete works an important political enterprise.

various programmatic pieces by Tomashevsky, Vinokur, Bondi, Yakubovich, and others, is found in Izmailov, "Tekstologiia," in Gorodetskii et al., *Pushkin. Itogi i problemy izucheniia*, 557–610, esp. 559n4.

12 The first volume (covering the years 1799–1826) of *Letopis' zhizni i tvorchestva A. S. Pushkina* appeared in 1951 after Tsiavlovsky's death. Tsiavlovsky's widow Tatiana Grigorevna then continued the work of her husband until her own death in 1978. The project, ultimately in four volumes, was completed and published many years later by N.A. Tarkhova in 1999. The new chronological divisions for the volumes are: 1 (1799–1824), 2 (1825–1828), 3 (1829–1832), 4 (1833–1837).

13 Useful background on the "large" Academy edition and on other aspects of Soviet Pushkin studies can be gleaned from Tomashevskii, "Sovremennye problemy istoriko-literaturnogo izucheniia" (1925); Tsiavlovskii, "Sovetskoe pushkinovedenie" (1947); Domgerr, "Sovetskoe akademicheskoe izdanie Pushkina" (1987).

14 An informal acronym derived from "*Gos*udarstvennoe *i*zdatel'stvo *kh*udozhestvennoi *l*iteratury" (State Publishing House of Artistic Literature).

15 The group of annotators included M.P. Alekseev, Bondi, N.V. Yakovlev, Oksman, A. Slonimsky, Tomashevsky, and Vinokur.

On the other hand, the "large" Academy edition's meticulous reconstruction of the textual histories, including datings, of all the known works of the poet and the arrangement of the latter into a definitive "canon" (what truly belonged to Pushkin and what represented contemporary scholarship's best idea of the text) was a milestone that all subsequent scholars have acknowledged, returned to, and built on.

As an aside to the history of the publication of the "large" Academy edition it is worth mentioning the fate of Yulian Grigorevich Oksman. An excellent scholar as well as ambitious administrator (he was deputy director of Pushkin House in the early 1930s), Oksman in effect oversaw the early stages of the preparation of the new edition. But when he was arrested in November 1936 on political charges and exiled into the camps the bulk of the editorial responsibilities shifted to Moscow and into the hands of Tsiavlovsky. This was clearly a blow not only to the talented Oksman (who upon his return from the camps would be forbidden for years from living in Leningrad and Moscow and would be permanently embittered by his exclusion from the publication he had once played such a prominent role in), but also to the prestige of the Pushkin House in general (another possible "Moscow-St. Petersburg" bone of contention) and to Tomashevsky, who while still active and definitely needed in the editing process saw his role reduced, in particular.[16]

Thereafter, as we enter the second half of the twentieth century, this positivist tradition ripens into the "mature" Pushkinists: a few individuals who stand alone in their excellence and who describe a kind of ultimate flowering of, and implied (and sometimes explicit) cross-fertilization among, the disciplines of textology, theory, and history/biography. In this latter group we meet the imposing trio of N.Ya. Eidelman (1930–1989), the resourceful documentary historian of Pushkin, Karamzin, and the Decembrists;[17] Yu.M. Lotman (1922–1993), the poet's biographer, the conceptual thinker behind the idea of Pushkin as supreme *homo semioticus* (the interplay between linguistic and behavioral codes in his life and works), the provider of illuminating commentaries to Eugene Onegin, and to many the greatest Pushkinist of them all;[18] and V.E. Vatsuro (1935–2000), the superb textologist and reader of Pushkin's lyric verse, the nonpareil expert on literary relations during the Pushkin era, and, again, to many the last and fullest refinement of Pushkin House empirical scholarship.[19] While the methodologies of these three scholars did not often intersect in their works (for example, Vatsuro's impeccable knowledge of sources and textual

---

16   My thanks to Ekaterina Larionova of the Pushkin House for some of the details of this reprise.

17   Eidelman's major works for our purposes are *Poslednii letopisets* (1983), *Pushkin i dekabristy* (1979), *Pushkin: Istoriia i sovremennost' v khudozhestvennom soznanii poeta* (1984), *Pushkin: Iz biografii i tvorchestva* (1987), *Stat'i o Pushkine* (2000). He was also a specialist on the Decembrists, with separate studies of Lunin, Pushchin, and Muravyov-Apostol.

18   Lotman's 1981 biography of Pushkin, his 1980 commentary to *Evgenii Onegin* as well as other important articles and publications have been col-

histories did not permit the sort of code-driven generalizing impulse often found in Lotman's more far-reaching studies, and vice-versa), the findings produced by them were extremely productive, especially when placed in creative juxtaposition with one another.

A second, parallel development in twentieth-century Pushkin studies (here more broadly defined) involves those individuals who, complementing the positivists, provided important new ways to conceptualize Pushkin. These thinkers, most of whom came out of the pre- and post-revolutionary formalist school or were tangentially related to it, were opposed to impressionistic criticism and to traditional "appreciations" of the poet. Their methodology gave the appearance of being rigorously scientific and was highly analytical, while their language was descriptive (the stress tending to fall on "functions" and "devices") and intentionally depersonalized. This does not mean, however, that their discoveries, despite the scientific cloaking, were not often ingenious, even idiosyncratic. Of these individuals, the most remarkable are, beginning with the eldest: R.O. Jakobson (1896–1982), the preeminent formalist-cum-Prague School linguist, whose long article on Pushkin's deployment of sculptural motifs (many autobiographically freighted with anxieties about marriage) in different genres and settings became a model of mature structural analysis;[20] and Yu.N. Tynianov (1894–1943), Jakobson's one-time ally, the Pushkinist and Pushkin period historical novelist who anticipated brilliantly Bloomian anxiety theory with his ideas about parody and about how "archaist" figures such as Katenin and Küchelbecker interacted with the initially "innovative" (Karamzinian) Pushkin, thus forcing him to deepen and complicate his language, his texts, and his characters.[21] From the next, slightly younger generation there is G.A. Gukovsky (1902–1950), perhaps the figure most responsible, as the author of *Pushkin i russkie romantiki* (Pushkin and the Russian Romantics, 1946) and *Pushkin i problemy realisticheskogo stilia* (Pushkin and Problems of the Realistic Style, 1957), for the powerfully (too powerfully) Soviet idea that Pushkin's creative path in the 1820s and 1830s ran ineluctably from

lected in one volume: *Pushkin* (1995).

19 Some of Vatsuro's finest work was done as a compiler, editor, and annotator of texts. Especially impressive in this regard is his painstaking editing of the first volume (*Stikhotvoreniia litseiskikh let, 1813–1817* [1994]) of a new academic Pushkin, which venture unfortunately seems to have stalled after his death. A sampling of his articles on Pushkin and his time are found in *Zapiski kommentatora* (1994) and *Pushkinskaia pora* (2000), but also see his various contributions in *A. S. Pushkin i kniga* (1982); *A. S. Pushkin v vospominaniiakh sovremennikov* (1974); "Arzamas" *Sbornik v dvukh khigakh* (1994); (with M. I. Gillel'son) *Skvoz' "umstvennye plotiny." Iz istorii knigi i pressy pushkinskoi pory* (1972); "Severnye tsvety" (1978) and *Pushkin v prizhiznennoi kritike, 1820–1827* (1996).

20 Jakobson, *Puškin and His Sculturol Myth* (1975); originally appeared in Czech in 1937 as "Socha v simbolice Puškinov" in the journal *Slovo a slovesnost* (#3).

21 See especially Tynianov's influential "Arkhaisty i Pushkin" (1926) in his volume *Pushkin i ego sovremenniki* (1968) and "Pushkin" in *Arkhaisty i novatory* (1929).

romanticism to realism. And from a still younger generation we find the already mentioned Lotman, who built conceptual bridges, in his numerous articles and commentaries on Pushkin, from formalism and structuralism to the "secondary modeling systems" (gambling, dueling, salon rituals, epistolary protocol, dress codes, etc.) of modern semiotics.

Among others contributing to but perhaps not dominating this stream of the "conceptual Pushkin" is L.Ya. Ginzburg (1902–1990), whose interest in the historically determined psychology of literary form bears the imprint of Gukovsky and whose astute comments about the impact of prosaic consciousness (the "verse prosaism"[22]) on the late lyrics of Pushkin (O lirike [On Lyric Verse, 1964]) owe something to her teacher Tynianov's notions about prose and poetry being "deformations" of one another. Then there is Tomashevsky, who coined the phrase "biographical legend" to treat only those facts from a writer's life (here Pushkin's) that have a meaningful place in his art and who, again whether consciously or no feeling the potent teleology of Gukovsky's ideas, saw Pushkin's increased interest in history (his "historicism"[*istorizm*]) as being tied to progress toward "realism."[23] Modern readers need to bear in mind that, inasmuch as Marxist determinism was the only view of history acceptable in the 1930s, those such as Gukovsky and Tomashevsky did not so much "discover" a master plot in Pushkin and his works as give this ready-made "macro" level credence through their subtle formal analyses.

Two important figures whose studies of Pushkin's language related them methodologically if not necessarily ideologically with the formalists are V.V. Vinogradov (1895–1969), the eminent linguist, and Vinokur, one of the founding members of the Moscow Linguistic Circle. Vinogradov's two books *Iazyk Pushkina* (Pushkin's Language, 1935) and *Stil' Pushkina* (Pushkin's Style, 1941) and Vinokur's articles are essential reading for anyone interested in the historical semantics and stylistic layering of Pushkin's verse. As suggested above, Vinokur was also a gifted editor, his textological decipherings of and extensive commentaries to *Boris Godunov* (in the Yakubovich 1935 trial volume) becoming a classic.[24] It goes without saying, however, that virtually all the formalists and "near" formalists, including those not already mentioned such as B.M. Eikhenbaum (1886–1959), V.B. Shklovsky (1893–1984), and V.M. Zhirmunsky (1891–1971; to be discussed below), wrote about Pushkin at one time or other, usually in ways that rubbed against the grain of accepted scholarly opinion. In this respect, it is just as impossible to imagine the sculptural myth study without Roman

22 See discussion in Ginzburg, *O lirike*, 2nd. ed. (Leningrad: Sovetskii pisatel', 1974), 172–242, esp. 215ff.

23 Tomashevskii, "Literatura i biografiia" (1923) and "Istorizm Pushkina" (1954).

24 See Vinokur, *Izbrannye raboty po russkomu iazyku* (1959), *Stat'i o Pushkine* (1999) and *Kommentarii k "Borisu Godunovu" A. S. Pushkina* (1999). The *Boris Godunov* commentaries were first published in 1935 as a trial volume (seven) in the planned "Jubilee" academic edition of the complete works. Vinokur was also an initiating figure in *Slovar' iazyka Pushkina*, 4 vols. (1956–1961).

Jakobson or the notion that literary "corporals" (Katenin) reveal "generals" (Pushkin) without Yury Tynianov as it is Jakobson and Tynianov without "their" Pushkins. Thus Russian cultural and intellectual thought has been infinitely enriched by this formula "Pushkin + scholarly innovation."

Another significant and always hotly debated trend in Pushkin studies has to do with the poet's biography.[25] Pushkin's life has been obsessively pored over by Russians not only because he is Russia's greatest cultural figure but also because, in the poet Vladislav Khodasevich's words, his was "the first Russian biography in which life is organically and consciously merged with art" and because "he was the first to live his life as a poet, and only as a poet, and for that reason perished."[26] What this means in the most basic terms is that virtually from the beginning the border between "fact" and "fiction" in Pushkin's biography has been contested territory. To tell a coherent life of the poet, or even to tell some crucial aspect of it (say, its ending), is to try to explain why things happened the way they did and thus to feel the pull toward interpretive narrative (psychologically emplotted story). Some scholars, among them S.L. Abramovich (1927–1996; on Pushkin's last years), L.P. Grossman (1888–1965), Shchegolev (on the events leading up to Pushkin's duel and death), Ariadna Tyrkova-Williams (1869–1962), and above all Lotman, have achieved this goal better than others.[27] At the same time there are those, most notably Lerner (whose *Trudy i dni* [the poet's "Works and Days," 1903] predated the Tsiavlovskys' project), the Tsiavlovskys, and V.V. Veresaev (1867–1945; the author of the compilatory *Pushkin v zhizni* [Pushkin in Life, 1st ed. 1926]), who have been drawn conceptually toward the opposite pole of pure chronicle (*letopis'*). And then there are those, such as the fine Silver Age thinker and author of *Mudrost' Pushkina* (The Wisdom of Pushkin, 1919) Gershenzon, who take up a principled position "in between." How one interprets, narrativizes, the known facts of Pushkin's life into a compelling yet believable, fully documented and substantiated text is an issue that has not lost its currency up to the present and will doubtless occupy the minds of leading Pushkinists well into the future.

25 An informative synopsis of the different approaches to Pushkin's biography up to 1966 is found in Levkovich, "Biografiia," *Pushkin. Itogi i problemy izucheniia*, 251–302. Although my emphasis in these pages is by design on the Russian language tradition of Pushkin scholarship, there are numerous biographies of the poet in western languages deserving of mention. To cite only English language exemplars: T. J. Binyon's *Pushkin* (2002), Robin Edmonds' *Pushkin: The Man and His Age* (1994), Elaine Feinstein's *Pushkin* (1998), David Magarshack's *Pushkin: A Biography* (1967), Ernest J. Simmons' *Pushkin* (1937), Henri Troyat's *Pushkin* (1950; original in French, 1946), Walter N. Vickery's *Pushkin: The Death of a Poet* (1968), and Serena Vitale's *Pushkin's Button* (1999, original in Italian, 1995). Of these, the recent study by Binyon is the most serious and impressive, while Vitale's highly eccentric treatment of the plots and scandals swirling around the poet in the last year of his life is the most interesting (and stylistically invigorating) reading.

26 Vladislav Khodasevich, "Pamiati Gogolia," *Literaturnye stat'i i vospominaniia*, ed. N. Berberova (New York: Chekhov, 1954), 89.

27 Abramovich, *Pushkin v 1836 godu* (1984) and *Pushkin v 1833 godu* (1994); Grossman, *Pushkin* (1939); Shchegolev, *Duel' i smert' Pushkina* (1916); Tyrkova-Williams, *Zhizn' Pushkina*, 2 vols. (1929, 1948).

Finally, as we survey the varied history of Pushkin studies three additional trends deserve mention. These are the "comparative Pushkinists," the "poet-Pushkinists," and the "metaphysical Pushkinists." As with so much else in twentieth-century Russian literary studies, important work for the first group was undertaken by individuals who got their start in or on the periphery of the formalist camp: Tomashevsky, whose *Pushkin i Frantsiia* (Pushkin and France, 1960) provides comprehensive treatment of Pushkin's intertextual relations with French literature; and Zhirmunsky, whose analysis of the poet's appropriation of Byron (*Bairon i Pushkin* [Byron and Pushkin, 1924]) was groundbreaking for its time. As one might expect, in both cases the authors demonstrably veer away from discussing the psychological mechanisms of "influence," preferring instead to focus on the descriptive results of appropriation: say, the *motifs* Pushkin borrowed from Byron's Oriental tales and then put in play in his Southern poems rather than any "anxiety" he might feel as he attached his own signature to the distinctive characters, plots, and linguistic subtleties of the genre. Other scholars making important contributions to the comparative study of Pushkin include M.P. Alekseev (1896–1981; Shakespeare, Chaucer, English literature), N.V. Yakovlev (1891–1981; English poetry), Yakubovich (Walter Scott), V.V. Sipovsky (1872–1930; Byron and Chateaubriand), and Vatsuro (Dante, French elegy).[28] Once again, the modern reader needs to be reminded how politically delicate, and hence potentially dangerous, the study of Pushkin in a comparative context could be during the Stalinist years. Pushkin is "our" poet, went the party line, and so it did not do to analyze connections that might place his originality in jeopardy, especially when foreign sources were automatically suspect to begin with. Against this forbidding background the accomplishments of someone like Alekseev, who was as meticulous as he was prolific, are all the more noteworthy.

The poet-Pushkinists are a special category: poets and creative writers who, in the seriousness of their essays and books, attempted to rival (and in several cases did rival) the academic Pushkinists. What is particularly noteworthy about the contributions of these individuals is the emphasis placed on Pushkin's *creative thinking* and on the subtle psychoerotic relations between his work and his life. While many poets and prose writers, from Marina Tsvetaeva to Andrei Bitov, have created their versions of "*Moi Pushkin*" (My Pushkin) or have interacted elaborately with the Pushkin myth in their own oeuvres, only four wrote studies that are routinely listed among the accomplishments of professional "Pushkinistika": Anna Akhmatova (1889–1966),

---

28 Alekseev, *Pushkin i mirovaia literatura* (1987) and *Pushkin: Sravnitel'no-istoricheskie issledovaniia* (1972); Iakovlev, *Pushkin v mirovoi literature* (1926); Iakubovich, "Kapitanskaia dochka i romany Val'ter Skotta" (1939), "Predislovie k Povestiam Belkina i povestvovatel'nye priemy Val'ter Skotta" (1926), "Reministsenzii iz Val'ter Skotta v *Povestiakh Belkina*" (1928); Sipovskii, *Pushkin, Bairon i Shatobr'ian* (1899); Vatsuro, "Pushkin i Dante" (1995) and "Frantsuzskaia elegiia XVIII-XIX vekov i russkaia lirika pushkinskoi pory" (1989). Although not strictly comparative (except for the Horatian subtext), Alekseev's greatest contribution

whose pieces on Washington Irving's presence in "The Tale of the Golden Cockerel" and on autobiographical echoes in *The Stone Guest* are scholarly criticism of a high order;[29] Valery Briusov (1873–1924), whose introductory essays for the Vengerov edition on such topics as Pushkin's first love (Ekaterina Bakunina), Pushkin in the Crimea, *Gavriiliada* (The Gabrieliad), *Egipetskie nochi* (Egyptian Nights), and Pushkin's verse technique show extensive knowledge of the subject;[30] Vladislav Khodasevich (1886–1939), perhaps the most serious poet-Pushkinist in the group, a meticulous close reader and aspiring (though ultimately unsuccessful) biographer, with two books (*Poeticheskoe khoziaistvo Pushkina* [Pushkin's Poetic Economy, 1924] and *O Pushkine* [On Pushkin, 1937]—the second based largely on the first) to his credit as well as many superb articles and notes;[31] and Vladimir Nabokov (1899–1977), whose translation of and voluminous commentaries to *Evgenii Onegin* are required reading (along with Lotman's volume) for anyone interested in the novel-in-verse, although the controversial work (especially valuable for its discussion of French sources) tells us as much about the translator and commentator as it does about its subject.[32]

Given the strong bias toward scholarly or "scientific" reasoning among the leading positivists and conceptualists in Pushkin studies, it is perhaps no surprise that the most controversial grouping in the tradition is what I have designated as metaphysical Pushkinists, a term that encompasses so-called *filosofskaia kritika* ("philosophical criticism") and that was adumbrated in several of the more famous pronouncements of Gogol and Dostoevsky but in fact goes back to the great turn-of-the-century religious thinker Vladimir Solovyov. In this tradition the question inevitably rises of Pushkin's calling—is it strictly poetic, or is it somehow more—religious, messianic, prophetic? Are his poems works of art *tout court* or are they semi-sacred texts and the speaker a vessel through which a higher power communicates? By the same token, this way of looking at Pushkin as the answer to Russia's self-doubts and as an expression of *Christian* (Orthodox) theodicy specific to the Russian people and the Russian nation has led to the establishment

---

as Pushkinist is his monumental *Stikhotvorenie Pushkina "Ia pamiatnik sebe vozdvig..."* (1967). This notion of the "comparative Pushkin" has been particularly actively studied in recent years in the works of such scholars as A.A. Dolinin (Pushkin and English literature), Yu.D. Levin (Pushkin and Shakespeare), and L.I. Volpert (Pushkin and French literature).

29 Akhmatova, "Posledniaia skazka Pushkina" (1933) and "Kamennyi gost' Pushkina" (1958).

30 Briusov's major articles and studies on Pushkin are collected in *Moi Pushkin: Stat'i, issledovaniia, nabliudeniia* (1929).

31 Khodasevich's voluminous Pushkiniana has been collected recently in Khodasevich, *Pushkin i poety ego vremeni*, ed. Robert Hughes, 3 vols. (Berkeley: Berkeley Slavic Specialties, 1999–).

32 Nabokov, trans. and comm., *Eugene Onegin: a novel in verse by Aleksandr Pushkin*, 4 vols. (1964).

of a series of powerful subterranean tensions and fault lines that evoke ancient myths and stereotypes: Moscow versus St. Petersburg, belief versus skepticism, essence versus form, and — while it is taboo to broach the subject in polite company (however much the tensions are still there and whatever else the interlocutors may be discussing this is the actual point of the dispute) — Christian versus Jew (a number of the leading formalists and Pushkin scholars over the past century have been ethnic Jews). To be sure, the metaphysical Pushkinists have not neglected the formal side of Pushkin's art, but in the end their episteme sees form and structure as in the service of not just meaning but *higher* meaning and Pushkin's life through art as a kenotic, and cathartic, example.

The most illustrious and articulate of the metaphysical Pushkinists are, in addition to the pivotal Solovyov (1853–1900): S.N. (Father Sergei) Bulgakov (1871–1944), G.P. Fedotov (1886–1951), and S.L. Frank (1877–1950). Various other Silver Age writers and thinkers, including Gershenzon, V.I. Ivanov (1866–1949) D.S. Merezhkovsky (1866–1943), V.V. Rozanov (1856–1919), and L. Shestov (1866–1938), contributed to the discussion, as did those who, like I. A. Ilyin (1883–1954), V. I. Ilyin (1891–1974), A. V. Kartashev (1875–1960), and P. B. Struve (1870–1944), continued to ponder the significance of Pushkin for Russia while living out their lives in exile, during the interwar period, especially around the time of the centennial of the poet's death in 1937.[33] What Solovyov accomplished was to pose the issue of the meaning of "Pushkin" in a new way. On the one hand, he faulted the man for giving in to his anger and wishing to kill his wife's suitor d'Anthès in a duel, thus creating a fate for himself where death was the only possible "correct" outcome (that is, Pushkin would not have been "Pushkin," the essential poet, if he had killed his rival and been forced to live with murder on his conscience. See "Sud'ba Pushkina" [Pushkin's Fate, 1897]). On the other, he demonstrated, with great sensitivity and deep exegetical grounding in the Bible, Koran, and other ancient texts and languages, how the first-person speaker at the center of "Prorok" (The Prophet, 1826), Pushkin's poem about the turn to higher calling (*vysshee prizvanie*), cannot be identified exclusively with either Mohammed or Isaiah, but is rather the poet, who for Solovyov is technically not a personage out of the Scriptures but is also patently more than a craftsman, in his ideal reflection ("Znachenie poezii v stikhotvoreniiakh Pushkina" [The Meaning of Poetry in Pushkin's Verse, 1899]). Taking up where Solovyov left off and evincing a fine sensitivity to Pushkin's texts and biography, Bulgakov

[33] A useful selection of works on Pushkin by the aforementioned authors is found in *Pushkin v russkoi Filosofskoi kritike* (1990).

argued that the failure of the poet to follow his true calling after the writing of "The Prophet" caused a dissipation of moral and psychological integrity that was restored only in the last days and hours of his life, after he had been mortally wounded by d'Anthes, when he experienced forgiveness and Christian transfiguration ("Zhrebii Pushkina" [Pushkin's Lot, 1938]). Likewise, Fedotov, writing out of a non-Soviet voice zone where discussions of philosophy and politics need not be Marxist and materialist, traced the life-long dialectic in Pushkin's works and thought between empire building and freedom in all its guises ("Pevets imperii i svobody" [Singer of Empire and Freedom, 1937]). And perhaps none of these metaphysicians wrote more persuasively and insightfully about Pushkin's inner world than Frank, whose different articles on the poet were collected as *Etiudy o Pushkine* (Studies on Pushkin, 1957). Of the latter, "Religioznost' Pushkina" (Pushkin's Religious Consciousness, 1933) and "Pushkin kak politicheskii myslitel'" (Pushkin as a Political Thinker, 1937) stand out particularly: the first because it acknowledges the poet's spiritual dimension without trying to fit him into a Procrustean bed of dogmatic belief; the second because it recognizes, again without the blinders of Marxist *parti pris*, Pushkin's prescient understanding of the full danger of a democratic tide that, uniting the half-educated with the uneducated and inchoate, threatened to inundate not only a reactionary monarchy but the educated classes as well.

In principle, genuine scholarship should bring together knowledge and discovery in a way that what is demonstrated becomes self-evident and capable thereafter of being returned to and built upon. The compilation of facts without analysis and the cognitive element is just as problematic as ingenious theorizing and "narrativizing" that remains at an abstract level and cannot enter into fruitful dialogue with actual texts and actual lives in their historical dimensionality. To an outsider, there is the sense that the highest and best contributions to Pushkin studies—Tomashevsky's textology, Vatsuro's commentaries, Lotman's biography—are milestones we can travel by: the wheel that is "Pushkin" need not and should not be reinvented. At the same time, political and social pressures, pressures that were omnipresent (if necessarily muted) during the Soviet period and that have come out into the open with a vengeance since 1991, have to be taken into account in any attempt to understand the *quo vadis* of Pushkin studies today. For my purposes here I would like to offer an illustration of how present-day Pushkin studies (again, the focus remains Russia) continues to relive the past even as it strives to move forward.

One of the great values of Soviet-period textology was that, to repeat, it gave every appearance of being thorough and scientific. To pore over all the different permutations of a Pushkin text — the rough drafts, the fair copy, the first published instance, subsequent publications (if there were such), relevant biographical and contextual data — and come to a decision about what should be definitive had the result, whether desired or not, of essentially forestalling further discussion. After all, who else other than the expert, especially one linked with the Pushkin House tradition such as Tomashevsky, had access to all the manuscripts and had the time and resources (not to mention *talent*) to complete a full "creative/compositional history" (*tvorcheskaia istoriia*) of the item in question. The textological method was especially successful when the issue was one of Pushkin's masterpieces that, either for political considerations (censorship) or personal reasons (too intimate, too potentially autobiographical), was not published during his lifetime: say, *The Stone Guest* or *The Bronze Horseman* or "I have erected for myself a monument." But the decision-making process became more vexed when the editor chose a manuscript variant (or more likely, some aspect thereof) over a lifetime published version, when published and unpublished redactions became "contaminated." In this case, it could be argued (and recently has been argued), that a certain "subjectivity" and "Soviet logic" enter the picture. And by "Soviet" one does not necessarily mean something as crude as individual lapses related to currying favor or making ethically questionable choices but something more general and insidious: the very notion that scholarly authority can and should be centralized.³⁴ For no one, no matter how subtle a scholar and thinker, can read Pushkin's mind, and what might seem in the published version an attempt by Pushkin to get around the censorship (which in the Soviet model inevitably repressed and distorted what the poet really wanted to say) could actually be what he, someone who had very complicated and by no means uniformly negative relations to the tsar and his censorship, desired.³⁵

Let us say Pushkin did not, for reasons of self-censorship, publish a poem in his lifetime, but that poem exists in a fair copy and has entered into the canon as such. And let us also say that one of the lines in the poem has two variants, one with an obscene word (the devil "farted") and the other, written in the margin, with a euphemism (he "popped"). Why should the euphemistic alternative enter into textological history as preferred (under Pushkin's poems of 1832, as the Dante-inspired lyric "I dale my poshli" [And we ventured farther]) while the more plain-speaking version is relegated to

---

34 See the excellent discussion in Boris Gasparov, "Questa poi la conoseo pur troppo," *Novoe literaturnoe obozrenie* 56. 4 (2002): 187–189.

35 As Pushkin once wrote in a draft version of "Puteshestvie iz Moskvy v Peterburg" (Journey from Moscow to Petersburg [1.841]), Pss, 11:235, "I am convinced [of the necessity] of censorship in a morally educated and Christian society, under whatever laws and governance the latter may dwell."

the variants? And why should we go along with Pushkin's self-censorship in this case, where it also dovetails conveniently with Soviet Victorianism about what is proper for the national poet to say or not say, when in other cases related to political topics the self-censorship can be "trumped" by a progressive viewpoint coming after that perceives what the poet really wanted to say.[36] These are the shoals upon which the textological tradition, once institutions understood as "Soviet" (again, whether rightly or wrongly is beside the point) came under attack and a modicum of free speech was restored to the process, were bound to founder. The situation, moreover, was not helped by the fact that Pushkin House specialists professed to a kind of insider's knowledge that could not, eo ipso, be disputed.

Recently heated polemics have swirled around just this problem of who owns the legitimate "copyrights" to how the post-Soviet Pushkin should be published and studied. Underlying this discussion is an important paper read by Lotman in Tartu in 1987: there the scholar outlines the five principles by which a new academic edition of Pushkin (if in 1987 a crying need, then by today even more so) should be undertaken. 1) The new edition should make every effort to restore the actual language of Pushkin (as distinct from the language in which editors "think" he wanted to express himself); 2) the lifetime editions of Pushkin's works, in particular the ones he held in his own hands, are to be considered authoritative, and only when such published versions are absent should editors resort to privileging alternative wordings in the manuscripts; 3) all aspects of Pushkin's language, even those instances where an editor may deem that the poet is using "substandard" grammatical forms, should be preserved; 4) the audience for such an academic edition should not be the "general reader" (*massovyi chitatel'*) but the "philologically literate" one (that is, "dumbing down" the text in this sort of serious undertaking does a disservice to Pushkin studies and Russian culture and should be avoided); 5) the "modernization" of Pushkin's language with regard to orthography should be applied only in those cases when the shift is absolutely straightforward and clear (say, from "-ago" to "-ogo" in the genitive case of the adjectival form).[37] While such principles may seem transparent and logically desirable, each addresses a potentially thorny issue: what if prior (pre-revolutionary) orthographic convention makes it impossible to choose between illegible homonyms that are, in context, equally meaningful? Which lifetime edition of the poet's given work

---

36 See discussion in M. Shapir, "Otpoved' na zadannuiu temu," 150–151. To be fair to the textologists, their reason for leaving the less colorful version in this particular poem could have to do with their well established procedures and not with squeamishness. As Larionova and Fomichev point out, here the textologist (N. V. Izmailov) is supposed to use the version that, in a situation where there is no clear choice, is the last one to be added by the poet "Nechto o 'prezumptsii nevinovnosti' oneginskogo teksta," 155.

37 See Iu. Lotman, "K probleme novogo akademicheskogo izdaniia Pushkina," *Pushkin* (St. Petersburg: Iskusstvo-SPB, 1995), 369–373. Orig. published in *Pushkinskie chteniia v Tartu: Tezisy dokladov nauchnoi konferentsii 13–14 noiabria 1987* (Tallinn, 1987).

is to be preferred since each represents its own "cultural moment"? What if a situation suggests that Pushkin actually has committed a solecism that renders the locution not merely "folksy" but patently incorrect? The devil, as the saying goes, is in the details.

Maxim Shapir,[38] the Moscow linguist and literature scholar who has built a following around his journal *Philologica*, entered the fray in 2002 when he published a provocatively sounding article entitled "Kakogo 'Onegina' my chitaem?" (Which 'Onegin' Are We Reading?) in the bellwether journal *Novyi mir* (New World).[39] Proceeding from his own experience as philologist Shapir made the argument that the 1833 version of *Evgenii Onegin* (the one Tomashevsky took for his basis) should not necessarily be preferred over the 1837 one (the last one appearing in the poet's lifetime) and that, even more important, alternate spellings and wordings reconstructed from the manuscript copies of the novel should not be allowed to "leak" into the otherwise "authorized" printed texts. This position elicited in turn a spirited (and in places bluntly dismissive) response ("Nechto o 'prezumptsii nevinovnosti' oneginskogo teksta" [A Little Something on the "Presumption of Innocence" of the Onegin Text]) in the same journal a letter from S.A. Fomichev and E.O. Larionova, two Pushkin scholars represented in *The Pushkin Handbook*.[40] What becomes obvious from such discussions, and the heated exchanges they have generated, is that Pushkin House scholars feel themselves under siege. They sense a sea change taking place, and like all such historical shifts the positive and negative, the pure ideas and their impure human residues, are mixed together as the tidal flux washes over the various institutions with their established practices. They cite their proud history of serving science when it wasn't popular to do so (the Oksman case and the famous example of the exclusion of the academic commentaries from the jubilee edition) and they tend to characterize those who question their methods or propose alternative ones as trendy and "unserious." In the words of senior Pushkin House scholar Vadim Rak, "At present academic Pushkin studies is being subjected to bitter attacks and energetically discredited by all means with the intention of driving it out of public view and of filling the vacated place with various 'Pushkinistikas' (journalistic, subjective-impressionistic, conceptual-interpretive, esoteric,

---

[38] Unfortunately, Maxim Shapir died unexpectedly in August 2006, as *The Pushkin Handbook* was being published.

[39] 6 (2002): 144–156. Shapir's other recent foray into Pushkin studies involved the 2002 publication, with extensive scholarly apparatus, of *Ten' Barkova* (Barkov's Shade), a scabrously playful narrative poem that a number of prominent Pushkinists, beginning with M. A. Tsiavlovsky, have attributed to the poet's juvenilia, though the most that other specialists will admit to is it belongs in the category of "Dubia." Shapir and his colleague I.A. Pilshchikov, using their painstakingly meticulous "new philological" approach, tried to demonstrate how the language of *Ten' Barkova* coincided lexically and stylistically with wordings in other poems from Pushkin's lyceum period. This work in turn elicited a mixed, but again mostly negative, response from Pushkin House scholars E.O. Larionova and V.D. Rak. See Larionova and Rak, "A. S. Pushkin. Ten' Barkova: Teksty. Kommentarii. Ekskursy."

[40] *Novyi mir* 12 (2000): 145–158.

etc. etc.), which relate not to science but to criticism, not to *studying* Pushkin... but to *teaching* how, in light of now prevailing social trends, aspirations, and morals, one ought to read his works."[41]

In an ideal world the Pushkin House positivist tradition would not be eliminated or "driven from public view" but would take its place among other approaches, perhaps (probably?) as first among equals, in a naturally evolving dialogic process. It would be a tradition whose right to exist depends on its merits. Describing all other "Pushkinistikas" as less than scholarly, with epithets ("journalistic," "impressionistic") that presuppose a lack of seriousness, does not advance discussion and comes across to non-participants as defensive. Rak is correct to fear an academic marketplace where standards are eroded by the blind pursuit of "new words." Those of us who study humanistic disciplines within a western, and more specifically American, academic framework certainly share those fears. But closing ranks and painting all alternative viewpoints with the same brush is not the answer. Shapir's reasons for challenging Tomashevsky's choice of the 1833 edition of *Evgenii Onegin* may not be a priori flawed (that is, according to Pushkin House logic, the poet was too caught up in the events of fall 1836 to think about this new edition, many of the same mistakes migrated unchanged from the 1833 to 1837 editions, and so on); time will tell if his rigorous philological analysis, almost microscopic in its ability to track tiny details, creates a new and viable "Pushkin" or merely reinvents an old wheel. By the same token, perhaps the distinguished linguist and semiotician Boris Gasparov is not displaying "striking carelessness" (*porazitel'naia nebrezhnost'*)[42] when he attempts to reconstruct the flow of Pushkin's thoughts and feelings and the attendant genre vectors guiding them through the use of different punctuation marks in the manuscripts.[43] While it is true Gasparov was not trained as a textologist and is bound to make some procedural mistakes, his idea of entering the poet's mind through a shorthand (semicolons mean one thing, commas another, etc.) that must be abandoned once the punctuation is regularized in a canonic text seems to this reader persuasive. Pushkin said famously in his great valedictory poem "Do not argue with the fool" (*ne osporivai gluptsa*), which is good advice for the scholar who is not writing for the moment, even if the line is suffused with a Karamzinian equanimity not typical of Pushkin and in this particular case dictated by the mood of ultimate stock-taking. But what if the interlocutor is not a fool? And what if the dialogue, or argument, is something we very much need? "I want to understand you, / I search for

---

[41] Rak, "O krizise akademicheskogo pushkinovedeniia," 198.

[42] S.A. Fomichev, "Tochka, tochka, zapiataia... ," *Novoe literaturnoe obozrenie* 56, (2002) 4: 183.

[43] See B. Gasparov, "Zametki o Pushkine," *Novoe literaturnoe obozrenie* 52, (2001) 6: 115–133; and "Questa poi la conoseo pur troppo," *Novoe literaturnoe obozrenie* 56, (2002) 4: 187–191.

your meaning" (Ia poniat' tebia khochu, / Smysla ia v tebe ishchu), writes Pushkin in another poem.

The other flank from which the Pushkin House tradition feels it is being attacked is not philological but philosophical: modern followers, including S.G. Bocharov,[44] V.S. Nepomniashchy, and I.Z. Surat, of the Solovyov-Frank-Bulgakov school of religious thought and "philosophical criticism." These latter scholars are concerned with teasing out of Pushkin's "creative path" (*tvorcheskii put'*) his "spiritual path" (*dukhovnyi put'*) and with establishing the latter through a careful parsing, *in chronological order*, of all the poet's written and biographical traces. Two basic rationales underlie these pursuits: 1) Pushkin's gradual move toward spirituality and belief in a higher intelligence has been downplayed or otherwise distorted by Soviet atheistic practice and needs to be corrected; and 2) the textological tradition, with its focus on different manuscript variants and on establishing a canon that supersedes the authority of the poet's lifetime publications, has blurred this chronological development. As examples of this "Moscow" methodology we have Surat's and Bocharov's new short biography of Pushkin and the "Nasledie" edition of the first volume of a new collected works.[45] Both publications have met with mixed responses, including again some sharp criticism on the part of Pushkin House scholars. One point of contention is how to measure chronology: does a work take its place in the story of the poet's path when it is first conceived, completed in fair copy published, or, as the case may be, republished (sometimes with changes)? Another serious issue is the attempt to bring Pushkin too close to doctrinaire belief when the absolute most that can be responsibly said is that he *desired* to believe, dearly *felt* (in a loose-fitting, nobleman's sort of way) the spiritual warmth of the Russian Orthodox tradition,[46] studied the Bible and other sacred writings (along with many other texts), tried mightily in his heart to humble himself toward the end of his life (even when his pride and *amour-propre* were very much in evidence during the months leading up to the fatal duel), and did by all accounts reach a kind of transfiguring

---

[44] Sergei Bocharov, a superb Pushkin scholar in his own right and someone else represented in *The Pushkin Handbook*, has written especially insightfully about Evgenii Onegin in an applied Bakhtinian vein. One suspects that, for Bocharov, Bakhtin is an important implied interlocutor in this ongoing dialogic process to, very subtly, "Christianize" the formal or code-driven (à la Lotman) elements in the poet's life and works.

[45] Irina Surat and Sergei Bocharov, *Pushkin: Kratkii ocherk zhizni i tvorchestva* (Moscow: Iazyki slavianskoi kul'tury, 2002); and Surat et al., ed., *Sobranie sochinenii Pushkina* (Moscow: Nasledie, 2000-).

[46] Here Bulgakov's and Frank's caveats are very much to the point: "We cannot but say that Pushkin's personal churchgoing [*tserkovnost'*] was not sufficiently serious and responsible; more accurately, it remained aristocratically superficial and included a paganism of class and epoch that Pushkin never overcame" (Sergei Bulgakov, "Zhrebii Pushkina" [orig. pub. 1938], in *Pushkin v russkoi filosofskoi kritike*, ed, E.G. Babaev et al. [Moscow: Kniga, 1990], 278); "The religious quality in a poetic worldview can of course never be contained within the bounds of a specific dogmatic content, especially with regard to Pushkin, who is always and in everything many-sided" (S.L. Frank, "Religioznost' Pushkina" [orig. pub. 1933], Etiudy o Pushkine (Moscow: Soglasie, 1999), 24).

peace in his last hours. But even so, to use religious and philosophical terminology ("ontology," "self-knowing," "hypostasis") to describe this most curious, impressionable, and physically and cognitively alive and probing of poets is, if carried too far, to diminish his "aura" in another direction. The Surat-Bocharov biography has some excellent formulations and individual readings,[47] but it too, in trying to "correct" Lotman's semiotic Pushkin, flattens out its subject by making him too metaphysical, too spiritual, and hence not worldly enough.[48] Poems and their makers are as much in the world as they are in mythical space, and Pushkin understood this better than anyone.

In 1966 the Soviet Academy of Sciences, under the editorship of distinguished scholars B.P. Gorodetsky, N.V. Izmailov, and B.S. Meilakh, published *Pushkin. Itogi i problemy izucheniia* (Pushkin: Achievements and Problems in the Scholarship[49]). The work was intended to provide a current assessment of Pushkin studies along with retrospective synopses of the salient trends and issues that had made the tradition so lively and so central to Russian culture of the previous one hundred fifty years. In general, the level of scholarship in *Pushkin: Achievements and Problems in the Scholarship* was very high and the thinking exhibited therein impressively grounded if often less than subtle. The different sections (with their internal chapters) in the large (663 page) volume were seemingly straightforward and self-evident yet also implicitly reflective of the interests and approaches of the time: "Pushkin in the History of Russian Criticism and Scholarship," "Pushkin and the Sociopolitical and Literary Movement of His Time," "Biography," "Creative Work," "Textology," "Source Study," and "Bibliography" While the volume

[47] An example of such fine individual reading, very much in the Gershenzon-Khodasevich "bioaesthetic" line of reasoning, is Surat's treatment of the 29 November 1825 pass or "internal visa" (bilet) that fell into the hands of Pushkinists in 1933 and that gives a physical description of two serfs who the landowner Praskov'ia Osipova (Pushkin's neighbor at Mikhailovskoe) asks be allowed to travel to St. Petersburg from her estate Trigorskoe on errands. (Those examining the document such as L. B. Modzalevsky strongly believed it was a forgery and the work of Pushkin himself.) One of the serfs, Alexei Khokhlov, possesses characteristics virtually identical to the Pushkin of the time. Surat's argument, which is elegant and makes good sense in the context of Pushkin's practice elsewhere, is that, having just completed Boris Godunov with its scene of the runaway monk Grishka Otrepev being pursued by authorities at an inn on the Lithuanian border and trying to trick them by misrepresenting his own physical traits in the document they have brought with them (they are illiterate) as applying to someone else in the company, Pushkin was in effect considering playing out in life— he very much wanted to "escape" from Mikhailovskoe—the episode he had just created in art. It is this fascinating interrelationship between the artistic text and the "text of life" that those interested in an "interior biography" of the poet pursue. See Surat, Pushkin: *biografiia i lirika* (Moscow: Nasledie, 1999), 116–117.

[48] A particularly persuasive (to this reader) expression of Surat's biographical method is found in her chapter "Problemy biografii Pushkina" (1997), in *Pushkin: biografiia i lirika*, 38–68, esp. 57–58, where she discusses Herzen's notion of the "soul's biography" (*biografiia dushi*) and the longstanding need for an "interior biography" (*vnutrenniaia biografiia*) of the poet.

[49] The correct literal rendering of this title is *Pushkin: Stages Reached and the Problems of Studying Him*, but I have gone with the closer-to-English *Pushkin: Achievements and Problems in the Scholarship*.

included a number of contributions that have not lost their value up to the present day, among them V.L. Levkovich's on the poet's biography and Izmailov's on textology and source study, it also, and quite understandably, bore the imprint of Soviet parochialism. In particular the separate chapters on the different genres of Pushkin's creative work, all uniformly informative, seemed to exist in a time capsule where the abiding ideology and teleology (Pushkin both is and is always becoming a "poet of reality" and all serious problems having to do with methodology in studying the poet's works were simply "waiting" for their resolutions in Soviet "scientific" thinking) had not yet been seriously challenged. Obviously in 1966 no genuine effort could yet be made to invite non-Russians (or most émigré Russians for that matter) into the discussion.

The Pushkin Handbook is an attempt both to build on the real accomplishments of *Pushkin: Achievements and Problems in the Scholarship* and to give some larger sense of the wealth of approaches and productive dialogic interchanges that can exist in a post-Soviet world. It grew out of a conference hosted by the Wisconsin Center for Pushkin Studies in Madison, Wisconsin in October 1996 (in anticipation of the bicentennial jubilee year of 1999). Undoubtedly our evocation of "pluralism" betrays its own American pretense to openness that is itself politically situated and not nearly as inviting and accepting as one might want. No word, as Bakhtin has taught us, can exist out of context, a principle we do not deny. And yet we feel the cognitive subtlety and multi-perspectival awareness displayed *The Pushkin Handbook*, a subtlety and awareness still routinely grounded in the texts and contexts, should provide food for future thought, especially in a design, as ours is, that intentionally brings together leading specialists from both the former Soviet Union and elsewhere.

Chapter 8 — Pushkin's Biography[1]

Introduction

As one considers any biographical treatment of Alexander Pushkin it is prudent to bear in mind the words of the eminent cultural historian, literary theorist, and biographer of the poet Yury Lotman. In his biography Lotman "wanted to show how, like the mythological King Midas who turned everything he touched to gold, Pushkin turned everything he touched into creativity, art. [But] Midas starved to death — his food became gold."[2] This metaphor is strikingly apropos when it comes to the facts of Pushkin's life. Let us take for an example the seemingly straightforward case of the poet's hair color. In the very early Lycée poem "Mon portrait" (1814) the fifteen-year-old Pushkin characterized himself in the following way:

> J'ai le teint frais, les cheveux blonds
> Et la tête bouclée.
>
> [I have a fresh complexion, blond hair
> And a curly head.]

Yet eyewitnesses claim that Pushkin's hair was always dark and, indeed, the lock of hair cut from the head of the dead poet and encased in a medallion now located in the Pushkin apartment-museum in St. Petersburg is dark brown with a reddish tinge. Pushkin's brother Lev explained why the poet's hair had "turned golden" in "Mon portrait": he was searching for a rhyme to go with the phrase "les plus longs" and "cheveux

---

[1] Co-authored with Sergei Davydov. The present essay is an expanded version of "Pushkin's Biography" in *Cambridge Companion to Pushkin*, ed. Andrew Kahn (Cambridge: Cambridge University Press, 2006), 11–25

[2] Iu.M. Lotman, *Pushkin* (St. Petersburg: Iskusstvo, 1995), 388. The citation comes from a 1986 letter to Lotman's friend Boris Egorov.

blonds" was what he found. Hence one is entitled to say with only a minimum of coyness that the task of the biographer consists in reversing the poet's Midas touch: we must try to turn the gold of art back into the actual food of the historical man.

Genealogy

Like Lord Byron, Pushkin took great pride in his own aristocratic ancestry. He was born into the family of Sergei Lvovich Pushkin and Nadezhda Osipovna Pushkina neé Gannibal, both of whose forebears played significant, though not in every case heroic, roles in Russian history. On his father's side Pushkin belonged to an ancient line of nobility dating back to the twelfth century (not thirteenth as Pushkin thought) whose names are cited twenty-one times in Karamzin's monumental history. The Pushkin clan managed to stay close to power through the Ryurik dynasty (i.e. up to the end of the sixteenth century), but under the Romanovs they fell from grace. Several ancestors were conspirators and mutineers and suffered in particular under Peter I. By 1799 (the year of the poet's birth) the Pushkin family had lost all of their influence and most of their fortune, and it is clear that, as he matured, Pushkin came to identify with their lot: "They were persecuted. And I am persecuted."[3] Inspired and encumbered by the past, Pushkin paid tribute to his ancestry on numerous occasions, most notably in the poem "My Genealogy" (Moia rodoslovnaia, 1830).

The maternal side of the family provides even more colorful material for mythopoetization. Pushkin's great-grandfather, Abram (originally Ibrahim) Petrovich Gannibal was born in Africa in 1696 and might have been the son of an Abyssinian prince, as Pushkin believed. At the age of seven he was taken (or sold) into captivity and shipped to Constantinople, where he was placed in the sultan's seraglio. From there he was smuggled into the hands of the Russian envoy, who sent him on to Russia to Peter the Great. The emperor had the blackamoor baptized, became his godfather, and kept him at his side. Abram was not merely an exotic ornament for the floorboards of Peter's carriage; he became the tsar's favorite and accompanied him as a drummer boy on military campaigns. He learned to read and write and soon became something akin to Peter's informal secretary. In 1716 Peter took the twenty-year-old Abram Petrov (as he was now called) with a group of other gifted young Russian men on a European tour, depositing him in 1718 in

---

3 A.S. Pushkin, *Pushkin's draft outline for a part of "Rejection of Criticisms." Polnoe sobranie sochinenii*, ed. V.D. Bronch-Bruevich et al., 17 vols. in 21 (Moscow: AN SSSR, 1937–59), XI:388. Henceforth "*Pss.*" *Pss*, 11:388.

France to study fortification. Abram participated in the French war against Spain and returned wounded to Paris. Constantly in need of money, he could not have participated in the social whirl of beautiful women and famous men (Voltaire, Montesquieu) that Pushkin imagined in his unfinished novel *The Blackamoor of Peter the Great* (*Arap Petra velikogo*, 1827). At Peter's request Abram returned to Russia in 1723; two years later he was promoted to the rank of lieutenant, which is also about the time he began assuming the name Gannibal (after the Carthaginian general) to boost his military image. After Peter's death in 1725, Gannibal fell out of favor, but with the ascension to the throne of Peter's daughter Elizabeth he progressed quickly through the ranks, eventually attaining the status of hereditary nobleman and being awarded several estates. He retired in 1762 at the rank of general-in-chief (*general-anshef*) and died at the ripe age of eighty-five in 1781, having outlived six monarchs.

Abram's private life was less happy. His first wife Eudoxia, forced into the marriage, was repulsed by his African features. When she gave birth to a white baby, Abram concluded that he had been cuckolded and constructed at his home "a private torture chamber complete with pulleys, iron clamps, thumbkins, [and] leather whips" to punish her.[4] Later on he had her incarcerated by the state (eventually she was forced into a nunnery) when, his divorce not yet final, he "married" another woman. This second wife then bore him eleven black babies. Little wonder that this colorful figure with ties to Russia's greatest tsar and with a story of meteoric rise out of literal "darkness" (but one punctuated by spells of sinister passion) captured the poet's imagination and played a role in his self-projection.

The next generation of Gannibals was much less illustrious, except for one son, Ivan, a naval hero. Indeed, several of Abram Gannibal's sons inherited his irascibility but not his self-discipline and curiosity for science and knowledge. Pushkin's grandfather Osip was the most profligate and willful of them all. While still married to the future poet's grandmother, Marya Alekseevna, he took a second wife by testifying that the first had died. It requird the intercession of Catherine the Great to annul the "marriage" and return to the lawful wife her property and her daughter, the three-year-old Nadezhda, who became Pushkin's mother.

Pushkin was proud of his "blue"- and "black"-blooded ancestry, accepting their heroic deeds and nobility (literal and figurative) along with the "taint" of their passions and penchant for self-destruction. Throughout his life he was sensitive about his "Negro ugliness" all the while understanding that his

4 V.V. Nabokov (trans.), *Eugene Onegin*, A Novel in verse by Aleksandr Pushkin, 4 vols. (Princeton: Princeton University Press, 1975), 3: 434. The account is from a *Russkaia starina* piece assembled by Stepan Opatovich in 1877 (vol. XVIII, 69–78). Cited also in Georg Leets, *Abram Petrovich Gannibal: Biograficheskoe issledovanie* (Tallin: Eesti raamat, 1984), 83.

"African temperament" could (and given his poetic fatalism probably would) develop an Othello-like plot in his own life.

1799–1811: Childhood

Alexander Pushkin was born on 26 May 1799 (old style) in Moscow. Though by no means wealthy the family endeavored to maintain aristocratic pretensions and therefore constantly lived beyond their means. Home life was on the chaotic side. Pushkin's father Sergei Lvovich was renowned for his Gallic wit and exquisite bon mots and could recite Molière by heart. In their literary salon the Pushkins entertained foreign and Russian celebrities. French was the lingua franca at home. The parents read French literature to their three surviving children (Olga, Alexander, Lev), but left their upbringing to foreign governesses and tutors. The pudgy and clumsy Sasha was the parents' least favorite child, something he felt keenly, but he found refuge and warmth with his grandmother Marya Alekseevna and his nurse Arina Rodionovna. From these two women the children learned Russian, a fact which Pushkin will recall in the poem "Sleep/Dream" ("Son," 1816), where "granny" and "nanny" merge into one appealing image. The children spent summers at their grandmother's estate in Zakharovo, near Moscow, where old-fashioned Russian life ruled. Pushkin will fondly remember this place in "Epistle to Yudin" ("Poslanie k Iudinu," 1815). To his nanny Pushkin addressed a number of moving poems,[5] and as the ultimate token of his affection he "lent" her to his favorite heroine Tatyana in *Eugene Onegin*. The other source of his early education Sasha found in his father's library of French classics. At the age of eight he began writing verses in French. When making an application for his son at the newly opened imperial Lycée in St. Petersburg, Sergey Lvovich could write without exaggeration that his son "had obtained rudimentary knowledge of Russian and French grammar, arithmetic, geography, history, and drawing."

1811–1817: Lycée

The Lycée was an exclusive boarding school, directly attached to the Catherine Palace in Tsarskoe Selo, the royal summer residence. The emperor himself inaugurated it with pomp on 19 October 1811 in the presence of the

---

5 E.g. "Confidante of Magical Olden Times" ("Napersnitsa volshebnoi stariny," 1822), "Winter Evening" ("Zimnii vecher," 1825), "To Nanny" ("Niane," 1826), "Again I have visited" ("Vnov' ia posetil," 1835).

court, the faculty, and the first class of thirty students. It was the most progressive liberal arts institution in Russia at the time.

Pushkin, nicknamed "the Frenchman," was a mediocre student whose main concern was to excel in sports and pranks. In 1812 the Lycée classmates were overtaken by a wave of patriotism and envy, as they watched guardsmen billeted nearby (some of them brothers) depart for the war against Napoleon. Pushkin continued to read avidly and began writing love elegies and verse epistles to friends. In the poem "The Little Town" ("Gorodok," 1814) the teenage poet lists his favorite authors: Homer, Virgil, Horace, Tasso, Molière, Racine, Voltaire, Rousseau, Parny, Derzhavin, Fonvizin, Karamzin, Dmitriev and Krylov — of these, however, Voltaire and Parny are granted exalted status. In 1814 Pushkin published his first poem "To a Poet-Friend" ("K drugu stikhotvortsu"), yet a more important debut was his public reading of "Recollections in Tsarskoe Selo" ("Vospominaniia v Tsarskom Sele") during the qualifying examination at the end of the junior course on 8 January 1815. The greatest Russian poet of the eighteenth century, Gavrila Derzhavin, was the guest of honor. He fell asleep during the examination and only when Pushkin began reciting his poem — a gentle parody of Derzhavin's style — did the ancient bard wake up. "Derzhavin was ecstatic; he asked after me, wanted to embrace me... They looked for me, but I was nowhere to be found," wrote Pushkin as he looked back on the event.[6] The moribund Derzhavin is alleged to have said, "I am not dead" and "Here is the one who will take Derzhavin's place."[7]

Pushkin's reputation grew by word of mouth and he was encouraged by poets and literati close to the Karamzin circle, such as Batiushkov, Vasily Zhukovsky, Prince Pyotr Vyazemsky, and Pyotr Pletnev, all of whom saw a bright future for the teenager. During these early years Pushkin was still known primarily as the nephew of Vasily Lvovich Pushkin, the author of scabrous verses. In 1817, however, Pushkin began his mock epic *Ruslan and Liudmila* which will bring him instant fame in 1820. The final examination in May 1817, at which Alexander I, by now the liberator of Europe, was present, was allegedly a sham — the students probably knew their questions in advance. Even so, Pushkin managed to graduate at the bottom of class, excelling only in Russian, French, and fencing. The Director of the Lycée V.V. Engelgardt gave him a less than flattering attestation:

> Pushkin's mind, possessing neither perspicacity nor depth, is a completely superficial, French mind. That's the best that one can say about Pushkin. His heart is cold and empty; in it

6 *Pss*, 12:158.
7 V.V. Veresaev, *Pushkin v zhizni*, 2 vols., 7th edition (Moscow: Sovetskii pisatel', 1936), 1:70–71, 77.

there is neither love nor religion. Perhaps it is as empty as any youthful heart has ever been.[8]

Still, Pushkin received at the Lycée the best available education in Russia at the time. Like other students, he was as if inoculated here with an acute awareness of personal freedom and independence and a firm belief in his own inherent worthiness. Most important, he found at the Lycée the real home he did not know with his parents; he made lifelong friends (Anton Delvig, Ivan Pushchin) and spent here perhaps the happiest time of his life. Pushkin would celebrate the day of the opening of the Lycée (19 October) in a number of anniversary poems.

After graduation some students embarked on high-profile military and civil-service careers, while others became involved in radical politics, eventually participating in the abortive Decembrist uprising (Pushchin and Küchelbecker). Pushkin dreamt of a military career in the Guards, but because the outfitting for the cavalry service was too costly his father chose instead for him a government post. The eighteen-year old Pushkin was assigned to the Ministry of Foreign Affairs in St. Petersburg, with the rank of Collegiate Secretary and a salary of 600 rubles per annum.

1817–1820: St. Petersburg, Arzamas, Green Lamp, Radicalism

Upon graduating from the Lycée Pushkin immediately took a vacation and spent time with his family at his mother's estate in Mikhailovskoe. He returned after two months to the capital but did not work. Among some aristocrats not to work was considered a political (i.e. anti-government) statement. Pushkin's post at the Ministry was purely nominal enabling him to lead an idle and dissipated life very much in the vein of his hero in chapter one of *Eugene Onegin*. He goes to the theater, has affairs with actresses, frequents brothels, contracts venereal disease, writes bawdy and politically provocative poems, fights several duels. Pushkin's friends and protectors become increasingly worried "As great as the Cricket's [Pushkin's nickname] talent is, he will squander it all" — and they recommend, not entirely facetiously, locking him up for three years in Göttingen and feeding him "milk soup and logic."[9]

While still at the Lycée Pushkin became involved with Arzamas, a literary-cum-dining society that took its name from the provincial town famous for its

---

[8] V.P Gaevskii, "Pushkin v listee i litseiskie ego stikhotvoreniia," *Sovremennik* 1863 (8):376; cited in P.V. Annenkov, *Pushkin v Aleksandrovskuiu epokhu* (Minsk: Limarius, 1998; orig., 1874), 42.

[9] K. Batiushkov's words, in Veresaev, 1:111.

geese. The club spawned a new generation of poets, including Zhukovsky, Batyushkov, Vyazemsky, Denis Davydov, and Vasily Lvovich Pushkin. They propagated a version of the literary language based on Karamzinian norms taken from French salon discourse. Their main occupation was to stage mock burials of the members of the Beseda Society,[10] guardians of the archaic sanctity of the language, with the chief targets being Admiral A.S. Shishkov, Prince S.A. Shirinsky-Shikhmatov, Prince A.A. Shakhovskoy, and Count D.I. Khvostov. All Arzamasians were thus by definition "gravediggers" and their burial protocols make for a hilarious reading. The clash of the two linguistic worldviews, known as the war of the "Innovators and Archaists," ended with the victory of the Karamzinians and with the Russian language codified as we know it today.

The other contemporaneous society to which Pushkin belonged was the Green Lamp (Zelenaia lampa), which was started in 1819 as a champagne and theater club with political overtones. Smart young military officers and men-about-town met "under the green lamp" at the home of Nikita Vsevolozhsky to discuss the great and the small — the contemporary theater, issues of freedom, equality and the need for a constitution, the beauty of ballerinas and the duplicity of the tsar. They also used the meetings to drink and gamble, which latter activity would become one of Pushkin's favorite and least successful pastimes. It was here to Vsevolozhky that Pushkin lost a manuscript of poems ready for print.

The liberal honeymoon of Alexander I's reign ("the beautiful beginning of Alexander's days," as Pushkin puts it in one of his Lycée anniversary poems) was followed by the repressive rule of Minister Arakcheev ("*arakcheevshchina*"). Pushkin was, for all practical purposes, one of the liberals of his day and enjoyed political posturing. Once, for example, he publicly displayed in the theater a portrait of Louis-Pierre Louvel, the assassin of the heir to the Bourbon throne, with the inscription "A Lesson to Tsars." Pushkin's friend A.I. Turgenev called his political bravado "vulgar free-thinking" while the real revolutionaries, grown weary of Pushkin's fidgety nature and dissipated lifestyle, did not trust him and never offered him membership in their secret societies. At the same time, Pushkin seemed to serve their cause well with such radical poems as "Liberty" ("Vol'nost'," 1817) and "The Village" ("Derevnia," 1819) and such jibes against the tsar and his minions as "Noël" (1818), "You and I" ("Ty i ia," 1817–20) and "On Arakcheev" ("Na Arakcheeva,"?).[11] These poems circulated privately and came eventually to the attention of the government.

---

10   Its full name was "Beseda liubitelei russkogo slova" (Colloquy of the Lovers of the Russian Word).

11   Its authorship has not been conclusively confirmed.

Arakcheev and Alexander I threatened to banish Pushkin to the remote Solovetsky Monastery on the White Sea or to Siberia. To add insult to injury, a malicious rumor was making the rounds in Petersburg that the poet had been flogged in the chambers of the secret police — a devastating blow to Pushkin's keen sense of honor, since a nobleman's person was sacrosanct. In April 1820 Pushkin was summoned to the office of the Petersburg governor-general Count M.A. Miloradovich who demanded to see the seditious poems. Pushkin, who had burned them in anticipation of a search, volunteered to write them down from memory, and the generous Miloradovich forgave Pushkin on the spot. It is useful to keep in mind that no matter how Pushkin may have disliked Alexander I, his political verse of this period advocated constitutional monarchy and the abolishment of serfdom by tsarist fiat — a not necessarily far-fetched prospect once entertained by Alexander I himself. Still, it took the intercession of several influential people, among them Miloradovich, Karamzin, and the emperor's mother, to prevail upon the tsar to commute Pushkin's exile to an administrative transfer to the south, where he would serve as translator to General Inzov, the senior military official of the colonies recently ceded to Russia by Turkey.

1820–1823: South Caucasus, Kishinev

In early May 1820 Pushkin left St. Petersburg unhappy but also relieved: to live further under the shadow of his rumored flogging would have been unbearable. In Ekaterinoslav (Dnepropetrovsk) he met General Raevsky, hero of the Napoleonic campaign, who was traveling with his family to the Caucasus, an exotic, newly conquered territory. With the consent of his new chief General Inzov, Pushkin passed a glorious three-month holiday with this charming family, admiring the mountains, the savage mountaineers, and reading his first Byron. Under the influence of Byron's "Oriental tales" Pushkin began the first of his three "Southern poems," *The Prisoner of the Caucasus* (*Kavkazskii plennik*, 1820–21). The group also visited the Crimea. On his way back to reunite with Inzov Pushkin fell ill with malaria and during his convalescence made a trip to Bakhchisarai, the former capital of the Crimean Khanate. The khan's harem became the setting for Pushkin's next Byronic tale, *The Fountain of*

Bakhchisarai (*Bakhchisaraiskii fontan*, 1821–23). In September Pushkin arrived in Kishinev, Bessarabia, whereto Inzov's headquarters had been transferred. He established an excellent rapport with the lenient and well-meaning Inzov. Here the poet befriended the division commander General M.F. Orlov, a member of the Union of Welfare, the group that was to form the basis of the more radicalized Southern Society preparing for an armed uprising to abolish the monarchy and all aristocratic privileges. Pushkin also spent two months at the Raevsky-Davydov estate in Kamenka, near Kiev, meeting other members of the secret society, among them V.L. Davydov and I.D. Yakushkin. In Kishinev Pushkin finally encountered the leader of the movement, Colonel Pavel Pestel, whom he proclaimed "a most original mind."[12] (After the unsuccessful uprising of December 1825 Pestel was one of the five executed leaders.)

No matter how much Pushkin may have wished it, the conspirators were not eager to initiate the hot-headed poet into their radical plans; either they did not trust him or they wanted magnanimously to spare him, deeming that his poems did enough for their cause.[13] Although Pushkin never became a member, his poem "The Dagger" ("Kinzhal," 1821) had been recited in the Secret Society of the United Slavs as a pledge of readiness for regicide.[14] Pushkin's political hopes were also fueled by the outbreak of revolutions in Italy, Spain, and Greece, but once these were suppressed he became quickly disillusioned. The poet knew personally Alexander Ypsilanti, the leader of the Greek revolt against Turks, whose cause Byron too soon would take up. While in Kishinev, in May 1821, Pushkin also became a member of the Masonic lodge "Ovid"; it had long been common knowledge that the Masonic lodges were breeding grounds for political unrest.

During his three years in Kishinev Pushkin fought several duels — all ending without bloodshed — for which he spent some weeks under house arrest. He also managed to have an affair with Calypso Polichroni, the Greek girl reputed to have been kissed by Byron. Here he saw in print *The Prisoner of the Caucasus* (pub. 1822) and finished *The Fountain of Bakhchisarai*, the most popular work published during his lifetime. In addition, he wrote "To Ovid" ("K Ovidiiu"), an elegiac paean to the Roman poet who too was exiled to Bessarabia. One of his most notorious achievements was the unprintable but widely circulating narrative poem *The Gabrieliad* (*Gavriiliada*, 1821), in which the sly and life-affirming poet, going much farther than Voltaire in *La Pucelle*, parodies the immaculate conception and provides a satanic father for Christ. Another risqué work is the mis-

12 "Kishinev diary," 9 April 1821, *Pss* 12: 303.

13 Cf. the words of K.F. Ryleev in M.A. Tsiavlovskii and N.A Tarkhova, comps., *Letopis' zhizni i tvorchestva Aleksandra Pushkina*, 4 vols. (Moscow: Slovo, 1999), 1: 348. Henceforth "*Letopis'*." See also V.L. Davydov's phrasing in V.E. Vatsuro et al., comps., *A.S. Pushkin v vospominaniiakh sovremennikov*, 2 vols. (Moscow: Khudozhestvennaia literatura, 1974), 2:317. Henceforth "*PvVS.*"

14 N. Eidel'man, *Pushkin. Iz biografii tvorchestva 1826–1837* (Moscow: Khudozhestvennaia literatura, 1987), 37. "Eidelman."

chievous fairy tale *Tsar Nikita and His Forty Daughters* (Tsar' Nikita i sorok ego docherei, 1822): here the forty princesses, all born without their most private parts, manage to get them installed through the services of an enterprising messenger. Most importantly, in Kishinev Pushkin began *Eugene Onegin*, his novel-in-verse loosely modeled after Byron's *Don Juan*, which will take him eight years to complete (1823–31).

1823–1824: Odessa

Thanks to the intercession of influential friends Pushkin was transferred in August 1823 to Odessa, a cosmopolitan European port on the Black Sea, where he was placed under the wing of governor general Count Vorontsov. This extremely rich, English-educated aristocrat was another hero of the Napoleonic wars and a well-known liberal who freed his serfs. The Count opened his house and his library to Pushkin and offered him a post on his office staff. Pushkin's salary of 700 rubles a year was insufficient to support his lifestyle, with the result that he was forced to rely on income from publishers. This need to haggle over money with publishers in a manner unbecoming a gentleman depressed and irritated Pushkin, producing the sardonic "Conversation between Bookseller and Poet" ("Razgovor knigoprodavtsa s poetom," 1824), where the poetic alter ego retorts "Inspiration can't be sold, but a manuscript can." Likewise, the setbacks in the revolutionary movements in Spain, Italy, and Germany, where the monarchies prevailed and the people betrayed their rebel sons, gave little reason for optimism at home. In the unpublished poem "Freedom's Lonely Sower" ("Svobody seiatel' pustynnyi," 1823) Pushkin lashes out at the idealists' squandered hopes and casts doubts on the people's readiness for liberty.

His heart emptied of revolutionary zeal, the resourceful poet refilled it with amatory ardor. Pushkin fell in love with three enchanting and (for him) tormentingly experienced women: the merchant's wife Amalia Riznich, the beautiful Polish double agent Karolina Sobanska (the dedicatee of Mickiewicz's *Crimean Sonnets* and the inspiration for some of Chopin's music), and the governor general's wife Countess Elizaveta Vorontsova. The names "Amalia" and "Eliza" we find on the famous "Don Juan list" that Pushkin penned in 1829. These "Odessan muses" were from different social backgrounds and classes but the intensity of what Pushkin felt for them and the manner in which he could encase that intensity in elegant, "breathing" language crossed all boundaries into the dark recesses of pure eros.[15]

In Odessa Pushkin was reunited with his friend, Alexander Raevsky, with whom he had traveled to the Caucasus, and who was, unbeknownst to the poet, Elise Vorontsova's favorite. It seems Raevsky was using Pushkin as a decoy in order to draw attention away from himself. Upon learning the truth the trusting but now jealous and deeply hurt Pushkin portrays Raevsky in the poems "Demon" (1823) and "Treachery" ("Kovarnost'," 1824). The relationship with Count Vorontsov now too became strained. The Count began to resent his subordinate's aristocratic tetchiness and his eagerness to court his lovely wife right under his nose. As tensions mounted the Count insisted on treating Pushkin as a petty civil servant, while the poet thought of his own six-hundred-year-old lineage and seethed at the icy putdown. Ultimately Vorontsov requested that the court remove this thorn in his side from Odessa. The last straw came when Pushkin was ordered to investigate some faraway crop damage caused by a swarm of locusts, something the poet found demeaning. Upon return from this latest imbroglio Pushkin handed in a request for retirement and mocked the Count in brilliantly barbed epigrams. To make matters worse, the authorities in Moscow intercepted Pushkin's letter to a friend in which he wrote that atheism is "unfortunately the most plausible" belief. By now Pushkin's fate was sealed: an offense against religion was tantamount to an offense against the state. The tsar decided to dismiss Pushkin from service and to banish him to his mother's Mikhailovskoe estate in northern Russia.

Elise was vacationing with her husband on their yacht in the Crimea when she learned of the tsar's decision. She quickly returned alone to Odessa to bid farewell to the poet. It was in this heated atmosphere that Elise and Vera Vyazemskaya devised a plan, ultimately unsuccessful, for Pushkin's escape to Constantinople. During the week of 25–31 July evidence indicates that a liaison, one which would engender a score of love poems and haunt the poet's imagination in his northern isolation, took place between Pushkin and Elise.[16] Thus, on 1 August 1824, dressed "in yellow nankeen wide trousers and Russian blouse," Pushkin left Odessa. In his luggage he was carrying the beginning of *The Gypsies* (*Tsygany*, 1824), the last and most complex of his three "Southern poems"; some 30 stanzas of chapter 3 of *Eugene Onegin*; and two gifts from Elise, a talisman-ring with a Hebrew inscription (Pushkin will wear it to his last duel) and a golden medallion with Elise's portrait.

15 To Amalia: "Under the blue sky of your native land" (Pod nebom golubym strany svoei rodnoi, 1826) and "For the shores of a distant fatherland" (Dlia beregov otchizny dal'noi, 1830); to Karolina: "I loved you…" ("Ia vas liubil…," 1829 and "What is my name to you" ("Chto v imeni tebe moem," 1830); and to Elise, a host of love poems, perhaps the most famous being "Preserve Me, My Talisman" ("Khrani menia, moi talisman," 1824) and "The Burned Letter" ("Sozhzhennoe pis'mo," 1825).

16 See T.G. Tsiavlovskaia, "Khrani menia, moj talisman" (1974), in *Utaennaia liubov' Pushkina*, ed. R.V. Iezuitova and Ia.L. Levkovich (Petersburg:

1824–1826: Exile in Mikhailovskoe

On 9 August 1824 Pushkin arrived in Mikhailovskoe where he was immediately placed under the surveillance of the police, the local abbot, and his own father. That Sergei Lvovich would consent to spy on his wayward offspring was especially humiliating to Pushkin, as the dishonor touched both the father and the son. After a stormy confrontation precipitated by the perusal of letters, the father ceased his shameful assignment and departed the premises. The residue of this confrontation would long taint Pushkin's relations with his father and find expression in his art in various plotlines involving paternal control and filial struggle, including, most famously, *The Covetous Knight* (*Skupoi rytsar'*, 1830).

Passionate longings for the Countess Vorontsova would not leave Pushkin in peace in the north. It can be argued that what Pushkin felt for Elise's special brand of high-born charm and complaisance he never felt for anyone else again. Whenever a letter sealed with a talisman-ring (the twin of the one Elise gave to Pushkin) arrived, the poet would lock himself in his room for a protracted period and end by burning the precious document.[17] From one of her letters Pushkin may have learned that Elise was pregnant and he was the father. In any event, approximately nine months after their last meeting Elise gave birth to a "swarthy" daughter. The theme of an out-of-wedlock child appears in a number of works of this period.[18]

Pushkin often grew bored in the country, passing the time by playing billiards with himself, riding, practicing his marksmanship, swimming (he joked of his "Hellespont"), and making plans to flee abroad by disguising himself as a neighbor's butler. Friends in the two capitals grew anxious that he might take to drink, but Pushkin was remarkably resilient and found a way, tapping deep into private reserves, to turn adversity into advantage and to grow miraculously as a thinker and artist during his Mikhailovskoe confinement. Often he would dispel his melancholy in the company of his old nurse, Arina Rodionovna, whose songs and tales he wrote down and later made into gems of stylized folklore. Another refuge was found in the nearby Trigorskoe estate of P.A. Osipova-Vulf, whose numerous daughters added a cheerful and much needed feminine touch to his now severe and stripped-down male world. He also enjoyed a dalliance with the serf girl Olga Kalashnikova. Not only did Olga's name show up later on Pushkin's Don Juan list but, on a more serious note, the lord of the manor made her pregnant and she bore a son Pavel, who died in infancy. Even as Pushkin

---

Akademicheskii proekt, 1997), 297–380.

[17] See "The Burned Letter" ("Sozhzhennoe pis'mo," 1825). Other poems related to Elise: "All is finished, between us there is no tie" ("Vse koncheno, mezh nami sviazi net," 1824), "The foul day has died down" ("Nenastnyi den' potukh," 1824), "Let the one crowned with love of beauty" ("Puskai uvenchannyi liubov'iu krasoty," 1824), "Preserve me, my talisman" ("Khrani menia, moi talisman," 1824), "All is sacrificed to your memory" ("Vse v zhertvu pamiati tvoei," 1825), "Talisman" (1827), "Farewell" ("Proshchanie," 1830).

[18] "To an Infant" ("Mladentsu," 1824), *The Gypsies*

tried to make light of the liaison in his correspondence with Vyazemsky his conscience seemed bothered by this turn of events: the echo of a fatal romance between a nobleman and a peasant girl appears in the unfinished verse drama *The Mermaid* (*Rusalka*, 1829–32).

The years 1824–1825 found Pushkin at a crossroads. Clearly he was chastened and the revolutionary South, the "free element" of the ever roiling, ever-changing sea, the fascination with Napoleon as romantic personage and the apprenticeship to Byron were all left behind (see the poem "To the Sea" ["K moriu," 1824]). While the secret societies were preparing for an armed insurrection in the capital, Pushkin, holed up deep in the Russian heartland, was learning a different and thoroughly anti-romantic lesson. He finishes *The Gypsies*, the last of his "Southern poems"; the cycle "Imitations of the Koran" ("Podrazhaniia Koranu," 1824), which paves the way for the "negative capability" of the poet's later religious consciousness; the great Shakespearean historical drama *Boris Godunov* (1825, pub. 1830); the witty epic *Count Nulin* (*Graf Nulin*, 1825), modeled after Byron's *Beppo* and parodying Shakespeare's *Rape of Lucrece*; and the chapters 4, 5, and 6 of *Eugene Onegin*. The sustained reading of Shakespeare, Karamzin's *History* and the Bible convince Pushkin that above individual will—noble or ignoble—ultimately stands a meaningful, if not always benign, historical destiny.

In November 1825 Alexander I died suddenly. His death caused confusion as to which of his two brothers (Constantine or Nicholas) should succeed him. Constantine had already relinquished his right to the throne, but for some reason this decision was not made public. In Petersburg the members of the Northern Society took advantage of the power vacuum and on 14 December mounted an armed insurgency. A group of officers commanding some 3,000 men refused to swear allegiance to Nicholas I and proclaimed their loyalty to "Constantine and Constitution." While the troops stood for hours in the cold on Senate Square, their leaders could not decide what to do next. Eventually the troops loyal to Nicholas opened artillery fire and the uprising was over. 120 mutineers were sent to Siberia (among them Pushkin's Lycée friends Pushchin and Kümchelbecker) and five leaders were hanged. Pushkin knew many of the rebels personally and was implicated because copies of his political verses were found among them. Yet he hoped that the interrogations of the insurgents would prove him innocent—after all, he was not a member of any secret society—and in May 1826 he appealed to the new tsar for a commutation of his exile. In July Pushkin learned about the execution of the rebel leaders, the first such execution in Russia since the quartering of Pugachev (in an expunged passage written in January 1825), and the autobiographically colored *The Blackamoor of Peter the Great* (the episode with the French Countess's black baby).

in 1774. In the manuscript of chapter 5 of *Eugene Onegin* we find sketches of gallows with five dangling corpses, accompanied by an inscription, "And like a fool, I too could have..." On 4 September 1826 a special courier arrived in Mikhailovskoe and whisked Pushkin away to Moscow.

1826–1829: After Exile, Nicholas I, 1828, Arzrum

Pushkin arrived in the Kremlin on 8 September. The first person the poet saw was the new tsar, who was still in Moscow after the coronation ceremonies. To the tsar's question, "Would you have taken part in the uprising of 14 December if you had been in St. Petersburg," Pushkin answered: "Undoubtedly, sire. All my friends were in the plot, and I could not have done otherwise. Only my absence saved me." The audience resulted in a truce of sorts. The tsar proclaimed Pushkin "Russia's most intelligent man," ended his exile and offered to be the poet's personal censor. For his part Pushkin presumably confirmed his pledge "not to contradict the accepted order," something he had expressed already in his May letter to Nicholas I.[19] Virtually overnight Pushkin became the darling of the Moscow beau monde and voiced his optimism for the new emperor in the poem "Stanzas" (Stansy, 1826). This did not endear him to his liberal compatriots who saw the poet's pas de deux with the tsar more as a faux pas unworthy of the author of "Liberty." Pushkin felt that he had gained a measure of the tsar's trust and that he could help him (as Karamzin had tried to help Alexander), and thus Russia. In any event, he paid dearly for the attempt to establish a union between poet and tsar. As the great civic critic Belinsky later put it, "All it took to suddenly lose the people's love was to write two or three loyalist [*vernopoddannicheskie*] poems and don the livery of a Gentleman of the Chamber."[20] In the poem "To Friends" ("Druz'iam," 1828) — the title is ironic — Pushkin was compelled to defend himself against the accusations that he had become a court toady.

It took some time before Pushkin fully realized that he had fallen into a trap. Ostensibly he was free, but actually he was the tsar's hostage under the supervision of General Benckendorff, the chief of the notorious "Third Department" and one of the tsar's closest aides. Without explicit permission the poet was not allowed to travel, publish, or hold public readings. One of Pushkin's first contretemps with the authorities involved the poem "André Chénier" (1825), presumed to contain a hidden reference

---

19 For a reconstruction of this audience see Eidel'man, 24–64.

20 V. G. Belinskii, *Polnoe sobranie sochinenii*, 13 vols. (Moscow: AN SSSR, 1953–1959), 10:217.

to the December uprising, although it was written some time before that and its subject was the fate of a poet in the French Revolution. Then, in 1828 the blasphemous *Gabrieliad* (written back in 1821) came to the attention of the Metropolitan of St. Petersburg. To save himself Pushkin kept denying his authorship; eventually, however, he confessed in a personal letter to Nicholas I, who forgave him and the matter was closed. Even so, 1828 was an exceptionally bleak year for Pushkin. On his birthday (26 May) he wrote his most despairing Job-like lament, "Gift futile, gift random, / Why, life, have you been given to me" ("Dar naprasnyi, dar sluchainyi"). In the same year Pushkin repeatedly asked permission to undertake some activity that would alter the circumstances of his trapped existence: to join the army in the war against Turkey, to travel to France, to take part in a diplomatic mission to China. All requests were denied. It was also during these difficult years (1828–30) that Pushkin was feverishly searching for a wife. His gypsy-like existence had become a burden to him; he longed for some rootedness, for a hearth and a family, yet he also realized that his reputation made him a less than attractive candidate for matrimony. Now he proposed to several women, yet each time was rejected. In 1828 at a Moscow ball he met the stunning sixteen-year-old Natalya Goncharova and proposed to her the following year in May. After an indefinite answer from Natalya's mother, which Pushkin perceived as another rejection, he bolted the same day for the Caucasus. There he visited his friends and his brother Lev at the front. Riding a Cossack horse in his frock coat and a top hat, lance in hand, he single-handedly "attacked" the Turks; luckily he was rescued by Russian Uhlans who not without reason took him for a mad German priest. (Throughout his entire life Pushkin had wanted to experience the thrill of battle.) In June Pushkin, along with the troops, rode into the newly conquered Turkish town Erzurum — this was the poet's first and last time abroad — where he remained until a plague epidemic chased him back across the Russian border. His suggestive travel notes would be published under the title *A Journey to Arzrum* (*Puteshestvie v Arzrum*, revised in 1835). Upon return he was duly reprimanded by Benckendorff for undertaking the journey without tsar's express consent.

To the most important works of the second half of the 1820s belong the lyrics "The Prophet" ("Prorok," 1826), "The Poet" (1827), "Arion" (1827), "Recollection" ("Vospominanie," 1828), "The Upas Tree" ("Anchar," 1828); the poetic dialogue "The Poet and the Crowd" ("Poet i tolpa," 1828); and the narrative poem *Poltava* (1828). Of these, "The Prophet" displayed the poet's newfound seriousness about his calling; "Arion"'s ambiguous title — the singer the shipmates conspire to throw overboard for his prize winnings but who is miraculously saved by a dolphin — may have been meant to tell former Decembrist friends that they nearly destroyed the poet; and "The Upas Tree," one of Pushkin's most beautifully executed works, delved into the origins of power. Pushkin considered *Poltava*, with its interweaving of tragic love story (the grizzled hetman Mazepa who uses the feelings of the innocent Maria to entrap and kill her father) and historical epic (Peter's defeat of Charles XII and the Swedes at the 1709 battle giving the poem its name), his best work so far in the *poema* (narrative/epic poem) genre. However, *Poltava* was received coldly by the reading public, a fact which clearly bothered Pushkin as he tried to find his way in a changing literary marketplace. Still revered as a man of letters and a figure of some importance, the poet knew his popularity was on the wane.

1830–1833: Boldino 1, Marriage, Historian, Pugachev, Boldino 2

On Easter Sunday 6 April 1830 Pushkin proposed again to Natalya Goncharova. This time his proposal was grudgingly accepted, and the couple were officially betrothed a month later. Now Pushkin had to provide a dowry for his bride, for such was the bizarre condition laid down by his future mother-in-law. The poet set off for Boldino in the province of Nizhny Novgorod (Gorky), to take possession of two villages and to mortgage two hundred souls — his father's wedding present to him. Upon arrival there Pushkin learned that a cholera epidemic had broken out and threatened to reach Moscow. Quarantines blocked his way back to his fiancée and he had to stay in this backwater, fearing the worst, for almost three months. Dreaming of Eros but surrounded on all sides by Thanatos the poet came under an unprecedented spell of inspiration during this "first Boldino autumn." He writes moving elegies in which he bids farewell to the female ghosts of prior love affairs; finishes the two last chapters of *Eugene Onegin* and burns chapter 10; inaugurates his "descent to prose" by penning the five experimental *Belkin Tales* (*Povesti Belkina*); and rethinks the concept of tragedy in four brilliant "dramatic sketches," which have come down to us as *The Little Tragedies* (*Malen'kie tragedii*). He also produces a metapoetically playful anecdote in ottava rima, *The Little House in Kolomna* (*Domik v Kolomne*), his first fairy tale in verse, "The Tale of the Village Priest and His Workman Balda" ("Skazka o pope i rabotnike ego Balde"), and over a dozen dazzling poems, among them, "The Devils" (Besy), "My Genealogy" (Moia rodoslovnaia), and "The Hero" (Geroi). Had Pushkin created nothing more than what he wrote during this first Boldino sojourn, he would still be Russia's greatest poet.

When he finally returned to Moscow Pushkin was confronted with the sad news that his closest friend from the Lycée days, Anton Delvig, was dead. On 18 February 1831 Pushkin and Goncharova were wed in the Ascension Church in Moscow. During the ceremony the cross and Scriptures fell from the altar and the candle Pushkin was holding went out: "Tous les mauvais augures," remarked the superstitious poet. Still, in the first blush of conjugal life the poet could remark to a friend that "I am married, and happy." Soon, however, the difficult presence of the mother-in-law drove the couple from Moscow. They moved in May to Tsarskoe Selo, where Pushkin had spent his happy Lycée years. Once in the vicinity of the capital Mme. Pushkina eclipsed all others with her exceptional beauty and became the smash hit of the social season. One of her admirers was none other than the emperor himself. If Pushkin believed in anything it was in the transfiguring power of beauty, whether the physical charm of Venus or the spiritual calm of the Virgin, and for him "Natalie," probably unbeknownst to her, was the embodiment of both. It was in the contemplation of such beauty that Pushkin dedicated to her the poems "Madonna" (1830) and the intimate "No, I do not prize stormy pleasure" ("Net, ia ne dorozhu miatezhnym naslazhdeniem," 1831?).

In Tsarskoe Selo Pushkin met Gogol for the first time—their relationship would become particularly fruitful for the latter. During a meeting with Nicholas I in July 1831 the tsar mentioned that he would like to obtain Peter the Great's house in Zaandam, Holland from the Dutch monarch. Always ready with a quip, Pushkin replied that should this happen he would be interested in the post of janitor. Instead the tsar appointed Pushkin court historiographer with the charge of studying in the archives and writing a history of Peter the Great. The poet, promoted now to the rank of titular councilor, began work on *The History of Peter the Great*, but was soon drawn to the Cossack rebellion of 1773–74, led by the notorious pretender Emelian Pugachev, who assumed the identity of Catherine's the Great assassinated husband, Peter III. Also, in 1831 Pushkin responded to the Polish uprising against Russian domination with two "patriotic" (i.e., anti-Polish, anti-European) verse invectives, "To the Calumniators of Russia" ("Klevetnikam Rossii") and "Borodino Anniversary" ("Borodinskaia godovshchina").

In fall 1833 Pushkin traveled to the Urals to collect oral histories of the rebellion. Eyewitnesses were dying out and he had to hurry. His research resulted in two very distinct versions of the rebel leader, an unvarnished (demythologized) one in the factual *History of Pugachev Rebellion* (1833) and a benevolent (romanticized) one in the historical novel *The Captain's Daughter* (1836). On his way home Pushkin stopped again at Boldino. As it happened, the poet had written little since his last stay. Now during his "second Boldino autumn" the need to write again overwhelmed him. Within six weeks he had finished the *History of Pugachev*, two fairy tales in verse, the brothers Grimm-inspired "The Tale of the Fisherman and the Fish" ("Skazka o rybake i rybke") and "The Tale of the Dead Tsarevna" (Skazka o mertvoi tsarevne); the verse adaptation *Angelo* (*Andzhelo*), based on Shakespeare's *Measure for Measure*, to become the poet's favorite work; and two of his greatest creations, the epic poem *The Bronze Horseman* (*Mednyi vsadnik*) and the prose tale "The Queen of Spades" (Pikovaia dama). In addition Pushkin wrote here the poetic "fragment" (*otryvok*) "Autumn" ("Osen'") and the haunting lyric "God grant that I not go mad" ("Ne dai mne Bog soiti s uma) and began the essay "Journey from Moscow to Petersburg" ("Puteshevtvie iz Moskvy v Peterburg," 1833–34).

In 1833 the first complete edition of *Eugene Onegin* came out. But the year ended on a sour note: on 31 December Nicholas I awarded Pushkin the court title "Gentleman of the Chamber" (*kameriunker*), something usually conferred on more junior scions of high aristocratic lineage. The no longer young poet (thirty-four years was already a substantial age for the time, and Pushkin looked every bit his age) felt humiliated, suspecting that the true reason why the tsar made him a courtier was to create a pathway of eligibility to his royal balls at Anichkov Palace for Mme. Pushkina.

1834–1836: Family man and Courtier

Pushkin did not hide the fact that his life as a courtier was a burden to him. Indeed, he hated his uniform, as it was a symbol of his humiliation ("a jester's motley," he would say) and he tried to avoid ceremonies where he was required to wear it. And at balls, whose social buzz once stimulated him, he would now demonstrably yawn, knowing that he had been cast in the despicable role of ugly husband to a beautiful wife and resenting the attention paid to her by admirers, first and foremost the tsar himself. The high-style living in the capital, the necessary appearances at court, the sartorial needs of his wife, the settling of debts accumulated by his spendthrift brother Lev — all this proved to be beyond the financial means of a professional writer and court historiographer. The poet was now forced to ask for subsidies and credit from Nicholas, just as it was not uncommon for him to turn to pawnbrokers for ready cash. By 1834 Pushkin was a father of two children (with two still to come) and, as if that weren't enough, two of Natalya's unmarried sisters had come to live with the family indefinitely. "If I die, my wife will be on the streets and my children in misery," he wrote to his brother-in-law in 1833.[21] By the time of his death his debts would number approximately 140,000 rubles.

In a 20 April 1834 letter to his wife Pushkin spoke with unguarded sarcasm of his court title. When he learned that this private letter was intercepted by the post and passed to the Third Department, the morally outraged husband handed Benckendorff his resignation. Pushkin later withdrew it under pressure from his friend and protector Zhukovsky, the tutor of the future Alexander II. Harassed by creditors, Pushkin made another request in 1835 for permission to retire for a time to his country estate in order to improve his financial situation. The request was not granted; instead, Pushkin was allowed to start a literary quarterly *The Contemporary* (*Sovremennik*), a venture which would sink him only further in debt. The theme of escape now figures prominently in poems such as "It's time, my friend, it's time" ("Pora, moi drug, pora," 1834) and "The Pilgrim" ("Strannik," 1835), a verse adaptation of John Bunyan's *The Pilgrim's Progress* (1678). In spite of his exhaustion and despondency the poet still managed to finish several important works, including: "The Fairy Tale of the Golden Cockerel" (Skazka o zolotom petushke, 1834), in which the Washington Irving source is used to encode feelings closer to home about a tsar reneging on his promise and stealing his stargazer-adviser's one wish, the beautiful maiden; "Songs of the Western Slavs" ("Pesni zapadnykh slavian," 1834); and *The Captain's Daughter* (1836), the superb historical novel about the Pugachev rebellion that reworks ingeniously the plot-line of Walter Scott's *Rob Roy*. He also continues to solicit and edit contributions for *The Contemporary*.

During the last summer of his life (1836) Pushkin turns to spiritual themes in a cycle of lyrics thematically arranged as steps along the *via dolorosa* of Holy Week: "Hermit fathers and immaculate women" ("Ottsy pustynniki i zheny neporochny"), "Imitation of the Italian" ("Podrazhanie italiianskomu"), "Secular Power" ("Mirskaia vlast'"), "When I, pensive, roam beyond the city" ("Kogda za gorodom, zadumchiv, ia brozhu"), and "I have erected for myself

[21] *Vremennik Pushkinskoi Komissii za 1970 g.* (Leningrad: Nauka, 1972), 7.

a monument not made by hand" ("Ia pamiatnik sebe vozdvig nerukotvornyi"). The poems "From Pindemonte" and "I have erected..." written that summer can be read as Pushkin's political and poetic last will and testament.

1836–1837: Duel and Death

Throughout 1836 George d'Anthès, a handsome Frenchman serving in the Russian Royal Guards, relentlessly pursued the poet's wife, who was, in his words, "la plus délicieuse créature de Pétersbourg."²² In February, in the seventh month of her pregnancy, the clearly not indifferent Natalya may have confessed to her suitor, as Tatyana had to Onegin, that she did love him but could offer him "no more than [her] heart, because the rest does not belong to [her]."²³ On 2 November 1836 d'Anthès succeeded in arranging a secret rendezvous with Mme. Pushkin (how much Natalya actually knew is open to question) at the house of Idalia Poletika, one of Pushkin's enemies. During the encounter d'Anthès allegedly pulled out a pistol and threatened to kill himself in front of the distraught woman if she would not give herself to him. Somehow Natalya managed to escape.²⁴ Two days later, on 4 November, Pushkin received an anonymous "diploma" stating that he had been unanimously elected to the post of Deputy Grand Master and Historiographer of the Most Noble Order of Cuckolds. Copies of the "diploma" were also sent to Pushkin's friends for forwarding to the poet—a gesture meant further to humiliate him. Pushkin then had a tête-à-tête with Natalya who admitted all: that d'Anthès had been pursuing her and that he had entrapped her just days before. At this point she also showed her husband d'Anthès's letters to her and told him that the Dutch ambassador, Baron Louis van Heeckeren, d'Anthès's adoptive father, had pleaded with her to acquiesce to his son's advances. Convinced that his wife was innocent and enraged at her treatment, Pushkin resolved to defend her (and of course his) honor. That same evening he challenged d'Anthès to a duel. The conditions were calculated to produce a lethal outcome, with the barriers set a mere ten paces apart. "The bloodier, the better," demanded Pushkin.²⁵ To shield his wife from the rumor mill Pushkin did not mention to anybody the entrapment at Poletika's.

But the course of events did not unfold as Pushkin had projected. The duel was postponed twice as d'Anthès suddenly claimed that he was actually in love with Natalya's sister Ekaterina and was preparing to propose to her. Pushkin

22 From d'Anthès's letter to Heeckeren, Janurary 1836, in S. Vitale and V.P. Stark, *Chernaia rechka* (St. Petersburg: Zvezda, 2000), 112. This is a bilingual edition of the d'Anthès-Heeckeren correspondence. Henceforth 'Vitale/Stark.'

23 D'Anthès' letter to Heeckeren of 14 Feb 1836, in Vitale/Stark, 125.

24 Reported by Vera Vyazemskaya to Bartenev, in P.I. Bartenev, *O Pushkine* (Moscow: Sovetskaia Rossiia, 1992; orig. pub. 1888), 384. See also S. Abramovich, *Pushkin: Poslednii god* (Moscow: Sovetskii pisatel', 1991), 396.

25 *Letopis'*, 4: 533.

tried to call d'Anthès's bluff, calculating that by compelling him to marry Ekaterina, the proposal would be perceived in society, and more importantly in the young man's regiment, as a cowardly ploy to sidestep the duel. The other likely reason why Pushkin did not believe that d'Anthès would propose to Ekaterina was the well-known rumor that Heeckeren had been having a homosexual liaison with his adopted son.[26] In order to diffuse this suspicion, which could seriously compromise his career in the Horse Guards, the (apparently bisexual?) d'Anthès sought a public affair with a brilliant society woman. Thus after Natalya rejected his suit, he began courting her sister. On 17 November d'Anthès formally proposed to Ekaterina and Pushkin, savoring victory, retracted his challenge. The kind-to-a-fault Zhukovsky then broke his word to Puskin to keep silent and informed Nicholas I about the events, after which the tsar summoned Pushkin for an audience on 23 November. Pushkin swore to Nicholas he would not fight; he also promised not to discuss the matter further and to inform the tsar in the event of any subsequent conflict. The marriage between d'Anthès and Ekaterina Goncharova took place on 10 January 1837. Pushkin did not attend the ceremony and refused to receive the couple at his home. He believed that he had made the dashing French officer look like a coward in the eyes of society and had punished him sufficiently by forcing him to marry the unloved, unattractive Ekaterina, who was three years his senior and quite possibly already pregnant with his child.[27] Pushkin's friends continued to receive the new couple and d'Anthès resumed his pursuit of Natalya. Now he was insinuating that he married Ekaterina in order to be closer to Natalya, his true love. Instead of being painted a coward d'Anthès became in the eyes of the beau monde a romantic hero who sacrificed himself in order to save the honor of the lady of his heart. Juxtaposed to such "chivalrous self-sacrifice" Pushkin's outbursts of jealousy and sullenness looked foolish in the eyes of society, including his own friends and well-wishers. Unable to forgive or forget the humiliating "diploma," Pushkin was fuming and on edge. Some friends saw his fits of rage, "demonic laughter," and "grinding of teeth," as signs of his "African temperament"—in a word, the reappearance of his Othello syndrome.

During a ball on 23 January 1837 d'Anthès publicly quipped to Natalya that, according to the chiropodist shared by the Goncharov sisters, "votre cor est plus beau que celui de ma femme" (your corn/body [cor/corps] is more beautiful than that of my wife's).[28] Pushkin was incensed when Natalya reported the remark to him, and the corn on the shapely lady's foot thus became the last drop causing the poet's gall-filled cup to overflow. On the

26 See P.E. Shchegolev, *Duel' i smert' Pushkina* (Moscow: Zhurnal'no-Gazetnoe Ob"edinenie, 1936), 269; A.A. Akhmatova, *O Pushkine* (Leningrad: Sovetskii pisatel', 1977), 128–129; Lotman, 384–386; and S. Vitale, *Pushkin's Button* (New York: Farrar, Straus and Giroux, 1999), 146.
27 Suggested by L. Grossman in "Zhenit'ba Dantesa," *Krasnaia niva* 24 (1929). See also Frans Suasso, *Dichter, dame, diplomat: het laatste jaar van Alexander Poesjkin* (Leiden,1988), and the new evidence in Vitale/Stark, 175, 177, 189, 221–223.
28 *PvVS*, 2: 305; Abramovich, 526.

next day (24 January) Pushkin pawned his sister-in-law Alexandra's silverware for 2200 rubles to purchase a pair of Lepage dueling pistols and a day later wrote an extremely insulting letter to Baron Heeckeren. Pushkin accused the Dutch Ambassador of acting like an "obscene old woman" and of playing the "pimp" for his "bastard" and "syphilitic" son who was also a "coward" and "scoundrel."[29] A duel was now inevitable. Since fighting was not an option for a foreign ambassador, Baron Heeckeren challenged Pushkin in the name of his adopted son.

On 27 January 1837 the duel took place on the Black River, not far from where the Pushkins had summered in the past. The poet arrived at the barrier before his rival, but d'Anthès got off the first shot. Pushkin was hit in the abdomen and collapsed in the snow. He then raised himself on his elbow, took aim at his adversary, and fired. When d'Anthès fell, Pushkin exclaimed "Bravo!" and tossed away his pistol. D'Anthès was wounded lightly, Pushkin mortally. On his death bed (in one account) Pushkin asked for Nicholas's forgiveness for breaking his word. "Tell him that I'm sorry to die and that I would have been all his."[30] He also asked that his second Danzas not be punished. When it was clear that the wound was mortal and there was no hope of recovery it was decided to perform the last rites. Those present bore witness to the excruciating pain that Pushkin experienced in his last days and hours, as doctors administered twenty-five leeches and gave him opium.[31] His final vision was one of ascent—he saw himself climbing out of his sickbed and "crawling around his books and bookshelves high above."[32] At 2: 45 p.m., on the 29th of January 1837, the poet's life ended.

Thousands of people came to mourn Pushkin's passing. In order to prevent demonstrations the government shifted the funeral from St. Isaac's Cathedral to the small Church of the Savior on Konyushennaya Street near Pushkin's home. The location was cordoned off by police and admission tickets were issued to court members and diplomats. On 2 February the coffin with the poet's body was sent secretly, at midnight, to Mikhailovskoe. It was accompanied by an old friend, A.Turgenev, who had helped with the poet's admission to the Lycée, the poet's aged butler, Nikita Kozlov, and a gendarme. Pushkin was buried on 6 February 1837 next to his mother in their family plot on the grounds of Sviatye Gory Monastery. Nicholas I generously took on Pushkin's debt and provided for the family, including granting pensions to the widow and daughters and allowances for the sons. He also promised to publish the poet's collected works at state expense for the benefit of the widow and children.

29   *Pss*, 16: 221–222.
30   *Letopis'*, 4:598.
31   T.J. Binyon, *Pushkin* (London: HarperCollins, 2002), 629.
32   *Letopis'*, 4: 601.

Chapter 9

Pushkin's Mythopoetic Consciousness: Apuleius, Psyche and Cupid, and the Theme of Metamorphosis in *Eugene Onegin*[1]

Pushkin was possessed of a richly mythopoetic consciousness. He was also, as numerous friends attest, intensely superstitious. Indeed, for a poet of Pushkin's range and energy, it is not surprising that some of his finest works are motivated thematically on the dual and interpenetrating notions that myths can, literally, come to life and that forces beyond one's control can prearrange one's destiny. Yet Pushkin never made the connection between certain crucial myths (or beliefs, superstitions) and his own unfolding biography *explicit*. He was protected from this not only by his own *amour propre* but by the carapace of what Lydia Ginzburg terms "genre consciousness."[2] Stories about the fortuneteller Kirchhof or the hare and the monk seen by the poet as he was preparing to depart for St. Petersburg on the eve of the Decembrist uprising are tantalizing facts of Pushkin's biography *(if* they are facts),[3] but their potential status in Pushkin's works, where everything having to do with the historical person is artistically

---

[1] First appeared as "Mifopoeticheskoe soznanie u Pushkina: Apulei, 'Kupidon i Psikheia' i tema metamorfozy v 'Evgenii Onegine'," in *Materialy po Pushkinskoi konferentsii v Stenforde* [Papers of the Pushkin Bicentennial Conference at Stanford], ed. D. Bethea, L. Fleishman, N. Okhotin, A. Ospovat, (Issledovaniia i materialy po russkoi kul'ture (Moscow: OGI, 2001), 208–232; also as "Pushkin's Mythopoetic Consciousness: Apuleius, Psyche and Cupid, and the Theme of Metamorphosis in *Evgenii Onegin*," in *Two Hundred Years of Pushkin*, vol. 2. (*Alexander Pushkin: Myth and Monument*), ed. Robert Reid and Joe Andrew (Amsterdam: Rodopi, 2003), 15–37.

[2] "Myshlenie zhanrovymi kategoriiami": see discussion in L. Ginzburg, *O lirike*, 2nd ed. (Leningrad: Sovetskii pisatel'), 183.

[3] The *locus classicus* in this case is Pushkin's friend S.A. Sobolevsky's article "Tainstvennye primety v zhizni Pushkina," first published in *Russkii arkhiv* in 1870 and subsequently excerpted (that is, the relevant section about Kirchhof's prophecy) in V.E. Vatsuro et al., eds., *Pushkin v vospominaniiakh sovremennikov* (St. Petersburg: Akademicheskii proekt, 1998), 2:9–11. See also I.S. Chistova, "K stat'e S.A. Sobolevsksogo 'Tainstvennye primety v zhizni Pushkina,'" in M.N. Virolainen, ed., *Legendy i mify o Pushkine* (St. Petersburg: Akademicheskii proekt, 1994), 249–56.

masked, is highly problematic. In other words, Pushkin could be as serious as he wanted within the bounds of a lyric poem, and given the date of composition of a work such as "The Prophet" (1826) it is hard to believe we as readers cannot make a connection between the violent change in the speaker and the shock of recognition in the real-life post-Decembrist Pushkin, but according to the rules of "genre consciousness" we cannot in good faith elide the historical man with the constructed voice. Thus we can speak of "The Prophet" as a poem of conversion, but any discussion of a converted "Pushkin" has to be placed in quotes.

There is a way, however, to get closer to Pushkin's mythopoeticizing consciousness and to see it in action, as it were. Pushkin used different angles of vision or "voice zones" — title, epigraph, dedication, text proper, and footnotes — to suggest ways of vectoring in on competing truths (romantic, historical, etc.) within one work, say, *Poltava*.[4] No one truth holds sway in *Poltava*; its "story" is the different truths' spirited coexistence within the bounds of a single text, which in turn is a model of the world. Likewise, we as readers can compare Pushkin's references to a single myth (or related myths) within a relatively short time period and from different generic voice zones. It would also help of course if the time period were one fraught with certain life choices and heightened by fear and anxiety. My purpose here is not to break down entirely the walls of "genre consciousness" (not that different from the precepts of New Criticism, after all) and engage in another instance of freewheeling postmodern intrusiveness, but rather to demonstrate, through a careful parsing of the evidence, that Pushkin *returned* to a certain mythopoetic core, let us call it the idea of *metamorphosis*, that he needed to guide some of his greatest works, including *Eugene Onegin*, and the creative life that fed them.

Two myths dominate Pushkin's thinking at the time of his marriage and his "descent to prose." These myths are complementary and they have one important structural element in common: metamorphosis, or a radical "change in form" that is simultaneously a change in substance. The first has to do with the female statue that comes to life (the Pygmalion story); the second has to do with the female soul in search of love and knowledge (the Psyche and Cupid story). It is important to note, with regard to different angles of vision, that the Pygmalion story, first appearing in Ovid's *Metamorphoses*, is told from the point of view of the legendary king/sculptor receiving the gift of the living statue, while the Psyche and Cupid story, first appearing in Apuleius' *Metamorphoses, or The Golden Ass*, is told from the point of view of the young princess

---

[4] See discussion in Iu.M. Lotman, "Posviashchenie 'Poltavy' (adresat, tekst, funktsiia)" and "K strukture dialogicheskogo teksta v poemakh Pushkina (problema avtorskikh premechanii k tekstu)," in *Izbrannye stat'i* (Tallinn: Aleksandra, 1992–93), 2:369–88.

who marries, unbeknownst to her, the god of love. My focus in this study will be primarily on the Psyche and Cupid story, as I have discussed the Pygmalion myth at some length elsewhere.[5] Briefly stated, the change that is the needy Pygmalion's gift is the one given the male narrator (or stylized "Pushkin") in *Eugene Onegin*, where the muse comes alive when a modest village maiden is "miraculously" transformed into a beautiful and wise princess; the change that is the equally needy Psyche's gift, on the other hand, is the one given the heroine Tatiana — *knowledge* of eros. How these changes relate to Pushkin the person (and bridegroom) will be noted in the course of my analysis.

During his first and most prolific Boldino autumn Pushkin was, as we know, simultaneously contemplating his upcoming marriage and anxiously corresponding across fourteen quarantines of a cholera epidemic with his fiancée in Moscow. He feared for himself, feared more for Natalie caught in the plague-infested city, and all the while wondered whether he, with his past (both its wander and its lust), was fit for domestic life with this exquisite beauty. Literal and figurative matchmakers and gravediggers/coffinmakers populate many of the works of this feverish period, from *Belkin Tales* to the *Little Tragedies* to the famous poem "The Devils" (*Besy*).[6] This was also the time Pushkin completed (except for Onegin's letter to Tatiana) the last chapter of *Eugene Onegin*. With this in mind, let us turn to another document Pushkin wrote that autumn. Referred to in the scholarly literature as "Refutation of Criticisms" ("Oproverzhenie na kritiki"), this piece was Pushkin's way of setting down his own responses to the faults others had found in his works over the years. His tone was often tetchy and much of what he wrote was never meant to be published. But one section he did publish the following year, in *The Morning Star* (*Dennitsa*), was both finished and important enough to see into print. The excerpt begins with reference as to why his *Poltava*, which he felt to be completely "original" and better than much of his earlier work, was a failure in the eyes of his critics. It was, first and foremost, because "no one has ever seen a woman fall in love with an old man and, therefore, Maria's love for the old hetman [Mazepa] ... could not have existed."[7] The paragraph that follows is key to my argument, so I will quote it in full:

> I couldn't remain content with this explanation: love is the most capricious of passions. I'm not even speaking about the ugliness and stupidity that are preferred daily to youth, intelligence, and beauty. Recall the mythological legends, the

---

5   See David M. Bethea, *Realizing Metaphors: Alexander Pushkin and the Life of the Poet* (Madison: University of Wisconsin Press, Madison, 1998), 10–17, 89–117.

6   See David M. Bethea and Sergei Davydov, "Pushkin's Saturnine Cupid: The Poetics of Parody in *The Tales of Belkin*," *PMLA* 96.1 (January 1981): 8–21.

7   A.S. Pushkin, *Polnoe sobranie sochinenii*, ed. B.V. Tomashevskii, 10 vols. (Leningrad: Nauka, 1977–79), 7:132. This edition will be referred to subsequently as *Pss*.

metamorphoses of Ovid — Leda, Philyra, Pasiphae, Pygmalion — and admit that all of these fantasies [vymysly] are not devoid of poetry. And Othello, the old Moor [negr], who captivated Desdemona with stories of his wanderings and battles ... And Myrrha, who inspired the Italian poet [Alfieri] with one of his best tragedies?[8]

How this argument implicates the speaker personally, who was obviously fretting over the May-December aspects of his union with the eighteen-year-old Natalie, is clear. As always with Pushkin, he speaks more about himself when he speaks about others. But this passage is also illuminating in the way that it presents Pushkin's deeply mythopoetic consciousness orienting itself toward the twin notions of metamorphosis and the writing of eros into life or "plot."

If we look a little closer, two things strike us about Pushkin's list proving love's "capriciousness." first, all the examples from Ovid involve females except one — Pygmalion.[9] And second, the story of Othello and Desdemona does not belong to Ovid at all, but to Shakespeare (via Cintio's *Ecatommiti*). The common denominator in all of these is the *unnaturalness* of the union. Leda is ravished by Zeus in the form of a swan; because Minos refuses to sacrifice the beautiful bull given him by Poseidon, the god causes Minos' wife Pasiphae to become enamored of the bull, with which she couples and gives birth to the Minotaur; likewise, Philyra lies down with Saturn, who has transformed himself into a horse, and produces the centaur Chiron. The unnaturalness in the case of Myrrha is that of incest: in the original Ovidian version, she conceives a fatal passion for her father Cinyras, tricks him into making love with her in the dark, is impregnated by him, and for her crime is transformed into the myrrh tree. The metamorphosis that Pushkin senses at the centre of *Othello* is for us especially pertinent: not only does the story involve the "inexplicable" love of the beautiful Desdemona for the "monstrous" Moor, with both family (Brabantio) and society (led by Iago) condemning the couple for "making the beast with two backs," but deeply implicated in the plot of the tragedy is Apuleius' tale of Psyche and Cupid, only in reverse. At the climax of Shakespeare's play it is the male spouse who, coming in the dark to murder the female one, is concerned with lamps ("Put out the light, and then put out the light"), lets fall on the comely sleeper (thus waking her) not a drop of boiling oil but his own hot tear, and, *contra* Apuleius (hence the tragedy), does succeed in killing what is most dear to him.[10] When Pushkin says that "these fantasies are not devoid of

8   Ibid.
9   Pushkin had at least three different editions of Ovid, two French and one Latin, in his library as catalogued by Modzalevsky: 1) *Amours mythologiques, traduits des Métamorphoses d'Ovide par De Pongerville*, second edition, Paris, 1827 (No. 1231 in catalogue); *Œuvres complètes d'Ovide*, ed. J.Ch. Poncelin, Paris, 1799 (No. 1232 in catalogue); and *Publii Ovidii Nasonis opera*, ed. J.A. Amar, Paris, 1822 (No.1233 in catalogue). See B.L. Modzalevskii, "Biblioteka A.S. Pushkina," in *Pushkin i ego sovremenniki. Materialy i issledovanii* 9–10 (1910): 304.

10   See commentary in P.G. Walsh, "Introduction" in Apuleius,

poetry," what he means is that desire is by definition unexpectedly, even shockingly, specific (a beautiful woman who, aroused, makes love to a bull or her father or an exotic blackamoor), just as it is both potentially "beautiful" and potentially "beastly."

How these stories link up to the actual Pushkin of the first Boldino autumn is, as we noted, fraught with conceptual problems, but perhaps not impossibly so. First, let it be said that, given his "protean" genius and the remarkable capaciousness of his imaginative empathy, Pushkin could insert himself, or his "textual desire," into multiple roles. One of the hallmarks of a Pushkin work is that the poet is everywhere and he is nowhere: he is Aleko and the Old Gypsy, Peter and Evgeny, Petrusha Grinev and Masha Mironova and even Pugachev himself. Indeed, at risk of contradicting myself, I would suggest that there are certain characters in Pushkin who are especially imbued with their author's desire: Grigory Otrepev, Tatiana, and Don Guan, for example. But this statement can be proved only by a methodical sifting of textual (artistically shaped) and non-textual (artistically unshaped and in many cases deriving from the observations of others) evidence that in any event is beyond the bounds of my analysis here. For now, suffice it to say that Pushkin was clearly smitten with the Othello story and read it into his own biography more than once in the second half of the 1820s, in the years leading up to his marriage: perhaps most persuasively for our purposes, he worked its major themes and plot peripeteias into his most autobiographically suffused narrative — *The Blackamoor of Peter the Great* (1827–28). In that unfinished (because it was too autobiographical?) historical novel we find a nexus of associations that is both familiar (Shakespearean) and new and specific (Pushkinian): passionate Abyssinian blood; family patriarch celebrated for his feats in battle;[11] love for a beautiful woman of the best society who is not only not put off but is actually aroused by the black man's "terrifying" exterior; a noble, trusting nature ("one that lov'd not wisely but too well" and "one not easily jealous, but being wrought / Perplex'd in the extreme") that, fearing betrayal, is nearly devoured by the "green-eyed monster." Add to this the evidence, presented convincingly by Tatiana Tsiavlovskaya, that Pushkin experienced the end of his affair with Elizaveta Vorontsova and his exile from Odessa to Mikhailovskoe as a kind of reenactment of his great-grandfather's story ("black-white" coupling, "Proserpinian" undercurrents of jealousy and betrayal, a natural child who is racially "unnatural," return to "Russia" and "Russianness" from "abroad"), and we begin to see how crucial this notion of a "beauty and the beast" metamorphosis was to Pushkin's interpretation of

---

The Golden Ass, intro. and trans. P.G. Walsh (Oxford: Oxford University Press, 1994), xlvi-vii.

  11 To be accurate, Abram [Ibrahim] Petrovich Gannibal's prowess as a military engineer (he eventually rose to the rank of general of the army [*generalanshef*] would come much later, and is not part of the storyline of *The Blackamoor of Peter the Great*. But as is clear from Pushkin's famous note to stanza 50 of the first chapter of *Eugene Onegin*, these exploits were well-known to the great-grandson and reinforced, as historical background or "horizon of expectations," the connection with the Othello story in the uncompleted *Blackamoor*. *Pss*, 5:430–31.

the facts given to him by the twin fates of biography and history.[12] That the Desdemona of Shakespeare was young, inexperienced, deeply in love with the Moor, and despite Iago's machinations, ultimately faithful was not lost on Pushkin. Where *Blackamoor* breaks off, that is, after Ibrahim has finally begun to get over his affair with the lovely yet anything-but-monogamous "Parisian"[13] Countess D. and to set his sights on the "unspoiled" and echt-Russian maiden of old boyar stock Natalya Gavrilovna Rzhevskaya, is also not far from the place that Pushkin the unlucky suitor had arrived with his own feelings by the late 1820s. The wishful thinking (artistic licence) that has Russia's greatest tsar assuring his godson of his inherent worth and dignity and informing the Rzhevsky family that it is the tsar's will that they make peace with the bridegroom they call a "black devil" strikes the reader as nothing short of divine intervention. It is as though this Othello has help from a fairy godfather as he prepares to win his homegrown Desdemona with tales of his adventures.

We know from a variety of sources, including his own private statements, that Pushkin was, from a very young age, sensitive about his appearance. But this knowledge gives the modern reader no special privilege, no psychoanalytic wedge, that pries open like a hinge the poet's "inner life." Pushkin's ugly-duckling appearance was no secret,[14] while that inner life was. His "blackamoorish ugliness" (arapskoe moe bezobrazie),[15] which some women found so repellent as to be attractive,[16] is simply a fact, though a not insignificant one, of his biography. What does concern us, however, is how Pushkin turned this perceived lack into gain by placing it at the center of his personal mythology through the theme of metamorphosis: undesirable transformed into desirable, nature rewritten as culture. Perhaps an example taken from his early verse can give a more vivid sense of what I have in mind:

> While I, an eternally frivolous scapegrace,
> An ugly descendant of Negroes,
> Raised in wild simplicity,
> Not knowing the sufferings of love,

---

12 T.G. Tsiavlovskaia, "Khrani menia, moi talisman," in R.V. Iezuitova and Ia.L. Levkovich, eds, *Utaennaia liubov' Pushkina* (St. Petersburg: Akademicheskii proekt, 1997), 295–380. Tsiavlovkaia's piece first appeared in *Prometei* 10 (1974): 12–84.

13 Elizaveta Ksarverevna Vorontsova ('Elise') was of Polish origin and Pushkin seems to have been playing off her "western" charms as he developed the figure of Countess D. in the novel. The same use of the Poles as western "others" plays an important role in *Boris Godunov*, for example.

14 'Vrai singe par sa mine' ('a real monkey in the face'), he writes while describing himself in the early Lycée poem "Mon Portrait," *Pss*, 1:80. "Mon Portrait," written in French, was not published in Pushkin's lifetime.

15 Letter to his wife of 14–16 May 1836, in *Pss*, 10:452.

16 As Countess Daria (Dolly) Fikelmon (Fiquelmont) wrote in her diary, "The writer Pushkin conducts a conversation in a charming fashion, without pretence, [but] with animation and fire. It is impossible to be more ugly: he is a mix of the exterior of a monkey and a tiger. He is descended from African ancestors and he has retained a certain blackness [chernota] in his complexion and something wild in his glance" (N.B. Izmailov, "Pushkin v dnevnike gr. D. F. Fikel'mon," *Vremennik Pushkinskoi komissii* [1962 (1963)]: 33).

17 "K Iur'evu" (To Iurev, 1820), *Pss*, 2:42: «А я, повеса

> I am pleasing to youthful beauty
> With the shameless fury of desire;
> With an involuntary flame in her cheeks,
> Not understanding herself [why],
> [So too] does a young nymph furtively
> Look at times on a faun.[17]

Here we see the principle of metamorphosis at work. The speaker, the stylized young "Pushkin" of 1820, is addressing his friend F. F. Iurev, a co-member of the Green Lamp society, who is dashing and handsome in all the traditional ways. With his black moustache and pleasing smile, this budding "Adonis" (Myrrha's son) and "favourite of Venus" (*baloven' Kipridy*) does not have to try in the games of love. Women's longing glances seem to "flock" (letiat) to him of their own accord. But in the second half of the poem, the portion cited above, the speaker creates an antithesis to Adonis as his own signature myth. This anti-Adonis is not beautiful on the outside, but rather an "ugly descendant of Negroes." There is something about him that is clearly "monstrous." And the monstrousness is in turn *transformed* into the attractive bestiality of the Pan-like faun, who, half-man and half-goat, is the epitome of lubricity and who is known to arouse irrepressible lust in women and to haunt them in their dreams. The nymph in the poem blushes because she wants the faun but does not know why and suspects that that desire is shameful or "unnatural."

Apuleius in Eugene Onegin

So far we have been discussing mainly the male attributes of desire.[18] The changes in the Tatiana of chapter 8, as she is transformed from village maiden to high society princess, are changes that arouse *him*. At some basic level she is his, the author-narrator's, creation: *he* explains her origins as the latest incarnation of his muse at the beginning of chapter 8, *he* "unveils" her at the "*svetskii raut*" (grand rout/reception), *he* makes this ice goddess both universally desirable and secretly passionate and needful, and at the end *he* withholds her ("my Tatiana") from the hero and gives her forever to the reader (which is to say, to himself). But in Pushkin's novel-in-verse the heroine is both the poet's creation and a psychologically realized character in her own right — she is both "poeticized" and "novelized." In this respect, and always keenly aware that turnabout is fair play, Pushkin was equally interested in

вечно праздный, / Потомок негров безобразный, / Взращенный в дикой простоте, / Любви не ведая страданий, / Я нравлюсь юной красоте / Бесстыдным бешенством желаний; / С невольным пламенем ланит / Украдкой нимфа молодая, / Сама себя не понимая, / На фавна иногда глядит».

18 For the purposes of this study I am speaking about *heterosexual* desire.

the female attributes of desire: he wanted to be able to imagine for himself and his readers (many of whom were women) a heroine who was not merely a male's Promethean self-projection but who really did appear to think and feel and need in a manner consonant with her "kind." For this Pushkin had to turn to another powerful story of metamorphosis, this one focusing on the female. In the very first lines of chapter 8 Pushkin takes us back to his poetic awakening at the Lyceum:

> In those days when in the Lyceum parks
> I insouciantly blossomed out,
> Read willingly Apuleius,
> But didn't read Cicero,
> In those days in the secret vales,
> In the springtime, to the calls of swans,
> Near the water glimmering in the quiet,
> The Muse began to appear to me.[19]

This reference to Apuleius is, arguably, one of many in a work that is throughout intertextual. In the drafts, for example, Pushkin also toyed with using as rhyme partner for "litseia" ("of the Lyceum") "Eliseia"("of Elisei"), another work replete with humor, bawdiness, and ancient gods and goddesses: Vasily Maikov's *Elisei, or Bacchus Enraged* (Elisei, ili razdrazhennyi Vakkh), 1771).[20] However, I submit that this return to the past is foregrounded in more than the usual way. In the end Pushkin opted for Apuleius as the one author he, or at least his stylized youthful self, read *with pleasure* during the sacred period of his Lyceum tutelage and brotherhood. And in yet another draft, this one dated December 24, 1829, he portrayed himself reading Apuleius not simply "willingly" (*okhotno*), as in the published version, but "on the sly" (*ukradkoi*), the idea being that there was something delightfully prohibitive about *The Golden Ass*—*ukradkoi* was the same word used to describe the nymph's blushing response to the faun—from the beginning.[21] The naturally evocative surroundings, the appearance of the Muse out of them, and the reading of Apuleius all go hand in hand. We are further entitled to consider the influence of *The Golden Ass* on the storyline of *Eugene Onegin*, especially its climax, because Pushkin was using the Psyche and Cupid story, mediated by Bogdanovich, to investigate another metamorphosing heroine's psychology in "Mistress into Maid," a story composed during the same Boldino autumn that the poet was completing his novel-in-verse. If the young noblewoman Liza Muromskaya is intrigued to see what it would be like to "become" a peasant in order to attract a handsome young squire

---

[19] *Pss*, 5:142: «В те дни, когда в садах Лицея / Я безмятежно расцветал, / Читал охотно Апулея, / А Цицерона не читал, / В те дни в таинственных долинах, / Весной, при кликах лебединых, / Близ вод, сиявших в тишине, / Являться муза стала мне».

[20] *Pss*, 5:460.

[21] *Pss*, 5:462.

(Alexei Berestov), then Tatiana can be seen to follow a similar course of self-reinvention, only in the opposite direction: from *uezdnaia baryshnia* (country maiden/miss) to mistress of the highest reaches of society.

So why was Apuleius potentially such an intriguing text to Pushkin?²² First of all, *The Golden Ass*, written probably in the first half of the second century A.D., was a novel. Rather than the mellifluous hexameters of Ovid's *Metamorphoses*, it was composed in a rather sophisticated prose framework that allowed for rapid shifts in tone, narrative irony, and the interplay between inserted texts and the outer storyline. But what must have attracted Pushkin most of all was its central theme of metamorphosis. Lucius, its hero, is turned into an ass when the too curious young man is drawn into sorcery experiments and given the wrong magic ointment. Thereafter he falls into the hands of robbers and undergoes a series of adventures, often being abused and variously humiliated. He feels intense mortification for his ugliness and brutishness and for the fact that he can no longer speak. In one later episode, which was sure to delight the same schoolboy Pushkin who read Barkov, Lucius the ass is called upon by his then keeper to have sex with a noble lady inflamed by his immense organ and willing to pay a large fee for his services. As opposed to Ovid, where similar "beauty and the beast" scenes are never explained or "fleshed out" with realistic motivations, here the accommodation of the beastly to the human is described in salacious detail.²³ At the end of the novel, in the now strangely rhapsodic (and much disputed) Book Eleven, Lucius is finally returned to his human form when he prays to the universal feminine deity Queen Isis and, blessed with a vision of her, agrees to serve her chastely for the rest of his life.

If *The Golden Ass* were just about the metamorphosis of Lucius, it would be entertaining but fairly one-dimensional. Its real liveliness comes from the inserted tales, which can span different books and create complex narrative structures, and Lucius' and other characters' reactions to them. It is also through these inserted tales that we find thematic allusions to other works by Pushkin, particularly *Ruslan and Liudmila* and its later sibling *Eugene*

---

22 Pushkin had two different editions of Apuleius' *The Golden Ass* in his library: *Œuvres complètes d'Apulée*, trans. M.V. Bétolaud (Paris: Bibliothèque Latine-Française publiée par C. L. F. Pannkoucke, 1835) (No. 613 in catalogue; Pushkin had the first two volumes, the ones containing *Métamorphoses*, of the four volume set); and *Apulei, Lutsiia Apuleia platonicheskoi sekty filosofa prevrashchenie, ili zolotoi osel*, trans.. Ermil Kostrov (Moscow: Universitetskaia tipografiia u N. Novikova, 1780–1). The Kostrov translation of Apuleius was one of the books that Modzalevsky determined to have been in Pushkin's library at one time but then subsequently lost. B. L. Modzalevskii, *Biblioteka A. S. Pushkina (Bibliograficheskoe opisanie)* (St. Petersburg: Tipografiia Imperatorskoi Akademii Nauk, 1910), 160; and B. L. Modzalevskii, *Biblioteka A. S. Pushkina: Prilozhenie k reprintnomu izdaniiu* (Moscow: Kniga, 1988), 12.

23 The episode takes place in Book Ten. See Apuleius, *The Golden Ass, or Metamorphoses*, intro. and trans. E. J. Kenney (London: Penguin, 1998), 184–86.

Onegin. For example, at one point during his captivity Lucius is brought together with a young captive, Charite, who relates to the robbers' ancient cook how she was kidnapped from her husband Tlepolemus on their wedding night: "a sudden invasion of armed men... burst straight into our room in a tightly packed mass... [and] snatched me, half dead with pitiful fright... That is how my marriage, like those of Attis and Protesilaus, was broken up and brought to nothing."[24] This sounds uncannily like the boisterous opening of *Ruslan and Liudmila*, especially if we take into account the fact that the wretched groom, like Ruslan, has lost his bride somehow shamefully, right at the moment of consummation, and is "loudly lamenting the rape of his beautiful wife and calling on the people to help him."[25] But the story of Charite and Tlepolemus frames the story of Psyche and Cupid, which is in turn told by the old woman: it ends on a tragic note of fidelity that interacts subtly both with the ultimately comic adventures of Psyche and with the low burlesque tales of concealed lovers and routine cuckoldry heard by Lucius on his asinine way.

In Book Eight, after Tlepolemus has heroically rescued Charite (and Lucius) from the robbers and begun, presumably, to live "happily ever after," we learn that the young husband has been killed by his friend Thrasyllus while boar hunting. The traitor, who wants Charite for himself, makes it look like the victim was gored by a boar, when in fact it was he who stabbed him. Shortly thereafter Tlepolemus comes to the grief-stricken Charite in a dream:

"Wife," he said. "I call you by the name which only I have the right to use, if any memory of me still remains in your heart. But if my untimely death has caused you to forget the ties of our love, marry whom you will and be happier than I could make you; only do not accept Thrasyllus' impious hand. Have nothing to do with him, shun his bed and board. Fly from the bloodstained hand of my assassin. The wounds from which you washed the blood with your tears are not those of the boar's tusks; it was Thrasyllus' spear that took me from you" — he told her the rest, revealing the whole enactment of the crime.[26]

This is the theme of the dead or absent husband/bridegroom in danger of having his conjugal rights usurped by an interloper, which runs through Pushkin's *oeuvre* like a red thread.[27] Pretending to reciprocate his advances, Charite then drugs Thrasyllus and plunges a hairpin deep into both his eyes, thus blinding him but leaving him alive. "This is how you have found favor with a chaste woman," rages the righteous wife, "this is how the marriage torches

---

24 Apuleius, *The Golden Ass*, 70–71.
25 Ibid., 71.
26 Ibid., 133.
27 The theme of a jealous speaker/hero in competition for a woman whose husband or fiancé has died is repeated throughout Pushkin's *oeuvre*, from the early poem "To a Young Widow" ("K molodoi vdove," 1817) to such mature works as *Boris Godunov* (1824–25) (the Pretender vying with the "ghost" of the murdered Tsarevich for the affections of Marina Mniszek), *The Stone Guest* (1830) (Juan trying to seduce Dona Anna in the presence of the statue of the murdered Commendatore), "The Blizzard" (1830) (the original

have lighted your bridal chamber. Your matrons of honour shall be the avenging Furies, and blindness your best man, and the prick of conscience will haunt you to eternity."[28] While Charite ends by stabbing herself and joining her husband in the grave, the careful reader notes how salient topoi from the preceding Psyche story are here reversed and, rather than erotically poeticized, rendered ironic and, so to speak, "novelized." Instead of the male's favored weapon, the sword, which Psyche takes up to kill the "monster" in her bridal bed, the female hairpin, which is then actually used; instead of the "male courage" Psyche pleads for, cunning female resourcefulness; instead of the marriage torches (cf. Psyche's oil lamp) lighting the way to the bridal chamber, the all-encompassing darkness of the blind; and instead of the prick of Cupid's arrow (eros), the prick of conscience that is synonymous with Thrasyllus' blindness and an everlasting reminder of his perfidy. So in a novel otherwise rife with tales of bawdy wives, simpleton husbands destined to wear horns, and bold lovers (the role the young Pushkin enjoyed imagining, and not only imagining, himself in), here was a story of fierce fidelity and vindication. But without doubt the sections of *The Golden Ass* most apt to draw the young Pushkin's attention were those describing the adventures of Psyche and Cupid: Books Four-Six. Just as Lucius' story has a metamorphosis (human beast) as its central conceit, and just as Charite's and Tlepolemus' story has certain "changeling" twists at its core ("Hæmus" appears to take command of the robbers' band only to turn into Tlepolemus and rescue Charite; Charite pretends to be in love with Thrasyllus in order to disguise her true intent as avenging fury), so does the Psyche and Cupid story have a shifting identity as its chief motivation, only in this instance the male hero does not become a beast but is revealed to be a god. More important, however, this story revolves around *the woman's* adventures, and misadventures, as she seeks self-knowledge, which is synonymous in the myth with not being kept in the dark about the true lineaments of her husband. Psyche is the traditional third, and loveliest, daughter of a king. But "for all her striking beauty, [she] had no joy of it ... Though all admired her divine loveliness, they did so as one admires a statue finished to perfection"; hence Psyche "stayed at home an unmarried virgin."[29] When the father, despairing over his daughter's unhappiness, prays to Apollo for help, the god answers:

and destined-to-die bridegroom Vladimir getting bizarrely lost on the way to his wedding while his bride Marya Gavrilovna is married, without her knowing it, to the stranger Burmin, and *Eugene Onegin* (in the drafts Lensky's shade may be aware that his beloved Olga has with unseemly haste fallen in love after his death with a handsome ulan officer). See *Pss*, 1:214–15; 5:242–43; 5:343; and 5:453. All of these instances may be summed up psychologically with Pushkin's own words, when he contemplates marrying the beautiful Natalie and then at some point in the future leaving her a widow: "God is my witness," he writes to his future mother-in-law on 5 April 1830, "that I am ready to die for her, but that I should die to leave a dazzling widow, free to choose a new husband tomorrow—this idea is hell." Alexander Pushkin, *The Letters of Alexander Pushkin, Three Volumes in One*, intro. and trans. J. Thomas Shaw (Madison: University of Wisconsin Press, 1967), 405–06; *Pss*, 10:217–18.

[28] Apuleius, *The Golden Ass*, 135.

[29] Ibid., 73–74.

> On mountain peak, O king, expose the maid
> For funeral wedlock ritually arrayed.
> No human son-in-law (hope not) is thine,
> But something cruel and fierce and serpentine;
> That plagues the world as, born aloft on wings,
> With fire and steel it persecutes all things;
> That Jove himself, he whom the gods revere,
> That Styx's darkling stream regards with fear.[30]

Thus Psyche, acting out the mythical fears of every nubile maiden commanded to enter into an arranged marriage and knowing nothing about her proposed spouse, is taken to the mountain top as "a living corpse." Believing her groom to be a monster, "something cruel and fierce and serpentine," she makes her approach to the place of sacrifice as one going "not to her wedding procession, but her own funeral."[31]

Rather than being ravished by the monster on the mountain top, however, Psyche is carried by the breath of Zephyr down into a deep valley, whereupon she falls "sweetly asleep." Now left alone, without her parents or sisters to advise her, Psyche's adventures begin in earnest. Once she awakes she proceeds to a magnificent palace, a "pleasure-house of some god" that holds the "vast treasure of the entire world" but is not secured by "a single lock, bolt, or guard."[32] "Becoming a little bolder," she crosses the threshold into the palace's empty splendor, where she is greeted by disembodied voices that tend her every whim. She examines the new surroundings in detail, is addressed as "mistress," and is informed that "all of it is yours." But as she is being prepared for her bridal bed Psyche is naturally uneasy. She "quails and trembles, dreading, more than any possible harm, the unknown." At last "there enters her unknown husband; he mounts the bed, makes her his wife, and departs in haste before sunrise. At once the voices that were in waiting in the room minister to the new bride's slain virginity."[33] The point of this marriage night description and indeed of the entire Psyche and Cupid story is *who* is this husband/lover. She does not know he is Cupid, a god, who has fallen in love with a mortal and who must conceal his identity because his mother, Venus, is jealous of Psyche's beauty. And she is faced with a dilemma: no matter how sweet this lover's embraces seem, is he a "monster," as Apollo's prediction suggested and as her jealous sisters subsequently insist, or is he the wonderful being that visits her in the dark? She has given herself, but there is something about him she is prohibited to know, and what this is is inextricably tied to her self-knowledge and "enlightenment."

---

30 Ibid., 74.
31 Ibid., 75.
32 Ibid., 78.
33 Ibid. For the sake of consistency in narration, I am rendering all the verbs in this passage and the ones to follow in the present tense.

As the invisible Cupid warns her, "their [the sisters'] one aim is to persuade you to try to know my face — but if you do see it, as I have constantly told you, you will not see it."[34]

Psyche's condition becomes archetypal of every woman who must depend on the male, on *who he is*, to define herself. She must disobey his prohibition and see things in the light because that is where her curiosity, which is more powerful than the urge to live in erotic captivity, however splendid, drives her. She must go back on her word — "As to your face, I ask nothing more; even the darkness of night does not blind me; I have you as my light"[35] — in order to *become herself*. So the sisters' arguments about the unknown husband being "an immense serpent, writhing in knotted coils, its bloody jaws dripping deadly poison" win out:

> For I have never seen my husband's face and I have no idea where he comes from; only at night, obeying his voice, do I submit to this husband of unknown condition — one who altogether shuns the light; and when you say he must be some sort of wild beast, I can only agree with you. For he constantly terrifies me with warnings not to try to look at him, and threatens me with a fearful fate if I am curious about his appearance.[36]

Torn between rage and despair, "in one and the same body … loath[ing] the monster and lov[ing] the husband," Psyche at last agrees that she must expose the unknown one's identity and kill him while he sleeps. But when she comes to do the deed and shines the light, "the secret of their bed becomes plain, [and] what she sees is of wild beasts the most soft and sweet of monsters, none other than Cupid himself, the fair god fairly lying asleep."[37] It is at this moment of *cognitio* in both the literal and figurative senses that Psyche inadvertently pricks herself with one of her husband's arrows and "without realizing it … through her own act falls in love with Love."[38] Immediately thereafter, that is, as she feels "ever more on fire with desire for Desire" and as she proceeds to "devour" her sleeping beauty with "quick sensuous kisses," she drops the boiling oil from the lamp on Cupid's right shoulder, causing him to wake and, as promised, fly away. Thus Psyche's desire for her husband is now inevitably linked with a forbidden knowledge that translates into separation. "But if you do see it [my face], as I have constantly told you, you will not see it."

Banished from her paradise, Psyche goes out in search of the Cupid she has, through her own act, forced to flee. The remainder of her story has to do with the trials, imposed by Venus, that she endures in order to remove the prohibition. Pan, seeing that she is "desperately in love," advises her to win

34 Ibid., 83.
35 Ibid., 84.
36 Ibid., 86.
37 Ibid., 88.
38 Ibid.

back her husband's favor "through tender service."[39] (Again, the parallel in the parent text involves the rehabilitation of Lucius, who can reassume his human form only after suffering various travails and then agreeing to worship unswervingly Queen Isis.) Whether sorting through a huge hill of seeds from different grains, or obtaining some golden wool from fierce sheep, or retrieving an urn of black water from a deadly spring on a mountain top, or finally journeying to the underworld to Proserpine and returning with a small casket filled with "beauty," Psyche rises to the occasion, showing courage and ingenuity. She is also of course aided by various magic helpers. But on her last assignment her "reckless curiosity,"[40] which is also a salient theme in Lucius' adventures, again gets the best of her: having made it safely in and out of the dark halls of Proserpine and succeeded in filling the box with its mysterious contents, she cannot restrain herself and opens the lid on her return trip, whereupon she immediately turns into a sleeping corpse.[41] She is revived, however, by another prick from Cupid's arrow, and the two lovers are at last reunited when Jupiter listens to the young god's plea and, cautioning him to curb his earlier hot-blooded pursuits, presides over the now official epithalamium. Psyche in turn is greeted into the ranks of the immortals and the daughter issuing from their union is called Pleasure.

Let us now return to *Eugene Onegin* and to the psycho-erotic arc of Tatiana's own adventures as a heroine. There are numerous moments in the novel that are revealing of Tatiana's character: her initial appearance, her dream, her name-day party, her wanderings in the countryside, her "sermon" to Onegin after receiving his letter, etc. But two in particular stand out as turning-points in the sense that they show Tatiana entering a *new* stage of self-knowledge. The first occurs in chapter 3 when she realizes she has fallen in love with Onegin and writes him a letter, and the second takes place in chapter 7 when she visits Onegin's library and learns something there that allows her to move on with her life, including in this case agreeing to be taken to Moscow to the "marriage market." In both instances the crux of Tatiana's engagement with the eroticized other has to do with that other's identity — who he is, what his motives are, why he has come into her life. And if in the first case what we see is Tatiana *falling in love with Love*, being *on fire with desire for Desire*, then in the second case what becomes clear is that she hasn't fallen out of love — indeed, far from it — but rather has learned something that translates knowledge of the heart into eternal separation.

To begin with, as an embodiment of the female "psyche," Tatiana shares certain traits with her mythological sibling:[42] she takes no joy in her beauty or in

---

[39] Ibid., 90.

[40] See ibid., xxvi, 104, 203. Lucius, for example, suffers from "ill-starred curiosity" (curiositas improspera).

[41] Again, this is strongly reminiscent of the scene in *Ruslan and Liudmila* when the heroine falls into a death-like sleep.

[42] Sisters of course in the Psyche myth.

those that admire it, she stays at home an unmarried virgin while her more gregarious and worldly sister succeeds in finding a mate,[42] and she is melancholy and lonely by nature. She is searching for something — something unavailable to her at home or in her known surroundings. When she meets Onegin she quickly falls in love, not with him specifically, because she hardly knows him, but rather with *the idea of love*.

> Tatiana listened with irritation
> At such rumours [of Onegin's interest in her]; but in secret
> With an inexplicable joy
> She thought involuntarily about it;
> And into her heart the idea sank;
> The time had come — she had fallen in love.
> Thus into the earth a fallen grain
> Is enlivened by the heat of the spring.
> For a long time her imagination,
> Burning with languor and melancholy,
> Had hungered for the fatal food;
> For a long time the longings of the heart
> Had constricted her young breast;
> Her soul ... awaited someone,
> And found him ... Her eyes were opened;
> She said, "It's him!"[43]

The point of this strophe, and of the enjambement of self-discovery that slips into the following one, is that Tatiana has for some time, and without really knowing why until now, been preparing to fall in love with Love. That her imagination is described as "burning with languor and melancholy" captures perfectly that state of being "on fire with desire for Desire" of Psyche's original self-inflicted wound (again, Cupid did not fire his arrow at her, but she found it, and pricked herself on it, on her own).

The parallels with Psyche become even stronger when Tatiana, increasingly inflamed, sits down in her nightshirt to write to Onegin. Suddenly she switches from the formal "vy" ("you") to the intimate "ty" ("thou," whose archaic flavor in English I have kept in the following literal translation):

> Another! ... No, to no one else on earth
> Would I give my heart!
> Such has been decreed in the highest council ...
> Such is the will of heaven: I am thine;
> All my life has been but a pledge

---

43 Pss, 5:50–51:
«Татьяна слушала с досадой / Такие сплетни; но тайком / С неизъяснимою отрадой / Невольно думала о том; / И в сердце дума заронилась; / Пора пришла, она влюбилась; / Так в землю падшее зерно / Весны огнем оживлено. / Давно ее воображенье, / Сгорая негой и тоской, / Алкало пищи роковой; / Давно сердечное томленье / Теснило ей младую грудь; / Душа ждала ... кого-нибудь, // И дождалась ... Открылись очи; / Она сказала: это он!»

Of a true meeting with thee;
I know thou hast been sent by God
And art my guardian to the grave ...
Thou appeared to me in dreams,
Unseen, thou wert very sweet,
Thy wondrous glance caused me to pine,
In my soul thy voice was sounding
Long ago ... no, it was not a dream!
As soon as thou entered, I recognized in an instant,
I was completely overcome, felt on fire
And in my thoughts said, "It's him!"
Isn't it true? I heard thee:
Thou spoke to me in the silence
When I was helping the poor
Or when I softened the anguish
Of my agitated soul with prayer?
And in that same instant
Didst thou not, sweet vision,
Flash by in the transparent darkness,
Press up quietly to my bedside?
Didst thou not, with joy and love,
Whisper words of hope to me?
Who art thou, my guardian angel
Or a perfidious tempter:
Resolve my doubts.[44]

As many commentators have noted, Tatiana's expression of desire is here far in excess of that allowed by the epistolary norms of her class and status as unmarried young lady.[45] Indeed, not only is Tatiana taking a great risk in initiating this correspondence in the first place, but the very way she addresses her interlocutor is tantamount to undressing before him. But even more than that, what we see here in this exchange of words is a spontaneous act of love, a soulful "coupling," that is highly eroticized in terms of the Psyche-Cupid encounter. This Cupid came to her in her dreams and, as the dramatic shift to "ty" signifies, "slew her virginity" well before he appeared in the flesh. That is why he is referred to as both "unseen" and a "sweet vision" that moves around her in the darkness and presses up against her bedside to whisper in her ear. The sexual nature of this love letter is never in question—for Tatiana the search for a soul-mate is never about

44 *Pss*, 5:61–62: «Другой! ... Нет, никому на свете / Не отдала бы сердца я! / То в вышнем суждено совете ... / То воля неба: я твоя; / Вся жизнь моя была залогом / Свиданья верного с тобой; / Я знаю, ты мне послан богом, / До гроба ты хранитель мой ... / Ты в сновиденьях мне являлся, / Незримый, ты мне был уж мил, / Твой чудный взгляд меня томил, / В душе твой голос раздавался / Давно ... нет, это был не сон! / Ты чуть вошел, я вмиг узнала, / Вся обомлела, запылала / И в мыслях молвила: вот он! / Не правда ль? я тебя слыхала: / Ты говорил со мной в тиши, / Когда я бедным помогала / Или молитвой услаждала / Тоску

sex per se or the offering or withholding of herself as partner—but what is in question is the identity of the phantom lover, the one who, in the Psyche myth, "enters [as the] unknown husband ... mounts the bed, makes her his wife, and departs in haste before sunrise." When Tatiana asks him, "Who are you, my guardian angel / Or a perfidious tempter: / Resolve my doubts," she is trying to learn whether he is, on the one hand, a Cupid, "of all wild beasts the most soft and sweet of monsters," or, on the other, "something cruel and fierce and serpentine" ("*kovarnyi iskusitel*'" has satanic connotations). To sum up our findings thus far, the Psyche-Cupid story is motivated by two turning points that are especially "magnetized" with female desire. These turning points happen at virtually the same instant in the text and are powerfully interrelated—indeed, each seems in a tantalizing way to be a mirror extension of the other. The first is when Psyche shines the lamp on her husband while he sleeps and, "curious as ever," takes an arrow from his quiver and tries the point on her thumb, but because her hands are trembling she applies too much force and pricks herself. This is the moment when she "falls in love with Love" and there is no turning back. It is important to realize that it is not the body of the god, however beautiful in its dormant state (for example, "golden hair," "rosy cheeks," "milk-white neck," "dewy-white wings"), that arouses Psyche until she is "carried away by joy and sick with love"; it is rather the point of the arrow, whose wound somehow "happens" of its own accord. The second turning point is likewise not the product of Psyche's volition:

> But meanwhile that wretched lamp, either through base treachery, or in jealous malice, or because it longed itself to touch such beauty and as it were to kiss it, disgorged from its spout a drop of hot oil on the right shoulder of the god. What! Rash and reckless lamp, lowly instrument of love, to burn the lord of universal fire himself, when it must have been a lover who first invented the lamp so that he could enjoy his desires for even longer at night! The god, thus burned, leapt up, and seeing his confidence betrayed and sullied, flew off from the loving embrace of his unhappy wife without uttering a word.[46]

The lamp, whose motives here are treated with mock-epic indignation, has a mind (and heart) of its own. It not only lights up the darkness, revealing the identity of what was hidden, but it spreads its scalding contents on the god of love, causing his flight. To want to know who, in the darkness of his soul, your lover is to chase him away. But then not to want, to *desire*, to

волнуемой души? / И в это самое мгновенье, / Не ты ли, милое виденье, / В прозрачной темноте мелькнул, / Приникнул тихо к изголовью? / Не ты ль, с отрадой и любовью, / Слова надежды мне шепнул? / Кто ты, мой ангел ли хранитель, / Или коварный искуситель: / Мои сомненья разреши».

45 See, for example, Iu.M. Lotman, *Roman A.S. Pushkina 'Evgenii Onegin': Kommentarii* (Leningrad: Prosveshchenie, 1980), 219–20, 230–31.

46 Apuleius, *The Golden Ass*, 88–89.

know is impossible—the lamp that is as essential to Psyche's identity as Cupid's arrow is to his *wills* it.

I would like to suggest in this last portion of my study that Tatiana's visit(s) to Onegin's library in chapter 7 is a novelized transposition of Psyche's adventures in Cupid's palace. During this visit Russia's favourite heroine displays the same "boldness" and "curiosity" as her mythological counterpart. She comes upon the "vacant castle" (*pustynnyi zamok*) as if by chance; she crosses over a threshold that is guarded by "wild animals" (barking dogs[47]); she enters the forbidden space of the male's living quarters while the master is absent; she is tended to by a servant, a "keeper of the keys" (*kliuchnitsa*), only this one is in the flesh; and she examines all the "priceless" items of this interior space, including a bed and a "dimmed lamp" (*pomerkshaia lampada*), as one "enchanted." Most convincingly, however, she has found her way to Onegin's home in order to discover at last, after various false starts, *who her lover is*. Where then is the wilful lamp, the scalding oil, and the fleeing god? This is a novel-in-verse, which means that Pushkin cannot play literally on mythical expectations, but must reflect and refract them through the alternating poeticizing and prosaicizing prism of his hybrid form. The light from Psyche's oil lamp has now become the reflected illumination of Onegin's *library*, his books, the windows to his soul in a modern world where you are, more and more, what you read.

After being left alone in the "silent library," Tatiana first has a long cry ("I dolgo plakala ona"), presumably over what might have been. But then she turns to the books themselves:

> At first she was not drawn to them,
> But their selection seemed
> Strange to her. Tatiana gave herself up
> To reading with a greedy spirit;
> And a new world opened up to her.[48]

The reader immediately notices that Tatiana is pulled along by her curiosity, by her will to know. Difference—the "strangeness" of the books' selection—plainly excites her. She doesn't rush in to apply her own categories of knowing to the new reading material, but rather allows the latter to draw her into its orbit. By the same token, the "greediness" she exhibits seems very close to the wellsprings of desire itself. And Tatiana is rewarded for her pursuit by seeing a "new world" open before her. On a literal level this is of course the contents of Onegin's favorite books—the stories by the "singer of the Giaour and Juan" as well as "two or three" contemporary novels that

---

[47] When Psyche first steps foot in Cupid's pleasure-house she sees "walls ... covered in embossed silver, with wild beasts and other animals confronting the visitor on entering"; and later, when she travels to the underworld to visit Proserpine, she is met at the palace threshold by a "huge dog [Cerberus] with three enormous heads, a monstrous and fearsome brute, barking thunderously" (ibid., 77, 103).

[48] *Pss*, 5:128: «Сперва ей было не до них, / Но показался выбор их / Ей странен. Чтенью предалася / Татьяна жадною душой; / И ей открылся мир иной».

we learn about in the next stanza. But it is not the identity of Byron or some fellow novelist of the time that is in question here, which is probably the reason why Pushkin left the account of the actual items in Onegin's library, after experimenting with more explicit versions, intentionally vague and underdeveloped.[49] No, Tatiana is interested in how Onegin reads these books (and their authors), what he shows about himself in the reflected light of his interactions with their texts. On a figurative level, this is the moment in the Tatiana-Psyche story when she, holding the lamp, sees her lover exposed.

What does she find? In the original Psyche and Cupid myth the heroine dramatically illuminates the physical form of the god of love: his hair, neck, cheeks, shoulders, wings. Now, in this later novelized version of the same myth, Tatiana casts her light on the *inner* physiognomy of her lover:

> On many pages were preserved
> The sharp mark of his fingernails;
> And the eyes of the attentive maiden
> Were trained on them ever more keenly.
> Now trembling, Tatiana sees
> With which idea or remark
> Onegin happened to be struck,
> With what he silently agreed.
> On the pages' margins she encounters
> The traces of his pencil.
> Everywhere Onegin's soul
> Involuntarily expresses itself
> With a short word, with a cross,
> With a question mark.[50]

Tatiana is "attentive" and her eyes are trained "keenly." The pages she is looking at "khranit'" (preserve) the outline of his spiritual movements as though he were an invisible body leaving fugitive impressions on its surroundings. She is discovering for the first time which ideas Onegin responds to as significant, which he questions, which he ignores and passes over. The hero's "soul" displays itself "involuntarily," which is to say, it lets out the secret it would prefer to keep to itself. And this new information causes the inquirer to tremble because it is intimate, it is like seeing the other lying undressed and asleep. The psychic energy of this revelation is caught in the alliterative scudding and internal rhyme—the k+r+s+t sounds of "To kratkim slovom, to krestom,/ To voprositel'nym

---

49 See Lotman, *Roman A. S. Pushkina 'Evgenii Onegin'*, 314–20.

50 *Pss*, 5:129: «Хранили многие страницы / Отметку резкую ногтей; / Глаза внимательной девицы / Устремлены на них живей. / Татьяна видит с трепетаньем, / Какою мыслью, замечаньем / Бывал Онегин поражен, / В чем молча соглашался он. / На их полях она встречает / Черты его карандаша. / Везде Онегина душа / Себя невольно выражает / То кратким словом, то крестом, / То вопросительным крючком».

kriuchkom"—of the last two lines. For Pushkin, and for Tatiana, perhaps his most self-referential character, nothing is more private and more revealing of one's core identity than one's reading habits.

But it is not until the next, climactic, stanza that the new information becomes understanding, *knowledge*:

> And little by little my Tatiana
> Begins to understand
> At last more clearly — thank God! —
> The one for whom she is fated
> To sigh by a powerful fate:
> A sad and dangerous eccentric,
> A creation of heaven or hell,
> This angel, this haughty devil,
> Who is he then? Could he really be an imitation,
> A paltry phantom, or even
> A Muscovite in Harold's cloak,
> An interpretation of others' fancies,
> A lexicon full of fadish words? ...
> Is he not just a parody?[51]

In the mythological world, which is also the world of poetic expectation (nymphs fall in love with fauns and gods of love fall in love with mortals), the "monster" is shown to be "of all wild beasts the most soft and sweet" and thus flies away when his changeling status is revealed. There is no burn on Cupid's shoulder in Pushkin's stanzas, but there are the marks of Onegin's pencil, which wound in their own way. To repeat, the notion of shifting identity/metamorphosis (the reader does not know that the monster is Cupid until Cupid is himself exposed) is tied both to the female's will to knowledge and to the idea of punishment and separation (male prohibition). In the world where "novel time" is emerging out of "poetry," the changeling identity of the hero is no longer between "monster" and "Cupid," devil and angel, but involves a third, more prosaic possibility: Onegin is an "imitation," a "parody," that interacts with its created alter-egos in a profoundly uncreative way. At this, for Tatiana pivotal, juncture in the plot, Onegin "copies" the texts that he reads into his life and merges all too neatly with the roles he encounters on the printed page. To say he is a "Muscovite in Harold's cloak" is to say that he tries to be like Childe Harold (that is his identity), which is a relation of lesser to greater, rather than being himself while still knowing Byron's text. The *"iasnee"* (to understand "more clearly") means that Tatiana at last

---

[51] *Pss*, 5:129–30: «И начинает понемногу / Моя Татьяна понимать / Теперь яснее —слава богу — / Того, по ком она вздыхать / Осуждена судьбою властной: / Чудак печальный и опасный, / Созданье ада иль небес, / Сей ангел, сей надменный бес, / Что ж он? Ужели подражанье, / Ничтожный призрак, иль еще / Москвич в Гарольдовом плаще, / Чужих причуд истолкованье, / Слов модных полный лексикон? ... / Уж не пародия ли он?»

sees what has lain hidden in her desire. This, I would suggest, is the precise moment in Pushkin's novel when Cupid leaves Psyche: "if you do see it [my face], as I have constantly told you, you will not see it." This is another way of saying that the "he" ("It's him!") who was Tatiana's male muse and the object of her most ardent desire still exists in her "psyche," but has from this point forth fled as something actively embodied in the person of Eugene Onegin. The myth of Psyche and Cupid has entered novelistic space and "my Tatiana," regardless of future trials, is not fated to be reunited with the sweet vision of her dreams.

The point about metamorphoses with which I began this discussion and to which I now return in conclusion involves the *unexpected*: the unnatural coupling of Pasiphae with a bull or Philyra with a horse (Saturn), the shocking passion of Myrrha for her father. It was Pushkin's very "poetic" understanding — "these fantasies [metamorphoses] are not devoid of poetry," as he said in "Refutation of Criticisms" — that every genuine desire is characterized by the quality of seeing (and feeling) something that others don't. The same holds true with the story at the center of Pushkin's most complicated and ambitious work. If in *The Golden Ass* Psyche goes to her marriage bed waiting to be ravished by a monster, she wakes up, so to speak, having made love, and now *wanting* to make love again, to a god. Yet in *Eugene Onegin* these expectations have been further undermined and frustrated: the hero is neither god nor monster, but an all too predictable human being, while the heroine still wants to sleep with the deity she imagined to be there. In the first Boldino autumn of 1830 Pushkin gives us not one but three competing versions of quintessentially female "Psyches" who learn secrets about the male embodiments of eros courting them: Dona Anna and Don Guan (*The Stone Guest*), the Tatiana and Onegin of chapter 8, and Liza Muromskaya and Alexei Berestov ("Mistress into Maid"). Not for nothing is each male lead closely tied to the Don Juan story or to "Byronism" (Onegin collects the works of the "singer of Giaour and Juan" and Alexei appears in the province suspiciously "gloomy and disenchanted" and wearing a death's-head ring) or to both. And likewise, given the author's personal concerns that autumn, it is not by chance that the heroines' anxieties and conflicts are intimately bound up with their sexual identities and with being true to themselves in different stages or statuses of life: maiden, wife, widow. (Recall again Pushkin's words to his future mother-in-law: "God is my witness that I am ready to die for her [Natalie], but that I should die to leave a dazzling widow, free to choose a new husband tomorrow — this idea is hell.") All of these plots, varying in tone from the tragic to the tragicomic to the comic, center on unexpected changes, metamorphoses that go to the center of a hero's or heroine's identity: Guan, the cynical and seemingly insatiable sexual athlete, claims to have become someone else, someone who has fallen in love for the first time and been reborn ("ia ves' pererodilsia"); Tatiana, freely admitting that she still loves Onegin yet not yielding to his entreaties, turns "miraculously" from pining provincial maiden to majestic princess; and Liza, following her thematic sibling Dushenka ("little Psyche"), keeps changing disguises until she is found out by Alexei and can at last just "be herself" ("In all costumes are you, Dushenka, pretty").[52]

Finally, both the inner (Psyche and Cupid) and outer (Lucius) storylines of *The Golden Ass* open with the theme of "ill-starred curiosity" (self-knowledge) and close with the theme of faithful service to a more elevated notion of love. And so it is with the magic-box structure of *Eugene Onegin*. Tatiana refuses to be simply the object of male desire, which of course makes her only more desirable. She loves to know and she knows to love and she will not accept a relationship where the erotic and the cognitive are decoupled. Her creative reading habits are precisely what her loved one's are not.[53] Onegin, for his part, cannot live in the glare of Tatiana's urge to know. And the narrator, the burnisher of the "magic crystal"? He is the force whose restless curiosity and will to know constantly challenge our expectations and eroticize all that they touch, including the provincial maiden who was prepared to give herself when she was not wanted and the *grande dame* who is no longer willing to give herself when she is. This source of energy lies somewhere between the golden ass who is crudely indistinguishable from his oversized organ (the bared device, so to speak) and the chaste priest who comes to pray to Queen Isis. Neither Psyche nor Cupid, he is closer to the prick of the arrow or the drop of the boiling oil. Which is to say, he is closer to desire *in the act of becoming*—a wanting that is articulate and that literally knows no end.

---

52 *Pss*, 6:99: «Во всех ты, Душенька, нарядах хороша» reads the epigraph from Bogdanovich to "Mistress into Maid."

53 Much of my argument about Tatiana's creative abilities in this essay has benefitted from the excellent discussion in Olga Peters Hasty, *Pushkin's Tatiana* (Madison: University of Wisconsin Press, 1999).

Chapter 10   "A Higher Audacity": How to Read Pushkin's Dialogue with Shakespeare in *The Stone Guest*[1]

The literary historian and poet Stepan Shevyryov was the first to identify what is doubtless a resonant intertextual echo of Shakespeare in Pushkin's *The Stone Guest*. Writing in the *Moskvitianin* in 1841, Shevyryov stated:

> The scenes with Don Guan and Dona Anna strongly recall the scene in *Richard III* with Gloucester (Richard III) and Lady Anne, the widow of Edward, Prince of Wales, right down to the detail of the dagger that Don Guan, like Gloucester, uses as a clever means for the coup de grace [*dlia doversheniia pobedy*]. The situation is precisely the same. It is not surprising that Pushkin, without imitating, without prodding his memory, coincided inadvertently [*soshelsia nechaianno*] in several traits with the world's leading dramatic genius.[2]

Since Shevyryov, a number of prominent Pushkinists, among them Mikhail Alekseev, Yury Levin, and, most recently, Lev Ospovat have commented on the plot similarities between Guan's wooing of Dona Anna and the dizzyingly rapid turn of events in act 1, scene 2 of Shakespeare's play.[3] As for the differences within the parallelisms, that is, how Pushkin presumably used Shakespeare in order to distinguish himself from him and to say something new about his erotically charged encounter, both Levin and Ospovat offer insightful points of reference. First Levin:

> But, while in large part following Shakespeare, Pushkin altered the situation, intensifying its psychological verisimilitude. The scene in *Richard III*, though very effective in a dramatic

---

1 First appeared as "'A Higher Audacity': How to Read Pushkin's Dialogue with Shakespeare in *The Stone Guest*," in *Alexander Pushkin's 'Little Tragedies': The Poetics of Brevity*, ed. Svetlana Evdokimova (Madison: University of Wisconsin Press, 2003), 211–228.

2 *Moskvitianin* 9 (1841): 246.

3 Alekseev, "A. S. Pushkin," *Shekspir i russkaia kul'tura*, ed. M.P. Alekseev (Moscow-Leningrad: Nauka, 1965), 162–200; Levin, "Pushkin," *Shekspir i russkaia literatura XIX veka*, ed. M.P. Alekseev (Leningrad: Nauka, 1988), 32–62; Ospovat, "'Kamennyi gost'' kak opyt dialogizatsii tvorcheskogo soznaniia," *Pushkin:*

sense, is deprived of psychological plausibility. [...] In Pushkin the seduction takes place gradually, in two scenes; what is more, Don Guan reveals his true name only at the end, when Dona Anna is already, in effect, won over by him. On the other hand, Richard the seducer, in the process of realizing his selfish ends, remains an evil-doer and hypocrite over the course of the entire scene — his influence on Lady Anne is one-sided. Don Guan, in the act of seducing Dona Anna, falls in love himself — the impact of the protagonists on each other is mutual.[4]

Then Ospovat: "In Shakespeare there is a duel of two powerful natures in which victory is won by the more powerful and perfidious side. In Pushkin there is, in essence, no duel at all: Dona Anna does not try to resist the love-blind [*osleplennyi liubov'iu*] Don Guan but rather goes forth to meet him — surreptitiously, she conquers the man while leaving him to think that he himself is the conqueror."[5]

Given the importance of "Our Father Shakespeare" to Pushkin,[6] I would like to probe beyond the essentially plot-based parallelisms asserted by earlier scholars in order to understand more fully what was at stake for the Russian poet, in terms of the psychology of creativity, by invoking act 1, scene 2 of *Richard III*. For to claim that Pushkin "coincided inadvertently" with Shakespeare in several particulars, or that his aim in invoking Shakespeare was to point up his own greater commitment to "plausibility" (*pravdopodobie*), or that Dona Anna is actually the more aggressive voice in this dialogue is, on the face of it, not very convincing. The essence of the intertextual challenge is not to isolate a "reminiscence" (*reministsentsiia*) in the chronologically younger text but to demonstrate why that echo is there and how it continues to generate meaning in dialogue with the older text. In this respect, what joins the erotic duels in Shakespeare and Pushkin seems more than "inadvertent"; what inspired Pushkin at this point to turn to Shakespeare was not "believability" per se, at least not in the sense of a normativity or typicality he felt he could improve on;[7] and what attracts Pushkin's Don Guan to his Dona Anna cannot be sufficiently contained in a description that underscores her "human ordinariness, even her commonplace quality."[8] In other words, in order to understand how Pushkin is conversing with Shakespeare in *The Stone Guest* we need to know what Anne signifies to Gloucester/Richard and why he feels compelled to woo her in this way, what Dona Anna signifies to Don Guan and why he needs to woo her the way he does, and, most important, what the *differences* between

---

Issledovaniia i materialy (Moscow-Leningrad: Izdatel'stvo Akademii Nauk SSSR, 1995) 15: 25–29.

4   Levin, "Pushkin," 54.

5   Ospovat, "'Kamennyi gost'," 56.

6   Alexander Pushkin, *Polnoe sobranie sochinenii*, ed. V.D. Bronch-Bruevich et al., 17 vols. (Moscow: Akademiia Nauk SSSR, 1937–58), 11: 66); hereafter cited as "*Pss.*"

7   Recall Pushkin's July 1825 letter to N. N. Raevsky *fils*, in which he states: "Read Sh[akespeare] [...] he never fears compromising his hero/character; he has him speak with all the naturalness of life because he is

these two acts of seduction could have meant for the Pushkin of the Boldino autumn in the context of the other *Little Tragedies*.

But first, the context of *The Little Tragedies*. As various commentators have pointed out, there is a richly interwoven unity to these four "dramatic sketches" that would have to be borne in mind while making statements about any one of them.[9] To cite only the most obvious parallels, all four works center on the interplay of Eros and Thanatos (perhaps the pivotal concern of the Boldino autumn); they involve a single powerful desire (which is also a desire for *power*) whose excessive expression leads to what, in the Christian worldview, is mortal sin (greed, envy, lust/adultery, despair); they show characters (the Baron, Salieri, Guan, and the Master of Revels) who are very near to experiencing a kind of consummation/climax (the erotic link is always there) but then are thwarted at the last possible moment by a higher authority; they repeat certain themes (retribution from beyond the grave, murder as a deadly sin, poison as inverted love potion, feasting as symposium–cum–death wish) that are then progressively "embodied"—made more and more literal; and they challenge the notion of a *giftedness or good fortune bestowed beforehand* (Albert's claim on his father's estate, Mozart's inborn artistic genius, Don Alvar's prior rights as husband to Dona Anna, the sanctity/gift of life itself) that does not seem "fair" under the circumstances. For our purposes, it is important that the theme of love, so crucial to Pushkin at this turning point in his life, is placed *after* the themes of wealth and art and *before* the theme of life itself; in other words, Pushkin is a "Renaissance man" and a "Shakespearean" in this regard as well, that in these four plays where the embodiment of desire becomes more and more pronounced, the dialogue does not stop at issues of personal aggrandizement (the Baron's gold) or chosenness (Mozart's musical genius) but spreads out into areas of greater and greater interpersonal and, finally, group risk.[10] Guan's ultimate incarnation and self-definition ("Mne kazhetsia, ia ves' pererodilsia") is *through a living other* (Dona Anna)—his essence cannot be captured by itself, as can the Baron's, through his treasure chests, or even Mozart's, through his splendid Requiem. It is little wonder that *The Stone Guest* is the longest of these plays and the one most dependent on dialogue and least dependent on monologue or soliloquy (cf., e.g., the long monologues of the Baron and Salieri). Likewise, but even more so, *A Feast in Time of Plague* is the most impersonal and the most indeterminate of the plays because its point of departure is Wilson's "another's words" (chuzhie slova) and because the notion of personal happiness and "ego gratification" has become so patently

certain that at the appropriate time and place he can make that hero find a language consistent with his character" (13: 198; original in French).

8   Ospovat, "Kamennyi gost'," 50. Here Ospovat is to some extent following Akhmatova, who tetchily dismissed Dona Anna as a "very coquettish, curious, faint-hearted woman full of false piety—a typical Catholic devotee" (Anna Akhmatova, *O Pushkine. Stat'i i zametki*, ed. Emma G. Gernshtein [Leningrad: Sovetskii pisatel', 1977], 163).

9   My discussion in the following paragraph owes much to Sergei Davydov's essay "Strange and Savage Joy: The Erotic as a Unifying Element in *The Little*

absurd in this situation. In these plays too, written at a time when Pushkin couldn't tell whether he or his fiancée would survive the cholera epidemic and be reunited across the quarantines, the author's trajectory recalls the Shakespeare who, in the words of a recent biographer, went to his grave "not knowing, and possibly not caring, whether *Macbeth* or the *Tempest* or *Anthony and Cleopatra* ever achieved the permanence of print."[11] It is not art as self-affirming perfection — what we might call the transcendence of the self through the recorded act of authorship — that Pushkin, perhaps the most technically refined of all poets, is concerned with here.

Which brings us to the role of Shakespeare in *The Little Tragedies* and in Pushkin's "life creation" as he contemplated marriage, turned increasingly from poetry to prose, and entered into the 1830s and his period of maturity. Pushkin made numerous references to Shakespeare in his correspondence and in publicistic articles and notes. Of these references, which make for fascinating reading in their own right, several stand out for the quality of their formulations: drafts of two letters to Nikolai Raevsky *fils*, one of 1825, the other of 1829; "Materials relating to 'Excerpts from letters, thoughts, and notes,'" ("Materialy k 'Otryvkam iz pisem, mysliam i zamechaniiam,'" 1827); "Letter of the editor of the *Moscow News*," ("Pis'mo k izdateliu 'Moskovskogo vestnika,'" 1828); "Drafts of the preface to *Boris Godunov*" ("Nabroski predisloviia k 'Borisu Godunovu,'" 1830); "On popular drama and the drama Martha the Governor / *Posadnitsa*," ("O narodnoi drame i drame 'Marfa Posadnitsa,'" 1830); and "Table-Talk" (1830s)."[12] Perhaps not surprisingly, 1830, the year of the first Boldino autumn, was also a time when Pushkin was returning repeatedly to thoughts of Shakespeare and to the latter's indwelling ways of knowing. *Boris Godunov*, written during the Mikhailovskoe exile, had finally passed the censorship and was due to be published at the end of that year.[13] Add to this the fact that *The Merchant of Venice* has been universally recognized as a key source for *The Covetous Knight* (i.e., Shylock's character has become split between that of the Baron and that of the Jew) and that there appears to be something very Iago-like in the remorseless plotting and deeply offended

Tragedies," in Svetlana Evdokimova, ed., *Alexander Pushkin's Little Tragedies: The Poetic of Brevity* (Madison: University of Wisconsin Press, 2003), 89–105.

10 The structural progression I speak of here is borne out by the dates of composition during the Boldino autumn: *The Covetous Knight* (*Skupoi rytsar'*) was completed on 23 October, *Mozart and Salieri* (*Motsart i Sal'eri*) on 26 October, *The Stone Guest* on 4 November, and *A Feast in Time of Plague* (*Pir vo vremia chumy*) on 6 November.

11 Samuel Schoenbaum, *William Shakespeare: A Compact Documentary Life*, rev. ed. (New York: Oxford University Press, 1987), 174.

12 See *Pss*, 13: 196–98; 14: 46–48; 11: 59–61; 66–69, 140–42, 177–83, 12: 159–61. The dates signify approximate or unconfirmed times of composition. The language in the 1825 and 1829 draft letters to Raevsky *fils* was used again in the 1830 draft preface to *Boris Godunov*.

13 *Boris Godunov* indeed appeared for the first time in print in St. Petersburg at the end of 1830, although the date of publication is recorded in the text as 1831.

amour propre of Salieri, and we begin to sense how Shakespeare was a guest, and not at all an inadvertent one, at Pushkin's magnificent autumnal feast. Pushkin's statements about Shakespeare tell us a great deal about his own view of literary tradition on Russian soil and about how he saw himself in that tradition. What Pushkin perceived in Shakespeare was, above all, a verbal daring, a willingness to break the rules of polite or civilized (read: French) discourse, beginning with the unities of neoclassical drama, in the name of a higher form of creativity and closeness to the life source. Pushkin also sensed this daring in Derzhavin, but perhaps because Derzhavin was his (Pushkin's) own chief precursor and because Derzhavin's very Russian, very un-Gallic excesses were better known to him,[14] it fell to Pushkin to become "Russia's Shakespeare," as Mickiewicz, Baratynsky, and others intimated was his role.[15] If Pushkin could praise Derzhavin for the vividness of his imagery—say, the diamond-studded mountain turned upside-down and falling from its heights that opens "The Waterfall" ("Vodopad," 1791–94[16])—then he could just as easily, if the forum permitted it,[17] criticize the older poet for lacking "style or harmony" and for not knowing the "rules of versification."[18] "Here is what is in him [Derzhavin]," wrote Pushkin in a letter to Delvig, "*thoughts, pictures, and movements which are truly poetic*; in reading him you seem to be reading a bad, free translation of some marvelous original. By God, his genius thought in Tatar—and he did not know the Russian ABC's from lack of leisure."[19] Why was this so, why was Pushkin more demanding of Derzhavin, less willing to admit his breaking of the "rules" (the Russian ABC's)? Because Derzhavin belonged to his tradition, the one in which he was trying to establish himself as the central figure, while Shakespeare was an "other" he could never completely master linguistically and thus could more freely "project upon." Or, to put it another way, the universality, the ability to transcend his "Englishness," that was Shakespeare's was not, in Pushkin's opinion, Derzhavin's. In this same essay, for example, Pushkin singles out those authors whose "bold locutions [...] powerfully and uncommonly convey to us a clear thought and poetic pictures;"[20] not

14 Shakespeare's dense Renaissance English would always be difficult for Pushkin, and it is hard to say how much he actually apprehended, either in the original or in a French translation.

15 See Bethea, *Realizing Metaphors: Alexander Pushkin and the Life of the Poet* (Madison: University of Wisconsin Press, 1998), 137–234; and "Aleksandr Pushkin: From Byron to Shakespeare," ed. Neil Cornwell *Reference Guide to Russian Literature* (London: Fitzroy Dearborn Publishers, 1998), 18–25.

Mickiewicz wrote in his Paris lectures, for example, "Et tu [Pushkin] Shakespeare eris, si fata sinant!" [And you (Pushkin) too would have been Shakespeare, if the fates had permitted!] (Adam Mickiewicz, *Dziela*, 16 vols. [Warsaw: Czytelnik, 1955], 5: 301). The Baratynsky reference (from a December 1825 letter to Pushkin) is cited below in the text.

16 *Pss*, 11: 60.

17 That is, a personal letter to a close friend like Delvig. Pushkin's public statements about Derzhavin were much more guarded and respectful.

18 Alexander Pushkin, *The Letters*, trans. and intro J. Thomas Shaw (Madison: University of Wisconsin Press, 1967), 225; original in *Pss*, 13: 182. The letter to Delvig was written in the first days of June 1825.

19 Ibid.

20 *Pss*, 11: 60–61.

fortuitously, Derzhavin heads the list of native writers, while Shakespeare heads the list of foreign ones. "There is," says Pushkin, "a higher audacity, an audacity of invention, creativity [*smelost' izobreteniia, sozdaniia*], in which the broad scheme [*plan*] is subsumed by creative thought." And it is this higher audacity, argues Pushkin further, that the. French, too constrained by issues of taste and the rules of individual word usage ("le bon mot"), totally lack.[21] The problem for Pushkin here, of course, especially the Pushkin who is contemplating setting off in new generic directions, is that his roots are much closer to French *bon goût* and restraint than he would like, and he knows it. As he acknowledged to his friend Prince Vyazemsky back in December 1823, "I hate to see in our primitive language traces of European affectation and French refinement. Rudeness and simplicity are more becoming to it. I preach from internal conviction, but as is my custom I write otherwise."[22] Now, in 1830, the poet was once again returning, inter alia, to the dramatic form and trying to realize that "higher audacity" that he linked both with the overcoming of his past and with the establishment of a living literary tradition. He was, we might say, trying to practice the "internal conviction" that he preached.

We can sense how much Pushkin saw himself as "Russia's Shakespeare" by the way those close to him, and particularly those whose aesthetic judgments he respected, ascribed that role to him. For example, Baratynsky, responding to news that Pushkin had completed *Boris Godunov*, wrote the following in a letter of December 1825:

> Don't think that I am such a marquis that I can't feel the heights of romantic tragedy! I love Shakespeare's heroes, almost always natural, always engaging, in the genuine attire of their time and with sharply featured countenances. I prefer them to the heroes of Racine; at the same time, I must give the great talent of the French tragedian its due. I will say more: I am almost certain that the French cannot possess a true romantic tragedy. It's not the rules of Aristotle that shackle them — from them [the rules] one can easily be freed — but [the fact that] they are deprived of the most crucial means of success: an elegant popular language. I respect the French classicists; they knew their language, they practiced the kinds of poetry that were characteristic to them, and they produced much that was wonderful. [But] their newest romantic writers are pathetic to me: it seems they have bitten off more than they can chew [*mne kazhetsia, oni sadiatsia v chuzhie sani*].

---

21 Citing examples of individual usage taken for "boldness" by the French in the language of Racine and Delille, Pushkin remarks sarcastically, "This is a wretched literature, that would obey such petty and capricious criticism" (11: 61).

22 Pushkin, *The Letters*, 146; original in *Pss*, 13: 80.

I'm dying to learn [*zhazhdu imet' poniatie*] about your Godunov. Our marvelous language is capable of everything — I sense this, although I can't myself make this happen [*ne mogu privesti v ispolnenie*]. This language is created for Pushkin, as Pushkin is for it. I am certain that your tragedy is filled with moments of extraordinary beauty [*ispolnena krasot neobyknovennykh*]. Go forth, complete what has been begun — you, in whom genius resides. Raise up Russian poetry to that level among the poetic works [literally, "poetries" (*poezii*)] of all peoples, just as Peter the Great raised up Russia among the nations [literally, "powers" (*derzhavy*)]. Complete on your own what he did on his own. Our business will be to stand by in recognition and wonder [*a nashe delo — priznatel'nost' i udivlenie*].[23]

Here we can see a friend and literary comrade in arms comparing Pushkin to the two giants — Shakespeare as the great master of popular, living language and the *auteur barbare* (La Harpe) most clearly embodying a *civilisation du Nord* (Guizot), and Peter as the great ruler of another "northern" people and the one responsible for leading his rough subjects onto the path of "European" consciousness — who hover at the edges of the poet's mature thinking as competing exemplars and challenges (linguistic versus political power). Baratynsky is challenging his friend to become through poetic words what Peter became through legendary tsarist deeds. That he makes these statements on the very eve of the epoch-defining Decembrist Rebellion could only have appeared foreordained to the letter's superstitious recipient.

The Stone Guest versus Richard III: The Meaning of Love

How exactly did the "higher audacity" I cited above manifest itself in Shakespeare or, more accurately, in the Shakespeare Pushkin believed he had discovered and endeavored to internalize? What the example of Shakespeare seems to have given Pushkin was, first and foremost, the *unpredictability* of personality, the ability to step out of a role assigned to a dramatic persona by the "unity of character." "In Molière," writes Pushkin in "Table-Talk," "the Miser is miserly, and that's it. In Shakespeare, [on the other hand,] Shylock is miserly, sharp, vengeful, fond of his children, witty. In Molière the Hypocrite chases after the wife of his benefactor by acting the hypocrite. In Shakespeare [...] Angelo is a

---

[23] *Pss*, 13: 253

hypocrite because all his public actions contradict his secret passions! What depth there is in this character!"[24] Hence in Shakespeare Pushkin first came face to face with a humanity capable of remaking itself at any moment, of shedding behavioral codes (stereotypes) imposed by convention, of genuinely *becoming* in a language fully appropriate to a history imagined as open-ended, as once existing in the present. This is where the boldness came in, for such a humanity—regardless of the role it played onstage—had less to lose, since it was by definition closer to the "people" and the raucous spectacle of the "square" (*ploshchad'*) and farther from the "court" with its aristocratic emphasis on "servility" (*podobostrastie*) and a strict rule-centered hierarchy.[25] Moreover, such unpredictability with regard to language and character was especially cherished by Pushkin for the reason that, as we know from his 1830 review of Polevoy's *History of the Russian People* (*Istoriia russkogo naroda*), the poet associated randomness, "chance"-ness (*sluchainost'*) with a Russian past too dominated by European versions of causality and specifically by French romantic historiography (Guizot, Thierry, Barante).[26] In other words, Shakespeare's linguistic consciousness was a happy example of that same unpredictability *as it applied to another people's history* that Pushkin was trying to capture for Russia in his novelistic and historiographic experiments of the 1830s (*The Captain's Daughter, The History of Pugachev*).

But let us now turn to *Richard III* and *The Stone Guest*. I begin again by reformulating the parallelisms between the two erotic duels, except now I focus on their internal contrasts, for it is here that Pushkin (consciously or no) *creates meaning*. First, both Gloucester and Guan tell why, either implicitly or explicitly, they are bent on wooing these women. At the same time, the "how," "when," and "to whom" they reveal their motivations are much different. Likewise different is the dramatic conceit underlying each case of disclosure. Gloucester addresses himself to the audience (who chance to "overhear" his private thoughts) in the optical illusion of the soliloquy:

> Was ever woman in this humour wooed?
> Was ever woman in this humour won?
> I'll have her, but I will not keep her long.
> What! I that killed her husband and his father
> To take her in her heart's extremest hate,
> With curses in her mouth, tears in her eyes,
> The bleeding witness of my hatred by,
> Having God, her conscience, and these bars against me,
> And I no friends to back my suit at all

---

24 Ibid., 12: 160.
25 See *Pss*, 11: 178–79, where these terms are glossed. It is here, for example, that Pushkin explains the difference between the "popular tragedy of Shakespeare" (*tragediia narodnaia, Shekspirova*) and the "court-sponsored drama of Racine" (*drama pridvornaia, Rasinova*).
26 For more on this topic, see the fine discussion in Svetlana Evdokimova, *Pushkin's Historical Imagination* (New Haven: Yale University Press, 1999), esp. chap. 1, "The Impediments of Russian History," and chap. 2, "Chance and Historical Necessity."

>   But the plain devil and dissembling looks?
>   And yet to win her! All the world to nothing!
>   Ha!²⁷

But Guan states his intentions to his servant Leporello in a dialogue:

>   DON GUAN: I didn't see a thing
>   Beneath those somber widow's weeds — just glimpsed
>   A bit of slender ankle as she passed.
>   LEPORELLO: Oh, that'll do. Your keen imagination
>   Will picture you the rest, I have no doubt;
>   It's defter than a painter's brush, I swear.
>   And never has it mattered where you start —
>   With forehead or with foot, it's all the same.
>   DON GUAN: O Leporello, you can be assured,
>   I'll know the lady soon.²⁸

More to the point, Guan says this in the play's opening pages, *before* the scenes where he progressively "exposes" himself to Dona Anna, while Gloucester's soliloquy comes at the end of scene 2, *after* he was won over Anne. And it is Leporello, Guan's interlocutor from the "people," and not simply his imagination that eggs him on, arouses him. That Guan is never "alone with himself" the way Gloucester is is crucial. Similarly, the urge that in Shakespeare is premeditated, malicious, and retaliatory ("All the world to nothing!") and that comes into focus only after the fact is in Pushkin purely erotic and spontaneous to begin with (the "narrow heel" whose "chance" sighting draws the *improvisatore* of love into the future and the hope of further embodiment). Or, to rephrase the opposition, Gloucester wants to "take" Anne in "her extremest hate"; Guan wants at some level *to be taken* —to feel the change in the other, from hate to love, that can, somehow, change him. Indeed, the way these two protagonists come at the challenge of winning the beautiful and faithful widow who has every right to hate her tormentor is strikingly different: Gloucester's intent is no more and no less than to vanquish the world through the power and magnetism of his (variously understood) "deformity"; Guan has no other ulterior goal than to sleep with this woman who should be, by all the rules of society and religion, inaccessible. In the one Eros is clearly the tool of power, politics, public display; in the other there is no power on earth greater than Eros itself.

Second, both Gloucester and Guan are referred to repeatedly as devils and their female counterparts as *angels*, and one has to assume that these appellations are not mere figures of speech, metaphors *tout court*. In other

---

27   William Shakespeare, *Richard III*, New Penguin Shakespeare, ed. E.A.J. Honigmann (London: Penguin, 1968), 1.2.227–38.

28   «[Дон Гуан:] Ее совсем не видно / Под этим вдовьим черным покрывалом, / Чуть узенькую пятку я заметил. / [Лепорелло:] Довольно с вас. / У вас воображенье / В минуту дорисует остальное; / Оно у вас проворней живописца, / Вас все равно, с чего бы ни начать, / С бровей ли, с ног ли. [Дон Гуан:] Слушай, Лепорелло, / Я с нею познакомлюсь» (*Pss*, 7:143).

words, the two heroes begin their wooings from positions *beyond* the laws of God and man. However, it is the righteously indignant Anne who changes in Shakespeare (she of course mistakenly thinks that Gloucester has committed his misdeeds out of love for her), while it is the supposedly damned Guan who changes (or who comes to believe he has changed — "*Mne kazhetsia, ia ves' pererodilsia*") in Pushkin. That Dona Anna eventually yields to Guan can be viewed either as a lack of fidelity on her part (a betrayal of her dead husband) *or* as a sacrifice of her "angelic" purity for the sake of this "demon" ("*Vy sushchii demon*") who needs her love in order to be "reborn." But even here there is a way to parse Dona Anna's behavior that stresses her essential difference (as opposed to her "ordinariness"). To repeat, Gloucester's soliloquy comes *after* Anne has been won, revealing all and removing any hint of risk or vulnerability in his prior words of love. Guan, on the other hand, has another dialogue with Leporello in scene 3, immediately after his first extended exchange with Dona Anna but *before* their ultimate meeting, this time in the presence of *the statue that nods*. In other words, Guan goes to his tryst with the wife of the dead husband–cum–statue in a real way knowing the risk, the sense that this is his personified doom coming for him, involved. And such an understanding would have to alter the dynamics of that tryst, making it maximally "open" and dangerous for both sides. In this respect, we could say that it is Anne who fails/"falls" in her reading of Gloucester (she is merely a pawn), but it is Guan who succeeds/"rises" in his reading of Dona Anna (he bets everything on the intercession of this "guardian angel"). The problem is that in Pushkin seduction (carnal love) is experienced simultaneously, *through dialogue*, as potential redemption (spiritual transfiguration) *and* damnation (judgment from beyond). Guan's carnality cannot be separated out from his need to be saved from his prior self and to change. It is not the hero's unworthiness (the story in Shakespeare) but the heroine's transformative beauty (the story in Pushkin) that is the issue. This is one of those indeterminacies typical of the mature Pushkin and often revolving around the theme of superstitious dread and the natural/supernatural opposition, where there is nothing internal to the text to help the critic solve the moral tensions of the situation.

Third, the most striking parallelism between the two seduction sequences is, as Shevyryov originally noted, the hero's presentation to the heroine of a weapon (a sword in Shakespeare, a dagger in Pushkin) by which she is invited to kill the speaker, who simultaneously acknowledges being the killer of her husband (and, in Anne's case, her father-in-law, the king). But this most glaring likeness carries with it an equally glaring difference: in Shakespeare, the revelation comes as no surprise, since Anne knows already with whom she is dealing; in Pushkin, however, this is a genuine revelation—Dona Anna has no idea that this man to whom she is attracted and who has already gone through one transformation in her eyes—from modest "monk" to passionate "Don Diego"—is indeed the diabolical Don Guan until this moment. At the time the respective weapons are unsheathed, the women are invited, or challenged, to kill not enemies per se but enemies changed into men in love. How this argument is smuggled into the two wooing scenes is telling. Gloucester explains that it was Anne's beauty that provoked him to kill ("I did kill King Henry—/ But 't was thy beauty that provoked me"[29]), whereas in Guan's case it is Dona Anna's beauty that, supposedly, saves him from his past:

> For all too many years
> I've been the most devoted slave of lust;
> But ever since the day I saw your face
> I've been reborn, returned once more to life.[30]

Thus, the revelation in Shakespeare is the exculpatory "why" of his crimes (they were committed "out of love"), while the revelation in Pushkin is the "who":

> I'm not Don Diego ... I'm Don Guan. [...]
> I killed your husband—and regret it not;
> I feel no true repentance in my soul.[31]

Guan takes full responsibility for the crimes before his chief victim, and he does so in the incarnation of the criminal. Then he, in effect, through the act of seduction (or love—we cannot tell the difference!), asks the victim to see him as someone other or better.

This is an extraordinary gambit on Pushkin's part, despite his greater commitment to so-called plausibility (*pravdopodobie*), and one worth pausing on for a moment. Recall that Shakespeare's character can use his stable identity as villain to break down Anne's defenses and make her see (even if this is duplicity) her part in his past crimes. Guan, on the other hand, has no equivalent rationale to fall back on. He, and he alone, is the author of his past. The moment at which he finally discloses himself to Dona Anna is also, and not fortuitously, the moment at which he transgresses the boundaries of verbal intimacy:

> DON GUAN: And what if you [*vy*] should chance
> To meet Don Guan?
> DONA ANNA: Why then I'd thrust a dagger
> Inside the villain's heart.

---

[29] Shakespeare, *Richard II*, 1.2.179–80.

[30] «Так, разврата / Я долго был покорный ученик, / Но с той поры как вас увидел я, / Мне кажется, я весь переродился» (*Pss*, 7: 168).

[31] «Я не Диего, я Гуан [...] Я убил / Супруга твоего; и не жалею / О том—и нет раскаянья во мне» (*Pss*, 7: 167).

> DON GUAN: O Dona Anna!
> Then thrust your [tvoi] dagger here!³²

The hero's statement of maximal honesty ("This is who I am!") is, once again, inextricable from a highly eroticized *cognitio* when he "takes" Dona Anna not only unawares but, as it were, emotionally *naked*. She is caught in the act of desiring the unspeakable: it is as though he pierces her psychological armor with the phallic dagger of his words in a manner that is more than figurative. "I am not Diego, I'm Guan" is, following immediately on the first usage of *tvoi*, not so much a disrobing of himself but of the chaste widow who has allowed herself to come this far.

How different this moment is from that in Richard III when Anne, in essence, backs down from Gloucester, refraining to strike him because she wants to believe he is telling the truth:

> ANNE: Arise, dissembler; though I wish thy death
> I will not be thy executioner.
> GLOUCESTER: Then bid me kill myself, and I will do it.
> ANNE: I have already.
> GLOUCESTER: That was in thy rage.
> Speak it again, and even with the word
> This hand, which for thy love did kill thy love,
> Shall for thy love kill a far truer love;
> To both their deaths shalt thou be accessory.
> ANNE: I would I knew thy heart.
> GLOUCESTER: 'Tis figured in my tongue.
> ANNE: I fear me both are false.
> GLOUCESTER: Then never was man true.
> ANNE: Well, well, put up your sword.³³

Anne yields ("put up your sword"), won over by Gloucester's staged eloquence yet still fearing he is not telling the truth. If one might put it this way, it is not so much her desire *for Gloucester* that has been "pricked" as it is her wish (however ambiguous and self-incriminating) to be the cause (inspiration) of his actions and therefore the power behind him. Here Anne, though her motivations are not so clearly drawn out and she is much more the victim, seems closer in her "desiring" to Lady Macbeth and, analogously, to Pushkin's Marina Mniszek. Eros for these Renaissance women cannot be separated out from the power and status their men possess. But Dona Anna is not attracted to Guan, in any of his incarnations, for his worldly power and prestige; quite the opposite,

---

32   «[Дон Гуан]: Что если б Дон Гуана / Вы встретили? [Дона Анна:] Тогда бы я злодею / Кинжал вонзила в сердце. [Дон Гуан:] Дона Анна, / Где твой кинжал? вот грудь моя» (*Pss*, 7: 166–67).

33   Shakespeare, *Richard III*, 1.2.184–96

in fact. In her, and in the way her being as a desiring woman has been awakened by this "demon" who has no right to "possess" her, Eros has become a free, open, and powerfully dialogic signifier: it is this process that is the "last word" and nothing outside it.

Which brings me to my final point about the Shakespearean lesson of the Boldino autumn. The unpredictability of human personality and the ability of genuine "romantic" drama to step outside the neoclassical unities and create a situation much closer to the "people" and to life "as such" are very much on Pushkin's mind as he considers all the possibilities at the denouement of *The Stone Guest*. Here is a Don Guan who, finally and fully revealed, can be reborn into something other than a "pure demon" of Eros; here is a Dona Anna who, starting out modest and faithful, can still experience desire and can therefore become other than her role as grieving widow; and here is a stone husband who, even in death, refuses to remain fixed in place and to play the role of unwitting cuckold. The "higher audacity" of this play consists precisely in these changes we cannot separate out from their dialogism (their always "triangulated" desire, as we might say today, after Girard) but understand nonetheless to be irreversible (the "tragic" quality). The Pushkin of the Boldino autumn and of *The Stone Guest* specifically is concerned above all with the *unlikely in love*. This is what he, the aging bridegroom and great-grandson of Peter's jealous blackamoor, needs. Despite the carping of critics, a young and impressionable Maria can fall in love with a grizzled Mazepa (*Poltava*), just as a Desdemona can fall in love with an Othello. All this Pushkin not only understood at some level but took as an article of faith (again, he *needed* to), as he discusses in another contemporaneous Boldino text, "Refutations of criticisms" ("Oproverzhenie na kritiki").[34] Yet there is one more strange metamorphosis of feeling, this one involving Ovid's Pygmalion, which is also mentioned by the poet in the same section of "Refutations" and which, I would argue, was crucial to his thinking about statues and Eros in *The Stone Guest*. Here we find a "classical" text, and one that Shakespeare himself was possibly engaging in *The Winter's Tale*, that takes the element of unpredictability in love to another, mythopoetic or "Promethean" level bound to appeal to Pushkin in this most anxious and creative of all autumns.

Pygmalion, we recall, was the legendary king of Cyprus who, unhappy in love, created a statue of such beauty that he became enamored of it and prayed

---

[34] *Pss*, 11: 158, September–October 1830.

to Aphrodite to give him a wife resembling his creation. Aphrodite not only heeded the supplicant but gave Pygmalion precisely *his own statue come to life*. It is my argument, developed at greater length elsewhere, that *The Stone Guest* is a reworking of this myth, with the following important differences: the statue come to life out of love (the "tranquille indifférence" of Natalya Goncharova that is figured in the play in the cool, "marble" beauty of Dona Anna) is tragically counterbalanced in this season of dread by the statue of death (the humiliated husband come to take the miscreant down to hell for his past crimes).[35] That the living statue is the poet's own, so to speak, is made clear in the other plot of love and marital fidelity being completed that fall: the concluding chapter 8 (originally 9) of *Eugene Onegin*, in which the village maiden, Tatiana, undergoes a "miraculous" metamorphosis to comme il faut high-society princess and muse (the poet's "creation"), so that her graceful presence now outshines even that of the legendary Nina Voronskaya, *with her marble beauty*.[36] In this reversal of the plot of *The Stone Guest*, Pushkin places the husband (the general), now neither dead nor cuckolded, in the virtuous and departing wife's boudoir at the climactic moment when the failed hero freezes on the spot: "She [Tatiana] leaves. There stands Evgeny / As though thunderstruck."[37]

Thus, in the erotic space of the Boldino autumn, as the poet contemplates being given Aphrodite's gift of his beautiful statue/muse come to life, he also imagines the full weight of his past crimes. Indeed, these crimes seem to be replayed when Guan, who being himself cannot help but enjoy an opportunity for male rivalry, *brings the other statue to life as well* by having Leporello invite it to take up its humiliatingly "erect" post and then refer to it, following the gender of *statuia*, as *ona* ("she") — the ultimate putdown. In this sense, the one statue ("female" grace) cannot exist without the other statue ("male" retribution) — hence the tragedy. As the ecstatic Guan says to this woman who has fallen for him despite his past,

35 See Pushkin's letter to his future mother-in-law of 5 April 1830, in which he refers to his fiancée's beauty in potentially "statuesque" terms ("the calm indifference of her heart") and claims that he has "nothing with which to please her" [Je n'ai rien pour lui plaire] (*Pss*, 14: 76). See the discussion in Bethea, *Realizing Metaphors*, 109–11.

36 *Pss*, 6: 172; Further corroboration that Pushkin had the Pygmalion myth squarely in mind as he "mused" about the source of erotic love is found in the first four stanzas of chapter 4 of *Eugene Onegin*, which were excluded (presumably for personal reasons) from the completed editions of the novel-in-verse but were still published separately as "Zhenshchiny. Otryvok iz 'Evgeniia Onegina'" (Women: An excerpt from *Evgeny Onegin*) in the *Moskovskii vestnik* in 1827. The second of these stanzas ends with the lines:

«То вдруг я мрамор видел в ней (в женщине), / Перед мольбой Пигмалиона / Еще холодный и немой, / Но вскоре жаркий и живой» (*Pss*, 6: 592).

37 «Она ушла. Стоит Евгений, / Как будто громом поражен» (*Pss*, 6: 189).

> No doubt you've often heard the man described
> As villain or as fiend. O Dona Anna ...
> Such ill repute may well in part be true:
> My weary conscience bears a heavy load
> Of evil deeds.[38]

I am suggesting that the Pushkin of *The Stone Guest* is *both* the Guan hoping to be reborn and the husband (his new role) protecting what is his by right. And his dialogic counterpart, that through which he experiences his own new incarnation? She is *both* the pagan living statue that comes to know passion (Ovid) *and* the spiritualized Christian beauty that confers grace through compassion/mercy (Dona Anna become Madonna).[39] When the recently married Pushkin wrote to Pletnev that "[t]his state [marriage] is so new to me that it seems I have been reborn [*chto kazhetsia, ia pererodilsia*],"[40] he was repeating, with the same joyous surprise, the sentiments of his hero.

The question of how Pushkin creatively adapted the principles of Shakespearean dramaturgy to his own tradition is only just being posed, despite all the excellent philological work done in the past on this topic. One is emboldened to assert this because the psychic mechanisms underwriting the works of the mature Pushkin lie somewhere between the Bloomian notion of influence ("strong," Oedipally challenged poets finding ways to say something new outside the shades/shadows of great precursors) and the depersonalized notion of intertext (a borrowing that is purely linguistic and exists in the absence of poetic fears, resentments, and "dodgings"). My guess is that Shakespeare, as the "barbaric northerner" whose magnificent language could never be fully absorbed by the "Gallically" restrained and elegant Pushkin, gave the poet the example he needed to transcend his own, and his immediate tradition's, past. As Akhmatova first insisted, Don Guan is not only a poet of love, he is also a poet in the more literal sense.[41] Thus as Pushkin, in that exceptional Boldino autumn, passed from poet to prose writer, illicit paramour to lawful husband, man who dreamed of muses to man who had to live daily with a muselike beauty come to life, he had as his "best man" the Bard whose shadowy biography, as opposed to Byron's, did not and could not stand athwart his path. Shakespeare more than any other writer, foreign or domestic, gave Pushkin this "higher audacity" he needed. How Pushkin took up this challenge is especially evident in *The Stone Guest* — in the way Dona Anna is different, more fully a dialogic partner, from Anne; in the way Guan wants to be desired

---

38 «Не правда ли—он был описан вас / Злодеем, извергом—о Дона Анна, / На совести усталой много зла, / Быть может, тяготеет» (*Pss*, 7: 168).

39 One thinks here of the "Marian" theme in poems such as "Zhil na svete rytsar' bednyi" (1829) and "Madona" (1830), Pushkin's lyric portrait of his fiancée.

40 *Pss*, 14: 154–55; cited in Akhmatova, "'Kamennyi gost'" Pushkina," *O Pushkine: Stat'i zametki*, 2: 268.

41 Ibid., 2: 260.

by this woman more than he wants the "power" that is the token of her submission; and in the language, so eroticized in its constant need to draw in and on the other, yet at the same time so pregnant with its own fatal "ontological rhymes" and with its implicit knowledge that the statue has its rights too and it will come.

Chapter 11. Stabat Pater: Revisiting the "Monumental" in Peter, Petersburg, Pushkin[1]

The present study is about Pushkin's Petersburg, what the city meant in the creative psychology of the poet. More specifically, it is about monuments — first, the famous equestrian monument to Peter I created by Etienne Falconet and unveiled on Senate Square by Catherine II in 1782 (the centennial of the great tsar's ascension to the throne); second, the city itself, which became synonymous in people's minds with the emperor's project to reshape and westernize Russia; and third, the narrative poem/epos (poema) by Pushkin, which took the statue as its title and central plot device.[2] It will be my argument that *The Bronze Horseman* (the poem) was designed from within to be its own kind of monument, a celebration of the city and its awesome materiality but also a profound reshaping, by other means, of Peter's original promethean handiwork. But before getting to Pushkin's words and ideas, some groundwork needs to be laid. To begin with, there is the idea of monument, which comes from the Latin *monumentum*. According to the dictionary definition the word can, depending on context, have multiple meanings:

> 1) A sepulchre, a burial place. 2) A written document, a record. Formerly also, a piece of information given in writing. 3) A structure or edifice intended to commemorate a notable person, action, or event; a stone or other structure built over

---

[1] First appeared as Stabat Pater: Revisiting the Monumental' in Peter, Petersburg, Pushkin," in special vol. of *Zapiski russkoi akademicheskoi gruppy v SShA* (on 300th anniversary of St. Petersburg), ed. Alexis Klimoff, 33 (2004): 3–21.

[2] The best single work on Falconet's monument is Alexander M. Schenker, *The Bronze Horseman: Falconet's Monument to Peter the Great* (New Haven: Yale University Press, 2003). The secondary literature on Pushkin's great poem is vast; useful places to start are the "Literary Monuments" (Literaturnye pamiatniki) edition A. S. Pushkin, *Mednyi vsadnik*, ed. N.V. Izmailov (Leningrad: Nauka, 1978); A.L. Ospovat and R.D. Timenchik, *"Pechal'nu povest' sokranit'"* (Moscow: Kniga, 1987); and, in English, Andrew Kahn, *Pushkin's "Bronze Horseman"* (London: Bristol Classical Press, 1998).

a grave or in a church etc. in memory of a dead person. Formerly also, a carved figure, a statue, an effigy. 4) An enduring thing, esp. a thing that by its survival commemorates a person, action, period, or event; a structure or edifice surviving from a past age; an outstanding survival of an early literature. [...] 5) A thing serving for identification; a thing that warns, a portent. [...]³

Virtually all of these meanings will have a place in the discussion to follow. What is most striking about the various connotations is that they may be, from the start, internally in conflict: something that celebrates *and* warns (from the verb *moneo*: "to remind, admonish, warn"); something that buries *and* raises up; something that is three-dimensional (an effigy, statue) and something that is two-dimensional (a written record). Of these ambiguities Pushkin himself was undoubtedly aware, as we know from his different uses of the Russian calque *pamiatnik*.⁴ When in his great valedictory poem he cites Horace's "Exegi monumentum," "I have erected a monument," he is playing off the literal meaning of the word, a three-dimensional physical artifact, by suggesting that his legacy, one made up of words, can be as real as a bust or a statue. This replacement of the literal and material by the figurative and airborne we will return to, but for now suffice it to say that a typical *monumentum*, whether the Great Pyramid, the Lincoln Memorial, or the Bronze Horseman, is meant to symbolize the permanence of the honoree's glory ("Krasuisia grad Petrov, i stoi / Nekolebimo kak Rossiia" ["Stay beautiful, city of Peter, and stand / Unshakeable like Russia] says Pushkin in the poem). If that monument is further anthropomorphized, as is the case with Falconet's statue of Peter, it can also become a kind of *genius loci*, the guardian spirit of a place.

Next, there is Pushkin's understanding of Peter the Great and his own status vis-à-vis the tsar. To put it mildly, Pushkin had exceedingly complicated feelings about Russia's greatest tsar and wrote about him on numerous occasions over the course of his short but intense creative life. Notes and essays, lyric poems, heroic epos, historical novel, history proper: Pushkin tried to vector in on Peter and his legacy in all these genres, each time capturing a different aspect of his subject. His understanding was also historically situated. Obviously, as we reach the 1830's, the last decade of Pushkin's life and the time period in which his relations with the then tsar Nicholas I are becoming the most difficult and personally humiliating, the poet's reading of Peter takes on a darker hue. The domesticated god-father of the 1827 *The Blackamoor of Peter the Great* (*Arap Petra Velikogo*) and the

3   *The New Shorter Oxford English Dictionary*, ed. Lesley Brown, 2 vols. (Oxford: Clarendon Press, 1993), 2:1823.

4   See *Slovar' Iazyka Pushkina*, gen. ed. V.V. Vinogradov, 4 vols. (Moscow: Gosudarstvennoe Izdatel'stvo Inostrannykh i Natsional'nykh Slovarei, 1956–1961), 3:270–71. Several of these meanings (1) something that reminds, 2) a commemorative structure or edifice, 3) remnants of the past) can also be found in *Tolkovyi slovar' zhivogo velikorusskogo Iazyka Vladimira Dalia*, 4 vols. (St. Petersburg-Moscow: Izdanie T-va M. O. Vol'f, 1912), 3:27.

larger-than-life field general of the 1828 epic *Poltava* becomes the avenging pagan idol of the 1833 *Bronze Horseman* (*Mednyi vsadnik*) and the author of brutal and arbitrary ukases in the 1835–36 *History of Peter I* (*Istoriia Petra*), a work that, while remaining unfinished at Pushkin's death in January 1837, was his longest manuscript and gave every indication of being his *magnum opus*.[5] More specifically, if the uncompleted historical novel presents Pushkin's Abyssinian great-grandfather in a special relationship with the tsar (something exclusively positive), and if the *poema* singles out the defeat of the Swedes in the 1709 battle as a turning point giving Russians confidence in Peter's policies (something also positive), then the latter two works are less than clear about the tsar's legacy. Hence, the Peter that Pushkin invoked in the 1826 lyric "Stanzas" ("Stansy") as an instructive model of hard work, enlightenment, generosity and mercy for the new tsar Nicholas had morphed by the mid 1830's into something much more ambivalent and difficult to read.

But the picture is even more complicated than this. To the above summary we can add the fact that Pushkin's own family had ancient noble roots and that one of his forebears (Fyodor Pushkin) had been executed as a result of his role in the Streltsy leader Tsykler's plot to overthrow Peter:

> A stubborn spirit undid us all.
> Irrepressible within his own family
> My ancestor didn't get on with Peter
> And for that got himself hung.[6]

Even if, on the one hand, Pushkin was genuinely proud of Russia's growing prominence among European nations following Peter's and Catherine's territorial expansions and Alexander I's role in subduing Napoleon, he was,

---

5 See the discussion of Pushkin's historiographical conception (*zamysel*) in *Isto-riia Petra* in Il'ia Feinberg's classic *Nezavershennye raboty Pushkina*, 7th ed. (Moscow: Khudozhestvennaia literatura, 1979), 11–180. On the one hand, several of those (e.g., the French writer Loeve-Veimars) who discussed Pushkin's project with him in the months leading up to the duel spoke after his death of how the poet, based on his careful research and *pace* Karamzin, was coming to see a chastening and moderating in Peter's character toward the end of his life (24–25). On the other, Pushkin was equally well aware of the tsar's propensity for using cruelty and arbitrary force to achieve his ends, his "writing of his ukases with the knout," in the poet-historian's famous phrase (44, 47, 53). All in all, even though Pushkin tried his utmost to understand Peter's character and its development, he never denied the tsar's inner contradictions (which he understood Russia to have inherited as a result) and the sense that, while the reforms (beginning with the destruction of the ancient hereditary nobility) may have been necessary, Peter's very impatience and impulsiveness set the wheels of state moving forward at a pace that the country was not yet ready for (44).

6 "Moia rodoslovnaia" (My Genealogy), not published in Pushkin's lifetime, in A.S. Pushkin, *Polnoe sobranie sochinenii*, ed. V.D. Bonch-Bruevich et al., 17 vols. (Moscow: Akademiia Nauk SSSR, 1937–1959), 3:262. This edition will be cited hereafter as "*Pss*." The Russian reads: «Упрямства дух нам всем подгадил. / В родню свою неукротим, / С Петром мой пращур не поладил / И был за то повешен им». For the record, Fyodor Pushkin was not hanged but beheaded. N. Eidel'man, *Pushkin: Istoriia i sovremennost' v khudozhestvennom soznanii poeta* (Moscow: Sovestkii pisatel', 1984), 324.

on the other, equally proud of his own family's martial prowess (he liked to compare in his mind Byron's admiral ancestors with his own people's victorious generals) and its reputation for challenging tsars and getting into trouble. For Pushkin the old, hereditary nobility (as opposed to Peter's new service nobility) had served a purpose: not all of them had lost their independent thinking as Appanage Russia gave way to the emerging Muscovite State, and they could serve as a check on the tsar's despotic tendencies when the occasion demanded. To make matters even more personal, Pushkin's friends, such as Baratynsky, had for years been saying that it was his role to do for Russia's linguistic consciousness what Peter in his reforms had done for the country's social, political, and military status:

> Our marvelous language is capable of everything [...] This language is created for Pushkin, as Pushkin is for it. [...] Go forth, complete what has been begun — you, in whom genius resides. Raise up Russian poetry to that level among the poetic works [literally, "poetries" (*poezii*)] of all peoples, just as Peter the Great raised up Russia among the nations [literally, "powers" (*derzhavy*)]. Complete on your own what he did on his own. Our business will be to stand by in recognition and wonder.[7]

Hence what needs to be factored into Pushkin's passionate admiration for Peter's daring in breaking a window into Europe and all but thrusting his countrymen through it is the countervailing disappointment and humiliation for his own class and of course for himself, that advisor-in-waiting the tsars now needed but could not be bothered to pay attention to. For what powerful ruler or politician has ever listened to the poet or intellectual of his day?

The remaining biographical trajectory is well known. Pushkin was exiled for six years by Alexander I and then suddenly pardoned by Nicholas I in the aftermath of the noblemen-led Decembrist Uprising (14 December 1825) and the interrogation and punishment (including in the case of the leaders execution) of the participants. Pushkin, trusting and impulsive by nature, had no way of knowing that the pardon was in fact the tsar's cunning way of keeping him on a very short leash. In the now famous audience with Nicholas taking place on 8 September 1826 the tsar told Pushkin that he was free to return to Moscow and St. Petersburg and that he, the sovereign himself, would henceforth be his personal censor. Nicholas had all the cards in his hand and he played them shrewdly. If Pushkin felt he could, à la the great historian Karamzin, serve as an advisor and mitigating force in the tsar's thinking, he was sorely mistaken. Accounts of the meeting with Nicholas

---

[7] «Чудесный наш язык ко всему способен [...]. Он создан для Пушкина, а Пушкин для него [...]. Иди, довершай начатое, ты, в ком поселился гений! Возведи русскую поэзию на ту степень между поэзиями всех народов, на которую Петр Великий возвел Россию между державами. Соверши один, что он совершил один; а наше дело — признательность и удивление». Letter of Baratynsky to Pushkin, December 1825, in *Perepiska Pushkina*, ed. V.E. Vatsuro et al., 2 vols. (Moscow: Khudozhestvennaia literatura, 1982), 1:417.

suggest that the tsar became uncomfortable when Pushkin started to express himself freely during the hour-long conversation. At its conclusion, when the poet had agreed to the terms of his release (i.e., he would do or write nothing that could be interpreted as undermining the autocracy), Nicholas was reputed to have said to those around him, "Gentlemen, this is my Pushkin."[8] Over the next decade, until his death in January 1837, Pushkin learned over and over again firsthand how little the tsar was willing to listen to him and how in fact this relationship was an elaborate, and brilliantly executed, ruse to keep him compromised and muzzled.[9] Grateful to be free, full of noble impulses, and constantly made aware of his promise of loyalty, he could not very well bite the hand that fed him.

So where does this leave us with the question of Peter, his city, the larger imperial project, and Pushkin's relationship to his own tsar's great forebear? Well, as a man of letters rather than a man of the sword or tsar's confidant, Pushkin had to create a space for himself in Russian history, a space that would be defined not by martial deeds but by words which brought, over time and often against the wishes of the reigning powers, an inner freedom and an inner sophistication to their readers and listeners. As he wrote in "On the Worthlessness of Russian Literature" ("O nichtozhestve literatury russkoi"), an essay completed in 1834, a year after *The Bronze Horseman*,

> For a long time Russia remained alien to Europe... The great epoch of the Renaissance had no influence on her. Chivalry did not inspire our ancestors with sublime feelings... Russia was assigned another high calling... Her boundless plains swallowed up the force of the Mongols and stopped their invasion at the very edge of Europe. These barbarians didn't dare to leave an enslaved Russia in the rear and so returned to their eastern steppes. The enlightenment then taking shape [in Europe] was saved by tortured and dying Russia... [During the period of the Tartar Yoke] the inner life of the enslaved people did not develop. The Tartars were unlike the Moors: having conquered Russia, they gave her no algebra or Aristotle. The overthrow of the yoke, [and with it] the squabbles of grand princes with the appanages, of single rule with the freedom of the cities, of autocracy with the boyars, and of conquest with what was unique and original to the people did not create conditions conducive to the free flowering of enlightenment. While Europe became flooded with an incredible multitude of epic poems, legends, satires, romances, and mystery-plays, our ancient archives and

---

8 V.E. Vatsuro et al., ed., *Pushkin v vospominaniiakh sovremennikov*, 2 vols. (St. Petersburg: Akademicheskii proekt, 1998), 2:61.

9 Up to and including the most personally humiliating of all — the perusing of Pushkin's private correspondence with his wife by government postal censors. See 18 May 1834 letter of Pushkin to his wife in *Pss*, 15:149–50.

libraries, with the exception of chronicles, offered almost no food for the curiosity of the researcher. [...]

Finally, Peter appeared. Russia entered Europe like a just launched ship, with hammers rapping and cannon thundering. But the wars undertaken by Peter the Great were beneficial and fruitful. The success at transforming the Russian people was an outcome of the battle of Poltava, and European enlightenment dropped anchor at the shores of the conquered Neva.

Peter did not have time to complete much of what he started. He died in the period of his manhood, in the full strength of his creative activity. He cast an unfocused yet penetrating glance on the world of letters. [...] The new literature, the fruit of a newly educated society, was soon to be born.[10]

Peter's epochal achievements are duly acknowledged by Pushkin, but they are also historically situated. The emperor "did not have time" to finish all his projects; his view of the world of letters was "unfocused yet penetrating"; the "new literature" that was to be the fruit of a "newly educated [i.e., enlightened] society" was "soon to be [but had not yet been!] born." There was, in short, much left to do, especially if we take into account that Peter's very impulsiveness, in Pushkin's judgment, set in motion certain forces that made it difficult to achieve enlightenment elsewhere. As Pushkin summed up these thoughts in a draft outline to this latter section of the essay, "Peter created the army, navy, learning, laws, but he couldn't create literature, which appears of its accord, from its own origins."[11] Thus, if in all the other areas of social and political life in which Russia was destined to become, in time, an enlightened, European nation Peter's reforms were absolutely seminal, "revolutionary" (we will also return to this notion of Peter the revolutionary in a moment), in the area of belles-lettres this sort of transformation could not be legislated or authorized by force of will. It had to grow and take root by itself, on its own schedule. It was free in a way at which the impatient autocrat could not get.

10 Pss, 11:268–69. «Долго Россия оставался чуждою Европе [...]. Великая эпоха возрождения не имела на нее никакого влияния; рыцарство не одушевило наших предков чистыми восторгами [...]. России определено было высокое предназначение... Ее необозримые равнины поглотили силу монголов и остановили их нашествие на самом краю Европы; варвары не осмелились оставить у себя в тылу порабощенную Русь и возвратились на степи своего востока. Образующееся просвещение было спасено растерзанной и издыхающей Россией. [...]. Но внутренняя жизнь порабощенного народа не развивалась. Татаре не походили на мавров. Они, завоевав Россию, не подарили ей ни алгебры, ни Аристотеля. Свержение ига, споры великокняжества с уделами, единовластия с вольностями городов, самодержавия с боярством и завоевания с народной самобытностью не благоприятствовали свободному развитию просвещения. Европа наводнена была неимоверным множеством поэм, легенд, сатир, романсов, мистерий и проч., но старинные наши архивы и вивлиофики, кроме летописей, не представляют почти никакой пищи любопытству изыскателей. [...]

Наконец, явился Петр. Россия вошла в Европу, как спущенный корабль, — при стуке топора и при громе пушек. Но войны, предприятые Петром Великим, были благодетельны и плодотворны. Успех народного преобразования был следствием Полтавской битвы, и европейское просвещение причалило к берегам завоеванной Невы.

When we think of Peter we usually think of him as a reformer, but the term is much too pallid to convey the inherently radical, often violent nature of the changes he imposed on the population. Pushkin writes for example in an 1830 outline for a work on the Russian nobility that "Pierre I est tout à la fois Robespierre et Napoleon (la révolution incarnée)" (Peter I is at one and the same time Robespierre and Napoleon [the revolution incarnate]).[12] In other words, in the Russian cultural psyche (of which Pushkin was to become the chief interpreter) Peter instituted a revolution *from above*: he *unleashed, unbridled* certain forces that virtually all other kings and emperors try to rein in, hence the typical Renaissance play on words involving "reigning" and "reining," as in reining in the body politic or, by contrast, the too ambitious courtier of the "hotspur."[13] In this instance it was the rider and not the mount that was, to old Russia at least, dangerous. At some level, from the boyars who had their beards shaved (but still wore hair-shirts under their "German" clothing to do penance for the sins their godless monarch was forcing them to commit), to the thousands of peasants who died miserably clearing the disease-infested swamps in a place unintended either by nature or God to be a capital, Peter goaded, *spurred on*, his subjects into this new world. Pushkin understood brilliantly the iconography of Peter's project and he insinuated its revolutionary message into the poem.

If Falconet originally thought of Peter's outstretched arm on the statue as being protective, a *main protectrice*, then Pushkin makes the same arm "menacing" or "threatening" in his drafts to the poem.[14] Likewise, the image of the slightly rearing horse, the concerto or "spark" Falconet took from Bernini,[15] was read by Catherine and her advisors to project plainly and simply dynamism and enlightenment—the great sovereign stamping out ignorance and envy (the snake underneath[16]), guiding his nation-steed, so that the horse seems both to be moving forward (or the rider's calm dressage suggests as much) and destroying almost as a matter of course what lies beneath.[17] However, this dynamic image was not erected into a vacuum. Earlier, in *Poltava*, Pushkin

Петр не успел довершить многое, начатое им. Он умер в поре мужества, во всей силе творческой деятельности. Он бросил на словесность взор рассеянный, но проницательный [...]. Новая словесность, плод новообразованного общества, скоро должна была родиться».

11 *Pss*, 11:495.
12 *Pss*, 12:205.
13 See discussion in David M. Bethea, *The Shape of Apocalypse in Modern Russian Fiction* (Princeton: Princeton University Press, 1989), 50–52. For the Renaissance context, see, e.g., Robert N. Watson, "Horsemanship in Shakespeare's Second Tetralogy," *English Literary Renaissance* 13 (1983): 274–300.
14 *Pss*, 5:467.
15 The idea of the rearing horse must owe something to the precursor Bernini, but Falconet himself didn't agree with how the latter had presented his sculpted steed ("he did not know how to make a horse") and insisted that his work was much more natural and authentic. See discussion in Schenker, *The Bronze Horseman*, 276.
16 On the image of the snake and its possible allegorical meaning(s) see Schenker, *The Bronze Horseman*, 277–280. Catherine herself at first did not like the addition of the snake (placed there by Falconet to help stabilize the monument) but grew to accept it under the sculptor's influence.
17 "Falconet's horse is usually described as galloping, even by the sculptor himself. Yet, it is shown in an attitude that

had concluded his epic about Peter's successful war with the Swedish King Charles XII, by celebrating the founding of St. Petersburg as the tsar's personal monument:

> A hundred years passed, and what's left
> Of those powerful, those proud men
> So full of willful passions? [...]
> Only you, Poltava's hero, have erected
> An enormous monument to yourself.[18]

However, the great Polish poet Mickiewicz, writing in the aftermath of the failed Polish revolution of November 1830, claimed in the *Digression* of Part III of his *Forefather's Eve* that Peter had erected the city not for the people but only for himself and that, while Rome was built by human hand and Venice by the gods, Petersburg was built by Satan. Moreover, Mickiewicz presented the equestrian iconography from a totally different, "Polish" perspective: in his poem Peter is seen as *letting go* of the reins and allowing his charger ("champing its bit unchecked, with slackened rein") to run *out of control*, the result being that both rider and steed, tsar and Russia, plunge off the cliff and into the abyss. To complicate the reading even further, Mickiewicz places this interpretation in the mouth of the "Russian bard" (i.e., Pushkin), who explains the scene to the "pilgrim" (i.e., Mickiewicz).[19]

Pushkin of course could not let these comments go unanswered. His celebration of the beauty and grandeur of the city in the Introduction to *The Bronze Horseman* ("I love you, creation of Peter, / I love your graceful, severe appearance") is just such a response. But perhaps even more important, in the climax of his poem Pushkin answers directly Mickiewicz's assertion that the horseman has let go of the reins: he asks, was it not you, Peter, who has "raised Russia up on her haunches," so that the steed/body politic does not know, is not yet aware, where its hooves will eventually land — a gesture both much more dramatic than Falconet's original intention and closer to how Pushkin perceived Peter's true character, its paradoxical center. Pushkin's horse is not out of control and yet its pose raises more questions than it answers.

has been referred to as rearing, although it does not raise itself high enough for the pose to fully qualify as such. More appropriate would be the French term *pose bondissante*, that is, a stance that resembles a levade in formal dressage." And "As for the *pose bondissante*, its symbolism may be deciphered in different ways. If one sees in it an animal recoiling from danger, it may be interpreted as an allegorical representation of the conservative forces opposing Peter's reforms, a role reserved usually for the trampled snake. If the rearing is viewed as a triumphant finale to a glorious ride, the horse may be said to be a mere instrument in Peter's hands, an ally in his mission to reform Russia. If the horse's stance is perceived in a moment of hesitation, which might end in a leap forward, a full stop, or a turnaround, it may express the Russians' doubts about the wisdom of Peter's attempt to steer the ship of state so abruptly onto a new course, with the winds high and the waters choppy." Schenker, *The Bronze Horseman*, 267, 276–77.

[18] *Pss*, 5:63: «Прошло сто лет — и что ж осталось/ От сильных, гордых сих мужей/ Столь полных волею страстей? [...]/ Лишь ты воздвиг, герой Полтавы,/ Огромный памятник себе».

[19] On the Polish perspective see especially Waclaw Lednicki, *Pushkin's "Bronze Horseman": The Story of Masterpiece* (Berkeley: University of California Press, 1955). In the section of the *Digression* where Mickiewicz describes the monument to Peter the Great and

> Where are you galloping, proud steed,
> And where will you set down your hooves?
> O, mighty master of fate!
> Was it not thusly that you, above the very abyss,
> On high, with iron bridle
> Raised Russia up on her hind legs.[20]

Now, when we turn to look more closely at Pushkin's poem and its "re-monumentalizing" of Peter's city, what does this yield? First and foremost, everything concerning the ethos and pathos of Peter's worldview, including the original inspiration for the city, is *pagan*.[21] How Peter treated the Orthodox church (he replaces the Moscow Patriarchate with a Holy Synod he can control), sacred ritual (he parodies and makes fun of it whenever he senses it is perpetuating ignorance and obscurantism), his subjects (he is no longer simply the divinely anointed *basileus*-tsar or *batiushka*-father but the pre-Christian "emperor"), time itself (he institutes a new calendar that begins in January rather than in September, when God had created the world)—all these facts and many more point to an image of Peter that is not merely new but new in a way that is old, ancient, pre-Christian, pagan. Pushkin captures all these fears in the loaded word *kumir*, which means "idol," and which was the one word that Nicholas fixed most on in his censoring role, for he understood that at some basic level to call Russia's greatest tsar a pagan idol was irreverent.

> And right there in the dark elevation,
> Above the fenced-in rock,
> The idol with extended arm
> Sat on his bronze steed.[22]

If not for that word (and the synonymous *istukan*) there is a good chance that Pushkin could have published his masterpiece during his lifetime. But by calling Peter, in the poem, *kumir na bronzovom kone*, "the idol on his bronze steed," Pushkin's intent is not necessarily to malign the city's founder. He almost never takes sides in this way and his best work is always *versts*

---

the two poets (i.e., Mickiewicz and Pushkin) musing over it, he compares the destructive riding of the Russian tsar (letting the reins go and plunging into the abyss) to the controlled riding of Marcus Aurelius, whose fiery steed is so becalmed under his hand that the people can come up to it to receive their blessing from the fatherly Caesar. Lednicki, *Pushkin's Bronze Horseman*" 120–22.

20 *Pss*, 5:147: «Куда ты скачешь, гордый конь, / И где опустишь ты копыта? / О мощный властелин судьбы! / Не так ли ты над самой бездной, / На высоте, уздой железной / Россию поднял на дыбы?»

21 Roman Jakobson was among the first to focus attention on the pagan element in the poem (in particular, the links with the word *kumir*, "idol") in his seminal "The Statue in Puškin's Poetic Mythology," in Jakobson, *Language and Literature*, ed. Krystyna Pomorska and Stephen Rudy (Cambridge, MA: Harvard University Press, 1987), 318–367, esp. 362–63. Jakobson's piece was originally published in Czech in 1937 as "Socha v symbolice Puškinove," in the journal *Slovo a slovesnost* (#3). See also Izmailov (A. S. Pushkin, *Mednyi vsadnik*), 219–225. Another perspective on the pagan thematics in the poem is found in Gary Rosenshield, *Pushkin and the Genres of Madness: The Masterpieces of 1833* (Madison: University of Wisconsin Press, 2003), 89–179, esp. 168–74.

22 *Pss*, 5:147: «И прямо в темной вышине/ Над огражденною скалою/ Кумир с простертою рукою / Сидел на бронзовом коне».

away from satire.²³ Yet Nicholas's instincts were also right. Peter represents virtue in its pagan incarnation. His "hardness" — the bronze of the statue, the granite of the pedestal, the stone corsetting the Neva and giving form, cosmos, to the city where there was formlessness, chaos — is not so much anti-human (a stance consciously taken) as *pre-human*, in the sense of existing before Renaissance humanism. Maybe Tiberius wasn't simply bloodthirsty, maybe he had to eliminate the popular Germanicus to keep order, as Pushkin argued earlier (1825–26) in his notes to Tacitus's *Annals*, where he takes the Latin historian to task for "satirizing" and de-historicizing the past.²⁴ In any event, in order to change Russia Pushkin's Peter must sacrifice individual lives and think of the collective good. He is not "evil" in any traditional sense, nor is he mad like Ivan the Terrible. But he lived through the numerous Streltsy revolts and "close calls" by his own flesh and blood (his sister Sophia) to wrest power and life from him as a young man; he could not, given Russia's state of development, act other than he did and retain power, as Pushkin readily understood. He often acted brutally, but the only means of survival in the given situation (running away to a monastery to avoid the assassins who had come for him) was to respond brutally.

Thus, when Pushkin describes in the *History of Peter*, in chapter after chapter, how the emperor accomplishes fantastic exploits (for example, he builds a new fleet, with 2506 cannon, 11 mortars, and 16,800 sailors, in only 3 years' time), he is foregrounding (after Golikov) Peter the *bogatyr'*-like doer and builder, the all-powerful, indefatigable prodder from above.²⁵ At the same time, in the yearly lists of ukases concluding these chapters, Peter emerges as arbitrary, cruel, a veritable eastern potentate or vizier caught in unseemly snapshots from below: for example — and here the reader can choose virtually at random — one ukase in 1705 describes the punishment for desertion of conscripts from the army — in groups of three, and deciding by lots, one is to be executed and the other two beaten with knouts and sent into hard labor; or in another ukase of 1708, those who sell wine in barrels will have their estates confiscated.²⁶ Obviously which Peter we see depends on whether we are looking at the chapter narratives or the list of ukases. He is both revolutionary *and* autocrat (if not tyrant). But the end result is Peter as yet has no time or inclination or, more to the point, opportunity to develop what lies between the greatness of the accomplished feat (the finished fleet) and the cruelty of the individual ukase (the hapless peasant deserter). Said in another way, Peter cannot yet attend to the issue of individual freedom, to those "natural rights" of mankind that was the legacy of 18th-century

23   One reason Pushkin dropped the Onegin-stanza format of *Ezersky* and moved to the "simpler" verse structure of *The Bronze Horseman* is that the sarcastic tone of the former was not the proper vehicle to present either the grandeur or the tragedy of the later work. Izmailov (A. S. Pushkin, *Mednyi vsadnik*), 189–90.

24   See analysis in Eidel'man, *Pushkin: Istoriia i sovremennost'*, 50–92.
25   *Pss*, 10:29.
26   *Pss*, 10:89, 126.

enlightenment thought and that Pushkin himself inherited from his training at the Lyceum. This turn from pagan to Judeo-Christian virtue would have to come from literature, the one sphere Peter could not take by force.

As generations of readers have noted, *The Bronze Horseman* is the tale of two wholly separate and inherently inimical worlds: the ode-like panegyric to Peter and his city in the Introduction and the diptych-like contrasting panels of the "story" (*rasskaz*) of the humble Evgeny that follows; the triumph of creating, ex nihilo, a beautiful city and the tragedy of the great flood of 1824 that is God's judgment on mankind's hubris; the process of male childbirth (couvade[27]) where Peter's mind, as he first surveys the site, grows pregnant with "great thoughts" (*velikie dumy*) versus the birth of destructive ideas of revolution, when the little man, now gone mad after the death of Parasha, rises up against the idol and tutelary spirit and challenges him ("Just you wait!" [*Uzho tebe!*]) for designing a world in which his dreams of simple domestic happiness are fated to perish; and the poetry (the iambic tetrameter lines of mixed alternating and adjoining rhyme) that is the effortless medium of Pushkin's telling and the prose that is the subject matter of the story (Evgeny is not a legitimate hero for an epos) and the non-stanzaic structure that is maximally unobtrusive (except at verse paragraph breaks, when punctuation becomes significant and some shift is about to happen).[28] These two worlds—master and subject, imperial plan and private daydream, rectilinear city and sinuous river, ode and sad tale—do not mesh, and that is precisely Pushkin's point. He forces us to see them in juxtaposition, and in thinking about that juxtaposition we as readers create that enlightened, more conscious "in-between" that Peter could not or would not be bothered with.

How this creation of an inner Petersburg exactly happens in the poem is probably the greatest stroke on the author's part. He teaches his readers, still insecure about their own contributions to world culture vis-à-vis their European counterparts, to think and desire for themselves, the seat of all poetry. He teaches them to want not just for Peter and for Russia in the abstract but also for Evgeny and for all those who do not merely want to be part of others' plans but to live for themselves, however modestly, on their own terms. In the first part of his story, Evgeny is worried that the flood waters are rising too quickly and his Parasha, who lives out on one of the islands with her mother, may be in danger. This is how Pushkin describes his hero who has taken refuge on a stone lion that, guarding one of the city's grand new homes, stands above the flood a little way off from the famous equestrian statue:

27 The term is used and developed in Daniel Rancour-Laferriere, "The Couvade of Peter the Great: A Psychoanalytic Aspect of *The Bronze Horseman*," in *Puškin Today*, ed. David M. Bethea (Bloomington: Indiana University Press, 1993), 73–85, 225–27.

28 On the conflicting readings of *The Bronze Horseman* see especially Ospovat and Timenchik, "Pechal'nu povest' sokhranit'," 5–16.

> Evgeny's desperate glances
> Were trained unblinkingly
> Toward one spot. Mountain-like,
> From the seething depths
> Waves rose up there and turned angry,
> There the storm howled, there debris
> Rushed by... Oh God, oh God! There also —
> Alas! — right by the waves,
> Almost at the very edge of the gulf,
> Stands an unpainted fence and a willow
> And a little old house: there they,
> The widow and the daughter, his Parasha,
> His dream [...]
> And he, as though bewitched,
> As though riveted to the marble,
> Can not get off! Around him
> All water and nothing more!
> And with his back turned to him,
> At an unshakeable height,
> Above the angry Neva
> Stands with outstretched arm
> The idol on his bronze steed.[29]

As readers we immediately note several details in this crucial passage (the concluding lines of part I). First, Evgeny's attention is anxiously focused on one thing: Parasha, "his dream," her tiny home which is far away from the imperial center of the city. Second, he is separated from Parasha by the very waters that Peter's plan was designed to control, rein in. Third, he is frozen on the stone lion (another statue) in a pose that forces him (or the reader — Pushkin doesn't say) to look at the Bronze Horseman, as the latter is in his field of vision. Fourth, the equestrian statue *has its back turned* to the humble viewer. Fifth, the statue of Peter rises above the flood into the *unshakeable* heights. And sixth, by having all these ominous impressions come at the very end of part I, Pushkin is suggesting an end to a historical saeculum: there is something about this scene that will cause a radical, apocalyptic shift in Russian history. As readers we already sense that Parasha will have perished, the waters will recede (they always do), Evgeny will descend the stone lion and begin to move about, the Bronze Horseman's pose (giving his back to Evgeny) will change because the little man himself will change places, the heights that were unshakeable will

---

29   *Pss*, 5:142: «Его отчаянные взоры / На край один наведены / Недвижно были. Словно горы, / Из возмущенной глубины / Вставали волны там и злились, / Там буря выла, там носились / Обломки... Боже, боже! там —/ Увы! близехонько к волнам, / Почти у самого залива —/ Забор некрашеный, да ива / И ветхий домик: там оне, / Вдова и дочь, его Параша, / Его мечта [...] / И он, как будто околдован, / Как будто к мрамору прикован, / Сойти не может! Вкруг него / Вода и больше ничего! / И, обращен к нему спиною, / В неколебимой вышине, / Над возмущенною Невою / Стоит с простертою рукою / Кумир на бронзовом коне».

become the roiling street level, and the pagan idol will have to do battle with the individual Christian soul, each instance of which is precious.

But there are several additional details in this highly theatricalized scene that deserve glossing before we move on. As I have argued elsewhere, the fact that Evgeny is sitting astride a stone lion is not merely another instance of Pushkin's using contemporary anecdotes to enliven his narration.[30] In a several-stanza length section of *Ezersky* where Pushkin describes the decline and fall of the hereditary nobility—in his mind the single greatest, and most damaging, change in Russian history brought about by the Petrine reforms—he ends his list of sarcastic laments with the lines, "'Tis a pity... / that the heraldic lion / by the ass's democratic hoof / now too is being kicked: / this is how far the spirit of the age has gone!"[31] As Pushkin moved from the too autobiographical character of Ezersky to the more muted and universalized Evgeny, this theme remained very much present though implicit: Evgeny is the end product of the downward spiral (there is now no old aristocracy left in mind or deed to challenge the arbitrary power of the tsar) whose image is the heraldic lion being kicked by the democratic ass. My interpretation is the word *heraldic*, here standing in for old and established (i.e., those with coats of arms), is powerfully marked by Pushkin, as is the word democratic. In his more subtle presentation in *The Bronze Horseman* he does not want to be so direct, so crude. But the lion is still there, as the guardian spirit ("l'vy *storozhevye*") of this new place, just as the democratizing ass has transmogrified into the powerful Petrine steed. *The Bronze Horseman* is set up to defeat utterly this lonely scion of a noble, "leonine" worldview now vanished. That Pushkin was linking this moment in *Ezersky* with the confrontation between the two "riders" at the end of part I is possibly confirmed by a line just above the reference to the "heraldic lion" in the former poem ("Chto v nashem tereme zabytom" [that in our abandoned tower]) that is repeated in the draft section of *The Bronze Horseman* where Evgeny is described on the stone lion.[32] It may be significant that the only hint of a "Christian" opposition to Peter's pagan force is Evgeny's pose (his arms are held "crosswise," *krestom*, which rhymes with *verkhom*, "astride" as a rider) and his fears, presented through the narrator, as "Oh, God, God!" (Bozhe, Bozhe!).[33]

On the basic level of plot, part II reconnects, in classic epistrophe fashion, the loose ends extended in part I. Evgeny hires a boat and goes to find Parasha and her mother; when he gets there the little house has been swept away

30 See David M. Bethea, "The Role of the *Eques* in Puškin's *Bronze Horseman*," in Bethea, *Puškin Today*, 99–118, 227–230. The anecdote refers to a certain Yakovlev who rumor had it saved himself during the flood of 1824 by taking refuge on one of the stone lions on the portico of A. Ia. Lobanov-Rostovsky's grand ("new") town house. This story circulated in the city and Pushkin probably picked it up that way. See A.V. Kochubei, *Zapiski (Semeinaia khronika)* (St. Petersburg, 1890), 203–05; cited in Izmailov (A. S. Pushkin, *Mednyi vsadnik*), 123–24.

31 Pss, 5:101: «Мне жаль... / Что геральдического льва / Демократическим копытом / Теперь лягает и осел: / Дух века вот куда зашел!»

32 Pss, 5:101, 463–64.

33 I argue in "The Role of the Eques" that Evgeny could be interpreted as representing here the "Moscow Horseman" (St. George), who is clearly Christian and Orthodox. Bethea, "The Role of the *Eques*," 110.

and there is not a trace of anything or anyone left (NB this total vanishing is to the common man's personal, private life the tragic inversion Peter's original creation-from-nothing of his imperial city, his collective, public monument); the poor fellow goes mad with grief, doesn't return home, and takes to the street as a vagrant; sometime later, probably toward the end of the following summer, in stormy weather reminiscent of the prelude to the flood, he returns by chance to the stone lions and the idol on the bronze steed (the exact words are repeated from the earlier passage); suddenly his deranged mind "clears up" with frightening thoughts; this is the moment of *cognitio* (*on uznal* = "he recognized") and we no longer know whether we are in Evgeny's brain or the narrator's; the elevated style, the repeated exclamation points, the capitalization of the god-like "He" who founded this fateful city, the acknowledgement that the idol's power is terrible/awesome, the famous question about where the Russian steed will lower its hooves—all this bespeaks its own privileged moment, its window broken through in the opposite direction, *back* onto Russian history and onto the Russian subject (in various senses) becoming aware, becoming consciousness in history; now Evgeny walks around to the front of the statue, trains his gaze at it from the street, shakes his fist and exclaims "Just you wait!"; then he runs away, pursued by the suddenly animate horseman, which leaps off its pedestal (or appears to) and gallops after the miscreant through the Petersburg streets; the following spring Evgeny's body is found on one of the islands, amid the wreckage of a tiny abode that is presumably Parasha's, and is buried, in the words of the narrator, *radi Boga* ("for God's sake"—i.e., out of charity).

Falconet's concetto for the statue was the idea of the rearing horse and of the great emperor who could rein in the steed's power and stamp out the snake of ignorance and opposition. What might we say is Pushkin's verbal concetto in his epic poem? For that we need to go to the story that may have been the kernel for Pushkin's.³⁴ In the words of Pushkin's early biographer Pyotr Bartenev,

> The idea for *The Bronze Horseman* came to Pushkin as a result of the following story, which was passed on to him by the well-known Count Vielgorsky. In 1812, as the danger of invasion threatened Petersburg, the Sovereign Alexander Pavlovich [i.e. Alexander I] proposed to remove from the city the statue of Peter the Great, and

---

34 Ospovat and Timenchik argue persuasively that the anecdote about Baturin was simply one of several that appeared *after the fact* of the writing of *The Bronze Horseman* and thus could not have played a role in the poem's conception. The idea here is that the poem gave birth to the anecdote (the myth of the Bronze Horseman was by now taking on a life of its own) and not the other way around. Prince Vyazemsky, for example, said near the end of his life that if such an anecdote had existed in the years after 1812 leading up to 1833, he would have known about it. Be that as it may, the fact that Bartenev recorded the story from Sobolevsky, who remembered it as preceding the poem, leaves the door of doubt still partly cracked. Thus I've included a discussion of the anecdote just in case Pushkin could have been aware of it. See Ospovat and Timenchik, "Pechal'nu povest' sokhranit'," 118–124.

35 Cited Izmailov (A. S. Pushkin, *Mednyi vsadnik*), 243–44: «Мысль о „Медном Всаднике" пришла Пушкину

for this purpose several thousand rubles were released to State Secretary Molchanov. [At this time] a certain Major Baturin took to visiting the reception-room of Prince A.N. Golitsyn, mason and spiritualist. Baturin obtained a meeting with the prince, who was a friend of the tsar, and told him that he, Baturin, was being haunted by one and the same dream. He sees himself on Senate Square. Peter's countenance turns. The rider descends from the rock and proceeds along the city streets to Stone Island, where the tsar resided. Baturin, drawn along by some wondrous power, hurdles after the rider and hears the clatter of bronze along the pavement. The rider enters the courtyard of the Stone Island Palace while out to meet him comes the sovereign, anxious and deep in thought. "Young man, to what have you brought my Russia," says Peter the Great to him. "As long as I am in place, the city has nothing to fear!" Then the rider turns around and once more there reverberates the heavy-sounding gallop. Stunned by Baturin's story, Prince Golitsyn, himself a seer of visions, passes on the dream to the sovereign. And at a time when many government treasures and institutions are being transferred to Russia's interior, the statue of Peter the Great is left in peace.[35]

If Pushkin was aware of this anecdote, his way of creating an inner space for his new reader by rearranging its parts is wonderfully subtle. He never openly psychologizes — that would be left to Dostoevsky, Tolstoy, and a later tradition — but instead takes a plot, twists it or inverts it, and then calls on his reader to fill in the gaps. The essential points of the legend are as follows: Peter the Great in his incarnation as Bronze Horseman wants to stay put — that is his role as *genius loci* and heavy, *immovable* force; the tsar turns his head and gallops through the streets because he is bothered by something (the notion that he will be moved and that his city will be left unprotected); this confrontation is between tsar and tsar, with the greater tsar "winning"; the "little man" (Baturin) who sees the dream and is carried along by the momentum of the galloping steed does not take part in it

вследствие следующего рассказа, который был ему передан известным графом М. Ю. Вильгорским. В 1812 году, когда опасность вторжения грозила и Петербургу, государь Александр Павлович предполагал увезти статую Петра Великого, и на этот предмет статс-секретарю Молчанову было отпущено несколько тысяч рублей. В приемную к н. А. Н. Голицыну, масону и духовидцу, повадился ходить какой-то майор Батурин. Он добился свидания с князем (другом царевым) и передал ему, что его, Батурина, преследует один и тот же сон. Он видит себя на Сенатской площади. Лик Петра поворачивается. Всадник съезжает со скалы и направляется по петербургским улицам к Каменному острову, где жил тогда Александр Павлович. Батурин, влекомый какою-то чудною силою, несется за ним и слышит топот меди по мостовой. Всадник въезжает на двор Каменно-островского дворца, из которого выходит к нему навстречу задумчивый и озабоченный государь. „Молодой человек, до чего довел ты мою Россию?", — говорит ему Петр Великий. —„Но покамест я на месте, моему городу нечего опасаться!" Затем всадник поворачивает назад, и снова раздается тяжело-звонкое скаканье. Пораженный рассказом Батурина, князь Голицын, сам сновидец, передает сновиденье государю, и в то время как многие государственные сокровища и учреждения перевозятся во внутрь России, статуя Петра Великого оставлена в покое».

(except to tell it) and is simply a bystander. But the deep-seated irony of the statue's movement and energetic intention is that its purpose is to be left alone, to remain in one place.

Everything in Pushkin is both reminiscent and reversed. The Bronze Horseman moves ominously off its pedestal, but now because Evgeny has himself circled around and confronted him face to face (he has dared to look into the face of divinity). It is the little man bystander, the one who had no role in this history of tsars, who steps forward and becomes a revolutionary actor. The statue's movement in Baturin's dream is to ensure its stasis, its constancy. Its same movement in Pushkin is the first token of its undoing — a sign that it cannot remain untouched by the swirling waters of natural disaster or manmade revolution. Its defeat of the little man — yes, Evgeny eventually perishes — is Pyrrhic, since it does not matter whether the statue has actually descended its pedestal in the poem (the fantastic) or the madman has imagined it as such (psychological realism). The point is the Horseman is incited to move by the little man, and the fact that this movement is presented in a space (the poem) where its existence cannot be disputed means that forever after it exists *in reality*. Evgeny's story is told, the second panel in the diptych takes its place beside the first, and the individual's fate, the life he could have lived, becomes important to every thinking and feeling person reading it. Evgeny is not buried by his and Parasha's grandchildren, as he had originally daydreamed, but by the narrator, who exclaims *sotto voce* into the space previously dominated by the bronze idol, that the poor man's remains were put to rest *radi Boga*.[36]

Thus, the lapidary forms that celebrate Peter and the city, whether the stone of the neoclassical architecture or the stately rhythm and rhymes of the panegyrical ode, cannot mean by themselves in Pushkin's world of the 1830's. They exist only in and through their foils: the déclassé hero (as Pushkin also saw himself), the prose tale, the air and water that cannot be contained by the stone. Pushkin wrote his wife at this period that he didn't want a portrait done of himself because it would capture, in a static pose, all his "Negroid ugliness."[37] He feared like the plague stasis and immobility. The monument that he erected to himself in one of his last poems is, following the unworldly temple that Christ promised to erect, "not made by hand." Because it is made of words, formed air, its alexandrines will live longer than the Alexandrian Column commemorating the other Alexander's victory over Napoleon that is mentioned in the poem. And it will continue, as long as there is recorded speech, to *inform* the ideas and perceptions of those individual Russians (and anyone else for that matter) who contemplates the beauty and brutality of Peter's greatest creation.

---

36 "For God's sake" can also of course be ironic, what is said in every such case and thus does not necessarily resonate with its original meaning. The *Slovar' iazyka Pushkina* (3:912) lists the meaning of something done, or paid for, "out of charity" as the primary one in the case of Evgeny's burial. Still, this phrase, which Pushkin could have imbued, and knowing his subtlety probably was imbuing, with multiple meanings, forms a neat book-end to the "Bozhe, Bozhe!" at the end of part

37 Letter of 14–16 May 1836 in *Pss*, 16:116.

Chapter 12

Slavic Gift-Giving, The Poet in History, and Pushkin's *The Captain's Daughter*[1]

> ... several things dovetailed in my mind, & at once it struck me, what quality went to form a Man of Achievement especially in Literature & which Shakespeare possessed so enormously — I mean *Negative Capability*, that is when man is capable of being in uncertainties, Mysteries, doubts, without any irritable reaching after fact & reason — Coleridge, for instance, would let go by a fine isolated versimilitude caught from the Penetralium of mystery, from being incapable of remaining content with half knowledge. This pursued through Volumes would perhaps take us no further than this, that with a great poet the sense of Beauty overcomes every other consideration, or rather obliterates all considerations.
>
> — *letter of John Keats to George and Tom Keats, 21, 27 (?) December 1817*

Preliminary Remarks

Like the bread and salt that are their folk embodiments, the values of generosity and hospitality are very old in the Russian mentality. And no writer is considered more "Russian" in this sense of spiritual generosity and inexhaustible "giftedness" than Alexander Pushkin. But what exactly does this mean, once one leaves the porous level of cultural myth? "There should not be any free gifts," writes the social anthropologist Mary Douglas, since each gift and each personality donating and receiving each gift belongs to a larger system of ongoing and mutually implicating relations. "Gift cycles

---

[1] First appeared as 'Slavianskoe darenie, poet v istorii "Kapitanskoi dochki" Pushkina' in Avtor i tekst. Sbornik statei, V.M. Markovich and Vol'f Shmid, eds. (St. Petersburg: Izdatel'stvo S.-Peterburgskogo universiteta, 1996), 132-149; also as "Slavic Gift-Giving, The Poet in History, and Pushkin's The Captain's Daughter," in Russian Subjects: Empire, Nation, and the Culture of the Golden Age, Monika Greenleaf and Stephen Moeller-Sally, eds. (Evanston: Northwestern University Press, 1998), 259-273

engage persons in permanent commitments that articulate the dominant institutions."[2] How can one in a precise and useful way apply the notions of donor, recipient, and gift to Pushkin's works and to the life he fashioned for himself in the interplay of his epoch's social and aesthetic codes?

Normally when one invokes the economy of gift-giving in the context of Pushkin there is, following Nabokov, a slight shift *upward* in stylistic register: from the concrete *podarok*, which seems too pedestrian for the riches of Pushkin's language and thought, to the lofty *dar*, with its implication of high calling (the Ur-text being "The Prophet" [Prorok]) and high (read "western") literary values.[3] This almost unconscious adjustment may be unfortunate, for, as I hope to demonstrate, Pushkin was himself exquisitely sensitive to the necessary concrete "containers" and quotidian psychological subtleties that gifts and gift-giving require. In this essay I will be examining, inter alia, Pyotr Grinev's famous present of a very Russian, very concrete hareskin coat (*zaiachii tulup*) to a chance peasant (Pugachev) as Pushkin's last and greatest expression of the gift-giving economy, in *The Captain's Daughter* (*Kapitanskaia dochka*).

It will be my argument that the Pushkin of the 1830's moved back in time, especially to the 18th century, to work his way free of the salon mentality of the 1810's and 1820's and to get closer to a sense of history that was more authentic, less "Karamzinian" — Karamzin being the author of the great "salon"[4] history that stood squarely in Pushkin's path.[5] Pushkin wanted to find a "poetry" in history that more closely reflected his view of reality, that was less moralizing, less harmonizing, less "sentimental." And as Pushkin moved back into the 18th century, he became increasingly interested in the historical situation where an individual's spiritual "charge" or *darovanie* (an inner "gift": a component of character) encounters a concrete situation requiring a gesture of outward generosity or *podarok* (a concrete "gift": a component of action or plot). Pushkin wanted to isolate the energy-releasing (or "inspiring") *move-outside-oneself* that redefines everything that has come before, from aspects of genre

---

2 In Marcel Mauss, *The Gift: The Form and Reason for Exchange in Archaic Societies*, trans. W.D. Halls, foreword Mary Douglas (New York: Norton, 1990), vii, ix.

3 On the frequency and possible levels of meaning of the word *dar* in Pushkin (in contrast to Mickiewicz), see Lawrence L. Thomas, "Toward a Contrastive Study of Word-Usage: Mickiewicz and Pushkin," in *Studies in Slavic Linguistics and Poetics*, ed. Robert Magidoff et al. (New York: New York UP, 1968), 261–69. It turns out, curiously, that *dar* is not used at all in *The Captain's Daughter*, while *podarok*, in the sense of concrete gift, is used twice: once in reference to the gift of the *zaiachii tulup* and once as incriminating evidence at Grinev's trial (i.e., reference is made to Pugachev's various "presents" to the hero), see A.S. Pushkin, *Polnoe sobranie sochinenii*, ed. B.V. Tomashevskii, 10 vols. (Leningrad: Nauka, 1977–79), 272, 362; hereafter cited as "*Pss.*" My thanks to Professor J. Thomas Shaw for drawing this to my attention and in general for his careful reading of the present study in draft form. I would also like to thank Professor Gary Rosenshield, Professor Caryl Emerson, Professor Sergei Davydov, and Mr. Dan Ungurianu for their helpful suggestions and corrections.

4 I use the term "salon" here merely as a shorthand. The intentional deployment of archaisms for dramatic effect in Karamzin's text as well as his massive agglutination of notes and scholarly apparatus would not have been emulated by Voltaire the historian, for example.

(one's art) to aspects of psychology (one's life). This latter has been described by Yury Lotman in one of his last and most adventuresome works as the moment of unanticipated *vzryv* (breakthrough), when the rules of a predefined "plot" (in life or in history) or the *predskazuemost'* (predictability) of established behavioral patterns are suspended and the future opens up as something full of multifarious potential: "The moment of explosion is simultaneously the place for the sharpest growth in new information across the entire system. The developmental curve here jumps onto an entirely new, unpredictable and more complex path... The moment when the explosion is exhausted is the turning point in the process. In the historical sphere this is not only the point of departure for future development, it is also the place where self-consciousness happens (*mesto samopoznaniia*)."[6] Pushkin's unparalleled ability to link this moment of *vzryv* both with the *sluchainost'* (chance) of history and the notion of gift goes to the heart of his later works and his growing sense of himself as the *poet in history*.

In the following study I would like to bring these various ruminations into focus by dwelling on three related concepts in the later Pushkin: 1) the gift-giving economy, particularly in its Slavic variety; 2) inspiration, or what I call "the poet in history" sensibility; and 3) the structure of reciprocal relationships in *The Captain's Daughter*. My hypothesis is that these three seemingly loose ideational threads form in fact a surprisingly dense, evocative weave in the Pushkin of the 1830's — a weave that constitutes, one might say, a kind of pattern in the poet's magic carpet and thus a unique vantage from which to investigate his last works. This relation between gift-giving and poetic inspiration can be seen to have significant theoretical implications for how Pushkin narrated the subject of history and the subject in history.

---

5   Recent scholarship has placed particular emphasis on the powerful connecting links between the aestheticizing ("harmonizing") codes of largely French-dominated polite society and salon culture, on the one hand, and the special self-awareness and insider status of Pushkin's literary language, on the other. See, e.g., William Mills Todd III, *Fiction and Society in the Age of Pushkin* (Cambridge: Harvard UP, 1986), which applies the ideas of such social theorists and critics as Erving Goffman (theatrical metaphors of the self), Clifford Geertz (culture as text), and Yury Lotman (culture as interpenetrating "semiospheres"). Also helpful for understanding the shifts in mythopoetic valences in Pushkin's language before and after 1825 (the Decembrist Uprising) is B.M. Gasparov, *Poeticheskii iazyk Pushkina kak fakt istorii russkogo literaturnogo iazyka* (Vienna: Wiener Slawistischer Almanach/Sonderband 27, 1992). Finally, let it be said that Pushkin's attitude toward Karamzin and his monumental history was exceedingly complex, especially after Karamzin died in 1826 and was "misremembered" in the various official eulogies: in his own statements and historical research Pushkin had to find some authentic middle ground where he could 1) praise Karamzin for the man's "honorable deed" (the famous phrase *podvig chestnogo cheloveka*) and reasoned independence in the face of ideological pressures from all sides, 2) write the kind of history that both built on Karamzin's scholarly scrupulosity and yet implicitly went beyond his enlightenment chronotope, and 3) serve Russia and its monarch (the office if not always the man) without debasing his own honor (*his "honorable deed"*). *The History of Pugachev* is Pushkin's most explicit response to that challenge.

6   Iurii Lotman, *Kul'tura i vzryv* (Moscow: 1992), 28, 30. My translation.

Pushkin and Slavic Gift-Giving

In an important article entitled "'Agreement'[7] and 'Self-Giving' as Archetypal Models of Culture" ("Dogovor' i 'Vruchenie sebia' kak arkhetipicheskie modeli kul'tury"), Yury Lotman advanced the thesis, primarily from within a Russian Orthodox worldview, that "a religious act has as its basis an unconditional act of self-giving" [*bezogovorochnoe vruchenie sebia vo vlast'*].[8] Lotman cites numerous examples to make his case that for Slavs religiously-inspired behavior is essentially *one-sided* and *non-compulsory*, that is, it must bear no signs of an implied quid pro quo. In this regard, the Slavic model differs radically from the western, largely Roman model for such behavior:

> In the West the sense of agreement, though having its remote origin in magic, had the authority of the Roman secular tradition and held a position equal to the authority of religion: in Russia, on the other hand, it was felt to be pagan in character... It is significant that in the Western tradition an agreement as such was ethically neutral. It could be drawn up with the Devil... but one might also make agreements with the forces of holiness and goodness... [In the Russian context, however,] an agreement may only be made with a Satanic power or its pagan counterpart.[9]

What Lotman is suggesting is that the sense of measurement, portioning-out, and calculated atonement that is part and parcel of the sin-and-redemption economy of the Roman Church (i.e., one's activities on earth, such as prayers, donations, etc., can affect one's relative placement on the terraces of Purgatory or in the rings of Hell in the other world) is essentially antipathetic to the Slavic religious mentality. The notion of agreement (quid pro quo) or of "supererogation" cannot coexist with the notion of genuine, free giving of one's self.[10] The Slav[11] enters into a religious transaction not as a "negotiating partner" (*dogovarivaiushchaiasia storona*) but precisely as the immeasurable — "a drop flowing into a sea" (*kaplia, vlivaiushchaiasia v more*). All that is required of the recipient of a gift or sacrifice in this case is that it acknowledge itself as the source of a higher power.

---

[7] "Agreement" is not a totally satisfactory translation for the Russian *dogovor*, which really means something akin to a "verbally agreed upon *contract*." But I have left Shukman's rendering both in order to avoid confusion and because the root of "agreement" does goes back both etymologically and psychologically to the notion of two different voices haggling over something and finally coming to rest at a mutually arrived upon spot ("dogovorit'sia"). Conversely, the Russian borrowing *kontrakt* is more recent and gives off resonances that are strictly legalistic.

[8] Yury Lotman, "'Agreement' and 'Self-Giving' as Archetypal Models of Culture," in *The Semiotics of Russian Culture*, ed. Ann Shukman (Ann Arbor: Michigan Slavic Publications, 1984), 125.

[9] Lotman, *Semiotics of Russian Culture*, 126–127.

[10] As "supererogation" refers to good deeds performed by a saint that are *over and above* what is strictly needed for one's salvation, we see that the notion of "over-payment" is interpreted in a legal manner here as well. Cf., e.g., Ernst Benz, *The Eastern Orthodox Church: Its Thought and Life* (Garden City: Anchor Books, 1963), 43–53: "From the beginning the West has understood the fundamental relationship between God and man primarily as a *legal* relationship" (43), while the focus in Orthodoxy has been on mysticism, apotheosis, and the primacy of love.

Lotman's arguments here compare and contrast in provocative ways with work done in the West on potlatch economies in archaic societies. The French social anthropologist Marcel Mauss has made the point, for example, that "the potlatch is an example of a total system of giving... each gift is part of a system of reciprocity in which the honour of giver and recipient are engaged. It is a total system in that every item of status or of spiritual or material possession is implicated for everyone in the whole community."[12] The system can incorporate rivalry (the Haida and Tlingit of the American Northwest), so that a gift must be returned "with interest," or it can be stable (Polynesia), so that exchanges are fixed within a hierarchy. But what is interesting is that Mauss's concept of sacrifice — "a gift that compels the deity to make a return: Do ut des"[13] — does not accord with Lotman's concept of one-sided, non-compulsory giving among Slavs. Above all, for Mauss and his Durkheimian tradition the potlatch seems to be about the notion of power, even when deities are involved, for humans and among humans. Even "voluntary" acts of destruction of wealth or lives are not necessarily self-abnegating but in fact can be self-asserting. "In certain kinds of potlatch one must expend all that one has, keeping nothing back... it is not even a question of giving and returning gifts, but of destroying, so as not to give the slightest hint of desiring your gift to be reciprocated... Such trade is noble, replete with etiquette and generosity."[14]

Hence regardless of whether the end result is acquisition or destruction of riches, the dispensing of precious items becomes a way of gaining and keeping prestige and control: presents are intended to challenge and obligate rivals in a continuously operating three-part system (to give, to receive, to reciprocate). The one who is afraid of or cannot reciprocate in kind becomes emotionally enslaved ("flattened") by his debtor status (cf. the Roman *nexum*).[15] However, in the conclusion to his study, even as he emphasizes the total and totalizing system of social relationships that is the potlatch ("All these phenomena are at the same time juridical, economic, religious," etc.), Mauss admits to one potentially important lacuna: "these institutions [i.e., potlatch, clans, tribes, etc. — DMB] have an important aesthetic aspect that we have deliberately omitted from this study."[16] It is the expenditure or destruction of an item of value that, qua gesture, is beautiful for its own sake and that cannot be completely subsumed under the desire for prestige and power within one's own group that leaves what Bakhtin would call a loophole (*lazeika*) in Mauss's otherwise elegant analysis.

[11] It should be stressed that I am not using the word "Slav" here in an ethnically precise way; a more rigorous scholarly treatment of the issue of *Slavic* gift-giving would need to take into account such non-orthodox (or non-Orthodox) distinctions as Slovenes, Czechs, and Poles.

[12] Douglas, in Mauss, *The Gift*, viii.

[13] Ibid., ix.

[14] Mauss, *The Gift*, 37.

[15] Ibid., 39, 42.

[16] Ibid., 79.

It is this *lazeika* that was then seized upon and amplified by the French writer Georges Bataille in his 1933 essay on "The Notion of Expenditure."[17] Here Bataille makes the distinction between a "restricted economy" and an "economy of loss" as the latter two relate to the expenditure of energy by human organisms. Weaving together a provocative tapestry of discourses (the Dostoevsky of the Underground Man, Nietzschean will to power, Freudian "excremental fantasy," Marxist disgust at bourgeois values, French anti-utilitarianism and anti-individualism) that both tellingly anticipates poststructuralism and is itself culturally conditioned, Bataille sets out to create a space in the potlatch and indeed in all gift-giving situations for *the self-destructive gesture that is beautiful*. Applying Mauss, Bataille explains most potlatch situations through their application of the principle of the restricted economy: any surplus of energy left over from a transaction is controlled or reinvested, but in any event it is eventually accounted for. In some situations marked by "unproductive expenditure," however, such as those involving "luxury, mourning, war, cults, the construction of sumptuary monuments, games, spectacles, arts, perverse sexual activity (i.e., deflected from genital finality),"[18] simple notions of production and acquisition cannot explain the seemingly extravagant expenditure of energy. These activities "have no end beyond themselves," meaning that an economy of loss has set in: here the requirement to receive a gift and then reciprocate is deliberately, and one assumes somehow *aesthetically*, preempted. What rises to the fore is the idea that the greatest gift is the one proffered without thought of remuneration or return on investment (in fact quite the opposite), so that, in a characteristically Bataillean move, power in its purest form becomes the "power to lose" and "glory and honor are linked to wealth" *through loss*.[19]

Bataille's thoughts about poetry and the poet as vehicles for unconditional expenditure will be useful to us in the context of Pushkin and his tradition, since many of the Frenchman's concerns about the lack of beauty in an increasingly dreary and utilitarian age were shared by the Pushkin who used the term *meshchanin* (petit bourgeois, Philistine) ironically to define himself (i.e., this is what he, with his aristocratic roots, was not) in his polemics with Bulgarin in the 1830's, and who, following Tocqueville, expressed dismay at democratic "leveling" in the John Tanner essay (1836). As Bataille writes,

> The term poetry, applied to the least degraded and least intellectualized forms of the expression of the state of loss, can be considered synonymous with expenditure; it in fact signifies, in the most precise way, creation by means of loss. Its meaning is

---

[17] Georges Bataille, *Visions of Excess: Selected Writings, 1927–1939*, ed. and intro. Allan Stoekl (Minneapolis: University of Minnesota Press, 1985), 116–29.

[18] Ibid., 118.

[19] Ibid., 122; Lest we forget, Pushkin lived in a period when Russian nobles were willing to gamble away not only entire fortunes but even, in one notorious example (A.N. Golitsyn ["Cosarara"], one's spouse! With regard to the biographical (as opposed to textual) Pushkin, one could say that "glory and honor are linked to wealth through loss" in his case by citing the famous episode when he lost the manuscript of his poems in a card game.

therefore close to that of sacrifice... [F]or the rare human beings who have this at their disposal, poetic expenditure ceases to be symbolic in its consequences; thus, to a certain extent, the function of representation engages the very life of the one who assumes it.[20]

Lotman's interpretation of Slavic gift-giving and Mauss's and especially Bataille's analyses of the potlatch psychology have some fascinating implications for the later Pushkin. The difference between Bataille and Lotman on the act of giving that is potentially destructive of the self is subtle and shows to what extent these matters are culturally determined and perhaps deeply embedded in ancient east-west binaries: the Dionysian gesture of unconditional expenditure in Bataille still focuses on *the self* (its honor, glory, nobility, etc.) even as that self is consumed, whereas in Lotman the emphasis — consider the traditional example of the beauty of the Russian Orthodox service — is on *the higher power* of the sea the drop of "I" is poured into. It is my working hypothesis, to be tested out below, that Pushkin, while more than any other Russian author before and probably since was aware of the subtle differences in a culture's gift-giving economy, finally comes closer to the Lotmanian than to the Bataillean model.

As Pushkin approached the historical theme, he seemed to become aroused, aesthetically and even as it were *erotically*, by the increased proximity to genuine risk, potential chaos, violent death, the lack of prefabricated literary plot. He was interested above all in the palpable seam separating legend and brute historical fact. He wanted to feel what was not his, what was not under his control. Yet Pushkin came to history and historiography not as a prose writer but, first and foremost, as a poet.[21] His *dominant*, his episteme, his way of organizing the world, was not the notion of "plot" or tellable *mythos* but the poetic or logosemantic *simultaneity* of sound's play with sense — the rhyme pair, paranomasia, the internal pun, etc. This is why the "metahistorical" theories of Hayden White or Arthur Danto, based as they are on notions of *emplotment*,[22] will not suffice to explain

---

20   Ibid., 120.

21   On the links between the "poetic" in Pushkin's prose and the "prosaic" in his poetry, see Wolf Schmidt, *Proza kak poeziia: Stat'i o povestvovanii v russkoi literature* (St. Petersburg: Akademicheskii prospekt," 1994), 9–34.

22   It can of course be argued that the "poetic" aspects (say the link between sound and sense) of Pushkin's prose, even his historiography, only beg the question of their "origins." Are they not too "metahistorical" in the Whitean sense? Here it can only be answered that Pushkin, who tried his best to be a meticulous historian in the wake of Karamzin, did not suffer anxiety about his language's ability to "tell the facts." What Pushkin associated with the falsely "poetic" and "contrived" (*vydumannoe*) at the time of the writing of *The History of Pugachev* was the notion of *literary* emplotment, of a story-line borrowed (perhaps unconsciously) from a novel and used to explain historical occurrences — something his own history writing could not be accused of. See his "Ob 'Istorii Pugachevskogo bunta'" in *Pss*, 8: 263–278. To reiterate: that Pushkin *arranged* the order of narration (the notion of *siuzhet*) even in his history-writing goes without saying, but that he himself viewed this arrangement as an aspect of novelistic fantasy and the *vydumannoe* is more open to question.

the internal mechanisms of Pushkin's historical thinking.[23] Like two poles in an electromagnetic field, the ontological rhyme pair *volia/dolia* (liberty, freedom/lot, fate) is at the center of the poet's consciousness.[24] Plot does not come first; what comes first is one's *dolia*, which fixes one within certain untransgressible conventions (honor, for example, or social class), and what comes second is the *volia* one exercises given those constraints. To express the verbal equivalent of unencumbered movement within a fixed rhyme scheme or to try one's fate while keeping one's honor intact are not identical (life does not "equal" art), but they are isomorphic statements: both go right to the heart of Pushkin's understanding of true creative risk. Moreover, the sense of arousal that plays at the edges of literary structure and takes pleasure in its transgressive potential has a name — "inspiration," about which I will have more to say below. But what is striking about this gradual evolution from various poetic genres through a novel-in-verse to artistic prose and ultimately to historiography is that Pushkin repeatedly imagined the seam between legend and fact as a liminal gift-giving situation. Inspiration, the creative process itself, gift-giving, the threat of death, punishment, and historical judgment are all telescoped, all point to that energy which gives of itself while asking nothing in return. Let us examine now a few examples before returning to *The Captain's Daughter*. Pushkin's poetic cycle "Songs About Stenka Razin" ("Pesni o Sten'ke Razine", 1826) celebrates the legendary leader of the Don Cossacks who fomented a major peasant rebellion in the towns along the Volga in 1670–71 (during the reign of Alexei Mikhailovich).[25] The personality and activities of Stenka fascinated Pushkin in a way that suggests unmistakably a dress

[23] As Hayden White, for example, has argued in *The Content of Form: Narrative Discourse and Historical Representation* (Baltimore: Johns Hopkins University Press, 1987), the "value attached to narrativity in the representation of real events arises out of a desire to have the real events display the coherence, integrity, fullness, and closure of an image of life that is and can only be imaginary" (24). Furthermore, this very impulse toward narrativity is, according to White, profoundly "moralizing": in its attempt to locate a "legal subject" (the Hegelian "State cognizant of Laws") and to address such topics as "law, legality, legitimacy, or more generally, authority" (*The Content of Form* 13), historiography can be distinguished from the "subject-less" writing of annals or chronicles. It is the argument of this essay that in Pushkin the "moralizing" aspect of narrativity underlying historiography is never prior to the "poetic" principle of sacrifice, generosity, and gift-giving. To repeat, Pushkin came to the genres of fiction and history through the genres of poetry.

[24] As Abram Terts (Andrei Siniavsky) says in *Progulki s Pushkinym* (London: Overseas Publications Interchange/Collins, 1975), «Несмотря на раздоры и меры предосторожности, у Пушкина было чувство локтя с судьбой, освобождающее от страха, страдания и суеты. „Воля" и „доля" рифмуются у него как синонимы. Чем больше мы вверяемся промыслу, тем вольготнее нам живется, и полная покорность беспечальна, как птичка» (48). Strictly speaking, the actual frequency of the *volia/dolia* pair in Pushkin's texts does not appear to bear out Siniavsky-Terts's provocative formulation: in all his basic texts the poet used the *volia/dolia* rhyme only twice and *voliu/doliu* once. In addition, the only time *volia/dolia* actually refers to Pushkin, or his lyrical I, as speaker is in "Pora, moi drug, pora," which as it turns out Pushkin did not publish in his lifetime. Even so, as a means of understanding Pushkin's psychology of creation and his somewhat superstitious tendency to see freedom as an inevitable extension of constraint, Terts's formulation strikes one as having much to recommend it. In a poet as subtle and self-concealing as Pushkin, frequency of usage may not be the only issue.

[25] For discussion of the historical and folkloric material

rehearsal for the later Pugachev studies. Indeed, in fall 1824 while in exile in Mikhailovskoe, Pushkin wrote his brother asking for a biography of Pugachev (*Zhizn' Emel'ki Pugacheva*) and then, virtually simultaneously, asked for information about Stenka, the "*edinstvennoe poeticheskoe litso russkoi istorii*" (the one and only poetical character in Russian history).[26] Clearly, the fates of Stenka and Pugachev were linked in Pushkin's mind, as were the notions of poetry and history.

The three-poem cycle revolves around different gift-giving situations, all important for what they do and do not say about the treatment of Pugachev in *The Captain's Daughter* and *The History of Pugachev*. In the first poem, realizing that he is in debt to his "mother" the Volga and that in his love for the captive Persian princess he has betrayed his greater love for the motherland, Stenka voluntarily drowns the beautiful *foreign* tsarevna and bows obediently to the *native* river.[27] In other words, Stenka gives the ultimate gift — something falling into the marked "exorbitant" categories of both beautiful and beloved — in a Slavic/Russian expression of quintessential *udal'stvo* (daring, boldness), or what Bataille would call an "economy of loss."[28] What is more, because Pushkin, according to Sergei Fomichev[29] composed the first and third poems of the cycle in spring 1825, under the influence of folk songs sung to him by his nanny Arina Rodionovna, his Russian popular hero is making this spiritually generous gesture at a time of maximal introspection for his author: recall that just months earlier, on the cusp of the move from Odessa to internal exile at Mikhailovskoe (late summer/early fall 1824), Pushkin had turned away from the two greatest representatives of western high literary values and historical drama — Byron and Napoleon — in another poem entitled, significantly, "To the Sea" ("K moriu").

The second poem is a mirror image of the first and, because of its probable later dating (between September 12, 1826 and July 20, 1827[30]), a post hoc turning point inserted into the cycle to give it shape and meaning.[31] Here Stenka, who has gone to Astrakhan' to barter goods at the market

serving as background to the cycle, see Dmitrii Blagoi, *Tvorcheskii put' Pushkina (1813–1826)* (Moscow and Leningrad: Izd. AN SSSR, 1950), esp. 515–31.

26   *Pss*, 10: 84, 86.
27   Pushkin obtained his information about Stenka's drowning of the Persian princess from the travel account of the Dutch sail-maker Jan Jansen Struys who was in Astrakhan' in 1669 and who witnessed Stenka after the latter's return from his Persian campaign." Struys's book, entitled in Russian *Puteshestvie*

Struisa, existed in an 1827 French translation in Pushkin's library as catalogued by Modzalevsky (one may assume in this instance Pushkin had access to an earlier copy of Struys, since the writing of "Pesni" dates to 1826). See Sergei Fomichev, "'Pesni o Sten'ke Razine' Pushkina: istoriia sozdaniia, kompozitsiia I problematika tsikla," in *Pushkin: Issledovaniia i materialy* 13 (1989): 4–20, esp. 6,10.

28   It is curious, though presumably fortuitous, that Stenka makes his sacrifice in a virtual lit-

eralization of the "drop in the sea" metaphor offered above by Lotman.

29   Fomichev, "Pesni," 17.
30   Ibid., 19.
31   For more on the structures of meaning in Pushkin's lyric cycles, see Fomichev, "Liricheskie tsikly v tvorcheskoi evoliutsii Pushkina," *Boldinskie chteniia* (Gor'kii, 1986).

(a potential conflict of the gift and market economies),³² is confronted by a *voevoda*. Not only does the *voevoda* break the rules of gift-giving by first demanding presents ("Stal voevoda / Trebovat' podarkov"), he then refuses the valuable damasks and brocades Stenka does offer ("Podnes Sten'ka Razin / Kamki khrushchatye, / Kamki khrushchatye —/ Parchi zolotye").³³ What the *voevoda* wants is for Stenka to *give* him (*otdat'*) the fur-coat (*shuba*) off his back, for if he doesn't the more powerful nobleman will hang the peasant from the nearest tree. This is an instance of a *forced gift*,³⁴ which in the Slavic mentality is no gift at all, and, moreover, since the *voevoda* is demanding it from the peasant, it is a shorthand for official oppression and a veiled explanation for the revolt.³⁵ Indeed, as Dmitry Blagoi has argued from evidence outside the poem which Pushkin presumably could have known, the *voevoda* in question eventually paid for the extorted gift with his life,³⁶ an implication apparently not lost on the censors and thus an important reason why the cycle was not published until 1881.³⁷ When Stenka finally says to the *voevoda* — "Voz'mi sebe shubu,/ Da ne bylo b shumu"³⁸ — he has shifted the center of gravity of the exchange situation from his *giving* (*otdat'*) to the stronger man's *taking* (*vziat'*), a move which, significantly, leaves no room for spiritual beauty.

In the third poem a personified Russian nature calls out to Stenka and, in an expression of folkloric wishful thinking and pure desire, returns all that has been lost and more to the peasant prince: in the first boat there is gold, in the second, silver, and in the third (the folklorically most "magnetized"), a beautiful maiden (*dusha-devitsa*), a replacement for the original sacrifice. Note that Stenka made his gift with no thought of recompense and note that nature's gifts, coming after history's trials, are *more* than was originally sacrificed. This amounts to a kind of potlatch, but what is important is that there is no rivalry (the urge for

---

32 "In being more directly cued to public esteem, the distributions of honour, and the sanctions of religion, the gift economy is more visible than the market" (Douglas, in Mauss, *The Gift* iv).

33 *Pss*, 2: 300–01.

34 The point here is that not only is a "forced gift" no gift at all, it is simply a tribute, a tax. The highly negative implications of "tax"—*nalogi*, that which is laid upon—in Russian culture, with its resonances of military extortion, not cooperative funding of social services, is, in its way, a polar opposite to *dar/padarok*.

35 The fact that Pushkin uses tonic or accentual (non-metered) verse in the first and third poems of the cycle but a kind of *raeshnyi stikh* (lines loosely dominated by trochaic clausulae) in the second is also possibly significant on the thematic level: the latter is often used for satiric or humorous purposes (thus emphasizing the crudity and lack of generosity in the *voevoda's* behavior), while the former, typical of the folk lyric, suggests Stenka large-spiritedness and *udal'stvo*. My thanks to Dr. Jennifer Ryan, a former graduate student in Slavic at the University of Wisconsin-Madison and now Associate Director of the CREECA program (Center for Russian, East European, and Central Asian Studies) there, for first bringing this to my attention.

36 «В этих взвешенных и неторопливых словах, которыми и заканчивается песня, явственно слышится закипающая ярость произносится продуманно-грозный и неотвратимый приговор над бессовестным и корыстным царским воеводой: действительно, в следующем 1670 г. Астрахань была взята Разиным и воевода убит» (Blagoi, *Tvorcheskii put'* 524).

37 Blagoi, *Tvorcheskii put'*, 525; Fomichev, "Pesni," 4.

38 *Pss*, 2: 301.

power) and that Stenka has not attempted to arrange this outcome with a force greater than himself. Note further, and most importantly, that the forced gift of the fur-coat to the nobleman in the second poem will be reworked *through inversion* by Pushkin in the famous gift-giving scene of *The Captain's Daughter*, where the nobleman (Grinev) will give, freely and generously, the hareskin coat to the peasant (Pugachev) — the first in a series of spontaneous overpayments that will constitute the salient links in the plot of the historical novel and that will bring the worlds of the nobleman and peasant together. And finally, note how the concept of gift-giving is linked with the theme of history (Stenka's uprising), violence (the death of the princess), and hints of possible betrayal (Stenka's initial guilt toward the Volga).

Pushkin never returned to the story of Stenka Razin. Instead his interest turned to the Pugachev Rebellion. One reason, we might hypothesize, is that Stenka's exploits were too thickly covered with the patina of legend, too removed to the distant and irretrievable past, not sufficiently complicated by the real carnage and chaos of the revolt, so that Pushkin could no longer feel that seam between myth and actual historical personage.[39] Pugachev, on the other hand, could still be recollected by eyewitnesses interviewed by the historian in fall 1833. Pushkin could put his hand right on the very seam, and this gesture both aroused and inspired him.

The Captain's Daughter, The History of Pugachev, and the Poet in History

Now, in the last part of my essay I would like to apply the notions of Slavic gift-giving and inspiration/arousal to the elements of fictional plot in *The Captain's Daughter* and to the factual account of events in *The History of Pugachev*. I will begin with a scene of terrible cruelty in the history, a scene which shows without the slightest doubt that Pushkin understood implicitly how blind *sluchainost'* (chance) and violence take over in real life when an oppressive government pushes the peasant masses beyond the breaking point. Recall that Pushkin had begun the history with a retelling of the sources of the conflict—the Iaik Cossacks of the Loginov faction had been complaining about the oppressive measures taken by the chancery officials whom the government had imposed on the Host (withholding of allotted wages, arbitrary taxes, infringement on fishing rights, etc.).[40] And when

---

[39] It is also true in this context that Pushkin presumably felt the Pugachev uprising offered a richer source of parallels to his own 1830's (violent unrest in the military colonies, Polish uprising, war with Turkey, cholera epidemic, etc.) than did the case of Stenka.

[40] *Pss*, 8: 113–14; see also A.S. Pushkin, *The Complete Prose Fiction*, trans., intro., and notes by Paul Debreczeny (Stanord: Stanford University Press, 1983), 366.

the Cossacks attempted to send their own men on a secret mission to the Empress to explain their position, they were found out, arrested, and further humiliated and antagonized (head-shavings). In any event, Pushkin understood that this violence had a cause and, moreover, when it erupted, it would have no fictional plot involving miraculous salvation — indeed, quite the opposite. This is how Pushkin describes the murder of Colonel Elagin and his family in the *History* (Elagin is the commander of the fortress at Tatishchev that Pugachev's forces overrun on September 27, 1773):

> The wounded Elagin [...] put up a desperate fight. At last the rebels charged into the fort's smoking ruins. The commanders were captured. Bulow was beheaded. Elagin, a corpulent man, was skinned [*S Elagina, cheloveka tuchnogo, sodrali kozhu*]; the scoundrels cut his fat out and rubbed it on their wounds. His wife was hacked to pieces. Their daughter, Kharlov's wife, widowed the day before, was led before the victor who presided over the execution of her parents. Pugachev was struck by her beauty and decided to make the poor woman his concubine [*i vzial neschastnuiu k sebe v nalozhnitsy*], sparing her seven-year old brother for her sake... [Then, somewhat later,] the young Kharlova had the misfortune of winning the pretender's affections. He kept her at his camp below Orenburg. She was the only person allowed to enter his covered wagon at any time, and at her request he gave orders to bury the bodies of all those hanged at Ozernaia at the time the fort was taken. She became suspect in the eyes of the jealous villains and Pugachev, yielding to their demand, gave his concubine up to them. Kharlova and her seven-year-old brother were shot. Wounded, they crawled up to each other and embraced. Their bodies, thrown into the bushes, remained there in each other's arms for a long time.[41]

What we see here in the history is, first of all, not the absence of an organizing intelligence[42] — after all, Pushkin is giving a narrative account of first why and then how the violence took place — but the absence of any positive source of energy (all urges and angers are immediately acted upon, nothing is stored up or left over) and of any sense of *siuzhet* as "happy ending" or deus ex machina. If one wishes, here is a straight and brutal quid pro quo: these victims, who are not recognized by Pugachev's men for their individuality or beauty or honor or rectitude, are the payment due for prior oppression. Note that here too are all the elements for Pushkin's fictional plot in *The Captain's Daughter*: the commander of the fortress, who fights bravely and

---

[41] *Pss*, 8: 123, 132; Debreczeny, *Complete Prose*, 376, 385.

[42] The metahistorical critics who consider the organizing intelligence of a work like *The History of Pugachev* isomorphic with the imposition of a literary *siuzhet* on an otherwise straightforward *fabula* are, in my judgment, overstating the case and extending quite different cognitive responses to reality over a broad and rather amorphous continuum.

[43] *Pss*, 8: 151.

who refuses to declare an oath to the impostor, is savagely murdered along with his wife, while his daughter becomes Pugachev's concubine. But Pushkin leaves room for excess energy and a positive gift-giving economy in the novel: Mironov is quickly hanged (not skinned alive), his wife is struck down with one blow, and his daughter, importantly, is only threatened with the possibility of concubinage. There is violence to be sure, but the child is spared, and the body lying grotesquely unattended is that of Vasilisa Egorovna and not that of Kharlova (a potential Masha) or that of her little brother. If Stenka had been too legendary for Pushkin, not real enough, then the Pugachev of the *History* is exactly the opposite—he is, in Bibikov's words, a "puppet" (*chuchelo*[43]) in the hands of his lieutenants, he quickly yields to their demands, he arrives drunk in battle, and so on. In the *History* there is no seam separating man from myth because there is no room for myth.

Now, if we look at an analogous crisis moment in the novel, one fraught with the specter of execution, a different principle exists. After Grinev has been spared the first time and is preparing to return to Orenburg, the meddling Savelich appears and demands recompense from Pugachev for the losses to his master's household incurred at the hands of the rebel forces.[44] According to the logic of the Slavic gift-giving mentality, Savelich's inventory is not only dangerously stupid, it is ungrateful, for it does not allow the other side the possibility of a *non-compulsory, unidirectional* gesture of generosity. Coming to the end of the inventory, Savelich exclaims, "And finally a hareskin coat given to Your Grace at the wayside inn, fifteen rubles." To which the angry Pugachev responds, "Hareskin coat! I'll give you a hareskin coat! Before you know it, I'll have you flayed alive and a coat made of your skin!" (Ia-te dam zaiachii tulup! Da znaesh' li ty, chto ia s tebia zhivogo kozhu veliu sodrat' na tulupy?).[45] These words resonate with the first song of the Western Slavs ("Videnie korolia"), a cycle that Pushkin composed at the time he was working on the history and the novel: here the betraying brother Radivoi (a potential Shvabrin), who bows down before the sultan (i.e., he does the equivalent of swearing allegiance to Pugachev), is made the ghastly gift of a kaftan stitched together from the flayed skin of his Orthodox brother (a potential Grinev).[46] Violence, gift-giving, and betrayal are again telescoped. However, with Savelich Pushkin has taken the terrible circumstances of Colonel Elagin's death (the flaying) and worked them into the fictional text only as threat. As any reader of a novel in Pushkin's time knew, to skin the good Savelich alive (or to hang his master, for that matter) would be to cross an impossible line comprised of genre, taste, and psychology. Instead

---

44 Savelich's list was based on a similar petition submitted by a certain Court Councillor Butkevich to the government. What is ironic is that Pushkin has a servant rather than a nobleman submit the *reestr* of lost or stolen items in the novel. He avoids the incident entirely in the *Istoriia*. See Iu. G Oksman, "Pushkin v rabote nad romanom *Kapitanskaia dochka*," in A.S. Pushkin, *Kapitanskaia dochka* (Moscow: Nauka ("Literaturnye pamiatniki"), 1984), 94–100; and Paul Debreczeny, *The Other Pushkin: A Study of Alexander Pushkin's Prose Fiction* (Stanford: Stanford University Press, 1983), 255.

45 *Pss*, 6: 319; Debreczeny, *Complete Prose*, 321.

46 *Pss*, 3: 266–68.

of carrying through with his threat, the fictionalized Pugachev does the opposite: "in a fit of generosity," he gives the departing duo a horse, the fur-coat (*shuba*) off his back (cf. Stenka), and a *poltina* (half-ruble).[47] Again, he overpays, and the historical plot-cum-potlatch continues.

But the question remains, is this a potlatch in the Maussian sense that Pugachev and Grinev are involved in an elaborate system that obligates and challenges the rival, or is the overpayment a symbol of something else? I would suggest, using Lotman's terminology, that the intersection (*peresechenie*) of events that first brought Pugachev and Grinev together in the snowstorm created an explosion (*vzryv*) in the fixed patterns of response typical of peasant and nobleman in their dealings with one another.[48] This explosion is full of potential energy; it forces each subject *out of itself* and into an intermediate space that is open, vulnerable, and no longer — at least no longer in the same way — "emplotted."[49] It is also, significantly, tied to the wonder or *chudo* of folk logic, which is crucial to understanding the "deep structure" of the novel and which serves, through the barge haulers' song ("Ne shumi, mati zelenaia dubrovushka"), the Kalmyk tale, and the chapter epigraphs taken from folk songs, to counterbalance the western plots and high literary values of the salon culture (cf. *Povesti Belkina*).[50] Pushkin is not saying that there is no meaning or communication in this space, in fact quite the opposite, but what he is saying is that this communication is maximally dangerous, "archaic" or unmediated by the veneer of civilization, very close (at least on Pugachev's end) to the subconscious urge for complete "barrierlessness," and, like the eagle of the Kalmyk *skazka* that would rather drink fresh blood and die than eat carrion and live 300 years, both dark and intoxicating.[51]

For Pushkin, the *sluchainost'* that underwrote the potlatch between Grinev and Pugachev lies at the heart of all history but especially of *Russian* his-

---

47 Ibid., 6: 320.

48 Lotman, *Kul'tura i vzryv*, 26–30.

49 Here Lotman's semiotic description of a paradigm shift has interesting links to what chaos theorists in the west term a "fractal"—a system that appears to behave unpredictably but nevertheless displays some order. Also close to Lotman's distinction between *predskazuemost'* and *nepredskazuemost'* in the *Kul'tura i vzryv* book is Arthur Danto's notion of "narrative predicates" in *Narration and Knowledge* (New York: Columbia University Press, 1985): those statements made by an historian (as opposed to fiction writer) which, when applied to objects, "do so only on the assumption that a future event occurs," and which are seen as "retrospectively *false*... if the future required by the meaning rules of these predicates fails to materialize" (349–50).

50 On the role of folk logic in *The Captain's Daughter*, see especially I.P. Smirnov, "Ot skazki k romanu" in *Istoriia zhanrov v russkoi literature X–XVII vv.* (Leningrad: Nauka, 1972), 305–20. The use of the Aesopian fable to read the Kalmyk *skazka* is treated in Michael Finke, "Puškin, Pugačev, and Aesop," *Slavic and East European Journal* 35.2 (1991): 179–92. Others who have touched on folkloric aspects in the novel include Iu.P. Fesenko, "Dve zametiki ob A.S. Pushkine i V.I. Dale," *Vremennik Pushkinskoi komissii* 25 (1993): 154–61; Marina Tsvetaeva, "Pushkin i Pugachev" in *Izbrannaia proza v dvukh tomakh*, preface J. Brodsky (New York: Russica, 1979), II: 280–302; Debreczeny, *The Other Pushkin* 258, 267–68; Viktor Shklovskii, *Gamburgskii schet* (Leningrad: 1928), 31; and V.D. Skvoznikov, "Stil' Pushkina," *Teoriia literatury* 3 (1965): 60–97, esp. 79–81. Fesenko makes the interesting point, for example, that Grinev withstands the four trials set to him in his meetings with Pugachev like the *dobryi molodets* of the barge haulers' song.

tory. Only the Grinev who lived to tell of his encounter with Pugachev can call this intersection the work of Providence (*Providenie*); to the young Petrusha at the time it is rather the work of *sluchai*. Indeed, the two words are joined in Grinev's mind as that very seam and energy source where what is private and anecdotally Russian becomes History: "A strange thought came to me: it seemed to me that providence, bringing me a second time to Pugachev, was presenting [*podavalo*; NB the notion of 'giving' or 'serving up'] me with the chance [*sluchai*] to turn my intention into action."[52] As epigraph to the *History* Pushkin took the words of Archimandrite Platon Liubarsky, which made sense of the impostor's military exploits not in terms of "rational considerations or military precepts," but in terms of "daring, happenstance [*sluchai*], and luck."[53] And in his 1830 review of Polevoy's *History of the Russian People* (*Istoriia russkogo naroda*) Pushkin was critical of Guizot's lack of appreciation of *sluchainost'* in historical events and insisted that it was precisely this possibility of chance and this avoidance of western emplotment that made Russian history different:

> But remember this as well: Russia has never had anything in common with the rest of Europe; her history requires a different [type of] thought, a different formula from those drawn out by Guizot from the history of Christian West. Don't say "It could not be otherwise." If that were so, then an historian would be an astronomer and the events in the life of humankind would be predicted in calendars, like solar eclipses. But providence is not algebra. The human mind, according to popular expression, is not a prophet, but a guesser; it sees the general course of things and can draw out from that profound suppositions, often confirmed in time, but it cannot foresee chance — the powerful, momentary instrument of Providence.[54]

In conclusion, the better Grinev gets to know Pugachev, the more articulate and even *inspired* become his answers to the risk-laden questions put to him by this human symbol of the historical id.[55] Pushkin gives to Grinev, who is no poet in terms of his artistic talent, that very quality of inspiration which distinguishes, in the author's own words, not the "prophet" but the fate-"guesser," the poet in history: "raspolozhenie dushi k zhiveishemu

---

51 Lotman has no doubts about where Pushkin's sympathies lie in the confrontation between the two camps (peasant/nobleman) when he writes in "Ideinaia struktura 'Kapitanskoi dochki,'" *Pushkinskii sbornik* (Pskov: Pskovskii Gos. ped. Inst., 1962), 3–20: «Было бы заблуждением считать, что Пушкин, видя ограниченность (но и историческую оправданность) обоих лагерей — дворянского и крестьянского — приравнивал их этически. Крестьянский лагерь и его руководители привлекали Пушкина своей поэтичностью [my emphasis — DMB], которой он, конеч но, не чувствовал ни в оренбургском коменданте, ни во дворе Екатерины. Поэтичность же была для Пушкина связана не только с колоритностью ярких человеческих личностей, но и с самой природой народной „власти", чуждой бюрократии и мертвящего формализма» (19).

52 *Pss*, 6: 332.

53 *Pss*, 8: 110; Debreczeny, *Complete Prose*, 362.

54 *Pss*, 7: 100. My translation.

priniatiiu vpechatlenii, sled[stvenno] k bystromu soobrazheniiu poniatii, chto i sposobstvuet ob'iasneniiu onykh" (a disposition of the soul toward the most vivid reception of impressions, and thus to the rapid apprehension of ideas, which process also promotes the clarification of these latter).[56] When asked by Pugachev during one of their several tête-à-têtes, "Don't you believe that I am your Sovereign Majesty? Give me a straight answer," Grinev hesitates before this particular riddle of survival and then answers in a way that shows he has broken through the irreconcilable binaries (*muzhik/barin*) of his historical situation. He answers both directly, in that he answers sincerely, and indirectly, in that he does not respond with a binary "yes" or "no." Like Ivan Kuzmich (Captain Mironov), the military man Grinev *père* would have said "You're not our sovereign, you, fellow, are an impostor and pretender," which is, from within that individual's system, undoubtedly correct.[57] But the son answers by not embracing the strict judgmental code of the father and by, as it were, seeing that code from the outside, as a range of potentials. He *tells Pugachev the truth* ("Listen, let me tell you the honest truth"[58]) by telling him that *God only knows who he is* and that his game, regardless of who he is, is a dangerous one. At the same time, Grinev again makes explicit his refusal to serve as one of Pugachev's officers, even adding that, if given his freedom, he cannot promise not to fight against his present benefactor.

In other words, Grinev is able to take in the impressions of his risky situation, to quickly understand their potential ramifications, and then to present them to his interlocutor so that, again, a breakthrough in communication takes place. The categories of public and private, peasant and nobleman, dissolve as each is forced to see the inherent rightness and necessity of the other's position.[59] Grinev is "inspired," as it were, to speak the truth in precisely this way. This is not a moment to lose oneself (the Küchelbeckerian/Derzhavinian *vostorg* [rapture]) but to find oneself. The hero's multivalent "sincerity" stuns Pugachev ("Moia iskrennost' porazila Pugacheva"[60]) because, like the gift that initiated their relationship, it is more than it needs to be. Grinev could fall on his knees before Pugachev in order to save his life (as Shvabrin will soon do), but then he will have lost his honor. He could also tell Pugachev the state's truth, that the latter is a *samozvanets*

---

55 For the psychological aspects of Petrusha's efforts to define himself against the various parent figures in the novel, see Caryl Emerson, "Grinev's Dream," *Slavic Review* 40.1 (1981): 60–76; and Debreczeny, *The Other Pushkin* 257–73. Pugachev is clearly a liminal figure, thus his eerie oneiric status to the hero, because he combines the role of "proxy father" (*posazhennyi otets*) and rebellious peasant son rising up against an authoritarian state symbolized by Catherine. See below.

56 *Pss*, 7: 29; see also Terts, *Progulki*, 63.

57 *Pss*, 6: 308; Debreczeny, *Complete Prose*, 311.

58 *Pss*, 6: 315.

59 Each feels, in Fomichev's formulation, a "korennoe dukhovnoe rodstvo pri vsei protivopolozhnosti svoikh klassovykh interesov" (*Poeziia Pushkina: Tvorcheskaia evoliutsiia* [Leningrad: nauka, 1986], 265). This is what Lotman calls their ability to see the "chelovecheskaia pravota" of a foil's position ("Ideinaia struktura," 14).

60 *Pss*, 6: 316.

(impostor), but by so doing he will have kept his honor by losing his life. He finds instead a third way. And after telling the truth, he puts the decision back in Pugachev's hands: "My life is in your hands: if you let me go, I'll be grateful; if you execute me, God shall be your judge; in any case, I've told you the whole truth."[61] Pugachev of course answers in kind, with his own brand of peasant generosity: "Be it so... Hang him or spare him: don't do things by halves [Kaznit' tak kaznit', milovat' tak milovat']."

At least one recent scholar has made a point of the "intergeneric dialogue" between *The Captain's Daughter* and *The History of Pugachev*, the implication being that for Pushkin each genre had its inherent rules and limitations and that the "truth" (the difference between the *vozvyshaiushchii obman* [the lie that uplifts] and the *t'my nizkikh istin* [the gloom of lower truths] of the famous "Hero" poem) should be sought in some extratextual vectoring of the two.[62] Details from the history can migrate, becoming tied to the fates of individual lives, into the novel, while the novel, again for reasons of genre, might refer the reader back to the history (with its broader, more impersonal sweep), as when Grinev demurs at describing the siege of the fortress: "I will not describe the siege of Orenburg, which belongs to history rather than to a family chronicle."[63] Both genres have their unique "observation points,"[64] and the dialogue that ensues takes place between and around, but not exactly in them. Thus Tsvetaeva's arch-romantic hierarchy of values is not necessarily Pushkin's: "V 'Kapitanskoi dochke' Pushkin-istoriograf pobit Pushkinym-poetom" (In *The Captain's Daughter*, Pushkin the historian is beaten by Pushkin the poet).[65]

---

61 *Pss*, 6: 316; Debreczeny, *Complete Prose*, 318.

62 In *An Obsession with History: Russian Writers Confront the Past* (Stanford: Stanford University Press, 1994), Andrew Wachtel writes, "The view of the Pugachev rebellion and the attitude toward history displayed in the novel are in no way meant to supersede the very different point of view of the history. Rather, Pushkin implies that the two works are meant to be read in tandem. The clash of their separate monologic narratives leads to an intergeneric dialogue that emphasizes the multiplicity of possible historical interpretations. Each belongs firmly to its own genre, but the two are linked to each other, and to all of Pushkin's work on historical themes by his conception of history as a series of possible stories" (83). My only reservation about this otherwise insightful argument is that it is a considerable impoverishment to describe a text as complex and cognitively challenging as *The Captain's Daughter* as a "monologic narrative." (One questions whether this is all Bakhtin meant by the term.) A similar but more nuanced approach is found in Dan Ungurianu, "Fiction and History in Pushkin's Portrayal of Pugachevshchina," (Article MS.), who divides the reception history of *The Captain's Daughter* into two basic groups: the genres as "separate but equal" (Sollogub, Strakhov, Emerson, Debreczeny) versus a "hierarchy of truths" (Vyazemsky, Katkov, Kliuchevsky, Iakubovich, Bliumenfeld, and, most vividly, Tsvetaeva). There is also a third "middle ground" group which, while acknowledging the rules of each genre, see *The Captain's Daughter* as a "continuation of the author's historical research (or search for the truth) but this time through artistic means which compensate for the lacunas in the documents": Annenkov, Cherniaev, Petrunina. See Ungurianu, "Fiction and History," 1–5.

63 *Pss*, 6: 325; Debreczeny, Complete Prose, 326; see Ungurianu, "Fiction and History," 6.

64 Ungurianu, "Fiction and History," 5.

65 Marina Tsvetaeva, "Pushkin i Pugachev," *Izbrannaia proza v dvukh tomakh* (New York: Russica, 1979), 2:300.

Yet this approach, while true enough, does not adequately account for how Pushkin energizes his verbal material from within, gives the gift of his own special brand of generosity to his own words. I claimed at the outset of my remarks that Pushkin came to every verbal structure, even those describing history, with the sensibility of the poet. I have tried in this paper to suggest that this sensibility operated on two levels *simultaneously* — that of sound and that of sense. The gift-giving moment that generates so much creative potential in *The Captain's Daughter*, Grinev's present of the hareskin coat, is, as Sergei Davydov first elegantly demonstrated, organized paranomastically or logosemantically: the p + l + t sounds in *"tulup"* are repeated in the thematically magnetized popular sayings (*poslovitsy*) in the text —"beregi *plat'e* snovu" and "dolg *platezhom* krasen".[66] What is more, this principle of phonetic similarity makes perfect semantic sense, inasmuch as these sayings bring together the theme of dress (*"plat'e"*) and the theme of (over)payment (the *"platezh"* is *"krasen"* because it is more than the initial investment), both crucial to the overall meaning of the novel.

Hence the *tulup* that existed in historical reality as an item of the pretender's clothing becomes "poeticized" as it passes into the novel. It does so not only because Pushkin has chosen to insert it into pre-existing plots or structures (Walter Scott's "wavering" heroes, the trapped wolf-turned-friend of folklore, the anecdote about how Pugachev freed the pastor who had earlier shown him kindness[67]), but because he has illuminated it from within with his own special genius, or "giftedness." Grinev gives the coat because he cannot give money; his gambling losses have forced him to cede control of his purse to Savelich, and he must honor his word.[68] The literal seams of the *detskii tulup*, now bursting with the body of the mysterious *vozhatyi*, become, as it were, the metaphorical seams of *sluchai* and *Providenie*. The very uselessness of the gift makes its expression more aesthetically marked, more "beautiful." Pugachev and Grinev instinctively understand this; that is their bond. Generosity of spirit, the essence of gift-giving, means that one should be willing to give the shirt off one's back, especially if that move, here taken by a nobleman to repay a peasant for his help, will create an alternative economy of mutual understanding. Perhaps it was wishful

---

66 Sergei Davydov, "The Sound and Theme in the Prose of A.S. Pushkin: A Logo-Semantic Study of Paromomasia," *Slavic and East European Journal* 27.1 (1983): 1–18, esp. 13.

67 *Pss*, 8: 178.

68 Virtually all the gift-giving situations in the novel arise as a *combination* of chance and honor. At another point, for example, Grinev, who has escaped from a skirmish with the rebels, goes back to save his faithful servant Savelich. Ironically, it is Savelich, whom Grinev would have allowed to stay behind in Orenburg and keep half of his money, who now, out of his own sense of duty, follows too slowly and thus gets his master caught. Grinev's decision to return, which in the *History* would most certainly have resulted in his death, is his moral obligation to carry out. But then all these "chance" circumstances translate into a new meeting with Pugachev and a new opportunity for extravagant gift-giving (the rescue of Masha and Pugachev's role as match-maker and "proxy-father").

69 *Pss*, 6: 370.

70 For more on the compositional symmetries in *The*

thinking or poetic desire, but Pushkin understood that by bringing these implacable enemies (*barin/muzhik*) together and by creating a flexible middle space where they could step outside their historical roles, one might undo the work of the *voevoda* in the earlier Stenka Razin poem and actually think one's way beyond the tragic alternative of revolt: "Ne privedi Bog videt' russkii bunt, bessmyslennyi i besposhchadnyi" (May the Lord save us from another such senseless and ruthless Russian rebellion).[69] Likewise, the notion of payment becomes altered when what is at stake is not justice but mercy and forgiveness ("one good turns deserves [more than] another" rather than "an eye for an eye and a tooth for a tooth").

I will close, therefore, with two final thoughts: first, it is fitting that Catherine's debt to the daughter of Captain Mironov should be repaid by the state in a coin — the generosity of *milost'*— that pleasurably echoes the (read *novelistically*) fatidic potlatch involving Grinev and the peasant tsar. So too is it proper that Catherine, the threat to the state eliminated and her matriarchy safely restored, should be wearing a *dushegreika* (lit. "soul-warmer," i.e., her sleeveless version of Pugachev's *tulup*) when Masha happens upon her in the park at Tsarskoe Selo. After all, this was the article of clothing that Vasilisa Egorovna was wearing when the rebels seized the fortress and she and her husband were so brutally murdered. With his remarkable sense of compositional symmetry, Pushkin now offsets the bearded cossack who had dressed himself in a simulation of imperial regalia (red caftan with gold tassels) with the empress who impersonates a simple woman.[70] Let Catherine the matriarch, who had her own way of using men, beware, says Pushkin, for a fate such as Vasilisa Egorovna's awaits her and her family if Russia's historical id, here portrayed as male, is too long repressed or, in political terms, oppressed.[71] Likewise, it is to be expected that the opposing parent figure in the novel, the peasant tsar himself and Catherine's mortal foe (because as long as he is alive as Peter III her legitimacy is in question), is brought to justice, that is, *payment for his crimes*, with variations on the same clothing motifs. The words, ironically, are from Dmitriev's memoirs and the place is the conclusion to Pushkin's *History*, but even so it is difficult to imagine a stronger contrast to the notion of soul-warming and mercy:

> At this moment the executioner gave a signal, and the headsmen rushed on Pugachev to undress him: they pulled off his white sheepskin coat [*sorvali belyi baranii tulup*] and started tearing at the sleeves of his crimson silk caftan [*stali razdirat'*

Captain's Daughter, see Lotman, "Ideinaia struktura" 12–13.

71 «Пушкин ясно видит, что, хотя „крестьянский царь" заимствует внешние признаки власти у дворянской государственности, содержание ее — иное. Крестьянская власть патриархальнее, прямее связана с управляемой массой, лишена чиновников и окрашена в тона семейного демократизма». (Lotman, "Ideinaia struktura" 9).

rukava shelkovogo malinovogo polukaftan'ia]. He clapsed his hands and fell backwards, and a minute later a head dripping with blood was raised high.[72]

The stripping or figurative flaying that accompanies Dmitriev's description of Pugachev's here at the end of *The History of Pugachev* will become, through the poet's own spiritual giftedness, the bestowal of the shirt off one's back that initiates the plot of *The Captain's Daughter*. How well Pushkin understood the laws of Clio and the laws of Calliope!

---

[72] *Pss*, 8: 248; Debreczeny, *Complete Prose*, 437.

Chapter 13

Pushkin's *The History of Pugachev*: Where Fact Meets the Zero-Degree of Fiction[1]

The *History of Pugachev* is, conceptually speaking, one of the most fascinating works in Pushkin's oeuvre. At the same time it is, belletristically if not historiographically, pretty much a flop, a point which has been made more than once over the past two centuries, most persuasively in recent decades by Marc Raeff.[2] Yet Pushkin was clearly up to something important here, in 1833–34, as he gained access to government archives and gathered materials, visited the sites of the 1773–74 rebellion in the Orenburg *guberniya*, took down eyewitness accounts, and drafted his history, a history which was intended to be read in tandem with the contemporaneously written and thematically isomorphic historical novel *The Captain's Daughter*. Obviously, the poet was trying to figure out, and approach, even get to, the epistemological limits of fiction and history, to test how meaning is made in the one as opposed to the other, and by so doing to arrive at what "really happened" during this chaotic period (the *pugachevshchina*) that almost brought down Catherine and her empire.

The present essay examines the different conceptual strands of Pushkin's "genre-driven" attitude toward, and understanding of, Emelyan Pugachev and the rebellion that he, Pushkin, felt was so richly representative of Russian history, past and present. To be sure, there are a multitude of ways "into" *History of Pugachev* and at some level it is true that we cannot understand what is happening in the history until we ascertain with some precision what is going on immediately *outside* it, that is, until we place in proper context and perspective the "epistemological edges" that Pushkin himself plied to vector in on his subject. Some of these edges and angles include: the poet's growth as historical thinker, from his remarks on Tacitus to his fascination with Peter (Tomashevsky, Eidelman); his 1830's

---

1   Originally appeared in Russian as "'*Istoriia Pugacheva*': na peresechenii fakta i nulevoi stepeni khudozhestvennogo zamysla," in *Slavic Helsingiensia* 41/*Studia Russica Helsingiensia et Tartuensia VIII* ("*Istoriia i istoriosofiia v literaturnom prelomlenii*") (Tartu, 2002), 102–133.

2   See, e.g., Marc Raeff, *Preconditions of Revolution in Early Modern Europe* (Baltimore: Johns Hopkins Press, 1970).

feelings toward Nicholas and the role those feelings played in what he did and did not include in his text; his professional and private attitude toward Karamzin as author of *The History of the Russian State*, whose massively authoritative text had been so influential in creating a historically aware readership and whose later volumes had inspired Pushkin at a turning point in his life (Vatsuro, Eidelman); the relationship of Karamzin's "Preface" to his history to Pushkin's "Preface" to his; the epic nature of Karamzin's text as opposed to the intentionally fragmentary, in various senses, nature of Pushkin's; the placement of Pushkin's history between Karamzin's moralizing and tsar-centered chronotope and Polevoy's more populist but slavishly westernizing and artificially "skeptical" viewpoint in the *History of the Russian People* (Bethea and Davydov); the structural devices — epigraphs, dedications, explanatory notes, etc. — that appeared earlier in works like *The Fountain of Bakhchisarai*, *Poltava*, and *The Belkin Tales* to provide alternative viewpoints on the main action (often ironic and aimed at problematizing the fiction) and that now serve to comment straightforwardly and "authentically" on the historical text (Lotman); the inadmissability of anything smacking of a literary or folkloric fiction (*vydumka*) in history proper, as Pushkin argued in his scathing assessment of *The History of the Don Cossack Host*, whose author, V.G. Bronevsky, had just attacked Pushkin's own scholarly bona fides in his Bulgarin-inspired review of *History of Pugachev*; Pushkin's principles of selection as he moved from his primary sources to his own narrative (G. Blok, Ovchinnikov), etc.[3] All these aspects and more are entirely legitimate as ways of understanding Pushkin's text in *History of Pugachev*. But rather than dwell on any of these aspects I would like to look more carefully at the internal texture of Pushkin's history and to try to locate that "zero-degree" of fiction that he was apparently after — that moment where he, as historian, in order to tell his subjects' story, cannot resort to any ready-made plots but must try to reconstruct meaning in the form that these subjects found it.

But this very move on Pushkin's part is fraught with its own set of problems, problems which are, one might say, as much ours as they are his and which show, again and again, how difficult it is to penetrate another's worldview

[3] See B.V. Tomashevskii, "Iztorizm Pushkina" (orig. 1961), in *Pushkin: Raboty raznykh let* (Moscow: Kniga, 1990), 130–78; N. Eidel'man, "Semnadtsat' vekov," in *Pushkin: Istoriia i sovremennost' v khudozhestvennom soznanii poeta* (Moscow: Sovetskii pisatel', 1984), 50–92; V.E. Vatsuro, "Podvig chestnogo cheloveka," in Vatsuro and M.I. Gillel'son, *Skvoz' umstvennye plotiny* (Moscow: Kniga, 1972), 32–113; N. Eidel'man, *Poslednii letopisets* (Moscow: Kniga, 1983); David M. Bethea and Sergei Davydov, "The (Hi)story of the Village Gorjuxino: in Praise of Puškin's Folly," *Slavic and East European Journal* 28 (Fall 1984): 291–309; Iu.M. Lotman, "K structure dialogicheskogo teksta v poemakh Pushkina (problema avtorskikh primechanii k tekstu)" (orig. 1970), in *Izbrannye stat'i v trekh tomakh* (Tallinn: Aleksandra, 1992–93), 2:381–88; G. Blok, *Pushkin v rabote nad istoricheskimi istochnikami* (Moscow-Leningrad: Izd. Akademii Nauk SSSR, 1949); R.V. Ovchinnikov: *Pushkin v rabote nad arkhivnymi dokumentami* ("*Istoriia Pugacheva*") (Leningrad: Nauka, 1969) and *Nad "pugachevskimi" stranitsami Pushkina* (Moscow: Nauka, 1981).

or episteme. By trying to reach the zero-degree of fiction and by trying to tell in words what really happened in fact, Pushkin and his text are flying in the face of the "metahistorical" viewpoint that has played so prominent a role in western critical debates about historiography in recent decades. For if that viewpoint has a common epistemological ground, it is the following: 1) that the "factual" and the "textual" cannot be disentangled from one another when invoking documentary evidence about the past; and 2) that therefore there is no such thing as a "neutral" telling of events. Here narrative itself, or more specifically what Hayden White has termed the *narrativizing* impulse,[4] is the culprit, for the historian, no matter how scrupulous, painstaking, and ideologically non-biased, is operating under a delusion if he believes, and writes as if he believes, that his version of events can provide meaning. Events do not simply, to rephrase Benveniste's witticism, *tell themselves*; rather, they *appear* to do so, and in that pretense of narrating without a narrator resides perhaps the chief optical illusion of previous historiographical texts.[5] Viewed in the context of this radical scepticism, the heretofore crucial difference between fiction writing, which is the narrating of imaginary events, and historiography, which is the narrating of actual events, becomes less important, a difference more of degree than of kind, than the larger, metacognitive category of narration itself.[6] But my point, which I will try to make in the discussion to follow, is that Pushkin was both sceptical and yet at some level believed that the events of the Pugachev rebellion could indeed *tell themselves*. What this means and whether the historian is correct in his assumption is the larger subject of my paper.

If Pushkin can do without the metastructure of either Western fictional plots or Eurocentric Enlightenment reasoning after the fact (post hoc, ergo propter hoc), then what is it that stands at the center of his historical telling as its moving force? The answer to this question comes in the final epistemological edge encountered by the reader before entering the history proper — the epigraph from Archimandrite Platon Liubarsky:

[4] "Historians do not *have* to report their truths about the real world in narrative form; they may choose other, non-narrative, even anti-narrative, modes of representation, such as the meditation, the anatomy, or the epitome. Tocqueville, Burckhardt, Huizinga, and Braudel, to mention only the most notable masters of modern historiography, refused narrative in certain of their historiographical works, presumably on the assumption that the meaning of the events with which they wished to deal did not lend itself to representation in the narrative mode... While they certainly *narrated* their accounts of the reality that they perceived, or thought they perceived, to exist within or behind the evidence they had examined, they did not *narrativize* that reality, did not impose upon it the for of a story" (Hayden White, "The Value of Narrativity in the Representation of Reality," in *On Narrative*, ed. W.J.T. Mitchell [Chicago: University of Chicago Press, 1981], 2).

[5] Emile Benveniste, *Problems in General Linguistics*, trans. Mary Elizabethe Meek [Coral Gables: University of Miami Press, 1971], 208; cited White, "The Value," 3)

[6] As White writes in this connection, "Far from being one code among many that a culture may utilize for endowing experience with meaning, narrative is a metacode, a human universal on the basis of which transcultural messages about the nature of a shared reality can be transmitted" (White, "The Value," 2).

To render a proper account of all the designs and adventures of this impostor would, it seems, be almost impossible not only for a historian of average abilities but even for the most excellent one, because all of this impostor's undertakings depended not on rational considerations or military precepts, but on daring, happenstance, and luck [*derzost', sluchai i udacha*]. For this reason (I think) Pugachev himself not only would be unable to recount all the details of these undertakings, but would not even be aware of a considerable portion of them, since they were initiated, not just by him directly, but by many of his unbridled daredevil accomplices in several locations at once.[7]

Several things about this epigraph leap out as if to announce its status as more than decorative. To begin with, it belongs to a clergyman-eyewitness and yet its message says nothing about divine intentionality, which is to say, this speaker does not represent the "monkishly simple" viewpoint of Pimen (or, for that matter, Karamzin). The difference, however, in this mini-window on the history, as opposed to earlier windows on fiction, is that irony, any kind of irony (romantic, aesthetic, etc.), has disappeared entirely. We can say this because it is precisely *derzost', sluchai i udacha* (daring, happenstance/chance, and luck) that will be the guiding force behind the amazing success of the popular revolt in its early and intermediate stages. As suggested in my opening comments, in his artistic works Pushkin is apt to use his epigraphs ironically or parodically, as a way to bracket the literary tradition of the *chuzhoe slovo* and then to play with or subvert it. Not in this instance, however. Archimandrite Platon Liubarsky seems to know something that all the academic historians do not.[8]

---

[7] Alexander Pushkin, *Complete Prose Fiction*, trans. and intro. Paul Debreczeny (Stanford: Stanford Univeristy Press, 1983), 362 (referred hereafter as "*CPF*"; A.S. Pushkin, *Polnoe sobranie sochinenii*, ed. B.V. Tomashevskii, 10 vols. (Leningrad: Nauka, 1977–79), 8:110 (referred to subsequently as "*Pss*").

[8] It is worth noting that the concept of *sluchai* had played a pivotal role in Pushkin's mock history, *Istoriia sela Goriukhina*. Recall that it was a *nechaiannyi sluchai* (unexpected/chance occurrence) that allowed Belkin to become the historian of the village Goriukhino in the first place: one of his serving women came upon an "old basket full of wood shavings, trash, and books" in his attic, and it was these latter, especially the old calendars (NB. the chronological principle), that then formed the basis of his "history" (*CPF*, 126; *Pss*, 6:122). Ironically, it was this same principle of *sluchai* that also gave Pushkin the opportunity to write his own history: as he wrote in an unsent letter (late May-early June 1833) to I.I. Dmitriev in which he broaches for the first time his intention to write *Istoriia Pugacheva*, "Happenstance [*Sluchai*] placed in my hands some important documents [i.e., the reference is to various papers in the Pugachev archive of the War College [*Voennaia kollegiia*]—DMB] relating to Pugachev (the personal letters of Catherine, Bibikov, Rumiantsev, Panin, Derzhavin, and others). I have put them in order and hope to publish them" (A.S. Pushkin, *Polnoe sobranie sochinenii*, ed. V.D. Bronch-Bruevich, 17 vols. [Moscow: Akademiia Nauk SSSR, 1937–59], 15:62).

It was also in his last (unpublished) review of Polevoy that Pushkin claimed that western historiographical models, such as Guizot's, faltered when applied to the Russian example because they routinely substituted reason and theory for "chance, the powerful, instantaneous tool of Providence" (VII:100). The full passage reads:

Guizot explained one of the events of Christian history: the European Enlightenment. He discovers its germ, describes its gradual development, and, shunting aside everything remote, everything extraneous, *accidental* [*sluchainoe*], brings it up to our time through the dark, bloody, rebellious, and, finally, enlightened [*rassvetaiushchie*] centuries. You have understood the great merit

Sluchai is the essence of the fragmentary in history.[9] It is what cannot be emplotted in any larger paradigm, coming, as it were, "out of nowhere." The element of chance in a literary plot, as Pushkin knew so well from his work on *The Belkin Tales*, is illusory: it is the artistic expression of unpredictability, which is to say, coincidence, what the author passes off as chance but knows, from his meta-perspective, is planned by the providential god of fiction. Burmin first appears out of the snowstorm that is synonymous with his name, then disappears at the "accidental" altar back into the elements, only to return for the ultimate epithalamium at the end. His actions are propelled forward by the happy ending that is his and Marya Gavrilovna's "fate." But the *sluchai* that the churchman invokes and that Pushkin attempts to present in the *History* is not already providential; it is the real thing. It is chance in all its terrifying presentness, unmediated by invention, stripped of any plot potential known in advance—the "unexpected" "now" that still, as it were, winks to and *expects* help from a backward-glancing "then." This is what the epigraphic voice means when it says that even the most accomplished historian would have difficulty telling the story of Pugachev. Nor, by the same token, would this task be any easier for the impostor himself. He is not about *sluchai*, he is it, the chance that carries chaos and death in its path for those that just "happen" to be in its way. When, for example, in Chapter 2 of the *History*, Major Kharlov, the Commandant of the Nizhne-Ozernaia Fortress, fires shots from his only two cannon in order to give courage to his troops during the early morning hours of 26 September 1773, this action frightens off the reinforcements under the command of Bilov who are at that very moment en route to the fortress,

of the French historian. But understand as well that Russia never had anything in common with the rest of Europe, that her history requires another way of thinking, another formula, than the thinking and formulas adduced by Guizot from the history of the Christian West. Don't say *it was impossible otherwise* [inache nel'zia bylo byt']. If that were true, then the historian would be an astronomer and the events in the life of mankind would be predicted, like solar eclipses, in calendars. But Providence is not algebra. The human mind, according to the popular expression, is not a prophet but a guesser; it sees the general course of things and can extrapolate from the latter profound assumptions, which are then often justified by time, but what it can't do is predict chance [*sluchai*], the powerful instantaneous tool of Providence (VII:100).

Pushkin's polemic with Polevoy, and with those, such as Guizot, Michelet, Thierry, and Niebuhr, who inspired him, was by no means delivered into a vacuum. The early 1830's were full of discussions about the necessary transcendence of chance by Providence in historical narration. Examples include Pogodin's essays in *Moskovskii telegraf* and parts of Gogol's *Arabeski*, both of which were heavily indebted to the "providential" theories of Herder, Schlozer, and Johann Muller. See Susan Fusso, *Designing Dead Souls: An Anatomy of Disorder in Gogol* (Stanford: Stanford University Press, 1993), 5–19, esp. 10–12.

In *The Captain's Daughter* as well this same *sluchai* will receive its ultimate embodiment in Pushkin's oeuvre: there the competing genre expectations of fiction (cf. *Povesti Belkina*), history (cf. *Istoriia Pugacheva*), and folklore/myth will conspire to produce the "poet in history's" most complex and profoundly simultaneous statement yet about survivorship and unpredictability.

9 In this regard, I disagree with the otherwise perceptive Wachtel, who argues that *sluchai* is less important in the history than in the novel: e.g., "The novel plays up the role of accident and coincidence in history, factors completely absent in the controlled and orderly narrative of *The History of Pugachev*" (Andrew Wachtel, *An Obsession with History: Russian Writers Confront the Past* [Stanford: Stanford University Press, 1994], 73).

thereby preparing the way for Pugachev's successful attack a few hours later.[10] Pushkin of course sees all the poignancy and existential absurdity of this *sluchai*, which leads to disaster rather than a tidy, comic denouement. The historian, however, as opposed to the fiction writer, is not allowed the droll wink.

The principles of Pushkin's un-Karamzinian historiography become evident as soon as we enter the world of the text. Everywhere there is a guiding intelligence, but it is a guiding intelligence that does not intrude on the private worlds of the historical figures, does not project from the documentation their possible inner dialogues in moments of crisis. Furthermore, there is no Karamzinian dialogue or tension between the "story" in the text and the occasional conflicting account of the primary source, left uncommented on, in the notes. Since the motive energy comes primarily from the unpredictable trio of *daring, happenstance, and luck* and not from the consistent exfoliation of one dominant psychological type (the tsar), there is no need to "find a place for everything" in the text. Instead, Pushkin's notes and appendices almost always provide pieces of *specific* or *personal* information that amplify and clarify but do not contradict the text: the fishing practices of the Yaik Cossacks, the exact location of a little-known garrison, the subsequent fate of one of the chief rebels, a personal letter from a military or civic leader explaining what is happening from his point of view, a longer version of the described event from a French source, etc. These supporting documents can show the reader aspects of an individual's inner psychological space, for example, A.I. Bibikov's reactions, as expressed to his family or friends, regarding the woeful state of affairs at the time of his arrival and what he and the others will need to do if they hope to restore order and confidence in the government's management of the uprising.[11] But never in the text itself does Pushkin splice together the previous accounts in an effort to speak from within Bibikov's own "voice zone," to step into his psychological shoes and reason for him, so to speak.

Pushkin's aim is thus both more modest and more ambitious than Karamzin's: to tell, without moralizing *razmyshleniia* (meditations), the verifiably accurate story of the *pugachevshchina* in a way that preserves its fatal energy — the ignitable combination of "daring, happenstance, and luck" — against the backdrop of an otherwise untellable cacophony of source materials (i.e., pro-government military archives, personal memoirs and family correspondence, folklore with its inevitable "poeticization," interviews with aging eyewitnesses and their relatives, etc.). Pushkin's narration, as opposed to Karamzin's, is

---

10 *Pss*, 8:122.

11 A typical example of Pushkin's more psychologically "chaste" treatment of his principal actors is found in the following statement about Bibikov's frame of mind after arriving in Kazan', a city on the verge of mass hysteria because of the rising tide of the *pugachevshchina*, on 25 December 1773: "Bibikov, in an attempt to raise the morale of the citizens and his subordinates, put on a show of equanimity and good cheer, but in fact worry, irritation, and impatience were gnawing at him. The difficulty of his position is vividly described in his letters to Count Chernyshev, Fonvizin, and his family" (*CPF*, 396; *Pss*, 8:144–45). Pushkin then goes on

as far from the "poetic" as can be imagined and still relate the (again, totally de-romanticized) energy of *pugachevshchina*. In it, in the text itself (and not just in the notes), verified fact and a popular energy that is in no way stylized or sentimentalized are absolutely contiguous—a remarkable feat for the Russian historical consciousness of the first third of the 19th century.

It would be a mistake, however, to assume that a literary intelligence as sensitive to issues of composition (*kompositsiia*) as Pushkin's would write a work, even a history, without some sense of cohering structure. *The History of Pugachev* does indeed possess an over-arching structure, but the point is that this structure came to the author from the flow of the events themselves, not from something external to them—what western critics might call a chronotope or an episteme. Description is, as it were, intelligible without being meaningful. There is, importantly, a clearly identifiable point of origin (the appearance of Pugachev on the scene) and point of conclusion (his execution) that the historian in no way has imposed on or "read into" the material. In this regard, the chapters form a parabolic arc describing the chronological rise and fall of the uprising. The first chapter gives the pre-history and origin of the troubles; the second and third chapters present the appearance of Pugachev, the rapid spread of his movement, and the general incompetence and ill timing of the government's response to it; the fourth and fifth chapters center on the efforts of Bibikov to turn the tide against the rebels and to reinstill confidence in the traumatized local population; and the sixth, seventh, and eighth chapters follow Pugachev, who has momentarily regrouped after Bibikov's death, toward his eventual ruin at the hands of the relentless Mikhelson and ultimately his capture and execution.[12] Logically, Pugachev is the personality who appears at the transition from Chapter One to Chapter Two (pre-history to history proper), while Bibikov is the figure who enters and departs the action on two other crucial "seams": the end of Chapter Three and beginning of Chapter Four, when the uprising is growing out of control and the government forces and loyal citizenry are in desperate need of a leader; and the end of Chapter five and the beginning of Chapter Six, when Pugachev's momentum is at last reversed and the baton of leadership is passed from the dying Bibikov to Panin/Mikhelson.

307.
Chapter 13

Immediately to quote at length Bibikov's 30 December 1773 letter to his wife which corroborates the inner states of "worry, irritation, and impatience" and shows him feverishly trying to mobilize his forces and asking the Almighty for help. In other words, there appears to be minimal distortion between the voice of the document (here Bibikov's) and the voice of the historian, whereas in Karamzin's case one could still sense on various occasions a discordance between the (often much earlier) time/worldview of the chronicle account and the overlaying "enlightenment chronotope" of the later historian.

12   Wachtel also points out the structure or compositional integrity of Pushkin's *Istoriia*, although our emphases and ultimate distribution of parts to whole are somewhat different (see below): "The uprising is presented as a completed and well-formed story consisting of a prologue (the historical overview, chapter 1), a beginning (the appearance of Pugachev and the start of the uprising, chapter 2), a middle (the actual course of the rebellion, chapters 3–7), and an end (the collapse of the rebellion and the

The basic narrative currency of this history is the chronological description of troop movements and battles, with their inevitable group dynamics and hence their merely passing interest in the fates of individuals (this latter being a "novelistic" as opposed to "historiographic" concern). The cast of characters is huge and their roles for the most part episodic. This structure, to repeat, cannot be called a plot in literary terms, for there is minimal distortion between what the Formalists would identify as *fabula* and *siuzhet*. Still, what is intriguing is that there is a potentially "poetic" or mythological structure (i.e., Bibikov as "savior" — see below) to the telling of these real events that, because Pushkin refuses to comment on, remains just that — *potential*, what a future poet might use but what the current historian simply includes as the texture of reported speech and perception. This impression of a "plotability"[13] not acted on or prosecuted in any strict literary sense is one of the tantalizing imponderables of Pushkin's narrative. In a text where the author builds his construction of events on the embedded quotations of others, can we rightfully say that this hidden structure is his or the eyewitnesses'? What history of a popular crisis can possibly be made in the first place without some ghostly or "mythological" structure being attached, virtually simultaneously and not necessarily by the historian, to the intentionality of the participants?

In Chapter One, Pushkin begins his history with the statement that "The Yaik River, renamed Ural by Catherine II's decree, issues from the mountains that have given it its present name." And in the last sentences of Chapter Eight, as the historian ends his history, he writes again, "Catherine, wishing to obliterate the memory of [this] terrible epoch, stripped of its ancient name the river whose banks had first witnessed the insurgence."[14] Thus our entry to and our exit from Pushkin's narrative form an epistrophe or conscious symmetry that could be termed "poetic" — i.e., it is the eye of the artist and not the scholar that organizes the material in this manner.[15] On the other hand, Pushkin's motivation for constructing this symmetry appears to be strictly historical or disinterestedly mnemonic: he wants now, between these two references to the renaming, to remind the reader what Catherine has decreed he should forget. This is a perfect example of one of those epistemological imponderables quite characteristic of *The History* and yet unlike anything else in Pushkin: can we say that the poet is here serving the scholar, or the scholar the poet? Whereas elsewhere in Pushkin the aesthetically structuring consciousness always asserts its primacy even as it points to its own "gaps" and unknowability, this simultaneity is of a

execution of Pugachev, chapter 8)" (*An Obsession with History*, 69).

[13] I borrow this term from the excellent discussion of the difference between historical and fictional emplotment in Dan Ungurianu's chapter on *The Captain's Daughter* in his *Plotting History: The Russian Historical Novel in the Imperial Age* (Madison: University of Wisconsin Press, 2007).

[14] CPF, 363, 438.

[15] This symmetry is mentioned as well in Wachtel, *An Obsession with History*, 69.

different order. The historian is seeing what is *already there* and what has happened *only once:* that is to say, the necessary contrast is not between "art" or literary tradition, which must repeat to become itself, and "life," but between "life" that has been forcibly returned to the status of the non-historical and "life" that has not. The absolutely straightforward and slightly dramatized (energized) words emanating from Pushkin's pen defy, as never before, precise ontological description.

Chapter One, as already mentioned, constitutes the necessary pre-history to the appearance of Pugachev. The rebel leader has to come from somewhere, has to grow out of certain concrete circumstances and contributing factors. In order to prepare the way for the principal actor, Pushkin gives a terse but factually rich account of the topography and ethnography of the area along the Ural (Yaik) River, in the general vicinity of Orenburg. He also provides brief sketches of the activities of several of the famous Cossack chieftains (*atamany*) prior to Pugachev: Gugnia, Stenka Razin,[16] Nechai and Shamai. He is careful, in this pre-history, to separate "poetic legend" (*poeticheskoe predanie*), such as that relating to how the roving Cossacks first decided to keep wives and children rather than abandon them, and documentable fact.[17] Into the latter category ("fact") rapidly enter all the evidence underlying the Cossacks' grievances against an arrogant and, in the case of their immediate superiors at the time of the Pugachev uprising, corrupt government: 1) in return for their initial decision to submit to his authority, Tsar Mikhail Fyodorovich granted these Cossacks a deed (*gramota*) to the Yaik River allowing them to take up residence on its banks as "free people" (*vol'nye liudi*); 2) thereafter, during the successive reigns of Peter I, Anna Ivanovna, Elizaveta Petrovna, and Catherine II, an effort was made to bring the Cossacks increasingly under "the general system of state governance,"[18] an effort that was resisted, however, because it traduced local tradition and subverted the well-established (essentially democratic, non-bureaucratic, pre-literary) forms of governance already in place; and 3) beginning in 1762, during the reign of Catherine, the situation became exacerbated when government functionaries imposed harsh new conditions on the Cossacks (withholding of wages, institution of arbitrary taxes, and, most important, infringement on essential fishing rights) that caused them, in 1771, to revolt in earnest. This revolt was quickly put down and the instigators punished. But Pushkin, citing the Cossacks' "just complaints" (*spravedlivye svoi zhaloby*),[19] which is to say, the as yet undissipated trajectory of their righteous anger, saw in retrospect that these feelings had to find some

---

16   Considered, as Pushkin points out, an enemy by the Yaik Cossacks.
17   *Pss*, 8:111.
18   *Pss*, 8:113.
19   Ibid.

violent outlet.[20] The "stern and necessary measures" to reestablish order could not keep the peace. As the aspiring historian wrote three years earlier in the Polevoy review, this was the general shape of events awaiting the specific embodiment of *sluchai*. The clipped, dramatic conclusion to the first chapter shows that Pushkin's voice is now on the verge of entering the wild, energetic stream of *sluchai*-in-motion: "Everything portended a new mutiny. Only a leader was missing. A leader was soon found."[21]

The beginning of Chapter Two, announced in the headings as "*poiavlenie Pugacheva*" (the appearance of Pugachev), changes the focus of Pushkin's history. The vague threatening atmosphere ("Everything portended a mutiny.") and the passive construction ("A leader was soon found.") at the end of Chapter One suddenly coalesce into the following: "In this time of trouble an unknown vagrant drifted about among the Cossack homesteads, taking jobs now with this, now with that master, and dabbling in all manner of handicrafts."[22] The Russian is far more expressive than the English here: the reference to *smutnoe sie vremia* (this time of trouble) conjures up immediately other episodes involving impostors and bloodshed in Russia's past, while the *nanimaias' v rabotniki* (hiring himself out in the absence of a fixed master) and the *prinimaias' za vsiakie remesla* (taking on odd jobs in the absence of a fixed trade) suggest that this was a faceless bundle of peripatetic energy looking for *something to attach to*. This sentence is indeed one of the most enigmatic and "pregnant" in the entire historiographical text. Pushkin commences by deliberately not naming this force, since it is *sluchai* incarnate, and the energy does not originate with it; rather, this "*unknown vagrant*" is the focus, the fulcrum, for what is about to happen.[23]

Pugachev is also the personal, yet largely unconscious, site, as it were, for those distillates of popular energy that allow the rebellion to come into being: daring, happenstance, and luck. The very first thing the historian remarks about Pugachev's behavior (as opposed to his movements) is "He was noted for the boldness [*derzost'*] of his statements—for heaping abuse on the authorities and inciting the Cossacks to flee to the lands of the Turkish Sultan."[24] An inspired, outrageous liar, Pugachev began by launching little flaming arrows of rumor and seeing if they would catch fire somewhere among the local populace: his assertions, for example, that, in order to subsidize the rebels' activities, he had amassed some 20,000 rubles in cash and 70,000 rubles

---

20 The Cossacks had been divided into two factions early in the 18th century: the "Ataman" (from Ataman Merkur'ev) and the "Longinov" (from Lieutenant-Colonel [*starshina*] Longinov), or "popular" (*narodnaia*). It was the latter that was the more unruly, so that eventually, by the time of the 1770's uprisings, the two were generally referred to as the "obedient" (*poslushnaia*) and "disobedient" (*neposlushnaia*).

21 *CPF*, 368; *Pss*, 8:115.

22 *CPF*, 368; *Pss*, 8:116.

23 Only much later in the paragraph, after setting up his dramatic appearance and detailing his initial movements and actions, does Pushkin write "This vagrant was Emelian Pugachev" (*CPF*, 371; *Pss*, 8:116).

24 *CPF*, 369; *Pss*, 8:116.

in goods at the border, and that "some pasha or other" was ready to provide another 5,000,000 upon the Cossacks' arrival; or his prediction that "around Christmas or Epiphany a riot [*bunt*] was inevitable." Luck and happenstance conspire as well from his earliest movements to prepare the way for his success: when caught in the village of Malykovka as one of the "disobedient" Cossacks, Pugachev was taken to Kazan for sentencing; yet just three days before the sentence (lashing followed by exile and hard labor in Pelym) was to be confirmed, on 19 June 1773, he was freed by his co-conspirators in a daring escape plot that itself must have been largely improvised. Pugachev and his confederates needed more than the ill-aimed darts of fantastic tales, however. They needed the sort of rumor that would give their undertaking legitimacy among the people. Because as a group they couldn't bear the thought of leaving their beloved Yaik and its familiar shores (the original idea of flight to Turkey), the conspirators lighted upon a second alternative: "Instead of fleeing, they decided to riot again. Imposture, they thought, would be a reliable motive force. All it required was a bold [*derzkii*] and resolute vagabond [*proslets*] not yet known to the people. Their choice fell on Pugachev."²⁵

So, the "strange rumors" (*strannye slukhi*) about a miraculously returned Peter III began to take root in the people's imagination.²⁶ And so too, predictably, as the Cossack Mikhailo Kozhevnikov testified at the time, did the "stranger" (*neznakomets*)²⁷ declare that not only was he "the Emperor Peter III" but that "*the rumors about his death were false.*"²⁸ In a twist of fate familar to readers of *Boris Godunov* but happening here indisputably in reality, the rumor of a resurrected tsar is substantiated by calling the fact of his death itself a rumor. The "facts" of history become hopelessly distorted and inverted in a popular "text" based much more on the dictates of suppressed desire than on those of logic or reason. This is of course what the people, at least the "disobedient" ones, had been waiting for—the torch to go with the powder-keg of their massive indignation. It mattered not that Pugachev's various declarations were, in the historian's words, a "ridiculous tale" (*nelepaia povest'*).²⁹ Nor did it matter that the powder-keg was lit by an utterly cynical

25 CPF, 372; Pss, 8:116.
26 Rumors continue to play a pivotal role in the unfolding rebellion. To give one of many such examples, Reinsdorp, the hapless governor of the Orenburg province, attempted to descredit Pugachev in one of his circulars by announcing that "the man engaged in villainous acts in the Yaik region *is rumored to be* [*nositsia slukh*] of an estate different from the one in which he truly belongs," when "in fact" he was none other than the Don Cossack Emelyan Pugachev, "who had been flogged and had his face branded for previous crimes" (CPF, 380; Pss, 8:127). However, this latter allegation was false—Pugachev had not been flogged, nor had he had his face branded for previous crimes. Thus the rebels could use the false rumors of the government to descredit the enemy who had been trying to diescredit them. And of course Reinsdorp does not help his cause by writing in "a tangled, obscure style [*temnyi i zaputannyi slog*]"— a style that seems to dominate government descriptions of events until the arrival of the sane and direct Bibikov.

27 Who, by the way, looked nothing as all like the deceased monarch, as Pushkin's precise physical description of the *samozvanets* (impostor) makes clear at this point.

28 CPF, 372; Pss, 8:118.
29 Pss, 8:118.

gesture (the Cossacks' idea to deploy the tactic of *samozvanstvo* [imposture]) and that Pugachev was himself more manipulated than manipulating, a "puppet" (*chuchela* [sic]), in Bibikov's perceptive phrase, in the hands of his lieutenants.[30] The point is that the people now had a legitimate lightning-rod for their frustration — a "good" tsar who had been deposed illegally by his "bad" spouse (what's more, a woman and foreigner!), thus making Catherine herself an impostor, and who had returned to undo the harm of the present unjust regime. The uprising was now ready to begin.

From the moment when Pugachev attacks his first fortress (Yaitsky Gorodok, on 18 September 1773) until the initial appearance of Bibikov in Kazan three months later (25 December), we follow a virtually unobstructed ascending line of rebel victories and government losses and blunders. One after the other the small towns and military garrisons either fall to savage enemy attack or sustain significant losses and teeter on the brink of catastrophe: Yaitsky Gorodok, Iletsky Gorodok, Rassypnaya, Nizhne-Ozernaya, Tatishcheva, Chernorechenskaya, Sakmarsky Gorodok, Prechistenkaya. Larger towns and cities such as Orenburg and Kazan are also under siege and dangerously susceptible to the rebels' flexible military tactics and shrewd psychological warfare. And all the while Pugachev's rag-tag forces are growing at an astonishing rate: from 300 to 3000 to 10000 to, eventually, upwards to 25000. It is in these pages of the *History* that Pushkin constantly tries to bring together various viewpoints simultaneously (i.e., in rapid juxtaposition) in an attempt to show how the *pugachevshchina* was being played out in the minds and activities of the various camps. Each attack or siege, for example, forms a single episodic link in a chain that is then connected by "joints" or "clasps" of contemporaneous information: how Pugachev performed the role tsar-*batiushka* after each victory (the ritual kissing of hand/blessing), how the defensive measures undertaken by Reinsdorp (the governor of the Orenburg *guberniya*) seemed ironically to play into the hands of the opposition, how Pugachev's army was recruited and paid, what the customary forms of address and behavior toward Pugachev were both within his immediate circle and in public, how the various leaders of the insurrection (Ovchinnikov, Shigaev, Lysov, Chumakov, Beloborodov, Padurov, Perfilev, Khlopusha, etc.) took on the names and ranks of tsarist generals and grandees in their kangaroo court, how the arrogant General Kar (Bibikov's predecessor) grossly underestimated the wiliness and resourcefulness of Pugachev, etc. Thus the "crisis time" of each individual confrontation with Pugachev, where the issue of life or death is decided quickly and brutally and

---

30 See Bibikov's letter to D.I. Fonvizin of 29 January 1774 in *Pss*, 8:397.

where the logic is strictly chronological (i.e., Pugachev's "path"), is framed by this extraordinary situation's version of "everyday time," where the reader learns what the participants were doing when they were not fighting or defending but where the next crisis always *feels* imminent.

One of the strikingly characteristic traits of Pushkin's—as opposed to Karamzin's—history is the description of a crisis situation with absolutely no reference to a larger enlightenment chronotope. By this one means that Pushkin is maximally interested in how an individual will react in the face of death, when this popular storm has now been, suddenly and "by chance," visited on him, and there is nowhere else to turn. Here the only options for an officer are "honorable death" (declaring one's oath of allegiance to Catherine and thereby incurring Pugachev's wrath) or "dishonorable life" (swearing a new oath of allegiance to the "people's tsar" and thereafter being viewed by the world as a coward and traitor). In this regard, one is judged in the eyes of "history" not by one's inner sensibility or positive virtues in everyday life (which in any event Pushkin couldn't know for the minor actors), but simply, and severely, by *what one does at the last*. Pushkin the historian seems to be almost obsessed by these "gallows revelations" of character: they are presumably, together with the recording of the progress of the revolt itself, among the most important traces of the past that his historiographical project has exhumed and fixed.

Considering, therefore, the author's own fastidious concern with matters of honor, particularly "honor under fire," it should come as no surprise that Pushkin seems closest to shedding his mask of roving camera-eye and, as it were, to "editorializing" precisely during these crisis moments. For instance, Pushkin presents the horrific violence of Pugachev's rampage during the rebel leader's first victories without the slightest hint of luridness or self-indulgence; instead, in direct, non-emotional language, which in this context is all the more powerful, he describes such scenes as Major Kharlov's[31] disfigured face prior to execution ("One of his eyes, poked out by a lance, dangled over his cheek"[32]) or Colonel Elagin[33] in the process of being skinned alive. These deaths are doubtless terrible and, if one likes, supremely "uncivilized," though the historian, to repeat, lets the details speak for themselves. But then, when the condemned are led to the gallows, one can detect Pushkin entering a foot or two on stage and proclaiming, "Not one of the victims betrayed a faint heart. Bikbai, a Muhammadan, crossed himself as he mounted the scaffold, and put his neck in the noose himself."[34] By the same token, toward the end of the same chapter (2), when reporting how Prechistenkaya fortress voluntarily surrendered (i.e., both the officers and

31 Kharlov was the commandant of the Nizhne-Ozernaya fortress and the husband of Elizaveta Kharlova, who subsequently became Pugachev's concubine for a time.

32 CPF, 376; Pss, 8:122.

33 Elagin was the commandant of Tatishcheva and the father of Elizaveta Kharlova (see note 31).

34 CPF, 376; Pss, 8:122.

the soldiers) to Pugachev, Pushkin writes that this was the first time that the rebel leader had "disgraced the officers by sparing them" (*v pervyi raz okazal pozornuiu milost' ofitseram*).³⁵ Just as *sluchai* is not attached to some higher positive novelistic consciousness in the *History*—i.e., it is not a "happenstance" to tie up loose ends but to unravel them further—so too is *milost'* (mercy) *pozornaia* (shameful) in the *History*, because it has been bought at too high a price—a price that in *The Captain's Daughter* would simply be part of a larger, generically "permissible" Christian framework.

Although Pushkin, as much as it is in his power, lets his documents speak for him, there comes a moment in the *History* when the reader feels the fictional equivalent of climax: first the rebel cause spreads out of hand; then it is met with a controlled resistance that slows the wave until one decisive victory turns the momentum in the opposite direction; and finally, although Pugachev escapes and continues uncannily to reassemble forces, the rebel leader's black-magical hold on the local population is broken and it is just a matter of time before the answering wave, itself now gathering strength, overtakes over him. This climactic turn is attached to one personality in the *History:* Alexander Ilich Bibikov. Pushkin's genre requires that the focus of his telling remain group-oriented: he cannot, needless to say, foreground Bibikov unduly at the expense of other participants. For this reason, Bibikov appears as the actual topic of extended discussion only three times in the text: at the end of Chapter Three, in the middle of Chapter Four, and at the end of Chapter Five. Nevertheless, Bibikov's presence is felt profoundly from the moment he appears on the scene until his death a few months later. He becomes the hero of this history, and he does so in a manner that cannot strictly be called fictional (everything is documented, at no time does Pushkin step into his familiar role as fictional god, etc.) and yet, strange to say, is *more* powerful than *vymysel* (invention), precisely because it holds up to its audience, *without showing it is conscious of it*, an example of the personal crossing over to the historical and the potentially mythical *simultaneously*. Pushkin is able to achieve this epistemological frisson (*what* is it we know here?) by using the primary sources to establish a synchrony: the timing of Bibikov's arrival and demise, the timing of the church calendar, and the timing of the shift in momentum in the campaign against the rebel forces. To repeat a crucial point, however, at no time does Pushkin comment in an authorial voice on the "coincidence" of these various calendars: *that* connection is left to the reader but is obvious from eyewitness accounts as constitutive of "meaning" for those undergoing the ordeal at the time. Hence, Bibikov is first mentioned by Pushkin

---

35 *CPF*, 378; *Pss*, 8:125.

36 *Pss*, 8:137.

37 *Unynie* (despair, loss of all hope) is the worst of all sins according to the Russian Orthodox faith.

38 *CPF*, 395; *Pss*, 8:144.

as one of the most remarkable (*zamechatel'neishii*) individuals of Catherine's epoch: courageous soldier and revered statesman, veteran of numerous military and political campaigns, known both for his loyalty and his honesty and independent thought. When asked by a smiling (but needful) Empress at a court ball to take on the assignment, Bibikov is reported to have responded with a quote from a folk song that shows beautifully his combination of loyalty, common-sense, and humor: "My sarafan, my dear sarafan! / Everywhere you come in handy; / And when you're not needed, sarafan, then just lie under the bench."[36] He then leaves St. Petersburg on December 9 and, passing through a tense Moscow, arrives in Kazan, at the center of the revolt, on December 25. Kazan is at this point a desperate, despairing (*unyvshii*)[37] city: those citizens that can have abandoned it and those that have remained have little hope. Bibikov brings the equivalent of the Christmas spirit to these countrymen (but again Pushkin never says this in his own words): on January 1 he helps the Archbishop (*arkhierei* Veniamin) celebrate a public prayer service, i.e., he encourages the city to "turn over a new leaf" that is fortunately (or *sluchaino*) synchronized with the coming of the New Year, and then he gathers all the nobles and delivers a speech (the first real effective use of language on the part of ruling class) that explains the present situation simply and directly and lays out a plan for what must be done to reverse the rising tide of anarchy. He calls on his compatriots to come to his aid and to supply new recruits. He also lets it be known that the Empress has "conveyed to the Kazan nobility her imperial favor, goodwill, and patronage," and in a separate letter to the general has offered to contribute to the effort and has signed herself symbolically "as a Kazan landowner."[38] These efforts immediately galvanize the people and seem to return hope to the devastated city, and yet the historian makes it clear in the very next paragraph of Chapter Four that Bibikov himself had grave doubts about his future course of action against the rebels.

Chapter Five provides the crucial turning-point in what many commentators, including some celebrated historians, have deemed a less than compelling, and in places *fragmented* to the point of being unreadable, narrative.[39] Unlike Karamzin, Pushkin makes very few concessions to the thirst for "prefiguring" (in White's sense) unity experienced by even exacting, scholarly readers. Be this as it may, Chapter Five is crucial because it comes physically half-way through the text, especially if we take into account the space devoted to pre-history in Chapter One, and because it contains the "break" (*perelom*) in Pugachev's momentum that suggests his wave has crested and is preparing to return in the opposite direction: still full of destructive force and capable of

---

39   Just to cite one example, the well-known emigre historian Marc Raeff, while praising Pushkin for his thorough research and documentation, considers the multi-perspectival narration of the *History* "boring"—the assumption being there is, amid all the descriptions of troop movements and battles, not enough "human" glue holding the larger scholarly enterprise together. See his chapter on "Pugachev's Rebellion" in *Preconditions of Revolution in Early Modern Europe* (Baltimore: Johns Hopkins Press, 1970).

stirring countless popular eddies, it is no longer on the ascendant. The long-awaited *perelom* takes place at the battle of Tatishcheva (22 March 1774). And although Pushkin of course makes no meta-commentary, this is precisely the moment in the text when fictional possibilities begin, one must assume, to swarm in his head: the night before, Pugachev, "with his typical *daring*, in a heavy *snowstorm*,"[40] had attacked Prince Golitsyn's vanguard, but had been repulsed by Majors Pushkin and Elagin (the latter, fighting bravely, as the historian hastens to add, was killed in this action). Then Pugachev, after first making a move toward Iletsky Gorodok, *suddenly* (note again: the element of *sluchainost'*) turned toward Tatishcheva and, upon entering the fortress, took up a fortified position there and waited for the arrival of his adversary. This was the head-on confrontation that Bibikov and his forces had been hoping for. At the same time, Golitsyn left his transport under the command of Lieutenant-Colonel *Grinev* before turning to face Pugachev.

Here, in one pregnant node of the text, we find the (potentially mythological) snowstorm motif (what Pugachev will emerge *from* in the novel) and the names of Pushkin, Elagin, and Grinev. The reader cannot help but recall—for who can forget this most gruesome scene in the entire *History*?—that it had been *Colonel* Elagin, the Commander of this same Tatishcheva, who had died such a horrible death defending his post the previous September and the fate of whose family provided such a tragic real-life shadowing for the fictional Mironovs (i.e., the husband flayed alive, the wife hacked to pieces, the daughter made into Pugachev's concubine and eventually, along with her little brother, murdered as well). In the novel Pushkin will send his own Grinev into the popular snowstorm; in that topsy-turny world where rebel tsars are folkloric wolves-turned-friends and "proxy fathers" (*posazhennye ottsy*), the hero will manage to save his Elizaveta (Elagina-)Kharlova, and she him. Peasant daring, which has its own version of honor, and a nobleman's honor, which has its own version of daring, will grow "miraculously" into extensions of one another beginning with that snowstorm. Now, however, the laconic historian can only be slightly aroused by the knowledge that he has arrived at the point in his story when, personalities aside, something momentous and pivotal is about to happen.

For the first time during the rebellion, Pugachev sustains a decisive defeat.[41] 1300 rebels die within the fortress walls alone, while outside their bodies are scattered across the countryside. 36 cannon are seized and more than 3000 insurgents taken prisoner. Somehow Pugachev manages to fight through the swarm of adversaries and make it to Berda with a handful of loyal Cossacks. There he and Khlopusha are momentarily held by Shigaev, another rebel leader, who plans to

---

40 *Pss*, 8:154.
41 "Victory [for the government forces] was decisive" (*Pobeda byla reshitel'naia*) (*Pss*, 8:155).

turn the former over to Reinsdorp to save his own head. But the governor fails to act quickly enough, and the two are suddenly released (another example of *sluchai* and *udacha*) by a group of sympathizing convicts that happen to be in Berda. Pugachev immediately flees with some 10 cannon and what is left of his mob-like army (approximately 2000 men), while Khlopusha, who sets off to save his family, is soon caught, returned to Orenburg, and beheaded in June. Bibikov, as Pushkin reports, is waiting anxiously for news of precisely this turning-point (*sei perelom*). He is enroute from Kazan to Orenburg, in order to be closer to the theater of battle, when he receives the news of "the total defeat of Pugachev" (*sovershennoe porazhenie Pugacheva*).[42]

It is at this juncture in his narrative, with Pugachev momentarily (though apparently ultimately) routed, that Pushkin turns to the mini-drama of Yaitsky Gorodok. The story of Yaitsky Gorodok is, like the *perelom* Bibikov had been waiting for, crucial to the history. It is so because it tells the trajectory of the larger tale in miniature and because it combines two contradictory "plot functions": it is the "cradle of the rebellion" (*pervoe gnezdo bunta*[43]) and it is also the fortress *that Pugachev never takes*[44] — i.e., through its sacrifice and its willingness to meet the peasant's "daring, happenstance, and luck" with a resistance, or "honor," equally powerful, it helps to turn the tide and comes to symbolize, when finally liberated, that the tide has been turned. Just as important, the siege of Yaitsky Gorodok lasts precisely as long as Bibikov's sacrificial command: from Christmas/New Year's to Easter. Pushkin bases his account of the siege on an *anonymous* eye-witness report that was published in P.P. Svinin's *Otechestvennye zapiski* (*Notes of the Fatherland*)[45] and that impressed him, as he says in a note, because it bore "the precious imprint of truth, unembellished and simple-hearted."[46] In order to tell the story of Yaitsky Gorodok, the historian has to back up a bit in time: a fact of narration that implies that pure simultaneity will not work here (i.e., the drama depends on build-up and retardation, frustrated expectations that are not the stock-in-trade of the novelist but that *really happened*). Thus, in a way, judging from Pushkin's telling, it would be a conceit for the modern reader to think of these plot functions as fictional or inventive; rather it would be closer to the truth to think of them as necessary categories of consciousness — the tools at hand that the besieged population used simply *to survive*. To put it another way, the slight difference between *fabula* and *siuzhet*, between seamless story-line and syncopated plot, is not here motivated (at least not primarily) by an author's proprietary urge for inventiveness or originality, but by an historian's urge to find in real life those shreds and fragments of "meaning" used by others as

---

42 *Pss*, 8:156.

43 *Pss*, 8:142.

44 "His wife [i.e., Pugachev's new wife Ustinia Kuznetsova] remained in Yaitsky Gorodok [i.e., after their marriage in early February], where he came to visit her every week. Each time he arrived there was a new attempt on the fortress. But the besieged did not lose heart. Their cannon never grew silent, and their sorties never ceased" (*CPF* 402; *Pss*, 8:152).

45 The title of the anonymous article was "Oborona laitskoi kreposti ot partii miatezhnikov" [The Defense of the Yaitsky Fortress against a Group of Rebels].

46 *Pss*, 8:224.

something unmistakably "historical" is happening around them and to them. The siege of Yaitsky Gorodok was a story that Pushkin did not author, but genuinely *edited*. It was a situation in which he, so used to ruses (authors passing themselves off as editors), must have felt quite at home.

Pushkin uses the eyewitness account to present the final six, most horrific weeks of the siege. The reader is prepared with the news that General Mansurov (one of Bibikov's commanders) has captured Iletsky Gorodok on April 6 or 7, has crossed the Bykovka River (where he successfully repelled a rebel attack) on April 15, and is headed in the direction of Yaitsky Gorodok.[47] Help appears to be on the way, although no one in the fortress is aware of this fact. Pushkin then moves into his long and detailed description of the siege, clearly the climax to Chapter Five, with the temporally retreating topic sentence "The fortress had been under siege since the very beginning of the year."[48] The following pages are among the most moving and tense in Pushkin's text: we learn how the trapped and desperate population was under constant threat from sappers; how their only form of defense were periodic sorties, which finally had to be stopped because they were met with ever greater ferocity on the part of the rebels (i.e., wounded soldiers were immediately cut down and beheaded); how they were terrorized with repeated rebel rumors about the imminent arrival (even more full of retribution) of Pugachev; how virtually no one was allowed to sleep (because of the fear of assault) and thus how everyone was driven to the point of utter exhaustion; how starvation became the rebels' principal weapon for unnerving the enemy, so that after eating all that was left of horse, dog, and cat meat, the fortress inhabitants invented a clay-based kissel, which provided no nourishment but partially alleviated the hunger pangs; how women begged the rebels to take mercy on them but then, after being held for a night, were driven back into the fortress, etc. All of these details, conveyed primarily in substantive nouns and verbs and almost in the total absence of emotional or "atmospheric" adjectives, add up to a picture of a community in maximal crisis, under threat of losing its last shreds of dignity or "civilization" before an enraged mob overruns it and destroys it. No wonder Pushkin repeats twice his use of the loaded word *unynie* (despair) in this context, for this is the Orthodox Russian sin (utter lack of hope) that these people are on the brink of committing as they ponder their final moves.

Again, one hesitates to claim, as usually happens in these circumstances, that Pushkin's telling is itself the master-key. It is, to be sure, but more importantly, the "facts" don't belong to him. The narrative symmetries and "coincidences" are not his, but these peoples' who lived these apocalyptic last weeks and

[47] *Pss*, 8:158.
[48] *Pss*, 8:158.

days. The rebels promised *pomilovanie* (mercy) if only the besieged would voluntarily surrender. This was how the wily insurgents tried to influence first the women and then, through them, the fortress leadership. But the commanders, rightly, did not believe this promise. Moreover, the leadership could not even bring itself to suggest that help was on the way (which ironically it was!), because they realized that their people could not suffer any further embitterment, any more *unynie*: "Nobody would even listen to them [i.e., the commanders talking about liberating reinforcements] without indignation: how embittered had their hearts become with the long futile waiting."[49] It is now that Pushkin comes to the existential denouement of the siege: those in the fortress, having fed themselves for 15 straight days on the ersatz kissel, decide that it is better to *die the honorable death of warriors* (*umeret' chetsnoiu smert'iu voinov*) than simply to starve. Thus, with no hope of victory but at least with a choice of how to die, they undertake to a man[50] a last desperate sortie. The "honorable" logic of the commanders wins the day: "They tried to arouse, in the souls of these unfortunate people, hope in God, all-powerful and all-seeing, and those sufferers who did manage to take heart repeated that it was better to give oneself up to His will than to serve a *villain* [*razboinik*]. And [indeed], during the entire time of the calamitous siege, there were, with the exception of two or three men, no deserters from the fortress."[51] It happens that the Tuesday (April 15) appointed for the final sortie occurs during Passion Week (*Strastnaia Nedelia*). Pushkin, in his historiographical "chasteness," gives the reader no help here: can God really be here somewhere or is this merely another example of chaotic "coincidence"? The crux of the siege, in its most basic, literal sense, involves the absence of "daily bread": the rebels are trying to break the adversary by denying him daily sustenance. One of the chief messages of Easter Week, naturally uncommented upon by Pushkin, is that Christ gave his body, in a symbolic last supper that provides renewal, so that others might live. These last paragraphs of the siege description are filled with references to bread, the most fundamental item of food (again, by implication, at the center of the communion ritual), that which the rebels have and that which the besieged desperately want. On the day of the sortie, the sentries placed on the church roof see that the rebels in town are full of confused activity and many are taking leave of each other and riding off into the steppe. Suddenly those in the fortress understand that an unexpected change may be at hand: "The beseiged had guessed that something extraordinary was happening and again gave themselves up to hope. 'All this gave us such courage,' says an eye-witness of the siege, who had withstood all its horror. '*It was as though we*

319.
Chapter 13

---

49 *Pss*, 8:160.
50 Only the totally exhausted and sick would be left behind. All others, it was agreed, would participate in the last-ditch sortie (*Pss*, 8:160).
51 *Pss*, 8:160.

had eaten a piece of bread'."⁵² But the horror is not over yet. After a time, the bustle passes and all returns to its besieged routine. "Despair [*unynie*], worse than before, took possession of the beleaguered people."⁵³ Then suddenly (*vdrug*), late in the day, all the remaining rebel forces and "disobedient" townspeople approach the fortress with their bound leaders in front: they are now surrendering to the fortress and begging for *pomilovanie* (mercy)! As tokens of their submission they bring loaves of bread (*kovrigi khleba*). Although Easter Sunday (*Svetloe Voskresenie*) is still four days away, this day becomes for the victors a holy/radiant/Easter holiday (*svetlyi prazdnik*), writes the eyewitness.⁵⁴ "Even those who had been unable to rise out of weakness and illness were *instanteously cured*."⁵⁵ Everyone in the fortress is renewed, full of energy, and most of all *thankful to God*. They learn that Orenburg has been liberated and that Mansurov, who will arrive two days later on April 17, is on the way. And Pushkin describes all this without once suggesting that he in any way *shares* the fragments of meaning in this "miraculous" deliverance.

His composition, however, seems to give him away. Or does it? "Such was the success (*uspekh*) of the orders/directives of the skillful, intelligent military leader. But Bibikov did not manage [*ne uspel*] to see through to the end that which he had begun,"⁵⁶ announce the opening sentences of the final paragraph of Chapter Five. Here Pushkin is playing with a type of success (*uspekh*) that implies force of will and that opposes the more accidental (*sluchainyi*) notion of good luck, the *udacha* that is not earned but "given" by fate, of Pugachev. And while the historian does not make the connection for the reader, this success comes at a cost — there is inevitably a sacrificial victim whose death *can be interpreted* as the price of Yaitsky Gorodok's liberation. The general comes down with a fever in Bugulma and dies on April 9, only 44 years old, "tired out by work, worry, and troubles, taking little care of his already failing health."⁵⁷ To the end Bibikov is carrying out his duties — putting his papers in order, informing the Empress of the liberation of Ufa, passing on his command to General Shcherbatov, etc. Pushkin pointedly ends Chapter Five with a description of this noble death which then expands into a summarizing eulogy, although chronologically the reader is already aware that Mansurov has arrived in Yaitsky Gorodok on April 17, that is, 8 days *after* his commander has succumbed. In other words, the news about Bibikov can be seen as the necessary conclusion and frame — of the *siuzhet* if not the *fabula* — for the Easter message: his heroic efforts, his concern for others coupled with his disregard for himself, in some mysterious way enabled the *perelom*. Pushkin organizes his telling so that this interpretation *must* be

52   Pss, 8:160.
53   Pss, 8:160.
54   Pss, 8:161.
55   Pss, 8:161.
56   Pss, 8:161.
57   CPF, 411; Pss, 8:161.

58   Pss, 8:162.
59   About Mikhel'son's first confrontation with the rebel leader near Varlamov on 22 May 1774 Pushkin writes, "This was the first time the pretender came face to face with the man who was to strike so many blows at him and was to put an end to his bloody enterprise" (CPF, 414; Pss 8:166).

60   E.g., in Chapter 6 Pushkin has a difficult time concealing his contempt for Major

present in the reader's mind in the context of the Eastertime liberation of Yaitsky Gorodok. Just as Simonov, the commandant of the fortress at Yaitsky Gorodok, accepts the townspeople in their plea for mercy and cannot believe his liberation (*izbavlenie*), which in the Christian context sounds close to salvation (*spasenie*), so does the city of Kazan want to inter its liberator (*izbavitel'*), again, a slightly secularized or military version of *spasitel'* (the Paschal Savior), in its cathedral. The message is transparent without being explicit, the meaning "real" without being fictionally "embellished." Last but not least, Bibikov's final words appear to be "Christian" in a way that the non-editorializing Pushkin would certainly approve: "I am not sorry for my wife and children; the Empress will look after them. I am sorry for [or I regret parting with] my fatherland."[58]

The remainder of *The History Pugachev* reflects the passing of this climax: P.I. Panin replaces Bibikov, and Mikhelson becomes the embodiment of Pugachev's "nemesis," the constant reminder that the *perelom* Bibikov had been waiting for has now happened and the "wave" is pursuing the rebel leader instead of bearing him aloft and drawing him forward.[59] There are numerous other instances of individual heroism and perfidy, each pregnant with private reckonings and each "chastely" commented upon by the honor-obsessed Pushkin,[60] but the group dynamics of the rebellion, its macro-plot, have altered. It is only a matter of time before Pugachev's confederates, sensing defeat and, with it, exposure and punishment, begin to entertain thoughts of betraying their "emperor." The historian duly records the fitful, zig-zag demise of Pugachev, where his very flight (*begstvo*) resembles an attack (*nashestvie*),[61] right up to the moment of his execution. These last chapters, especially six and seven,[62] by far the shortest in the History, while "conscientious" (the *dobrosovestnyi* of the Preface), lack narrative energy. It is as if Pushkin has solved for himself the riddle of the *pugachevshchina*, including its deadly confrontation between *sluchai* and *chest'*, and is now eager to conclude his labor. The personal can become historical in these chapters only in the category of victim, but not as agent of change. And whereas heroism and

Skrypitsyn, who had been sent by Brant to defend the fortress at Osa (18–20 June 1774) (*Pss*, 8:169). When Pugachev surrounded and stormed the fortress, Skrypitsyn asked for a day to consider the options, then surrendered to the rebel forces. He accepted Pugachev into the fortress *on his knees*, with the requisite icons and the offering of bread and salt—for Pushkin a humiliation worse than the loss of one's life. Skrypitsyn believed he could trick Pugachev by writing a letter in which he explained his action and then retaining the letter on his person, in the hope that the liberating forces would exculpate him. He tried, in other words, to explain his "dishonorable" action by appealing to the weight of circumstances. But one of his co-conspirators, Second Lieutenant Mineev, denounced Skrypitsyn to Pugachev, who quickly had him hanged. In the eyes of history, as recorded by Pushkin, Skrypitsyn lost *both* his honor and his life, a double insult resulting from his attempt to "cheat" in a matter of honor. See also Pushkin's reference to the *shameful apology* (*postydnoe izvinenie*) of the disabled officers in Kurmysh, who swore allegiance to Pugachev out of "fear of death" (*smertnyi strakh*) in Chapter 8 (*Pss*, 8:181).

61   *Pss*, 8:179.

62   Chapter 8, which details, among other things, the betrayal, capture, and execution of Pugachev, has its own internal drama, so that the historian seems to revive his narrative "energy," as it were, especially toward the end.

sacrifice are always real, such as the courage of Mikhelson and the faith of Archbishop Veniamin,[63] they no longer seem to affect the momentum of events — hence the historian's "impatience." They seem, instead, only to embody it further.

In conclusion, one of the implicit aims of this essay has been to suggest how a constructive dialogue between the best traditions of Russian/Soviet "philological" research (say, Ovchinnikov's careful tracing of Pushkin's sources as he worked on *History of Pugachev*) and Western "new historicism" with its "metahistorical" emphasis on any history's impulse to narrative framing (Hayden White, W.B. Gallie, Arthur Danto, Morton White, and others) may help us to pose the issue of Pushkin's "historical consciousness" in new and useful ways. To return to the powerful description of the siege of the Yaik Fortress (Yaitsky Gorodok), when Pushkin ties the liberation of the desperate inhabitants to the events of Easter Week and then, in the conclusion of the chapter, tells of the death of Bibikov — *which happened before the actual liberation*—in sacrificial terms, is this a "poetic" plotting of events? Can we use the term "poetic" in this way? Is Pushkin, within his own time-space, being simply an editor and "splicer" of facts, or is he crossing the line into the realm of art and *vymysel* (fictional emplottedness)?[64] As M.L. Gasparov has argued eloquently in the context of post-Bakhtinian studies, it is by no means as simple as we think to "enter into dialogue" with a mind like Pushkin's — to engage him *on our terms* ("metahistory") as if he understands, or cares to understand, the questions we pose him. Would Pushkin, in the manner of a Roland Barthes or a Hayden White, call the arrangement of others' accounts that went into the telling of the siege of the Yaik Fortress a "fiction"? Presumably not. The suffering, the starvation, the loss of the last vestiges of "civilization," the omnipresence of death—all this was not "fiction." The historian could foreground or dramatize, but *he could not invent*. Narrative organization, simply because it came later, was not for that reason more "real" than the words of the fortress inhabitants trapped and preparing to die. What we out of academic scepticism may call "poetic" Pushkin may perceive as the minimal cognitive texture enabling any historical understanding — what separates pure chronology (the *fabula* of the *letopis'* [chronicle]) from the meaning-generation possible in any *siuzhet* (a position on the outside that allows for *re*-arrangement and closure).

63 This holy man, the Archbishop (*arkhierei*) of Kazan, was the same one who had conducted a prayer service (*molebstvie*) at the beginning of the New Year after Bibikov's arrival. His steadfast behavior during the assault on Kazan, as described by Pushkin in Chapter 7 (*Pss*, 8:173), would have appealed to the historian on several counts, not least because it did not leave Veniamin even when the latter subsequently fell into disfavor: i.e., for a time Catherine apparently believed the wrongful slander being circulated about him by one of the rebels (Aristov). Eventually, however, the priest's name was cleared in a letter from the Empress herself, who rewarded him with the title of Metropolitan. See Pushkin's note 2 to Chapter 7 (*Pss*, 8:226–27).

64 See discussion in Svetlana Evdokimova, *Pushkin's Historical Imagination* (New Haven: Yale University Press, 1999), 23–24.

PART III
Reading Russian Writers Reading Themselves and Others

Chapter 14   *Sorrento Photographs:*   323.
            Khodasevich's Memory Speaks[1]

The Russian poet Vladislav Khodasevich (1886–1939), who spent the last seventeen years of his life in Western Europe, wrote a total of five books of verse: the first two, Youth (*Molodost'*, 1908) and The Happy Little House (*Shchastlivyi domik*, 1914), are largely derivative and, by the poet's own admission, immature;[2] the last three, Grain's Way (*Putem zerna*, 1920), The Heavy Lyre (*Tiazhelaia lira*, 1922), and European Night (*Evropeiskaia noch'*, 1927), form the limited body of his mature work.[3] It is on the basis of the last three collections that Khodasevich's modest reputation has been established. It is ironic that the relative obscurity of Khodasevich's best work bears witness to the vagaries of exile about which he often wrote. Indeed, in 1922, the year Khodasevich left Russia, Valéry published *Charmes*, Proust died while polishing his novel, Eliot founded the journal *Criterion* and printed *The Waste Land* in its pages, and Joyce's *Ulysses* was released in a small Parisian edition. While the twenties were roaring in European capitals and the great modernists of world literature were finding an audience, Khodasevich (among others) met with a silence in many ways more hostile than the literary politics which had beleaguered him in Moscow and St. Petersburg.[4]

In 1928, Wladimir Weidlé described Khodasevich as a "wingless genius" (*beskrylyi genii*).[5] As the phrase cleverly suggests, a special relationship existed between Khodasevich and the "wings of poesy." Weidlé attached his image to the poet's use of irony, so apparently consistent and pervasive as to evolve out of a rhetorical device into an all-encompassing attitude. Whether comparing the soul to iodine or contrasting the

---

[1] First appeared in *Slavic Review* 39 (March 1980): 56–69. New information added since the time of original publication is in bold.

[2] Because he considered them "immature" (*iunosheskie*), Khodasevich did not include *Molodost'* and *Shchastlivyi domik* in his *Sobranie stikhov* (Paris: Vozrozhdenie, 1927). See Vladislav Khodasevich, "Predislovie k Sobraniiu stikhov 1927 g.," *Sobranie stikhov*, ed. N. Berberova [Munich: Izd. I. Bashkirtsev, 1961], 7. Hereafter, unless otherwise stated, all references to Khodasevich's verse will be to the 1961 Munich edition.

[3] *Evropeiskaia noch'* did not appear under separate cover but was included in the 1927 Paris edition of Khodasevich's *Sobranie stikhov*.

[4] Khodasevich had difficulty adapting to the compromises of Soviet literary life (see Nina Berberova, *The Italics Are Mine*, trans. Philippe Radley [New York: Harcourt, Brace, 1969], 79–149).

[5] V.V. Veidle, "Poeziia Khodasevicha," *Sovremennye zapiski* 34 (1928): 468.

clamoring of poetic feeling to the calming effect of headache tablets, Khodasevich punctuated his later verse with swift descents into the banal, and many of his poems, particularly those written after leaving Russia, end with an ironic about-face.[6] But Khodasevich's irony is not universally bitter.[7] When the element of play is added to the poet's dismantling eye, what emerges in his art is the moment of "moving stasis"—the verse, stanza, or entire poem in which a balance is struck between the ponderous and the light, the romantic and the threadbare, and the timeworn world of history and the timeless world of art. Perhaps it is this sort of moment, which occurs less and less frequently in the frustrated atmosphere of exile, more than the elegant expression of acedia and spiritual defeat that offers us evidence of Khodasevich's significance as a poet.

The view of Khodasevich often found in the émigré press throughout the 1920s and 1930s, and for the most part still current in the West, is not totally unjustified.[8] As a critic for *Vozrozhdenie*, Khodasevich could be sarcastic and prickly, and as a poet of a lost generation he could be cheerless, at times almost doggedly so.[9] Still, this view seems to overlook something. It limits Khodasevich to an angular profile where he might be seen at some point, poetically at least, *en face*—the creator of a number of works whose tone is both serious and playful and whose irony is both dark and light.[10] The purpose of this essay is, therefore, twofold: to explore the use of irony in one of Khodasevich's finest works and, on the basis of those findings, to propose, if only for the brief moment held in suspension by the work, another view of the poet.

6 See "Probochka" (The Cork) and "Khranilishche" (The Storehouse) in Khodasevich, *Sobranie stikhov*, 87 and 148.

7 Khodasevich's irony has traditionally been described as "bitter" or "malicious" (*zloi*) (see Iurii Ivask, "Poeziia 'staroi' emigratsii," in Nikolai P. Poltoratzky, ed., *Russian Émigré Literature: A Collection of Articles with English Résumés* [Pittsburgh: Pittsburgh University Press, 1972], 49). Zinaida Shakhovskaia, former editor of *Russkaia mysl'*, writes in her memoirs that, while still in Russia, Khodasevich was nicknamed "formic acid" (*murav'inyi spirt*) (see Zinaida Shakhovskaia, *Otrazhenlia* [Paris: YMCA, 1975], 184).

8 When this article first appeared in 1980 the renewed interest in Khodasevich was just beginning to intensify. Over the past three decades the poet has been republished in various editions and studied in numerous articles, dissertations, and books. Of the dissertations and monographs one could cite: Sarah Clovis Bishop, "The Book of Poems in Twentieth-Century Russian Literature: Khodasevich, Gippius and Shvarts" (PhD diss., Princeton University, 2004); Jane Ann Miller, "Creativity and the Lyric 'I' In the Poetry of V.F. Xodasevič" (PhD diss., University of Michigan, 1981); Kristen Elizabeth Welsh, "Crisis of Poetry: Nabokov, Khodasevich, and the Future of Russian Literature" (PhD diss., Yale University, 2005); Julia Zarankin, "The Literary Memoirist as Necrographer: Khodasevich, Tsvetaeva, Nabokov, and Proust" (PhD diss., Princeton University, 2004); Inna Broude, *Ot Khodasevicha Do Nabokova: Nostaligicheskaia Tema V Poezii Pervoi Russkoi Emigratsii* (New York: Hermitage, 1990); Henry Gifford, Khodasevich and Tradition (New York: Grand Street, 1988); Frank Göbler, *Vladislav F. Chodasevič: Dualität Und Distanz Als Grundzüge Seiner Lyrik* (Munich: O. Sagner in Kommission, 1988); I.Z. Surat, *Pushkinist Vladislav Khodasevich* (Moskva: Izd-vo Labirint, 1994). Recent studies of Sorrento Photographs include: Jason Brooks, "'Directing the Reader: Khodasevich's 'Sorrento Photographs' and Montage The Comparatist 28 (May 2004): 39–51 and Margarita Nafpaktitis, "Multiple Exposures of the Photographic Motif in Vladislav Khodasevich's 'Sorrentinskie fotografii'," SEEJ 52.3 (Fall 2008): 389–413.

9 See Roger M. Hagglund "The Adamovič-Xodasevič

Though found in his last and darkest collection, *Evropeiskaia noch'*, Khodasevich's most intriguing verse narrative bears the sunny title Sorrento Photographs (*Sorrentinskie fotografii*). The work presents unique opportunities for reviewing the poet's use of irony.[11] Its sage and sometimes enigmatic speaker, its personal as well as national themes, and its Petersburg setting (among others) suggest that this ironic *poema* has its headwaters — more remote than a direct comparison can justify — in Pushkin and *The Bronze Horseman*. Indeed, while Khodasevich's earlier poems in blank verse have been described as replies to *The Little Tragedies*, in *Sorrento Photographs* we can only suspect that Pushkin was an abiding presence in the modern poet's mind.[12] Yet the liminal reference to Pushkin becomes more apparent when we notice that the perfectly modulated iambic tetrameter, the fluid, seemingly effortless enjambments, the ingenious rhymes, and the generally limpid style recall Pushkin's language perhaps more than anything else Khodasevich wrote.[13]

Nevertheless, *Sorrento Photographs*, one of the most Pushkinian of all Khodasevich's works, could only belong to a modern ironist. The central images, for one, are a double-exposed snapshot and a motorcycle. Manifestly, the concerns of a premodern age of poetry have now, some one

Polemics," *Slavic and East European Journal* 20.3 (Fall 1976): 39–52.

10 For varying degrees of playful seriousness" and "serious play" in Khodasevich's work, see the following poems in Khodasevich, *Sobranie stikhov*: "Look for Me" ("*Ishchi menia*" [1918], 40), *Noon* (*Polden'* [1918], 45–47), *The Encounter* (*Vstrecha* [1918], 48–49), "To Aniuta" (*Aniute* [1918], 57), "Without Words" ("*Bez slov*" [1918], 59), *Music* (*Muzyka* [1920], 63–64), and "The Cloak of Hidden Maia" ("*Pokrova Maii potaennoi*" [1922], 113).

11 Khodasevich wrote several verse narratives. Not, strictly speaking, *poemy*, they are also far from traditional lyrics. Each tells in blank verse and with a profusion of realistic detail an experience pivotal to the poet's life. See, for example, the following in Khodasevich, *Sobranie stikhov*: *The Episode* (*Epizod* [1918], 35–37), *The Second of November* (*2-go noiabria* [1918], 41–44), *Polden'*, *Vstrecha*, *The Monkey* (*Obez'iana*

[1919], 50–52), *The House* (*Dom* [1919–20], 53–55), and *Muzyka*. See also Khodasevich's parody of the ballad form in *John Bottom* (*Dzhon Bottom* [1926], 167–76).

12 Veidle, "Poeziia Khodasevicha," 456.

13 The significance of Pushkin for Khodasevich cannot be overstated. Several critics, including Andrei Belyi (in "Tiazhelaia lira i russkaia lirika," *Sovremennye zapiski* 15 [1923]: 371–88), have compared Khodasevich to Pushkin, though perhaps not always for the right reasons. (The formal similarities are not as revealing as the differences in tone and mood.) Khodasevich wrote two monographs on Pushkin, *Poeticheskoe khoziaistvo Pushkin* (Leningrad: Mysl', 1924) and *O Pushkine* (Berlin: Petropolis, 1937), and Pushkin seems to have been for him the very embodiment of a now disappearing Russia. This feeling for Pushkin is encountered in Khodasevich's speech, "The Shaken Tripod" ("Koleblemyi

trenozhnik"), delivered on February 14, 1921 to the Petersburg Writers' Club (in Carl R. Proffer, ed., *Modern Russian Poets on Poetry*, trans. Alexander Golubov [Ann Arbor: Ardis, 1974], 60–70): "Moved back into the 'smoke of centuries,' Pushkin will arise in gigantic stature. National pride in him will flow into indestructible bronze forms — but that spontaneous closeness, that heart-felt tenderness with which *we* loved Pushkin will never be known to the coming generations. They will not be granted this joy. ...The heightened interest in the words of the poet which was felt by many people during the past several years arose, perhaps, from a premonition, from an insistent need: partly to decipher Pushkin while it is not yet too late, while the tie with his time is not yet lost forever; and partly, it seems to me, it was suggested by the same premonition: we are agreeing to what call we should answer, how we should communicate with each other in the oncoming darkness."

hundred years later, been replaced by those of a modern one. The tone of Khodasevich's poem reflects in turn the elusive position of the modernist. With its emphasis on imagination and memory, this work partakes of the playful, avowedly "artificial" world of artistic patterning and of the world of historical inexorability. The *poema's* ironic tension arises from the superimposition of the former world on the latter. In a word, *Sorrento Photographs* is seriocomic, Khodasevich managing that balancing act which few, if any, Russian poets other than Pushkin have managed to do. This may be one reason why Robert Hughes calls the work "one of Khodasevich's most successful — if untypical — efforts,"[14] since he feels its tone is alien to the ubiquitous gloom of *European Night*. Yet, superimposing past on present, imagination on history, and the comic, morning mood of "To Aniuta" ("Aniute") on the somber, evening mood of "An Mariechen," *Sorrento Photographs* stands at the center of Khodasevich's oeuvre.[15]

Sorrento Photographs was written in three installments, Khodasevich tells us:

> The first seventeen lines [were composed] in Saarow [Sorrento], at the beginning of 1925 (March 5). Then [I continued working] in Chaville, in February 1926. I finished it, hurriedly, in February [1926] in order to read it at the Tsetlins (I had promised). I wrote efficiently, every day, sometimes to this end going into Paris to the Cafe Lavenue [sic]. At times I wrote with great enthusiasm. As regards their sound, these are my favorite verses. "[Written] from within" — no, not exactly. Everything here is told just as it was.[16]

The praise that Khodasevich himself gives these verses is significant. He rarely praises his own poetry, and thus his definite preference for the sound of *Sorrento Photographs* suggests a new benchmark in his work.[17] It is curious that the *poema*, so balanced in its use of iambic tetrameter, was written at a time when Khodasevich was deliberately deflating the sound of poetry in "Windows to the Courtyard" ("Okna vo dvor," 1924), "Poor

---

[14] Robert Hughes, "Khodasevich: irony and dislocation: A poet in exile," *TriQuarterly* 27 (Spring 1973): 64.

[15] Irony is a salient feature in Khodasevich's three mature collections. But what is often a bright, matinal irony in the poems, such as "Aniute," of *Putem zerna*, develops gradually through *Tiazhelaia lira*, a book whose poems generally show a more trenchant, angular variety of irony, until the desperate, bitter, and hence "nocturnal" irony of the poems, such as "An Mariechen," of the last collection. *Sorrentinskie fotografii* is unique because, while located in *Evropeiskaia noch'*, it seems to retrieve briefly the mood of *Putem zerna*.

[16] Notes to *Sorrentinskie fotografii*, in Khodasevich, *Sobranie stikhov*, 221. In the first line, "Saarow" is an obvious error in the 1961 edition and should read, as indicated, "Sorrento." The Tsetlins are Mikhail Osipovich and Mar'ia Samoilovna, who had a literary and political salon in Paris. Mikhail Tsetlin was a minor émigré poet and critic (see Berberova, *The Italics Are Mine*, 584).

[17] Though Khodasevich himself often records the praise of others in notes, he praises his own work only one other time, referring to "Zvezdy" ("The Stars") as "very good verses" (*ochen' khoroshie stikhi*), in his notes to "Zvezdy" (Khodasevich, *Sobranie stikhov*, 221).

[18] Khodasevich, *Sobranie stikhov*, 160–61, 162, 164–65, 167–76. There are times in these poems when Khodasevich combines light, jocular rhymes with exceptionally flat or even grotesque content.

Rhymes" ("Bednye rifmy," 1926), "Ballad" ("Ballada," 1925), and *John Bottom* (*Dzhon Bottom*, 1926).[18]

Sorrento Photographs is a very difficult work, integrating various surfaces on a large scale as several of Khodasevich's earlier lyrics had integrated them on a smaller one.[19] The work's initial source was Khodasevich's eight-month retreat (September 1924–April 1925) in Maxim Gorky's villa in Sorrento and the memories surrounding that visit. The more recent memories constitute the work's narrative frame, and the literal and figurative vehicle of the narrative is young Maxim's (Gorky's son's) motorcycle, which speeds through the Italian hills near Sorrento with the poet in its sidecar. As often happens in the ironist's world, he is allowed to go along for the ride, to observe the countryside from his privileged seat, and to fantasize freely, while the driving is left to someone else. But the stereoscopic theme of *Sorrento Photographs* does not stop here. Instead, it presents the memory of the poet's life in Moscow and St. Petersburg *within* the memory of his life in emigration.[20] Thus, throughout the *poema* the speaker, seemingly playing with the knobs on a viewfinder, brings one surface into focus while removing the other surface to the background. Considering that one is dealing with poetry not prose, the result is a remarkable application of the principles of narrative irony and point of view, bringing to mind the "mirror gallery" technique (that is, the author observing the author observing) of André Gide's *Les Faux Monnayeurs*.

The first two stanzas of the poem set the tone for what follows, and therefore I shall quote them in full:

>   Воспоминанье прихотливо
>   И непослушливо, оно —
>   Как узловатая олива:
>   Никак, ничем не стеснено.
>   Свои причудливые ветви
>   Узлами диких соответствий
>   Нерасторжимо заплетет —
>   И так живет, и так растет.
>   Порой фотограф-ротозей
>   Забудет снимкам счет и пленкам
>   И снимет парочку друзей

---

19 The mature Khodasevich, like Mallarmé in "Les Fenêtres," loves to work with surfaces — windows, polished floors, mirrors, anything which reflects. As with concepts of largeness and smallness, it often happens in his poetry that the irony of existence is best revealed by contrasting concepts of depth, both spatially and emotionally, with what passes lightly over a surface (see "Ishchi menia" in Khodasevich, *Sobranie stikhov*, 40).

20 Khodasevich's mature poetry is associated with three different locales. *Putem zerna* was written primarily in Moscow between 1914 and 1920; *Tiazhelaia lira* primarily in Petrograd between 1920 and June 22, 1922, the date of the poet's emigration; and *Evropeiskaia noch'* in various European cities, including Venice, Berlin, and Paris, between 1922 and 1927.

На Капри, с беленьким козленком —
И тут же, пленки не сменив,
Запечатлеет он залив
За пароходною кормою
И закопченную трубу
С космою дымною на лбу.
Так сделал нынешней зимою
Один приятель мой. Пред ним
Смешались воды, люди, дым
На негативе помутнелом.
Его знакомый легким телом
Полупрозрачно заслонял
Черты скалистых исполинов,
А козлик, ноги в небо вскинув,
Везувий рожками бодал...
Хоть я и не люблю козляток
(Ни итальянских пикников) —
Двух совместившихся миров
Мне полюбился отпечаток:
В себе виденья затая,
Так протекает жизнь моя.²¹

Set at what seems a safe distance from the reality of revolution and exile, these lines generalize from a few comic particulars and constitute an amusing prologue to the sense of loss that will follow. In the opening line, Khodasevich introduces the theme of memory which is the fulcrum of the entire work. The growth and organic intuition of the olive tree, simultaneously gnarled and beautiful, suggest the artistic process. To grow the tree must unite two elements, earth and air, just as the poem *in posse* unites memory, which is rooted in past experience, and imagination, which ramifies freely. A symbol of life and peace, the olive tree seems strangely out of place in the deadly landscape of *European Night*. And the branches,

21 Khodasevich, *Sobranie stikhov*, 150–51. The plain translations of Khodasevich's Russian which follow the text are mine. Memory is capricious / as well as contrary — / like the knotty olive, / it cannot be hemmed in. / Inextricably it weaves / in knots of farfetched correspondences / its whimsical branches — / and so it lives, and so it grows. / At times a scatterbrained photographer / will lose count of shots and film / and snap a pair of friends/ on Capri, beside a little white goat — / and on the spot, not changing film, / he will print over them the bay / beyond the steamer's stern / and the sooty stack / with a shock of smoke on its forehead. / This winter one of my friends / did just that. Before him / water, people, and smoke intermingled / on the turbid negative. / His friend in half-transparency / hid the features of rocky giants / with his light body, while / the little goat, its legs flung skyward, / was butting Vesuvius with its tiny horns... / Though I'm not in love with little goats / (or Italian picnics) — / that imprint of two worlds/ telescoped caught my fancy: / concealing in itself a vision, / so does my life flow by.

which intertwine like a series of coincidences, imply that the poet's life has been patterned by forces he admires but cannot understand.[22] There is more wonder and play in this eight-line frontispiece than in all of Khodasevich's last collection.

The second stanza presents what will become the overarching image of the double-exposed snapshot. The language is again playful ("scatterbrained photographer" [*fotograf-rotozei*], for example), simple, and more or less conversational. There is light humor as well in the aside "or Italian picnics" (*Ni ital'ianskikh piknikov*). Yet there is more here than meets the eye, and the movement of these apparently straightforward lines presents the same problem of focus as the scatterbrained friend's picture. First, Khodasevich is blurring various levels of reality — the world of things, of animals, of people which he has done numerous times in his work. Next and more vital, through the agency of his memory he is perceiving two moments of time almost simultaneously, and consequently retrieving the present which exists in the past and the past which exists in the present, that is, the Proustian *entre deux* first associated with such verse narratives as *Noon* (Polden') and *The Encounter* (*Vstrecha*).[23] Khodasevich seems to relate the past, or the province of tradition and memory, and the future, or the province of prophecy and imagination, as tinder to spark — there is no flame until both are brought together. And as he often opined, Soviet art was bound to fail as long as it ignored the tradition and collective memory of pre-Revolutionary culture.[24] Thus, imagination is not free to be wholly inventive or innovative and depends, in large part, on the "memory" of the poem's opening and on what the poet has actually lived through. As an ironist, Khodasevich maintains his distance, however, and he does not explore the kinetic energy of the actual present. Rather, he only hints at the potential for poetic fire as well as historical holocaust, here associated with the "smoky" surface of events and Mount Vesuvius, to which he will return in the poem's climax.

[22] Note that Khodasevich manages to tangle the branches ("vetvi") in the knots of correspondences ("sootvetstvii") and the living ("zhivet") and growing ("rastet") in the inextricable ("nerastorzhimo") weaving.

[23] See Khodasevich, *Sobranie stikhov*, 45–47, 48–49. T.S. Eliot explores the meaning of history and develops a similar concept of "pure time" in *Four Quartets*: "The historical sense involves a perception, not only of the past, but of its presence… This historical sense, which is a sense of the timeless as well as of the temporal and of the timeless and temporal together, is what makes a writer traditional" (see "Tradition and the Individual Talent," in T.S. Eliot, *Selected Essays* [New York: Harcourt, Brace, 1950], 4).

[24] For Khodasevich's views on Soviet art and letters, see his "Dekol'tirovannaia loshad'," *Vozrozhdenie*, September 1, 1927; "O formalizme i formalistakh," *Vozrozhdenie*, March 10, 1927; "O Sovetskoi literature," *Vozrozhdenie*, May 20, 1938; and "Proletarskie poety," *Sovrernennye zapiski* 26 (1925): 444–55.

The speaker has two memories of Russia, triggered in turn by two different locations, in or near Sorrento, which he passes through on the motorcycle. The first memory, that of the funeral of Savelev, a Moscow floor-polisher, is superimposed on the scenery of the Amalfi Pass, and the second memory, that of St. Petersburg, the Neva, and the angel on the Peter and Paul Cathedral, is reflected at dawn in the Bay of Naples with Mount Vesuvius in the background. Serving to foreshorten the "distant" viewpoint of these two memories is the "nearer," more recent, viewpoint of a third memory, sandwiched in between, describing a Roman Catholic procession that takes place in the streets of Sorrento on Good Friday. The two distant memories suggest themselves as Khodasevich's swan song to imperial Russia, the Russia with which the poet identified. Through these memories the poet is possibly bidding farewell to the people, in the peaceful body of Savelev, and to Russian Orthodoxy and the state, in the proud figure of the guardian angel high atop the Peter and Paul Cathedral. Hence, it would seem initially that Khodasevich has replaced Pushkin's Evgeny with his own Savelev and the Bronze Horseman with the angel on the Peter and Paul Cathedral. And the parallel is reinforced, if only superficially, by the fact that the "little man" has an unhappy fate and the angel (guarding Peter's tomb), like Peter's statue, changes poses. But here difference is more important than similarity, for history, both personal and national, has entered another era: Savelev does not die in the flood of history *during* the poem. When we meet him, he is already dead. Russia's guardian angel does not move the forces of history, but is moved by them.

Savelev's funeral is a simple, private affair. The speaker seems almost to be eavesdropping on his own recollection:

> Раскрыта дверь в полуподвал,
> И в сокрушении глубоком
> Четыре прачки, полубоком,
> Выносят из сеней во двор
> На полотенцах гроб дощатый,
> В гробу — Савельев, полотер.[25]

Khodasevich has selected an artisan for this death scene. Dressed in a worn jacket and carrying on his breast the traditional icon, Savelev lies in his coffin with an air of benign indifference. By keeping the narration on a homely and personal level, the poet skirts a tragic interpretation. He does not allow us to know why Savelev died, since it is apparently not important.

25 Khodasevich, *Sobranie stikhov*, 152.
A door is open wide into a basement flat, / and, in acute grief,/ four washerwomen turn half-sideways / to carry from the entry to the courtyard / a deal coffin on towels;/ in the coffin [lies] Savelev, the floor-polisher.
I have translated *polupodval* as "basement flat." Actually, it is a humble dwelling, perhaps one room, located partly below ground. From within the inhabitants can see the feet of passers-by through the windows. The towels are probably not simple ones, but decorative ones reserved for this occasion, and serve here in ritual allusion to the *vynos* (bearing-out

The speaker's gentle, nearly avuncular prodding of one of the keening washerwomen, perhaps the widow — "Now, Olga, that's enough. Come out." (*Nu, Ol'ga, polno. Vykhodi.*) — likewise undercuts the implicit tragedy of the situation. Indeed, the image of Savelev and his coffin, swaying through the agaves of the mountainous region near Amalfi, is light and soothing to the eye:

> И сквозь колючие агавы
> Они выходят из ворот,
> И полотёра лоб курчавый
> В лазурном воздухе плывет.²⁶

Finally joining the funeral procession in an olive grove, the speaker follows behind, tripping somewhat unceremoniously on the alien stones.

Before describing the second memory, which is closer to the actual present and hence strikes the reader as more immediate, Khodasevich turns the knob of his viewfinder. He bridges vast areas of time and space, the "before" and "after" of the Revolution, with the device of the motorcycle which, turning this way and that, its headlights dancing on the rocky road, suggests the ironist's answer to a time machine. When the second memory does come into focus, it has a new orientation: instead of a funeral procession for one man, it is something large and public — a reenactment of Christ's Passion with a throng of believers. Proximity is juxtaposed to remoteness; a tradition that is alive in Italy and that relives Christ's death in order to celebrate his resurrection is set against a tradition over whose funeral Khodasevich will preside in the closing stanzas of the poem. The second memory expands gradually, and, as the speaker observes the streets of Sorrento in the nocturnal calm, there is little hint of what will follow:

> В страстную пятницу всегда
> На глаз приметно мир пустеет,
> Айдесский, древний ветер веет
> И ущербляется луна.
> Сегодня в облаках она.
> Тускнеют улицы сырые.
> Одна ночная остерия
> Огнями жёлтыми горит.
> Ее взлохмаченный хозяин
> Облокотившись полуспит.²⁷

The padrone does not know his part in memory's play, yet he will, like Shakespeare's John Bottom, humorously enter the action a little later. Now the singing of the

f Christ's *plashchanitsa* (shroud). *polotentse* and *plashchanitsa* have the same etymology: the former taking the more prosaic Russian form and the latter the more elevated Old Church Slavic form.

26 And through the prickly agaves/ they come out of the gate,/ and the floor-polisher's curly forehead / sails along in the azure air. Ibid.

27 Always, on Good Friday, / the world grows noticeably empty, / an ancient, Hadean wind blows, / and the moon wanes. / Tonight the moon is in the clouds. / The damp streets grow dim. / Only an inn/ burns its yellow lights. / Its tousled padrone / half dozes on his elbows. Ibid., 153

procession grows more distinct and the crowd comes into view. Above their heads the people hold a sculptured likeness of the Virgin Mary. The "She" of these lines presses palm to palm and wears an immobile expression on her face. Akin to Mona Lisa and perhaps reminiscent of Blok's Beautiful Lady and his feminine Jesus, the Virgin is distant and unapproachable. With the wisdom of one who understands human frailty and who speaks from the far side of fervent ideals, the poet asks rhetorically whether this inaccessibility is not what the people want:

> Но жалкою людскою дрожью
> Не дрогнут ясные черты.
> Не оттого ль к Ее подножью
> Летят молитвы и мечты,
> Любви кощунственные розы
> И от великой полноты —
> Сладчайшие людские слезы?[28]

But Khodasevich the ironist turns away from the Blokian theurgy. Here the prosaic *padrone* surfaces, and the speaker, describing the gap between man and divinity in comic terms, wryly inserts:

> К порогу вышел своему
> Седой хозяин остерии.
> Он улыбается Марии.
> Мария! Улыбнись ему![29]

Only an onlooker, the poet does not follow but watches the Virgin pass.[30] Then in a radiant light and under a thunderous choir of voices, she enters a cathedral. As dawn breaks over Sorrento, the worshippers seem transfigured in the light. This mood, as one might expect, cannot be sustained for the *eiron*, however. The romantic crescendo and ellipsis —

> Яснее проступают лица,
> Как бы напудрены зарей.
> Над островерхою горой
> Переливается Денница...[31]

—are cut short by the image of the veering motorcycle, which introduces the third memory.

The poet's last memory is perhaps the most intriguing. On the one hand, he sets it in the background of Vesuvius, the legendary volcano that perennially consumes and renews itself:

> В тумане Прочида лежит,
> Везувий к северу дымит.

---

28 But Her serene features will not move / with the people's pathetic trembling. / Is this not why their prayers and dreams, / the blasphemous roses of their love, / and, out of [the heart's] great fullness, / their sweetest tears fly to Her pedestal? Ibid., 154.

29 The gray-haired *padrone* / has come out to the threshold. / He smiles to Mary! / Mary! Smile back! Ibid.

30 Though born to Russified Polish parents and raised a Catholic, Khodasevich in some ways felt closer to the traditions of Russian Orthodoxy than to those of the Church of Rome. One reason was his

> Запятнан площадною славой,
> Он все торжествен и велик
> В своей хламиде темно-ржавой,
> Сто раз прожженной и дырявой.³²

Like history's periodic convulsions, there is something constant in the volcano's destructive power. So Vesuvius stands out in the Italian countryside as a reminder of our great potential for self-annihilation. The other figure in the background is Naples which, in ironic opposition to the image of Petersburg soon to follow, stands up (*vstaet*) and out of the morning fog. The speaker locates his memory of Petersburg *after* the fall, that is, following the volcanic eruption of 1917. Treated as *nature morte*, there are no battle scenes or cannon fire. The smoke of a once vital tradition, a tradition generally associated with Falconet's magisterial statue and Pushkin's *poema*, has dispersed forever. But Khodasevich turns from the Russia epitomized by the equestrian figure of the tsar-conqueror. Instead, he returns to the poem's opening as he telescopes once again the past and the present — from the founding of St. Petersburg in 1703 at the walls of the fortress, through that fortress's dark and enigmatic history as both prison and royal burial vault, to the final collapse of imperial Russia in the chill November of 1917 — with the image of the angel holding the cross:

> Я вижу светлые просторы,
> Плывут сады, поляны, горы,
> А в них, сквозь них и между них —
> Опять, как на неверном снимке,
> Весь в очертаниях сквозных,
> Как был тогда, в студеной дымке,
> В ноябрьской утренней заре,
> На восьмигранном острие,
> Золотокрылый ангел розов
> И неподвижен — а над ним

Russian nurse (see V. Khodasevich, "Mladenchestvo," *Vozdushnye puti* 4 [1965]: 100–119, and "Ne mater'iu, no tul'skoiu krest'iankoi," in Khodasevich, *Sobranie stikhov*, 66–67).

31 The faces stand out more clearly, / as though made up by the dawn. / Above the mountain's sheer peak / the Morning Star spills its light…/
Khodasevich, *Sobranie stikhov*, 154. *Dennitsa* (Morning Star), as Nina Berberova has told me, may belong to a symbolic system combining the Virgin Mary and Lucifer. This would account for the curious transition from the Easter procession's promise of new life to the fall of Russia's guardian angel. The link between the Morning Star and Lucifer is made, for example, in V. Dal', *Tolkovyi slovar' zhivogo velikorusskago iazyka*, 4th ed., vol. 1 (St. Petersburg-Moscow: Izd. T-va M.O. Vol'f, 1912), 1059. The *ostroverkhaia gora* prepares us for the poem's climactic image, the angel atop the *vos'migrannoe ostrie* (eight-faceted point).

32 Procida lies in the mist, / Vesuvius is smoking to the north. / Sullied by the fame of the marketplace, / the volcano is, in its dark rust-colored / chlamys, a hundred times scorched and full / of holes, still solemn and grand.
Khodasevich, *Sobranie stikhov*, 155.

Вороньи стаи, дым морозов,
Давно рассеявшийся дым.
И отражен кастелламарской
Зеленоватою волной,
Огромный страж России царской
Вниз опрокинут головой.
Так отражался он Невой,
Зловещий, огненный и мрачный,
Таким явился предо мной —
Ошибка пленки неудачной.³³

Russia's guardian is reflected upside down in the Gulf of Castellammare. Stood on its head, the world as Khodasevich knew it can never be righted. Nevertheless, Khodasevich, a master of understatement, here reduces all the anguish and chaos to an optical illusion, a mistake on a photograph.³⁴ Khodasevich ends his masterpiece on a whimsical note. Balancing the serious and the playful and presenting straightforwardly what is deceptive, he "closes" with something that can only cause new beginnings — a question. This, after all, is one answer appropriate for the modern ironist:

33 I see bright expanses, / gardens, glades, and mountains sailing by, / yet in them, through them, and between them, / once more, as on the muddled photo, / all in transparent outline, / [I see] how then, in the freezing haze / of a November dawn, / a top its eight-faceted point, / the golden-winged angel was pink / and still, while above it / [moved] flocks of crows, and frosty / smoke long since dispersed. / And reflected in the greenish waves / of the Gulf of Castellammare, / the huge guardian of tsarist Russia / is toppled [there] headfirst. / Ominous, fiery and brooding, / so had the Neva reflected him [then], / so had he appeared to mean / error of the unlucky film.

Ibid., 155–56. Cf. *Pamiatniki arkhitektury Leningrada*, N.N. Belekhov, gen. ed. (Leningrad: Gos. izd-vo lit-ry po stroitel'stvu, arkhitekture i stroit. materialam, 1958), 21, 24, 32. These lines clearly refer to the angel on the Peter and Paul Cathedral — not, for example, to another famous angel on the Alexandrine Column — because the figure is gilded, thus "golden-winged," and it stands on the cathedral's faceted spire (the Alexandrine Column, on the other hand, is round). It is "huge" because it is the tallest (122.5 meters) landmark in central Petersburg, and it is "ominous, fiery and brooding" because it looms over a place known for its dark history and because it bears witness to the cataclysmic November of 1917. I am grateful to Jane Miller of Middlebury College (**now an independent scholar/translator**) and John Malmstad of Columbia (**now of Harvard**) for pointing me in the direction of the angel on the Peter and Paul Cathedral. Thanks are due as well to Nina Berberova for corroborating this interpretation.

Note how Khodasevich has removed even the angel's grammatical agency through the use of passive constructions: *otrazhen, oprokinut,* and *otrazhalsia.*

34 Of all the media available to modern man, the photograph is perhaps by nature the most impersonal and the most open to irony. See, for example, Susan Sontag, *On Photography* (New York: Farrar, Straus, Giroux, 1977), 158: "Photography has powers that no other image-system has ever enjoyed because, unlike earlier ones, it is not dependent on an image maker. However carefully the photographer intervenes in setting up and guiding the image-making process, the process itself remains an *optical-chemical* (or electronic) one, the workings of which are automatic, the machinery for which will inevitably be modified to provide still more detailed and, therefore, more useful maps of the real. The *mechanical* genesis of these images, and the literalness of the powers they confer, amounts to a new relationship between image and reality. And if photography could also be said to restore the most primitive relationship — the partial identity of image and object — the potency of the image is now experienced in a different way. The primitive notion of the efficacy of images presumes that images possess the qualities of real things, but our inclination is to attribute

> Воспоминанье прихотливо.
> Как сновидение — оно
> Как будто вещей правдой живо,
> Но так же дико и темно
> И так же, вероятно, лживо...
> Среди каких утрат, забот
> И после скольких эпитафий
> Теперь, воздушная, всплывет
> И что закроет в свой черед
> Тень соррентинских фотографий?[35]

Sorrento Photographs occupies a unique position in Khodasevich's work. It shows the poet at his best, if not his most typical, and it shows his irony at its most "forbearing" and least bitter. History becomes within its complex framework something chaotic, imprisoning the poet in the time and space of a meaningless present. But art is equally important, for it applies the various lenses and camera angles of memory and imagination to what moves within two distinct dimensions — Russia in the presence of revolution and life abroad in the absence of Russia — achieving the brief focus that, while "capturing" history, is also outside and free of it.

Sorrento Photographs also encourages, as much as one work of its scope can, a reevaluation of the poet. Born too late to be a full-fledged Symbolist and too early to be an Acmeist, in his poetry Khodasevich gradually moved toward what at the level of the word and the image was specific, "realistic," and in turn deliberately unpoetic and ironic. But at the same time he did not forswear out of hand the largely Symbolist ideals of his youth. Another world, seen through the details of this one, is a force in his art to the end. And it coexisted, unwillingly as time went on and crowded in, with the poet's irony. Yet in Khodasevich's finest work, of which *Sorrento Photographs* is an example, this tense coexistence finds moments of perfect balance, the eyes in the storm of

---

[...]o real things the qualities of an [...]nage" (emphasis added).

35 Memory is capricious. Like a dream, it seems / alive [w]ith prophetic truth, / but is [j]ust as wild and obscure / and, [p]robably, just as false... / Amidst [w]hat losses and troubles, / [a]nd after how many epitaphs, / [n]ow, belonging to the air, will it [s]urface, / and what shall overlay [i]n turn / the shadow of Sorrento [p]hotographs?

Khodasevich, *Sobranie [s]tikhov*, 156. Note that the [vi]sion" (*viden'e*) hidden by memory in the poem's opening and rooted in the tradition of a once vigorous culture is now likened to and contained in the "dream" (*snovidenie*).

revolution and exile. Perhaps it is, or should be, in the contemplation of such moments that Khodasevich's poetry is rescued from the European night falling around it.

Chapter 15 — Nabokov's Style[1]

For a prodigiously gifted *homo scribens* such as Vladimir Nabokov, there is nothing more precious or distinctive about his constructed persona than his style. Indeed, the written trace is, to a degree potentially disturbing to some readers, that aspect of personhood Nabokov most valued. It was *what remained behind*, always under his control, to be wielded with consummate elegance and grace even as the enemy, time itself, took from him his homeland, his loved ones, and eventually his own life. "Summer *soomerki*—the lovely Russian word for dusk. Time: a dim point in the first decade of this unpopular century. Place: latitude 59° north from your equator, longitude 100° east from my writing hand,"[2] writes the autobiographer of the time-place coordinates of his childhood. If words are vessels of spirit, then such statements are pure "Nabokov": the poetic quality of the Russian *soomerki* (more evocative in English with the resonant "oo" than with the squat "u" of standard transliteration), coupled with an exact placement in memory that is also a subtle chess move vis-à-vis the reader ("your" vs. "my"), then finished off with the playful, winking flourish of the "east of my writing hand." Nabokov's writing hand knows no occident, no dying into the west.

Style was then, one could say, Nabokov's *linguistic personhood*: because it allowed him to join within one created structure the natural world of precise scientific observation and the abstract world of metaphysics and consciousness, it was his pledge of immortality, his active participation in the patterns of divine mimicry. Several recent commentators have argued that Nabokov's style is infectious not in the sense that it can be imitated but in the sense that its demands on the reader *uplift the latter*, challenge him or her to a fuller, more conscious and generous humanity. This claim is absolutely central to Nabokov's entire project as a writer and needs to be questioned further. Does this man's mastery of words inspire or dispirit us, raise us up to a potential we did not know was there, or cast us down into the "galley slave" role of many *littler* Nabokovs? Nabokov's style clearly shows on those who write about him, beginning with his biographer. When,

---

[1] Originally appeared as the chapter "Style" in *The Garland Companion to Vladimir Nabokov*, ed. Vladimir Alexandrov (New York: Garland Pub., 1995), 696-704.

[2] Vladimir Nabokov, *Speak, Memory: An Autobiography Revisited* (New York: Putnam, 1967), 81.

for example, Brian Boyd writes that "Nabokov the scientist never ceased to wonder at the elaborateness of nature's designs, the regularities at every level from atoms and crystals to clouds and comets. He knew how the forms of life branched out from willowherb to bog orchid, waxwing to grebe, elm to paulownia, cichlid to sea-squirt,"[3] he is not only borrowing a trick — seeing the world in its marvelous specificity — from the old master. He is, the reader senses, *energized* by that typical Nabokovian oscillation back and forth between the precisely named and the generalizing abstract. If we can locate the bog orchids, grebes, and cichlids within the elaborateness of nature's designs and celebrate through language the consciousness that put them there, we are, in our ulteriority or outsideness, a bit like God Himself on the seventh day of creation.

Nabokov turned the tables on — *ironized* — Romantic irony. It is a trope that he played with constantly in his mature work but at some level took seriously: because his personhood resides so completely in his written, as opposed to biographical, traces, Nabokov the author resembles a god (or the God). He demands that we look for him *in his creation*. The artistic house of cards does not come tumbling down because its creator is in the hands of a higher creator. No, the game becomes worth playing precisely because its first rule is to turn the infinite regress of Romantic irony on its head. Rather than a humanoid butterfly transfixed by a mocking lepidopterist God, we have the forever twitching antennae of cognitive and creative potential. In a modernist reprise of the act of divine Logos (the word-become-flesh) central to the poetics of his Symbolist youth, the three-dimensional writer enters the two-dimensional printed page as a consciousness that then coalesces and reascends, transfigured, into the shadowy intimation of four-dimensional ("divine") cognition. Nabokov's style is the fullest and most revealing expression of the two chief, competing quiddities of his personality: his seeming invulnerability, which at moments of hyperconsciousness or "cosmic synchronization" in the novels approaches God's position on the outside,[4] and his real — though exquisitely disguised — vulnerability, which was an extension of his love for others that, despite his great gifts, was subject to the wages of time. In the pages that follow we will investigate the different qualities of Nabokov's style as formal indices of his mature psychology and personhood and as means of engaging his reader.

Recent scholarship, especially the books and articles of Vladimir Alexandrov, Brian Boyd, Alexander Dolinin, Ellen Pifer, Pekka Tammi, Sergej Davydov, and Elizabeth Beaujour, has focused attention on Nabokov's style (broadly

---

[3] Brian Boyd, *Vladimir Nabokov: The Russian Years* (Princeton: Princeton University Press, 1990), 297.

[4] See Vladimir E. Alexandrov, *Nabokov's Otherworld* (Princeton: Princeton University Press, 1991), 26–29.

defined) as a way to reevaluate and enrich possible strategies of reading the novels. Alexandrov, for example, has made perhaps the strongest case yet for a direct link between the formal aspects of Nabokov's style and what he calls the "hermeneutic imperative":

> The experience [of epiphany in Nabokov's art] is ... structurally congruent with a characteristic *formal* feature of his narratives, in which details that are in fact connected are hidden within contexts that conceal the true relations among them. This narrative tactic puts the burden on the reader either to accumulate the components of a given series, or to discover the one detail that acts as a "key" for it; when this is achieved, the significance of the entire preceding concealed chain or network is retroactively illuminated. This process of decipherment that Nabokov imposes on his readers has far-reaching implications. Since the conclusion that the reader makes depends on his retaining details in his memory, he appears to have an atemporal insight into some aspect of the text's meaning; he is thus lifted out of the localized, linear, and temporally bound reading process in a manner resembling the way characters' epiphanies remove them from the quotidian flow of events within the world of the text.[5]

In fact, as Alexandrov goes on to argue, all the various qualities that critics have traditionally subsumed under the rubric of "style" in Nabokov's case — onomatopoeia and alliteration, anagrams, patterns of imagery, tampering with viewpoint and other narrative ploys, etc. — are placed in the text in the service of this hermeneutic imperative ("deception through concealment"). Even the so-called "phrasal tmesis" — the very Nabokovian "I'm all enchantment and ears" or "the Arctic no longer vicious circle" (*Ada*) — is, in Lubin's formulation, the author's "greater deception writ small. The mind apprehends the terminal words which it expects to find juxtaposed, and then must accommodate the alien phonemes thrust between."[6] The point is that Nabokov, in a manner reminiscent of the early Russian Formalists' emphasis on "making strange" ("ostranenie"), constantly interrupts the flow of his narrative in order to stimulate his reader *to see better*, with increased alertness and cognitive engagement.[7]

A significant added benefit of the studies of Alexandrov, Boyd, and Davydov is that they have introduced greater balance between the notorious "metaliterary" Nabokov (the arch postmodernist *avant la lettre* and the lesser-known "metaphysical" Nabokov clearly more modernist than postmodernist). If the stylist

5   Ibid., 7.
6   Alexandrov, *Nabokov's Otherworld*, 13–14; Peter Lubin, "Kickshaws and Motley," Alfred Appel, Jr., and Charles Newman, eds, *Nabokov: Criticism, Reminiscences, Translations, and Tributes* (Evanston: Northwestern Press, 1970), 193–96.
7   See Ellen Pifer, *Nabokov and the Novel* (Cambridge: Harvard University Press, 1980), 24–26; A.A. Dolinin, "Pogliadim na arlekinov: Shtrikhi k portretu V. Nabokova," *Literaturnoe obozrenie* 9 (1988): 19.

is so controlled and controlling that even memory itself becomes, as Robert Alter has argued, voluntary and "un-Proustian," then the metaphysician has let it be known that somewhere there could be a higher presence, a "to whom it may concern," whose fatidic fingers turn the pages of Nabokov's own life.[8] The reorientation has been aptly formulated by Boyd, first in his book on *Ada* and now more recently in his massive biography: "Independence and pattern function like the complementary twin hemispheres of Nabokov's mind."[9] But what precisely does this mean for Nabokov's style? What in his style represents independence and what pattern? And is there a genuine tension in Nabokov's scriptive traces between independence and patterns, and if so, where does it reside?

For the purposes of discussion, I will cite an excerpt that displays Nabokov's style in its typically stunning way. In *The Gift*, Nabokov's greatest Russian novel, the autobiographical hero Fyodor Godunov-Cherdyntsev gets his passion for scientific observation and naming from his father, the naturalist explorer. Here he recalls some of the lessons imparted to him by this remarkable man:

> The sweetness of the lessons! On a warm evening he would take me to a certain small pond to watch the aspen hawk moth swing over the very water, dipping in it the tip of its body. He showed me how to prepare genital armatures to determine species which were externally indistinguishable. With a special smile he brought to my attention the black Ringlet butterflies in our park which with mysterious and elegant unexpectedness appeared only in even years.... He taught me how to take apart an ant-hill and find the caterpillar of a Blue which had concluded a barbaric pact with its inhabitants, and I saw how an ant, greedily tickling a hind segment of that caterpillar's clumsy, sluglike little body, forced it to excrete a drop of intoxicant juice, which it swallowed immediately. In compensation it offered its own larvae as food; it was as if cows gave us Chartreuse and we gave them our infants to eat. But the strong caterpillar of one exotic species of Blue will not stoop to this exchange, brazenly devouring the infant ants and then turning into an impenetrable chrysalis which finally, at the time hatching, is surrounded by ants (those failures in the school of experience) awaiting the emergence of the helplessly crumpled butterfly in order to attack it; they attack — and nevertheless she does not perish.[10]

The passage is a tour de force, and yet it is standard fare for the mature Nabokov. *The Gift* is absolutely full of such brilliant patches.[11] Without commenting

---

[8] See Robert Alter, "Nabokov and Memory," *Partisan Review* 58.4 (1991): 620–29.

[9] Boyd, *Nabokov: Russian Years*, 9.

[10] Vladimir Nabokov: *The Gift*, trans. Michael Scammell (New York: Capricorn, 1963), 109–10; *Dar* (orig. 1952; Ann Arbor: Ardis, 1975), 124–25.

[11] While crucial to any discussion of the writer's style, we will leave aside, in the interest of space, the fascinating question of the *Russian* versus the *English* Nabokov. As Jane Grayson has remarked, "The brilliance of Nabokov's later English style owes not a little to his viewpoint as a foreigner. He sees the English language through

for the moment on *where* the author who makes these observations might be situated vis-à-vis his reader, let us begin by analyzing the passage on the basis of internal evidence. First of all, the *quality* of observation, its overpowering visual acuity — as if the viewer were wearing special magnifying glasses — is immediately striking.[12] The moths and butterflies are expertly named and their activities minutely described. Their colors, sizes, and shapes are lingered over as in a finely drawn illustration for a scientific journal. Their tactile characteristics are brought to life, as though on the reader's own skin, through references to temperature and habitat. This entire naming process is, to repeat, itself empowering, for the wonder engendered by watching the insects' activities does not appear to disable or "strike dumb" the observer; quite the opposite, by giving everything its proper name, the scientist learns to see how the natural world fits together, how its patterns make "artful" rather than "common" sense.[13] The wonder, we are led to believe, makes the boy not less but more alert. As the narrator says a few pages later, the father was "happy in that incompletely named world [the Tyan-Shan mountain range] in which at every step he named the nameless."[14] The point here presumably is that to catch butterflies in this way is to "catch" a momentary glimpse into the meaning of existence. The person who can name these things is, again, like God: *nomen est cognitio*. Unlike the ants, which are *not* distinguished as to their roles in their society, the *singular* butterfly is, in the father's words, "calm and invulnerable."

Even so, the naming is not the cool, disinterested naming of the naturalist, and this is crucial, for it is what gives Nabokov's style its magical, transformative quality. From the exclamation point of the opening sentence to the emotionally colored gestures (the father's "special smile") and qualifiers (the "mysterious and elegant" unexpectedness of the black Ringlets' appearance), to the subtle incursions of anthropomorphizing descriptions (the "barbaric pact" concluded by the Blue, the "greedy tickling" of the ant, etc.), we are dealing with a naming that is drenched in human viewpoint and aesthetic sensibility. The precision of the naturalist gives the creatures their proper

different eyes. He sees patterns of sound and potential meanings in words which the [monoglot] native speaker, his perception dulled through familiarity, would simply pass over. He deviates more readily from set modes of expression and conventional registers of style, inventing new and arresting word combinations, employing high-flown, recherché vocabulary alongside the most mundane colloquialisms" (Jane Grayson, *Nabokov Translated: A Comparison of Nabokov's Russian and English Prose* [Oxford: Oxford University Press, 1977], 216; cited Elizabeth Klosty Beaujour, *Alien Tongues: Bilingual Russian Writers of the "First" Emigration* [Ithaca: Cornell University Press, 1989], 105). The issue of Nabokov's bilingualism as it affects his writing style is treated with considerable insight in Beaujour, *Alien Tongues*, 81–117.

[12] "I think I was born a painter — really! — and up to my 14th year, perhaps, I used to spend most of the day drawing and painting" (Vladimir Nabokov, *Strong Opinions* [orig. 1973; New York: Vintage International, 1990], 17); and "As a writer, I am half-painter, half-naturalist" (in Peter Quennell, ed., *Vladimir Nabokov: A Tribute* [New York: William Morrow, 1980], 13).

[13] See Alexandrov, *Nabokov's Otherworld*, 17–18, 45–46, 53–57.

[14] Nabokov: *Gift*, 119; *Dar*, 136.

names; the sensibility of the artist shows how these names interact in a way that makes life appear planned, cognitively invigorating, *meaningful*. That is why we are infected by the thrill of the narrator who learns that some higher intelligence sends certain butterflies to their park only on even years — a kind of otherworldly chess move. And that is why the contract between ants and the Blue is also satisfying *on an aesthetic level*: the caterpillar of the Blue is "programmed" to eat the ant larvae (aesthetically, ants count less in God-the-artist's scheme of things, and the best they can do is serve as nourishment for beauty), while the ant gets to drink the "wine" secreted by the "sluglike body" before the latter decomposes and recomposes as butterfly.

But most of all, that is why "one exotic species of Blue" can protect itself against the attacking ants by catching them in the sticky substance while it, calm and invulnerable, is given sufficient time for its wings to strengthen and dry. One has to be careful not to read too much into such passages, but there is the temptation to see the strong caterpillar-become-exotic Blue as a kind of Sirin substitute (*sirin* itself being a rara avis): the hoi polloi are not allowed, thanks to the great artist's protective coloration, to get "at him," to paw him with their dirty limbs, to prey on him with their ant-hill psychology. Nabokov's style, despite its remarkable Tolstoyan and Buninesque lucidity and passion for naming, is the sticky substance that prevents the "vulgar" from attacking the "helplessly crumpled butterfly" before it is ready to fly. All that has to do with the hive or social life — the uncontrollable, open-ended aspects of any biography; dialogue in everyday space that can move in any direction and depends on a real interlocutor; the prosaic that is not poeticized; the inevitable pain and even boredom that go with loving another human being, etc. — is seemingly banished as the verbal Nabokov disappears into the "impenetrable chrysalis" of style.

The real-life Nabokov felt these things, to be sure. He knew and freely acknowledged, for example, that he was not a good impromptu speaker.[15] Self-conscious and not naturally warm and gregarious in large groups, he was made uncomfortable by the role of featured guest at a gathering or party, where conversation "flowed" spontaneously and he could not, with his native wit and eloquence, get outside and shape it. And the death of his father, whom he dearly loved and passionately admired, was one of the few genuine turning points in his life. But such matters were not to be smuggled into his art so

---

15 "Formed and delivered in a moment, likely to be forgotten soon after, spoken language smacked to Nabokov of the prison of the present. The very nature of written language meant something special to him: an opportunity to revisit the impulse of a past instant from which time has forced us to march on, a sort of access to a more elastic time where one can loop back on an idea and develop it to maximum power and grace. In the 1960s he began to refuse interviews unless questions were submitted well in advance and answers could be fully prepared in writing. That may look like mere personal vanity, but he was simply hyperconscious of the difference between his spoken language ('I speak like a child') and what he could achieve given that rubbery time of revision" (Boyd, *Nabokov: The Russian Years*, 312).

that others could explain how caterpillar pupated into butterfly. If they were there at all, they were displaced, inverted, concealed.[16] To quote Pushkin, with whom Nabokov shared a fastidious scorn of the mob: "'He [the artist] is small like us [the mob]; he is loathsome like us!' You are lying, you scoundrels: he's small and he's loathsome, but not the way you are — differently."[17] Sociability is inevitably a mark of vulgarity (*poshlost'*) in Nabokov: negative characters, such as M'sieur Pierre in *Invitation to a Beheading*, tend to be full-bodied, crudely gregarious and ingratiating, while positive characters, such as Cincinnatus in the same novel, tend to be lithe and fine-featured (to the point of being virtually "disembodied"), shy and standoffish, and self-enclosed in their world and in their gift. In a recent study Julian Connolly has commented astutely on the tension between self and other in Nabokov's world: "While [Nabokov's characters] seek to gauge the efficacy of their personal visions through contact with another, they also evince a persistent anxiety — the fear that their unique individuality will be lost through expropriation or finalization by an impersonal other. Desperate to assert their worth in the face of others, many of Nabokov's characters either try to subordinate others to their own designs or withdraw entirely from meaningful interaction with another....Nabokov eschewed the 'social' of 'general' in favor of the personal."[18] Positive characters often possess a secret knowledge (gnosis), as does Fyodor's father in *The Gift*, a knowledge that makes them virtually impenetrable to all, including their loved ones: "It sometimes seems to me nowadays that — who knows — he might go off on his journeys not so much to seek something as to flee something, and that on returning, he would realize that it was still with him, inside him, unriddable, inexhaustible. I cannot track down a name for his secret, but I only know that that was the source of that special — neither glad nor morose, having indeed no connection with the outward appearance of human emotions — solitude to which neither my mother nor all the entomologists of the world had any admittance."[19] "Style," in this case Fyodor's father's, resides in the secret (his place in a pattern that is out of this world?) and is perhaps indistinguishable from it. Style is something that belongs to the private individual; its secret is not tellable (nor should it be) and the charisma it endows cannot be shared. To put the paradox of his gift another way, style gave Nabokov the time that life took away. Here, to quote Boyd, "we can sense the author beyond, making *his* choices in that special space that writing and rewriting afford just outside time, taking advantage of first thoughts, second thoughts, third thoughts to allot his character the illusion of a mind that...remains wonderfully free

---

16 See Dolinin, "Pogliadim arlekinov," 17.

17 In a letter of November 1825 to his friend P.A. Vyazemsky; see Alexander Pushkin, *The Letters*, trans. and intro. J. Thomas Shaw (Madison: University of Wisconsin Press, 1967), 264.

18 Julian Connolly, *Nabokov's Early Fiction: Patterns of Self and Other* (Cambridge: Cambridge University Press, 1992), 6–7.

19 Nabokov: *Gift*, 115; *Dar*, 131.

to dart this way and that."²⁰ Style, moreover, gave Nabokov the control over history that life as an exile denied. Conveniently, the ants in the above passage lack the butterfly's "imagination"; they are, like so many Soviet *udarniki truda* (*shock troops of labor*), "failures in the school of experience." They cannot, from their vantage (spatial and cognitive), make a splendidly unexpected statement such as "it was as if cows gave us Chartreuse and we gave them our infants to eat." It takes the flight of the Blue to reverse common sense. Almost involuntarily, we are taken in by the logic of Nabokov's style: we want the world to be meaningful, the beautiful to survive and fly off, the scientific to be embalmed with artistic blood, the smallest creature to be part of a larger benign pattern, the predatory to be stupid, the engineers of human souls to fail. We want, in short, to be privy to this secret knowledge.

But Nabokov's hermeneutic imperative also instructs us not to look for the knowledge that transforms its seeker in obvious places, beginning with the social activities of the ants. Knowledge of this sort cannot be taught. Mimicry has a "vertical" dimension, while brute imitation is purely "horizontal": the former is the chosen metaphor for Nabokov's style because it both mocks ("mimics") the reader who tries to explain its secret in terms of obvious external — biographical, "Freudian," etc. — evidence and inspires the reader who sees the subtle camouflaging of small to large as *more* than it needs to be. It always contains a surplus of creative energy that expands consciousness. Mimicry is nature's version of parody (Nabokov's favorite trope), but parody that uplifts because it celebrates its unique placement vis-à-vis a source that is superior to itself.²¹ As the narrator sums up the father's (and Nabokov's) position a little farther on, "He told me about the incredible artistic wit of mimetic disguise, which was not explainable by the struggle for existence (the rough haste of evolution's unskilled forces), was too refined for the mere deceiving of accidental predators, feathered, scaled and otherwise (not very fastidious, but then not too fond of butterflies), and seemed to have been invented by some waggish artist precisely for the intelligent eyes of man (a hypothesis that may lead far an evolutionist who observes apes feeding on butterflies)."²²

Nabokov knew very well that the beautiful butterfly was fed upon, if not by the ants, then all too often by the apes of history. The author's father, V.D. Nabokov, was an heroic and very much engaged political figure; he was plainly not saved from the clutches of the "worker ants" when he was murdered in 1922, by right-wing extremists while trying to protect his rival Pavel Miliukov during an assassination attempt at a public meeting. Here

20 Boyd, *Nabokov: Russian Years*, 313.

21 Cf. Nabokov "always favored rhymed verse for the surprises that could be found within natural sense, and mimicry he once defined as 'Nature's rhymes'" (Boyd, *Nabokov: The Russian Years*, 298); and "the spirit of parody always goes along with genuine poetry" (*Gift*, 12; *Dar*, 18).

22 Nabokov: *Gift*, 110; *Dar*, 126; cf. *Strong Opinions*, 125.

the authorial chess move is that the biographical son "rescues" the father by making him into a naturalist more interested in the society of insects than in the society of human beings. Then, in something which is closer to a move-to-the-second-power than to a second move, the father, from his position in the other world, helps the son find the "keys" to love (Zina) and to calling (Russian literature).[23] This particular move is at the center of Nabokov's style and all his art: the dead are resurrected through the secret knowledge that they guide the living to the patterns of transcendence. The writing hand is moved by a symbiotic consciousness both in (the son's) and out of (the father's) this world. This is Nabokov's most fiercely guarded article of faith. "Nabokov's textual patterns and intrusions into his fictional texts emerge as imitations of the otherworld's formative role with regard to man and nature: the metaliteray is camouflage for, and a model of, the metaphysical."[24] Nabokov is absolutely right to resist a crudely Freudian logic that has him writing his greatest work *in compensation for* the loss of his father and his childhood. Such logic, which makes the author just another human being, "small and loathsome like us," cannot *get inside* the miracle of creative pupation. It can only explain, by likeness and analogy, after the fact. Nabokov's style was, therefore, his way not simply to gain time but — and here is the metaphysical check-mate — to defeat it.

Let us close with a brief summary and parting sideways glance. It is hard to imagine a more self-conscious and controlled artist than Vladimir Nabokov. And yet, this control is coupled with a gratitude that acknowledges a consciousness more capacious and non-contingent than anything humans can imagine (the author's favorite metaphor for this being a kind of free-floating eyeball capable of turning 360 degrees). If we read the patterns creatively, goes the logic of hermeneutic imperative, we will puzzle our way to greater cognitive "independence." Nevertheless, this poetics of gratitude (ours to Nabokov, his to "to whom it may concern") needs to be questioned as a constructive principle. Nabokov, born exactly 100 years after Pushkin, was fond of invoking the father of Russian literature when it came time to construct his own stylistic and historico-literary genealogy. When the narrator says of Fyodor's preparations for his father's biography that "Pushkin entered his blood. With Pushkin's voice merged the voice of his father,"[25] we are entitled to challenge the difference (species) within the sameness (genus). Pushkin's *Journey to Arzrum*, with its roving curiosity for all manner of alien human subject and its intense interest in the rituals, behaviors, and interpersonal hierarchies of other societies, is a

23 See Boyd, *Nabokov: Russian Years*, 471–78.
24 Alexandrov, *Nabokov's Otherworld*, 18.
25 Nabokov: *Gift*, 98; *Dar*, 111.

much different document than the fictive biography it supposedly models. Nabokov's scientific cast of mind, his visual acuity together with his love of puzzles and shifting planes and all that is cognitively challenging, suggests a great affinity with the "positivist" and detail-laden Tolstoy than with his professed favorite, the superstitious, risk-loving, and more laconic Pushkin. Nabokov's games were chess and the hunt for the rare, or better, unnamed butterfly; Pushkin's games were the more socially embedded and ultimately dangerous duel, gambling, and the affair of the heart. There are structures a-plenty in Pushkin's created world, but they are probably not "keyed" to a benign transcendental aesthete. The risks in Pushkin are more real, both to the author and to his reader, the connections to biography, despite the exquisite masking and play, "hotter" and more vulnerable. Both in style and substance, Pushkin is more the poet than Nabokov; poems of the former such as "The Prophet" ("Prorok") or "Memory" ("Vospominanie," 1828) or the Stone Island cycle would be literally unthinkable to the latter. Pushkin's ties to the eighteenth century and his fabled Apollonian restraint notwithstanding, he clearly had access to a poetic "id" (a genuine "lyric I") and to language as disturbing (or arousing) sound as well as enlightening sight and sense. (Nabokov, on the other hand, was apparently tone deaf and had little appreciation for music.) And his biography, both always on display and concealed, required a diet of the unfamiliar and even the threatening. Pushkin was more open to the random or chaotic in life, less interested in words as "impenetrable chrysalis"—he would not, for example, encode himself in his work as a vulnerable butterfly under attack by worker ants. He would be as interested in the future Pugachevs among the hoi polloi as he was in the sensitive artist.

Nabokov, as I have attempted to suggest in this essay, is a rather different breed. Both above the fray and ever unwilling to "let go," encased in the diaphanous armor of his winged verbal creatures, he is Russians literature's supreme superego, and it is doubtful than any naming under the sun could do his transmogrifications justice.

Chapter 16   Sologub, Nabokov, and the Limits of Decadent Aesthetics[1]

One of the more fascinating aspects of Nabokov's artistic method is the way he "covers his tracks" when referring to potential intertextual sources or "influences." He prefers his readers to believe that each work has emerged fully formed from the broad forehead (as opposed to dark loins) of his Zeus-like consciousness. Or so the prefaces to his novels, with their disclaimers as to matters of genealogy and their repeated references to the "Viennese delegation," would have us think. It is not that Nabokov hesitates to engage in intertextual punning or name-dropping, which practice clearly enriches the links within his own works to the classics of world literature and culture—to those names, titles, characters, lines of verse, emplotted situations, titbits of literary (and nonliterary) history, and so on, whose subtle interweaving makes Nabokov, like Joyce, one of the central figures in twentieth-century high modernism. However, to judge by the master's *obiter dicta*, this intertextual play is not meant in any serious way to undermine the originality of a novel's or story's central idea. Cincinnatus C. is not, despite the many intriguing parallels, an intertextual brother to Joseph K., since at the time (1934) he wrote *Invitation to a Beheading* (*Priglashenie na kazn'*), Nabokov-Sirin supposedly "had no German, was completely ignorant of modern German literature, and had not yet read any French or English translations of Kafka's works."[2] My own point in these preliminaries is not to gainsay Nabokov, as he may be telling the truth,[3] but rather to underscore his expressed need to distance himself from Kafka and to assert his own independence (the one influence he will admit being of course "the melancholy, extravagant, wise, witty, magical, and altogether delightful Pierre Delalande, whom I [Nabokov-Sirin] invented").[4] In this respect, Nabokov beats his *bête noire*, the Freudians, to the punch: even as he "protests too much" about how critics have hurled the "harmless missiles" of "Gogol, Tolstoevski, Joyce, Voltaire, Sade, Stendhal, Balzac, Byron ... [the list goes on to include other greats as well as fictional authors]"[5] in his direction as sources for his style and ideas, he wins. Either he is wholly

---

1 Originally published in *The Russian Review* 63 (January 2004): 48-62.

2 Vladimir Nabokov, *Invitation to a Beheading* (New York, 1965), 6.

3 At least his biographer thinks so. Brian Boyd, *Vladimir Nabokov: The Russian Years* (Princeton: Princeton University Press, 1990), 415: "Nabokov denied that he had been influenced by Kafka, and there seems no reason whatever to doubt his disclaimer."

4 Nabokov, *Invitation*, 6.

5 Ibid.

original, a colossus unto himself, or he is in the company of some of the most extravagantly gifted literary minds the world has ever known. In chess parlance, this comes under the classification of anticipating the next move. The purpose of the present essay is to retrace Nabokov's steps, and uncover his intertextual tracks, in the very "American" *Lolita*, by returning to one of the central texts of Russian Symbolism, Fyodor Sologub's *The Petty Demon* (*Melkii bes*, 1907).[6] My argument will be that, rather than looking at the more obvious intertextual clues in *Lolita*, such as those involving Poe, Mérimée, Shakespeare, Joyce, Cervantes, or Hugo,[7] which point to Western sources and are more easily recoverable by the author's primary (anglophone) audience, the genuine or deeper structural sibling in this case comes from a source closer to home—the *fin de siècle* Russian Symbolist/Decadent movement that Nabokov experienced at a still impressionable age and that, to a degree he often hinted at but was not willing to admit outright, was powerfully formative.[8] Of Blok, for example, undoubtedly a stronger influence on him in his early years than Sologub, Nabokov wrote Edmund Wilson in 1943, "I am glad you are studying Blok—but be careful: he is one of those poets that gets into one's system—and everything else seems unblokish and flat. I, as most Russians, went through that stage some twenty-five years ago."[9] What I will be suggesting is that in Lolita Nabokov is not merely invoking Sologub in a mockingbird game of "trivial pursuit," but actually engaging *The Petty Demon* at a deeper striation, with the result that the central concerns of Sologub's novel are precisely those of Nabokov's, *but in reverse*.[10] At issue here then is not intertextuality at a "micro" but at a "macro" level. Nabokov, as I will try to demonstrate, is returning to some of the key aesthetic and

6 *Melkii bes* was written 1892–1902, excerpted serially in *Voprosy zhizni*, and published separately in 1907. For the purposes of the present study I am using the following edition of Sologub and the translations of his work are, unless otherwise indicated, my own: Fedor Sologub, *Melkii bes. Stikhotvoreniia. Rasskazy. Skazochki* (Moscow, 1999).

7 I take these names from some of those that appear in Appel's annotations to the opening pages of the novel. See Vladimir Nabokov, *The Annotated Lolita*, ed. Alfred Appel, Jr. (New York, 1970), 321–36. Other names, such as Rimbaud, Verlaine, and Maeterlinck, could be added virtually at random, simply by leafing through Appel's annotations. But a pattern (certain figures—Poe, for example—seem freighted with greater meaning and "emplottedness" than others) does appear to emerge: one could call it primarily "French" (Poe was a favorite among the French Symbolists) and "symbolist" and/or "romantic." This is because Nabokov, raised in the atmosphere of Russian Symbolism, imbibed the latter through its filtering and enthusiastic "russianizing" of Poe, Baudelaire, Verlaine, Rimbaud, and numerous other (mostly French) Symbolists, all of whom were translated by those such as Briusov and Balmont. On this last point see especially the astute remarks in A. Dolinin, "Bednaia 'Lolita'," in Vladimir Nabokov, *Lolita*, ed. A. Dolinin (Moscow, 1991), 6.

8 Though he has denied the influence of the Russian Symbolists upon him in an interview, Nabokov says that he had digested 'the entire population' of the 'so-called' Silver Age in the soft-cover ivory Sirin volumes which he purchased at a certain table at Volf's, a large St. Petersburg bookstore" (Andrew Field, *Nabokov: His Life i[n] Part* [New York, 1977], 95).

9 Simon Karlinsky, ed., *The Nabokov-Wilson Letters, 1940–1971* (New York, 1979), 94. In the Russian version of *Lolita*, Nabokov gave the name of Quilty's anagrammatical biographer as "Vivian Damor-Blok" (= Vladimir Nabokov), whereas in the English version this biographer is camouflaged as "Vivian Darkbloom." The point is that Blok's shadow, the shadow o[f] the greatest and most "infectious[ly]" Russian Symbolist, is present as Nabokov's "co-author" (parodied

ethical problems with which he got his start in prerevolutionary Russia: How does one approach ethically the human incarnation of beauty? Is the Beautiful Lady (of Solovyov, Blok, and Bely fame) an angelic or demonic (or daemonic—Nabokov plays with the different spellings) presence in the life of the beholder? Is the world (and word) structure that filters everything we see and do really Manichean or still perhaps Judaeo-Christian? In the pursuit of beauty, at which point does one's aesthetic seeing and feeling (the lovely patterns on a butterfly's wing, the way the human body moves gracefully in a young person) intersect and implicate one's ethical seeing and feeling? What are the rules of *zhiznetvorchestvo*, that very Symbolist game of "life creation" that incorporates others, often unbeknownst to them, in making myth (or mythos, literary plot) out of one's personal life? But then, having returned to these formative issues, Nabokov again brilliantly covers his tracks, by projecting them onto an American literary-cultural chronotope that has no memory of *The Petty Demon* (Sologub does not seem to be directly cited in the text of *Lolita*) or of a young Russian's first encounter with it.

Sologub's *The Petty Demon* was clearly a book the young Nabokov read and pondered. According to Andrew Field, it was one of the period volumes in Nabokov père's library.[11] More to the point, as one of the most celebrated (and notorious) of Symbolist texts, it was, along with Blok's lyrics and Bely's *Petersburg*, bound to strike a resonant chord in the adolescent Nabokov. Intriguingly, we have virtually no references by Nabokov himself to Sologub or his novel in his surviving correspondence.[12] Moreover, one of the very few times Nabokov said anything about Sologub in print was a characteristically dismissive judgment that, if taken at face value, could only suggest that the decadent author would

of course) in the creation of the diabolical double Quilty. Vladimir Nabokov, *Lolita*, trans. ?. Nabokov (New York, 1967), n.p.; Nabokov, *Annotated Lolita*, 6. One should also mention in this regard the five "B"s (Blok, Belyi, Briusov, Bal'mont, and either Bunin or Baltrushaitis) of the "new" Russian poetry that the autobiographical hero Fyodor had accepted with ecstatic approval "voskhishchenno, blagodarno, polnost'iu, bez kriticheskikh zatei") in his adolescence in *The Gift* (Vladimir Nabokov, *Dar* [Ann Arbor: Ardis, 1975], 85).

10 The well-known Cold War-generation Slavist Ernest Simmons once tossed off a formulation that was more prescient than he realized: Sologub introduces into the novel [*The Petty Demon*] the extensive episode of the seduction of the handsome young schoolboy Sasha by the erotic and sadistically-minded *demi-vierge* Liudmila. It is a *Lolita* situation in reverse, and the scenes are wantonly delightful and flecked with humor and not a little satire" (Fyodor Sologub, *The Petty Demon*, trans. Andrew Field [Bloomington, 1970], xii). At the time (1962, in the translation's first edition) Simmons made the comparison of the seduction scenes in *Lolita* and *The Petty Demon*, one has to assume that his point was not one of literary genealogy (that is, Nabokov is actually engaging Sologub in his American novel) but one of "typology," of fortuitously parallel structures. Other than this brief remark by Simmons, the precise links between *The Petty Demon* and *Lolita* have not, to the best of this reader's knowledge, been studied in a systematic way.

11 "Apart from an occasional best-seller such as Fyodor Sologub's *The Petty Demon* and some old Solovyov and Rozanov the library [of V D. Nabokov] contains very few of the Sirin books, the publishing house which printed most of the modernists of the time" (Field, *Nabokov: His Life in Part*, 95).

12 An exception is a brief discussion of a Sologub poem with Andrew Field in Vladimir Nabokov, *Selected Letters, 1940–1977*, ed. Dmitri Nabokov and Matthew J. Bruccoli (San Diego, 1989), 487.

be the last person Nabokov would take seriously or deem worthy of returning to: "that very minor writer for whom England and America show such an unaccountable predilection."[13] On the other hand, we also have a number of fairly significant intertextual allusions to Sologub in general and *The Petty Demon* in particular in Sirin's early Russian work, allusions which to a significant degree counteract *The New Republic* assessment and could be seen to imply that he saw the earlier writer as a part of the tradition he was wrestling with and trying to make his own.[14] In *Mary* (*Mashen'ka*, 1926), for example, Nabokov-Sirin's first novel, the unsavory character Alferov spits out a piece of chocolate that then sticks to the wall of the pension, a probable reference to Peredonov, who both likes sweets and is notorious for spitting on the walls in *The Petty Demon*.[15] And in *Invitation to a Beheading*, as Vladimir Alexandrov has pointed out, the symbolic representation of children (compare the proto-Lolita Emmie as well as the young Cincinnatus) comes very close to that found in Sologub.[16] Most convincing, however, are the numerous allusions to *The Petty Demon* in *Despair* (*Otchaianie*, 1936), a novel that, with its emphasis on the aesthetics of crime, doubles, and the obsessive behavior and potential madness of a first-person narrator, provides a powerful precedent for the thematics and architectonics of *Lolita*.[17] Here we encounter a character named Ardalion (Peredonov's first name), a cane/walking stick that gets turned against its owner (a motif in both novels), a reference to a *melkii demon* (an obvious play on *melkii bes*), another character called Perebrodov (vs. Peredonov), a case of spitting straight in the face of a less-than-hygienic girlfriend (Lida vs. Varvara), and various other explicit reminders of the Sologubian genesis of Hermann's type of "petty" evil.[18] In other words, Nabokov may have successfully

13   Vladimir Nabokov, "Cabbage Soup and Caviar," *New Republic* 110 (17 January 1944): 92.

14   Although relatively little has been written on Nabokov-Sirin's intertextual relations with Sologub in the 1920s and 1930s, two recent exceptions to this trend should be cited: Ol'ga Skonechnaia, "*Otchaianie* V. Nabokova i *Melkii bes* F. Sologuba: K voprosu o traditsiiakh russkogo simvolizma v proze V. V. Nabokova 1920–1930-kh gg.," in *Vladimir Nabokov-Sirine: Les Années Européenes*, ed. Nora Buhks (Paris, 1999), 133–43; and Iu. Leving, "Rakovinnyi gul nebytiia (V. Nabokov i F. Sologub)," in *Vladimir Nabokov: Pro et contra*, vol. 2, ed. D. K. Burlaka (St. Petersburg, 2001), 499–519. Both of these pieces make strong cases for the presence of Sologub (particularly *Melkii bes* and *Tiazhelye sny*) in such Nabokov-Sirin works as *Otchaianie* (*Despair*), *Priglashenie na kazn'* (*Invitation to a Beheading*), and *Dar* (*The Gift*).

15   See Vladimir Nabokov, *Sobranie sochinenii russkogo perioda v piati tomakh*, vol. 2 (St. Petersburg, 1999), 120, 697. The edition also cites the lamb dinner being served at the *pension* as a possible reference to the character Volodin in *The Petty Demon*, who is regularly likened to a *baran* ("ram") and who, like Alferov, is set up as a sacrificial victim, but the allusion strikes this reader as somewhat far-fetched (pp. 56, 693).

16   Vladimir E. Alexandrov, *Nabokov's Otherworld* (Princeton, 1991), 107. Alexandrov cites the following important passage from *Melkii bes* as evidence: "Only the children, those eternal, tireless vessels of God's joy in the earth, were alive, and ran, and played. But sluggishness was beginning to weigh even upon them, and some faceless and invisible monster, nestling behind their shoulders, peered from time to time with eyes full of menace into their faces, which suddenly went dull" (Sologub, *Melkii bes*, 88 [Alexandrov's translation]). Much of the Gnostic or Manichean structure of *Invitation to a Beheading* can also be seen to interact in productive ways with Sologub's major fiction, including *Melkii bes*.

17   Again, for more on the numerous connections between *Despair* and *The Petty Demon*, see the discussion in Skonechnaia, "*Otchaianie* V. Nabokova i *Melkii bes* F. Sologuba."

reinvented himself for his American audience in *Lolita*, but there is every reason to believe that, if we can slow down his conjuror's tricks to a speed visible to our reader's eye, we will see that the differing roles and interrelationships of Sologub's Peredonov, Sasha, and Liudmila are being replayed through Humbert's crime of seduction, his "safely solipsizing" of the heroine, in *Lolita*. First, the literal level of meaning in Sologub's text. *The Petty Demon* is the story of an evil presence (hence the title) in a provincial Russian town at the turn of the century. One of the central ironies of the novel and one Sologub cultivated in his various prefaces is to whom or what exactly the title refers: Is it the protagonist, Peredonov, who gradually goes out of his mind, commits murder, and himself appears as the incarnation of petty evil (and who was thought by some critics to be an autobiographical portrait of the sadistic teacher Teternikov)? Is it the subplot revolving around Alexander (Sasha) Pylnikov, whose appearance in town seems somehow to incite Peredonov's mad acts (note how the *nedotykomka* begins to appear to Peredonov shortly after the latter first sees Pylnikov in church and, curiously, whenever the *nedotykomka* is on stage Pylnikov is absent, and vice-versa[19]) and whose tutelage in amoral paganism and eroticism at the knee (literally) of the Rutilova sister Liudmila can be viewed in terms of traditional Christian teaching as itself "demonic"? Is it the atmosphere of the entire town, which seems "possessed" by *poshlost'* (vulgarity, pettiness), which produces victims (Peredonov in the first instance) that are symptomatic of the problem without necessarily being the source of it, and which is embodied in the gray, indeterminate, yet forever moving and tormenting *nedotykomka*? Or is it, finally, in a Gogolian reading Sologub encouraged, the "petty demon" that resides in Russia as a whole and that, to borrow Baudelaire's line, is the still larger implicit target: "Hypocrite lecteur,—mon semblable,—mon frère"?[20]

Thus, the ontological nature of evil is a, perhaps the, crucial starting point in Sologub's novel.[21] It is so because all actions and reactions by the narrator and characters, all perceptions and conclusions as to why the world is the way it is, are filtered through that starting point. (By the same token, it is this

18 See Nabokov, *Sobranie sochinenii* 3:415/759, 431/762, 453/766, 458/766, 463/767, 465/768, 483/770, 498/771, and 522/776.

19 Mentioned in Tomas Venclova, "K demonologii russkogo simvolizma," in *Christianity and The Eastern Slavs, III*, ed. Boris Gasparov et al. (Berkeley, 1995), 152–53.

20 "It is true, people love to be loved. They like it when the elevated and noble sides of the soul are depicted... And that's why they don't believe it when the depiction in front of them is reliable, precise, gloomy, evil. They want to say, 'He's speaking about himself.' No, my dear contemporaries, it is about you that I have written my novel about the *Petty Demon* and its terrifying Nedotykomka, Ardalion and Varvara Peredonov, Pavel Volodin, Darla, Liudmila, and Valeria Rutilova, Alexandr Pylnikov, and others. It's about you" (Sologub, *Melkii bes*, 14). Baudelaire was a favorite of the Symbolists.

21 A lone escapist from humble origins who knew poverty and humiliation firsthand, Sologub did not begin with any of the initial idealism of a Blok or Bely. The biographical and historical reasons mediating (but not necessarily explaining) Sologub's special brand of aesthetic Symbolism lie beyond the scope of this essay.

same starting point from which Nabokov, *mutatis mutandis*, will initiate his plot about malign intent in *Lolita*.) What this means on a metaphysical level is that Sologub's universe is, a priori, Manichean and false, created not by a benevolent God but by a Gnostic demiurge.²² Likewise, as Tomas Venclova has elegantly argued, it is ruled by *demony pyli* (demons of dust), these carriers of spiritual entropy first introduced by Briusov in his 1899 poem by that name (Sologub was present among the audience in St. Petersburg when Briusov first read the verses in public) and then developed conceptually by Merezhkovsky, who saw in this foregrounding of the diabolical as lukewarm and petty an obvious continuation of Gogol (*Gogol' i chert* [1906]), and Vyacheslav Ivanov, who personified this disintegration of spiritual light/energy as the deity Ariman (as opposed to Lucifer, the grand demonic personality) (*Rodnoe i vselenskoe* [1917]).²³ In Venclova's words, "the correlation of demonism with formlessness, feebleness, disintegration and, concretely, with dust became an important myth-generating model of Russian Symbolist literature."²⁴ And it is this conjoining of the image of dust with the notion of the demonic that powerfully informs all aspects of Sologub's contemporaneous novel, from issues of characterization to issues of plot, language, and symbolic patterning. Just as the town is constantly described in terms of dirt and dust — "Again the weather was overcast. The wind blew in gusts and bore funnels of dust [*pyl'nye vikhri*] along the streets. Everything was illuminated by a sad, almost un-sun-like light cast through the cloudy mist" — so too are its inhabitants Grushina's skin is said to be "all covered with wrinkles that were fine and as if filled with dust [*zapylennye*]."²⁵ Even the *nedotykomka* seems to appear, and, paradoxically, draw its haunting strength from, the debilitating presence of dust, disorder, indeterminacy, shape-shifting:

> The *nedotykomka* ran under the chairs and into the corners and began to let out a shriek. It was dirty, evil-smelling, disgusting, terrifying. It was by now clear that it was inimical to Peredonov and that it had turned up precisely on his account, and that previously it had not existed at any time or in any place. ... Here it is alive, sent to terrorize and destroy Peredonov, magical, of differing shapes; it follows after Peredonov, tricks him, laughs at him, now rolling on the floor, now pretending to be a rag, a piece of ribbon, a branch, a flag, a cloud, a dog, *a column of dust on the street* (*stolbom pyli*), and all the while crawling and running after Peredonov, exhausting him, wearing him out with its shimmering dance.²⁶

22 For a Gnostic reading of *Melkii bes* see Irene Masing-Delic, "Peredonov's Little Tear'—Why Is It Shed," in Fyodor Sologub, *The Petty Demon*, ed. Murl Barker (Ann Arbor, 1983), 333–43. The article first appeared in *Scando-Slavica* 24 (1978): 107–24.
23 See Venclova, "K demonologii," 134–60, esp. 134–42.
24 Ibid., 138 (original in Russian).
25 Sologub, *Melkii bes*, 88 41. This last instance is cited in Venclova, "K demonologii," 146.
26 Sologub, *Melkii bes*, 228 (emphasis added). Compare this passage and the immediately subsequent phrasing (for example,

the secret knowledge or gnosis that the parodically questing character (here Peredonov, "the Don [Quixote] done over"[27]) seeks is everywhere covered by the demonic dust particles. Indeed, in Sologub's pessimistic worldview, the secret is the dust. There is no transcendence. Princess Volchanskaya is a Beautiful Lady who will never come. Varvara, whose debauched head belongs to Aldonsa and whose weirdly beautiful (bewitched?) torso belongs to Dulcinea ("the body of a tender nymph"[28]), is the bride as both cousin (the taboo of incest) and slut. "And this is how it often happens, for in truth it is the lot of beauty in our time to be trampled and cursed."[29]

Into this fallen world comes Sasha Pylnikov. He is a beautiful child with epicene features,[30] a veritable young Dionysus, while the dancing, drinking Rutilova sisters are his maenads. Physically, he is distinguished by luxuriant hair (especially his dark eyelashes), a trademark of Dionysus. And from the very beginning he is associated with ecstatic religion and ritual:

> Peredonov moved forward, toward the middle rows [of the church]. There, at the very end of the row, to the right, stood Sasha Pylnikov. He was praying in a modest fashion and often getting down on his knees. Peredonov looked at him: it was particularly pleasant to see Sasha on his knees, as though someone being punished, looking forward at the radiant altar doors, with a concerned and beseeching expression on his face, with entreaty and sadness in his black eyes, shaded as they were by long, blue-black eyelashes. He was dark-complected, gracefully slender [*stroinyi*]—a fact especially obvious when he sat, calm and erect, on his knees, as if under somebody's sternly observant glance—and with a high and broad chest. He seemed to Peredonov the very image of a maiden.[31]

Note here, before any of the action surrounding the Sasha-Liudmila subplot gets underway, the chasteness of Sasha's young body coupled with the sincerity/purity of his inner world, his soul. It is this "intact" quality, seen against the backdrop of its potential sadistic defilement (Sasha on his knees, his modesty, his position as one being punished, and the like), that attracts the demonic Peredonov to him. Other motifs that point unmistakably to the myth of Dionysus are: women helpers as snake handlers (Liudmila's dream) and flower bearers (the scents from Liudmila's perfumes); the reversal of social roles during Dionysian festivals, including cross-dressing by boys and men (Liudmila's clothing of Sasha in female attire); and the appearance of the young Dionysus as beardless (Liudmila praises Sasha's lack of *usiki* and

---

'hot' by kto-nibud' izbavil, slovom akim ili udarom naotmash'") with Sologub's 1899 poem (written a few months after hearing Briusov's 'emony pyli") "Nedotykomka seraia" [Fedor Sologub, *Stikhotvoreniia*, ed. . I. Dikman [Leningrad, 1975], 234).

27 Andrew Field, "Preface," in Sologub, *Petty Demon*, trans. Field, xix.
28 Sologub, *Melkii bes*, 62.
29 Ibid.
30 Note how the very first reference to him by Grushina describes him as a "disguised maiden" (*pereodetaia baryshnia*). He is also alluded to repeatedly by this superstitious community as a "shape-shifter" (*oboroten'*). See Sologub, *Melkii bes*, 109–10.
31 Ibid., 114–15.

boroda) and partially nude (Liudmila eventually strips Sasha to the waist).³² And finally, of course, there is the climactic scene of the masquerade ball, where the "geisha girl," à la Dionysus, is "torn apart," or nearly (hence the parody), by the mad celebrants.

While the myth of Dionysus is central to the "pagan" subplot in *The Petty Demon*, just as the myth of the nymph (or "nymphet") will be significant to the nontranscendent world of Humbert Humbert, I would like to pause here for a moment to focus on the function of the aesthetic realm in Sologub (and, by implication, Nabokov). As stated, there is no escape from the *poshlyi* (vulgar, petty) world of Sologub's demiurge. However, through their erotic play, which is essentially *foreplay*, Sasha and Liudmila come as close as is humanly possible to exiting this prison. Following the Symbolist notion of the sexual/procreative act itself as degradation and animality (Solovyov, the Merezhkovskys, Blok and Bely, and so on), Sologub raises *the art of making love without performing intercourse* to a new level. (Again, to leap ahead of ourselves a little, it is precisely this line that Humbert crosses and ethically criminalizes in his "solipsizing" of Lolita.) For example, Liudmila is interested in Sasha first and foremost because he is *not mature*:

> "The best age for boys," said Liudmila, "is fourteen-fifteen years old. He [Sasha] still can't do anything and doesn't understand fully, but he already has a presentiment of everything, absolutely everything. And he doesn't have a disgusting beard. ...
>
> "You [Liudmila's sisters] don't understand a thing. I don't love him at all in the way you think. To love a boy is better than falling in love with a vulgar mug with a moustache. I love him in an innocent way. I don't need anything from him."³³

It is precisely this notion of "staged" eroticism — the combination of physical youth and beauty, bright colors, exotic smells, limited caressing or touching, the ritualized exchange of pleasure and pain (the sadomasochistic theme), the playing at sacred boundaries/taboos (child abuse, the undercurrent of incest), and so on — without "penetration" or mature heterosexual relations that is Humbert Humbert's dream, only with the roles reversed. "I am not concerned with so-called 'sex' at all," says Humbert. "Anybody can imagine those elements of animality. A greater endeavor lures me on: to fix once for all the perilous magic of nymphets."³⁴ The enchanted hunter even goes so

---

32 See Simon Hornblower and Anthony Spawforth, eds., *The Oxford Classical Dictionary*, 3d ed. (Oxford, 1996), 480–81: "Typical features of Dionysus and his religion — including wine and ivy; divine epiphanies and ecstatic forms of worship; women dancing, handling snakes, or holding flowers; the divine child and nurturing females; and bulls with and without anthropomorphic features — all are prominent in Aegean, especially Cretan religion and art. ... Festivals of Dionysus were often characterized by ritual licence and revelry, including reversal of social roles, cross-dressing by boys and men, drunken comasts in the streets, as well as widespread boisterousness and obscenity. ... No other deity is more frequently represented in ancient art than Dionysus ... later [after 430 BC] he usually appears youthful and beardless, effeminate, and partially or entirely nude."

33 Sologub, *Melkii bes*, 165–66.

34 Nabokov, *Annotated Lolita*, 136.

far as to define, in terms of temporal boundaries, the exact parameters of his mythic prey (the "nymphet"), just as Liudmila (in the above quote) had been quite precise about the age of her young Dionysus:

> Now I wish to introduce the following idea. Between the age limits of nine and fourteen there occur maidens who, to certain bewitched travelers, twice or many times older than they, reveal their true nature which is not human, but nymphic (that is, demoniac); and these chosen creatures I propose to designate as "nymphets."
> ... You have to be an artist and a madman, a creature of infinite melancholy, with a bubble of hot poison in your loins and a super-voluptuous flame permanently aglow in your subtle spine (oh, how you have to cringe and hide!), in order to discern at once, by ineffable signs—the slightly feline outline of the cheekbone, the slenderness of a downy limb, and other indices which despair and shame and tears of tenderness forbid me to tabulate—the little deadly demon among the wholesome children; she stands unrecognized by them and unconscious herself of her fantastic power.[35]

Perhaps the key to the attraction that the younger partner holds for the older one in both relationships, other than the fact that the bashful epicene and the nymph-like tomboy[36] are as physically lovely as they are sexually ambivalent, is that they are unaware of their beauty or "daemonic" (projecting an inner spirit) status. Stated simply, they are viewed as blank pages to be written on, which inevitably raises the issue of art and the role of the older partner as artist or shaper of this virgin material. Thus, the emphasis on punning and proto-poetry that goes with the seduction scenes in both novels is part and parcel of this foreplay, the sense that these neophytes are being introduced into a kind of game that is verbal and erotic at the same time and that does not necessarily lead anywhere, except back to itself (the aesthetic principle): Liudmila asking Sasha "*Kto zhelaet?*" (Who wishes/desires?) but then teasing him with the same phrase parsed differently "*Kto zhe laet?*" (Who is that barking?), or even better her *double entendre* on *rozochki* (meaning either "roses" or "birch rods"—that is, the source of pleasure or pain); Humbert singing along with Lolita the "Carmen/barmen" ditty (presumably Lolita does not know who the original Carmen is) at the moment that her legs are extended across his lap.[37]

35 Ibid., 18–19.

36 Just as Sasha's sexual identity is made deliberately ambiguous/androgynous by Sologub (that presumably is part of his charm), so too is Lolita's by Nabokov: she wears a "boy's shirt" and "tomboy clothes," has "boy knees" and "little doves" for breasts, and so on (ibid., 48, 50, ..., 122).

37 Sologub, *Melkii bes*, 157; Nabokov, *Annotated Lolita*, 60–64. There are numerous instances of punning as erotic foreplay in the Liudmila-Sasha relationship. It can be argued that this more subtle use of language is a positive counterpoint to the linguistic degeneration in the Peredonov plot—for example, the idiotic rhyming of Tishkov (Sologub, *Melkii bes*, 87). Intriguingly, the reference to Carmen in *Lolita*, with its theme of female "possession" and jealousy, was an habitual topos among the Symbolists, Nabokov's favorite Blok in particular. See footnote 9 above.

The structural parallels between the two plots reach an apogee in their respective "lap" scenes. The notion of lap (*lono* in Russian, but also *na koleniakh*, as in sitting "on [someone's] knees") is suggestive in both cultural contexts, as Nabokov (if not Sologub) was well aware. It evokes connotations of nurture and comfort, as of a mother holding a smaller child "on her lap" or "at her breast" (*lono* can mean figuratively both "lap" and "bosom"), but it also can become eroticized, particularly when the place being offered is male and close to the genitals (as in Humbert's case).[38] The figure doing the sitting is symbolically in a more vulnerable or submissive position (note the link here between Sasha in church "on his knees, as though someone being punished," and his repeated pose later in the text on Liudmila's knees). The fact that we see the child shift its status before our eyes from someone traditionally protected to someone explicitly eroticized and fetishized, while sitting on a "protector's" knees, is precisely what has made the two stories so controversial. So-called moral outrage (again, something Sologub rightly or wrongly seems not at all concerned about) meets aesthetic titillation in an exceptionally potent brew. Furthermore, it is during these lap scenes qua pseudo-epiphanic moments that the adult characters declare (Liudmila openly to Sasha, Humbert significantly only to himself) their fervent faith in their pagan religions: Liudmila tells Sasha she is a *iazychnitsa* (pagan) and he is her *otrok-bogoravnyi* (god-like youth); Humbert exclaims, as he surreptitiously masturbates against the pressure of Dolly's body, that Lolita has been "safely solipsized."[39] And it is during these very lap scenes, I would argue, that the notion of crime, which is absent in Sologub's text, enters the picture in Nabokov's, exposing what could be called, at least for the younger writer who had lived through the excesses of Symbolist myth-making, the limits of decadent aesthetics.

Looking more closely, what exactly is at stake in these parallel lap scenes and what are the significant affinities, and inversions, shaping them? First of all, with regard to Sologub, a strong argument can be made for the total absence of an ethical realm. Gorky understood this implicitly and this is what so incensed him about the unregenerate "decadent."[40] What I mean by absence of ethics is that no one is immune to the "demonic" in Sologub's world—there is no one who is ethically above the fray. Liudmila and Sasha are, for the time they have together (and clearly Liudmila understands that these days are numbered), god-like aesthetically, that is, Sasha is the *otrok-bog* and Liudmila his guide and worshiper, but not ethically. Their virtue has nothing to do with kindness or goodness or self-abnegation, but with beauty

---

[38] In the Russian version of the novel Nabokov repeatedly uses the term *lono* to describe Dolly's "seat" on Humbert that Sunday morning. See Vladimir Nabokov, *Lolita* (Russian version), 48.

[39] Sologub, *Melkii bes*, 238–39; Nabokov, *Annotated Lolita*, 62.

[40] See discussion in S.D. Cioran, "Introduction," in *Petty Demon*, ed. Barker, 17–18.

and form and self-affirmation. Likewise, Peredonov and all the denizens of his lower world are "evil" not because they hurt or torment others (which they do), but because they defile and disfigure — that is, they contribute to the absence of beauty and form. Hence the ethical is simply not a category that is engaged in *The Petty Demon*. Moreover, this *a priori* understanding affects the intimate scenes involving Sasha and Liudmila in intriguing ways, particularly when certain details are juxtaposed with Nabokov's presentation. For example, the closest we come to force or coercion in Sasha and Liudmila's erotic foreplay is the time Liudmila wants her young god to disrobe to the waist:

> [Liudmila] drew Sasha to herself and began to unbutton his shirt. Sasha tried to fight her off, grabbing hold of her hands. His face took on a frightened look and shame akin to fear overcame him. And because of this it seemed as though he momentarily lost his strength. Liudmila knitted her brows and with determination began to undress him. She took off his belt, then somehow pulled off his smock [bluza]. Sasha fought her off more and more desperately. They struggled, circling around the bedroom and bumping into tables and chairs. An intoxicating sweet smell came from Liudmila and went to Sasha's head and overpowered him.
>
> With a swift shove in the chest Liudmila toppled Sasha onto the sofa. A button popped off the shirt at which she had been tugging. Liudmila quickly exposed Sasha's shoulder and then began to pull his arm out of this sleeve. Fighting back Sasha struck Liudmila by mistake on her cheek with the palm of his hand. Of course he hadn't wanted to hit her, but the blow, which landed on her cheek with all his strength, was powerful and loud. Liudmila shuddered, wobbled a bit, turned blood red, but did not release Sasha.
>
> "You wicked boy, fighting [like this]," she screamed with a choking voice. Sasha was terribly embarrassed, dropped his hands, and guiltily looked at the whitish stripes, the traces of his fingers, imprinted on Liudmila's left cheek. Liudmila took advantage of his confusion. She rapidly pulled his shirt off his shoulders down to his elbows. Sasha came to his senses, tried to pull away from her, but it turned out even worse for him — Liudmila nimbly jerked the sleeves from his arms, and the shirt fell down to his waist. Sasha felt the cold and a new rush of shame, clear and merciless, which caused his head to spin. Now Sasha was exposed to his waist. Liudmila held him firmly by the hand, and with a trembling hand slapped him several times on his naked back, then looked

into his lowered and, beneath the blue-black eyelashes, strangely twinkling eyes.[41]

This is really the climax of the Sasha-Liudmila relationship. Though they both break down in tears due to their respective struggles — Sasha from shame and Liudmila from her young god's momentary recalcitrance — within a few paragraphs Sasha begins to understand the depth of Liudmila's feelings and Liudmila confides to him her pagan *profession de foi*. The experience is not presented in any way as a "deflowering" of Sasha by the older aggressor; if anything, it brings them both closer to an impossible, because finally unfulfillable, desire. There is no room, no space, for the relationship to develop beyond this *status* of the young Dionysus naked to the waist in the presence of his adoring female worshiper/bacchante: "Liudmila hastily kissed Sasha's arms from his shoulders to his fingers, and Sasha didn't pull them away, now aroused, now plunged as he was in passionate and cruel dreams. Liudmila's kisses were warmed with adoration, and now it was as if not a boy, but a youthful god was being kissed in secret and trembling worship of flowering flesh."[42] By the same token, there will be no rape, no penetration, for that is not what Liudmila wants (she cannot in any event "enter" him) or what (though he has intimations) Sasha is capable of.

Thus, as the inner logic of these scenes seems to dictate, the *pyl'* that is in Sasha's name (*Pylnikov*) and is in the pollen-sprinkled (pollen being flowers' "dust" — "tsvetochnaia *pyl'*") aromas that refine and aestheticize their trysts (Liudmila uses a "ras*pyl*itel'" or atomizer to spray her scents) is the positive flip-side of Peredonov's negative "dirty" and "dusty" (*pyl*'nyi) world. Based on these semantic ties, some scholars have argued that Sasha and Liudmila's world is essentially no different from Peredonov's — that is, it too is demonic, fallen, a kind of alluring mirror inversion of the *nedotykomka*'s realm, with which it alternates.[43] It is also true that Sasha begins to experience demonic tendencies because of what Liudmila has awakened in him: when his aunt comes home to his "mad" cavorting about the house (while thinking about Liudmila and "what she wants" he is overcome by "wild gaiety") she accuses him of "acting possessed [by the devil]" ("besnovat'sia") and "going mad" ("*besit'*sia").[44] Be this as it may, Sasha and Liudmila are extremely ambiguous, yet for the most part positive, figures in the novel: they are the closest of all the characters to gods (pagan ones) and the divine; they turn their dust (*pyl'*) into beauty (flowers); they are trapped in the demiurge's prison but they try for something better; they learn a pleasure laced with pain that is not degrading but refining; and

41 Sologub, *Melkii bes*, 237.
42 Ibid., 239.
43 See, for example, Venclova, "K demonologii," 150–55.
44 Sologub, *Melkii bes*, 240.

45 "I am unable to foresee and to fend inevitable attempts to find in the alembics of *Despair* something of the rhetorical venom that I injected in a much later novel. Hermann and Humbert are alike only in the

they embody an aesthetic principle that is as far as possible from social amelioration and Christian conscience (the ethical principle). Similarly, it is this version of total aestheticism in the absence of an identifiable morality that Nabokov confronts in his "lap scene" and its aftermath in *Lolita*. If one could identify the central difference in how Sologub and Nabokov treat the erotic foreplay-cum-aestheticization of reality in their novels it would be this: what happens to Sasha at the hands of Liudmila is, all things considered, a positive "awakening." Whether Sasha cannot physically be "abused" by this older (though still young) woman, or whether the lessons that he learns from her are the best his fallen world can yield up, it is clear that their playing at the religion of Dionysus is not a conventional morality tale. If Sasha obeyed his inhibitions, succeeded in fending off Liudmila's overtures, and simply went back to being a chaste and dutiful youth, there is absolutely no indication in the text that this outcome would produce either a happier or psychically more fulfilled young protagonist. Quite the opposite. In their coming close to, or perhaps even achieving, the truth of pagan worship — the glimpsing of a god in the flesh — there is no identifiable irony. For the moment he has with Liudmila, before he becomes a hirsute, pomaded, and dumbly "penetrating" *samets* (male adult of the species), Sasha could be Dionysus. That seems to be Sologub's point. Not that he will not inevitably become another feckless prisoner in Peredonov's world (the Manichean theme), but that for this brief interlude he and Liudmila, celebrating the beauty of their bodies without having sex, can taste something "other." With Nabokov the issue of what Humbert does to Dolly Haze is much less ambiguous, the morality of his actions much clearer. First and foremost, by reversing the sex roles and making Humbert considerably older than Liudmila, Nabokov brings the theme of what today is termed "child abuse" much closer to the surface. Humbert knows he is a criminal and realizes the depths of his degradation (which makes him superior to Hermann in *Despair*[45]), yet the fact that he supposedly "cannot help himself" does not mitigate the crime in his ethically staunch creator's eyes. For what is not consummated in Sologub's world is in Nabokov's: first Humbert masturbates (presented with elaborate verbal pyrotechnics and circumlocution—a parody of aesthetic foreplay[46]) as he "safely solipsizes" his prey on the sofa, then he eventually has sex with Lolita after her mother has died and he has "captured" her for the night (to be repeated again and again elsewhere) at the Enchanted Hunters hotel. The point is that by displacing the real Dolly to a safe solipsistic remove and making her permanently into Lolita Humbert has affirmed the girl's semi-

sense that two dragons painted by the same artist at different periods of his life resemble each other. Both are neurotic scoundrels, yet there is a green lane in Paradise where Humbert is permitted to wander at dusk once a year; but Hell shall never parole Hermann" (Vladimir Nabokov, "Foreword," *Despair* [New York, 1965], 9).

46 Nabokov, *Annotated Lolita*, 59: "I want my learned readers to participate in the scene I am about to replay; I want them to examine its every detail and see for themselves how careful, how chaste, the whole wine-sweet event is if viewed with what my lawyer has called, in a private talk we had, 'impartial sympathy.'"

divine, semi-daemonic status by denying her personhood: she exists not as amoral foreplay, where both parties participate equally in the pagan worship, but as the unwitting (hence manipulated) situational rhyme partner with Annabel. In effect, Nabokov takes Sologub and moralizes him by showing the inherent dangers in using other human beings as material to realize one's private dreams (the *zhiznetvorchestvo* theme), whether "wet" or innocent, no matter how refined or verbally dressed out. Nabokov also builds off the dangerous inwardness of the situation by linking it directly to masturbation (solipsistic behavior = playing with oneself) and then, eventually, to actual sex, penetration, which Lolita complains of as hurting her (first physically but then, and more pervasively, emotionally, psychologically):

It was something quite special, that feeling: an oppressive, hideous constraint as if I were sitting with the small ghost of somebody I had just killed.

As she was in the act of getting back into the car, an expression of pain flitted across Lo's face. It flitted again, more meaningfully, as she settled down beside me. No doubt, she reproduced it that second time for my benefit. Foolishly, I asked her what was the matter. "Nothing, you brute," she replied. "You what?" I asked. She was silent. Leaving Briceland. Loquacious Lo was silent. Cold spiders of panic crawled down my neck. This was an orphan. This was a lone child, an absolute waif, with whom a heavy-limbed, foul-smelling adult had had strenuous intercourse three times that very morning. Whether or not the realization of a lifelong dream had surpassed all expectation, it had, in a sense, overshot its mark — and plunged into a nightmare. ...

"You chump," she said, sweetly smiling at me. "You revolting creature. I was a daisy-fresh girl, and look what you've done to me. I ought to call the police and tell them you raped me. Oh, you dirty, dirty old man."

Was she just joking? An ominous hysterical note rang through her silly words. Presently, making a sizzling sound with her lips, she started complaining of pains, said she could not sit, said I had torn something inside her. ...

She appeared at last [from the filling-station restroom]. "Look," she said in that neutral voice that hurt me so, "give me some dimes and nickels. I want to call mother in that hospital. What's the number?"

"Get in," I said. "You can't call that number."
"Why?"
"Get in and slam the door."
She got in and slammed the door. The old garage man beamed at her. I swung onto the highway.
"Why can't I call my mother if I want to?"
"Because," I answered, "your mother is dead."[47]

The irony everywhere present in Nabokov is totally absent in Sologub (at least with regard to the Liudmila-Sasha episodes). This irony is felt because there is obviously a dissonance between the point of view of Humbert and that of the implied author. Earlier, during the Sunday sofa scene, Humbert's behavior had been precisely not "chaste" (despite his disclaimers); indeed, such phrases as "learned readers" lend themselves to the somewhat buffoonish, tongue-in-cheek tone, as if at some level Humbert does not believe himself (which is probably true). Now again, at this crucial juncture in the text (intercourse has finally been accomplished, Part Two is about to begin), Humbert's words constantly comment ironically on themselves. His jocose melodrama and overstatement ("small ghost," "Loquacious Lo," "cold spiders," "absolute waif," "heavy-limbed, foul-smelling adult," and so on), which might seem in other circumstances to take the edge off the seriousness of the moment, here only cause us to see through their smokescreen to the real pain being glossed underneath. On the very day that Humbert realizes his obsession by crossing the final boundary, "[tearing] something inside her" through his brute act of penetration, he informs her of the actual condition of her orphanhood, and in so doing tears something else inside her. He has, in a cruelly literalized metaphor, "overshot [his] mark." What is more, Lolita now has "absolutely nowhere else to go" except back into the clutches of her captor, the "pentapod monster."[48]

In conclusion, we might say that the *pyl'* that is the dust and dirt of Peredonov's realm but also the pollen and flowering scents of Liudmila's and Pylnikov's has become the "haze" (the unfortunate Dolly's and Charlotte's surname) of Humbert's enchanted, but deeply immoral (not amoral) story. Indeed, if Sasha's counterpart in *Lolita* is the young heroine, then Humbert's partner in Sologub is not so much Liudmila as Peredonov himself—a more refined and cultured and, yes, occasionally sympathetic Peredonov, but still one trapped in his own obsessions and blindly buffeted about by his lower urges. The grotesque and ontologically tautological "Double Don" (Perédónov) has become the innerly beastly and identically two-beat, tetrasyllabic "Humbert Son of Humbert" (Húmbert Húmbert).[49] Likewise, Symbolism/

---

47 Ibid., 142–43.
48 Ibid., 144, 286.
49 As Nabokov says in his 1964 *Playboy* interview, "the double rumble is, I think, very nasty, very suggestive. It is a hateful name for a hateful person. It is also a highly kingly name, but I did need a royal vibration for Humbert the fierce and Humbert the Humble. Lends itself also to a number of puns" (cited in Nabokov, *Annotated Lolita*, 321–22).

Decadence, *zhiznetvorchestvo*, and Russia have given way to post-symbolism, the morning after, and a Nova Zembla called America. The hazy, pseudo-exculpatory logic (after all, the miscreant does deserve one evening a year in the alleyways of Paradise) and alluring language (comic and lyric by turns) of Humbert's cautionary tale ostensibly belong to the madman in his cell. But the sure sense we readers get that this tale is cautionary and that the place Humbert's hypertrophied longings must go is, despite the aesthetic foreplay, where they must always go in such cases belongs to the enveloping sanity of Humbert's creator.

More to the point, the very vulgarity, *poshlost'*, that lies at the heart of Humbert's lifelong project — for what is *poshlost'* in Nabokov's mind if not the penchant for dragging others into one's indecent and all-too-predictable dreams? — is the same profound lack of originality that confuses the hero with the author[50] (also Sologub's problem) and condemns the text as pornographic when what it is is a masterfully executed send-up of the expectations that go with literary titillation. This, the *poshlost'* embedded in much symbolist *zhiznetvorchestvo*, is what Nabokov took from Sologub, the exquisite aesthete, and turned on its head. And the symbolist magic moment, the coming of a Beautiful Lady or Sophia (an eroticized Holy Wisdom) to a uniquely privileged mortal? It is nothing more and nothing less than a coming of the most basic biological sort. Thus, if in *The Petty Demon* the one bright spot is the young Dionysus and his bacchante *before* they become the same defiled lovers as Peredonov and Varvara, then in *Lolita* the picture of the young nymph, no matter how mesmerizing to the hunter, simply cannot exist in the reader's eye without the countervailing image of the "hugely pregnant" and soon-to-die Mrs. Richard F. Schiller. The phrase "Lolita had been safely solipsized," surely the most pregnant in the novel, was rendered tellingly by Nabokov himself in the 1967 Russian version as "Real'nost' Lolity byla blagopoluchno *otmenena*"[51] (Lolita's reality had been safely *cancelled out*). It is this cancelling out that lies behind all the intertextual gamesmanship and gives to the work what could otherwise be mistaken for mockingbird lightness and brightness a true humanity and moral *gravitas*.

---

50   See, for example, Skonchenaia, "*Otchaianie* V. Nabokova i *Melkii bes* F. Sologuba," 142, where the scholar explains how both Adamovich and Sartre, identifying/confusing the hero of *Despair* (Hermann) with the author in their moral judgment of the latter, show themselves criminally "drawn into the world of Nabokov's obedient characters" (*okazalis' vtianuty v mir poslushnykh nabokovskikh personazhei*).

51   Nabokov, *Lolita*, 49.

Chapter 17 — Exile, Elegy, and Auden in Brodsky's "Verses on the Death of T. S. Eliot"[1]

"Death," writes Joseph Brodsky in his 1982 essay on Akhmatova, "is a good litmus test for a poet's ethics. The 'in memoriam' genre is frequently used to exercise self-pity or for metaphysical trips that denote the subconscious superiority of survivor over victim, of majority (of the alive) over minority (of the dead). Akhmatova [in her poetic cycle *Requiem*] would have none of that."[2] This statement, as self-regarding as it is self-effacing, is itself a kind of litmus test for the author's own ethics and aesthetics. Versions of it reappear at strategic moments in Brodsky's important essays on Tsvetaeva and on Auden,[3] and its central notion plays a conceptual and configural role in several of his finest elegiac efforts. Yet the in memoriam genre did not always occupy pride of place in Brodsky's oeuvre. Only when the boundaries symbolized by a poet's death were elided with the borders of a national poetic tradition, only when the issues of exile, whether physical or psychic, and elegy became extensions of each other, could this happen. A number of early texts foreground this process, but perhaps the most famous was written in January 1965, when the young Brodsky was located in internal exile in the far northern village of Norenskaya (Arkhangelsk province).[4] In view of the time and place of composition, 'Verses on the Death of T. S. Eliot' ("Stikhi na smert' T.S. Eliota") is a crucial text not only in Brodsky's career but in the history of post-Stalinist Russian poetry. Here the poet consciously demonstrates what will become a basic principle of his mature *ars poetica*: he speaks of the death of one Western poet (Eliot) in the "mourning tongue" and elegiac form borrowed from another (Auden) and, in this way, keeps "the death of the poet... from [the poet's] poems."[5] Brodsky goes out of his native tradition in order, as it were, to reinvent it.

1   First published in *PMLA* 07 (March 1992): 232-245.
2   Joseph Brodsky, *Less Than One: Selected Essays* (New York: Farrar, Straus, Giroux, 1986), 50.
3   Ibid., 195-96, 361.
4   Background on this period of Brodsky's life can be found in various sources: e.g., Ralph Blum, "A Reporter at Large: Freeze and Thaw: The Artist in Soviet Russia-III," *New Yorker* 11 Sept. 1965: 192–217; Anatolii Naiman, *Rasskazy o Anne Akhmatovoi* (Moscow: Khudozhestvennaia literatura, 1989), 5–226; and Valentina Polukhina, *Joseph Brodsky: A Poet for Our Time* (Cambridge: Cambridge University Press, 1989), 20–30. The court proceedings involving Brodsky, preserved through Frida Vigdorova's stenographic notes, are reproduced in: "Zasedanie suda Dzherzhinskogo raiona goroda Leningrada" [A Session of the Court of the Dzherzhinsky District of the City of Leningrad] (Russian-language transcript of Brodsky's trial), *Vozdushnye puti* [Aerial Ways] 4 (1965): 279–303; and "The Trial of Iosif Brodsky" (English-language transcript of Brodsky's trial). *New Leader* (31 Aug. 1964): 6–17.
5   Polukhina treats "Verses on the Death of T. S. Eliot" at some length (81–88); but see as well Gerald Janecek, "Comments on Brodskij's 'Stixi na smert' T. S. Eliota,'" *Russian Language Journal* 34 (1980): 150–53 and Kline's notes on the poem in Brodsky, *Selected Poems*, trans. George Kline (New York: Harper, 1973), 102, 195. In one interview Brodsky briefly mentions what he

How and why was Brodsky drawn to these non-Russian poets, especially Auden? The topic is, prima facie, fraught with all manner of Bloomian overtones. If poetic influence is "a disease of self-consciousness" and if every "strong" poet is "condemned to learn his profoundest yearnings through an awareness of *other selves*,"[6] then Brodsky should, by all rights, be feeling considerably under the weather. No other Russian poet of the post-Stalinist era is a better candidate for the Bloomian flu, with its "history of anxiety and self-serving caricature, of distortion, of perverse, wilful revisionism."[7] In fact, readers have to go back to the 1930s and the high modernism of Mandelstam to find another poet as bent on domesticating the foreign and the "other" to create his or her own niche within the mainstream, or at least on the margins, of Russian-Soviet letters. "The Russian language," remarks Mandelstam in his essay "On the Nature of the Word" (1922), "just like the Russian national spirit, is formed through ceaseless hybridization, cross-breeding and foreign-born [*chuzherodnykh*] influences."[8] That Mandelstam was a Jew whose family had come to Russia from Central Europe and whose own generation suffered from what the poet called, in *The Noise of Time* (1925), "congenital tongue-tie" are facts that have not been lost on Brodsky, whose debt to this precursor as outsider is very great indeed.[9]

The question of the outsider does not stop here, however, and that is precisely the point. If we recall that Auden, Brodsky's source, was himself a kind of outsider who labored under the weight of his debt to Yeats and that Eliot, Brodsky's subject, was a man "who lived in a condition of permanent exile... as if isolation or aloneness were something he was compelled to choose,"[10] then we begin to sense how potentially complex the issue of

was trying to achieve in the poem ("The Muse in Exile: Conversations with the Russian Poet, Joseph Brodsky," with Anne-Marie Brumm, *Mosaic* 8 [1974]: 232), and in another he comments on Auden's and Eliot's "fling" with Christianity, favoring the more existential Auden ("The Art of Poetry XXVIII: Joseph Brodsky," with Sven Birkerts, *Paris Review* 83 [1982]: 110–11). My study differs from Polukhina's in several ways but chiefly in its emphasis on Auden, rather than on Eliot, as the primary formal as well as philosophical source for the poem. Polukhina's attempts to trace Brodsky's use of water imagery to Eliot's *Four Quartets*, especially to "The Dry Salvages," are, according to Brodsky himself, misplaced, since in 1965 he did not know that work. (See, in addition, Janecek, "Comments," 152.) At that time Eliot was to Brodsky more a symbol of forbidden Western fruit, of a modernism denied poets like himself. Hence the water imagery, despite its superficial affinity to Eliot's, is Brodsky's own (Telephone interview, 14 Feb. 1990).

Another supposedly, but not certainly, fortuitous convergence of Eliot, Auden, and Brodsky occurs in their respective treatments of Simeon, the old man who "should not see death before he had seen the Lord's Christ" and who represents the transition in thought between the Old Testament and the New (Luke 2.22–36). See Eliot's "Song for Simeon," Auden's "Meditation of Simeon" (in his *For the Time Being*), and Brodsky's "Nunc Dimittis" («Сретенье»).

6 Harold Bloom, *The Anxiety of Influence* (New York: Oxford University Press, 1973), 26–29.
7 Ibid., 30.
8 Osip Mandelstam, *The Complete Critical Prose and Letters*, ed. Jane Gary Harris, trans. Jane Gary Harris and Constance Link (Ann Arbor: Ardis, 1979), 120; *Sobranie sochinenii* Vol. 2, ed. Gleb Struve and Boris Filipoff (Washington: Inter-lang. Lit. Assocs., 1972), 245.
9 See Jane E. Knox, "Iosif Brodskij's Affinity with Osip Mandel'štam: Cultural Links with the Past." Diss. University of Texas, 1978.
10 Frank Kermode, *An Appetite for Poetry* (Cambridge: Harvard University Press, 1989), 109.

cross-breeding and foreign-born influences is for this Russian poem and the elegiac tradition it represents.[11] Auden, as we know, excised the sections of "September 1, 1939" that sounded too much like the Yeats of "Easter 1916." In fact, he wrestled with the Yeatsian presence to the point where, in this text at least, he surrendered — acknowledging that something inauthentic had permeated to the core of the poem and could no longer be included in his collected verse.[12] Similar analogies could be drawn between the famous Yeatsian occasional elegy "In Memory of Major Robert Gregory" and Auden's "In Memory of W. B. Yeats." By the time Auden emigrated to America on the eve of the Second World War, he so feared and resented this symbolic scion of the "last romantics" ("Coole Park and Ballylee, 1931") and the voice Yeats could ventriloquize from afar, against the will of the younger poet, that it is fair to speak of "a kind of obsession."[13] Later, referring to Day Lewis's debt to Hardy, Auden wrote, "I wish I could say the same about Yeats' influence on me. Alas, I think it was a bad influence, for which, most unjustly, I find it difficult to forgive him."[14] How much of this background was Brodsky aware of when he wrote his poem in 1965 and then his prose eulogy of Auden, "To Please a Shadow," in 1983? On the one hand, he seems to have managed the specter of his belatedness and the oedipal demons of prior traditions with the aplomb of a cultural conquistador. One of his greatest achievements, presumably in his own mind and certainly in the collective opinion of the Russian intelligentsia, is that he has opened up traditions that, because of the suspended animation of Stalinism, were either insufficiently known or prematurely forgotten. He has never, as far as we can tell by his interviews and written statements, seemed upset that Donne or Auden or Milosz "got there first." Indeed, Brodsky has gone on record — and defiantly so — as denying the kind of anxiety that Bloom describes;[15] and his disclaimers have the ring of authenticity about them, although the psychoanalytic critic could argue that any such statements are really defense mechanisms and thus, a fortiori, proof of anxiety.

Could it be, on the other hand, that these traditions were not his to begin with and that, in discovering these poets for the Russians, Brodsky is not a latecomer but, rather, a newcomer? Strong poets, once "ephebes" (in Bloomian terminology), always wrestle with precursors, but that struggle is a good deal less polemical when the alien tradition of the father does not make the son belated in his own native tradition. The "misprision" or "swerve" (clinamen) from, or

[11] Brodsky claims that in January 1965 he knew relatively little about the biographies of Eliot and Auden or, more important, about the outsider-insider issue in those biographies (telephone interview, 14 Feb. 1990). These categories may nonetheless have been operating on some level, for in part 2 of "Verses," he personifies the responses of England and America to Eliot's death, and in part 3 he invokes Horace (in a later essay he refers to Auden as "our transatlantic Horace" [Brodsky, *Less Than One*, 382]).

[12] Edward Callan, *Auden: A Carnival of Intellect* (New York: Oxford University Press, 1983), 156.

[13] Ibid., 144.

[14] "Letter of Introduction," in *C. Day Lewis, the Poet Laureate: A Bibliography*, comp. G. Handley-Taylor and Timothy d'Arch Smith (London: St. James, 1968), v-vi, in Callan, *Auden*, 144.

[15] Knox, "Iosif Brodskij's Affinity," 383.

[16] Edward W. Said, "The Mind of Winter: Reflections on Life in Exile," *Harper's* (Sept 1984):

the "completion" (tessera) of, the original model works in a Bloomian universe where the later poet, say Auden, feels the full weight — in his own language and native tradition — of the precursor's, say Yeats's, word. But what becomes of that weight and the vexed issue of poetic priority when the model itself is experienced as a word that could not have been one's own to begin with?

Exile

From early on Brodsky gave evidence of the "nomadic, decentered, contrapuntal" poetic imagination that Edward Said and others have identified as characteristic of the exile.[16] In January 1965 Brodsky was in internal exile in the Arkhangelsk province of northern Russia; the previous year he had been tried and sentenced on charges of "social parasitism" (*tuneiadstvo*) and had now begun serving his sentence of five years' hard labor (subsequently commuted after twenty months). And yet despite, or perhaps thanks to, his nearly total isolation in the north, he was able to advance substantially as a poet.[17] Indeed, although Brodsky himself rejects the notion of turning points, at least in his own life,[18] it can be argued that this experience was crucial in the formation of the new, more expansive, odic voice that emerged from the frozen chrysalis of the north in the mid-sixties. This growth can now be linked, at least in part, to his reading of modern Anglo-American poetry, Auden in particular. Brodsky had first read English poetry in Russian translation at home in Leningrad, but exile, he reports in "To Please a Shadow," gave him a chance to become more familiar with it:

> It so happened that my next opportunity to pay a closer look at Auden occurred while I was doing time in the North, in a small village lost among swamps and forests, near the polar circle. This time the anthology that I had was in English, sent to me by a friend from Moscow. It had quite a lot of Yeats, whom I then found a bit too oratorical and sloppy with meters, and Eliot, who in those days reigned supreme in Eastern Europe. I was intending to read Eliot.[19]

55. The secondary literature on the exilic condition is substantial. Works that I have found helpful, particularly in treating the relation in Brodsky between the existential category of exile and the aesthetic category of elegy, include Brodsky, "The Condition We Call Exile," *New York Review of Books* (21 Jan. 1988): 18; Harry Levin, "Literature and Exile," *Refractions: Essays in Comparative Literature* (New York: Oxford University Press, 1966), 62–81; Czeslaw Milosz, "Notes on Exile," in "The Writer in Exile," spec. sec. of *Books Abroad* 50.2 (1976): 281–84; Said, "Mind" and *The World, the Text, and the Critic* (Cambridge: Harvard University Press, 1983), 1–30; Michael Seidel, *Exile and the Narrative Imagination* (New Haven: Yale University Press, 1986), 1–16; and Joseph Wittlin, "Sorrow and Grandeur of Exile," *Polish Review* 2.2–3 (1957): 99–111. See as well "The Writer in Exile," spec. sec. of *Books Abroad* 50.2 (1976): 271–328; *The Literature of Exile*, spec. issue of *Mosaic* 8.3 (1975).

17 Cf. Sandler's illuminating remarks on the exiled Pushkin's relations to his readership (Stephanie Sandler, *Distant Pleasures: Alexander Pushkin and the Writing of Exile*, [Stanford: Stanford University Press, 1989], 1–15) and Said's analysis of the benefits of exile, with specific reference to Auerbach's writing of *Mimesis* in Istanbul (*World*, 5–9).

18 Brodsky, *Less Than One*, 17.

19 Ibid., 361; The equally important connection with

elaborate on Brodsky's Auden connection later, but for now let us note (1) that Brodsky was in physical exile; (2) that he was drawn at this time to reading Eliot above all other English-speaking poets; (3) that Eliot's death in January 1965 led him to write a poem modeled on Auden's "In Memory of W. B. Yeats," a work about the death of another major figure in another January (1939); and (4) that all the poets implicated in this specific concatenation of the in memoriam genre were in some sense outcasts or exiles—Yeats an Irish nationalist writing in English, Eliot an American who had emigrated to England and Anglicanism, Auden an Englishman who had emigrated to America (and its quintessential city, New York), and Brodsky a Russian Jew in internal exile who was beginning a poetic emigration to the Anglo-American tradition.[20] All these border crossings were playing at the edges of Brodsky's mind. If they were not yet present explicitly, the poet was, in his choice and treatment of subject, feeling his way toward them. Characteristically, Brodsky seems to come closest to defining the term *exile* on an occasion when he distances himself from it. Discussing Auden's "September 1, 1939" he refers to the lines "Exiled Thucydides knew / All that a speech can say / About Democracy" and describes the attempts of a modern Thucydides to muffle self-pity:

> "Exiled" is a pretty loaded word, isn't it? It's high-pitched not only because of what it describes but in terms of its vowels also... Now, what in your opinion makes our poet think of Thucydides and of what this Thucydides "knew"? Well, my guess is that it has to do with [Auden's] own attempts at playing historian for his own Athens [prewar England]; ... he too is doomed to be ignored. Hence this air of fatigue that pervades the line, and hence the exhaling feeling in "exiled"—which he could apply to his own physical situation as well, but only in a minor key, for this adjective is loaded with a possibility for self-aggrandizement.[21]

"Exile" is, for Brodsky, at least in its explicit hypostasis, ultimately a nonissue, a dead center off which to move rather than a dead end, which permits no further movement. He views exile in this way largely because of its po-

---

John Donne and the English Metaphysicals came earlier, in 1963, when Brodsky first began to read English poetry, primarily in translation. Not only did Brodsky render into Russian (among other works) "A Valediction: Forbidding Mourning" (see *Ostanovka v pustyne*, [New York: Chekhov, 1970], 224–25), he wrote "Large Elegy to John Donne," a major poem focusing on the soul's extended monologue at the moment of Donne's death.

For more on the influence of English-language sources on Brodsky, see, for example, his interview with the Swedish Slavist Bengt Jangfeldt (*Expressen* [3 Apr. 1987]): "English has certainly influenced my Russian. It's difficult to determine how, but I've noticed, for example, that unwittingly I try to apply to Russian the precise analytical mechanism characteristic of English. I used to write without deliberation; now I ponder every line."

20 On the Jewish theme and its importance to Brodsky's status as an exile, see Bethea, "Mandelstam, Pasternak, Brodsky: Judaism and Christianity in the Making of a Modernist Poetics," in *Russkaia literatura XX veka: Issledovaniia amerikanskikh uchenykh* [Russian Literature of the Twentieth Century: Studies by American Scholars], ed. Boris Averin and Elizabeth Neatrour (St. Petersburg: "Petro-RIF," 1993), 362–399.

21 Brodsky, *Less Than One*, 327–28.

tential for cliché.²² No poet in the twentieth century can use the topos of his own loneliness and exile status without first disarming that loaded term, introducing the motif, if at all, only in a minor key, which deflects attention from the speaker. Brodsky returns to these thoughts in his essays on Tsvetaeva and on Auden, the poets who represent to him the purest essence of elegy and on whose behalf he raises his own eulogistic voice a note higher than he does anywhere else in *Less Than One*. According to Brodsky, it should be remembered, Tsvetaeva and Auden managed multiple acts of self-creation through self-effacement in their famous works on Rilke "New Year's Greeting" (*Novogodnee*) and Yeats ("In Memory of W. B. Yeats"). In these poems "self-aggrandizement" that might attend any mention of personal exile is transmuted into the disinterested contemplation of the psychic exilium confronting us all in the passing of a great poet. The lyrical element (the personal loss of a loved one) elides with the metaphysical element (the theme of death as universal border crossing) to produce the distilled essence of elegy, what Brodsky calls "the most fully developed genre in poetry."²³

Brodsky is most revealing on the connection between physical estrangement (exile) and poetic estrangement (elegy) in analyzing Tsvetaeva's speaker in "New Year's Greeting." By looking at the world abandoned by Rilke at his death and forcing herself to see it as if through the eyes of his soul, she develops the capacity to "look at herself at a distance,"²⁴ to deflect her grief by becoming the other. This stratagem, as any reader would readily acknowledge, is also the Brodskian trope par excellence. Tsvetaeva turns the tables of habitual cognition or reader expectation by making us the exiles, the ones stranded in the here and now as Rilke's soul wanders in the empyrean beyond. This is a bold gambit on her part, for we are accustomed to mourning the dead by visualizing the loss from our point of view, through our sorrow at another soul banished from this world (i.e., the bel canto, self-aggrandizing element Brodsky so fears). Tsvetaeva, who certainly possessed an ego of monstrous proportions, forestalls this possibility by separating her self from the other mourners and repositioning that self as the eye "'see[ing]' Rilke 'seeing' all of this."²⁵ Brodsky attaches primary importance to this stance:

> The knack of estranging — from reality, from a text, from the self, from thoughts about the self — *which may be the first prerequisite for creativity*... developed in Tsvetaeva's case to the level of instinct. What began as a literary device became the form (nay, norm) of existence... Estrangement is at the same time both the method and the subject of this poem.²⁶

---

22 "For art doesn't imitate life if only for fear of clichés" (Brodsky, *Less Than One*, 41). It is in this issue of poetic cliché more than anywhere else that we can sense Brodsky's anxiety of influence. He will go to great lengths, if not to avoid saying what has already been said, at least to say it in a totally new way (see Mikhail Kreps, *O poezii Iosifa Brodskogo* [Ann Arbor: Ardis, 1984], 2–3).

23 Brodsky, *Less Than One*, 195.
24 Ibid., 216.
25 Ibid., 219.
26 My emphasis; ibid., 219–21; At the end of the essay, as if to raise the ante one last

Elegy

Let us now take a closer look at how the notion of exile is reworked in Auden's and Brodsky's elegies. A cursory examination yields the following thematic and compositional similarities: (1) each poem is divided into three complementary parts, with a distinct progression from first to last; (2) each treats the death, in January, of another poet; (3) each uses the properties of rhyme to "domesticate" the sense of loss; (4) each blends elements of the traditional pastoral elegy and love lyric into its descriptions of a modern cityscape; and (5) each self-consciously situates itself against the notions of a national poet or bard and a national elegiac tradition.

Auden begins "the decade's elegy"[27] by describing not the dying Yeats but the world as it might be seen responding to the news of that dying:

> He disappeared in the dead of winter:
> The brooks were frozen, the airports almost deserted,
> And snow disfigured the public statues;
> The mercury sank in the mouth of the dying day.
> O all the instruments agree
> The day of his death was a dark cold day.[28]

The first verb in the poem is a euphemism, what de Man would call a *prosopon*—a mask or face that talks around the subject but does not name it.[29] It is intimately linked to the later exclamation "O all the instruments agree...," which resembles the trope of apostrophe and has ties to an older, more rhetorical tradition. In other words, although the poem is ostensibly about Yeats's death, in actuality it is not. To say that the poet has disappeared is to say that he has gone elsewhere, that he has emigrated. The attributes of death fall instead on this world—on the frozen brooks, deserted airports, and snow-covered statues. Even Auden's rhetoric, the sudden surfacing of the

---

time, Brodsky makes a statement that borders on self-revelation, with specific application to "Verses on the Death of T. S. Eliot": "is precisely on account of its destructive rationalism [Brodsky's favorite mode] that 'Novogodnee' falls outside Russian poetic tradition, which prefers to resolve problems in a key that while not necessarily positive is at least consoling... It might be more reasonable to say that 'Novogodnee' does not fall outside Russian poetic tradition but expands it." (Brodsky, *Less Than One*, 263).

27 Samuel Hynes, *The Auden Generation: Literature and Politics in England in the 1930s*, (Princeton: Princeton University Press, 1972), 351.

28 Auden, *The Collected Poetry of W. H. Auden*, (New York: Random, 1945), 48–49; I am using the version of the poem that Brodsky read and responded to in 1965, although several lines were either emended or removed in the final edition that Auden approved—the changes once again reflecting Auden's increasing anxiety of influence in the face of his subject. It is intriguing to note that these lines, including "O all the instruments agree" and the pivotal "time worships language," were precisely the ones that originally attracted Brodsky to Auden. Hence Auden's "anti-heroic" posture (Brodsky, *Less Than One*, 367) seems to have possessed enough lyricism to influence the twenty-four-year-old Russian poet but too much to satisfy the author himself, at least the author of the final version. The older Auden, for example, changed the penultimate line in the quoted passage to the more informal "What instruments we have agree," thus rejecting the influence of an older tradition, as explained below.

29 Paul de Man, "Lyric Voice in Contemporary Theory: Riffaterre and Jauss," *Lyric Poetry: Beyond the New Criticism*, ed. Chaviva Hosek and Patricia Parker (Ithaca: Cornell University Press, 1985), 57.

iambic cadence in "O all the instruments agree," sounds hollow, as though the traditional participation of nature in a poet's death is by this point in literary history an overly conscious and awkward convention, little more than an attempt to calibrate our loss on a thermometer. It follows, therefore, that what is defunct in the line "The *day* of his *death* was a *dark* cold *day*" is not, in spite of the wording, the poet (he has simply disappeared) but the traditional language of elegy (the "grand" style). That language, Auden seems to say—the heavy, alliterative thud of the *d*'s evoking the organ bass of a funeral dirge—no longer rings true.

Lest these remarks sound too much like the idle play of the signifier, I quote Auden himself on the way his work reflected Yeats. In a 1964 letter to Stephen Spender, Auden wrote, "I am incapable of saying a word about W. B. Yeats because, through no fault of his, he has become for me a symbol of my own devil of authenticity, of everything which I must try to eliminate from my own poetry, false emotions, inflated rhetoric, empty sonorities."[30] To ensure his own authenticity, to distance himself from false emotions and inflated rhetoric, Auden surrounds the Yeatsian voice in his elegy with the slight whiff of parody. Only through parody can the genuine Yeats, the one who has disappeared beyond the threshold of January 1939, be preserved from the dangers of self-aggrandizement.[31]

One would expect the twenty-four-year-old author of "Verses on the Death of T. S. Eliot" to be free of the anxiety of influence that plagued Auden. Brodsky confirms such suspicions by telling us exactly how he first responded to the formal features of Auden's poem, which he encountered in an anthology of English poetry sent to him in exile by a Moscow friend:

> By pure chance the book opened to Auden's "In Memory of W. B. Yeats." I was young then and therefore particularly keen on elegies as a genre, having nobody around dying to write for.... I soon realized that even [the poem's] structure was designed to pay tribute to the dead poet, imitating in reverse order the great Irishman's own modes of stylistic development, all the way down to his earliest: the tetrameters of the poem's third—last—part.[32]

There is almost no room here for parody, for the complex polemical relationship that Auden felt as he tried to do justice to Yeats without losing his own voice. In recognizing that the poem's structure pays "tribute to the dead poet" by adopting his "modes of stylistic development," Brodsky appears, at first glance, not to see that tribute as vexed.

It is not surprising then that Brodsky's tone carries over into his poem, whose

---

30 Charles Osborne, *W. H. Auden: The Life of a Poet* (New York: Harcourt, 1979), 280.

31 If, as Lawrence Lipking remarks in his study of the poem, "Yeats enjoys picturing himself dead [and] expects to lose none of his authority in the grave," then it is Auden's role, first and foremost, to rob "Yeats of property rights in his own death" (Lipking, *The Life of the Poet: Beginning and Ending Poetic Careers* [Chicago: University of Chicago Press, 1981], 152–54).

Two texts that shed light on Auden's understanding of Yeats after January 1939 are his prose dialogue "The Public vs. the Late Mr. William Butler Yeats" (1939) and his *Elegy for Young Lovers* (1961). The first, in

sonority and ponderous beauty seem entirely "on the level":

> Он умер в январе, в начале года.
> Под фонарем стоял мороз у входа.
> Не успевала показать природа
> ему своих красот кордебалет.
> От снега стекла становились уже.
> Под фонарем стоял глашатай стужи.
> На перекрестках замерзали лужи.
> И дверь он запер на цепочку лет.[33]

We are immediately impressed by the simple syntax of the stanza: only one sentence extends beyond the boundary of a line, and there is not a single dependent clause. The style here is a far cry from the remarkably dense, almost baroque composition evident even in Brodsky's early works. The reason is, presumably, that the Russian stanza follows the sentence structure of the English original, where each line (except the last two) represents its own self-enclosed thought. Brodsky may also intend the form to reinforce the notion of border crossing (hence exile): just as sentence and line boundaries are coterminous, so too is each thought realized through a threshold image (the frost at the entrance, the ballet on stage, the windows framed in snow, the intersections reflected in puddles, the closing door, etc.). All these thresholds, of course, grow out of the irony inherent in the opening line: the end of a life comes at the beginning of a new year, and the difference between the one and the other is a caesura, a pause for breath, an invisible stepping off or over. Brodsky's rhyme scheme (AAAbCCCb) is as formally complex as Auden's is nonexistent. There are, however, no slant or partial rhymes, which often surface in Brodsky's works in moments of existential doubt and irony; and all the rhyme words, with the exception of *úzhe* ("narrower, thinner"), are nouns — another rarity. Against Auden's vers libre Brodsky counterposes iambic pentameter, a meter that "throughout much of the twentieth century... has rivaled the iambic tetrameter" in popularity among Russian poets.[34] The overall effect is one of simplicity and grandeur. Clearly Brodsky

---

which the "Public Prosecutor" and the "Counsel for the Defence" present pro and con cases for Yeats's "greatness," has particular relevance to "In Memory of W. B. Yeats." See the discussions in Callan, *Auden*, 143–62; Hynes, *Auden Generation*, 349–53; and Pköping, *Life of the Poet*, 151–60. See also Brodsky's recollection of a conversation with Auden: "[Auden:] 'I have known three great poets, each one a prize son of a bitch.' I: 'Who?' He: 'Yeats, Frost, Bert Brecht'" (Brodsky, *Less Than One*, 374).

32 Brodsky, *Less Than One*, 361–62.

33 He died at start of year, in January. / His front door flinched in frost by the streetlamp. / There was no time for nature to display / the splendors of her choreography. / Black windowpanes shrank mutely in the snow. / The cold's town-crier stood beneath the light. / At crossings puddles stiffened into ice. / He latched his door on the thin chain of years.

The Russian quotations from Brodsky's poem are taken from *Ostanovka v pustyne* [A Halt in the Desert] (New York: Chekhov, 1970), the English passages from *Selected Poems*, 99. Kline's relatively faithful translation preserves the original meter but makes no attempt to reproduce the elegant rhyme scheme.

34 Barry P. Scherr, *Russian Poetry: Meter, Rhythm, and Rhyme* (Berkeley: University of California Press, 1986), 52.

does not yet sense that the prosodic structures of his language, in this elegiac context, are in danger of casting his enterprise into overstatement or "inflated rhetoric." The marked presence of adjoining rhyme, which would almost certainly sound parodic in modern English, only adds to the poem's acoustic splendor (i.e., sonority is not perceived as empty). The same may be said of alliterative effects: the "*kr*" sound in "emu svoikh *kr*asot *k*o*r*debalet" and particularly the ст sound in "*Ot snega stekla stanovilis' uzhe*" and "*Pod fonarem stoial glashatai stuzhi*," the last two seeming to announce in advance the naming of the poet ("*Tomas Sterns*") in the third part.

Auden's opening stanza has three examples of what might be called figurative language: the pun on "dead of winter," the "disfigurement" by snow of the public statues, and the striking "The mercury sank in the mouth of the dying day," a line that Brodsky calls "astonishing."[35] Brodsky's more elaborate figures, in contrast, despite the coolness of the occasion and the tempo, hide a certain exuberance, especially the ballet image and the perfectly epigrammatic "I dver' on zaper na tsepochku let." Perhaps because Brodsky is writing in Russian about the death of a foreign poet, there is a sense of fullness, of balance, between the formal and semantic features, whereas the same features in Auden suggest an emptying out of tradition. Brodsky, in effect, like the Tsvetaeva of "New Year's Greeting," can reinvigorate his native elegiac tradition through a kind of defamiliarization:

> If... the subject [of a Russian elegy] was the demise of a preeminent figure belonging to another culture (the death of Byron or Goethe, for example), its very "foreignness" seemed to give added stimulus to the most general, abstract kind of discussion, viz.: of the role of the "bard" in the life of society, of art in general, of, as Akhmatova put it, "ages and peoples."[36]

If there is a difference so far in the two elegies, it is in the added stimulus inherent in Brodsky's poem.

This reading is borne out and amplified as the two poems unfold. Auden hews to his tone of studied understatement and irony: life, epitomized by the wild, unmindful wolves and the "peasant river" of stanza 2, runs on even as the great man dies. "By mourning tongues," that is, by the words of those left behind, "[t]he death of the poet [is] kept from his poems." The poem expresses no interest in the state of Yeats's soul or its present whereabouts (that would be too Yeatsian a gesture); the speaker's perspective remains relentlessly tethered to the here and now. The cityscape of stanza 1 is reassembled in stanza 3, only on this occasion the urban metaphors refer specifically to the

---

35 Brodsky, *Less Than One*, 362.
36 Ibid., 196–97.
37 Auden, *Collected Poetry*, 49.
38 Brodsky is not enamored of the symbolists' imprecise diction and self-importance (though he owes much to their thematics), but he has great respect for the acmeists (especially Mandelstam and Akhmatova) and for Tsvetaeva.
39 Lev Loseff, "Iosif Brodskii's Poetics of Faith," *Aspects of Modern Russian and Czech Literature: Selected Papers of the Third World Congress for Soviet and East European Studies*, ed. Arnold McMillin (Columbus, OH: Slavica, 1989), 190.

poet and to the absence of what was once a powerful, magnetic personality:

> The provinces of his body revolted,
> The squares of his mind were empty,
> Silence invaded the suburbs,
> The current of his feeling failed: he became his admirers.[37]

For Auden what is important, therefore, is the threshold at which the man "becomes his admirers," the poet his poems. And this threshold is broached only when there is total absence on one side—for example, empty squares, silent suburbs, and failed current. The emigration or exile is completed in stanza 4 as the poet "is scattered among a hundred cities" and given over exclusively to the world of "alterity," one no longer his—the "unfamiliar affections," the "happiness in another kind of wood," and the "foreign code of conscience." In short, Auden's elegizing is, at least thus far, anti-Tsvetaevan; we do not see the poet seeing Yeats's soul seeing us. Instead, Yeats becomes his poems (a notion he himself expresses in his Byzantium pieces), but in the process the active, difficult, protean self that gave birth to the poems is, in a sense, exiled from them, deprived of any say in what the words mean. "The words of a dead man / Are modified in the guts of the living."

Brodsky, like Auden, raises the traditional issue of poetic, or secular, immortality—that is, of the poem that lives on in the world after the poet's death. But, unlike Auden, he is not against mentioning the nonsecular aspect of that immortality. Here one should note that Auden, in 1939, has wearied of the symbolist heritage and grown impatient with Yeats's numerous "dialogues of self and soul." Brodsky, however, is writing in 1965, in a world starved for the higher values of a now distant silver age.[38] Willing to do battle with facile, state-sponsored atheism, he states in another context that his reintroduction of the word *dusha* (soul) into the Russian lyric lexicon, in a serious and "nonpartisan" framework, is his greatest achievement as a poet.[39] In, stanza 3 of his elegy, Brodsky makes the same distinction between life and art, between the bard (*pevets*) and the bard's word (here *slog*), that Auden does:[40]

> Без злых гримас, без помышленья злого,
> из всех щедрот Большого Каталога
> смерть выбирает не красоты слога,
> а неизменно самого певца.[41]

But it is at this point that Brodsky's and Auden's visions of a dying poet part company. In the last two stanzas of part 1 Brodsky produces a masterly scenario of what it would feel, look, and sound like for the soul of a great poet to depart this world. Note that our angle of vision is directed, except

40 Auden, however, would be unlikely to use the word bard except in an ironic context. *Poetry* (*poeziia*), the central noun in stanza 2, and *death* (*smert'*), the central noun in stanza 3, can be seen here to complement and define each other. Both nouns are feminine, and the substitution of pronouns in the second half of each stanza acts to reinforce this notion of complementarity.

41 With neither grimace nor maliciousness / death chooses from its bulging catalogue / the poet, not his words, however strong, / but just—unfailingly—the poet's self. (*Ostanovka v pustyne*, 139; *Selected Passages*, 99).

for the final line of stanza 5, entirely on the receding Eliot, and that we, à la Tsvetaeva's speaker, set out with him on his journey:[42]

> На пустырях уже пылали елки,
> и выметались за порог осколки,
> и водворялись ангелы на полке.
> Католик, он дожил до Рождества.
> Но, словно море в шумный час прилива,
> за волноломом плеснувши, справедливо
> назад вбирает волны — торопливо
> от своего ушел он торжества.
> Уже не Бог, а только время, Время
> зовет его. И молодое племя
> огромных волн его движенья бремя
> на самый край цветущей бахромы
> легко возносит и, простившись, бьется
> о край земли. В избытке сил смеется.
> И январем его залив вдается
> в ту сушу дней, где остаемся мы.[43]

These verses, regardless of the role of the Auden original, are metaphysical poetry of a high order. Stanza 4 breaks into two four-line sentences: in the first, we see details of the Christmas season (another threshold [*porog*], this one of course symbolizing the miracle of the divine word become flesh) that Eliot, a believing Anglican, "lived til" ("Katolik, on dozhil do Rozhdestva"); in the second, we see the now dead poet, or presumably his soul, riding the ebbing waves away from his "solemn victory." Indeed, the entire stanza is itself in the shape of a wave, with its crest in the center, at the break between "*do Rozhdestva*" and "*No*." The last line—"*toroplivo / ot svoego ushel on torzhestva*"—is Brodsky's moving, "russified" version of Auden's more matter-of-fact "he became his admirers." That Eliot's soul blends with the vital movement of the sea, which "justly" (*spravedlivo*) recalls its waves from the shore, suggests that there is a divine intentionality or essential rightness to this process. Auden's Yeats, merging with his admirers, is thereby lost, at least as a responding self; Brodsky's Eliot looks back at his creation as he is borne away on the wave of time.[44]

Part 2 of each poem contains a figurative statement (Brodsky's is allegorical) about the poet's relation to his country or countries. These statements function as mid or turning points in the elegies, enabling us to pause momentarily as our attention shifts from the literal fact of death in part 1 to the triumphant,

---

42 The speaker and the point of view here can be compared with those in Brodsky's 1963 elegy to Donne.

43 Used Christmas trees had flared in vacant lots, / and broken baubles had been broomed away. / Winged angels nested warmly on their shelves. / A Catholic, he lived till Christmas Day. / But, as the sea, whose tide has climbed and roared, / slamming the seawall, draws its warring waves / down and away, so he, in haste, withdrew / from his own high and solemn victory. // It was not God, but only time, mere time / that called him. The young tribe of giant waves / will bear the burden of his flight until / it strikes the far edge of its

cathartic cadences of part 3. Significantly, Auden departs from the pure vers libre of his initial stanzas by beginning, almost imperceptibly, to use "Yeatsian" slant rhyme (another ironic filter). Perhaps, he seems to say, the lyrical elements, the melos, in the elegiac tradition have to be broken down (through parody) before they can be reassembled. The poet has to be purged from his poems (as he is in part 1) before his poetry, as poetry, can be celebrated. Brodsky's response—a modified version of a Petrarchan sonnet—is, characteristically, more formally complex, in keeping with the possibilities of an inflected language.

Auden calls Yeats "silly like us," presumably for believing in his own mythology and willfully blurring the boundaries between life and art. This error in turn led Yeats—as it did the young Auden, now looking back self-critically at his Marxist phase—to posit a causal relation between poetry and politics.[45] But by 1939, with the world on the verge of another great war, Auden can say in all seriousness that "poetry makes nothing happen," a position that Yeats, with his Irish nationalism (albeit complicated by various contradictory feelings), could apparently not maintain. "Mad Ireland," therefore, may have "hurt [the poet] into poetry," but that poetry did not hurt, or for that matter console, Ireland back. Auden's profound existential denial of the symbolist ethos and all it stands for is the emotional low point in his elegy. Yeats's legacy was founded on a lie—the "parish of rich women [e.g., Lady Gregory], physical decay, / Yourself"—that conspired in an unconscionable way to identify poetical truths with historical ones. Yet—and here Auden quietly begins to turn back from his despair—Yeats's art was somehow not compromised by the lie on which it was founded: his "gift survived it all." By the end of this brief part, a mere ten lines, we have managed, perhaps like Auden writing about England from America in 1939, to distance ourselves from history, the world, and the high-modernist logic (poets can be prophets) that brings the world to war and have begun, sotto voce, to speak of survival and grace. Poetry has no raison d'être beyond itself; it is always and only a "way of happening, a mouth"—that is, a disembodied voice—

lowering fringe, / to bid a slow farewell, breaking against / the rim of the earth. Exuberant / in strength, it laughs, a January gulf in that dry land of days where we remain. (*Ostanovka v pustyne*, 50; *Selected passages*, 99–100).

44 This opposition between Auden's and Brodsky's elegiac perspectives finds its ultimate expression at the end of Brodsky's stanza 5, when the waves carry the poet to the end edge of the earth ("*krai zemli*"), break over this threshold, and send him, joyfully, on his way to the great beyond, only to come crashing back as January into "that dry land of days where we remain."

45 "In the first version of 'In Memory of W. B. Yeats' Auden had written that time would pardon writers like Kipling and Claudel for their right-wing views; the implication was that the left-wing views held by Auden and his audience were consonant with the force of history and would need no forgiveness whatever. Auden soon found this less easy to believe than he did when he wrote it, and was less willing to encourage such complacency in his readers" (Edward Mendelson, "Auden's Revision of Modernism," *W. H. Auden*, ed. Harold Bloom [New York: Chelsea, 1986], 118). Mendelson is excellent on Auden's gradual move away from the tenets of high modernism, including the poetics of Yeats, a prime example of how issues of life and art, politics and aesthetics, could be confused and manipulated under the force of rhetoric (esp. 114–19). See as well Callan, *Auden*, 148–51.

and for this reason "it survives." Auden is at last ready for the rhymed tetrameters of the concluding part.

Brodsky, as already noted, has a less polemical relationship to his subject, T. S. Eliot, in the Russia of 1965 than Auden has to Yeats in 1939. Auden left England to avoid the inbred traditionalism and nationalist sentiment, the parish of rich women and the physical decay, that he associated with Yeats. The Anglo-Irish political tensions driving much of Yeats's poetry, especially the "terrible beauty" of a work such as "Easter 1916," were precisely the stuff of the poet-prophet's mentality that Auden, now an outsider residing in America, wished to escape. But for Brodsky, Eliot was *equally* foreign whether viewed as an American expatriate or as a British citizen. Only much later, presumably, did Brodsky fully understand the ironic, inversely symmetrical contrast between Eliot, the naturalized British subject, and Auden, the naturalized American citizen. In any event, as we have seen, Brodsky's perspective in his 1965 poem is not the same as that of his 1983 essay on Auden. Hence Brodsky's part 2 contains none of the withering irony and despair of its counterpart in Auden's elegy. There is nothing, for example, to correspond to the stylistic descent of "silly like us" or the bitter resignation of "poetry makes nothing happen." Instead, Brodsky's sonnet enacts a solemn pantomime or shadow play[46]: in the octet, two unnamed female mourners stand silently beside the poet's grave; in the sestet, the allegory is decoded and their identities divulged—one is England, the other America. Because the two are equally bereft and because Eliot's poetic identity is an indeterminate composite of both, he belongs to neither. Rather, he becomes, like Brodsky himself, a citizen of the republic of letters, with his grave "bordering" not on any single country but on the world:

Но каждая могила —
край земли.[47]

Each poem concludes with a third part containing an "exegi monumentum" to its subject (the Horatian subtext—"I have completed a monument"—is explicitly alluded to in Brodsky).[48] In these lines the respective tones of the poems dovetail for the first time. The authors have arrived at this point of catharsis and celebration by different paths: Auden, the troubled insider, has moved for the moment beyond England and its politics, although, ever the skeptic, he cannot ignore what lies behind:

---

[46] The first two lines of Brodsky's sonnet could, presumably, be read as tongue-in-cheek, although their irony, if that indeed is what it is, seems bright and non-threatening: «Читающие в лицах, маги, где вы? / Сюда! И поддержите ореол» [Where are you, Magi, you who read men's souls? / Come now and hold his halo high for him] (140; 100). I read these lines as serious, however.

[47] But each grave is / the limit of the earth. (*Ostanovka v pustyne*, 140; *Selected poems*, 100.).

[48] Here Auden could be recalling Yeats's self-epitaph in "Under Ben Bulben," with the important difference that the younger poet is invoking the healing powers of verse in a time of strife while the older poet is, among other things, settling scores and "scorn[ing] the sort [of poet, including presumably Auden] now growing up / All out of shape from toe to top, / Their unremembering hearts and heads / Base-born products of base beds." In this last part, in other words, Auden's parody is meant not to challenge or polemicize but to forgive and reconcile—his (ultimately Christian) way of exorcizing the "anxiety of influence."

> In the nightmare of the dark
> All the dogs of Europe bark,
> And the living nations wait,
> Each sequestered in its hate.[49]

Brodsky, the young poet marginalized and exiled in his own country, has cast his admiring glance at Eliot from a not-so-beautiful afar. The two poems express their celebration through identical trochaic meters and rhyme schemes (aabb). Both temper the severity of winter cityscapes by introducing pastoral elements. Auden, in fact, returns the meaning of "verse" to its Latin etymology (versus "furrow"):

> With the fanning of a verse
> Make a vineyard of the curse ...[50]

And Brodsky, playfully circumlocuting the *urozhai* 'harvest' of socialist-realist fame, informs his poet that he need not fear time's harvest even in its most primordial guise:

> Томас Стернс, не бойся коз!
> Безопасен сенокос.[51]

Still, despite the numerous formal similarities and the final notes of triumphant lyricism, there remains a basic difference between the two poems. Auden appears, as it were, congenitally unable to make a positive statement about the power of art without first qualifying it with a reference to its tragic origins: the poet must pursue his truth "to the bottom of the night" before he can "persuade us to rejoice"; "healing fountain[s]" must spring up "in the deserts of the heart"; and ultimately the "free man" must learn how to celebrate within "the prison of his days." (In this regard Auden, despite his intention to distance himself from his subject, comes intriguingly close to the essence of the mature Yeats's tragic vision. Or perhaps this is the point after all?[52])

Although Brodsky is certainly one of the most ironic and questioning of modern Russian poets, the spirit of skepticism is absent from the conclusion to his elegy. The poet, like love, must always leave this world:

> Так любовь уходит прочь.
> Навсегда. В чужую ночь.
> Прерывая крик, слова.
> Став незримой, хоть жива.[53]

---

[49] Auden, *Collected Poetry*, 51.
[50] Ibid.
[51] Thomas Stearns, don't read the sheep, / or the reaper's deadly sweep. (*Ostanovka v pustyne*, 141; *Selected poems*, 101).
[52] See Hynes, *Auden Generation*, for a discussion of what Yeatsian and un-Yeatsian about the last part of Auden's poem (351–52). The unmotivated joy in the face of tragedy recalls Yeats's beggar-fools ("The Three Hermits," "Tom O'Roughley," "Two Songs of a Fool," "Another Song of a Fool," "The Hero, the Girl, and the Fool," "Tom the Lunatic," "Tom at Cruachan," "Old Tom Again," etc.) and, of course, the "Chinamen" of "Lapis Lazuli," looking "on all the tragic scene" with their "ancient, glittering, [and] gay" eyes.
[53] "Thus it is that love takes flight. / Once for all. Into the night. / Cutting through all words and cries, / seen no more, and yet alive." (*Ostanovka v pustyne*, 141; *Selected poems*, 101).

Yet that departure is more than a death, with implications for there as well as for here. Love may not be visible, but it is, wherever it is, alive. Brodsky seems able to affirm, with his final reference to *krai*, what Auden could not: that we call the other world a "kingdom of darkness" only out of envy, because it is closed to us, and that the world, like a lyre (cf. "Shum shagov i liry zvuk / buden pomnit' les vokrug" [Forests here will not forget / voice of lyre and rush of feet]), will continue to reverberate with, and hence to "remember," Eliot's music, just as a body still feels the touch of a loved one who has left.

> Ты ушел к другим. Но мы
> называем царством тьмы
> этот край, который скрыт.
> Это ревность так велит!
> Будет помнить лес и луг.
> Будет помнить все вокруг.
> Словно тело — мир не пуст! —
> помнит ласку рук и уст.⁵⁴

Aude

Brodsky learned a great deal by tracking his elegiac sentiments at the time of Eliot's death through the filter of Auden's poem on Yeats. I conclude by noting that the lesson consisted of several main points, all converging ultimately on what I term poetic authenticity.⁵⁵ First, on the issue of language and its relation to historical time, Brodsky recalls that Auden's lines "Time [worships] language and forgives / Everyone by whom it lives" (from part 3) struck him with the force of revelation:

> I remember sitting there in the small wooden shack, peering through the square porthole-size window at the wet, muddy, dirt road with a few stray chickens on it, half believing what I'd just read, half wondering whether my grasp of English wasn't playing tricks on me.... But for once the dictionary didn't overrule me. Auden had indeed said that time (not the time) worships language, and the train of thought that statement set in motion in me is still trundling to this day. For "worship" is an attitude

---

54 "You have gone where others are. / We, in envy of your star, / call that vast and hidden room, / thoughtlessly, "the realm of gloom." / Wood and field will not forget. / All that lives will know you yet — / as the body holds in mind / lost caress of lips and arms." (*Ostanovka v pustyne*, 141, *Selected poems*, 101–102.).

55 In the original version of this paper, I created a pun, *Audentichnost'* 'Auden-ticity,' which seemed to me to work well in Russian, inasmuch as the only difference in that language between it and the word for authenticity (*autentichnost'*) already quite foreign sounding to the native, is a "d" in place of the voiced "t." But in preparing the article for a broader readership, I was convinced by the Editorial Board of *PMLA* that the pun did not work nearly as well in English. Let me simply add that this sort of play between English and Russia is not a little Brodskian and is in the spirit of his work, on the borders of two cultures.

of the lesser toward the greater. If time worships language, it means that language is greater, or older, than time, which is, in its turn, older and greater than space. That was how I was taught, and I indeed felt that way.[56]

It is difficult to say whether the notion that language is prior to history originated with Auden, since Brodsky repeats it often in his essays on other poets, but he seems to claim as much, and one would like to think so. In any event, it is the one cardinal, a priori belief that has accompanied Brodsky through all his wanderings in and out of other belief systems, including Christianity

The second point, which issues directly from the first, has to do with Auden's attitude toward language and toward the voice uttering that language.[57] It is an attitude that seems to have crystallized in the intervening years (1965–83) and is much more explicit in Brodsky's essay "To Please a Shadow" than in his "Verses on the Death of T. S. Eliot." Here one cannot state too strongly that the qualities Brodsky found in Auden left their indelible signature on his post-1965 persona. For example, the Englishman delivers his most profound truths (e.g., "time worships language"), Brodsky says, in an "offhand, almost chatty" style — "metaphysics disguised as common sense, common sense disguised as nursery-rhyme couplets"; there is a "touch of irrelevance" to everything Auden says; he is "a new kind of metaphysical poet, a man of terrific lyrical gifts, who disguise[s] himself as an observer of public mores"; his "mask" is dictated not by a single creed but by "his sense of the nature of language"; the drama of his voice is not personal but "existential"; he is a master of "indirect speech"; his sensibility is a unique "combination of honesty, clinical detachment, and controlled lyricism."[58] All these qualities could, in one form or other, be imputed to the speakers of Brodsky's mature works. In short, Brodsky found in Auden a poet whose "anti-heroic posture" was "the *idée fixe* of [Brodsky's] generation."[59] That Auden was a foreigner in whose language and culture the metaphysical poetic tradition was born only added to his already mythical status.

Last but not least, Auden played the role — first unwittingly, then wittingly — of Virgil in Brodsky's passage into the world of Anglo-American poetry. He, with his indirect speech and antiheroic posture, came to represent the future of a poetic tradition that Brodsky would soon, unbeknownst to him, inherit. We know this because Brodsky, on reflection in the 1983 essay, casts Yeats in the role of the past ("too oratorical and sloppy with meters"), Eliot in the

---

56 Brodsky, *Less Than One*, 363.

57 In this regard one would do well to compare Auden's notions on "writing," "reading," and the poetic craft in the early essays of *The Dyer's Hand* (*The Dyer's Hand and Other Essays* [New York: Random, 1948] with Brodsky's statements in *Less Than One* and in interviews and articles. The two poet-critics have many beliefs in common: poets are dependent on the language they inherit; they must be philologists; "sincerity," in the sense of "honest feelings," is less important than "authenticity" in a work of art; poets must master rhymes, meters, and stanza forms; they must understand intuitively the difference between poetry and prose; to learn and absorb verse properly, they must memorize it in large quantities; and so on.

58 Brodsky, *Less Than One*, 364–65, 369.

59 Ibid., 367.

role of the present (he "reigned supreme in Eastern Europe" in 1965), and Auden in the role of what Brodsky had still to learn:

> I had yet to read my Auden. Still, after "In Memory of W. B. Yeats," I knew that I was facing an author more humble than Yeats or Eliot, with a soul less petulant than either, while, I was afraid, no less tragic. With the benefit of hindsight I may say that I wasn't altogether wrong.[60]

When we remember, too, that the aging Auden took Brodsky under his wing immediately after the younger poet's exile to the West in 1972 and looked after Brodsky's affairs "with the diligence of a good mother hen,"[61] we begin to see what this man symbolized, and symbolizes, to Brodsky. He was nothing less than the sole reason that Brodsky began, in 1977, four years after Auden's death, to write in the English language ("to find myself in closer proximity to the man whom I consider the greatest mind of the twentieth century"[62]). It was he, not Eliot, as in the poem, whom Brodsky truly considered "our transatlantic Horace."[63] What is remarkable then is that Auden, a foreigner, has come to occupy a niche in Brodsky's pantheon as prominent as that of the native Tsvetaeva.[64] Not only is this evaluation a tribute to Auden; it is a tribute to Russia's greatest living poet, who also happens to be his tradition's most defiant *homo duplex* and unreconstructed cosmopolitan.

---

60   Ibid., 364.
61   Ibid., 377.
62   Ibid., 357.
63   Ibid., 382.
64   The Russian émigré's last mental picture of his hero is at a dinner party at Stephen Spender's shortly before Auden's death: to compensate for a chair that is too low, Auden accepts from the mistress of the house two volumes of the *OED* as a makeshift throne. Brodsky concludes his prose eulogy with the claim that he "[is] seeing the only man who [has] the right to use those volumes as his seat" (Brodsky, *Less Than One*, 382). In identifying Auden with Horace, Brodsky may be echoing Auden's line from "The Cave of Making" in *About the House*: "I should like to become, if possible, / a minor Atlantic Goethe" (Auden, *About the House* [New York: Random, 1965], 10). The Horatian temper of much of Auden's later poetry has often been remarked on (see, e.g., George T. Wright, *W. H. Auden* [New York: Twayne, 1969], 146–48), but the important links between Brodsky and Horace have yet to be studied. Brodsky has written two elegies to Auden, one in English ("Elegy to W. H. Auden," 1974) and one in Russian ("York," 1977). Both show how much Brodsky's diction had changed since 1965 and how much it continued to change thereafter (see Polukhina, *Joseph Brodsky*, 90–101).

Chapter 18

Joseph Brodsky and the American Seashore Poem: Lowell, Mandelstam and Cape Cod[1]

The two anglophone poets who exercised the greatest sway over the young exiled Russian poet Joseph Brodsky in the early 1970's were W. H. Auden and Robert Lowell. In retrospect, this influence should not be puzzling, inasmuch as these two established older poets took the younger one under their wings after his forced expulsion from the Soviet Union in June 1972, extended him various kindnesses as he tried to adapt to a new linguistic environment, and then both died soon thereafter—Auden in 1973, Lowell in 1977—leaving Brodsky, an obsessive elegist, to consider their passing in the light of his fast-developing "Americanization." (Brodsky himself, as fate would have it, would die prematurely of long-standing heart problems in January 1996.) Other English-language poets, including Donne, Frost, Eliot, Yeats, Larkin, and more recently Derek Walcott, would play important roles in the poetic thinking and practice of Brodsky over the years, but it was these two, Auden and Lowell, who left an indelible *personal* residue on Brodsky and his language at a very vulnerable and impressionable time, and whose deaths inspired elegies whose *translation*—in various senses—from a Russian to an Anglo-American context was necessarily implied. The Auden connection, especially with regard to Brodsky's wonderful "Verses on the Death of T. S. Eliot" ("Stikhi na smert' T. S. Eliota"), which uses Auden's "In Memory of W. B. Yeats" as its formal model, has been investigated elsewhere. Here I would like to take a closer look at Brodsky's debt to Lowell, which has gone, as far as I know, virtually unattended.

Before turning to the specific nature of the Lowell inheritance in Brodsky, I would like to propose a model for understanding Brodsky's use of tradition, a use which in some ways is quite "Russian" and which, if it possesses any generalizing power at all, suggests that Harold Bloom's model of obsessive anxiety before great precursors may itself be culturally conditioned. Bloom's reading of the Freudian family romance into questions of poetic genealogy, his singling out of the swerves and misprisions in a tradition as evidence of the thrust and counterthrust of parental domination and filial rebellion, may itself be peculiarly "American," or at least not, to judge by Brodsky's case,

[1] Originally published as "Joseph Brodsky and the American Seashore Poem: Lowell, Mandelstam, and Cape Cod," *Harvard Review* 6 (Spring 1994), 5–122.

"Russian." Grand oracular formulations such as "the history of fruitful poetic influence" [in Western poetry since the Renaissance]... is a history of anxiety and self-saving caricature, of distortion, of perverse, willful revisionism"[2] do not really describe, unless it is at some fabulously buried remove, the way the majority of Russian poets have imagined tradition. The term I have proposed elsewhere for Brodsky's remarkably capacious attitude toward tradition is "triangular vision."[3] What is meant by this is that Brodsky, one of the most cosmopolitan poets in the history of Russian poetry and certainly the one most at home in the Anglo-American tradition, constantly looks *both ways*, both to the West and to Russia. His vision can be called triangular in that a Russian source, say Mandelstam, is subtly implanted within a Western source, say Dante, so that both sources comment on each other, but as they do so they also implicate a third source — Brodsky himself. This ingenious triangularity happens often enough to be, for the mature Brodsky, a kind of signature. Moreover, it serves as an over-arching frame for other notions of exile, including ethnic origins, geographical homeland, national tradition, and personal relationships. In essence, Brodsky constantly "outflanks" his own marginal status through cultural triangulation.

In the interests of concision I will give only one preliminary example. Perhaps Brodsky's boldest triangular statement to date comes from his essay and travelogue "Flight from Byzantium" (1985). As Tomas Venclova has pointed out, the essay "enters into two textual spaces."[4] That is to say, the English-language version, with its emphatic *from* in the title, is meant to enter into polemical dialogue with the golden bough, the singing bird, and the "artifice of eternity" of Yeats's ideal poetic culture in "Sailing *to* Byzantium" and "Byzantium." Conversely, the Russian-language version, which is translated as "Journey to Istanbul" ("Puteshestvie v Stambul"), invokes an entirely different tradition: the philosophical travel sketches of Alexander Radishchev (*Journey from Petersburg to Moscow*), Alexander Pushkin (*Journey to Arzrum*), and, of course, Osip Mandelstam (*Journey to Armenia*).[5] Last but not least, however, the essay enters into a third textual space — that of Brodsky's own work on the interrelations of time, space, poetry, and empire. It turns out to be a way of reading Brodsky himself.

Brodsky's haunting odyssey is based on a controversial assumption. What happens if the Yeatsian destination is achieved and we are delivered into the hands of "orientalist" myth — in this instance the original seat of Eastern Christianity and the source of both Russian Orthodoxy and the Russian historical imagination? Well, it depends on which side of the myth one is

---

2   Harold Bloom, *The Anxiety of Influence: A Theory of Poetry* (Oxford: Oxford University Press, 1973), 30.

3   This notion of "triangular vision" is discussed at length in my *Joseph Brodsky and the Creation of Exile* (Princeton: Princeton University Press, 1994).

4   Tomas Venclova, "Journey from Petersburg to Istanbul," in Lev Loseff and Valentina Polukhina, eds., *Brodsky's Poetics and Aesthetics* (New York: St. Martin's, 1990), 135.

5   Ibid., 136.

situated. Raised in the *kosnost'* (sluggishness) and *zastoi* (stagnation) of the aging Soviet empire, Brodsky has no illusions about his country's roots. Indeed, the essayist is terrified and repulsed by what he sees as the — pace Yeats — "formlessness" (*bezobrazie*) of the East. In this idiosyncratic reading, the formlessness expressed itself first and foremost as a disregard for the individual: "Socrates would have been impaled on the spot, or flayed, and there the matter would have ended. There would have been no Platonic dialogues, no Neoplatonism, nothing."[6] Brodsky's preference for the many voices of paganism over the one voice of monotheism, and for the individualism of the Greeks over the anti-individualism of the Romans, is, again, unmistakably akin to the Mandelstam who was influenced by the famous classicist Tadeusz Zielinski and who authored the essay "Pushkin and Scriabin." Significantly, the transformation of the Hagia Sophia (also the title of one of Mandelstam's famous cathedral poems) into a mosque by the mere erection of four minarets on each side of the cathedral is, for Brodsky, an ominous metaphor for the triumph of the crescent over the cross and "for profound Eastern indifference to problems of a metaphysical nature."[7] the travelogue is read against Yeats, Mandelstam, and especially Brodsky, the following formula emerges: poetry is the temporalization (or dematerialization) of space, while empire, including social utopias and applied Christianity (e.g., Marxism), is the spatialization of time. Hence Mandelstam, the sacrificial victim of empire (the triumph of space), wrote verse whose "heavily caesuraed" lines give the "viscous sensation of time's passage" and whose words and even letters "are almost palpable vessels of time."[8] In the end Brodsky comes to Istanbul not as a Western tourist or journalist but as a belated representative of Mandelstam's Hellas. He is confronting the specter of those same despotic "Eastern" roots that banished him from his homeland and swallowed Mandelstam whole. His occidentalism, nearly as hard-earned as his great forebear's, is a counterweight to the romantic (and in his opinion false) orientalism of Yeats. The golden bough and the bird singing out of time of the latter become the tragically caged goldfinch of Mandelstamian song, about which Brodsky writes movingly in his fine poem "December in Florence."

Brodsky first met Robert Lowell in 1972, the year of his exile from Russia. Lowell had offered to help Brodsky by reading the latter's poems in English while the author recited them in Russian at the International Festival of Poetry. Additional meetings took place three years later at the Five Colleges in Massachusetts[9] and at Lowell's home in Brooklyn.

6 Joseph Brodsky, *Less than One: Selected Essays* (New York: Farrar, Straus, Giroux, 1986), 413.

7 Ibid., 431–32.

8 Ibid., 125–26.

9 Where Brodsky taught at Mount Holyoke until his death in January 1996.

Conversations seemed to have centered primarily around Dante, a favorite of both Lowell and Brodsky. It was in this same year of 1975 that Brodsky wrote one of the major pieces of his early émigré period, *Lullaby of Cape Cod* (*Kolybel'naia Treskovogo Mysa*). *Lullaby* was then translated by Brodsky himself into English in 1976. When Lowell died suddenly of a heart attack in a taxi while returning home from Kennedy Airport in 1977, Brodsky was moved to write one of his very first English-language elegies; his only previous attempt to set down in his adopted language a poetic dialogue with a departed colleague was the simply titled and in Brodsky's own opinion completely unsuccessful "Elegy," a poem written back in 1973 on the occasion of his beloved Auden's death. Brodsky rightly concluded that in 1973 his English was not yet up to the task of paying homage to Auden in the appropriate coin; thus the Russian-language "York" ("Iork", 1977), written several years later, was his preferred medium for reaching the now distant ears of the poet he calls "our transatlantic Horace." ("Sometimes I even think I *am* W. H. Auden," Brodsky has gone so far to say in one interview.)

Chronology is not irrelevant as we chart Brodsky's reactions to Lowell the man and the poet. 1975, to repeat, was the year Brodsky wrote *Lullaby* and the year he got to know Lowell better. The notion of the seashore as backdrop to larger ruminations on time, space, history, and the fate of man was not new to Brodsky or to the Russian tradition that fed his personal mythology; indeed, prior to his exile he had traveled often to Yalta and had written poems filled with the imagery of the Crimea that resonated with earlier works by Pushkin, Mandelstam, and, of course, Ovid before them. In other words, it would be wrong to suggest that Brodsky came to Cape Cod with only Robert Lowell on his mind. Moreover, by 1975 he was certainly aware of such major American seashore poems as Eliot's "Dry Salvages" and Stevens' "The Idea of Order at Key West" and when writing, even in Russian, would expect the Ovid-Pushkin-Mandelstam constellation to be evoked in the reader's mind along with the Eliot-Stevens constellation of his new homeland. The reason, however, that we can fix more or less firmly on Lowell as privileged source is that the English-language elegy written two years later cites specific image clusters from Lowell's poetry, suggesting that Brodsky was awash in Lowell texts in the mid-1970s.[10] Particularly poignant is the fact that there are direct *translations* from the Russian of 1975 into the English of 1977, which means that Brodsky's poem about linguistic adaptation and survival is directly implicated in the later poem, now in his new language, about

[10] I am indebted to Adam Weiner, formerly a graduate student at the University of Wisconsin and now a professor at Wellesley College, for many of the intertextual ties between Lowell and Brodsky offered in the discussion below. Mr. Weiner worked out these connections in an ingenious seminar paper he wrote for my fall 1991 "Brodsky and the West" course. That paper was subsequently published as Adam Weiner, "Influence as Tribute in Joseph Brodsky's Occasional Poems: A Study of His Links to Modern English-Language Poets," *Russian Review* 53.1 (1994): 36–58.

death. If it can be put this way, Brodsky's Russian lullaby about migration into the English language and American empire anticipates and frames — but only to those readers who understand *both* contexts — the English prayer for the dead.

Lullaby of Cape Cod is a long and complicated poem in twelve parts, but its central trajectory is as follows: the speaker describes, in exquisitely ironic and metaphysically ulteriorizing terms, his humiliating departure from one empire and his equally inauspicious entry into another; he tries to come to terms with these changes as he strolls without purpose in the nocturnal heat among the shops and then along the shoreline of Cape Cod. The ubiquitous realia of American life and pop culture — a neon Coca-Cola sign, the Unknown Soldier, a pool hall, the sounds of Ray Charles — flow over the receptive speaker, leaving their flotsam and jetsam on the beach of his consciousness. English words, "breeze" and "fish," make their way grotesquely into the Russian language environment of the poem. Everywhere the poet espies his own increasing diminution as a person and subjective entity holding these warring thoughts and emotions together. He is lonely, and the woman he longs for is separated from him by oceans, continents, and time zones. The only thing he has left is language itself, but he is understandably fearful of the ebbing away, like the tide, of his own Russian and of his organic, living grasp on native tradition. This is a situation, apparently, where there is everything to lose and not much to gain. Two years later in "Elegy: for Robert Lowell," however, Brodsky marshals the same imagery, all taken from the Lowell of such poems as "For the Union Dead," "In Memory of Arthur Winslow," and "The Quaker Graveyard in Nantucket," to compose a tribute that is, while far from buoyant or serene, clearly "un-Lowellian" in its triumphant emphasis on cultural continuity, the transcendent power of language, and the absolute lack of a Calvinist/Puritanical urge to judge, damn, and rage at pettiness and evil. What precisely has happened between *Lullaby of Cape Cod* and "Elegy: for Robert Lowell"? I would suggest that Brodsky has quietly "Russianized" the elegiac tradition of his arch Bostonian and rebellious Puritan precursor. How and why does this happen, one might ask?

The persevering reader might turn up a striking palimpsest in this instance. The "Shoals of cod and eel / that discovered this land before Vikings or Spaniards still / beset the shore," a stanza from the elegy, turns out to be a direct translation from *Lullaby* (V:1). The cod did not originate there, however; instead it goes back still further to Lowell's own morbid fascination with the intrusion of lower forms of life into American culture and with the deeply ironic "weathervane cod" in "For the Union Dead." (The weathervane then resurfaces at the end of Brodsky's elegy in the "false song of the weathercock.") The point here is *how* should one interpret the rather humbling fact that the continent was not discovered by valiant explorers but by schools of cod and herring. Brodsky and Lowell, each in his way quite representative of a tradition, come to this information, as we shall see, from different and, ultimately, telling perspectives. Other themes, images, and locales shared by either or both Brodsky poems with Lowell include: Logan Airport and the Charles River; the crab as fit survivor as well as *memento mori* (symbolizing both a lower form of life and the disease of cancer that kills Lowell's grandfather in "In Memory of Arthur Winslow"); glittering eyes as stones worn white on a beach ("Near the Ocean"); an empire or republic in decline ("For the Union Dead"); the sea as graveyard ("Quaker Graveyard"); the loss of a Christian salvational economy ("Near the Ocean"); a creeping, soulless mechanization where automobiles, the new fish, will inherit the earth ("For the Union Dead"); the cape itself as a grotesque foreskin symbolizing both the *limen* separating sea and land and the thwarting of man's procreative power before the onslaught of teeming sea life ("Waking Early Sunday Morning"); and so on.

Although Brodsky builds both *Lullaby* and "Elegy" with the bricks and mortar of Lowell's thought and imagery, the resulting edifice does not belong to the subject it celebrates. As Lawrence Lipking has formulated the dynamics of the elegiac relation within his own Western, primarily Anglo-American context: "The living poet always wins the day, of course. The dead cannot choose their own monuments...Characteristically, the tombeau incorporates many reminiscences of the poet it memorializes—style, verse forms, images, specific lines—and may even try, eerily, to impersonate his voice."[11] But Brodsky would never pose the issue of elegiac dialogue in terms of winning and losing, again, with their implication of Freudian anxiety, fear of belatedness, and filial rebellion. Nowhere in his work has Brodsky suggested that he is in a position of strength vis-à-vis a departed parent figure, in fact quite the opposite; and nowhere has his language registered the sort of adjusting parody, when ventriloquizing the voice of an Akhmatova, Mandelstam, Tsvetaeva, Donne, or Auden, that takes pleasure in its belatedness or in its ability, to quote Auden on Yeats, to modify the words of a dead man in the guts of the living. There is adjustment, to be sure, but there is no "winning," no sense of getting the last, because the later, word. This is because, to put it crudely, Brodsky and his tradition have always felt

---

[11] Lawrence Lipking, *The Life of the Poet: Beginning and Ending Poetic Careers* (Chicago: University of Chicago Press, 1981), 140.

the overpowering weight of the past, of Russia's conflicted and "orphaned" status in the context of European culture, and of a future that was never "open" and that never could be imagined as a newly erected shining city on a hill. Within this tradition, the poet was, for better or worse, the martyred conscience of a nation; his words became sacred texts and his biography inevitably, because the state always cooperated in its violence and cruelty, the stuff of public myth. The Oedipal struggle, if there was one, was between the poetic word of the rebellious son (or daughter) and the stern symbolic order of an Ivan the Terrible, Peter the Great, or Joseph Stalin. The economy was as crudely efficient as it was biblically apocalyptic, and of course no one, including the martyrs, as Brodsky himself would be the first to admit, was entirely free of complicity. Everyone participated, at various levels of consciousness, in what the poet Vladislav Khodasevich once called, following Pushkin, the culture's "bloody repast" (*krovavaia pishcha*).

rodsky has one central article of faith in his attitude toward poetic language, it is the following: language is older than the state and prosody is the seat of time in language, its distillate, so to speak. We need not agree with Brodsky on this score, particularly in the wake of much postmodern discourse, but that he takes this position seriously and writes out of a deep conviction in it is beyond doubt. The attitude itself is profoundly "Acmeist," and indeed the young poets and cultural figures Brodsky grew up with in Leningrad in the late 1950's and early 1960's came under the sway of Mandelstam and Akhmatova and could be called, in their own way, "neo-Acmeists." The point is that Brodsky, following Mandelstam, believes in a Christian aesthetics that, leaving questions of God and theodicy aside (questions which Brodsky has wrestled with many times in his work), telescopes the notion of divine Logos and the miracle of poetic speech. In Mandelstam's and Brodsky's tradition, the best and perhaps only example we have of the word-become-flesh and of genuine Christian behavior in the modern world is the poem itself, where words reach their own flash point through the spontaneous combustion of prosodic form and where the poet, the locus for this activity, sheds his lower, needful human self in an *askesis* that is reminiscent of *imitatio Christi*. No matter how cynical, cryptic, ironically bemused, and self-mocking the poet may be, this is the deeply Mandelstamian Brodsky who wrote first *Lullaby of Cape Cod* and then "Elegy: for Robert Lowell."

, to return to the poems under discussion. *Lullaby of Cape Cod* is, as mentioned, a kind of verbal petri dish of images and phrases out of Lowell from which the recently arrived poet will construct his hybrid self. If read in a Lowellian key, the thoughts on the sea as watery grave or threatening primordial hatchery are only negative and hopeless.[12] And yet, situated in the midst of these musings is the opening line from one of Mandelstam's great poems, "Preserve my speech" ("Sokhrani moiu rech'"). Mandelstam, already by 1931 seeing his martyr's fate clearly before him, asks that he be allowed to become the axe-handle in his own execution provided the charismatic contract, the words themselves, be preserved. It is Mandelstam at his most incantational and haunting, and the forlorn speaker of *Lullaby* intones the line like a mantra. Brodsky summons this father as he contemplates his rebirth into American letters. The line can be read several ways: as a preservation of Brodsky's own precious Russian, now under seige in an alien environment; or as a preservation of *poetic* speech *tout court*, regardless of the flesh that the word decides to enter, in this case presumably the poet's adopted, "hybrid" English.

In this context, Lowell's lines in "For the Union Dead"—"I often sigh still / for the dark downward and vegetating kingdom / of the fish and reptile"— uttered as the speaker considers the demolition of the old South Boston Aquarium to make way for a parking lot and the answering judgment of the facing statue of Civil War hero Colonel Robert Gould Shaw, need to be read against nearly identical lines from Mandelstam's poem "Lamarck" (1932). In the latter, contemporaneous with "Preserve my speech," Mandelstam celebrates the renegade scientist and embraces his theories of the sea as point of origin in a massive evolutionary chain. For Mandelstam, intuitive poetic language is the only key, inversely and retrospectively applied, to the "phylogeny recapitulates ontogeny" formula. Poetic language is no more and no less than the life force itself, and it matters not *which* particular life form it animates. Mandelstam is eager to take his place on the lowest rung of the Lamarckian evolutionary ladder because that is where this life force lies, distilled, undifferentiated, pre-conscious and pre-vertebrate, in its cradle. Hence, the fact that we are linked to these lower forms of life actually gives hope to the little tramp who by the early 1930's was an endangered species in Stalinist Russia. Likewise, Brodsky's speaker in *Lullaby* is energized by the oxygen of these native and foreign precursors. In the poem's seriocomic finale, he is visited on his threshold by an erect cod that asks for a drink and directions. This alter-ego, this fish out of water with no sure sense of how to breathe in his new incarnation, has nonetheless risen linguistically out of the sea and is ready to pass, presumably in some reptilian form, into the broad continent

---

[12] This idea presumably goes back in American culture to Thoreau, who describes the sea as both a "womb of life" and a "vast morgue" in *Cape Cod*. See Willard H. Bonner, *Harp on the Shore: Thoreau and the Sea*, ed. George R. Levine (Albany: SUNY Press, 1985), 9.

of American letters. When the speaker points out the way to the cod, he is also, of course, pointing out his own destiny or, as Russians say, his *tvorcheskii put'* (creative path).

In conclusion, let me simply remind the reader that there are many fascinating links between Lowell and Brodsky still remaining to be explored: their obsession with aging, diminished sexual prowess, and death; their orientation toward the Metaphysicals and toward formal patterns in verse (this applies primarily to the early Lowell); their visits (for different reasons, of course) to insane asylums; their interest in the Roman classics, etc. Be all this as it may, Lowell's view of tradition appears to have been profoundly "American": the rising up against his Boston Brahmin family (recall the speaker's shame and rage at striking down his father in "Charles River"); the trampling of his Protestant heritage with his 1941 conversion to Roman Catholicism; the Calvinist taint of his recurring feelings of remorse and guilt; his fascination with Jonathan Edwards and the latter's thoughts on madness, torture, and death; his Jobean anger at the failure of the American Dream and the ubiquitous intrusion of Philistine values; and perhaps above all his fierce attachment to issues of character.

As much as Brodsky admires Lowell's poetry and indeed has learned from it, he, understandably, cannot share fully in the insider's pessimism at the tawdry failure of the American experiment. Brodsky is virtually without guilt and experiences no regret that one generation has performed its ethical duty worse than another generation. His view is so long and his preference for the distant past so abiding that it is sometimes difficult to imagine how he can be touched by present events. There was never any clean start after which the Russian experience could be equated with something called "the Russian Dream." Language does not reside in character, but character in language. The pragmatism, work ethic, self-reliance, earnestness and moral authority that many see as our inheritance from the Puritans Brodsky would locate in the syntactic structures of the language itself. He even goes so far as to say that the English language is not *structured* to accept the data of Russian experience: "It's been my impression that any experience coming from the Russian realm, even when depicted with photographic precision, simply bounces off the English language, leaving no visible imprint on its surface."[13] Thus, when Brodsky writes in the last stanza of his elegy, "In the sky with the false/song of the weathercock/your bell tolls/— a ceaseless alarm clock," he is paying Lowell the ultimate compliment.

13   Brodsky, *Less Than*

The "weathervane cod" of "For the Union Dead" has become the weathercock, whose song is false because it comes and goes with the wind, with time, history, and the inevitable passage of human life. But the false song is nevertheless interrupted by the Donnean bell of Lowell's poetic word — an alarm clock that continually awakens us to the miracle of creation. Brodsky has preserved Lowell's speech in his own, affirming the tradition of this tormented pilgrim soul and of the generosity of spirit that grants him, an outsider, a place in it. If this be poetic anxiety, one wonders where to look for poetic health.

Chapter 19 — Joseph Brodsky's "To My Daughter" (A Reading)[1]

Joseph Brodsky is a bundle of contradictions. This statement might be problematic if he were a philosopher, but his consistent inconsistency makes perfect sense to those studying his primary status — that of poet. Stoic toward the arbitrariness of the world order (or disorder), deeply melancholic (if not corrosively skeptical) about "human nature," yet passionately believing in language's ontological priority as the only *thing* (note this word) in human existence approaching a genuine God-term, Brodsky could be maddening in the sheer outrageousness, the "demanding-the-maximum-and-the-hell-with-the-rest" quality, of his metaphorical thinking. But that is what poets, especially great poets, do — they challenge our cognitive, emotional, aesthetic and metaphysical constants with their sprung logic. And Brodsky could do this with the best of them, including his teachers Mandelstam and Tsvetaeva, whose own metaphorical thinking and contrary, "vertical" argumentation the younger poet extended not only into the texture of his verse but also into that of his prose essays.

As Lotman, following Jakobson, has suggested with his characteristic precision, there are only two ways to make meaning ("new information") out of language: either we can assert a similarity between two different things or we can assert a difference between two things taken to be similar.[2] In both cases, however, we are dealing with a process akin to rhyme — the *coexistence* of similarity within difference. But poets and poetry, roughly speaking, begin by scaling the metaphorical axis, which means that they are drawn to see the sameness in items or ideas that most of us would not choose to link up otherwise. This accounts for both the inspiring "shock of recognition" (this is really bold and fascinating) and the deflating "realization of improbability" (this is more ingenious than it is real) that often go with our responses to poetic, that is, metaphoric logic. Along the so-called metonymic axis, on the other hand, the one we generally associate with novelistic thinking, there is "contiguity," which is to say there exists an a priori attitude toward things and ideas which before now we might have seen as "alike" by virtue of their proximity in time and space but which now we begin to distinguish among and to see as "nuanced," as different. Operating in his primary mode (which is only a tendency), the novelist will give you five different names for

---

[1] Originally appeared as "Joseph Brodsky's 'To my Daughter'" in *Joseph Brodsky: The Art of a Poem*, eds. Lev Loseff and Valentina Polukhina (New York: Palgrave, 1999), 240-257.

[2] See Iurii M. Lotman, *The Structure of the Artistic Text* (Ann Arbor: Michigan Slavic Contributions, 1977), 45.

a window when describing *how to see a house* ("meaning" is created by understanding the different nuances among windows — *that* is "reality"); operating in his mode (which is also only a tendency), the poet will tell you that the window is an eye to the universe ("meaning" is created by understanding that there is a genuine parallel between inorganic glass and organic tissue — *that* is "reality"). Neither of these viewpoints ever "wins," but it is important to realize before turning to Brodsky's concrete practice as a poet that everything he believed in and dedicated his life to (and, while he often went on record as saying that he would prefer if we didn't mention it, *suffered* for) relates to the "truth" of poetic thinking. Poets live in heroic simultaneity, since few people would be willing to stake their lives on the proposition that a window is an eye; it is simply too hard, too risk-laden, to believe in this as a way of being in the world. It is far easier to live in a world of prosaic distinction, where everything is both part of something else, either prior in time or adjacent in space, and a "logical" extension of it.

But let us return to the "matter" (Brodsky's pun, as we shall see) at hand. In order to understand a Brodsky poem, it is crucial to understand first something about his thinking, or, as he would have said it, "vector." He himself might have denied this or argued something to the effect that the poem "speaks for itself," but here I think he is being as ever the contrarian: Brodsky, at least the Brodsky of his later years, is not very understandable "on his own." His metaphors have coalesced into a kind of "system," but one whose verbal layering and retrieval, whose archaeology if you will, is consistently non-rational, paradoxicalist, fragmentary (both in image and method), and defiant of any explanation from origins. In this respect, his poems need his essays, his essays need his poems, and even then the reader needs to come to his words with a certain amount of additional information in tow. His words always make us think, and that is good, but it is even better if we have enough information so that our thinking is at least on the right track. For example, here is a sentence from Brodsky's late essay "A Cat's Meow": "Now, matter, I believe, comes to articulate itself through human science or human art presumably only under some kind of duress."[3] This statement is, I would argue, completely incomprehensible to most non-specialist readers. How can matter, which whether organic or inorganic is as far as we know pre-conscious, come to articulate itself, i.e. to perform a conscious act? How can it experience duress? In what sense does matter articulate itself through science or art? In short, these words seem intentionally riddling, too clever by half, arch, and possibly insincere —

3   Joseph Brodsky, *On Grief and Reason: Essays* (New York: Farrar, Straus & Giroux, 1995), 310.

i.e. made for effect rather than for their truth value. However, as I will try to demonstrate in the remainder of this essay, these words make perfect sense in the context of Brodsky's "voice zone," prior history, and the larger Russian lyric tradition that gave him his start. They even make sense, albeit highly idiosyncratic, in terms of the Anglo-American tradition (Auden, Lowell, Frost, Hardy, etc.) that he eventually made his own. Not only are these words not insincere, they are an article of faith, incredibly "hot" while giving every appearance of being maximally cool (metaphorical thinking, as we have been saying, forces powerful differences into cohabitation), and the "reason" (or Logos) underlying the belief that allows the poet to keep his love alive in that most vulnerable of all positions — when the dying father has to say goodbye to the baby daughter who will never know him outside of some "wooden" words.

Let us begin with the poem itself, published by Brodsky in the *Times Literary Supplement* on 2 December 1994:

To My Daughter[4]

Give me another life, and I'll be singing	1
in Cafe Rafaello. Or simply sitting	2
there. Or standing there, as furniture in the corner,	3
in case that life is a bit less generous than the former.	4
Yet partly because no century from now on will ever manage	5
without caffeine or jazz, I'll sustain this damage,	6
and through my cracks and pores, varnish and dust all over,	7
observe you, in twenty years, in your full flower.	8
On the whole, bear in mind that I'll be around. Or rather,	9
that an inanimate object might be your father,	10
especially if the objects are older than you, or larger.	11
So keep an eye on them always, for they will no doubt judge you.	12
Love those things anyway, encounter or no encounter.	13
Besides, you may still remember a silhouette, a contour,	14
while I'll lose even that, along with the other luggage.	15
Hence, these somewhat wooden lines in our common language.	16

There are certain skeletal "facts" about this poem that one should have in mind before taking the first step toward understanding or "interpreting" it. First of all, these verses are, as the title says, written to the poet's daughter — Anna Maria Alexandra, who was born on 9 June 1993, to Brodsky and his wife Maria Sozzani. Thus at the time of this writing, the little girl, named in honor of Anna Akhmatova and Brodsky's parents

---

4   After its initial appearance in *TLS*, "To My Daughter" was then collected in Brodsky's book of verse *So Forth: Poems*, published posthumously in 1996 by Farrar, Straus & Giroux (New York).

(Maria and Alexander), was a year and a half old, while the father had little more than a year to live (Brodsky would die of longstanding heart problems on 28 January 1996).

Second, the poem is, technically speaking, written in a cadence that could be called a loose heroic hexameter, one which Brodsky would be familiar with from both the Russian and the English: most lines have six metrical stresses (exceptions: ll. 1, 2 and 10), the anacrusis (the unstressed syllable[s] leading up to the first stress) "wanders" here (cf. the Russian hexameter should have zero anacrusis), the intervals between metrical stresses are normally one to two syllables (typical for the Russian), and the clausula (the unstressed syllable[s] following the last stress) is constantly one syllable (also typical for the Russian). While the Russian practice of hexameter use avoids rhyming, Brodsky's English practice here does not: instead of unrhymed feminine endings (the "heroic" or "Gnedich" expectation), we have rhymed ones, deployed in a symmetrical, 4-quatrain scheme of aabb (the exception being l. 12). Brodsky's rhymes are often not "pure" but slant and quite ingenious. His use of enjambment, especially in the poem's opening lines, is striking, and begs to be "semanticized" in the context of slipped metrical stresses. Likewise, his use of intonational pauses (the "caesura") skips around in this poem, which is more typical for English practice, while it would have remained in one place (i.e. it would have been part of the meter) in Russian. We will return to these formal issues, and most pointedly to that of English versus Russian hexameter, in a moment.

And third, in terms of diction or stylistic register, this poem is as "matter-of-fact," as implicitly "unlyrical," and as apparently stripped bare of high culture (often Brodsky's trademark elsewhere), as is its primary theme of furniture and inorganic "thingness." The only factual curiosity in the poem, other than the speaker's tendency to project himself into the future not only as deceased but precisely as an "inanimate object," is the reference to Cafe Rafaello. There is indeed such a place in Manhattan, on 7th Avenue South, near where Brodsky, himself clearly a product of a century that could not manage without caffeine or jazz, once lived in Greenwich Village. The Italian resonances in its name would not be lost on a poet who had written so much about and "to" Venice, Rome, antiquity, classical poets, thinkers and statesmen, and who was now contemplating his own demise and entry into history from precisely this location.

These facts are what we need to get started on the poem. But they don't yet "mean." And in this respect, it is the "typical" critic's move from the one to the other, from the inanimate/descriptive (the "form" of a hexameter or a chair) to the animate/conscious (these things' inner illumination through an unexplained and unexplainable use of language), that the poet in Brodsky always resisted. Even when he spoke about others' verse, say Frost's or Hardy's in *On Grief and Reason*, he always minimized the biographical element (all the while giving his students or his readers enough to ground his statements in something) and tried to show how poetic language worked from the inside. So "To My Daughter" doesn't mean, doesn't become a poem, because the speaker is soon to die and his daughter is starting life, or because the Cafe Rafaello is near his old home in Greenwich Village. Nor does the knowledge alone that his words are framed in hexameters make his poem mean either, although this is, technically speaking, closer to the truth. Facts, and biographical facts *a fortiori*, do not "cause" meaning (the—to Brodsky—much-detested explanation from origins); they merely give it a place to be born. How these facts become meaning is through language. Thus, such vintage Brodsky "one-liners," already familiar to readers of *Less than One*, as "to make a long story short, a poet shouldn't be viewed through any prism other than that of his poems"; or "it is language that utilizes a human being, not the other way around"; or "The last bastion of realism, biography is based on the breath-taking premise that art can be explained by life"; or, if "what critics do" is to "subordinat[e] literature ... to history," what poets do is the opposite.[5]

In a word, Brodsky had a romantic view of the poet, but one that he tempered with large doses of adoptive democratic spirit, irony and humor (another paradox). He shared with Tsvetaeva her disdain for the critic as the *poète manqué*, the one whose definitions and terms inevitably fail because they can never get to the vantage of the other. The poet was special, but not because he was uniquely endowed in a way he could take personal credit for or enjoy or use in and as "life." Rather, he was nothing more or less than the site where language, in its mythical role as something older and greater than the State or History (note the explanation from origins doing flips over itself here), brought meaning to life. A poem that succeeds is, therefore, according to Brodskian sprung logic, literally an inanimate life form. By the same quirky token, poetic language is permanent, but not because it can be preserved on papyri or computer disks. It is so because it is the intersection of the finite and the animate, i.e. the human being, on the one hand, and the infinite and the inanimate, i.e. matter *per se*, on the other. Don't look for meaning in anyone's life, including the poet's; human history is hopelessly anthropomorphic and solipsistic; better, as the poet

[5] Brodsky, *On Grief and Reason*, 315, 333, 85, 313. Cf. similar remarks by Brodsky in his first book of essays *Less than One: Selected Essays* (New York: Farrar, Straus & Giroux, 1986): "This is also why her [Akhmatova's] verses are to survive whether published or not: because of the prosody, because they are charged with time in both these senses. They will survive because language is older than the state and because prosody always survives history" (52); "Writing is literally an existential process; it uses thinking for its own ends, it consumes notions, themes, and the like, not vice versa. What dictates a poem is the language, and this is the voice of the language, which we know under the nicknames of Muse and Inspiration" (125).

once told the graduating class at Dartmouth College, to learn "the lesson of your total insignificance" vis-à-vis the universe, and so on.[6] "Meaning," then, if not an illusion, is what the poetic soul experiences as it sees and feels, in a process it can't control or summon but none the less lives for, its life being transformed into the matter of language. Note that the stress here is not language's vague anthropomorphic immortality (Yeatsian birds keeping drowsy emperors awake, etc.) but precisely its character as materiality, as something that has outgrown human pain but is able — indeed fated — to contain it. Rather than the miracle of Christian Logos, the word-become-flesh, it is, again quite literally and along a trajectory that Brodsky repeated obsessively in his mature verse, the flesh-become-word, or, to use another familiar metaphor, the poet become his own "part of speech."[7]

But where, finally, do Brodsky's views on poetic language, as opposed to the poetic locutions themselves, come from? And if language is the God-term, then what, if any, is its creed? The answers to these questions provide a segue back into "To My Daughter" and its enigmatic meaning. Brodsky saw a poem's prosodic manifold as a virtual memory bank whose contents could be drawn upon to invoke an entire tradition. This was especially true of his work as a Russian lyric poet: in general, the Russians have been much more aware of the links between the history of a prosodic form and its semantic and thematic "aureole" than have their English-speaking colleagues. For Brodsky, as for Mandelstam before him, Mnemosyne (mother of the Muses) and the memory of — "musing" about — prior poetic forms each of which allows one to say certain things in a certain way are synonyms or at least collateral hypostases. Such is "history" from a poet's point of view and such is the notion Brodsky has in mind when he writes of poetic language as "restructured time" and as possessing, despite its indifference to human tragedy, the attributes of a "personality" or a (Mandelstamian) soul/psyche. In any event, when the poet once said goodbye to another child, his son Andrei, in a poem that was written on the eve of his exile to the West, the form that he invoked in "Odysseus to Telemachus" ("Odissei Telemaku," 1972) was blank verse (unrhymed iambic pentameter). The form had an interesting Russian genealogy that went back to various instances in Zhukovsky, Pushkin, Ogaryov, Blok, Gumilev, Khodasevich, Knut, Akhmatova and Brodsky himself (e.g. "A Halt in the Wilderness" ("Ostanovka v pustyne," 1966).[8] Its thematics, established (as so much else) irrevocably when Pushkin rewrote Zhukovsky's "Perishability" ("Tlennost'," 1816), itself a rather pale translation from the German (Hebel), into the great

---

[6] Brodsky, *On Grief and Reason*, 109.

[7] Again, these thoughts are by no means new for Brodsky and have been repeated often in *Less than One*, *On Grief and Reason*, and in numerous uncollected essays, reviews, and interviews. See, e.g., *Less than One*, 123: "[Poetry] is spirit seeking flesh but finding words. In the case of Mandelstam, the words happened to be those of the Russian language."

[8] My comments here owe much to the discussion in chapter two of Michael Wachtel, *The Development of Russian: Meter and its Meanings* (Cambridge: Cambridge University Press, 1998).

"Again I Have Visited" ("Vnov' ia posetil," 1835), seemed to "feel" the form by attaching itself to ruminations on death, generational passage, and a speaker's reactions as he returns to a place of prior activity. But it was with the startling fusion of the lyrical and the prosaic (the unrhymed quality, the simpler, more straightforward diction, etc.) that Pushkin set the semantic and thematic "tone" for the form on Russian soil. Moreover, the longer "breath" of the line, a concept dear to both Mandelstam and Brodsky, had in this case not only the more obvious "Shakespearean" associations (i.e. the source for blank verse models in Pushkin). In Brodsky's "A Halt in the Wilderness," for example, the return motif had definite classical or "antique" markings as well — what had once been a Greek Orthodox Church (with its potential links to both Hellenism and Christianity) had now become a modern "concert hall"; thus Pushkin's affirmation of mortality and of the necessary ascendance of youth has turned in Brodsky into something ironic and skeptical — the ghastly Sovietism *kontsertnyi zal*. And similarly, the application of a classically stylized biography in "Odysseus to Telemachus" is meant both to show (not without a certain irony) the ancient in the modern and to foreground the poet's culture and sophistication in an otherwise barbarous state. The Greeks, Circe, Poseidon, Palamedes, Oedipus, etc. — these are the reference points out of which the poet constructs his tale of betrayal and exile, and his method has clear antecedents in the high modernist tendencies and neo-classicist display of such exemplars as Mandelstam, Akhmatova and Tsvetaeva. But here the return to the scene of the action is not a homecoming but a pause before banishment.

The Brodsky who writes "To My Daughter" is a very different creature, however. Or to be precise, he is the same Brodsky, but he has moved so far along his original "self-estranging"[9] trajectory as to be virtually unrecognizable to all but his most persistent readers.[10] Thus, instead of a high modernist "martyrological" biography (the poet — Mandelstam and Akhmatova — as Christ or Mary figures) that once implicated him (the "Christ child"[11]), the eschewal of biography altogether as a category of poetic understanding;[12]

9   Cf. Brodsky's statement that as an artist he has set himself the goal of "trying to see how human [he] can become and still remain a human being" ("The Acceleration of the Poet," with Peter Forbes, *Poetry Review* 1 [1988]: 4).

10   In this respect, he has, as it were, turned his life into a metaphor for metaphorical thinking, by which I mean nothing postmodern, but simply that he has, by his own example, personalized and heroicized the very impersonality of language. Here too he has remained a kind of "Old Testament" son: cf. the Isaac of his great early long poem *Isaak i Avraam*. The poet is tested by a Yahweh, the Yahweh of language, who is not a loving parent and has not made man in his own image, but has given him, in the wilderness of an arbitrary world order, speech.

11   See Nunc Dimittis ("Sreten'e," 1972) and discussion in David Bethea, *Joseph Brodsky and the Creation of Exile* (Princeton University Press, 1994), 166–73.

12   This does not mean, by the way, that Brodsky denies his heroes (Mandelstam, Akhmatova, Tsvetaeva, Auden, etc.) the possibility of inspiring lives; always the contrarian, he simply does not want that criterion (an uplifting biography that is read together with one's works) applied to himself. See, for example, his comments in his Nobel speech: "It is precisely their [the "heroes" mentioned above] lives, no matter how tragic and bitter they were, that make me often — evidently, more than I ought — regret the passage of time" (Lev Loseff and Valentina Polukhina, eds., *Brodsky's Poetics and Aesthetics* [Basingstoke: Macmillan, 1990], 1).

instead of the marked presence of Russian models (with a stray Auden or Montale) in *Less than One*, the defining role of adoptive "others," in particular an Anglo-Saxon autodidact and skeptic (Hardy) and an American individualist (Frost), in *On Grief and Reason*; instead of busts, torsos, Ovidian candlesticks, and, in general, disfigured fragments/"ruins," with their ties to Mandelstamiam *toska po mirovoi kul'ture* (nostalgia for world culture), the last frontier of furniture, particles of dust, and of decultured "matter as such";[13] and instead of a Russian Mnemosyne as the mother of prosodic form (the blank verse of "Odysseus to Telemachus"), an English-language understanding of hexameter, but one whose ears, significantly, were once Russian.[14] It is this Brodsky, then, who starts with the words,

>   Give me another life, and I'll be singing
> in Cafe Rafaello. Or simply sitting
>   there. Or standing there, as furniture in the corner,
> in case that life is a bit less generous than the former.

What, now that we have come this far, could they possibly mean? To begin with, that the poet knows his days are numbered but that were he to be granted a stay of execution ("another life"), he would nevertheless choose to return to these familiar surroundings and to his role as singer.[15] Singing and returning, taken together, imply the notion of rhyme, or poetic echo. The opening two lines are, for this reader, terribly poignant and already storing up a lifetime of meaning because they implicate a return as inanimate matter—language—even as they hint at, with the "falling-off" of their repeated enjambments ("singing/in" and "sitting/there") and the insufficiency of their metrical stresses (5 instead of the soon-to-be-established hexametric 6, with only 4 realized in l. 2),[16] the arrival of death itself. So painful is it for this poet to get a full "breath," so weak is this heart that skips beats, that by the time his language stabilizes into a pattern (l. 4),[17] "he" will no longer be there. He will, instead, with the help of the caesural (i.e. temporally refining) "or's," be turning into something, or some thing: from "singing" poet, to "sitting" bystander, to furniture "standing" in the corner. Thus, the "another life," or

---

13 One almost imagines Brodsky, an inveterate punster, reprising the Biblical "flesh-become-word" as "flesh-become-wood."

14 Cf. the marvelous hexameters in such well-known Mandelstam lyrics as "Sestry—tiazhest' i nezhnost'—odinakovy vashi primety" ("Sisters, heaviness and tenderness, identical are your tokens).

15 And he would do so, as we know from other works, out of gratitude. See, for example, the lines concluding the poem Brodsky wrote on the occasion of his 40th birthday «Что сказать мне о жизни? Что оказалась длинной. / Только с горем я чувствую солидарность. / Но пока мне рот не забили глиной, / Из него раздаваться будет лишь благодарность» (*Uraniia* [Ann Arbor: Ardis, 1987], 177); translated by the poet as "What should I say about life? That it's long and abhors transparence. / Broken eggs make me grieve; the omelette, though, makes me vomit. / Yet until brown clay has been crammed down my larynx, / only gratitude will be gushing from it" (*To Urania* [New York: Farrar, Straus & Giroux, 1988], 3).

16 Line 1: *__*__*__*__*__* line 2: __*__*__*__*__

17 Line 3 has 6 metrical stresses, but the 5th is omitted: *_*_*_*____*_. Thus, l. 4 is the first line with all 6 stresses fulfilled: _*_*__*_*_*_*

life-after-death, may not be in anything resembling human form — in this sense, it may be "less generous than the former."

The next stanza projects the poet's new status as "dead-wood" into the future:

> Yet partly because no century from now on will ever manage
> without caffeine or jazz, I'll sustain this damage,
> and through my cracks and pores, varnish and dust all over,
> observe you, in twenty years, in your full ower.

It is important that as Brodsky is saying goodbye to his daughter, he is doing so in terms of a new-world urban culture that he has made his own and that is hers by birthright — New York, a cafe atmosphere, the stimulation of caffeine, the improvisation of jazz. This is a culture that, for better or worse, does not look back ("no century from now on") and seems to thrive on free and open forms. What is left out of course is the dialogue between father and daughter that will never take place. For what possible need could there be for poetry, for Mnemosyne and her prosodic memory bank, in this atmosphere? The "damage" here is thus not only to the eventual petrification of the poet's memory as man and father, but to his language, which is not "native," not completely "fluent." It, Brodsky's English-language verse, is in some crucial sense inorganic: it will have to strain through the wages of time and a palpable artificiality, "through my cracks and pores, varnish and dust all over," with their fusion of human and inhuman wounds, in order to be present at the very organic blossoming of the daughter's young adulthood ("in your full flower"). Given all this, how is it then that the poet will not only not mind that he has died but that he has become furniture, and neglected, if not downright abused, furniture at that?

At this point, it might be helpful to recall that Brodsky completed several essays at the same time he wrote "To My Daughter," all of which shed considerable light on this and the following quatrains.[18] Of these, perhaps the long Hardy piece, "Wooing the Inanimate," is the most germane. Hardy turns out to be a remarkably congenial figure to Brodsky, and the fact that the latter was thinking about this "pre-modern" near the time of his death is by no means coincidental. Hardy's status as autodidact, along with his compensatory passion for reading Greek and Roman classics, were definitely Brodsky's.[19] So too were the "predominance [in Hardy] of the rational over

---

18 For example, "Wooing the Inanimate: Four Poems by Thomas Hardy" (On Grief and Reason, 312–75) is based on a series of lectures delivered to students in a poetry course ("Subject Matter in Modern Lyric Poetry") at Mount Holyoke in fall 1994; "On Grief and Reason" (On Grief and Reason, 223–66), the last essay, was also written in 1994; "A Cat's Meow" (On Grief and Reason, p 299–311), Brodsky's talk on the sources of creativity, was delivered at a symposium organized by the Foundation for Creativity and Leadership and held in Zermatt, Switzerland, in January 1995. "To My Daughter," to repeat, was published in TLS on 2 December 1994.

19 On Grief and Reason, 321. On the autodidact's interest in "essences" over "actual data," with what I take to be self-reference, see On Grief and Reason, 362–63.

emotional immediacy," the "practiced self-deprecation," the "abhorre[nce] [of] the smooth line" together with the "crabby syntax," the interest in the formal qualities of verse,[20] the linking of a poem's "length" with its "breath," the notion "that language flows into the human domain from the realm of nonhuman truths and dependencies, that it is ultimately the voice of inanimate matter," the "general stylistic nonchalance" (definitely felt in "To My Daughter") and love of paradox, and perhaps most of all the courageous insistence on "a full look at the worst."[21] Add to this the facts that Hardy married for a second time late in life and that his place in the tradition — as poet rather than as prose writer — has never been properly understood, and we begin to see why Brodsky, the Poet Laureate whose reputation in the anglophone world is at best mixed, was so taken with him precisely at this juncture.[22]

Interestingly, however, the parallels do not stop at this level of abstraction. The last Hardy poem that Brodsky discusses is "Afterwards." The teacher here has presumably saved the best for last: it is this poem, written near the end of Hardy's life, that serves as a kind of *exegi monumentum* — what will be left behind after the poet is gone. Hardy has mapped his absence onto the four seasons in their natural habitats (Hardy was as much a nature poet as Brodsky was urban), each presented in a quatrain that ends (both Hardy and Brodsky are famous for their "punch lines") with an enigmatic statement about how this disappearance might be registered as either meaning or non-meaning. The "overall sensation," as Brodsky says, is suffused with the "future perfect tense."[23] But it is Brodsky's comments on the interrelationship of form to meaning that is most apposite to our discussion of "To My Daughter":

> These twenty hexametric lines are the glory of English poetry, and they owe all that they've got to hexameter.[24] The good question is to what does hexameter itself owe its appearance here, and the answer is so that the old man can breathe more easily. Hexameter is here not for its epic or by the same classi-

[20] For example, Brodsky would have felt great affinity for what he calls Hardy's "eye/ear/mind-boggling stanzaic designs unprecedented in their never-repeating patterns" (On Grief and Reason, 319–20).

[21] Brodsky, On Grief and Reason, 319, 322, 331, 332, 333, 348, 361.

[22] The connection between "birdlike" and "bardlike" (Brodsky's pun) in Hardy's self-portrait gave him something in common with Mandelstam, one of Brodsky's heroes. See, for example, ""An aged thrush, frail, gaunt, and small, / In blast-beruffled plume" [a line from Hardy's poem "The Darkling Thrush"] is, of course, Hardy's self-portrait. Famous for his aquiline profile, with a tuft of hair hovering above a bald pate, he had indeed a birdlike appearance — in his old age especially, judging by the available photographs" (On Grief and Reason, 330). Cf. similar bird/bard ruminations in the Frost essay (On Grief and Reason, 227–32). On Mandelstam's birdlike appearance and Brodsky's use of it in his own work, see Bethea, Joseph Brodsky, 68–70.

[23] On Grief and Reason, 367–8.

[24] Calling Hardy's lines "the glory of English poetry" demonstrates once again how willing Brodsky was to go against critical commonplace (i.e. Hardy's stature as an interesting but not "great" pre-modern) if the latter did not correspond to what he, as a poet, *heard and felt* (whether Hardy sounded better in English to Brodsky's russophone ears is a fascinating imponderable).

cal token elegiac connotations but for its trimeter-long, inhale-exhale properties. On the subconscious level, this comfort translates into the availability of time, into a generous margin. Hexameter, if you will, is a moment stretched, and with every next word Thomas Hardy in "Afterwards" stretches it even further.[25] his gloss on "Afterwards," is, I submit, the point of departure for Brodsky's poem, or vice versa: either way, Brodsky was thinking about Hardy's death-defying hexameters set in nature as he devised his own set in a Manhattan coffee house. The "generous margin" that the hexameters give is precisely what is needed *in case that life is a bit less generous than the former.* They are the breath the (prematurely) "old man" in Brodsky is looking for. That Hardy's, and English-language verse's, hexameters rhyme, while their Russian counterparts do not, shows Brodsky making the bold (that is, self-estranging) gesture of immortalizing himself in a formal pattern that was not his to begin with.[26] Everything he says about the formal character of Hardy's "auto-elegy" could be said about his own: "the stressed words here are two and three syllables long," "the unstressed syllables play the rest of these words down with the air of a postscript or an afterthought," the caesuras are "bravely shifted," etc.[27] In fact, "Afterwards," with "all its peregrination of stresses," its "self-referential metaphor" of "an interrupted yet resuming sound," and its "thirst for the inanimate," could be called an extended rhyme partner to "To My Daughter."[28] And as strange as it may sound, "Give me another life, and I'll be singing / in Cafe Rafaello" is a kind of translation, transposed into Brodsky's new world idiom, of the late Victorian "When the Present has latched its postern behind my tremulous stay," the first line of "Afterwards."

ith this lengthy aside, we are now ready for the third stanza of Brodsky's poem:

> On the whole, bear in mind that I'll be around. Or rather,
> that an inanimate object might be your father,
> especially if the objects are older than you, or larger.
> So keep an eye on them always, for they will no doubt judge you.

ne might not make so much of the formal aspects of Brodsky's verse here if he himself had not drawn attention to similar issues in Frost and Hardy. In the entire poem, there are only three lines (1, 2 and 10) in which the number of metrical stresses is fewer than 6 (the hexametric expectation). The line "that an inanimate object might be your father" is one of them: $\_ \_ \_ ^* \_ \_ ^* \_ \_ ^* \_ ^* \_$. Indeed, in this line not only are the metrical stresses fewer (5, with the first being omitted), but the actual number of fulfilled

25 *On Grief and Reason,* 6.

26 Note that Brodsky anges Hardy's rhyme scheme om abab to aabb) —this is ; way of answering his hero's allenge."

27 *On Grief and Reason,* 367, 370.

28 *On Grief and Reason,* 373.

ictuses (4) is fewer still, making this, along with line 2, the least stressed, least "hexametrically felt" section of the poem. Why? Because these are the parts of the poem where the theme of metamorphosis — man/father to furniture/inanimate object versus child/daughter to "in full flower" — comes most palpably to the surface, where the father reaches out to the daughter first from "this side" of the change, i.e. as he senses the "petrification" coming on, then from the "far side," after he has already become the inanimate object and is no longer recognizable, except in the "wooden" language itself.[29] As Brodsky says at the end of the Hardy essay, in a statement repeated verbatim in "A Cat's Meow": "language is the inanimate's first line of information about itself, *released to the animate.*"[30] If the daughter would like to know who the father was and where "he" is now, she should ponder these lines.[31] For he is passing on to her what might be termed the "long view," the sense that it is not we who judge and possess the world ("things"), but the other way around ("for they will no doubt judge you"). "To put it perhaps less polemically," concludes Brodsky in "A Cat's Meow," "language is a diluted aspect of matter. By manipulating it into a harmony or, for that matter, disharmony, a poet — by and large unwittingly — negotiates himself into the domain of pure matter — or, if you will, of pure time — faster than can be done in any other line of work."[32] This is what the poet means when he says, in his typical offhand way (e.g. "on the whole"), that he will "be around." Why "judge you" is the only non-rhyme in the poem is a tantalizing puzzle. My guess is that while inanimate matter, including the particles that were once her father, will one day judge Anna Maria Alexandra, the speaker of these lines cannot yet, while he is still alive, include her in this ontological echo-chamber, where birth inevitably leads to its rhyme partner, physical dissolution and death. That is not yet thinkable, and thus she, so animate and vulnerable, is not yet part of this process. The judgment that is literally in the phrase has not been, as it were, poeticized — its clock has not begun ticking.

Brodsky ends his poem with the self-deprecating wit that has always been his special signature as a poet. Hardy's "Afterwards" concluded with lines invoking one of Brodsky's favorites, John Donne and his famous "and therefore never send to know for whom the bell tolls; it tolls for thee":

And will any say when my bell of quittance is heard in the gloom,
And a crossing breeze cuts a pause in its outrollings,
Till they rise again, as they were a new bell's boom,
"He hears it not now, but used to notice such things?"

---

29 Note that Brodsky returns to the same caesural use of "or" ("Or rather") in the preceding line (9) that he had used in the opening lines (2 and 3) of the poem.

30 *On Grief and Reason*, 311, 374; my emphasis.

31 Cf. the following excerpts from "A Cat's Meow": "what human inquiry indeed boils down to is the animate interrogating the inanimate"; "Ideally, perhaps, the animate and the inanimate should swap places"; "For the only opportunity available for the animate to swap places with the inanimate is the former's physical end: when man joins, as it were, matter";

question in Hardy shows his irony, his pessimism, his willingness to take, in his phrase, "a full look at the worst." The bell is, to repeat, the "self-referential metaphor," the notion of "interrupted yet resuming sound," that is the poet's principal legacy—his poetry itself. But will anyone notice the bells' tolling, and if they do, will they link them with the consciousness that first pondered them and gave them verbal form? Brodsky was clearly a reader who heard the tolling of Hardy's bells, and so now he looks for an analogous listener in his own posterity:

> Love those things anyway, encounter or no encounter.
> Besides, you may still remember a silhouette, a contour,
> while I'll lose even that, along with the other luggage.
> Hence, these somewhat wooden lines in our common language.

Hardian irony is there, the sense that what the poet was as a human being and what he lived for could possibly be lost entirely—no one may notice the sounding bells that were his consciousness.[33] This inanimate-to-animate encounter with his beloved offspring may, after all, not take place, since there may not be enough left of "him"—or the particles that were once him, the "even that"—to register her animation on his total lack of it. But despite all that, he urges gratitude and willing sacrifice: "Love those things *anyway*." Her remembering, if she can manage it after all the years, would be a return on the level of life (her domain): the "silhouette" or "contour" of a small child's murky memories of a departed father. His return, however, is the more heroic, since he knows beforehand that he will have lost everything and have joined ontological forces with his final rhyme pair: luggage/ language. Still, he celebrates. The "hence" is the "explanation" we have been waiting for. His response to becoming "luggage" is the slightest shift of breath, and the last word—"language." The puns, the ability of the words to say two or more things at once, in "these somewhat *wooden* lines" and "in our *common* language" give the reader parsing them after the poet's death the feeling that he is still with us. For these lines *are* wooden, in the sense that they are intentionally flat (unlyrical) and at the same time they *are not*: their lack is full of love, pain, feeling. The joke at his own expense makes the wood

---

y would the infinite keep an e on the finite? Perhaps out he infinite's nostalgia for its n finite past, if it ever had e? In order to see how the poor finite is still faring against rwhelming odds?" 1 *Grief and Reason*, 304–05). at's Meow," to repeat, was ivered as a talk in January 95, approximately a month er the appearance of "To My ughter" in *TLS* (2 December 94).

32 *On Grief and Reason*, 311.

33 Another potentially self-referential passage from the Hardy essay comes to mind here: "The real seat of poetry for him [Hardy] was in his mind... With Hardy, the main adventure of a poem is always toward the end. By and large, he gives you the impression that verse for him is but a means of transportation, justified and even hallowed only by the poem's destination. His ear is seldom better than his eye, but both are inferior to his mind, which subordinates them to its purposes, at times harshly" (*On Grief and Reason*, 321, 329). Similar statements could easily be made about Brodsky's own English-language poetry, and he knew it. Whether the same could be said about his Russian-language poetry is more debatable, however.

almost organic, as though it were the tree, altogether innocent, before it has been converted into the rood of time.[34] By the same token, the language is common, as in shared, and also common, as in maximally "undistinguished" (Brodsky may have put these feelings differently in Russian), but all the same it is highly *uncommon* — this willingness to shed oneself in order to (in various senses) "become" oneself. It is on this note that the last line of the poem returns to the first ("I'll be singing"), and the tolling bell-cum-woodwind is heard by posterity, and the "contrary to fact" quality of Brodsky's metaphorical thinking may be, in the end, a "matter of fact," may be, for all we know, right.

---

[34] Cf. this passage describing an American poet's attitude to time and space (as opposed to a European's) in the Frost essay ("On Grief and Reason"): "When an American walks out of his house and encounters a tree it is a meeting of equals. Man and tree face each other in their respective primal power, free of references: neither has a past, and as to whose future is greater, it is a toss-up. Basically, it's epidermis meeting bark" (*On Grief and Reason*, 225–26). One wonders whether Brodsky could be recalling Frost and his voice as "American" poet when he describes "epidermis meeting bark" in the "somewhat wooden lines" of this farewell poem.

Chapter 20

Brodsky, Frost, and the Pygmalion Myth[1]

> All that we've got together,
> what we've called our own,
> time, regarding as extras,
> like the tide on pebble and stone,
> grinds down, now with nurture,
> now with a chisel's haste,
> to end with a Cycladean sculpture,
> with its featureless face.
> You walk out right
> into the leaves' soft clapping,
> into the U.S. night.
>
> Brodsky, "Strophes"

Central to any understanding of Joseph Brodsky as poet and thinker is his myth of language, his belief in words, and not just any words but specifically poetic words, ability to restructure time and to outwit states, tyrants, history itself. "Prosody is simply a repository of time within language,"[2] writes Brodsky in a statement repeated many times over in different guises and contexts. Poetic words, by their very nature, got there, and are always still getting there, first. Indeed, what makes this idea a myth in the first place, that is, something larger than the life it explains, is these "chosen" words a priori *consciousness* of their role. If God exists, then He exists through language and through what language does to those who accept its divinity. No other idea comes closer to an article of faith on Brodsky's part than this conviction that the human is being acted on and through by words *that choose him*, which is to say by an Old Testament deity of Logos who, despite the modern dress, is rather close to Yahweh and who is not all that moved by what such a choice does, personally, existentially, to its receptacle.

Brodsky's world, then, *language thinks the poet*, not the other way around. I start with this premise because Brodsky, by the second half of his career, had begun to operate in two separate linguistic environments and poetic traditions, the Russian and the Anglo-American, and had applied a similar mythopoetic function (God = language) to both. English became a language with its own personality and history for Brodsky; it could say things that

[1] Originally appeared in *Russian Literature* 42 (2000): 9–305.
[2] Joseph Brodsky, *Less Than One: Selected Essays* (New York: Farrar, Straus, Giroux, 1986), 52.

Russian couldn't, and vice versa. And English had its own personality not only as the language of such favorite British poets as Auden and Hardy, but also as the language of Robert Frost, who Brodsky came to regard as somehow echt-American. In this essay I would like to investigate what Brodsky meant when he referred to Frost's special brand of "autonomy" and "restraint." I will do this by dwelling on the myth of Pygmalion and Galatea, which Brodsky consciously incorporated into "On Grief and Reason" (1994), his essay on Frost's great narrative poem "Home Burial," as well as into his own English-language lyric, "Galatea Encore" (1983).[3] It is in this latter lyric, I will argue, that the Russian poet can already be seen progressing rapidly toward that (literally and figuratively) "petrifying"[4] autonomy and that striking blend of "grief and reason" that was to become so intertwined with the personal myth of his last years and that he associated with the American and with Frost in particular. If *Less Than One* (1986) had paid homage first and foremost to the "poetics of subtraction" in Brodsky's Russian background and cultural experience, then *On Grief and Reason* (1995), his second, and as it happened last, book of essays, proceeded quite consciously under the banner of Frost and the author's adopted status as American man of letters.

Let us begin with Brodsky's thoughts on Frost as expressed in his interview with Solomon Volkov (fall 1979 — winter 1982). It is in this mid-career interview, for example, that Brodsky makes several explicit statements about the inherent capabilities and blind spots of English and Russian as mediums of poetic thought, as well as about the "translatability" of English poetry into Russian and vice versa. Here the notion of what it would take to "Russian" Frost (as well as "English" himself) is constantly tugging at the surface:

> It's easier to translate from English into Russian than the reverse. It's just simpler. If only because grammatically Russian is much more flexible. In Russian you can always make up for what's been omitted, say just about anything you like. Its power is in its subordinate clauses, in all those participial phrases and other grammatical turns of speech that the devil himself could break his leg on. All of that simply does not exist in English. In English translation, preserving the charm is, well, if not impossible, then at least incredibly difficult. So much is lost. Translation from Russian into English is one of the most horrendous mindbenders. There aren't all that many minds equal to this. Even a good, talented, brilliant poet who intuitively understands the task is

---

[3] "Galatea Encore" first appeared in the *New Yorker* 61.33 (October 7, 1985): 38. Its date of composition is given as 1983 in *To Urania* (New York: Farrar, Straus, and Giroux, 1992), 97.

[4] See, e.g., "Mr. Frost is the most petrifying, most terrifying poet this earth ever bore. And he is 100 per cent American" (in Missy Daniel, "Interview with Brodsky," *Threepenny Review* 11 [Fall 1990]:23–24). Later on in this essay I will be developing the idea of Frost's influence as petrifying in both the figurative ("terrifying") and literal ("turning to stone") senses. My guess is

incapable of restoring a Russian poem in English. The English language simply doesn't have the moves. The translator is tied grammatically, structurally. This is why translation from Russian into English always involves straightening out the text.[5]

Note that Brodsky launches into the question of Frost's American English in typical baroque fashion — by telling us what English, and American English a fortiori, can't manage. "Doesn't have the moves" is a lovely dodge, as it explains through the sprung logic of metaphor, for avoiding the rigor, and boredom, of philology. This passage recalls in the staccato rhythms of its oral genre the brilliantly perceptive and funny Russian-to-English impasse first conjured up by Brodsky in "Less Than One" (1976): "At least it's been my impression that any experience coming from the Russian realm, even when depicted with photographic precision, simply bounces off the English language, leaving no visible imprint on its surface."[6] And "One [i.e., the anglophone speaker] gets done in by one's own conceptual and analytic habits — e.g., using language to dissect experience, and so robbing one's mind of the benefits of intuition. Because, for all its beauty, a distinct concept always means a shrinkage of meaning, cutting off loose ends. While the loose ends are what matter most in the phenomenal world, for they interweave."[7] Hence "loose ends" have an up-side, in that they teach their poetic weavers to see the world associatively, and a down-side, in that they engender irony, scepticism, and double-voicing (duplicity's sibling). "I merely regret the fact that such an advanced notion of evil as happens to be in the possession of Russians has been denied entry in [the anglophone] consciousness on the grounds of having a convoluted syntax. One wonders how many of us can recall a plain-speaking Evil that crosses the threshold, saying: 'Hi, I'm Evil. How are you?'"[8] The "convoluted syntax" of Brodsky's native language translates into a convoluted way of seeing the world, with the result that "Evil" (the ethical imperative) is recognizable in all its glittering nuances and asides, even causing (in Brodsky's own phrase) the devil himself to break his leg, but nothing can be said simply, straightforwardly. By the same token, the reason Brodsky opted to eulogize his parents in English ("In a Room and a Half") was because he wanted something different: the text about their lives and deaths to be, as it were, "straightened out."[9]

This is where Frost enters the picture as a poet with, in Brodsky's mind, a distinctly American virtue: "reticence." "The main difficulty in translating from English into Russian is the reader's lack of cultural preparation. For instance, what in English is called 'reticence' can be restored in Russian,

that Brodsky has chosen his words very carefully here.

5   Solomon Volkov, Conversations with Joseph Brodsky, trans. Marian Schwartz (New York: Free Press, 1998), 86.

6   Brodsky, Less Than One, 30.
7   Ibid., 31.
8   Ibid.
9   Ibid., 460–461.

too, but the Russian reader is incapable of evaluating this reticence on its merits."[10] Why is it so difficult for the Russian speaker to "get" Frost's reticence? For the same reason that it is hard for the American speaker to comprehend in any way other than the metaphorical what Brodsky means by "loose ends." Yes, such essential traits may exist, but they can't be "felt" outside an intimate understanding of their opposite. In other words, Russians, at least Russians prior to Brodsky, can't really experience and "know" Frost.

> Metrically, Frost is close to Russian poetry because formally, Frost is not that varied or interesting, but in spirit it would be hard to find anything more opposite. Frost is the representative of an art that simply doesn't exist in Russian. A Russian poet uses verse to pour out his soul. Even the most abstract, the coldest, the most formal of Russian poets. Unlike Russian poets, Frost never splashes himself out on the piano [...] Almost all modern poetry owes its existence to some degree or another to the romantic lineage. Frost has absolutely no connection to romanticism. He is located as far outside the European tradition as the national American experience is from the European.[11]

This is a very powerful statement on Brodsky's part. To be sure, Brodsky seems to single out similar traits in Auden ("anti-heroic posture")[12] and in Hardy ("audial neutrality" and "the predominance of the rational over emotional immediacy"),[13] but in these musings about Frost there is something different. In Frost Brodsky has found a poet who possesses "European" culture, yet prefers not to display it. One may choose to derive Frost's origins by connecting the poet to notions of the "pastoral" and the "eclogue," or to the Virgil of the *Bucolics* and the *Georgics*, or to the Lake School, or even to the Dante of the *selva oscura* ("Come In"),[14] but these are not connections that Frost himself ever seems to foreground. Frost's relation to the world, to nature (his "farmer" mask) and to man, is more stripped down, more existentially bare, than anything Brodsky can

---

10   Volkov, *Conversations*, 86–87.

11   Ibid., 93. Here I think it could be argued that Brodsky either didn't know his Frost all that well or that he was, for effect, overdoing Frost's "American" individualism and autonomy. For example, not only has Frost been placed rather convincingly in the tradition of American Pragmatism (Emerson, C.S. Peirce, William James, John Dewey, George Satayana, G.H. Mead, etc.), he has also been seen as consciously post-romantic. As Denis Donoghue puts it, "In my reading of [Frost], he is a post-Romantic poet, more specifically post-Wordsworthian and post-Shelleyan. It is surprising how often his poems allude to poems by Wordsworth, Shelley, and other English poets he first read in Palgrave's *Golden Treasury*. 'The Most of It' may have started from Wade Van Dore's 'The Echo,' but its deeper source is Wordsworth's 'The Boy of Winander.' 'Spring Pools' reimagines Shelley's 'To Jane.' The main difference between Frost's sense of life and Wordsworth's is that Frost regularly insists, as Wordsworth only occasionally does, on finding the daily sublime in his own mind rather than in the given world." ("Frost: The Icon and the Man," *The New York Review of Books* 66.16 [October 21, 1999] 20–21).

12   Brodsky, *Less Than One*, 367.

13   Joseph Brodsky, *On Grief and Reason* (New York: Farrar, Straus, Giroux, 1995), 32

discover among the greatest Russian and European poets. Only Tsvetaeva is the exception: "Where are the qualitatively new world views in twentieth-century literature, though? In Russia, the most interesting phenomenon is, of course, Tsvetaeva, and outside Russian culture—Frost."[15] Thus Frost never "cultivates" nature, places it within history, the way a European might. As Brodsky, citing his beloved Auden, tells us in the "On Grief and Reason" essay, "When an American walks out of his house and encounters a tree it is a meeting of equals. Man and tree face each other in their respective primal power, free of references; neither has a past, and as to whose future is greater, it is a toss-up. Basically, it's epidermis meeting bark."[16] I'll return to this restrained or stripped-down quality in Frost in a moment, but for now suffice it to say that what we experience in Frost, at least in Brodsky's reading of him, is not a lack (of culture, of experience of the world), but rather a conscious holding back, a "simplicity" that is extremely complex and that has decided on its own not to tell too much, especially with regard to matters personal and autobiographical. Clearly Brodsky found this reticence very appealing as he continued to grow and reinvent himself in his adoptive homeland.

Brodsky's Frost also has much in common with the Frost first announced by Randall Jarrell and Lionel Trilling—the "dark" Frost, the "poet of existential horror,"[17] the one that Trilling toasted on his eighty-fifth birthday as a "terrifying poet."[18] This Frost certainly exists, but he is not necessarily the only Frost, nor is he even the most important one. There is also, in William Pritchard's more balanced cataloguing, the "elevated" (yet consistently playful) Frost, the "homey" and "ingratiating" Frost, the "anecdotal" Frost of the longer fables and narratives, and the "entertainer" Frost.[19] But the main thing from our perspective is that Brodsky fixed on, and apparently *needed* to fix on, this dark Frost singled out by Trilling. When he says to Volkov, for example, that "Frost senses the utter isolation of his own existence. He has no one for his helper. Incredible individualism, right? But individualism not in the romantic, European version, not the repudiation of society," he is operating within the parameters of the Jarrell-Trilling definition. Equally important, however, Brodsky is thinking about himself, and the challenges Frost has set him, as he is doing the talking. In point of fact it can just as easily be argued that "no personality, no special posture or tone of voice,

14   See Brodsky's own very thorough "high culture" analysis in *On Grief and Reason*, 233–236.

15   Volkov, *Conversations*, 93.

16   Brodsky, *On Grief and Reason*, 225–226.

17   Volkov, *Conversations*, 89.

18   Brodsky, *On Grief and Reason*, 224–225. See discussion in William H. Pritchard, *Lives of the Modern Poets* (Hanover: University Press of New England, 1997, 113–114. Denis Donoghue suggests intriguingly that it was not Trilling's now famous statement that Frost was a "terrifying poet" that caused such a stir among friends and supporters at the Waldorf-Astoria testimonial dinner on March 26, 1959, but more the fact that Trilling, the very urban (and urbane) critic, was mounting a full-scale assault on Frost's version of pastoral America ("Frost: The Icon and the Man," 20).

19   Pritchard, *Lives*, 132.

can be identified as characterizing. these moments of impersonal perception or insight [in Frost's poetry]."[20] The "terrifying" Frost is a projection not of what is said but of what is not said. And it is here, in how Brodsky "comes at" Frost, that we get one of those illuminating triangulations typical of his mature work, where the outsider is striving to redefine the inside and where one of the most urban, textually complex, and "European" poets in the history of Russian letters is testing out his credentials as inheritor of American pastoral understatement.[21] This challenge, if we look a little further, also leads directly into the myth of Pygmalion and Galatea.

In "On Grief and Reason" the Pygmalion-Galatea relationship is the guiding leitmotif of the piece. For anyone interested in Brodsky, that mythopoetic relationship seems to cry out for interpretation: one wants to know why Brodsky has chosen it for his special optic on Frost and where exactly he is going with it. In the earlier Volkov interview, however, which in many ways is a rambling dress rehearsal for the essay, there is no direct reference to the myth. But the myth, I would argue, is still implicated. How it is implicated, *through Pushkin*, sheds light both on the essay and, ultimately, on "Galatea Encore," Brodsky's own creation as poet:

> Brodsky. [...] In Frost it comes out like this: "Good fences make good neighbors." That is, it is a statement replete with unresolved horror. Once again, we are dealing with the understatement of the English language, but this understatement rather directly serves its own purposes. The distance between what ought to have been said and what actually was said is reduced to a minimum, which, however, is expressed with maximum restraint. By the way, if you forget about particular devices and purposes, you can find a general similarity between Frost and Pushkin's *Little Tragedies*.
>
> Volkov. A surprising comparison.
>
> Brodsky. What is most interesting in Frost are the narrative poems written between 1911 and 1926. The main power of Frost's narration is not so much his description as his dialogue. As a result, the action in Frost takes place within four walls. Two people talking (and the whole horror is what they *don't* say to each other!).[22]

One of Frost's narrative poems written between 1911 and 1926 that Brodsky clearly has in mind in these musings is "Home Burial," which first appeared in *North of Boston* (1914), the book of verse that, together with *A Boy's*

---

20 Ibid., 123.

21 See David M. Bethea, *Joseph Brodsky and the Creation of Exile* (Princeton: Princeton University Press, 1994), 48–73.

22 Volkov, *Conversations*, p. 90.

23 The classic text on this subject in Roman Jakobson, *Pushkin and His Sculptural Myth*, ed. and trans. John Burbank (The Hague-Paris: Mouton, 1975). My own reading is found in "Jakobson: Why the Statue Won't Come to Life, or Will It," in *Realizing Metaphors: Alexander Pushkin and the Life of the Poet* (Madison University of Wisconsin Press, 1998), 89–117.

24 "Home Burial" has often been interpreted as autobio-

Will (1913), firmly established the poet's status among contemporaries. Brodsky doesn't say which of the *Little Tragedies* he is referring to, but the one that comes to mind, especially in the context of "Home Burial," is *The Stone Guest* (Kamennyi gost', 1830). This blank verse narrative in dialogue form (Frost's signature as well) is the most "Pygmalionized" of all Pushkin's texts, including "The Bronze Horseman." It is both highly autobiographical — Pushkin's anxieties about marriage and his fears surrounding the cholera epidemic during the first Boldino autumn, his future wife's "statuesque" and seemingly unreciprocating beauty, his many previous failures in love, the sins of his "atheistic" past coming back to haunt him, etc. — and it tells the story of how a duel of words can turn the chaste widow (Donna Anna, the Galatea incarnation) into desiring subject and the mobile "poet of love" (Guan, the Pygmalion incarnation) into petrified object. The Ovidian metamorphosis devoutly to be wished happens precisely at the moment when the nemesis-husband's statue takes the erotic "sculptor's" hand in its stony grip, hence the "tragedy."[23]

was, then, this Pushkinian erotic dialogue that Brodsky had in mind as he engaged Frost's "Home Burial" in "On Grief and Reason." Both works have the same prosodic form and the same sense, of restraint/understatement on the part of the creating intelligence, both seek to "overcome" an autobiographical element linking death and marriage (in Frost it is the death of an infant that comes to symbolize the death of communication in the marriage),[24] both focus on the ancient duel/dialogue between the "male" and the "female," and both thwart ironically the Ovidian expectation of happy metamorphosis (although in Frost this metamorphosis is almost

aphically freighted. The Frosts, for the record, lost their first-born child, Elliott, to cholera at age four in 1900. Whether this link between cholera in Frost's case and in Pushkin's case (the Boldino autumn of 1830) triggered any thoughts by Brodsky, who seems to have known aspects of Frost's biography well however much he downplayed the use of biography in the study of poetry), is open to speculation.

24 "Galatea Encore" has been recently interpreted as a poem very much in the European tradition of intertextual palimpsest, with predecessors including: the Tenth Book of Ovid's *Metamorphoses*, Shakespeare's *The Winter's Tale* (1610–1611), Rousseau's *Pygmalion* (1762), Hazlitt's *Liber Amoris, or The New Pygmalion* (1823), Morris's *Earthly Paradise* (1868–70), and Shaw's *Pygmalion* (1914). See Leon Burnett, "'Galatea Encore'," in *Joseph Brodsky: The Art of the Poem*, eds. Lev Loseff and Valentina Polukhina (New York: St. Martine's, 1999), 150–176, especially 152–153. By the end of his article Burnett comes to the conclusion that the metamorphosis alluded to by mention of the myth is one that, by the late twentieth century, is wholly, and in its way hollowly, *linguistic*: "The name of the beloved female is included in the title of the poem and sets up its own expectations for a reader at the end of the twentieth century. The face, first glimpsed partially in the reference to the mercury 'under the tongue' and then fully 'when your countenance starts to resemble weather', becomes the focus of the reader's attention in the process of animation within the first half of the poem. And finally, as the reader comes to recognize, the voice heard in the 'return to language' is one that is superimposed upon the poem, for Galatea remains silent and the lyric persona, as I have already argued, creates *in absentia*" (169). While Burnett's densely intertextual reading is quite revealing, including his references to Brodsky's beloved and statue-crowded Venice and the play with reflecting surfaces and inner depths in *Watermark* (1992), I have chosen in the analysis to follow to pursue a more "Frostian" angle, one that minimizes the "culture" and maximizes the existential horror and the dialogic impasse of the so-called metamorphosis. But I should like to stress that, given the hermetic quality of Brodsky's poem, various readings are possible.

impossibly implicit — in fact, if it is there at all, it is because of Pushkin and Brodsky's use of him). With this in mind, let us now turn to "Galatea Encore" and attempt a reading of it through the lens of "On Grief and Reason."[25]

> Galatea Encore
>
> As though the mercury's under its tongue, it won't
> talk. As though with the mercury in its sphincter,
> immobile, by a leaf-coated pond
> a statue stands white like the blight of winter.
> After such snow, there is nothing indeed: the ins
> and outs of centuries, pestered heather.
> That's what coming full circle means —
> when your countenance starts to resemble weather,
> when Pygmalion's vanished. And you are free
> to cloud your folds, to bare the navel.
> Future at last! That is, bleached debris
> of a glacier amid the five-lettered "never."
> Hence the routine of a goddess, neé
> alabaster, that lets roving pupils gorge on
> the heart of the color and temperature of the knee.
> That's what it looks like inside a virgin.

Several things can be said about "Galatea Encore" by way of preliminaries. It is, all else aside, an intensely unlyrical lyric, even for this very ironic poet. Indeed, it is as close to being denuded of "feeling" (the restraint, the understatement) and "culture" (the statue's very ambiguous placement or framing) as anything Brodsky ever wrote. Yes, the classical or "European" heritage is there, in the references to Galatea (the title), the statue/goddess, and Pygmalion (who has vanished), but this heritage is mentioned only to be stripped away. It seems to offer no comfort to the speaking voice, which is outside it and which is dissecting it with its own blend (to be discussed in a moment) of "grief and reason." If this is not "epidermis meeting bark," then it is certainly "epidermis meeting stone/alabaster." The slant-rhymed accentual verse, with four and five ictuses per line and the intervals between beats appearing irregularly, comes mesmerizingly close to the cadences of conversational speech, and is again defiantly un-*bel canto*-like.[26] Only the occasional iambs ("And you* are free*/ to cloud* your folds*, to bare* the na*vel") threaten to break the spell of petrification with their reminder of poetic culture going gradually, as it were, to seed. The poem is also, in its

26 ["As though* the mer*cury's un*der its ton*gue, it won't / talk*. As though* with the mer*cury in its sphin*cter, / immo*bile, by a leaf*-coated pond* / a sta*tue stands white* like the blight* of win*ter. / Af* ter such snow*, there is no*thing indeed*: the ins* / and outs* of cen*turies, pe*stered hea*ther. / That's* what co*ming full cir*cle means* — / when your coun*tenance starts* to resem*ble wea*ther, / when Pygma*lion's va*nished. And yo are free*/ to cloud* your folds,* to bare* the na*vel. / Fu*ture at last*? That is, blea*ched debris* / of a gla*cier amid* the five*-lettered 'ne*ver'. / Hen*ce the routine* of a god*dess, née* /

way, a kind of ironic or anti-pastoral, a theme which should put the reader in the vicinity of Frost's voice zone.

Brodsky initiates his analysis of "Home Burial" with the statement that "The opening line ['He saw her from the bottom of the stairs / Before she saw him'] tells you as much about the actors' positions as about their roles: those of the hunter and the prey. Or, as you'll see later, of Pygmalion and Galatea, except that in this case the sculptor turns his living model into stone."[27] All art and all eros are about the "hunter's" projection onto the "prey" of a meaning one hopes is there. When that prey is reduced to a physical body or anatomical object, and the cloak of cultivated desire is pulled aside, then we are left not with projection (where there is the idea of some space — the "soul" — in between), but penetration *tout court*. "Having pulled up the beauty's dress, / you see what you were looking for, and not any new marvel of marvels," as Brodsky himself put it in "The End of a Beautiful Epoch."[28] Pygmalion turns his living subject to stone when he projects onto her a role that "isn't her" and that therefore she rejects. If in Ovid the impenetrable statue is supposed to be, through sufficient worship of Aphrodite (the mother of Eros), the flesh-and-blood, and ultimately penetrable, mate, then in Pushkin, Frost, and "Galatea Encore" the process is reversed. And not only is it reversed, it is so with a vengeance: from eros that stops just short of consumption (the promise of Donna Anna's "cold kiss" and her willingness to shift to the intimate *ty*), to eros that is now laden with the painful memories of family life (the "'Don't, don't don't / don't,' she cried" that is a wife's anger and disgust at her husband's insensitivity but that also conceals something sexual), to eros that seems to have passed beyond the pale and to have no concrete referent left in sight (only the "ins and outs of centuries").[29] My point here is that the "encore" in the title is also Brodsky's wry way of "going one better" his great rivals and predecessors. The metonymic thermometer that opens the poem does nothing to measure human health or to prod the statue to life, but merely underscores the latter's silence ("the mercury's under its tongue") and immobility ("with the alabaster, that lets roving pupils gorge on / the heart of the color and temperature of the knee. / That's what it looks like inside a virgin."]

27 Brodsky, *On Grief and Reason*, 236.

28 Iosif Brodskii, 'Konets prekrasnoi epokhi', in *Konets prekrasnoi epochi* (Ann Arbor: Ardis, 1977), 59: "Krasavitse plat'e zadrav, / vidish' to, chto iskal, a ne novye divnye divy."

29 Brodsky implies such a progression in the Volkov interview when he returns, a few pages after the initial mention of Pushkin, to the links between the *Little Tragedies* and Frost's verse "plays": "I've already spoken of the possible parallel to Pushkin's *Little Tragedies*, but Frost's 'plays' are much more horrible and simple. After all, our sense of tragedy is linked to the notion that something went wrong, and the result is a tragic situation. According to Frost, everything is as it should be, everything is in its proper place. Frost shows the horror of everyday situations, simple words, undemanding landscapes. Herein lies his uniqueness" (Volkov, *Conversations*, 94). My guess is that Brodsky is attempting to fit himself into this progression as a later, and even more stripped down, version of the "horror" that somehow attends on "everything [being] in its proper place."

mercury in its sphincter"). It pretends ("as though") to penetrate orifices, but then the role of this slightly absurd mini-phallus is to demonstrate, paradoxically, the absence of desire, the stasis that comes when Galatea has "come full circle."

We can get a better idea of the impression Brodsky is trying to create if we read a little further on in "On Grief and Reason":

> Scrutiny and interpretation are the gist of any intense human interplay, and love in particular. They are also the most powerful source of literature: of fiction (which is by and large about betrayal) and, above all, of lyric poetry, where one is trying to figure out the beloved and what makes her/him tick. And this figuring out brings us back to the Pygmalion business quite literally, since the more you chisel out and the more you penetrate the character, the more you put your model on a pedestal. An enclosure — be it a house, a studio, a page — intensifies the pedestal aspect enormously. And depending on your industry and on the model's ability to cooperate, this process results either in a masterpiece or in a disaster. In "Home Burial" it results in both. For every Galatea is ultimately Pygmalion's self-projection.[30]

Brodsky is telling us here that every artist (Pygmalion) is trying to "figure out" the source of his inspiration (Galatea). The phrase is well chosen, as it is both seemingly offhand (American conversational speech) and quite precise, or "chiseling," in its use of metaphor — to place the other into "figures" that are "out" there and are a resolution of some sort. And this trajectory works on its own to place the model higher and farther away, so that the more the words seem to "penetrate the character" (this is not sex, but the distillation of eros on the printed page), the more that probing translates into distance ("on a pedestal"). If in Pushkin and Frost we have words presenting confrontations between "real" men and women, in Brodsky we have a confrontation between the lyrical speaker and a statue, which is at least a second (if not an infinite) remove from the flesh-and-blood model inspiring it. Furthermore, the "model's ability to cooperate" is a crucial phrase in this case, since the implication is that most models do not. The artist needs to project, the model needs to step down off the pedestal and back into the frame where she cannot be "figured out", and these competing needs eventuate in a "disaster" of communication that may also be a "masterpiece" of art.

---

30 Brodsky, *On Grief and Reason*, 237.

pastoral element is smuggled into "Galatea Encore" in a manner that has become even colder, "frostier" as it were. Again, what Brodsky writes in "On Grief and Reason" could be applied to the creative logic driving his own poem:

> Actually "Home Burial" is not a narrative; it is an eclogue. Or more exactly, it is a pastoral — except that it is a very dark one. [...] Invented by Theocritus in his idylls, refined by Virgil in the poems he called eclogues or bucolics, the pastoral is essentially an exchange between two or more characters in a rural setting, returning often to that perennial subject, love. Since the English and French word "pastoral" is overburdened with happy connotations, and since Frost is closer to Virgil than to Theocritus, and not only chronologically, let's follow Virgil and call this poem ["Home Burial"] an eclogue. The rural setting is here, and so are the characters: a farmer and his wife, who may qualify as shepherd and shepherdess, except that it is two thousand years later. So is their subject: love, two thousand years later.[31]

a leaf-coated pond," "white like the blight of winter," "After such snow, there is nothing indeed," "pestered heather," and "bleached debris / of a glacier" are about as uncozy and "unpastoral" as one can get. This is not a nature that is felt to respond to man's attempts to cultivate and domesticate it. Rather it is a nature that couldn't care less about our efforts to write on it, chisel it, project upon it. Indeed, it is difficult to tell exactly what is "inside" and what "outside" in Brodsky's poem: only the "leaf-coated pond" seems an exact portrait of some landscape; all else has entered the domain of language, Of metaphor and simile, so that the reader cannot really say if "white like the blight of winter" refers simply to the statue's color or to actual weather conditions — is it *any* winter (a figure of speech) or is it specifically this winter (the scene framing the statue)? Moreover, in order to wrest his poem from the "European" tradition where space automatically becomes place, Brodsky won't let us know when or how or in what spot this picture grew into words — again, "epidermis meeting bark." Finally with regard to Brodsky's definition of the eclogue cited above, I would suggest that "Galatea Encore" contains, however deeply embedded and rhetorically minimalized ("restrained"), "an exchange between two or more characters in a rural setting, returning [...] to that perennial subject, love." But now that rural love story has evolved not

---

31 Ibid., 234–235.
32 Or that, to return to ⟨Bro⟩dsky's formulation in the ⟨Vol⟩kov interview, "According to ⟨Fro⟩st, everything is as it should ⟨be⟩, everything is in its proper ⟨pla⟩ce?" (Volkov, *Conversations*, 94). In this sense, Brodsky, following Frost, seems to be trying to get at a notion of tragedy that is not Greek, in that it is plotless (it can't be tied to events) and purely existential. I would add only that there is an event—the death of a first-born—implicated in "Home Burial," however much Brodsky wants to argue that that death is not constitutive of Frost the poet's treatment of it. See below.

only two thousand years, from Virgil to Frost, but almost a century (if not cultural light years) beyond that, from Frost to Brodsky. This Pygmalion and this Galatea don't appear to have a biography, a point which their creator (the intelligence outside both figures) seems insistent on making. In fact, if there is any metamorphosis in this cold landscape, perhaps that is it — that the human exchange/story supposedly underlying the art is no longer necessary?[32]

As in almost everything Brodsky wrote, there is the sense that his ideas came to him via the indwelling structures, beginning with prosody, of language itself. In analyzing "Home Burial," he argues that the work's framing is built around the couple's simultaneous positions on the staircase (the visual) and in the dialogue (the poetic): "Each piece of information in this narrative poem comes to you in an isolated manner, within a pentameter line. The isolation job is done by white margins framing, as it were, the whole scene, like the silence of the house, and the lines themselves are the staircase. Basically, what you get here is a succession of frames."[33] Likewise, "Galatea Encore" could have been laid out on the page (Brodsky's frame or "pedestal") as four quatrains, three of which (1, 3, and 4) would end with a full stop: the periods after "winter," "never," and "virgin." Again, the reason the poet runs these quatrains together on the page is presumably his desire to muffle his own poetic culture and to set off more starkly his own words against the "snow" of the page. The only exception to this pattern of enclosure would be "stanza" 2, which is where the negative metamorphosis takes place ("when your countenance starts to resemble weather") and which ends not by closing the frame but by extending it into the next scene/quatrain: "when Pygmalion's vanished." I suspect this breaking of the mold is significant on the poet's part, for this is also exactly where the "it" of the opening lines is replaced by a very ambiguous "you" (the only hint of dialogue or "exchange" in the poem) and where the iambs suddenly creep into what up to now has been a syncopated rhythm.

If we read Brodsky, and Brodsky on Frost, correctly, two things have to happen for this shift from "it" to "you" to take place. First, the artistic vector has to be established as inevitable. Which is to say, the love-starved Pygmalion doing the self-projecting has to realize that this very process, which is at the heart of all desire and culture, also has something profoundly *dehumanizing* about it, and that to keep looking in this way is nothing less, in existential terms, than staring into the countenance of Medusa:

[33] Brodsky, *On Grief and Reason*, 238.

> His [Pygmalion's] fascination is not with what he sees but with what he imagines it conceals — what he has placed there. He invests her [Galatea] with mystery and then rushes to uncloak it: this rapacity is always Pygmalion's double bind. It is as though the sculptor found himself puzzled by the facial expression of his model: she "sees" what he does not "see."[34]

What is potentially tragic is that, regardless of biography or "life," he and she never "see" the same thing. He looks for a meaning that he has projected and that lies concealed in her; she sees a meaning, or seems to see a meaning (he never knows), that is other. Indeed, her very lack of cooperation fuels his movement further and further away from issues of biography and human connectedness: "The model refuses to cooperate. [...] Yet the lack of cooperation here *is* cooperation. The less you cooperate, the more you are Galatea. For we have to bear in mind that the woman's psychological advantage is in the man's self-projection."[35]

The second thing that must transpire before the metamorphosis can become a "fact of life" is the acknowledgment that Pygmalion's vector is not only inevitable but now irreversible — there is no going back. This is why Brodsky believed that life never creates art, that poems never simply arise out of biographical facts or events:

> Imagine, for instance, that the story line [in "Home Burial"] has been drawn from experience — from, say, the loss of a firstborn. What does all that you've read thus far tell you about the author, about his sensibility? [...] The answer is: he is very free. Dangerously so. The very ability to utilize — to play with — this sort of material suggests an extremely wide margin of detachment. The ability to turn this material into a blank-verse, pentameter monotone adds another degree to that detachment. To observe a relation between a family graveyard and a bedroom's four-poster — still another. Added up, they amount to a considerable degree of detachment. A degree that dooms human interplay, that makes communication impossible, for communication requires an equal. This is very much the predicament of Pygmalion vis-a-vis his model. So it's not that the story the poem tells is autobiographical but that the poem is the author's self-portrait. That is why one abhors literary biography — because it is reductive. That is why I'm resisting issuing you with actual data on Frost.[36]

---

34 Ibid., 239.
35 Ibid.
36 Ibid., 245.

In other words, Brodsky refuses categorically to admit, as a matter of faith and experience, that "Home Burial" is in any meaningful way about how "Robert Frost" argued with "Elinor Frost" over the death of "Elliott."[37] No, the poem is about the intelligence, hopelessly "beyond" and in the grip of language, that can present "his" reason and "her" grief in a dialogue of pentameters that is both viewpoints at the same time and something else as well. "Would you like to meet Mr. Frost? Then read his poems, nothing else,"[38] concludes Brodsky.

I think these ideas about Frost in "Home Burial" give us the best available clue to the metamorphosis at the center of Brodsky's poem. To repeat, the "it" (the statue) of lines 1–2 becomes silently the "you" and "your" of lines 8–10 (presumably the Galatea of the title), while the "Pygmalion" of line 9 *implies* an "I" (otherwise, who is addressing the "you"?) that is, significantly, never named (i.e., the absence of biography). "That's what coming full circle means —/ when your countenance starts to resemble weather, / when Pygmalion's vanished" conjures a change that is also a return ("encore"). The female statue has become so chiseled, so figured out, so placed on a distant pedestal that it no longer recalls the human being it was modeled upon. "Her" features are now so remote that they have come to resemble the weather itself. So far into poetic outer space have the speaker's self-projections cast him that he, for the "her" that once upon a time had a biographical counterpart, has vanished, making her thereby free. The "coming full circle" signifies that this is a process whose trajectory, if followed out to the end, will restore its human actors to primal nature —the dark pastoral of Frost. Likewise, "And you are free / to cloud your folds, to bare the navel. / Future at last!" announces, as it were, a total capitulation on the part of this unnamed Pygmalion: Galatea can take any pose she likes, and he cannot reach her with his instruments, and this is the future she wished for, hence the exclamation. Or, in the words of the essay, "The man is groping for understanding. He realizes that in order to understand he's got to surrender — if not suspend entirely — his rationality. In other words, he descends. [...] She wants to stay impenetrable and won't accept anything short of his complete surrender."[39] All the speaker has left from his vanishing act are the iambs briefly breaking to the surface and hinting, however wanly, at some linguistic organization of the pain. There is no color in this post-Frostian eclogue ("bleached debris / of a glacier") just as there is no temporal perspective ("five-lettered 'never'") because all hope of contact has ended. Pygmalion has not been given a statue come to life

---

[37] To be sure, it is also possible that Brodsky, who had seen his own "heroic" biography used to explain his poetry in an over-determined way, is simply defending his favorite American poet from similar "decodings," only from the opposite end of the spectrum: i.e., the accusations of personal spite and pettiness that explode the icon of "genial farmer" and that serve as corrosive metacommentary on the poems in Lawrence Thompson's famous multi-volume biography of Frost See Volkov, *Conversations*, 94–95.

[38] Brodsky, *On Grief and Reason*, 245.

[39] Ibid., 250.

at his touch, as in Ovid's original, but a human being he, in acting out the dictates of his own linguistic fate, has turned to stone (alabaster). Hence this ice goddess cares not that "roving pupils gorge on / the heart of the color and temperature of the knee." She has become what she wanted, totally impenetrable, and, in a fitting conclusion to the false penetrations of the opening lines, she has shown her mate, through the speculum of poetic language that still leaves her free and intact, "what it looks like inside a virgin."

In conclusion, we cannot say how closely, if at all, Brodsky had Frost in mind as he composed "Galatea Encore." It does strike me, however, that his prominent use of the Pygmalion-Galatea myth in "On Grief and Reason" and his thinking of the dialogic forms in Pushkin and Frost provided a momentum that he, ever mindful of tradition and "new words," would want to tap and redirect after his own fashion. It is also not at all clear to whom the "Galatea" and the "Pygmalion" refer in his poem, although I have tried to make the case, one against the use of a biographical (or autobiographical) parsing, that this ambivalence is quite intentional on Brodsky's part. It doesn't matter who is the source of "grief" and who "reason"; the poem is what the author looks like. Or to allow Brodsky the last word:

> So what was it that he [Frost] was after in this, his very own poem? He was, I think, after grief and reason, which, while poison to each other, are language's most efficient tool — or, if you will, poetry's indelible ink. Frost's reliance on them here and elsewhere almost gives you the sense that his dipping into this ink pot had to do with the hope of reducing the level of its contents: you detect a sort of vested interest on his part. Yet the more one dips into it, the more it brims with this black essence of existence, and the more one's mind, like one's fingers, gets soiled by this liquid. For the more there is of grief, the more there is of reason. As much as one may be tempted to take sides in "Home Burial," the presence of the narrator here rules this out, for while the characters stand, respectively, for reason and for grief, the narrator stands for their fusion. To put it differently, while the characters' actual union disintegrates, the story, as it were, marries grief to reason, since the bond of the narrative here supersedes the individual dynamics — well, at least for the reader. Perhaps for the author as well. The poem, in other words, plays fate.[40]

40 Ibid., 260.

420. What Brodsky was after in "Galatea Encore" was something similar: a Russian émigré poet's American self-portrait, another marriage of grief to reason with no one "taking sides," and a hidden story about ice goddesses, snow sculptors, and a less than fairytale "Grandfather Frost."[41]

---

[41] The pun, involving the Russian version of Santa Claus, "Grandfather Frost" (Ded Moroz), was not lost on Brodsky. See Volkov, *Conversations*, 95.

Index

Abramovich, S. L., 193
Abrams, M. H., 76, 79n115
Acmeism, 335, 373n38, 387
Akhmatova, Anna, 12, 33–34, 39, 99, 115–16, 125, 126n66, 194–95, 251n8, 263, 363, 372, 373n38, 395n5, 386–87, 393, 396–97;
"'Kamennyi gost' Pushkina," 111n24, 115–16, 119n53, 263;
Requiem, 39, 363
Aksakov, Konstantin, 68
Alaric I, 55
Alekseev, M. P., 126n66, 189n15, 194, 249
Alexander I (emperor), 109, 125, 126n68, 208–9, 211–12, 217–18, 267–68, 278, 280
Alexander II (emperor), 223
Alexander III (emperor), 89
Alexander the Great, 86
Alexander, Victoria, 128, 136–7
Alexandrov, Vladimir, 25, 338–39, 345, 350
Alexis (tsar), 58, 61, 63, 288
Alter, Robert, 340
Anna Ivanovna (empress), 309
Annenkov, P. V., 186–7
Anuchin, D., 92
apocalypse, 15, 19;
genre of, 45–48, 79–80;
Judeo-Christian tradition of, 42–50, 52–54;
myth of, 42–50, 55, 59, 75;
in Russian history, 50–69, 276
apocalyptic fiction, 10, 69–86, 99;
typology of, 72–83
apocalyptic thinking, 14, 44–45, 387
apocalyptic plot, 32, 39, 69–83;
elements of, 77–83
apocalyptic steed, 86–100
Appel, Alfred, 348n7
Apuleius, 23, 227–30, 233–248. See also Pushkin: Cupid and Psyche myth
Arakcheev, Count A. A. (minister), 211–12
Arina Rodionovna (Pushkin's nanny). See Yakovleva
Ariosto, Ludovico, 90
Arzamas (literary society), 67, 116n42, 210–11
Auden, W. H., 185, 363–80, 381, 384, 386, 393, 397n12, 398, 406, 408–20;
"In Memory of W. B. Yeats," 365, 367–80, 381
Augustine, Saint, 43–44, 48–49, 56, 63, 90;
City of God, 43–44, 49
Avraamy (monk), 58–59

Avvakum (archpriest), 34, 38, 52, 56–58, 61–62, 70
Babel, Isaak, 33, 99
Baehr, Stephen L., 96n156
Bakhtin, Mikhail, 9, 17, 20–22, 71n101, 72–73, 81, 84, 102–103, 161n31, 170, 172, 202n44, 204, 286, 297n62, 322
Bakunin, M. A., 68
Bakunina, Ekaterina, 195
Balmont, Konstantin, 348n7
Balzac, Honoré de, 347
Baratynsky, Evgeny, 253–55, 268
Bartenev, P. I., 186–7, 278–79
Barthes, Roland, 70n100, 72–73, 169, 172, 322
Bataille, Georges, 286–87, 289
Batiushkov, Konstantin, 209–11;
"The Song of Harold the Brave," 94n153
Baudelaire, 348n7, 351;
"Les Chats," 105–106
Beardsley, Aubrey, 171
Beaujour, Elizabeth, 338
Beckett, Samuel, 99n167
Behe, Michael, 131–32, 135
Belinsky, Vissarion, 37, 68, 218
Belobotsky, Andrei, 63
Belousov, A. F., 109n21,
Bely, Andrei (B. N. Bugaev), 33, 40, 59n60, 74–76, 84, 98–99, 139, 187, 325n13, 349, 351n21, 354;
Petersburg, 32, 57n54, 73–74, 78–84;
The Beginning of the Century, 75n108;
Between Two Revolutions, 75n108
Benckendorff, Count Alexander von (general), 218–19, 223
Benois, Alexander, 185
Berberova, Nina, 323n4, 326n16, 333n31, 334n33
Berdyaev, Nikolai, 32, 50, 57, 61, 66, 93, 99;
The Russian Idea, 32, 57
Bergson, Henri, 139
Bernini, Giovanni, 87–88, 271
Beseda Liubitelei Russkogo Slova (literary society), 211
Bestuzhev-Marlinsky, A. A., 175
"Saatyr," 94n153
Bilibin, Ivan, 185
Bitov, Andrei, 194
Blackmore, Susan, 128n5, 140
Blackwell, Stephen, 128
Blagoi, D. D., 188, 288n25, 290
Blake, William, 76

INDEX

Blok, Alexander, 25, 33, 39–40, 59n60, 75, 92–93, 99, 187, 332, 348–49, 351n21, 354, 355n37, 396;
  The Twelve, 32, 40
Bloom, Harold, 9, 17, 19–20, 24–25, 102n3, 169, 173–76, 181–184, 186, 191, 263, 364–66, 370, 376n48, 381–82
Bobrov, Semyon, 67
Bocharov, S. G., 202–3
Bogdanov, Alexander, 53n40
Bogdanovich, Ippolit, 234, 248n52
Bologna, Giovanni, 87
Bondi, S. M., 188–89
Borges, Jorge Luis, 93–94
Boyd, Brian, 128, 135, 337–40, 343n15, 343–44
Briusov, Valery, 75, 187, 195, 348n7, 348n9, 352
Brodsky, Joseph, 9, 15, 17, 25, 33, 99, 130, 182;
  "Elegy: For Robert Lowell," 385–89;
  exile, 363, 366–69, 371–74, 380, 381–82, 384–86, 388–89, 420' "Flight from Byzantium" ("Puteshestvie v Stambul"), 382–83;
  "Galatea Encore," 405–20;
  Less than One, 41, 363, 365–370, 372, 379, 380n64, 383, 389, 395–98, 405, 407;
  Lullaby of Cape Cod (*Kolybel'naia Treskovogo Mysa*), 381–390;
  On Grief and Reason, 392, 395–403, 406, 409–20;
  Pygmalion and Galatea myth, 410–19;
  "To My Daughter," 391–404;
  "Verses on the Death of T.S. Eliot," 363–80, 381;
  "York" ("Iork"), 384
Browning, Robert, 173
Bulavin, Kondraty, 59
Bulgakov, Mikhail, 33, 75–77, 98, 99n167;
  The Master and Margarita, 32, 37, 39, 73–74, 78–83, 84
Bulgakov, Father Sergei, 53n39, 196–97, 202
Bulgarin, F. V., 67, 175, 286, 302
Bultman, Rudolph, 183
Bunin, Ivan, 25, 342, 348n9
Bunyan, John, 90, 223
Burnett, Leon, 411n24
Burton, Robert, 90
Byron, George Gordon, Lord, 114, 122, 174–78, 180–4, 194, 206, 212–14, 217, 244–47, 263, 268, 289, 347, 372;
  Beppo, 217;
  Childe Harold, 175, 246;
  Don Juan, 175, 180, 214, 244

C: Calvin, John, 58n58
Campanella, Tommaso, 50
Cassedy, Steven, 151
Catherine II ("the Great"), 59, 87, 90, 107, 110, 207, 221, 265, 267, 271–72, 299, 301, 308–9, 312–15, 322n62
Cerularius, Michael, 55
Cervantes, Miguel de, 348;
  Don Quixote, 97n157, 353,
Chaadaev, Pyotr, 35, 68
Chaplin, Charlie, 182
Chateaubriand, François-René de, 194
Chaucer, Geoffrey, 90, 194
Chekhov, Anton; "The Peasants," 96
Chénier, André, 141
Cherniavsky, Michael, 54n42, 56, 60, 70
Chernyshevsky, Nikolai, 30, 33;
  biography of in Nabokov's *The Gift*, 127n2, 136, 138, 144n45;
  What is To Be Done?, 30, 35, 37, 67;
  "The Russian at the Rendezvous," 75n108
Chetverikov, Sergei, 133n13
Chomsky, Noam, 109
Chopin, Frédéric, 214
Cixous, Helen, 17
Clark, Katerina, 77
Cohn, Norman, 48, 51n35, 56
Coleridge, Samuel Taylor, 76, 281
Collins, John C., 79–80
Comte, Auguste, 50
Condorcet, M. J. A. N. C., 53n40
Connolly, Julian, 343
Cumont, Franz, 44

D: Dante Alighieri, 23, 44n10, 90, 103, 131n8, 173–74, 182, 185, 194, 198, 382, 384, 408;
  The Divine Comedy, 14, 149–166
d'Anthès, Georges, 113n30, 196–7, 224–26
Danto, Arthur, 69–71, 287–88, 322
Darwin, Charles, 11, 13–14, 24, 127n1, 130–32, 135, 137, 148;
  Darwin-Mendel synthesis, 132, 135. *See also* evolution
Davydov, Denis, 211,
Davydov, Sergei, 205–226, 251n9, 298, 302, 338–39
Davydov, V. L., 213
Dawkins, Richard, 9, 24, 129n5, 130, 135n15, 138–140, 147
de Bonald, Louis, 68
Decadent movement. *See* Symbolism
Decembrists, 67, 110, 190, 213, 217–20, 227–28, 255
Delille, Jacques, 254n21
Delius, Juan, 129n5
Delvig, Anton, 143, 210, 221, 253
de Maistre, Joseph, 68

de Man, Paul, 11, 369
Dennett, Daniel, 130n6, 140
Derrida, Jacques, 11, 17
Derzhavin, Gavrila, 17, 34, 91n141, 110–111, 209, 253–54, 296–97;
"The Chariot," 94n153;
"Felitsa," 35;
"Monument," 126;
"The Waterfall," 253
Dickens, Charles, *David Copperfield*, 28
Dimitry of Rostovsk, Saint, 61–64
Dmitriev, I. I., 299–300, 304n8
Dmitriev, Mikhail, 67, 209
Dmitriev-Mamonov, Matvei, 67
Dobroliubov, Nikolai;
"What is Oblomovism?", 37;
"When Will the Real Day Come?", 17n108, 37
Dobuzhinsky, Mstislav, 185
Dobzhansky, Theodosius, 133–36, 147
Dolinin, Alexander, 142n37, 143n42, 144, 338
Donatello, 87
Donne, John, 365, 366n19, 374n42, 381, 386, 390, 402–3
Dorosh, Efim, 99
Dostoevsky, Fyodor, 22, 28, 31, 33, 36, 50, 53, 61, 66, 68–69, 75–76, 91n141, 91n143, 97–98, 185, 195, 279, 286;
The Brothers Karamazov, 30–31;
The Devils, 32;
Crime and Punishment, 27–28, 96;
The Idiot, 30–31, 39, 73–74, 78–84, 90, 97;
Notes from the Dead House, 35
Douglass, Mary, 281–82
Eco, Umberto, *In the Name of the Rose*, 49
Edmundson, Mark, 11
Edwards, Jonathan, 389
Efremov, P. A., 186–87
Eidelman, N. Ya., 190–91
Eikhenbaum, B. M., 192
Einstein, Albert, 13, 150, 153–5, 160, 166
Eliade, Mircea, 42, 44, 62–63, 84, 92
Eliot, T. S., 172–73, 323, 329n23, 363–64, 366–67, 370–80, 381, 384
Elizabeth (empress), 207
Emerson, Caryl, 16, 84;
Introduction by, 17–26
Emerson, Ralph Waldo, 173, 408n11
Engelhardt, E. E., 111
Engelgardt, V. V., 209–210
Ephrem the Syrian, 62
Erofeev, Venedikt, *From Moscow to the End of the Line (Moskva-Petushki)*, 98
Escher, M. C., 71, 139, 153
Esenin, Sergei, 33, 92, 99;
"Sorokoust," 98

Etkind, Efim, 10
Euclidean geometry, 151, 153, 155, 157, 160, 164
Euripedes, 90
evolution, 127, 130–137, 145–148
F: Falconet, E. M., 87–91, 265–66, 271, 273, 278, 333
Favorsky, Vladimir, 153
Fedotov, G. P., 196
Filaret (metropolitan), 144,
Fisher, Ronald, 132
Flaubert, Gustav, *Madame Bovary*, 30
Florensky, Father Pavel, 23, 31, 33, 37, 75, 150–166;
Imaginary Spaces in Geometry, 150–161, 164
Fomichev, S. A., 200, 289
Fonvizin, Denis, 209
Formalism, 9, 104–105, 191, 308, 339
Frank, S. L., 196–7, 202, 203n46
Freud, Sigmund, 9, 11, 17, 19, 90n135, 102–3, 123, 136, 173–74, 176, 182–84, 286, 344–45, 347, 381, 386
Frost, Robert, 381, 393, 395, 398, 404n34, 406–420;
"Home Burial," 406, 410–19
Funkenstein, Amos, 43–44
Futurism, 104
Fyodor Ivanovich (tsar), 88
Fyodorov, Nikolai, 33, 40, 61, 75;
The Philosophy of the Common Cause, 69
G: Gannibal, Abram Petrovich, 206–7, 231n11, 267
Gannibal, Marya Alekseevna, 206–8
Gasparov, Boris, 201–2
Gasparov, M. L., 322
Gatsev, Alexei, 53n40
Gauss, Carl Friedrich, 153–4
Genet, Jean, 99n167
Genette, Gerard 169, 172
Gershenzon, M. O., 187, 193, 196, 203n47
Ginzburg, Lydia, 101–102, 192, 227
Girandoux, Jean, 99n167
Girard, René, 108
Gladkov, Fyodor, *Cement*, 37, 77
Glinka, Mikhail, 185
Gnedich, Nikolai, 394
Goethe, Johann Wolfgang, 372
Gogol, Nikolai, 33, 66, 74, 91n141, 92, 195, 221, 347, 351;
Arabesques, 304n8;
"The Carriage," 94n153;
Dead Souls, 32, 35, 93–94;
"Diary of a Madman," 94n153;
Marriage, 94n153;
"Nevsky Prospect," 94n153

Goncharov family, 107, 119–121, 219, 225–26
Goncharov, Ivan, *Oblomov,* 37
Goncharova-Pushkina, Natalia Nikolaevna. *See* Pushkin: marriage
Goodwin, Brian, 136
Golikov, Ivan, 274
Gorky, Maksim (Alexei Peshkov), 33, 327, 356;
Mother, 30, 32, 37, 77
Gorodetsky, B. P, 203–4
Gould, Stephen J., 11, 13, 132, 134–5, 148
"Green Lamp" society (Zelenaia lampa), 116, 211, 233
Griboedov, Alexander, 170;
Wit from Woe (*Gore ot uma*), 37, 94–95
Grigoriev, Apollon, 185
Grossman, L. P., 193
Grot, Ia. K., 186–7
Gruzinov, I. I., 99
Gudov, I., 99
Guizot, François Pierre Guillaume, 142, 255–56, 295–96, 304n8
Gukovsky, G. A., 191–2
Gumilev, Lev, 39
Gumilev, Nikolai, 39, 396
Haldane, J. B. S., 132
Hardy, Thomas, 365, 393, 395, 399–402, 406, 408;
"Afterwards," 400–402
La Harpe, Jean-François de, 255
Hasty, Olga Peters, 248n53
Hawthorne, Nathaniel;
"The Celestial Railway," 97n158;
The House of Seven Gables, 97n158
Hazlitt, William, 411n25
van Heeckeren, Baron Louis, 224–25
Hegel, G. W. F., 67, 68, 76, 83
Heidegger, Martin, 151
Heine, Heinrich, 71n103
Herbert, George, 90
Herzen, Alexander, 35, 37, 68, 75n108;
Who Is to Blame?, 37;
From the Other Shore, 75n108;
Endings and Beginnings, 75n108
Hesiod, 43
Hilarion (metropolitan), 64;
"Sermon on Law and Grace," 38, 52
Hirsch, E. D., 169, 183
Hitler, Adolf, 50
Hoffman, E. T. A., 71n103
Hölderlin, Friedrich, 76
Homer, 149–51, 209
Ulysses, 149–151
Horace, 126n68, 194n28, 209, 266, 365n11, 376, 380, 384
Hugo, Victor, 348

Humphrey, N. K., 140
Ilenkov, V., *The Driving Axle,* 98
Ilyin, I. A., 196
Ingarden, Roman, 151
Intelligent Design debates, 16, 24, 127, 131–133
Inzov, I.K. (General), 212–213
Ionesco, Eugène, 99n167
Irving, Washington, 195, 223;
A History of New York, 126n66,
"Legend of the Arabian Astrologer," 125
Iskoz, A. S., 187
Ivan III, 55n45 (tsar)
Ivan IV ("The Terrible") (tsar), 39, 54, 56, 58n57, 60, 274, 387
Ivanov, Vyacheslav, 99, 196, 352;
Furrows and Boundaries, 75n108
Izmailov, N. V., 188, 203–4
Jakobson, Roman, 9, 17, 102–126, 178n20, 191–3, 273n21, 391;
aphasia, 104;
dominant, 103, 105, 108;
"On a Generation that Squandered its Poets," 104;
poetic function, 103–104, 140;
"Poetry of Grammar and Grammar of Poetry," 105;
Puškin and His Sculptural Myth, 107–111, 115–6, 123, 192–3, 411n23
James, Henry, 34, 71n101,
Jarrell, Randall, 409
Jefferson, Thomas, 185
Joachim of Fiore, 48–50, 74
John of Damascus, Saint, 165
Jonson, Ben, 90
Joyce, James, 172–73, 323, 347–48
Kachenovsky, M. T., 67
Kafka, Franz, 347
Kalashnikova, Olga, 216–17
Kant, Immanuel, 136, 153
Kantemir, Antiokh, 64, 91n141
Kapiton (monk), 57–58
Karamzin, Nikolai, 18, 34, 35, 54, 114, 125, 171, 190–91, 202, 209, 211–212, 218, 267n5, 268, 282, 302, 304, 306;
History of the Russian State, 35, 206, 217, 302, 306–7, 313. *See also* Lotman, Yu: *The Creation of Karamzin*
Kartashev, A. V., 196
Katenin, Pavel, 191, 195;
"An Old True Story," 125n65
Keats, John, 173, 281
Kermode, Frank, 73, 76
Khlebnikov, Velimir, 33, 104;
Ladomir, 75n109
Khodasevich, Vladislav, 15–17, 25, 34, 193, 195, 203n47, 323–336, 387, 396;

"Sorrento Photographs" ("Sorrentinskie fotografii"), 16–17, 325–336
Khomyakov, Alexei, 61, 68
Khvostov, Count D. I., 211
Kiprensky, Orest, 185
Kireevsky, Ivan, 67, 68
Kliuev, Nikolai, 33, 92, 99
Knut, Dovi (D. M. Fiksman), 396
Korvin-Piotrovsky, Vladimir, 99
Kozlov, I. I., "The Nocturnal Ride," 94n153
Kozlov, Nikita, 226
Kristeva, Julia, 17, 74, 169, 172
Krylov, I. A., 209;
"The Rider and the Steed," 94n153
Küchelbecker, V. K., 170, 191, 210, 217, 296–97;
"Sviatopolk," 94n153;
"Rogday's Hounds," 94n153
Kurbsky, Prince Andrei, 39, 60
Kutuzov, A. M., 67
Lacan, Jacques, 11
Lamarck, Jean Baptiste Pierre Antoine de Monet de, 130, 388
Larionova, E. O., 200
Larkin, Philip, 381
Larson, Edward, 132–133
Lawrence, D. H., 74, 99–100
Lazhechnikov, I. I., 67
Leach, Edmund, 84–85
Leibniz, Gottfried Wilhelm, 153
Lenin, Vladimir, 41, 67, 70, 77, 89
Leontiev, K. N., 69, 97
Lermontov, Mikhail, 33, 91n141, 95–96;
A Hero of Our Time, 95
Lerner, N. O., 187, 193
Leskov, Nikolai, "The Enchanted Pilgrim," 96
Lessing, G. E., 50
Levi-Strauss, Claude, 106
Levin, Yury, 249, 350n14
Levkovich, V. L., 204
Lipking, Lawrence, 386
Liubarsky, Platon (archmandrite), 295, 303–4
Lotman, Yury M., 9, 17–20, 32–33, 50–51, 62, 99, 102–103, 139n30, 149–172, 174, 182, 283–85, 287, 289n27, 294, 391;
and Bakhtin, 22;
The Creation of Karamzin (*Sotvroenie Karamzina*), 167–172, 174, 182;
on Pushkin, 190–2, 195, 197, 203, 205, 302;
semiosphere, 24, 28, 149;
structuralism, 22–23;
The Universe of the Mind, 149–151, 154–8, 160–1, 164–6
Lowell, Robert, 381, 383–90, 393
Löwith, Karl, 44

Lubin, Peter, 339
Luther, Martin, 58n58, 90
M: Maeterlinck, Maurice, 348n7
Maikov, L. V., 187
Maikov, Vasily, *Eslisei, or Bacchus Enraged*, 234
Malinowski, Bronislaw, 42
Mallarmé, Stéphane, 182
Mandelstam, Nadezhda, 36
Mandelstam, Osip, 14, 33, 36, 39, 99, 130, 172–73, 182–3, 364, 382–84, 386–87, 391, 396–98, 400n22;
"Concert at the Station," 98;
"Conversation about Dante," 103, 131n8;
Journey to Armenia, 382;
"Lamarck," 388;
"Pushkin and Scriabin," 382;
"Preserve my speech," ("Sokhrani moiu rech'"), 388
Mann, Thomas, *The Magic Mountain*, 82
Manuel, Frank and Fritzie, 47n25, 28n27, 53n40
Marcus Aurelius, 86, 88n130, 91
Marcus Curtius, 87
Mariengof, A. B., 99
Marx, Karl, 50, 53n40, 77–78, 81, 83, 183, 192, 197, 286, 383
Mauss, Marcel, 285–87
Mayakovsky, Vladimir, 33–34, 40, 104
Medvedev, Silvester, 61
Meilakh, B. S., 203–4
memes, 16, 24, 129–130, 136, 139–140, 145–148
Mendel, Gregor. See Darwin-Mendel synthesis
Mercier, Sébastian, 53n40
Merezhkovsky, Dmitry, 50, 74–75, 196, 354
Mérimée, Prosper, 348
Mickiewicz, Adam, 91–92, 214, 253, 272
Mikhail Fyodorovich (tsar), 309
Milosz, Czeslaw, 365
Miloradovich, Count M. A., 212
Milton, John, 173
Mitsishvili, N., 64n76
Mochi, Francesco, 87
Modernism, 99, 172–73, 323, 326, 338–39, 347349, 364, 375n45, 376, 397
Modzalevsky, B. L., 187–8
Modzalevsky, L. B., 188, 203n47
Moebius, A. F., 153;
Moebius strip, 139, 144, 153, 160, 165
Molière (Jean Baptiste Poquelin), 208–9, 255
Montesquieu, Charles de Secondat, baron de, 207
Moore, Thomas, 175–76
More, Sir Thomas, 47n25

Müntzer, Thomas, 50
Musil, Robert, 74
Musorgsky, Modest, 185
myth, 14–15, 27–29, 34, 41–43, 54, 382–83;
apocalyptic, 42–50, 54, 59;
Cupid and Psyche, 14–15, 23, 228–48;
erotic/national, 38–40;
eschatological/utopian, 32;
in opposition to history, 42–43, 55;
of Moscow and Petersburg, 38;
Pygmalion, 14–15, 19, 117–19, 122–23, 143, 177–83, 228, 261–64, 401–19
mythopoesis, 10–12, 14–15, 17, 25, 40, 108–26, 410–12;
definition of, 14;
and apocalypse, 41–100;
and Pushkin, 108–26, 174–84, 227–48, 249–64;
vectors of in Russian literature, 27–40

Nabokov, Vladimir, 15, 17, 25, 127–31, 133–48, 172–73, 185, 195, 282, ;
Ada, 339–40;
and butterflies, 24–25, 127–29, 133–37, 140, 143–46, 338, 340–44, 349;
Despair, 350, 359, 362n50;
The Gift (Dar), 127, 129n5, 130, 133–48, 340–45, 348n8, 350n14;
and Intelligent Design, 16, 24, 127, 133–45;
Invitation to a Beheading, 141, 343, 347, 350;
Lolita, 347–56, 359–62;
Mary (Mashen'ka), 350;
Pale Fire, 362;
Strong Opinions, 135;
style, 337–46
Napoleon I (emperor of France), 67, 126n68, 143, 209, 214, 217, 267, 271, 280, 289
Nekrasov, Nikolai;
"The Railroad," 96n156;
About the Weather, 96
Nepomniashchy, V. S., 202
New Criticism, 171–72, 228
New Enlighteners, 61–64
Newton, Isaac, 153
Nicholas I (tsar), 68, 96n156, 109, 125, 217–18, 221–23, 225–26, 266–69, 273–74, 302
Nicholas II (tsar), 67n87
Nijhout, Frederik, 136–7
Nietzsche, Friedrich, 286
Nikon (patriarch), 38, 52, 58, 61
Odoevsky, Vladimir, 67, 185
Ogaryov, Nikolai, 396
Ognyov, Nikolai, 33;
"Eurasia," 75n109
Oksman, Yu. G., 188–90, 200

Old Believers, 32, 38, 51, 56–62
Olesha, Yury, *Envy*, 31
Origen, 43
Orlov, M. F., 213
Orlovsky, B. I., 143
Ospovat, Lev, 249, 251n8
Ostrovsky, A., *The Storm*, 97n159
Ovid, 117–19, 122, 177–83, 213, 228–30, 235, 261–63, 384, 398, 411, 413, 418–19. *See also* Myth, Pygmalion
Panchenko, A. M., 61–62
Paley, William, 131
Parny, Evariste, 209
Pasternak, Boris, 33, 34, 39, 64n76, 75–77, 98, 99n167;
Doctor Zhivago, 32, 35, 40, 73–74, 78–83, 84
Paszkiewicz, Henryk, 60n62
Pecherin, Vladimir, 67
Perugino, 179
Pestel, Colonel Pavel, 213
Peter I ("the Great") (tsar/emperor), 32, 36, 38, 57, 59–65, 87–91, 97, 175, 206–7, 220–21, 255, 265–75, 279, 309, 387
Peter III, 221, 299, 311
Philo Judaeus, 90
Philotheus (monk), 54–56
Pifer, Ellen, 338
Pilnyak, Boris, 59n60
Plato, 43, 47n25, 90, 382
Platonov, Andrei, 33, 59n60, 75–76, 98;
Chevengur, 32, 73–74, 78–84, 97n157
Pletnev, Pyotr, 209, 263
Plutarch, 90
Poe, Edgar Allen, 348
Pogodin, M. P., 67, 304n8
Polevoy, Nikolai, 67, 305;
History of the Russian People, 142–43, 25, 295, 302, 304n8, 310
Postmodernism, 12, 40, 147, 165, 173, 183, 228, 339, 387,
Poststructuralism, 172
Pritchard, William, 409–10
Prokopovich, Feofan, 64
Propp, F. Ya., 74
Proust, Marcel, 323, 340
Prudentius, 90
Psychoanalysis, 9. *See also* Freud
Pugachev, Emelyan, 32, 59, 217–18, 221, 223, 289–92, 301, 304–21. *See also* Pushkin, works, *The Captain's Daughter*; *The History of Pugachev*
Pushchin, Ivan, 109n17, 210, 217
Pushkin, Alexander Sergeevich;
biography, 40, 177–78, 182, 192–93, 196–97, 202–4, 205–26, 251, 286n19, 41
Boldino autumn, 18, 24, 26, 114, 119,

180–82, 220–22, 229–31, 247–48, 261–263, 410–11;
and Byron, 114, 122, 174–8, 180–4, 194, 206, 212–14, 217, 244–47, 263, 268, 289;
Cupid and Psyche myth, 14–15, 23, 228–48;
death, 33, 196–97, 203, 224, 269;
exile, 33, 109n21, 119n52, 177, 203n47, 212–18, 252, 268, 289;
genre consciousness, 18, 22–23, 26, 34, 35, 190–91, 227–28, 253, 275, 282–83, 288, 291–300, 302–4, 306–7, 319–22;
influence on later writers, 10, 25, 34, 74, 129, 138, 140–44, 182, 185, 343, 345–46, 382–84, 387, 396–97, 410–13, 419;
inspiration, 23–24, 283, 288, 291, 296;
and history, 32, 67, 141–2, 256, 283, 287–300, 301–22;
and mythopoesis, 11–12, 14, 108–26, 174–84, 227–48, 249–64, 410–13;
marriage, 12, 40, 107–8, 110, 113–14, 117–24, 141, 178–81, 191, 219–26, 228–31, 247–48, 252, 261–63, 280, 410–11;
Pygmalion myth, 14–15, 19, 117–19, 122–23, 143, 177–83, 228, 261–64, 401–13;
statue-come-to-life motif, 11–12, 17, 19, 107–8, 114–26, 143, 177–83, 191–93, 228–48, 261–64, 278–80, 410–13;
study of, 9–10, 15–18, 21–22, 105, 107–110, 170, 185–204, 297n62, 301–2, 322;
superstition and religious sensibilities, 11–12, 89n133, 109–112, 179, 202–3, 215, 221, 223–24, 227, 295, 304n8, 319–21;
works: "Again I Have Visited" ("Vnov' ia posetil"), 208n5, 396–97;
"And the weary wanderer grumbled at God" ("I putnik ustalyi na boga roptal"), 110n22;
"And we ventured further" ("I dale my poshli"), 198–99;
"André Chénier," 141, 218–19;
Angelo (*Andzhelo*), 222;
"Arion," 219–20;
"Autumn" ("Osen'"), 222;
Belkin Tales (*Povesti Belkina*), 21, 23, 180, 220, 229, 234–35, 236n27, 247–48, 294, 302, 305;
The Blackamoor of Peter the Great, 207, 231–32, 261, 266;
Boris Godunov, 31, 114, 138, 192, 203n47, 217, 231, 236n27, 252, 254–55, 267, 304;
"Borodino Anniversary" ("Borodinskaia godovshchina"), 221;
The Bronze Horseman (*Mednyi vsadnik*), 15, 32, 89–92, 94, 96n156, 107, 124, 198, 222, 231, 265, 269, 272–280, 325, 330, 411;

The Captain's Daughter (*Kapitanskaia dochka*), 21, 142, 222–23, 231, 256, 281–83, 288–300, 301, 304n8, 314, 316;
"Confidante of Magical Olden Times" ("Napersnitsa volshebnoi stariny"), 208n5;
"Conversation between Bookseller and Poet" ("Razgovor knigoprodavtsa s poetom"), 214;
The Covetous Knight (*Skupoi rytsar'*), 216, 220, 229, 251–52, 325, 410–11;
Count Nulin (*Graf Nulin*), 217;
"The Dagger," ("Kinzhal"), 213;
"Demon," 215;
"The Devils" ("Besy"), 94n153, 109n21, 221;
Egyptian Nights (*Egipetskie nochi*), 195;
"Epistle to Yudin" ("Poslanie k Iudinu"), 208;
Eugene Onegin (*Evgenii Onegin*), 14, 17–18, 35, 37, 39, 115, 122–23, 175–77, 180–81, 190, 195, 200–201, 208, 210, 214–18, 220, 222, 224, 228–36, 240–48, 262;
Exegi monumentum ("Ia pamiatnik sebe vozdvig"), 16, 198, 202, 223–24, 265;
Ezersky, 273n23, 277;
"The Fairy Tale of the Golden Cockerel," ("Skazka o zolotom petushke"), 107, 124–26, 223;
Feast in a Time of Plague (*Pir vo vremia chumy*), 220, 229, 251, 325, 410–11;
"Fonvizin's Shade" ("Ten' Fonvizina"), 111n26;
"Foreboding" ("Predchuvstvie"), 109n21;
The Fountain of Bakhchisarai (*Bakhchisraiskii fontan*), 212–13, 302;
"Freedom's Lonely Sower" ("Svobody seiatel' pustynnyi"), 214;
"From Pindemote" ("Iz Pindemonti"), 224;
The Gabriiliad (*Gavriiliada*), 12, 112–13, 115, 195, 213, 219;
"Gift futile, gift accidental" ("Dar naprasnyi, dar sluchainyi"), 109n21, 143–44, 219;
"God grant that I not go mad" ("Ne dai mne bog soiti s uma"), 222;
The Gypsies (*Tsygany*), 215, 217, 231;
"Hermit fathers and immaculate women" ("Ottsy pustynniki i zheny ntporochny"), 223;
"The Hero" ("Geroi"), 221, 297;
The History of Peter the Great, 124, 221, 267, 274;
The History of Pugachev (*Istoriia Pugacheva*), 21, 125, 142, 222, 256, 291–300, 301–22;
The History of the Village Goriukhino, 125–6, 304n8;
"I loved you" ("Ia vas liubil"), 105;
"Imitation of the Italian" ("Podrazhanie italiianskomu"), 223;
"Imitations of the Koran" ("Podrazhaniia Koranu"), 110n22, 217;

"It's time, my friend, it's time" ("Pora, moi drug, pora"), 223;
"A Journey from Moscow to Petersburg" ("Puteshestvie iz Moskvy v Peterburg"), 198n35, 222;
A Journey to Arzrum, (*Puteshestvie v Arzrum*), 219, 345–46, 382;
"The Last Relative of Jeanne d'Arc" ("Poslednii iz svoistvennikov Ioanny d'Ark"), 112–13;
"Liberty" ("Vol'nost'"), 211, 218;
The Little House in Kolomna (*Domik v Kolomne*), 220–21;
"The Little Town" ("Gorodok"), 209;
The Mermaid (*Rusalka*), 217;
"Madonna," 122, 179, 221;
"Mon portrait," 205–6;
Mozart and Salieri, 220, 229, 251, 325, 410–11;
"My genealogy" ("Moia rodoslovnaia") 206, 221, 267;
"No, I do not prize stormy pleasure" ("Net, ia ne dorozhu miatezhnym naslazhdeniem"), 118, 178–79, 221;
"Noël," 211;
"On Arakcheev" ("Na Arakcheeva"), 211;
"On the Worthlessness of Russian Literature" ("O nichtozhestve literatury russkoi"), 269–70;
"The Pilgrim" ("Strannik"), 223;
"The Poet," 219;
"The Poet and the Crowd" ("Poet i tolpa") 219;
Poltava, 119, 180, 219–20, 228–30, 261, 267, 272, 302;
"The Prisoner" ("Uznik"), 387;
The Prisoner of the Caucasus (*Kavkazskii plennik*), 212–13;
"The Prophet" ("Prorok"), 33, 113–14, 196–97, 219–20, 228, 282, 346;
"The Queen of Spades" ("Pikovaia dama"), 222;
"Recollection" ("Vospominanie"), 219, 346;
"Recollections at Tsarskoe Selo" ("Vospominaniia v Tsarskom Sele"), 110, 209;
"Refutations of Criticisms" ("Oprovezhenie na kritiki"), 118–19, 180, 229–30, 247, 261;
Review of Polevoy's *History of the Russian People*, 142–43;
Ruslan and Liudmila, 209, 235–36;
"Secular Power" ("Mirskaia vlast'"), 223;
"Sleep/Dream" ("Son"), 208;
"Songs about Stenka Razin" ("Pesni o Sten'ke Razine"), 288–91, 294, 299;
"Songs of the Western Slavs" ("Pesni zapadnykh slavian"), 223, 293;
"Stanzas" ("Stansy"), 125n65, 218, 267;
The Stone Guest (*Kamennyi gost'*), 11, 107, 111, 115–17, 123–24, 179–81, 195, 198, 220, 229, 231, 236n27, 247–48, 249–264, 325, 410–11;
"Table-Talk," 252, 255;
"The Tale of the Dead Tsarevna" ("Skazka o mertvoi tsarevne"), 222;
"The Tale of the Fisherman and the Fish" ("Skazka o rybake i rybke"), 222;
"The Tale of the Village Priest and His Workman Balda" ("Skazka o pope I rabotnike ego Balde"), 221;
"To the Artist" ("Khudozhniku"), 143;
"To the Calumniators of Russia" ("Klevetnikam Rossii"), 221;
"To Friends" ("K druziam"), 218;
"To Iurev" ("K Iur'evu"), 232–33;
"To Licinius" ("Litsiniiu"), 91n139;
"To [My] Nanny" ("Niane"), 109n21, 208n5;
"To Ovid" ("K Ovidiiu"), 119n52, 213;
"To a Poet-Friend" ("K drugu stikhotvortsu"), 209;
"To the Sea" ("K moriu"), 217, 289;
"To a Young Widow" ("K molodoi vdove"), 111, 236n27;
"Treachery," ("Kovarnost'"), 215;
Tsar Nikita and His Forty Daughters (*Tsar' Nikita i sorok ego docherei*), 213–14;
"The Upas Tree," ("Anchar"), 219;
"Verses composed at night during insomnia ("Stikhi, sochineyyne noch'iu vo vremia bessonitsy"), 109n21, 202;
"The Village" ("Derevnia"), 211;
"What is there in my name for you" ("Chto v imeni tebe moem"), 105;
"When I, pensive, roam beyond the city" ("Kogda za gorodom, zadumchiv, ia brozhu"), 223;
"Winter Evening" ("Zimnii vecher"), 109n21 208n5;
Women (*Zhenshchiny*), 177;
"You and I" ("Ty i ia"), 211
Pushkin House (Pushkinsky Dom), 188–91 198–202
Pushkin, Lev Sergeevich (brother), 208, 219, 223
Pushkin, Sergei Lvovich (father), 206, 208, 216
Pushkin, Vasily Lvovich (uncle), 209, 211
Pushkina, Olga Sergeevna (sister), 208
Pushkina, Nadezhda Osipovna (neé Gannibal) (mother), 206–7
Pynchon, Thomas, 99n167

R: **Racine, Jean,** 209, 254, 256n25
Radishchev, Alexander, 33;
Journey from St. Petersburg to Moscow, 75n108, 382

Raevsky, Alexander, 176, 215
Raevsky, General Nikolai (father), 212–13
Raevsky, Nikolai (son), 252
Rak, Vadim, 200–201
Razin, Stenka, 32, 59, 288–91, 293, 309.
See also Pushkin, A. S.: works, *Songs about Stenka Razin*
Realism, 22, 27, 36, 91, 191–92, 280, 395
Reeves, Marjorie, 49
religious imagination, Russian, 29–32
  writer in, 33–34, 387
  gift vs. agreement, 284–87, 290, 293
Rilke, Ranier Maria, 368
Remizov, Alexei, 75
Repin, Ilya, 185
Ricoeur, Paul, 169, 183
Riemann, Bernhard, 153–54
Riffaterre, Michael, 172
Rimbaud, Artur, 348n7
Rimsky-Korsakov, Nikolai, 185
Riznich, Amalia, 113n30, 214–15
Romanticism, 71n103, 76, 114, 129, 191–92, 338, 408
Rousseau, Jean-Jacques, 209, 411
Rozanov, Vasily, 40, 75, 196, 349n11
Sade, Marquis de, 347
Said, Edward, 366
Saussure, Ferdinand de, 11, 172
Savonarola, Girolamo, 50
Schelling, F. W. J., 67, 76
Schlegel, Friedrich, 72
Scott, Walter, 194, 298
  Rob Roy, 223
Serafim, Saint, 67
Shakespeare, William, 11, 90, 114, 185, 194, 217, 249–264, 281, 331–32, 348, 397, 411n25;
  Hamlet, 14;
  Henry IV, 144n45;
  Macbeth, 252, 260;
  Measure for Measure, 222, 255;
  Merchant of Venice, 252;
  Othello, 119, 230–32, 252–53;
  Rape of Lucrece, 217;
  Richard III, 249–51, 255–260;
  Sonnet 129, 105–108;
  A Winter's Tale, 261
Shakhoskoy, Prince A. A., 211
Shalamov, Varlam, 33, 34
Shapir, Maxim, 200
Shaw, George Bernard, 411
Shchegolev, P. E., 187, 193
Shelley, Percy Bysshe, 173, 408n11
Shershenevich, V. G., 99
Shestov, Lev, 196
Shevyryov, Stepan, 249, 258–59
Shirinsky-Shikhmatov, Sergei, 67, 211

Shishkov, Admiral A. S., 211;
  Shishkovites, 211
Shklovsky, V. B., 192
Sholokhov, M. A., 99
Sidney, Sir Philip, 90
Simchenko, O. V., 99
Simeon of Polotsk, 61–64
Simmons, Ernest J., 349n10
Sinyavsky, Andrei, 33–34, 288n23
Sipovsky, V. V., 194
Sirin. *See* Nabokov, Vladimir
Skonechnaia, Ol'ga, 350n14, 362n50
Slavophiles, 68, 75
Smith, Marie (neé Charon la Rose), 111
Sobolevsky, S. A., 227n3
Sobanska, Karolina, 214
Socialist Realism, 75, 77–78, 99, 377
Sokol, Alan, 147
Solger, Karl, 71n103
Sologub, Fyodor, 33;
  The Petty Demon, 347–62
Solovyov, Alexander, 60
Solovyov, S. M.
Solovyov, Vladimir, 33, 39, 40, 50, 66, 69, 74–75, 148, 195–96, 202, 349
Solzhenitsyn, Alexander, 33, 34;
  The Gulag Archipelago, 35;
  "Matryona's Homestead," 98
Sontag, Susan, 334n34
Southey, Robert, 76
Spender, Stephen, 370, 380n64
Spenser, Edmund, 90, 97
Stalin, Joseph, 387–88
Stendhal (Marie-Henri Beyle), 347
Stepnyak-Kravchinsky, Sergei, *Andrei Kozhukhov*, 30
Stevens, Wallace, 173, 384
Stirner, Max, 68
Structuralism, 9, 10, 22–23, 50, 72, 102, 172, 192
Struve, P. B., 196
Sumarokov, A. P., 91n141
Surat, I. Z., 202–3
Symbolism, 75, 76n110, 99, 139, 152, 155, 161, 335, 338, 348–56, 373n38
T: Tammi, Pekka, 338
Taranovsky, Kirill, 169, 172–73
Tasso, Torquato, 209
Tchaikovsky, P. I., 185–86
Teilhard de Chardin, Pierre, 50
Tertz, Abram. *See* Sinyavsky, Andrei
Thompson, D'Arcy Wentworth, 136
Tieck, Ludwig, 72
Tiutchev, Fyodor, 61
Todorov, Tzvetan, 72–73
Tolstoy, Leo, 22–23, 27–28, 30, 66, 96, 279, 342, 346;

Anna Karenina, 27, 39, 95;
The Kreutzer Sonata, 40;
War and Peace, 34, 35, 97n159
Tomashevsky, B. V., 72–73, 88–90, 192, 194, 197–98, 200–201, 301
train, 97–100
Trediakovsky, Vasily, 33, 91n141
Trilling, Lionel, 409
Trubetskoy, Paolo, 89
Tsiavlovskaya-Zenger, T. G., 188–89, 193, 231
Tsiavlovsky, M. A., 188–90, 193
Tsvetaeva, Marina, 33–34, 39, 99, 194, 297–98, 363, 368, 380, 386, 391, 395, 397, 409;
"New Year's Greeting," 368, 372–74
Turgenev, Alexander, 211, 226
Turgenev, Ivan, 68, 95–96, 104n7;
Fathers and Sons, 37;
"First Love," 95;
"Living Relics," 30;
On the Eve, 75n108;
Rudin, 37
Turing, Alan, 136
Tynianov, Yury, 105, 170, 191–93
Tyrkova-Williams, Ariadna, 193
U: Ungurianu, Dan, 297n62, 308n13
Uspensky, Boris, 38–39, 51, 155–6
V: Vasily III (grand prince), 56
Vatsuro, Vadim, 126, 190–91, 194, 197, 302
Venclova, Tomas, 352, 382
Vendler, Helen, 106–8
Vengerov, S. A., 187, 195
Verlaine, 348n7
Verrochio, Andrea del, 87
Versaev, V. V., 193
Vesyoly, Artyom, Russia Drenched with Blood, 98
Villon, François, 182
Vinogradov, V. V., 192
Vinokur, G. O., 188–89, 192
Virgil, 209, 408, 415–16
Vladimir, Saint, 64
Volkov, Solomon, 406–9, 420
Voloshin, Maximilian, 75, 93, 99
Voltaire (François-Marie Arouet), 30, 89n133, 110, 112–3, 207, 209, 213, 282n4, 347
Vorontsov General Mikhail (count), 214–15
Vorontsova, Elizaveta (countess), 176, 214–16, 231, 232n13
Vsevolozhky, Nikita, 211
Vyazemsky, P. A. (prince), 61, 120, 175, 209, 211, 217, 254;
"Again the Troika," 94n153;
"Pyotr Alekseevich," 96n156

W: Wachtel, Andrew, 297n62, 305n9, 307n12
Walcott, Derek, 381
Weiner, Adam, 384n10
White, Hayden, 287–88, 303, 322
Whitman, Walt, 173
Wilson, Edmund, 130, 348
Wimsatt, W. K., 171
Wordsworth, William, 76, 173, 408n11
Wright, Sewall, 132–33, 146
Y: Yakovlev, N. V., 194
Yakovleva, Arina Rodionovna, 208, 216, 28
Yavorsky, Stephan, 61
Yakubovich, D. P., 188–89, 192, 194
Yakushkin, I. D., 213
Yakushkin, V. E., 187
Yeats, W. B., 364–70, 372–80, 381–83, 386
Ypsilanti, Alexander, 213
Z: Zablotsky, Nikolai, 33;
Columns, 75n109;
The Triumph of Agriculture, 75n109
Zagoskin, M. N., 67
Zamyatin, Evgeny, 33, 93;
We, 32
Zenkovsky, V. V., 163
Zhirmunsky, V. M., 175, 192, 194
Zhukovsky, V. A., 61, 211, 223, 225, 396;
"Perishability" ("Tlennost'"), 396;
"The Song of the Arab [Sung] over the Grav of his Horse," 94n153;
"Svetlana," 94n153;
"Lenora," 94n153;
"The Knight Rollon," 94n153
Zielinski, Tadeucz, 383
Ziolkowski, Theodore, 82
Zosimius (metropolitan), 55
Zwingli, Huldreich, 58n58

www.ingramcontent.com/pod-product-compliance
Lightning Source LLC
Chambersburg PA
CBHW071356300426
44114CB00016B/2082